# Implementing and Administering Cisco Solutions: 200-301 CCNA Exam Guide

Begin a successful career in networking with 200-301 CCNA certification

**Glen D. Singh**

BIRMINGHAM—MUMBAI

# Implementing and Administering Cisco Solutions: 200-301 CCNA Exam Guide

**Commissioning Editor**: Vijin Boricha

**Senior Editor**: Rahul Dsouza

**Content Development Editors**: Ronn Kurien and Nihar Kapadia

**Technical Editor**: Sarvesh Jaywant

**Copy Editor**: Safis Editing

**Project Coordinator**: Neil Dmello

**Proofreader**: Safis Editing

**Indexer**: Rekha Nair

**Production Designer**: Jyoti Chauhan

First published: November 2020

Production reference: 1151020

Published by Packt Publishing Ltd.
Livery Place
35 Livery Street
Birmingham
B3 2PB, UK.

ISBN 978-1-80020-809-4

www.packt.com

Packt.com

Subscribe to our online digital library for full access to over 7,000 books and videos, as well as industry leading tools to help you plan your personal development and advance your career. For more information, please visit our website.

## Why subscribe?

- Spend less time learning and more time coding with practical eBooks and Videos from over 4,000 industry professionals

- Improve your learning with Skill Plans built especially for you

- Get a free eBook or video every month

- Fully searchable for easy access to vital information

- Copy and paste, print, and bookmark content

Did you know that Packt offers eBook versions of every book published, with PDF and ePub files available? You can upgrade to the eBook version at packt.com and as a print book customer, you are entitled to a discount on the eBook copy. Get in touch with us at customercare@packtpub.com for more details.

At www.packt.com, you can also read a collection of free technical articles, sign up for a range of free newsletters, and receive exclusive discounts and offers on Packt books and eBooks.

# Contributors

## About the author

**Glen D. Singh** is a cybersecurity and networking instructor, InfoSec author, and consultant. His areas of expertise are penetration testing, digital forensics, network security, and enterprise networking. He has many certifications, including CEH, CHFI, and 3xCCNA (cyber ops, security, and routing and switching). He loves teaching and mentoring others, and sharing his wealth of knowledge and experience as an author. He has written books on Kali Linux, Kali NetHunter, and CCNA Security.

Glen has trained many professionals in various sectors ranging from ISPs to government agencies in the field of cybersecurity. As an aspiring game-changer, Glen is passionate about increasing cybersecurity awareness in his homeland, Trinidad and Tobago.

*I would like to thank Rahul Nair, Suzanne Coutinho, Ronn Kurien, and the wonderful team at Packt Publishing, who have provided amazing support and guidance throughout this journey. To the technical reviewers, Aaron Caesar and Jessie James Araneta, thank you for your outstanding contribution to making this an amazing book.*

# About the reviewers

**Aaron Caesar** holds a BSc. in Computing and Information Systems and other professional certifications in networking and security. His career in technology spans 16 years, including technical support and teaching at various private and public sector agencies. Currently, he is employed at a multinational ISP, providing specialist support to a wide cross-section of the company's corporate customers. Aaron has a passion for learning about information and communication technologies that he continues to pursue daily.

Above all, however, he is a father, husband, son, brother, and friend.

> *I would like to thank my beautiful wife, Abbigail, for all the support she has provided to me during this process; and all the people who believed in me and my growth. I would also express my gratitude to the author and the team at Packt for giving me this great opportunity to contribute to this excellent book.*

**Jessie James** is a licensed electronics engineer and a Cisco Certified Network Associate. His experience and specialization is mobile and fixed network operation for telecommunications. During the development of this book, he has been working for Etisalat UAE as Operations Field Support – Fixed Network.

> *I'd like to thank God first, for His almighty guidance on whatever decisions I made. I'd also like to thank Packt Publishing for the opportunity to review this wonderful book. To my parents, siblings, relatives, friends, and mentors (you know who you are), thank you for guiding and supporting me. Lastly, I'd like to thank Bonie for the love and support while reviewing this book.*

# Packt is searching for authors like you

If you're interested in becoming an author for Packt, please visit `authors.packtpub.com` and apply today. We have worked with thousands of developers and tech professionals, just like you, to help them share their insight with the global tech community. You can make a general application, apply for a specific hot topic that we are recruiting an author for, or submit your own idea.

# Table of Contents

**Preface**

# Section 1:
# Network Fundamentals

## 1

## Introduction to Networking

| | | | |
|---|---|---|---|
| Understanding the evolution of networking and the internet | 20 | Layer 3 switches | 50 |
| | | Routers | 50 |
| Understanding network sizes – SOHO, LAN, and WAN | 22 | Next-generation firewalls and IPS | 51 |
| | | Access Points | 55 |
| Learning about network protocol suites | 25 | Cisco Wireless LAN Controller (WLC) | 56 |
| | | Endpoints and servers | 57 |
| OSI reference model | 25 | Cisco DNA | 58 |
| Understanding the TCP/IP protocol suite | 41 | | |
| | | **Network topology architectures** | **58** |
| **Understanding the functions of network devices** | **42** | 2 Tier | 60 |
| | | 3 Tier | 63 |
| Hubs | 42 | **Summary** | **65** |
| Layer 2 switches | 45 | **Further reading** | **68** |

## 2

## Getting Started with Cisco IOS Devices

| | | | |
|---|---|---|---|
| **Technical requirements** | **70** | Virtual CCNA Lab | 77 |
| **Building a Cisco lab environment** | **71** | Physical labs | 89 |
| Cisco Packet Tracer | 71 | **Getting started with Cisco IOS** | |

devices                                    90
Boot process                               90

Accessing a Cisco IOS device               92
Configuring the Cisco IOS                  96
Setting up a small Cisco network           98

Performing troubleshooting
procedures                                117
Summary                                   118
Questions                                 119
Further reading                           120

# 3

## IP Addressing and Subnetting

Technical requirements                    122
The need for IP addressing                122
Characteristics of IPv4                   125
Composition of an IPv4 packet             126
Converting binary into decimal            129
Converting decimal into binary            132
Transmission types                        137

Classes of IPv4 addresses                 140
Public IPv4 address space                 141
Private IPv4 address space                142

Special IPv4 addresses                    144
Loopback address                          145
Test-Net                                  145
Link Local                                145

Subnet mask                               146
Network prefix                            146
Identifying the Network ID                148

Subnetting                                150

Step 1 – Determining the appropriate
IP address                                152
Step 2 – Creating new subnets
(subnetworks)                             154
Step 3 – Assigning subnets to each
network                                   157
Step 4 – Performing Variable-Length
Subnet
Masking (VLSM)                            159

IPv6                                      162
Types of IPv6 addresses                   165

Lab – Configuring IPv6 on a
Cisco IOS router                          168
Lab – Configuring IPv6 on a
Windows computer                          170
Testing end-to-end connectivity
                                          172
Summary                                   172
Further reading                           173

# 4

## Detecting Physical Issues, Wireless Architectures, and Virtualization

Technical requirements                    176
Understanding network switch

functions                                 176
Detecting physical issues                 178

Wireless technologies                187
2.4 GHz versus 5 GHz                 189
Wireless bands                       192
SSID, BSSID, and ESS                 193

## Cisco wireless architectures      195

Autonomous                           196
Cloud-based                          197
Split-MAC                            198

## AP modes                          199

## Wireless components and management 200

Lab – accessing a Cisco WLC GUI      201
Lab – configuring a wireless network using

a Cisco WLC                          203

## Virtualization fundamentals       209

Type 1 hypervisor                    210
Type 2 hypervisor                    211

## Cloud computing                   213

Cloud services                       215
SaaS                                 215
PaaS                                 216
IaaS                                 216
Cloud delivery models                216

## Summary                           217
## Questions                         218
## Further reading                   221

# Section 2: Network Access

## 5

## Implementing VLANs, Layer 2 Discovery Protocols, and EtherChannels

Technical requirements               226
Understanding VLANs                  226
VLAN ranges                          232
Types of VLANs                       233
Trunk interfaces                     236
Inter-VLAN routing                   239
Lab – implementing VLANs             242
Lab – creating trunk interfaces      248
Lab – configuring inter-VLAN routing 252

Layer 2 Discovery Protocols          255

Cisco Discovery Protocol (CDP)       255
Link-Layer Discovery Protocol (LLDP) 257

Understanding and configuring EtherChannels   259
Lab – implementing EtherChannels     263

Summary                              265
Questions                            266
Further reading                      268

# 6
## Understanding and Configuring Spanning-Tree

| | | | |
|---|---|---|---|
| Technical requirements | 270 | PVST+ | 281 |
| What is Spanning-Tree | | Rapid-PVST+ | 286 |
| Protocol? | 270 | Lab – implementing Rapid-PVST+ on a Cisco network | 288 |
| Bridge Protocol Data Unit | 273 | | |
| Root bridge and secondary root bridge | 274 | Lab – configuring PortFast and BPDUguard | 291 |
| Spanning-tree standards | 277 | Summary | 293 |
| Port roles and states | 277 | Questions | 293 |
| Determining the root bridge and port roles | 278 | Further reading | 295 |

# Section 3: IP Connectivity

# 7
## Interpreting Routing Components

| | | | |
|---|---|---|---|
| Technical requirements | 300 | Administrative Distance | 311 |
| Understanding IP routing | 300 | Routing metrics | 314 |
| Components of the routing table | 306 | Gateway of last resort | 317 |
| Routing protocol codes | 306 | Summary | 318 |
| Prefix and network mask | 309 | Questions | 318 |
| Next hop | 310 | Further reading | 320 |

# 8
## Understanding First Hop Redundancy, Static and Dynamic Routing

| | | | |
|---|---|---|---|
| Technical requirements | 322 | Lab – configuring static routing using IPv4 | 332 |
| Understanding static routing | 322 | Lab – configuring an IPv4 default route | 337 |
| Do we need static routing? | 324 | Lab – configuring static routing using | |
| Types of static routes | 325 | | |

IPv6                                          340

## Understanding dynamic routing
                                              345

Types of dynamic routing protocols           346
Open Shortest Path First                      349
Lab – configuring OSPFv2                      363
Validating OSPF configurations               366

Understanding first hop
redundancy                                    370
Various FHRPs                                 372

Summary                                       384
Questions                                     384
Further reading                               386

# Section 4:
# IP Services

## 9
## Configuring Network Address Translation (NAT)

Technical requirements                        390
The challenge of using IPv4 on
the internet                                  390
Understanding NAT                             391
Understanding NAT operation and
terminology                                   393

Types of NAT                                  395
Static NAT                                    395
Dynamic NAT                                   397
Configuring PAT                               399

Lab – implementing NAT
overload (PAT)                                403
Lab – implementing static NAT
with port forwarding                          406
Lab – implementing dynamic
NAT                                           409
Summary                                       412
Questions                                     413
Further reading                               415

## 10
## Implementing Network Services and IP Operations

Technical requirements                        418
Understanding NTP                             418
Lab – configuring NTP                         421

Understanding DHCP                            426
DHCP operations                               426
Cisco's DHCP configurations                   429
DHCP relay                                    430

Lab – configuring DHCP and DHCP
relay                                         432

Domain Name System                            435
DNS root servers                              437
DNS record types                              438
Lab – configuring DNS                         439

Understanding the benefits of

using Syslog                                   442
Syslog severity levels                         443
Lab – configuring Syslog                       445

Simple Network Management
Protocol                                       448
SNMP versions                                  451
Management information base                    451
Lab – configuring SNMP                         453

QoS traffic classification                     456
QoS terminologies                              458
Traffic type characteristics                   459
QoS queuing algorithms                         461
QoS policy models                              462
QoS implementation methods                     464

Summary                                        466
Questions                                      467
Further reading                                469

# Section 5:
# Security Fundamentals

## 11
## Exploring
## Network Security

Technical requirements                         474
Security concepts                              474
The CIA triad                                  475
Threats                                        478
Vulnerabilities                                482
Exploits                                       495
Attacks                                        496

Authentication, Authorization,
and Accounting                                 503

Lab – Implementing AAA                         506
Elements of a security program
                                               509
Wireshark 101                                  509
Lab – Analyzing packets                        514

Summary                                        516
Questions                                      516
Further reading                                518

## 12
## Configuring Device Access Control
## and VPNs

Technical requirements                         520
Device access control                          520
Securing console access                        520
Securing an AUX line                           525

VTY line access                                527
Securing Privilege Exec mode                   535
Encrypting all plaintext passwords             539

Virtual Private Networks                       540

Site-to-Site VPNs                                541
Remote access VPNs                               543
IPsec                                            544
Lab – Configuring a site-to-site VPN             545
Lab – Configuring a remote access VPN  551

Summary                                          558
Questions                                        558
Further reading                                  560

# 13

# Implementing Access Control Lists

Technical requirements                           562
What are ACLs?                                   562
Benefits of using ACLs                           563

ACL operation                                    564
ACL wildcard masks                               568
Calculating the wildcard mask                    569
ACL guidelines and best practices                571

Working with standard ACLs                       573
Creating a numbered standard ACL                 573
Implementing a named standard ACL                575
Deleting an ACL                                  576

Lab – implementing a standard
numbered ACL                                     576
Lab – configuring a standard named
ACL                                              580
Lab – securing VTY lines using ACLs              583

Working with extended ACLs                       588
Creating a numbered extended ACL                 588
Implementing a named extended ACL                589
Lab – implementing extended ACLs                 591

Summary                                          596
Questions                                        596
Further reading                                  598

# 14

# Implementing Layer 2 and Wireless Security

Technical requirements                           600
Types of Layer 2 attacks on a
network                                          600
Network attacks                                  601
Defense in depth                                 603
Layer 2 threats                                  606

Protecting against Layer 2
threats                                          621
Port security                                    621

DHCP snooping                                    634
Dynamic ARP inspection                           641

Wireless network security                        645
Authentication methods                           647
Lab – implementing wireless security
using a WLC                                      649

Summary                                          655
Questions                                        656
Further reading                                  658

# Section 6: Automation and Programmability

## 15
## Network Automation and Programmability Techniques

| | | | |
|---|---|---|---|
| Understanding automation | 662 | Understanding network configuration management | 676 |
| Understanding data formats | 663 | | |
| eXtensible Markup Language | 665 | Fabric, overlay, and underlay | 682 |
| JavaScript Object Notation | 666 | Cisco DNA Center | 685 |
| YAML Ain't Markup Language | 668 | Summary | 686 |
| Understanding APIs | 670 | Questions | 687 |
| Types of APIs | 670 | Further reading | 689 |
| RESTful APIs | 671 | | |

## 16
## Mock Exam 1

## 17
## Mock Exam 2

## Assessments

## Other Books You May Enjoy

## Index

# Preface

*Implementing and Administering Cisco Solutions: CCNA 200-301 Exam Guide* is an excellent book that focuses on a range of Cisco technologies that will help you gain a firm understanding of networking, IP connectivity, IP services, security, network programmability, and automation.

Throughout this book, you will be exposed to various networking components and discover how they all work together in an enterprise network. You will also learn how to configure Cisco devices using the **command-line interface (CLI)** to provide network access, services, security, connectivity, and management.

During the course of this book, you will come across different hands-on labs with real-world scenarios that are designed to help you gain essential on-the-job skills and experience. Furthermore, this book will guide you and teach you networking technologies and solutions to implement and administer enterprise networks and infrastructure using Cisco solutions.

By the end of this book, you will have gained the confidence to pass the CCNA 200-301 examination and be well-versed in a variety of network administration and security engineering solutions.

## Who this book is for

This guide is targeted at every IT professional looking to boost their network engineering and security administration career. Users interested in certifying in Cisco technologies and starting a career as network security professionals will find this book useful. Readers with no knowledge about Cisco technologies but some understanding of industry-level network fundamentals will have an added advantage.

# What this book covers

*Chapter 1, Introduction to Networking*, introduces various network protocols, devices, and components, and network topology architectures.

*Chapter 2, Getting Started with Cisco IOS Devices*, introduces **Cisco Internetwork Operating System (Cisco IOS)**. You will learn how to access the device, perform initial configurations, and learn how to verify the device's settings. Additionally, you will learn how to build your personal learning environment to reduce your expenditure in terms of purchasing expensive equipment.

*Chapter 3, IP Addressing and Subnetting*, covers different classes of IP addresses and their assignments. The second half of the chapter will teach you how to use subnetting to break down a large network into smaller subnetworks.

*Chapter 4, Detecting Physical Issues, Wireless Architectures, and Virtualization*, covers various Layer 1 issues and takes a deep dive into understanding Cisco Wireless Architectures and deployment models. Additionally, this chapter covers the concept of virtualization and virtual machines.

*Chapter 5, Implementing VLANs, Layer 2 Discovery Protocols, and EtherChannels*, introduces you to **Virtual Local Area Networks (VLANs)**, configuring and troubleshooting VLANs on a Cisco network, setting up inter-switch connectivity by configuring Trunk links, and configuring inter-VLAN routing to allow multiple VLANs to inter-communicate. Additionally, you will learn how to use various Layer 2 discovery protocols to map devices on a network and use EtherChannels to perform link aggregation.

*Chapter 6, Understanding and Configuring Spanning-Tree*, covers the importance of designing a proper switch network showing devices should be interconnected to ensure redundancy. Furthermore, the chapter introduces you to a Layer 2 loop prevention mechanism known as the **Spanning-Tree Protocol (STP)**. You will learn about the operations, configurations, and troubleshooting of STP in a Cisco environment.

*Chapter 7, Interpreting Routing Components*, focuses on the importance of routing and discusses how routers make their forwarding decisions. You will learn all about the components of the routing table and the factors that help a router to choose a preferred path for forwarding packets to their destination.

*Chapter 8, Understanding First Hop Redundancy, Static and Dynamic Routing*, continues the discussion on routing but takes a more technical approach, such as demonstrating how to implement static and dynamic routing protocols to ensure IP connectivity between multiple networks in a Cisco environment.

*Chapter 9, Configuring Network Address Translation (NAT)*, focuses primarily on **Network Address Translation (NAT)**. The chapter will take you from an introduction to use cases onto the configuration of various types of NAT and troubleshooting techniques.

*Chapter 10, Implementing Network Services and IP Operations*, introduces you to various network and IP services that are required on almost all enterprise networks and are required knowledge for network engineers. This chapter covers technologies such as NTP, DHCP, DNS, Syslog, and QoS.

*Chapter 11, Exploring Network Security*, discusses various topics, such as cybersecurity threats and issues many professionals face each day, such as threats, vulnerabilities, exploits, user training, security awareness, and countermeasures.

*Chapter 12, Configuring Device Access Control and VPNs*, focuses on securing your Cisco switches and routers and configuring secure device access. Additionally, this chapter introduces you to remote access and how to configure **Virtual Private Networks (VPNs)**.

*Chapter 13, Implementing Access Control Lists*, covers ACLs, which are a mandatory topic for everyone who is starting or is already in the field of networks or security. ACLs are Layer 3 security controls. When implemented on a route, they create a firewall-centric device to filter unwanted traffic.

*Chapter 14, Implementing Layer 2 and Wireless Security*, introduces you to various Layer 2 attacks on an enterprise network and explains how to implement countermeasures to create a secure network environment.

*Chapter 15, Network Automation and Programmability Techniques*, broaches the fact that the world of networking is moving toward automation and network engineers will now need to learn how automation can improve efficiency in network deployment and management. This chapter introduces you to network automation techniques and programmability.

*Chapter 16, Mock Exam 1*, includes a simple mock test containing questions that will help you to prepare for the Cisco CCNA 200-301 examination and will help you identify any topics you need to spend additional time learning about and practicing.

*Chapter 17, Mock Exam 2*, includes another mock test containing questions that will help you to prepare for the Cisco CCNA 200-301 examination and will help you identify any topics you need to spend additional time learning about and practicing.

# To get the most out of this book

All configurations were done using a Windows 10 operating system running Cisco Packet Tracer version 7.3.0.

| Software/Hardware covered in the book | OS Requirements |
|---|---|
| Cisco Packet Tracer 7.3.0 | Windows, macOS, and Linux (Any) |
| GNS3 2.2.5 (optional) | Cisco IOSv (optional) |
| GNS3 VM server 2.2.5 (optional) | Cisco IOSvL2 (optional) |
| Oracle VirtualBox (optional) | Cisco CSR1000v (optional) |
| VMware Workstation 15 Pro (optional) | |
| Wireshark | |
| Nessus Essentials | |

**If you are using the digital version of this book, we advise you to type the code yourself or access the code via the GitHub repository (link available in the next section). Doing so will help you avoid any potential errors related to the copying and pasting of code.**

After completing this book, using your imagination, attempt to create additional lab scenarios using Cisco Packet Tracer. This will help you to continue learning and further develop your skills as an aspiring network engineer.

# Download the example code files

You can download the example code files for this book from GitHub at `https://github.com/PacktPublishing/Implementing-and-Administering-Cisco-Solutions`. In case there's an update to the code, it will be updated on the existing GitHub repository.

We also have other code bundles from our rich catalog of books and videos available at `https://github.com/PacktPublishing/`. Check them out!

# Code in Action

Code in Action videos for this book can be viewed at `https://bit.ly/30fYz6L`.

# Download the color images

We also provide a PDF file that has color images of the screenshots/diagrams used in this book. You can download it here: `http://www.packtpub.com/sites/default/files/downloads/9781800208094_ColorImages.pdf`.

# Conventions used

There are a number of text conventions used throughout this book.

`Code in text`: Indicates code words in text, database table names, folder names, filenames, file extensions, pathnames, dummy URLs, user input, and Twitter handles. Here is an example: "If you use the `show flash:` command in privilege mode on a Cisco IOS switch, you will see the `vlan.dat` file."

When we wish to draw your attention to a particular part of a code block, the relevant lines or items are set in bold:

```
Branch-B(config)#ip route 10.1.1.0 255.255.255.0 10.2.1.5
Branch-B(config)#ip route 172.16.1.0 255.255.255.0 10.2.1.10
Branch-B(config)#ip route 192.168.1.0 255.255.255.0 10.2.1.20
```

Any command-line input or output is written as follows:

```
SW1(config)#interface FastEthernet 0/1
SW1(config-if)#switchport mode access
SW1(config-if)#switchport access vlan vlan-ID
SW1(config-if)#no shutdown
SW1(config-if)#exit
```

**Bold**: Indicates a new term, an important word, or words that you see onscreen. For example, words in menus or dialog boxes appear in the text like this. Here is an example: "Select **System info** from the **Administration** panel."

> **Tips or important notes**
> Appear like this.

# Disclaimer

The information within this book is intended to be used only in an ethical manner. Do not use any information from the book if you do not have written permission from the owner of the equipment. If you perform illegal actions, you are likely to be arrested and prosecuted to the full extent of the law. Packt Publishing does not take any responsibility if you misuse any of the information contained within the book. The information herein must only be used while testing environments with proper written authorization from the appropriate persons responsible.

# Get in touch

Feedback from our readers is always welcome.

**General feedback**: If you have questions about any aspect of this book, mention the book title in the subject of your message and email us at customercare@packtpub.com.

**Errata**: Although we have taken every care to ensure the accuracy of our content, mistakes do happen. If you have found a mistake in this book, we would be grateful if you would report this to us. Please visit www.packtpub.com/support/errata, selecting your book, clicking on the Errata Submission Form link, and entering the details.

**Piracy**: If you come across any illegal copies of our works in any form on the Internet, we would be grateful if you would provide us with the location address or website name. Please contact us at copyright@packt.com with a link to the material.

**If you are interested in becoming an author**: If there is a topic that you have expertise in and you are interested in either writing or contributing to a book, please visit authors.packtpub.com.

# Reviews

Please leave a review. Once you have read and used this book, why not leave a review on the site that you purchased it from? Potential readers can then see and use your unbiased opinion to make purchase decisions, we at Packt can understand what you think about our products, and our authors can see your feedback on their book. Thank you!

For more information about Packt, please visit `packt.com`.

# Section 1: Network Fundamentals

This section introduces you to the world of networking, starting with how devices intercommunicate. It then discusses the various types of networking devices along with their functionality. This section also covers popular networking protocols and services that allow a network to share a resource with other devices. Additionally, you will learn about IPv4 and IPv6 addressing, and subnetting techniques.

This section contains the following chapters:

- *Chapter 1, Introduction to Networking*
- *Chapter 2, Getting Started with Cisco IOS devices*
- *Chapter 3, IP Addressing and Subnetting*
- *Chapter 4, Detecting Physical Issues, Wireless Architectures, and Virtualization*

# 1
# Introduction to Networking

Beginning a journey in the field of networking is an exciting one for everyone. I'm sure you are interested in learning about the operations of a computer and especially how the internet, the largest network, functions and grows. Networking is an ever-demanding field in **Information Technology** (**IT**); each day, organizations from healthcare providers, educational institutions, government agencies, and other industries are continuously expanding and improving their network infrastructure to support newer services and network traffic. Almost everyone is connected to the internet. Educators and businesses are using various online collaboration platforms to extend their reach to students and potential customers in a global market. All these amazing technologies are made possible by computer networks.

The **Cisco Certified Network Associate** (**CCNA**) 200-301 certification is designed to prepare you for associate-level networking roles in the IT industry. CCNA is one of the most popular certification requirements for almost every network engineering job, and there is a very good reason why. The CCNA certification is a foundational level certification with a lot of essential information; I know part of the name contains the word "associate", but that's just in the Cisco certification hierarchy structure since the next level is Cisco Certified Network Professional and so on. The CCNA is one of the most recommended certifications you can follow to begin your networking journey.

The CCNA will teach you how to design, implement, configure, and troubleshoot small- to medium-sized enterprise networks. You will learn to efficiently implement network access, IP connectivity, IP services, and security through an enterprise network. Additionally, gaining your CCNA certification will open up a whole new world of career opportunities as the certification itself is well-respected in the networking field.

Throughout this chapter, you will learn about the important history of how computer networks were developed and the era before the internet. Then, we will cover the early and current generation of the internet and explore how networking has become part of our daily lives. You will learn about communication technologies and networking protocols that are designed to help us connect with our loved ones, friends, and colleagues. You will also learn about the various sizes of networks and components such as routers and switches, which move messages from one device, across a network, to another person. Lastly, you'll learn about the various protocol suites that are built into each operating system and network device that sets the protocol for exchanging messages.

In this chapter, we will cover the following topics:

- Understanding the evolution of networking and the internet
- Understanding network sizes – SOHO, LAN, and WAN
- Learning about network protocol suites
- Understanding the functions of network devices
- Network topology architectures

# Understanding the evolution of networking and the internet

In the pre-internet age, scientists, institutions, and other experts were working to create a network that could allow them to connect computers on a worldwide scale. Computer scientists began working on a model; the initial prototype was known as the **Advanced Research Projects Agency Network** (**ARPANET**).

ARPANET was developed in the 1960s. It was funded by the US **Department of Defense** (**DoD**) with the idea it would be used to connect universities and research centers. The network technology used on this prototype was packet switching. This allowed connected computers to send and receive data on a single network. However, ARPANET was not resilient enough to allow multiple channels of communication on the network.

The US **Defense Advanced Research Projects Agency (DARPA)** developed the **Transmission Control Protocol/Internet Protocol (TCP/IP)** suite, which was adopted by ARPANET in the early 1980s. The US DOD called it the official standard computer networking. With the adoption of TCP/IP, ARPANET began to evolve into much larger networks, allowing other organizations to be interconnected, and became what we commonly refer to as the internet today.

The internet is a worldwide collection of many interconnected networks, such as **Wide Area Networks (WANs)** and **Local Area Networks (LANs)**. Each organization or person who connects a device to the internet simply extends the network (internet), so the internet is continuously growing as more devices are going online. Later in this chapter, we will take a deeper dive and discuss various types and sizes of network topologies.

The internet itself is not owned by any one person or organization in the world. However, there are many groups and organizations that help maintain the stability and set standards for intercommunicating on the internet and private networks.

As an upcoming network engineer, it's good to know a little about the following organizations and groups:

- **Internet Engineering Task Force (IETF)**. Its mission is simply to make the internet work better for all. You can find more information about IETF on their website at www.ietf.org.

- **Internet Assigned Numbers Authority (IANA)** is responsible for the assignment, coordination, and management of **internet protocol (IP)** addressing, internet protocol resources, and the **Domain Name System (DNS)** Root Zone. You can find more information about IANA on their official website at www.iana.org.

- **Internet Corporation for Assigned Names and Numbers (ICANN)** contributes to the internet's sustainability by coordinating and managing the internet's numerical spaces and namespaces to ensure its stability. You can find more information about ICANN on their official website at www.icann.org.

Now that we have covered the history of the internet, we'll look at how various network sizes differ in the next section.

# Understanding network sizes – SOHO, LAN, and WAN

Let's imagine we have a few devices that are all interconnected in a single network, sharing files between themselves without having the user (human) physically walk around with a portable storage device such as a flash drive to copy and paste files. Users access a centralized file server within the company's network from their local computer.

The following diagram shows a small network with both a network-shared printer and file server:

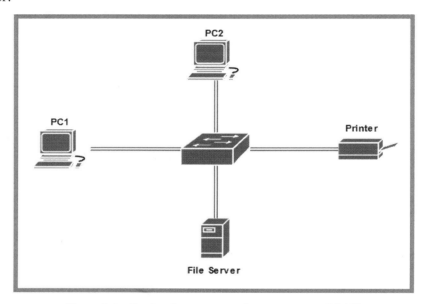

Figure 1.1 – Devices interconnected to create a small LAN

This type of network is commonly referred to as a LAN. A LAN is defined as a small computer network that does not exceed the physical space of a home or a single building. To help you understand this, we're going to use a simple analogy. Let's imagine you work for ACME, a fictional-based organization that has a single branch. Within the branch (that is, the physical building), ACME has a LAN that is used to interconnect all their devices – computers, servers, printers, and so on. This LAN allows employees to sit at their workstations and send documents to print via the network to the local printer and access the file server to store and copy files for their projects. Let's call this office location **HQ**.

The following diagram shows a typical LAN with interconnected devices within the **HQ** building:

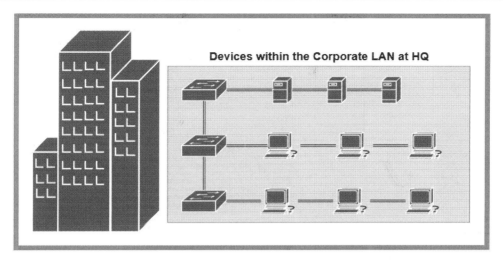

Figure 1.2 – A building containing a LAN

One day, ACME wants to open a new branch in another city to provide services to new and potential customers; however, there is a challenge. We shall refer to the new branch as **BranchA**. The new location, **BranchA**, is many miles away and the staff at **BranchA** need to access resources such as the application server, **Customer Relationship Management** (**CRM**) database, and other important resources that are located at the HQ location. One solution would be to create a clone of the servers from **HQ** to the new location, **BranchA**; however, this means each time new records and data is updated at the **HQ** location, it will take a long time to replicate the data on the servers at **BranchA**. This may create inconsistency issues when employees try to access the most up-to-date files and records at **BranchA**.

> **Important note**
> In our scenario, **BranchA** is typically known as a **Small Office/Home Office** (**SOHO**). This type of network is generally smaller than the main corporate office of a company, but it enables the users to connect or access the resources that are centrally shared on the corporate network (**HQ**).

A better approach is to create a WAN. A WAN is used to simply extend a LAN over a large geographic distance. A company such as ACME would definitely benefit from using this technology within their organization. By implementing a WAN between their branches, **HQ** and **BranchA**, the servers and main resources can simply stay at **HQ** while employees are still able to access the resources, files, and records across the network at their **BranchA** location.

The following diagram shows a depiction of a WAN connection between the **HQ** location and the new branch office:

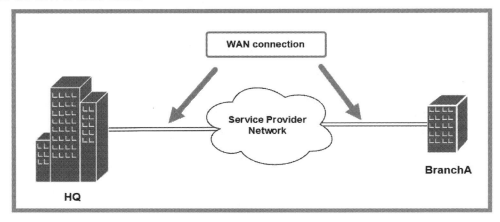

Figure 1.3 – A WAN connection between two buildings

In modern times, WANs are managed by **service providers (SP)** and **Internet Service Providers (ISPs)**. WANs can extend your LAN beyond cities, countries, and even continents. ISPs offer a range of WAN services to their customers, such as the following:

- **Metro Ethernet (MetroE)**
- **Virtual Private LAN Service (VPLS)**
- **Multiprotocol Label Switching (MPLS)**

As a simple example, MetroE enables customers of a service provider to establish a WAN between branches, functioning like a very huge LAN within the service provider network. This means a company can interconnect multiple branches using a MetroE service within the service provider network. On the customer's end, the network functions as if it were on a large LAN.

Another type of WAN service is MPLS, which provides us with the functionality to extend an organization's network beyond the local service provider's network. Imagine having a WAN circuit starting from the HQ location and passing through multiple ISP networks until the connection is terminated at a remote branch in another country.

With that, we have covered the fundamentals of SOHOs, LANs, and WANs. In the next section, we will learn about the components that help us build and extend networks.

# Learning about network protocol suites

Thanks to various technology companies, we can break down communication barriers between people who speak different native languages. We can simply install an app on our smartphone such as Google Translate and translate a foreign language into our own and vice versa.

For a device to communicate with another on a network, it requires a set of protocols or a protocol suite. A protocol suite is a common format that devices can use by following a set of rules for exchanging messages with other devices on a network. A protocol suite enables devices to speak a common, universal language that allows all networking devices to understand each other.

Years ago, computer manufacturers made their own protocol suites, which, in most instances, allowed only same-vendor devices to communicate and exchange data on a network. Some of these protocol suites were AppleTalk and Novel Netware (IPX/SPX), which were proprietary to the vendor and not suitable for consumers on a large scale.

Then came the **Open Systems Interconnection** (**OSI**) reference model and the **Transmission Control Protocol/Internet Protocol** (**TCP/IP**) suite. In the following subsections, we will further discuss and compare both the OSI model and TCP/IP protocol suite.

## OSI reference model

The OSI reference model is a seven (7) layer model that was developed by the **International Organization for Standardization** (**ISO**) in the 1970s. It was intended to be a fully operational protocol suite to allow all devices on a network to intercommunicate using a mutual language. However, it was never actually implemented in any systems.

You may be wondering, if it's not implemented in any operating systems and devices, why is it important we learn about the OSI reference model? Each layer of the OSI model has a unique functionality associated with a computer network. This allows network engineers to better understand what happens on each layer when performing troubleshooting tasks.

During the development of the OSI model, it was noted the model consisted of seven layers. These are as follows:

- Layer 7: Application
- Layer 6: Presentation
- Layer 5: Session
- Layer 4: Transport

- Layer 3: Network
- Layer 2: Data link
- Layer 1: Physical

Why are there so many layers? Each layer of the OSI model has a particular responsibility for ensuring a device is able to successfully exchange messages with other devices on a network. In the following sections, we are going to learn the essentials of each layer and how they help us understand network operations. This enables us to better identify and troubleshoot network-related issues in the industry.

> **Tip**
>
> We can take the first letter of each layer of the OSI model to create an easy-to-remember phrase: **A**ll **P**eople **S**eem **T**o **N**eed **D**ata **P**rocessing.

As an example, when a device such as a computer wants to send a message (data) to another device either on a local or remote network, the data has to flow downward in the OSI model, passing through each layer. During this process, a specific set of rules, encoding, and formatting is applied. This is known as encapsulation. Whenever a recipient is processing a message, it goes upward, passing each layer, and parts of the message are stripped away. This is known as de-encapsulation.

The following diagram shows the typical flow of a message through the OSI model when one device is sending a message and another device is accepting and processing an incoming message:

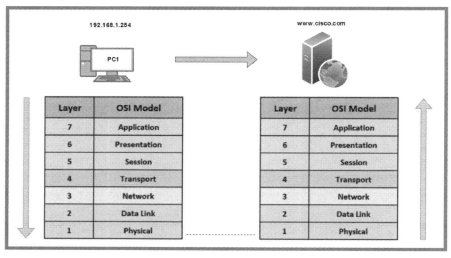

Figure 1.4 – Visual representation of traffic flowing through the OSI model

In the field of networking, a device such as a computer creates a **Protocol Data Unit** (**PDU**), sometimes referred to as a *datagram*. This is the raw data to be sent across a network to another device. At each layer of the OSI model, the PDU has a different name. These names are used to reference the characteristics of the PDU at a particular layer. In your exam, it's important to use this terminology. The following diagram shows a table containing the layers of the OSI model and the name of the PDU at each layer:

| Layer | OSI Model | PDU |
|-------|-----------|-----|
| 7 | Application | Data |
| 6 | Presentation | Data |
| 5 | Session | Data |
| 4 | Transport | Segment |
| 3 | Network | Packet |
| 2 | Data Link | Frame |
| 1 | Physical | Bits |

Figure 1.5 – PDUs at each layer of the OSI model

To get a better understanding about each layer of the OSI model and the characteristics of PDUs as they are passed between layers, we will discuss the role and function of each layer in the following sections. Let's take a closer look.

## Layer 7 – Application layer

The application layer (Layer 7) is the closest layer to the user within the protocol suite. It provides an interface for communication between the applications running in a local system and the underlying network protocols. To further explain, imagine you would like to get a bit more information on the **Cisco Certified Network Associate (CCNA)** certification. In today's world, internet access is readily available to us, either on mobile data plans that utilize 4G and LTE technologies or internet cafes and coffee shops with free internet access via their Wi-Fi network. Whichever method we use to access the internet, we always need an important application: a web browser to view web pages in a graphical interface, which helps us navigate the internet easily.

Let's continue with our analogy. One action you may want to perform is to visit Cisco's website at www.cisco.com to research the examination objectives and better prepare yourself for the certification.

Opening your favorite web browser, you enter the URL www.cisco.com and hit *Enter*. Within a couple of seconds, the Cisco website is displayed within the browser's interface. Looking closely at the address bar in the browser, we can see that the **Hypertext Transfer Protocol Secure (HTTPS)** protocol has been involved by the web browser, as shown in the following image:

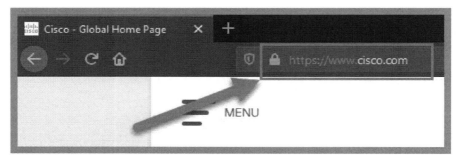

Figure 1.6 – HTTPS protocol used in web browser

Keep in mind that the web browser is simply an application running on our computer or smart device that allows us, the user, to use an application layer protocol such as HTTPS to exchange messages (encoded in web languages) between our computer and a web server. This makes the HTTPS protocol one of many application layer protocols.

The following are some commonly known application layer protocols:

- **File Transfer Protocol (FTP)**
- **Simple Mail Transfer Protocol (SMTP)**
- **Domain Name System (DNS)**
- **Dynamic Host Configuration Protocol (DHCP)**
- **HyperText Transfer Protocol (HTTP)**

In reference to the OSI model, the web browser (application) creates the raw HTTPS message. At this point, the **PDU** is known as data. Data has no additional encoding or formatting as it is simply the raw (bare) message the application has generated. However, in this state, the PDU can only be recognized and interpreted by another similar application that understands HTTP/S.

When the application layer has finished its job, it passes the PDU onto the lower layer, known as the presentation layer.

# Layer 6 – Presentation layer

A very important factor in communication is how content is presented. We must always try to ensure the format in which the message is written or spoken can be interpreted by the recipient very clearly. Imagine an ambassador who only speaks English is traveling to a foreign country on diplomatic business where the foreign nationals do not speak English. This will be a challenge for the ambassador; it can negatively affect some of the communication that they have with the locals during their visit. Having a dedicated person as a translator will assist the ambassador in communicating clearly with the foreign nationals.

We can apply this analogy to a network. There are many protocols that exist both inside and outside of a computer system; some are on the network itself, while others are on the operating systems of a server or desktop computer. Furthermore, as previously mentioned, each layer of the OSI reference model has its own set of protocols, which aid in the transmission of data between devices.

When an application layer protocol such as HTTPS sends the raw data to the network, it passes through the presentation layer (Layer 6), which has to perform some tasks before sending it to the lower layers. The presentation layer is responsible for the following functions:

- Data formatting
- Data compression
- Data encryption and decryption

Most importantly, data formatting ensures the raw data is presented or formatted into a compatible format for both the lower layers and the recipient's device(s) to understand. It's a bit like creating a universal language on a digital network.

Let's look at a simple analogy to further explain this concept. Imagine having to write a letter to a friend who resides in another country. After writing your letter, you securely enclose it within an envelope and insert the correspondence destination address before dropping it off to the local mail courier. Since the letter is intended for international shipping, the local courier will attach an international shipping label containing a universal format for the addressing information. This means the local courier company may need to pass the letter onto another courier until it reaches the intended destination. During this process, each courier will be able to read and interpret the information printed on the universal shipping label because its format is standardized. The same applies to messages passing to the lower layers of the OSI model, hence the importance of the presentation layer.

Another function of the presentation layer is compressing data before it is placed on the network and decompressing it on the recipient's device. Lastly, the presentation layer encrypts data before transporting it between the sender and receiver over a network. On the receiving device, the presentation layer is responsible for the decryption of the encrypted message.

At the presentation layer, the **PDU** is still known as data. Next, the PDU is passed on to the session layer.

## Layer 5 – Session layer

The session layer (Layer 5) has a simple responsibility. At this layer, there are three main functions that work together with a device to ensure datagrams (messages) can be exchanged across a network. These are as follows:

- Create or build a session between a sender and receiver.
- Maintain the established session during the transmission of messages between the sender and receiver devices.
- Terminate a session when both parties indicate they no longer want to communicate with each other.

Keep in mind that, at the session layer, the PDU maintains the same name as the upper layers: data.

## Layer 4 – Transport layer

The transport layer (Layer 4) is responsible for moving datagrams between the upper layers (application layer) onto the network itself. At the transport layer, the PDU has a new name, **Segment**.

At the application layer, there are many applications (programs) that generate network traffic, such as HTTP or SMTP, at any time. When each application layer protocol sends their datagram to the network, the transport layer has the responsibility of tracking these conversations as they occur.

Whenever a device wants to send a message across a network, the transport layer prepares the datagram (message) and separates it into manageable pieces for delivery. This is due to the fact that networking devices such as switches and routers, together with client machines such as desktop and server operating systems, have limitations regarding the amount of data that can be put in an IP packet. Therefore, the transport layer handles how to segment and reassemble these messages between the sender and the receiver.

As mentioned previously, there are many protocols at the application layer that handle data in different ways. Web traffic uses HTTP and HTTPS, which is formatted differently from email traffic, which uses the SMTP application protocol. Each protocol is designed to interpret its own type of traffic just fine, but if foreign traffic enters its application, it would be malformed and foreign in nature and therefore be discarded. One of the most important roles of a transport layer is to ensure data is passed to the corresponding applications. In other words, if a web browser is sending HTTP(S) traffic to a device on a network, the recipient application protocol on the destination device is expected to be running HTTP or HTTPS, such as a web server.

The transport layer ensures each datagram is sent to its corresponding application or application layer protocol by assigning a unique port number to the PDU, therefore creating a transport layer header. This process is known as encapsulation.

To get a better understanding of this process, let's use a simple analogy of a commercial tower whose tenants are various companies sharing the same physical infrastructure: the building. Typically, the main public area is the lobby, displaying a directory listing of each company and their floor number.

Let's think of the building as an **operating system (OS)**. According to RFC 6335, there are 65,535 logical network ports within an OS. These ports are categorized as follows:

| Port Ranges | Category |
|---|---|
| 0 - 1,023 | Well-Known Ports |
| 1,024 - 49,151 | Registered Ports |
| 49,152 - 65,535 | Private/Dynamic Ports |

Figure 1.7 – Network port number ranges

The well-known ports are those that are commonly used by application layer protocols, which are as follows:

- File Transfer Protocol: 20, 21
- **Secure Shell (SSH)**, **Secure Copy (SCP)**: 22
- Telnet: 23
- SMTP: 25
- DNS: 53
- DHCP: 68, 69

- HTTP: 80
- POP: 110
- IMAP: 143
- HTTPS: 443

Each application layer protocol/service uses a unique port that they send and receive their traffic type to and from. For example, all HTTP traffic will be sent to a device running a web server application (IIS, Apache, or Nginx) with open port 80. For HTTPS traffic to enter the web server, port 443 is the default port that must be open.

Registered ports are used by software and other vendors who want to use a specific port only for their application. These dynamic ports are used temporarily when a device is sending traffic and are sometimes referred to as ephemeral ports. For example, if a PC wants to send traffic to a web server, we know the web server will have port 80 and/or 443 open by default. However, the PC must use a source port. This means a dynamically generated port (ephemeral) between 49152 to 65535 will be used.

---

**Tip**

For more information of service names and port number assignment, please see the following URL: https://www.iana.org/assignments/ service-names-port-numbers/service-names-port- numbers.xhtml.

---

Getting back to our analogy, each person (datagram) who is entering the building (OS) has the intention of visiting a specific company (application protocol/service). They are instructed to take a specific elevator or staircase (transport layer) to reach the destination company in the building. When the individual (datagram) exits the elevator or staircase, they are faced with a few doors (network ports) to different companies on the same floor. Walking through a door (port) will carry the individual to a specific company. Within the OSI model and TCP/IP protocol suite, the transport layer inserts its own header, which contains the source port number of the sender and the destination port number of the recipient to ensure the datagram goes through the correct network port (doorway). This way, it can reach the relevant application layer protocol to be processed.

The following diagram represents the encapsulation of data. The transport layer inserts our header, which contains the source and destination port addresses:

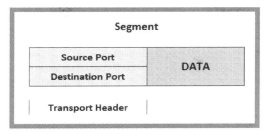

Figure 1.8 – Transport header information

Within the transport layer, there are two protocols that are responsible for the delivery of messages between a sender and a receiver over a network. These are the **Transmission Control Protocol (TCP)** and the **User Datagram Protocol (UDP)**.

## Transmission Control Protocol

TCP is often referred to as a **connection-oriented** protocol that guarantees the delivery of a message between a sender and a receiver. Before messages are exchanged between two devices, a **TCP three-way handshake** is established.

The following diagram shows the TCP three-way handshake process:

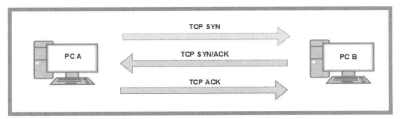

Figure 1.9 – TCP three-way handshake

The following is a live capture I took while using **Wireshark**. Look closely and you'll notice the sender, 172.16.17.14 (Client A), has sent a TCP **Synchronization (SYN)** packet to a destination address of 172.16.17.18 (Client B). By default, Client B responds with a TCP acknowledgement but additionally with a TCP SYN because it also wants to communicate with Client A. Hence, a **TCP SYN/ACK** packet gets returned. Finally, Client A receives the **TCP SYN/ACK** packet and responds with a **TCP ACK** to establish the TCP three-way handshake, as shown here:

| Source | Destination | Protocol | Length | Info |
|---|---|---|---|---|
| 172.16.17.14 | 172.16.17.18 | TCP | 62 | 59403 → 49152 [SYN] Seq=0 Win=64240 Len=0 MSS=1460 S |
| 172.16.17.18 | 172.16.17.14 | TCP | 62 | 49152 → 59403 [SYN, ACK] Seq=0 Ack=1 Win=14600 Len=0 |
| 172.16.17.14 | 172.16.17.18 | TCP | 54 | 59403 → 49152 [[ACK]] Seq=1 Ack=1 Win=64240 Len=0 |
| 172.16.17.14 | 172.16.17.18 | HTTP | 2... | GET /▮▮▮▮▮▮▮▮▮▮1 HTTP/1.1 |

Figure 1.10 – TCP three-way handshake shown in Wireshark

Once this process is complete, whenever each message is delivered to the recipient, a **TCP ACK** packet is sent back to the sender, indicating a successful delivery. However, if a sender does not receive a **TCP ACK** response from a recipient after a certain time, the sender will resend the message until a **TCP ACK** is received. This is how TCP ensures the delivery of messages on a network. However, due to the high overhead of TCP ACK packets on the network, not all application layer protocols uses TCP as their preferred choice of transport protocol. Some use UDP instead.

### User Datagram Protocol

The UDP is a connectionless protocol, known for its best-effort delivery methods. Best-effort simply means the UDP protocol will send the message but will not provide reassurance during delivery. This means that if the message is lost during transmission, UDP will not attempt to resend it. Unlike TCP, it does not provide any message delivery guarantees. If an application layer protocol such as DNS uses UDP for transporting its messages, the transport layer will send it off to its intended destination without any prioritization or any reliability during the message's transmission on the network.

Unlike TCP, UDP does not provide any delivery confirmation, though some application layer protocols prefer UDP for its low overhead and speed on the network.

### Layer 3 – Network layer

The network Layer, (Layer 3) is responsible for the logical address on the network and the encapsulation of the IP header, which adds both the source (sender) and destination (receiver) **IP version 4 (IPv4)** and/or **Internet Protocol version 6 (IPv6)** addresses to the packet.

This layer provides the following functions:

- Logical addressing of end devices
- Encapsulation and de-encapsulation of datagrams
- Routing (moving packets between networks)

The **Internet Protocol (IP)** operates at this layer. IP is a connectionless protocol, which means the protocol itself does not establish a session with a recipient before attempting to send or receive messages. In a similar way to the UDP of the upper layer (transport layer), it is also sent using best-effort mechanisms, thus providing no delivery guarantee for IP packets. Lastly, IP can function independently from the medium on the network (copper, fiber optic, or even wireless). Since IP does not have any reliability, the responsibility of ensuring packet delivery depends on the transport layer.

Furthermore, the network layer provides the functionality of directing traffic flows using routing protocols, which operate using the IP. At this layer, routers operate as they have the ability to read and understand IP addressing and the contents of a packet.

When the PDU is passed down to the network layer, it is encapsulated with an IPv4 or an IPv6 header to provide logical addressing, as shown here:

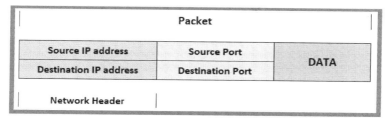

Figure 1.11 – Packet header

Keep in mind that the source and destination IP addresses do not change during their transmission between devices on a network. However, there is one exception: the source IP address changes when it passes a NAT-enabled router, which is configured to change a private IPv4 address into the public IPv4 address of the router's internet-facing interface. We will cover **Network Address Translation** (**NAT**) in *Chapter 9, Configuring Network Address Translation (NAT)*.

At this state, the PDU is called a **Packet**. In later chapters, we'll discuss IPv4 and IPv6 in greater detail.

## Layer 2 – Data link layer

The data link layer (Layer 2) of the OSI model is responsible for allowing the messages of the upper layers to access the physical network. It also controls how data is placed and received on the physical network (media), and it handles error detection and flow control. Within the data link layer, there are two sublayers. These are the **Logical Link Control** (**LLC**) and the **Media Access Control** (**MAC**).

### Logical Link Control

LLC encapsulates the packet that's received from the network layer into a frame by adding a Layer 2 header containing the source (sender) and destination (receiver) MAC addresses. At the end of the frame, a trailer is added. The trailer of a frame contains the **File Check Sequence** (**FCS**). The data link layer creates a hash value to represent the contents of the frame; this is known as the **Cyclic Redundancy Check** (**CRC**) hash value. The CRC value is located in the FCS field of the trailer. The recipient device(s) use this value to determine whether the frame was corrupted or modified during its transmission between the sender and the receiver.

## Media Access Control

For a device to connect and communicate on a computer network, a **Network Interface Card** (**NIC**) is required. The NIC allows the device to establish a connection to the physical network, regardless of whether the medium is copper or fiber optic cabling, or a wireless connection such as Wi-Fi. The NIC enables a device to exchange messages with another device while using the media (or medium) as the highway.

The MAC address is **48 bits (6 bytes)** in length and is presented in the format of hexadecimal values; that is, 0 1 2 3 4 5 6 7 8 9 A B C D E F. An example of a MAC address is 12 : 34 : 56 : 78 : 9A : BC. The first 24 bits of the MAC address are known as the **Organization Unique Identifier** (**OUI**). The OUI identifies the manufacturer of the **Network Interface Card** (**NIC**) and the second 24 bits are assigned by the manufacturer. The MAC address is also known as a **burned-in address** (**BIA**) since it is hardcoded onto the hardware and, theoretically, can't be changed.

The following diagram represents a datagram known as the **Frame**. It contains both a **Data Link Header** and a **Trailer**:

| Frame | | | | | |
|---|---|---|---|---|---|
| Preamble | Source MAC Address | Source IP address | Source Port | DATA | File Check Sequence (FCS) |
| | Destination MAC Address | Destination IP address | Destination Port | | |
| | Data Link Header | | | | Trailer |

Figure 1.12 – Frame header

Notice that an additional field inserted called the **Preamble**. The **Preamble** is a 7-byte field used on an Ethernet frame to indicate the start of the frame, its sequencing, and its synchronization. Before the data link layer places a message on the physical layer, it needs to break it up into smaller piece called **bits**. Each bit will contain the addressing headers, trailers, and the preamble, which contains a sequence for each bit.

The following diagram represents a depiction of two computers. **PC A** is sending some messages to **PC B** and since the blocks represent the message, it has been segmented into small bits. These are then sent across the network to the recipient:

Figure 1.13 – Bits moving across the physical layer

When the bits are received on the destination device, the sequence numbers of each bit will help the recipient reassemble the bits into a message.

To check the MAC address of your network adapters on a Microsoft Windows operating system, use the following instructions:

1.  On your Windows computer, use the keyboard combination *Windows Key + R* to open **Run**.

2.  Enter cmd and click **OK**.

3.  The **Windows Command Prompt** window will appear; enter ipconfig /all to display the current settings of all the network adapters on your device.

    The following screenshot shows the output after running the ipconfig /all command:

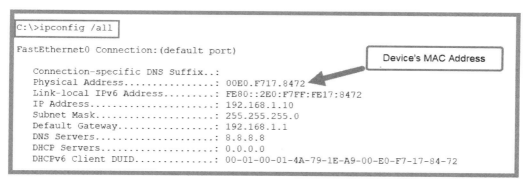

Figure 1.14 – MAC address on a Windows device

On Microsoft Windows, the **Physical Address** is the MAC address of the NIC.

> **Important note**
>
> On some operating systems, the MAC address is shown in XX:XX:XX:XX:XX:XX, XXXX.XXXX.XXXX, or XX-XX-XX-XX-XX-XX format.

Additionally, if you would like to determine the manufacturer of the device, use the following steps:

1.  Open your web browser and go to https://www.wireshark.org/tools/oui-lookup.html. You can enter the search term mac vendor lookup to discover more OUI lookup websites on the internet.

2.  Enter the MAC address of the NIC in the search field and start the search.

The following is the OUI search results:

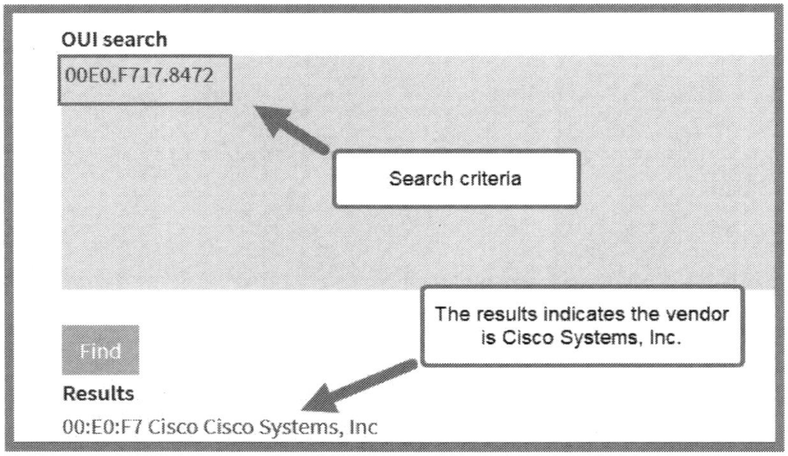

Figure 1.15 – MAC vendor lookup

Now that you know about the data link layer, how to determine the MAC address, and how to perform a vendor lookup, let's take a look at the physical layer.

## Layer 1 – Physical layer

The physical layer (Layer 1) is used to transport the messages that are created by the host device using network media. When messages are placed on the media, they are converted into signals such as electrical, light, and radio frequency, depending on the medium (copper, fiber, or wireless). At this layer, the PDU is known as **bits**.

### Network components

In very network there is some form of media that's used to transport messages (signals) between devices. **Ethernet** is the underlying technology standard that describes how messages (signals) are transmitted over a cable at a defined speed. Ethernet is part of a family of communication standards developed by the **Institute of Electrical and Electronic Engineers (IEEE)**.

> **Important note**
> Specifically, Ethernet is defined by IEEE 802.3.

Furthermore, Ethernet has standards for both copper and fiber optic cabling and supports speeds ranging from 10 **Megabits per second (Mbps)** to 10 **Gigabits per second (Gbps)**. Keep in mind that these speeds may vary based on various variables, such as the length of the cable, the type of cable, and whether the signals are transmitted through copper or fiber.

There are two main types of cabling that are used on an Ethernet network: copper and fiber. In the following sections, we will outline the characteristics of each type and their use cases.

Copper cabling is very cheap and easy to implement in almost all environments. There are two popular types of copper cables: **Unshielded Twisted Pair (UTP)** and **Shielded Twisted Pair (STP)**.

> **Important note**
> STP cables provide protection from **electromagnetic interference (EMI)** compared to the UTP cable. However, due to this added feature, the cost of STP cables is a bit higher because a metal shielding is used during the manufacturing process and this needs to be grounded.

Each of these cables contains a total of eight copper wires, each of which has their own color code, as follows:

- Green
- White and green
- Orange
- White and orange
- Blue
- White and blue
- Brown
- White and brown

With copper, there are a number of cable categories. The following are the characteristics of various cables:

- **Cat 3**: Contains two pairs of twisted wires and supports 10 Mbps at a maximum distance of 100 meters
- **Cat 5**: Contains four pairs of twisted wires and supports up to 100 Mbps at a maximum distance of 100 meters.

- **Cat 5e**: Contains four pairs of twisted wires and supports up to 1,000 Mbps at a maximum distance of 100 meters.

- **Cat 6**: Supports up to 10 Gbps from up to 37 to 55 meters.

- **Cat 6a**: Supports up to 10 Gbps from up to 100 meters.

- **Cat 7**: Supports up to 10 Gbps from up to 100 meters.

Copper cables are all susceptible to **attenuation**. Attenuation is the loss of signal over a great distance. In the field of networking, when a device is sending a signal over the wire, the longer the distance the signal has to travel, the more likely the signal will deteriorate (get weaker) as it's moving along the wire.

Nowadays, ISPs are rolling out fiber-optic cables between their head offices and their customers' locations to provide increased bandwidth and other services. You may be wondering, what is fiber optic? Fiber uses light pulses to exchange messages in the form of bits. These light pluses are generated using **light-emitting diodes** (**LEDs**) rather than electrical signals used in the regular network cables we are accustomed to. Since fiber cables uses light pulses, this creates a major benefit for network and telecommunication professionals.

The core material a fiber cable is made with is either glass or plastic. The plastic core is cheaper to manufacture and therefore the fiber cable itself is cheaper to the customer. Additionally, it is less fragile compared to a cable with a glass core. The glass core allows for higher throughput due to its less dense material. Keep in mind that neither a glass or plastic core can be bent; both cores can be broken easily with very light force.

Fiber has some benefits; for example, much larger throughputs of network traffic can be supported, signals can travel along a fiber cable for many kilometers without experiencing signal loss, it's immune to EMI and RFI, and it allows service providers to transport more services and bandwidth to customers. However, there are a couple of disadvantages. The cost of fiber is a lot higher than the cost of copper cables because of the material composition. Also, the fragile nature of the fiber optic core (glass or plastic) makes the cable susceptible to damage.

Fiber optic cables can operate in two modes: single mode fiber and multi-mode fiber. The following are the characteristics of these two modes:

Single-mode fiber has the following characteristics:

- Small core

- Suited for long distances

- Uses laser as the light source

- Produces a single straight path for light
- Commonly used to interconnect cities

Multi-mode fiber has the following characteristics:

- Has a larger core
- Suited for long distance but shorter than single-mode fiber
- Uses LEDs as the light source
- Commonly used on LANs
- Allows multiple paths for light

With that, we have covered all the layers of the OSI reference model in detail. Now, let's take a look at the TCP/IP protocol with reference to each network layer.

## Understanding the TCP/IP protocol suite

As mentioned in the earlier sections of this chapter, the TCP/IP was developed by the US Department of Defense and has been implemented in all networking devices since its approval. The protocol suite is currently maintained by the **Internet Engineering Task Force (IETF)**.

Unlike the OSI reference model, the new updated TCP/IP protocol suite has five layers. The following diagram displays the five layers, along with their alignment to the OSI model:

| Layer | OSI Model | PDU | TCP/IP Stack | Layer |
|-------|-----------|-----|--------------|-------|
| 7 | Application | Data | Application | 5 |
| 6 | Presentation | | | |
| 5 | Session | | | |
| 4 | Transport | Segment | Transport | 4 |
| 3 | Network | Packet | Internet | 3 |
| 2 | Data Link | Frame | Data Link | 2 |
| 1 | Physical | Bits | Physical | 1 |

Figure 1.16 – OSI model and TCP/IP protocol suite comparison

To compare, the upper layers of the OSI model (application, presentation, and session) are equivalent to the application layer (Layer 4) of the TCP/IP protocol suite. The transport layer of the OSI model remains the same for TCP/IP; however, the data link and physical layers are also equivalent to Layers 1 and 2 of the TCP/IP suite.

Keep in mind that TCP/IP has been implemented in all network-connected devices, ranging from end devices and smartphones to servers and network devices.

# Understanding the functions of network devices

On almost every network, there are a range of different devices that can be found, each with a unique function and purpose. In this section, we will discuss the functions of various network components. At the end, you will understand the roles each network device plays to ensure we have end-to-end connectivity over a network.

In the following subsections, we will discuss the functions and features of a Hub, Switch, Router, Firewall, **Intrusion Prevention System (IPS)**, **Access Point (AP)**, Cisco-based network controllers such as Cisco DNA and **Wireless LAN Controller (WLC)**, and endpoints and servers.

## Hubs

In today's world, you won't really find too many Hubs on enterprise networks. Hubs are a very old type of network intermediary device, used to interconnect computers, servers, printers, and other end devices to create a network. However, Hubs are now obsolete and are no longer recommended to be used in any network.

Let's take a look at how Hubs operate on a small network. Firstly, Hubs are devices used strictly for repeating any incoming signals they may receive on any of their physical interfaces. To get a better understanding of how Hubs forward traffic on a network, take a look at the following diagram:

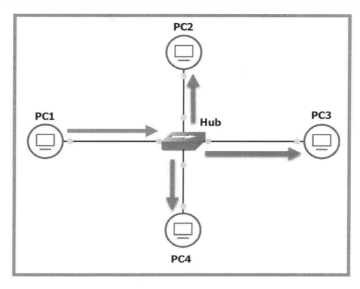

Figure 1.17 – Operations of a Hub

As shown in the preceding diagram, there are four computers connected to a unique physical interface (port) on the hub. In our scenario, **PC1** wants to send a message to **PC4**. **PC1** sends the message to the hub since it's the intermediary network device. The message is sent as an electrical signal along the network and to the hub. When the hub receives the signal, it rebroadcasts it out of all other ports, except the incoming port.

This means the message is also sent to unintended devices on the network, which is both a networking and security concern. First, let's understand the performance issues we can encounter if there are too many hubs as part of the network infrastructure. Any signal a hub receives is simply rebroadcasted out its other physical interfaces. Let's imagine there are multiple hubs being used on a single LAN for a building, where each hub is used to extend the physical network in order to interconnect all devices, such as network printers, desktop computers, and servers. Each time a device sends a message (signal) in a Hub's interface, it rebroadcasts it out of all the ports. This same signal will propagate to all the other interconnected hubs and do the same in the same manner, thus causing unnecessary broadcast (noise) traffic, which, in turn, will create network congestions. Think of it as a roadway being filled with too many vehicles, resulting in heavy traffic.

The following diagram shows the replication of the broadcast traffic through a small network:

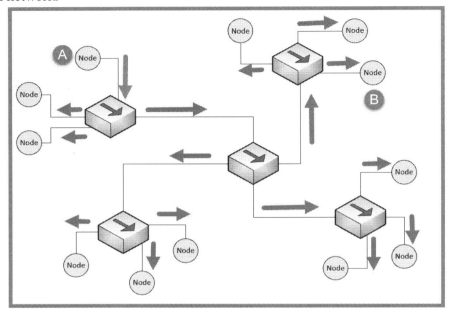

Figure 1.18 – Broadcast messages created by a Hub

Here, we can see that **Node A** sends a message to **Node B** but that the signal is being rebroadcast throughout the entire network.

What if you have two or more devices (nodes) transmitting messages at the same time over a Hub-based network? The result is the same as two vehicles colliding; in a network, this is known as packets colliding, which results in packets being corrupted. This means to ensure there is almost no collision, only one device should send their message at a time on the network. This creates a challenge because all the end devices on the network will be fighting to use the medium, thus creating a **contention-based** network.

To overcome such challenges, **Carrier-Sense Multiple Access with Collision Detection (CSMA/CD)** is used to help end devices such as computers to determine whether the media is clear (available) to transmit data (send a signal). Let's use a real-world analogy to explain how CSMA/CD works on a network. Imagine that, one day, you are shopping in the city and you want to visit various shops and stores. There are roadways separating them. Imagine the roadway is the media (wire) and you have to cross the road to reach the other store. Before crossing the road, you look both ways (left and right) a few times to ensure there are no vehicles (signals) passing and that it's safe to cross the street. Therefore, you are checking the media to ensure no vehicles (signals) are passing. When the media is clear, you proceed to walk across to the other side (transmit).

CSMA/CD ensures a device checks the media for a signal. If a signal is found on the media, the device waits and tries again at a later time. If the media is free, the device proceeds to transmit its message across the network.

However, network switches overcome this issue and devices do not have to check the media before transmitting their messages. In the next section, we will learn about the characteristics of switches.

## Layer 2 switches

Switches are considered to be smart devices compared to hubs. Switches are devices that network professionals use to interconnect end devices (PCs, printers, servers, and so on) and extend the network infrastructure, typically extending a LAN within a building. As you may recall, in a hub, any incoming signal is rebroadcasted out all other ports. However, with a network switch, this is no longer the operational state. With a switch, when a device wants to send a message to another device, the switch directly forwards the message to the intended recipient.

The following diagram shows a small LAN where **PC1** is transmitting a message to **PC4** and the switch forwards the message only to **PC4**:

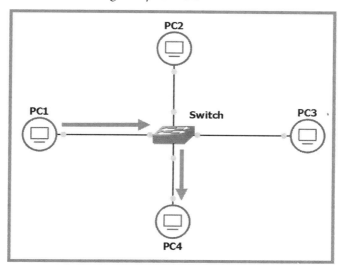

Figure 1.19 – Functions of a switch

You may be wondering, how is this possible? How does a switch defer from a hub? How does the switch determine which interface (port) the recipient is connected to? To put it simply, switches operate at the data link layer (Layer 2) of the OSI reference model. As you may recall, at the data link layer, the MAC addresses are inserted into the Layer 2 encapsulation header of the frame.

Switches are able to read the Layer 2 header information found in frames and create a table to temporarily store the MAC addresses it learned about on its interfaces. This table is known as the **Content Addressable Memory (CAM)** table in Cisco switches. Whenever a frame enters a switch's interface, the source MAC address of the frame is stored in the CAM table and is associated with the incoming interface.

To further understand how a switch populates the CAM table, let's imagine we have three PCs, all connected to a network switch to create a small LAN, as shown in the following diagram:

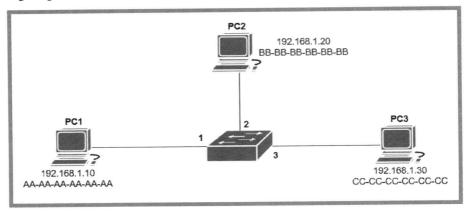

Figure 1.20 – Devices interconnected using a switch

Whenever a switch boots up, the CAM table is empty because its content is stored in **Random Access Memory (RAM)**. Therefore, the content is lost whenever the device is powered off or rebooted. To begin, the CAM table is currently empty until end devices begin to exchange messages on the network.

Let's assume **PC1** wants to send a message to **PC3**. Typically, we think both devices would use the IP addresses of each other to communicate on a local network, but this is not the case when it comes to working with network switches. Switches are only able to read the Layer 2 header of a frame, which contains source and destination MAC addresses, not IP addresses. There is no way for a network switch to read an IP header unless it's a Layer 3 switch; we will discuss Layer 3 switches in the next section.

**PC1** knows the IP address of **PC3** but not its MAC address. Therefore, **PC1** sends an **Address Resolution Protocol (ARP)** request message on the network, requesting the IP address 192.168.1.30.

**Important note**

**ARP** is used to resolve IP addresses to MAC addresses on a network. Remember, for communication that happens on a local network, messages are exchanged via switches. This means each device uses MAC addresses to communicate with other devices on the same network.

The following diagram shows an ARP Request being sent through a network:

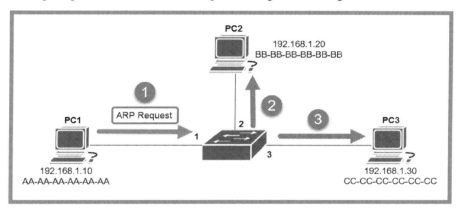

Figure 1.21 – ARP Request message

Each device on the LAN will receive the **ARP Request** message via a broadcast (all devices on the LAN receive the same message). At this point, the switch receives the ARP Request message on **Interface 1** and populates the source MAC address on the CAM table, as shown here:

| Interface | MAC Address |
|-----------|-------------|
| 1 | AA-AA-AA-AA-AA-AA |
| 2 | |
| 3 | |

Figure 1.22 – CAM table

Only the device who has the IP address of 192.168.1.30 will respond with an **ARP Reply**, as shown here:

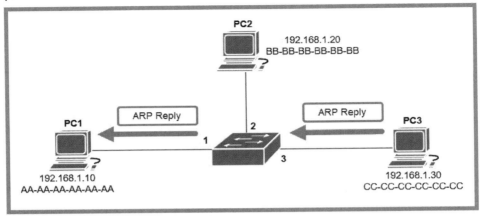

Figure 1.23 – ARP Reply

The **ARP Reply** message is a unicast transmission (device to device) and is sent directly to **PC1**. Keep in mind that the switch reads the frame header and populates the source MAC address into its CAM table, as shown here:

| Interface | MAC Address |
|---|---|
| 1 | AA-AA-AA-AA-AA-AA |
| 2 | |
| 3 | CC-CC-CC-CC-CC-CC |

Figure 1.24 – CAM table

Additionally, the end devices also have their own ARP cache that temporarily records IP-to-MAC binding information. If there are no messages being exchanged between a MAC address for a predefined time interval, the operating system removes them from its ARP cache. On Cisco devices, the CAM table maintains a default inactivity timer of 300 seconds (5 minutes); this value can be modified.

> **Important note**
> To view the contents of the CAM table on a Cisco IOS switch, use the show mac address-table command.

To view the ARP cache on a Microsoft Windows operating system, follow these steps:

1.  Open the Command Prompt.

2.  Use the `arp -a` command and press *Enter*.

    The following snippet shows the ARP cache's contents on a Windows host computer on my network:

```
C:\>arp -a

Interface: 10.10.10.100 --- 0xc
  Internet Address      Physical Address      Type
  10.10.10.10           00-0c-29-7e-37-58     dynamic
  10.10.10.255          ff-ff-ff-ff-ff-ff     static
  224.0.0.22            01-00-5e-00-00-16     static
  224.0.0.252           01-00-5e-00-00-fc     static
  239.255.255.250       01-00-5e-7f-ff-fa     static
```

Figure 1.25 – ARP cache on a Windows machine

To view the ARP cache on a Linux operation system, use the following steps:

1.  Open the Terminal.

2.  Use the `arp` command and press *Enter*.

The following snippet shows the ARP cache's contents on a Linux (Debian) host computer on my network:

```
root@kali:~# arp
Address                 HWtype  HWaddress           Flags Mask        Iface
10.10.10.100            ether   00:0c:29:a0:b0:6a   C                 eth0
_gateway                ether   00:0c:29:2b:29:7f   C                 eth0
root@kali:~#
```

Figure 1.26 – ARP cache on a Linux machine

In both snippets, we can see that the ARP cache contains both IP-to-MAC address bindings of the other devices that exchanged messages.

Now that we have an understanding of how Layer 2 switches function, let's take a look at Layer 3 switches.

## Layer 3 switches

Layer 3 switches have all the same functionalities as the Layer 2 switches. However, these devices come with an additional feature. They can read the information within an IP packet header, as well as the source and destination IP addresses. This enables the Layer 3 switch to interconnect two or more networks together and allows basic routing of IP packets between networks.

Keep in mind that Layer 3 switches do not have all the features of a Cisco router. In the next section, you will learn about the features and characteristics of a Cisco router.

## Routers

A router is a device that is used to interconnect two or more different IP networks. These devices observe the destination IP address within the header of an IP packet, then check its local **routing table** for an available path to the destination's network when making its decision to forward the packet to the recipient.

Since routers can read and understand IP. They are considered to be Layer 3 devices due to their capabilities of reading IP information from packets. Without routers, end devices would not be able to communicate with devices residing on another IP network. The following diagram shows two IP networks, 192.168.1.0/24 and 172.16.1.0/16. Devices on the 192.168.1.0/24 network will only be able to intercommunicate between themselves; the same goes for the devices on the 172.16.1.0/24 network:

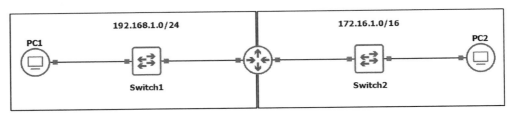

Figure 1.27 – Router interconnecting different networks

To allow both networks to exchange messages, a Layer 3 device such as a router is required. The router is used to interconnect these two different networks together. Additionally, the router acts at the default gateway for each of the networks. This means that if **PC1** wants to send a message to **PC2**, the message must be sent to *the doorway that leads to another network*. This is the router in this scenario.

As a real-world example, your network at home is a private network and uses technologies a bit differently than those that are used on the ISP network and the internet. The following diagram shows a home network that is connected to the internet:

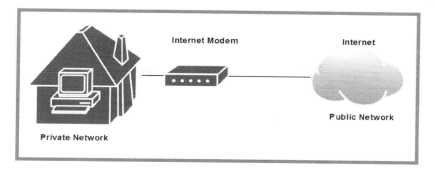

Figure 1.28 – Internet connection to a house

The private network uses a very different address space than what is used on the internet (public network). To allow communication between these networks, the ISP provides you with a modem, which has the capabilities of a router. This allows the ISP network to interconnect to your home (private) network. Lastly, the modem in this scenario acts as the default gateway for all your devices, providing a path to the internet.

Now that you have learned about the fundamentals of routers, let's cover the importance of implementing a firewall on an enterprise network.

# Next-generation firewalls and IPS

A firewall is a network security appliance that is designed to filter malicious traffic, both inbound (entering a network) and outbound (leaving a network). Firewalls have an important role to play in networks of different sizes. These appliances typically sit at the network perimeter of an enterprise network, carefully inspecting all incoming and outgoing traffic, looking for any security threats and blocking them.

To get a better understanding of the benefits of using a firewall, let's use a simple analogy. A vehicle such as a car has a physical component called a firewall, which is the place between the cabin and the engine. The purpose of this component is important in the event of the engine of the car catching fire; the firewall will prevent most (if not all) the fire or heat from entering the cabin where the passengers are seated. Another analogy is a castle being surrounded by a moat and a single drawbridge that provides people with a single entry and exit point. In the event an opposing side wants to invade the castle, the drawbridge can be raised, and the moat will prevent the enemy from entering.

It is highly recommended to implement a firewall on your network. The internet contains millions of useful resources, from training videos to cooking recipes. However, there are many threats, such as malware and hackers, that roam the internet and attempt to infect and compromise systems. The firewall will act as the first line of defense against these threats.

The following diagram shows the typical deployment of a firewall on a network:

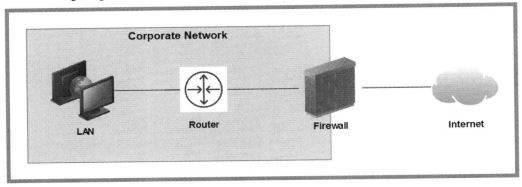

Figure 1.29 – Perimeter firewall deployment

**Next-generation firewalls (NGFW)** are designed to be superior in many ways, such as protecting the network and users from advanced threats, providing **Deep Packet Inspection (DPI)**, preventing ransomware from entering the network, and having **Virtual Private Network (VPN)** features.

A firewall, by default, will allow traffic originating from the internal private network to go to all other networks, such as the internet. However, any traffic that is initiated from the internet to the internal corporate network is blocked by default. The firewall uses the concept of a *security zone* to help determine the level of trust it has for a logical network. When deploying a firewall, the security engineer must configure the interfaces of the firewall as a security zone with a trust level.

The following diagram shows the default security level for a Cisco **Adaptive Security Appliance (ASA)** firewall:

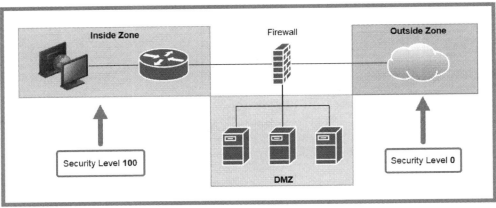

Figure 1.30 – Security zones of a firewall

The Inside Zone is usually your private, internal network, which is supposed to be a fully trusted and safe environment for all devices in the corporate network. This *zone* will normally hold a security level of 100 to indicate it's a fully trusted security zone. The firewall will allow all traffic originating from the Inside Zone with a security level of 100 to all other zones that have lower security levels. The internet as we know it is the most unsafe network in existence, being filled with extremely malicious malware and hackers, so the internet is usually assigned a security level of 0 as a Zero Trust zone. Any traffic that has been initialized from the internet to the Inside Zone will be blocked by default on the firewall. However, keep in mind that if a user on the Inside Zone has initialized a connection to the Outside Zone, the firewall will allow it by default, and if there is any returning traffic, the firewall will allow it as well. For example, as you open a web browser to visit www.google.com, the firewall will allow the **HTTP GET** message to the web server, and then the web server will send a response back the user's computer. In this case, the firewall will only allow the returning traffic.

> **Important note**
> Please note that the security-level schemes mentioned in this book are based on the Cisco technologies.

The **Demilitarized Zone (DMZ)** is a semi-trusted zone that's attached to the firewall on the corporate network. This zone is created to place servers that are accessible from the internet and the Inside Zone. The following are some guidelines for creating a DMZ on your network:

- The traffic initiating from the DMZ should not be allowed to access the Inside Zone.

- Rules should be created on the firewall to allow specific traffic to flow to the servers within the DMZ only. If there is a web server, then incoming HTTP and HTTPS traffic should be sent only to the web server.

- Ensure traffic initiating from the Inside Zone can access the DMZ.

Lastly, the security level of the DMZ should be between the value of the Inside and Outside Zones. However, within an organization, there many multiple trusted zones that have a security level closer to 100. There may be additional trusted zones, so the DMZ should have a security level of 50.

## Intrusion Prevention Systems

An **Intrusion Prevention System** (**IPS**) is a component that is used to **detect and block** malicious traffic. In a traditional deployment, the IPS appliance usually sits in line of all incoming traffic and behind the firewall on the network. This type of deployment ensures the IPS can inspect all traffic as it passes through the appliance.

The following diagram shows the traditional IPS deployment model on a network:

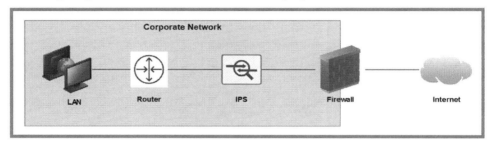

Figure 1.31 – Traditional IPS deployment

Traditional IPS appliances are deployed behind the firewall within the corporate network. Their purpose is to inspect any traffic and catch both suspicious and malicious traffic the firewall may have missed. Years ago, the IPS appliance was a separate physical device. However, with the advancement of technologies and innovation, Cisco has integrated the IPS into their next-generation firewall appliances as a module. The benefits of this are a less physical appliance and a firewall interface that provides a single management dashboard for both the Cisco IPS and firewall all-in-one appliance. This allows a firewall administrator to enable the IPS feature with the use of a license key provided by Cisco systems.

**Next-generation IPS** (**NGIPS**) inspects and filters traffic a bit differently to a firewall. The IPS downloads a database of malware signatures from TALOS, Cisco's Security Intelligence and Research Group. It uses this information to closely inspect all traffic flowing through it to identify any malicious traffic. Additionally, the IPS can be manually configured with predefined rules created by a security engineer. It can also automatically learn the behavior of the network to catch abnormal traffic types. The awesome benefit of having an IPS on a network is that if it detects any malicious traffic, it can stop it in real-time, preventing the attack.

> **Tip**
> If you're interested in building your own IPS device, check out **Snort** at www.snort.org. Snort is an open source intrusion prevention system application.

On the other hand, IDSes are considered to be reactive devices compared to IPSes. An IDS is configured to receive a copy of the network traffic, detect security threats, and send alerts. IDSes are not implemented in-line with network traffic, so they do not have the capability to stop an attack as it happens on a network. Furthermore, the IDS only sends an alert after an attack has happened, which makes it reactive in nature.

Now that we have learned about the functions of firewalls and IPSes, let's take a look at a device that allows us to extend a wired network into a wireless one.

## Access Points

An **Access Point (AP)** is a device that allows you to extend a wired network into a wireless frequency, allowing wireless-compatible devices to connect and access the resources on the wired network.

This provides many benefits, such as the following:

- Increases the mobility of users and roaming within a compound
- Reduces the need for physical cabling
- Increases ease access to a network

Wireless APs use a wireless radio frequency, which is broadcast from the AP using the 2.4 GHz and/or 5 GHz channels. This allows mobile devices with a compatible wireless NIC to listen on these frequencies and connect to an AP. Most commonly, the 2.4 GHz APs are found almost on every wireless network due to the fact it was the first type of AP produced and a lot of organizations and home users invested in the technology.

> **Important note**
> The 2.4 GHz channel provides a lower frequency and gives a greater distance.

As there are so many building and homes equipped with a 2.4 GHz AP, the radio airways of 2.4 GHz are now a very saturated space, where each device is trying to transmit their data to clients without causing interference. This has become almost impossible now. The 2.4 GHz band uses a total of 11 channels; however, it is recommended to use channels 1, 6, and 11 to ensure there is no overlapping.

The following diagram shows the recommended clean channels of the 2.4 GHz channels:

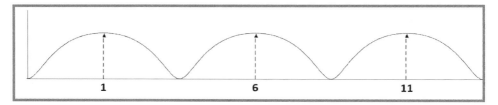

Figure 1.32 – Wireless channels range

However, even this recommendation is no longer beneficial. An AP can be using channel 2, 4, or even 8, which will create an overlap (interference) between the recommend channels (1, 6, and 11).

The 5 GHz frequency provides a lot more channels, thus creating less interference among nearby Access Points that are operating on the 5 GHz frequency. The downside of using 5 GHz is the short distance the signal can travel. However, this may be a benefit. Let's imagine that a company with multiple floors in their building are deploying the 5 GHz frequency Access Points; because the 5 GHz frequency travels much shorter distances, this means the possibility for one AP's signal to interfere (overlap) with another AP who is using the same frequency has been reduced.

> **Important note**
> In later chapters of this book, we will discuss wireless architectures in more depth.

Having covered the purpose of using Access Points, let's take our discussion a bit further and describe how to improve the management of our corporate wireless network.

# Cisco Wireless LAN Controller (WLC)

**Wireless LAN (WLAN)** is simply defined as a wireless network containing either a single Access Point at home for personal use or an organization containing multiple Access Points to provide wireless connectivity between employees' mobile devices (smartphones, tablets, and laptops) and the wired network infrastructure. With the increase of wireless networking, a lot of companies are implementing a **Bring-Your-Own-Device (BYOD)** policy to ensure an acceptable level of security is established and maintained. However, for network engineers, this means the wireless network needs to be able to support the large number of portable devices that are connecting and exchanging messages on the WLAN.

This will result in network professionals having to implement a robust wireless network with multiple **APs** throughout the organization, on each floor and room where a wireless signal is needed or required. Let's imagine that our fictional company, ACME Corp, own a 10-storey building and that the network administrators have to implement Access Points. One key aspect is to maintain the consistency of each AP's firmware, configurations, and security settings. Imagine that, after the deployment of the wireless network, the network administrator has to make a change on the WLAN that will affect all Access Points. It's definitely not efficient to log into each Access Point and manually make the changes in the device's configuration as this is time-consuming and prone to human error.

A WLC allows a single management interface for the entire wireless network. This device enables you to control any number of **APs** on a network. Therefore, you can simply log into a WLC and configure the entire WLAN, providing a centralized management platform for network professionals. In later chapters, we will cover various deployment models for Access Points and wireless LAN controllers in more detail.

## Endpoints and servers

So far, we have been talking about intermediary devices that connect us to a network and the internet. However, we must not forget about the simple yet cool devices that allow us to communicate on a network and provide resources to others: endpoints and servers.

Servers are devices that run specialized applications that enable them to provide resources to users on a network. To get a better idea of the functionality of a server, let's imagine you work for a small business with approximately 30 employees, all residing in a single building. Each employee has their own company-issued laptop or desktop computer fitted with all the relevant software applications for each person to complete their duties efficiently. Each day, employees may be creating new documents and files that have to be shared with others in the organization; however, emailing each file to a user or group may not always be the best way to efficiently collaborate on a project.

In this case, a centralized file server can be set up within the company's network to allow various persons or all employees to centrally store their work-related files on the file server, rather than storing them locally on their computers (endpoints). In this scenario, the server is hosting files for the organization or the client (endpoint) devices to access.

Keep in mind that client devices (endpoints) are usually devices that are connected to a network to access a resource. These might be laptops, smartphones, tablet computers, desktop computers, and so on.

## Cisco DNA

The **Cisco Digital Network Architecture** (**DNA**) is an IP-based software solution designed by Cisco Systems to provide engineers with applications they can use to manage, automate, and gather intelligence analytics, as well as monitor security, on a Cisco network across multiple devices and platforms.

# Network topology architectures

One of the tasks you may have to perform as a network engineer is to design an optimal network for a customer. How do we get started with planning and designing a network? To get started with such a task, you need to determine some important key details about the customer's needs. The following are some key guidelines to help you plan your network:

- Meet with the customer to determine their needs and expectations.

- Understand the budget the customer has planned for the solution.

- Ensure your team has the right skillset and certified professionals to work on the project.

- Determine the type and quantity of the networking devices required for the implementation.

> **Important note**
> Please note that these are just a few typical questions; your planning phase should not be limited to the points mentioned here.

The first point is very important. As a professional in the field, you do not want to assume anything about the customer's needs. Ensure you have a proper discussion and take note of exactly what the customer needs and their expectations. If you think the service or solution should be added on to what the customer needs, suggest it to the customer, providing its pros and cons, and gather their feedback.

Ensure you understand the budget for the project before choosing the type or quantity of network equipment to purchase. To determine the right device(s) to purchase, use the following steps as a guide:

1. Go to Cisco's website at www.cisco.com.

2. Navigate to **Products | Networking**. Here, you will see subcategories such as **Switches**, **Wireless**, **Routers**, and so on.

3. Select **Switches**. Under **Products**, you will see that Cisco has made it simple for us to determine the type of network switch based on its purpose on a network. You'll see that there are network switches for **LAN Access**, **Distribution and Core switches**, **Data Center**, and even **Small-business** switches.

4. Click on **Catalyst 1000 Series**. When the new page loads up, click on **Models**. Here, you will see an overall description of each model belonging to the Catalyst 1000 line of products. However, your research does not stop here.

5. Scroll down until you see the **Resource** section. You will see the **Data Sheet** for the models; click on it. The Data Sheet provides the exact specifications for a variety of devices within the product family. It provides the type and number of physical interfaces, unlink capacity, bandwidth capacity, and the physical dimensions and weight of the device.

Using the same concept, other devices such as wireless, routers, and firewalls will be very useful as you determine the right model of device(s) needed for the deployment of a project.

You may be wondering, what about the actual network design? Do we design all networks from the ground up? What makes our network design optimal? To answer all these questions, the experts at Cisco Systems have created a Design Zone containing tons of Design Guides. These are known as **Cisco Validated Design** (**CVD**) guides.

> **Important note**
> Cisco Validated Design can be found at `https://www.cisco.com/c/en/us/solutions/design-zone.html`.

Keep in mind that there is a **CVD** for almost every type of network and deployment for various type of industries. These design guides will provide you with guidance, recommended devices, design models, and full descriptions of their solutions. Such design guides eliminate the need to *reinvent the wheel* when there are experts who have already created both approved and accredited designs.

Cisco has created both a 2 Tier and 3 Tier network architecture, which is recommended for enterprise networks. In the following sections, we will discuss each of these architectures in greater detail.

# 2 Tier

When designing a LAN for a building or an organization that has multiple buildings near each other, we are indeed designing a campus LAN. Within a campus LAN, there are multiple network switches that are all interconnected. Sometimes, in the industry, you may see network switches interconnected in a fashion of chaining one switch to another. This is referred to as *daisy chain* or *daisy chaining*.

The following diagram shows multiple switches in a daisy chain model:

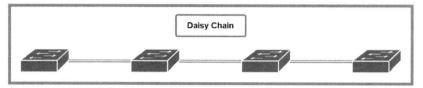

Figure 1.33 – Daisy chaining

For IT professionals, this may be a workable approach to extend their local area networks within a building. However, a major disadvantage to using such a design is that there is no redundancy in the event a cable or device fails. A fault cable or switch within the daisy chain can cause a disruption in network operations, which will affect all the devices that are connected to the faulty segment. Hence, such practices are not recommended when designing a campus LAN.

When designing a network, ensure it is **hierarchical** when creating various tiers to help you understand the roles of each device in the network. Ensure that the design is **modular** and improves the network's scalability, allowing you to expand the network and its services easily. Consider implementing **resiliency** and **flexibility** to ensure the user has a great experience while they execute their daily tasks in the organization. In other words, you don't want your users to experience a network failure that will disrupt daily transactions. Lastly, flexibility will ensure traffic is distributed between paths and devices efficiently.

> **Important note**
> In *Section 5, Security Fundamentals*, we will cover various security topics and techniques we can use to improve the security posture of a Cisco network.

This is where the Cisco 2 Tier architecture comes in to save the day when designing a LAN for a building – a campus LAN. This design creates two layers of switches: the distribution layer and the access layer.

The access layer provides a means of connecting end devices (computers, servers, printers, and so on) to the network. At the access layer, there is no form of redundancy between the end device and the access layer switch; this is due to most end devices usually having only a single NIC for LAN connectivity. However, each access layer switch is connected to two or more distribution layer switches, thus providing redundancy to the remainder of the network.

> **Tip**
>
> To see the Cisco Access layer switches, please visit the following URL:
> `https://www.cisco.com/c/en/us/products/switches/`
> `campus-lan-switches-access/index.html`.

The following diagram shows the Cisco 2 Tier architecture within a building (campus LAN):

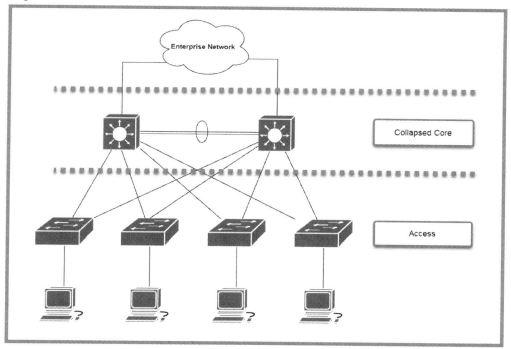

Figure 1.34 – Cisco 2 Tier architecture

In a Cisco 2 Tier architecture, the distribution layer is known as the **Collapsed Core**. The distribution layer is responsible for the following roles and functions on a campus LAN:

- Providing **Quality of Service (QoS)** to prioritize network traffic

- **Access Control Lists (ACLs)** to filter network traffic

- Basic routing functions

The distribution layer also provides redundancy for interconnecting multiple access layer switches to expand the campus LAN.

> **Tip**
> To find out more about the Cisco distribution layer switch, please visit the following URL: `https://www.cisco.com/c/en/us/products/switches/campus-lan-switches-core-distribution/index.html`.

Keep in mind that the Cisco 2 Tier architecture is typically used within a building. This brings about the question, how do we interconnect multiple buildings that each have a Cisco 2 Tier architecture? One method is to simply interconnect the distribution switches of one building with another.

The following diagram shows multiple branches interconnected using the 2 Tier model:

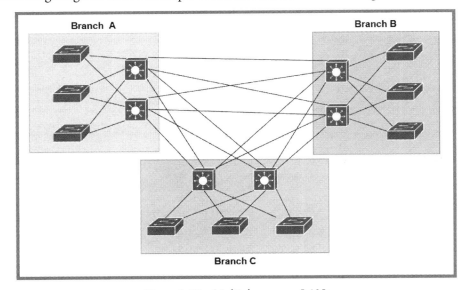

Figure 1.35 – Multiple campus LANs

As you may have noticed, each distribution layer switch is connected to each other distribution layer switch in each of the campus LANs. As the network grows and more branch offices (campus LANs) are created, there will be too many inter-branch connections and the design will not be efficient.

To solve this issue, Cisco have designed a 3 Tier hierarchical model.

## 3 Tier

In the Cisco 3 Tier architecture, there are three layers. There is now a core layer. The core layer is defined as the high-speed backbone of the network. These core layer switches are used to forward traffic as quickly as possible between networks, which are geographically separated. To put this simply, the core layer switches are used to interconnect each campus LAN to the others in a more efficient way.

The following diagram shows a simplified version the Cisco 3 Tier model:

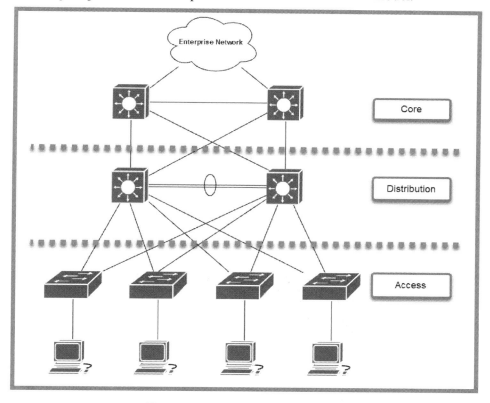

Figure 1.36 – Cisco 3 Tier architecture

The core layer plays a vital role in an enterprise network. To get a better idea of how the connections are made in a real-world scenario, let's take a look at the following diagram:

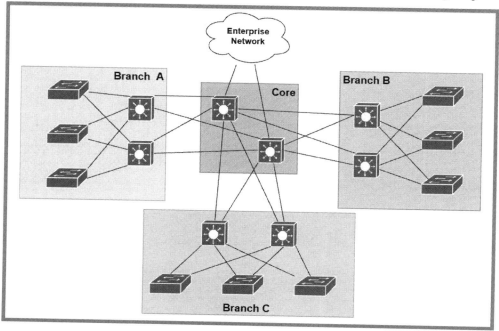

Figure 1.37 – Cisco 3 Tier architecture interconnecting multiple branches

As you can see, there are three campus LANs (branches). Each campus LAN has its own access layer switches that allows end devices to access the network. There is the distribution layer, which provides redundancy to the access layer, via multiple paths to each end device.

> **Important note**
> In the 2 Tier architecture, the collapsed core plays the role of both the distribution and core layers as one.

The core layer ensures each campus LAN (branch) is interconnected. If a branch has to send network traffic to another branch office, the traffic goes up to the distribution layer and then to the core layer for forwarding. Additionally, the core layer connects to the routers of the enterprise network. These routers provide internet and WAN connectivity.

The Cisco 3 Tier hierarchy has the following benefits:

- Improves network performance
- Improves the scalability of the network
- Creates better redundancy between paths
- Improves network management

The following is a summary of the functions and characteristics of each layer of the Cisco 3 Tier model:

- The core layer is the high-speed backbone of the network. These switches are used to forward traffic as quickly as possible between networks, which are geographically separated.
- The distribution layer is responsible for providing a boundary by implementing access control lists and other types of application filters and policies. The distribution layer is made up of Layer 3 switches.
- The access layer is used to interconnect end devices such as computers, printers, and servers.

Having completed this section, you are now able to identify the functions and purposes of each layer of both the Cisco 2 Tier (collapsed core) and 3 Tier architectures.

# Summary

In this chapter, we learned about the evolution of networking and how the internet came into existence. Then, we learned about two important protocol models: the OSI reference model and the TCP/IP protocol suite. However, only TCP/IP is implemented on devices, which allows messages to be exchanged across a network. Furthermore, we looked at the roles and functions of various networking components and how they forward messages between devices. Lastly, we covered the essentials of the Cisco 2 Tier and 3 Tier architectures in detail to help you understand how to design a campus LAN for an organization.

I hope this chapter has been informative for you and that it will be helpful in your journey toward learning how to implement and administrate Cisco solutions and preparing for the CCNA 200-301 certification. In the next chapter, *Getting Started with Cisco IOS Devices*, we will learn how to access and configure Cisco IOS devices while building a small network.

# Questions

Here's a short list of review questions to help reinforce your learning and help you identify gaps in your knowledge:

1. Which layer of the OSI reference model is responsible for encapsulating the physical address of a device?

    A. Internet

    B. Data link

    C. Network

    D. Link

2. An employee uses Microsoft Outlook on their client PC to send and receive emails to/from others. Which is the highest layer of the OSI model?

    A. Presentation

    B. Internet

    C. Session

    D. Application

3. The physical address of a device is made up of how many bits?

    A. 32

    B. 42

    C. 48

    D. 52

4. Which layer of the TCP/IP protocol suite is responsible for computing the checksum (hash) and determining whether a frame is damaged?

    A. Network access

    B. Data link

    C. Physical

    D. LLC

5. In which layer of the TCP/IP protocol suite does routing occur?

   A. Network

   B. Internet

   C. Router

   D. Data link

6. What does a Cisco switch use to make the decision to forward a message across a network?

   A. Destination IP address

   B. Destination MAC address

   C. Source MAC address

   D. Source IP address

7. Which network protocol is used to resolve the MAC address to the IP address of a host on the same local area network?

   A. ARP

   B. HTTP

   C. TCP

   D. UDP

8. Which device is used to extend a network to another room or floor of a building?

   A. Router

   B. Firewall

   C. Switch

   D. Hub

9. Where does a Cisco switch store MAC addresses?

   A. RAM

   B. HDD

   C. ROM

   D. CAM

10. Which layer of the Cisco Campus LAN architecture is responsible for interconnecting different branch offices?

    A. Router

    B. Core

    C. Distribution

    D. Access

    E. All of the above

# Further reading

The following links are recommended for additional reading:

- TCP/IP overview: `https://www.cisco.com/E-Learning/bulk/public/tac/cim/cib/using_cisco_ios_software/linked/tcpip.htm`

- Cisco 3 Tier architecture: `https://www.cisco.com/c/en/us/td/docs/solutions/Enterprise/Campus/campover.html`

- Understanding network port numbers: `https://hub.packtpub.com/understanding-network-port-numbers-tcp-udp-and-icmp-on-an-operating-system/`

# 2
# Getting Started with Cisco IOS Devices

You must be thrilled to start your journey of learning about Cisco technologies, especially learning how to implement and administer Cisco solutions in an enterprise organization. One of the key components to ensure your success is gaining a lot of hands-on experience with technologies. This hands-on experience will help you grasp the concepts we'll be talking about easily, while demonstrating the effect of configurations during the implementation phases. However, a major challenge for most beginners is getting hands-on experience during their learning and examination preparation phases. Another concern is getting access to Cisco equipment after classroom training hours or even when a training session has ended.

To solve these challenges, I am dedicating this chapter to demonstrate how to build a Cisco lab environment to get the hands-on experience you need, at your convenience.

In this chapter, we will cover the following topics:

- Building a Cisco lab environment
- Getting started with Cisco IOS devices
- Accessing a Cisco IOS device
- Configuring the Cisco IOS
- Performing troubleshooting procedures

# Technical requirements

To follow along with the exercises in this chapter, please ensure that you have met the following hardware and software requirements:

**Core**:

- A computer
- PuTTY

**Virtual lab environment**:

- Cisco Packet Tracer 7.3.0
- GNS3 2.2.5
- GNS3 VM server 2.2.5
- VirtualBox 6.1
- VMware Workstation 15 Pro (optional)
- Cisco IOSv
- Cisco IOSvL2
- Cisco CSR1000v (optional)

**Physical lab environment**:

- Cisco 2911 routers
- Cisco 2960 switches
- 1 x Cisco 3560 switch or Cisco 3650 switch
- 1 x Cisco console cable
- 1 x RS-232 to USB converter cable
- A few network patch cables (straight-through and crossover)

The code files for this chapter are available here: `https://github.com/PacktPublishing/Implementing-and-Administering-Cisco-Solutions/tree/master/Chapter%2002`.

Check out the following video to see the Code in Action: `https://bit.ly/36OOdeo`

# Building a Cisco lab environment

It's very important to get a lot of hands-on practice when pursuing a technical Cisco certification. You can do this by *labbing up* everything, whereby you practice by putting everything you've learned for the certification in practice labs along the way.

In the following sections, you will learn about the various methods of building a Cisco environment using both virtual and physical equipment.

## Cisco Packet Tracer

You may be wondering, what is **Cisco Packet Tracer**? Years ago, Cisco Systems created their own online learning platform using a variety of e-learning and collaboration tools for some of their certification programs. In doing so, they also created a very lightweight network simulator tool that allows users to build, design, and troubleshoot a Cisco enterprise network. Its purpose is to allow students to sharpen their skillset while learning and preparing for the CCNA certification.

Just a few years ago, the Cisco Networking Academy released Cisco Packet Tracer to the internet, allowing everyone to officially download and install the application on their personal computers. However, now, you must enroll in the Cisco Networking Academy's *Intro to Packet Tracer* online course.

> Tip
> The *Intro to Packet Tracer* course is designed to teach you all about the functionality and operations of the application as a learner. Enrolling is beneficial as the course will show you how to simulate real-world networking environments using Cisco solutions.

Is it better than other network simulators? Cisco has designed Cisco Packet Tracer as a lightweight network simulation application that allows learners to sharpen their skillset at the CCNA level. The simulator is not perfect compared to a physical Cisco IOS switch or router, but it provides the environment you need to configure and troubleshoot networks within its interface, allowing you to save money on purchasing physical equipment.

Why use Cisco Packet Tracer rather than physical equipment? While it's, of course, preferable to use physical equipment, we must remember that physical devices cost money and not everyone has a budget to support this cost. You can definitely get used and refurbished Cisco devices from various online retailers, but when purchasing such equipment, keep in mind that you will not able to update the **Internetwork Operating System (IOS)** on those devices in future without having a service contract or valid licensing details from Cisco Systems. Cisco IOS 15 has many newer features compared to Cisco IOS 12 and prior. Therefore, Cisco Packet Tracer is the most efficient method in gaining hands-on experience, allowing you to put almost everything at the CCNA level into labs.

If you are concerned with whether the configurations used within the devices in Cisco Packet Tracer may be different from those used on the physical equipment, don't worry – the configurations are exactly the same.

One of the cool things I like about Cisco Packet Tracer is its ability to build a network and copy device configurations from the application, and then simply paste them onto the command-line of a physical Cisco IOS device that's the same model. The physical device will accept the configurations seamlessly.

To get your hands on the Cisco Packet Tracer application, use the following instructions:

1.  Go to www.netacad.com.

2.  Click on **Courses** to expand the drop-down menu. Then, select **Packet Tracer**.

3.  Scroll down until you see the online, self-paced course called **Intro to Packet Tracer**. Click on it.

4.  Click on **Sign up today!**.

    A new enrollment page will open. Be sure to complete the required fields to register for the course.

5.  Once you have enrolled, log into www.netacad.com using your newly created username and password.

6.  Click on **Resources** to expand the drop-down menu. Then, click on **Download Packet Tracer**, as shown in the following diagram:

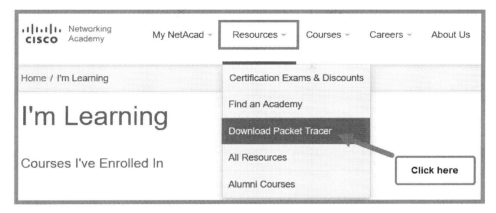

Figure 2.1 – Drop-down menu of the Resource page

7.  Next, the **Cisco Packet Tracer** download page will open. Download the version specific to your operating system and install it using all the default settings.

Now that you have Cisco Packet Tracer installed on your computer, go through the **Intro to Packet Tracer** online course as it contains a lot of help tutorials, tips, and tricks so that you can get the most out of the application as a learner.

To get started quickly with Cisco Packet Tracer, use the following steps:

1.  Open **Cisco Packet Tracer**.

2.  In the bottom-left corner, you will see two short rows of icons. The upper row contains the parent category of the network components, while the lower row contains the subcategories. The following image shows the parent category:

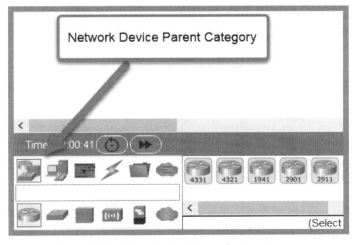

Figure 2.2 – Cisco Packet Tracer device category

3.  Click on each parent category, thus displaying the subcategory in the second row, as shown in the following image:

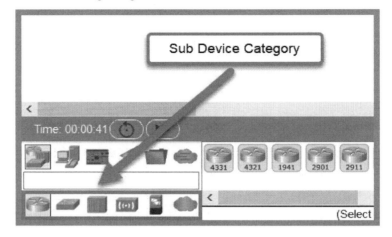

Figure 2.3 – Sub Device Category

4.  Upon selecting a subcategory, you'll see some Cisco devices appear, as shown in the following image:

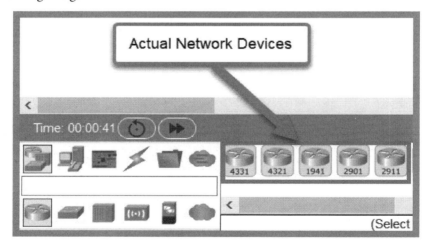

Figure 2.4 – Network devices in Cisco Packet Tracer

5.  To access a device, select a Cisco 2911 model router and drag it to the main layout in Cisco Packet Tracer.

6.  Next, select the **End Devices** category and drag a PC onto the layout.

7.  Select the **Connection** category (the one with the lightning bolt symbol) and select the **console** cable.

8.  Click on the PC. A list of available ports will appear. From here, choose the **RS-232** port.

> **Important note**
> We will discuss the importance of the console cable and the RS-232 port in the *Accessing a Cisco IOS device* section.

9.  Then, drag the cable to the router. After, click and select the **Console** port.

    The following diagram shows the typical connection that we have established within Cisco Packet Tracer:

Figure 2.5 – PC to router within Cisco Packet Tracer

10. To access the command line of the Cisco IOS router, click on **PC**. Select **Desktop | Terminal**, as shown here:

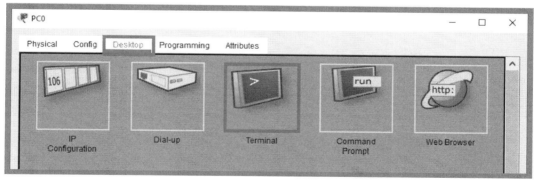

Figure 2.6 – Terminal within Cisco Packet Tracer

11. The **Terminal** application will open like so. Click on **OK** to access the CLI:

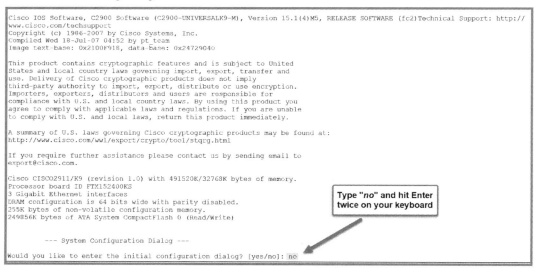

Figure 2.7 – Terminal settings

Next, you will see that the Cisco operating system is decompressing and that the device is booting.

The following image shows the user interface for Cisco IOS devices:

```
Cisco IOS Software, C2900 Software (C2900-UNIVERSALK9-M), Version 15.1(4)M5, RELEASE SOFTWARE (fc2)Technical Support: http://
www.cisco.com/techsupport
Copyright (c) 1986-2007 by Cisco Systems, Inc.
Compiled Wed 18-Jul-07 04:52 by pt_team
Image text-base: 0x2100F918, data-base: 0x24729040

This product contains cryptographic features and is subject to United
States and local country laws governing import, export, transfer and
use. Delivery of Cisco cryptographic products does not imply
third-party authority to import, export, distribute or use encryption.
Importers, exporters, distributors and users are responsible for
compliance with U.S. and local country laws. By using this product you
agree to comply with applicable laws and regulations. If you are unable
to comply with U.S. and local laws, return this product immediately.

A summary of U.S. laws governing Cisco cryptographic products may be found at:
http://www.cisco.com/wwl/export/crypto/tool/stqrg.html

If you require further assistance please contact us by sending email to
export@cisco.com.

Cisco CISCO2911/K9 (revision 1.0) with 491520K/32768K bytes of memory.
Processor board ID FTX152400KS
3 Gigabit Ethernet interfaces
DRAM configuration is 64 bits wide with parity disabled.
255K bytes of non-volatile configuration memory.
249856K bytes of ATA System CompactFlash 0 (Read/Write)

        --- System Configuration Dialog ---

Would you like to enter the initial configuration dialog? [yes/no]: no
```

Type "*no*" and hit Enter twice on your keyboard

Figure 2.8 – Command-line interface (CLI) of a Cisco IOS device

Now that you have an idea of setting up Cisco Packet Tracer on your personal computer, let's learn how to use a more robust application to emulate Cisco devices, appliances, and end devices.

# Virtual CCNA Lab

**Graphical Network Simulator 3 (GNS3)** is an emulator for many network and security appliances. It uses the official operating systems and firmware of devices and creates a virtualized environment. This allows you to run the real operating systems of vendor devices on your laptop or desktop computer without having to purchase physical devices. Additionally, you can have a portable, software-based networking lab environment on the go.

Why is GNS3 better than Cisco Packet Tracer or physical equipment? It's convenient to have virtualization networks and security devices right on your desktop computer. The benefit of using GNS3 is that it allows you to install the official Cisco operating systems into its application, which means you will be able to access the full functionality of the virtual Cisco router, switch, and firewall devices.

The only downside to using virtualization technologies is you'll need to have a good CPU that supports virtualization and a sufficient amount of RAM. When you start a virtual machine, in our case, it'll be a virtual appliance or device. They use the same amount of RAM as a physical device. This means that if a Cisco IOS router uses 1 GB of RAM, a virtual Cisco router within GNS3 will most likely be the same.

Another downside of using GNS3 is that you will need to use official Cisco IOS images within GNS3. Unlike Cisco Packet Tracer, which is a simulated environment, GNS3 creates an emulated working environment for official operating systems.

> **Important note**
> Cisco IOS images can be obtained from Cisco's website if you have a service contract that allows image downloads, you have a valid license agreement from Cisco Systems, or you purchase them directly from Cisco.

However, the benefit of using GNS3 is that you get very close to the real-world experience of the actual Cisco IOS devices. This includes the time it takes to converge the network and how all the Cisco commands work with operating systems (the switch, routers, firewalls, and so on).

To set up a GNS3 environment, use the following instructions:

1.  To download **GNS3 client** and **GNS VM**, go to www.gns3.com and click on **Sign Up** to create a user account on the website.
2.  After creating your user account, log into the website.

3.  Click on **Download**.

    You will see a **Download** button on the left-hand side of the screen. Click it to download the GNS3 standalone client. Additionally, download the GNS3 **VM** (**virtual machine**) by clicking the **Download VM for GNS3** hyperlink, as shown in the following image:

Figure 2.9 – GNS3 download links

The GNS3 VM is recommended with the GNS3 client as it improves performance.

When you click **Download VM for GNS3**, you'll be provided with multiple options to download a virtual image specific to your hypervisor of choice: VirtualBox, VMware Workstation and Fusion, VMware ESXi, and Microsoft Hyper-V platforms. I would recommend Oracle VirtualBox as it's a really good hypervisor and it's free. However, I'll demonstrate how to set up the environment using both Oracle VirtualBox and VMware Workstation.

4.  Download **Oracle VirtualBox** by going to www.virtualbox.org and clicking on **Downloads**. Choose the VirtualBox package for your operating system. Once the file has been successfully downloaded onto your computer, install it using all the default settings.

5. This step is optional as VMware Workstation is a commercial (paid) product. To get **VMware Workstation Pro**, go to `https://www.vmware.com/products/workstation-pro.html` to make an official purchase of the product.

6. Install the GNS3 standalone client on your computer using all the default settings within the installation wizard.

7. Right-click on **GNS3 VM**, select **Open with**, and choose **VirtualBox** or **VMware Workstation** to import the virtual machines into the hypervisor, as shown in the following image:

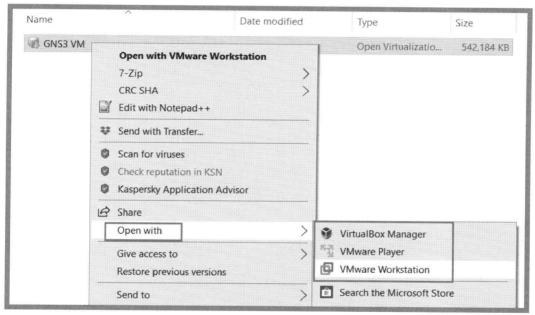

Figure 2.10 – GNS3 VM import options

8. If you are using **VMware Workstation**, the **Import Virtual Machine** wizard will open. Click **Import** to begin the process.

The following screenshot shows the import window on VMware Workstation:

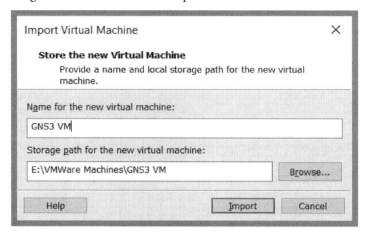

Figure 2.11 – VMware Workstation import window

9. When the importing process has been completed on **VMware Workstation Pro**, click the **Edit virtual machine setting** link to adjust the CPU and RAM on **GNS3 VM**, as shown in the following image:

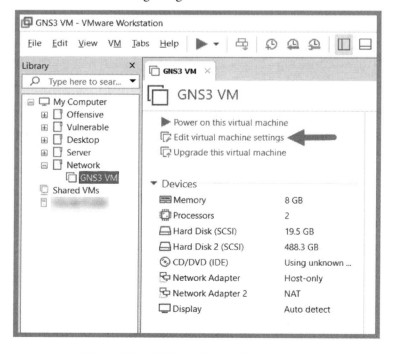

Figure 2.12 – VMware Workstation overview

I would recommend using the following settings on the GNS3 VM:

--Memory (RAM): 8 GB,

CPU:

--Number of processors = 1,

--Number of cores per processors = 2.

Enable any additional virtualization features found on the CPU tab.

When you're finished, click on **OK** to save the setting on VMware Workstation Pro.

10. If you are using **Oracle VirtualBox** to import **GNS3 VM**, you will see the following window; click on **Import**:

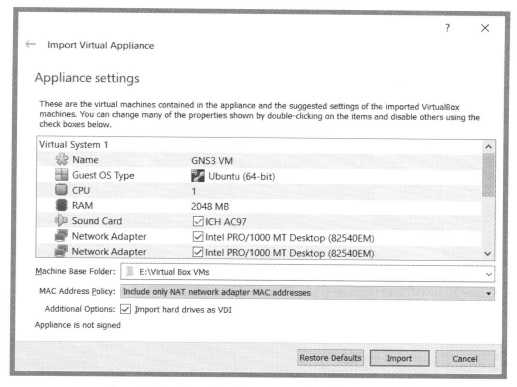

Figure 2.13 – VirtualBox Import Virtual Appliance window

11. After **GNS3 VM** has been imported into VirtualBox, select the virtual machine and click on **Settings** to adjust the CPU and RAM specifications.

12. Next, open the **GNS3 standalone client** application. Select **Edit** to expand the drop-down menu and click on **Preferences**, as shown in the following screenshot:

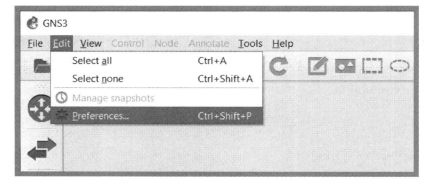

Figure 2.14– GNS3 Edit menu

13. Click on the **GNS3 VM** tab. Then, set the options shown in the following image to connect **GNS3 client** to **GNS VM**:

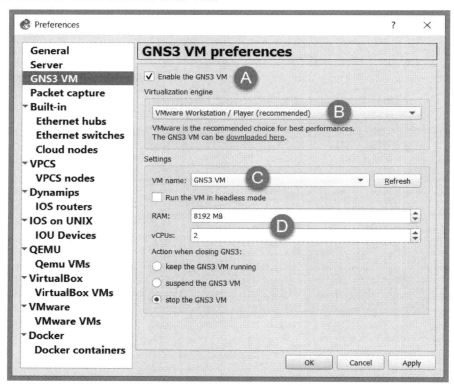

Figure 2.15 – GNS3 VM configuration

If you are using **Oracle VirtualBox**, set **Virtualization Engine: VirtualBox**.

14. Click **Apply** and then **OK** to save these settings.

Now that we have configured the GNS3 VM so that it works with the GNS3 standalone client, on the GNS3 client user interface, on the right-side, under **Servers Summary**, **GNS3 VM** should appear, as shown in the following screenshot:

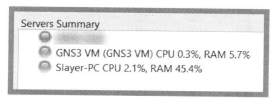

Figure 2.16 – GNS3 Servers Summary

To add an official Cisco IOS image in GNS3, use the following instructions:

1. Ensure both the GNS3 client and **GNS3 VM** are up and running. To add a **Cisco IOSv** router appliance, click on the **Router** icon and then **New template**, as shown in the following image:

Figure 2.17 – GNS3 interface

2.  Select **Install an appliance from the GNS3 server** and click **Next**, as shown here:

Figure 2.18 – New template window in GNS3

3.  Search for Cisco IOSv to quickly find the template and click **Install**, as shown here:

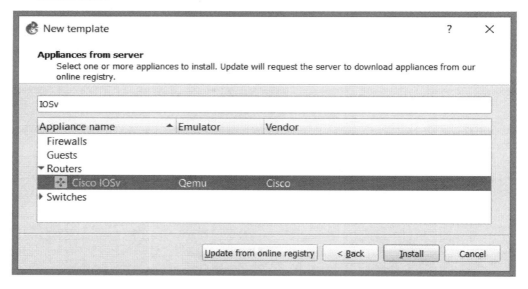

Figure 2.19 – Appliance template window in GNS3

4. Select **Install the appliance on the GNS3 VM** and click **Next**, as shown here:

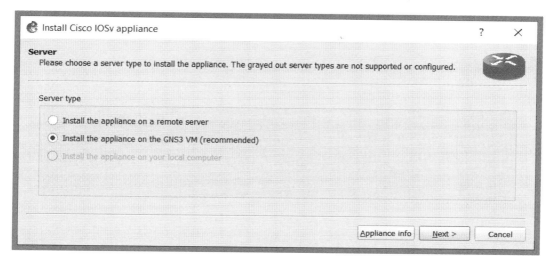

Figure 2.20 – Install Cisco IOSv appliance window in GNS3

5. The **Qemu binary** options will be automatically selected. Click **Next**, as shown here:

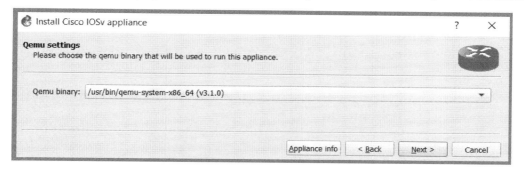

Figure 2.21 – Qemu setting in GNS3

Set the required **IOSv version** based on the IOSv image you got from Cisco and click **Import**:

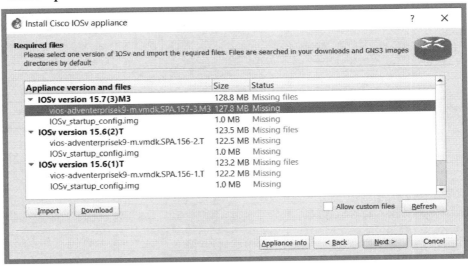

Figure 2.22 – Install Cisco IOSv Appliance window on GNS3

After importing the Cisco IOSv into **GNS3 VM**, you should see that the status shows that the image has been found.

6.  Next, select **IOSv_startup_config.img** and click **Download** to retrieve the file that's required to complete the installation:

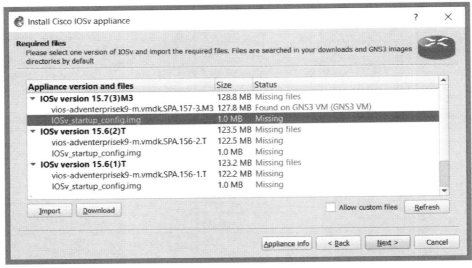

Figure 2.23 – Install Cisco IOSv missing file status

7. Once both the **IOSv** and **startup-config** files have been uploaded to **GNS3 VM**, the status of the IOSv router appliance will change to **Ready to install**. Click **Next**, as shown in the following screenshot:

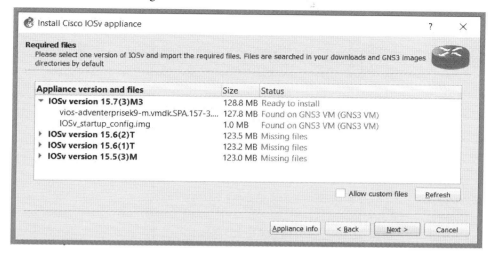

Figure 2.24 – Cisco IOSv ready to install window on GNS3

8. When the installation is completed, click **OK** to accept the message of a successful installation and click **Finish** to close the wizard, as shown in the following screenshot:

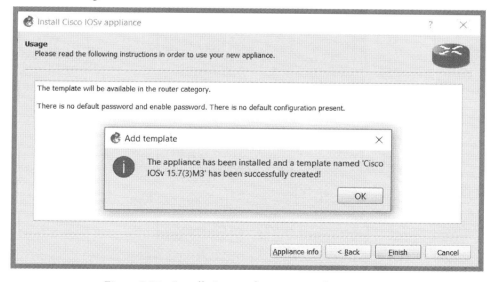

Figure 2.25 – Installation confirmation window in GNS3

To add a Cisco IOSvL2 switch to GNS3 VM, follow the same procedure mentioned previously. Don't forget that when you have reached *step 3*, search for IOSvL2 instead as it's a Cisco switch rather than a router.

To add and access devices within GNS3, please use the following instructions:

1.  In GNS3, click **File** to open the drop-down menu and select **New Blank Project**.

2.  Create a project name and choose a location to save the project files. Then, click **OK**.

3.  On the left of the GNS3 window, click the **Router** icon to show all available devices.

4.  Drag the newly created router onto the center of the **GNS3** layout.

5.  Click the **Play** icon to start the device in **GNS3**.

    The following image shows the **Play**, **Pause**, and **Stop** icons for controlling the device:

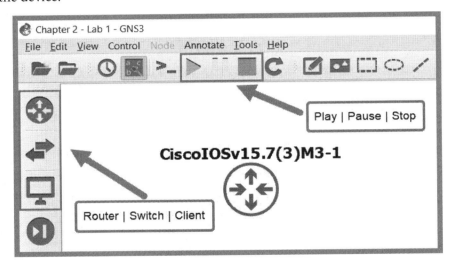

Figure 2.26 – GNS3 controls

Now, on the right-hand side of GNS3, under **Topology Summary**, you should see that the router icon has now turned green to indicate it's currently active.

6.  To access the command-line interface of a device within **GNS3**, simply double-click on the device's icon on the main layout. This will open PuTTY or the default Terminal program on your computer.

7.  If you add more devices to **GNS3**, you can click the **Cable** icon to use the same method to interconnect devices.

> **Important note**
>
> During the installation of the GNS3 standalone client, Putty was included during the installation phase.
>
> When you are finished, be sure to click the **Stop** icon to power down all the virtual devices within GNS3. Additionally, closing the GNS3 client will automatically power-off the GNS3 VM as well.

Now, you know how to create a virtual environment to sharpen your skills for the CCNA certification. Let's take a dive into understanding the requirements for acquiring a physical lab.

# Physical labs

As I always say, there is no greater experience than using the real, physical equipment. The benefit of using physical equipment, especially for network engineering, is the fact you see everything in action. Please note that I'm not saying you won't see it in a virtualized environment, but there is something irreplaceable about using physical equipment – perhaps it's the thrill.

The following is a list of devices I recommend using if you are interested in building a physical lab:

- Cisco 2911 routers

- Cisco 2960 switches

- Cisco 3560 switch or Cisco 3650 switch

- 1 x Cisco console cable

- 1 x RS-232 to USB converter cable

- A few network patch cables for interconnecting devices

The quantity of these devices will depend on how large you wish to scale your physical lab. Ideally, having two devices, such as two laptops, to test end-to-end connectivity is highly recommended. Lastly, ensure each Cisco device is running the latest version of its operating system. This ensures the essential features are available to you when needed.

Having completed this section, you have gained the essential skills you need to build your very own Cisco lab environment. We'll take a deep dive into learning about the Cisco operating system in the next section.

# Getting started with Cisco IOS devices

Nowadays, almost all electronic devices have some form of firmware to help them execute tasks. In most instances, there is an operating system that's used to provide the user with a lot of functionality. Similar to a typical laptop computer or a smartphone, there are hardware components such as a **Central Processing Unit** (**CPU**), also referred to as the processor, that are used to execute arithmetic calculations and provide control over the computer. There is also **Random Access Memory** (**RAM**), which is used to temporarily store data while the CPU accesses it, and there is a storage unit where you can store the operating system and other types of data while the device is powered off.

However, without an operating system such as Windows, MAC, or even Linux, the components of the computer will not be able to work together to execute functions defined by the user. To put it simply, the operating system provides a process for controlling the hardware components of the device and allows you, the user, to tell the computer/device what to do.

Cisco Systems created their own proprietary network operating system for their switches and routers called the **Cisco Internetwork Operating System** (**Cisco IOS**). The Cisco IOS allows you to configure and manage their devices via a **command-line interface** (**CLI**).

You read that correctly – its' a command line. Don't be worried – I'll share a little insight into my personal experience. When I started my journey to get my first CCNA certification some years ago, I was feeling a bit apprehensive. I was accustomed to **Graphical User Interfaces** (**GUI**) on all devices and the thought of learning code was cool, but at the same time, very new to me. However, to this day, I love working on device systems and devices using command lines as I have realized how powerful CLIs can be in any device.

Throughout this book, I'll ensure you will be able to understand the purpose of each command we use to execute a function and build an optimal Cisco network.

## Boot process

In any computer or mobile device, the operating system needs to be stored in an area of memory on the device when it is powered off. In computers, we use either a **hard disk drive** (**HDD**) or a **solid-state drive** (**SSD**) to hold the operating system and other important data (files). The benefit of having an HDD/SSD is that when the device is turned off or restarts, its content is not lost. However, on a Cisco switch or router, there is no local hard disk drives or solid-state drives, so where is the Cisco IOS stored?

The Cisco IOS is stored in a location called **Flash**. Data that is written to **Flash** memory is not lost when the device is turned off or rebooted.

> **Important note**
>
> This type of memory is referred to as **non-volatile random access memory (NVRAM)**.

To get a clear understanding of the actual boot process of a Cisco IOS device, let's look at the following stages:

1. Upon powering on a Cisco device, a **Power-on Self Test (POST)** is executed by the device's firmware to check for the possibility of any hardware failure prior to loading the Cisco IOS. If everything seems fine, the firmware loads the Bootstrap, which is located in **Read-only Memory (ROM)**.

2. The **Bootstrap** checks in the **Flash** memory for the Cisco IOS file. If found, the Cisco IOS is loaded into RAM.

3. If the Cisco IOS is not found in the Flash memory, the device checks for a local **Trivial File Transfer Protocol (TFTP)** server on the network. One common practice in the industry is that networking professionals remove the Cisco IOS file from the devices and place them on a local TFTP server. This creates the effect that each time a device boots up, it will pull the Cisco IOS across the network from a TFTP server and load it into its RAM.

4. If the Cisco device is unable to locate a TFTP server on the network, it loads a scaled-down version of the Cisco IOS into the RAM. The scaled-down version provides the essential functions that allows the device administrator to troubleshoot and reload the Cisco IOS file into its Flash memory, therefore restoring the device into a workable state.

5. Once the Cisco IOS is loaded into the RAM, the bootstrap will check the contents of **NVRAM** for previously saved configuration files; this file is known as `startup-config`. If a `startup-config` file is found, it is loaded into the RAM.

6. If a `startup-config` file is not found, the device loads its default configurations into the RAM as `running-config`.

The contents of the RAM are known as `running-config`. This `running-config` are the device's current configuration as the device is powered on. However, keep in mind that if the device loses power or gets rebooted, the content of its RAM is lost.

> **Important note**
>
> `running-config` does not automatically save into NVRAM. The device's configurations need to be saved manually as this creates or updates the `startup-config` file.

The following is a flow chart to give you a better visual representation of the boot process of a Cisco IOS device:

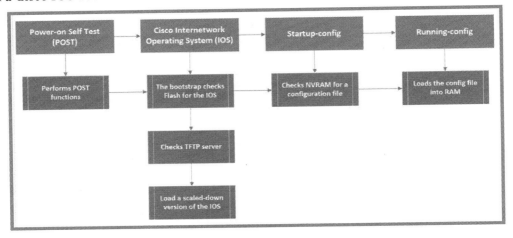

Figure 2.27 – Cisco IOS device boot process

Now that we have covered the essentials of the Cisco IOS boot process, let's cover the various methods a person can use to access a Cisco IOS device.

# Accessing a Cisco IOS device

Unlike a computer or smartphone, a network intermediary device such as a router or switch does not have a display screen that shows you the user interface for managing the operating system. Whenever you purchase a new Cisco IOS device, within the packaging of the box, you will usually find a blue cable; this is called a console cable or rollover cable.

The following is an image of a console cable:

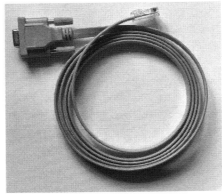

Figure 2.28 – Cisco console cable

On one end, there's a DB-9 (RS-232) interface, which is used to connect to a computer's DB-9 (RS-232) port. However, modern-day computers and laptop manufacturers no longer make devices with these interfaces. However, you can get an RS-232 to USB converter cable from an online or local computer store. This converter cable enables you to use the console cable over a USB connection.

The following is an image of the RS-232 to USB converter cable:

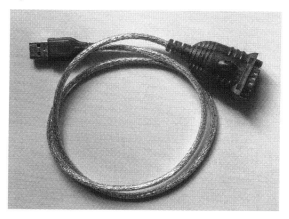

Figure 2.29 – USB to RS-232 converter cable

At the other end of the console cable, you'll see the cable terminates using a RJ-45 (registered jack). This end of the cable is to be inserted only into the console port of the Cisco IOS device. The console is typically located at the back of a device or sometimes on the front. For us to quickly identify the console port, Cisco has printed a label on it.

> **Important note**
> There are additional methods for accessing a Cisco IOS device, such as **Secure Shell (SSH)** and Telnet. These will be covered in later sections on this book.

The console port provides physical management of the device. However, the console port is typically used to configure the device with initial configurations until it's deployed on the network for remote access management. Network professionals can also use the console port as a management interface when performing maintenance procedures.

The following photo shows the console port on the back of a Cisco IOS device:

Figure 2.30 – Console port on the back of a Cisco IOS router

Upon making the connection between the PC and the Cisco IOS device using the console cable, a serial connection is created between the PC and the device via the RS-232-to-USB cable. To access the CLI of the Cisco device, we will need a terminal emulation application on our computer.

The following is a brief list of terminal emulation applications:

- PuTTY (free)
- SecureCRT (commercial)
- Tera Term (free)

To access the CLI, please use the following steps:

1. Connect the console cable to your laptop and the Cisco IOS device. This will create a serial connection.
2. Open **Control Panel** and click on **Device Manager**.
3. Expand the **Port (COM & LPT)** category to see the COM interface being used.

    The following screenshot shows the details listed under the **Ports** category:

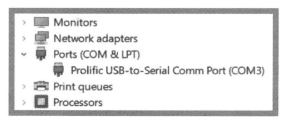

Figure 2.31 – Device Manager on Windows

At the time of writing, **COM3** was used for the serial connection. This information will be useful for the next few steps. Please keep in mind that the **COM** port is dependent on your computer and availability. Be sure to verify the **COM** port before moving on to the next step.

4. Download **Putty** (`www.putty.org`) and open it. Use the following settings on the terminal emulation application:

--**Connection Type**: `Serial`

--**Serial Line**: `COM3`

--**Speed**: `9600`

--**Data bits**: `8`

--**Parity**: `None`

--**Stop bit**: `1`

--**Flow control**: `None`

The following screenshots show the user interfaces for both PuTTY and SecureCRT:

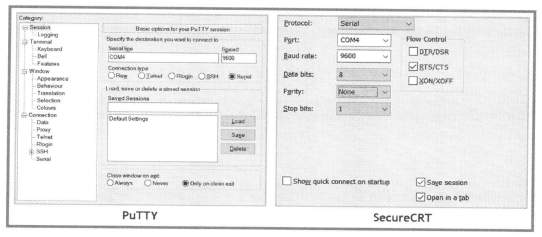

Figure 2.32 – PuTTY and SecureCRT interfaces

5. Click on **Open** or **Connect** on the terminal emulator to access the command line of the device.

The following image shows the typical welcome screen when connecting to the IOS:

```
Cisco CISCO2911/K9 (revision 1.0) with 491520K/32768K bytes of memory.
Processor board ID FTX152400KS
3 Gigabit Ethernet interfaces
DRAM configuration is 64 bits wide with parity disabled.
255K bytes of non-volatile configuration memory.
249856K bytes of ATA System CompactFlash 0 (Read/Write)


        --- System Configuration Dialog ---

Would you like to enter the initial configuration dialog? [yes/no]: no


Press RETURN to get started!

                         ┌─────────────────┐
                         │  User Exec mode  │
                         └─────────────────┘
Router>
```

Figure 2.33 – CLI of a Cisco IOS router

Now that we you have learned how to access a Cisco IOS device using the console cable, let's take a look at how to navigate the Cisco IOS and learn some Cisco commands.

# Configuring the Cisco IOS

The Cisco Internetwork Operating System (Cisco IOS) is a full-fledged operating system that provides you with an interface to control the hardware and the device. The Cisco IOS has many security features to ensure you are able to secure a network environment and the device as well. One such security feature is that the Cisco IOS has many command modes. This separates the management access interface into the following modes:

- **User Exec**
- **Privilege Exec**
- **Global configuration mode**

When you establish a console connection to a Cisco IOS device, you are taken directly into the **User Exec** mode by default. **User Exec** mode provides very limited capabilities for a user as it allows for basic troubleshooting and monitoring commands such as ping and traceroute.

**User Exec** mode can be easily identified with the > prompt, as shown here:

```
Router>
```

**Privilege Exec** mode allows the user to perform many more commands within the Cisco IOS. In this mode, the user can configure the system clock, perform many troubleshooting or "show" commands, and access the global configuration mode.

To access privilege mode from **User Exec** mode, simply enter the enable command.

**Privilege Exec** mode can be easily identified with the # prompt, as shown here:

```
Router#
```

To exit privilege mode, use the disable command. This takes you back **User Exec** mode.

**Global Configuration** mode allows a user to make changes to the entire Cisco IOS. Any configuration entered in this mode affects the operations of the entire device immediately. Other command modes are accessible from **global config** such as **interface** modes, **line configuration** modes, **router** mode, and many more. In the remaining chapters of this book, you will learn about other modes and advanced configurations to help you build and design an enterprise network.

From **Privilege Exec** mode, you can use the configure terminal command to access **Global Config**.

**Global Config** mode can be easily identified, as shown here:

```
Router(config)#
```

To exit **Global Config**, use the exit command. This will take you back to privilege exec mode.

> **Tip**
>
> In any mode that is *global config* or higher, you can use *Ctrl + Z* on your keyboard as a shortcut to take you back into *privilege exec* mode. Additionally, you can use the *Tab* button on your keyboard to automatically expand your typing of a command. Cisco IOS also accepts short typing of commands, such as show ip interface brief, which can be typed as sh ip int bri; both are acceptable.

The following diagram provides a visual representation of the navigation process within the Cisco IOS:

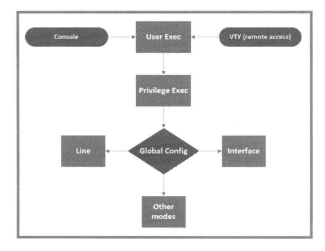

Figure 2.34 – Cisco IOS navigation path

Now that you have learned how to perform basic navigation within the Cisco IOS, let's *take it up a notch* and build a small network using Cisco devices.

## Setting up a small Cisco network

When building a network, it's always recommended to start with a network diagram called a network topology. A topology is used to show the logical and physical connections between devices on a network, as well as basic IP addressing assignments.

For our exercise, we are going to build the following network topology:

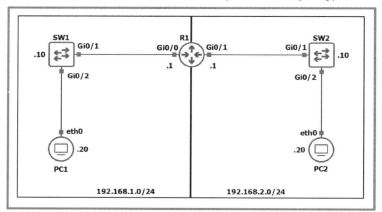

Figure 2.35 – Lab 1 – network topology

As you can see, there are two networks: 192.168.1.0/24 and 192.168.2.0/24. These are interconnected using a Cisco 2911 router. Each of these networks has a Cisco 2960 switch (**SW1** and **SW2**) to extend their LAN. Additionally, each LAN has a single PC attached with the purpose of checking end-to-end connectivity when our lab is fully configured and operational.

You can use either physical equipment, GNS3, or Cisco Packet Tracer to complete this task. Simply interconnect the devices as shown in the preceding diagram.

The objectives of this lab are as follows:

- Learning how to navigate the Cisco IOS
- Configuring IP addresses on Cisco devices
- Securing administrative and remote access

The following are the situations where you should use a copper straight-through cable:

- PC to switch
- Switch to router
- Switch to server

The following are the situations where you should use a copper crossover cable:

- PC to PC
- Switch to switch
- Router to router
- Router to PC
- Router to server

If you are using Cisco Packet Tracer, your topology should look as follows:

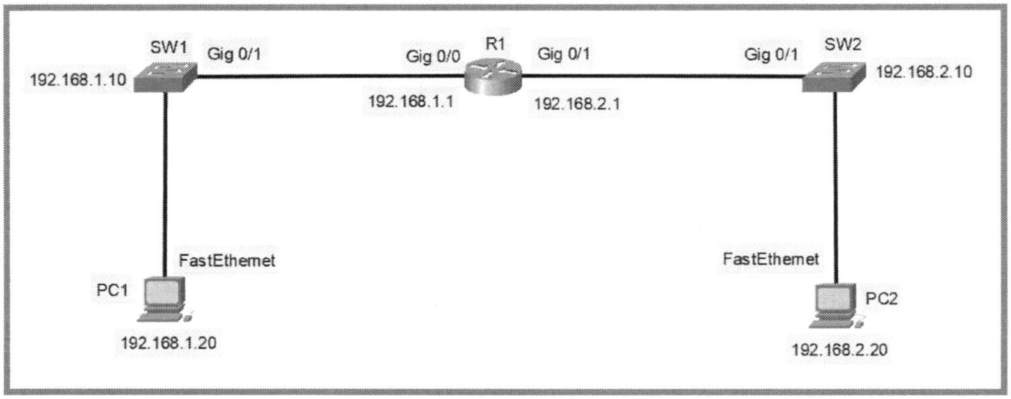

Figure 2.36 – Lab 1 – Network topology in Cisco Packet Tracer

To help make your learning experience better, we shall describe and demonstrate how to find our way around the Cisco IOS.

## Task 1 – Learning how to navigate the Cisco IOS

To learn how to use the Cisco IOS and all its features for CCNA, please use the following instructions:

1.  When you boot up a Cisco IOS router for the first time, you'll receive the following interactive message:

    ```
    --- System Configuration Dialog ---
    Would you like to enter the initial configuration dialog?
    [yes/no]:
    ```

2.  Type no and hit *Enter* on your keyboard a couple of times until you see the **User Exec** prompt.

    > **Important note**
    >
    > The interactive dialog is designed to help non-technical users configure the device. However, as an upcoming networking professional, you should not use the interactive wizard as it's better to perform manual configurations on the device so that it fits your expected outcome. In other words, as much as the interactive dialog may be helpful, it may also install configurations onto the device that we may not want.

3. At this point, you should be in **User Exec** mode (>). To access **Privilege Exec** mode, use the `enable` command, as shown here:

```
Router>enable
Router#
```

Notice that the Command Prompt has changed to a pound or hash symbol (#).

4. To go back into **User Exec**, use `disable` to revert back to the previous command mode, as shown here:

```
Router#disable
Router>
```

The Cisco IOS is able to temporarily store the most recent commands executed on the device. Using the *Up* and *Down* keys on your keyboard will allow you to cycle through recently used commands for your current command mode. Therefore, if you are in **Privilege Exec**, you will only be able to see the most recent commands that are used with **Privilege Exec**.

5. Another cool feature is that the Cisco IOS has the ability to recognize a Cisco IOS command by simply typing the mode part of the command itself. To further understand this concept, in **User Exec** mode, type the following command and hit *Enter*:

```
Router>en
Router#
```

Notice that the Cisco IOS accepts the `en` command as `enable` and carries you to **Privilege Exec** mode.

6. Next, let's learn how to use both `context-sensitive help` and the command syntax checker feature. To determine the correct syntax of a command, type part of the command and enter a question mark (?) right after.

The following is an example of a context-sensitive help that's used to determine what commands begin with en in **User Exec** mode:

```
Router>en?
enable
Router>
```

The Cisco IOS provides a list of commands that begin with en and return you to your current command mode. In our example, enable is the only Cisco IOS that begins with en in **User Exec** mode. This is helpful if you have forgotten the spelling or the correct syntax to use during device configuration.

To explore this further, head on over to **Privilege Exec** mode on the router. As mentioned previously, this mode allows us to execute a lot of troubleshooting commands. These commands usually begin with show, followed by additional commands.

7.  To see a list of available syntax that goes after the show command, place a ? after show. The following is an example of the expected results:

| Router#show ? | |
| --- | --- |
| aaa | Show AAA values |
| access-expression | List access expression |
| access-lists | List access lists |
| acircuit | Access circuit info |
| adjacency | Adjacent nodes |
| aliases | Display alias commands |
| --More-- | |

The column on the left shows available commands that can be paired with show. Additionally, the column on the right provides a description of each corresponding syntax on the left.

When the Cisco IOS has to output multiple lines of code, it temporarily breaks by indicating a --More-- syntax at the end. Using the *Enter* button on your keyboard will display an additional line of output, while the *Spacebar* key will display another page of output on your screen.

> **Tip**
> The Cisco IOS is filled with tons of commands that allow you to perform many tasks, such as routing, switching, security, and many more. However, we do not need to learn every syntax. We'll just concentrate on those that are needed for the CCNA certification.

Now that you have a better idea of how to navigate the Cisco IOS, let's get right into configuring our small network topology.

## Task 2 – Changing the hostname

One of the very first tasks during initial device configuration is changing the hostname of the device. Each device on your network should have a unique hostname. Many organizations usually have a standard for naming conventions that are used on devices on the network. Additionally, when remotely accessing a device, the hostname is usually one of the first things that's used to identify you have logged onto the correct device.

The following are some guidelines for configuring a hostname on a Cisco IOS device:

- Ensure there are no spaces in the actual hostname.
- The hostname should not be longer than 64 characters.
- start with a letter.
- Hostnames can end with a letter or number.

Let's change the hostname on each device so that it matches the network topology shown in *Figures 2.35* and *2.36*. Use the `hostname` command, shown as follows, to change the default hostnames for each of the corresponding devices:

### SW1

```
Switch>enable
Switch#configure terminal
Switch(config)#hostname SW1
SW1(config)#
```

### SW2

```
Switch>enable
Switch#configure terminal
Switch(config)#hostname SW2
SW2(config)#
```

### R1

```
Router>enable
Router#configure terminal
Router(config)#hostname R1
R1(config)#
```

As you may have noticed, any command entered in global configuration mode takes effect immediately. In this exercise, the change took effect immediately after executing the hostname configuration on each device.

## Task 3 – Configuring IP addresses on Cisco devices

Before placing an IP address on an interface, it's recommended to check both the number and type of interfaces available on a device. On the router and switches, we can verify the type and number of interfaces available on the device by using the `show ip interface brief` command, as shown here:

```
Router#show ip interface brief
Interface            IP-Address      OK? Method Status                Protocol
GigabitEthernet0/0   unassigned      YES unset  administratively down down
GigabitEthernet0/1   unassigned      YES unset  administratively down down
GigabitEthernet0/2   unassigned      YES unset  administratively down down
GigabitEthernet0/3   unassigned      YES unset  administratively down down
Router#
```

Figure 2.37 – Summary of interfaces on a Cisco router

The `show ip interface brief` command provides us with a summary of each interface's status on the device:

- The **Interface** column tells us the interface's type and port number on the device.

- The **IP-Address** column tells us whether the interface has an IP address or not.

- The **OK?** and **Method** columns tells us how the IP address was set on the interface, such as DHCP, unset, and manual.

- The **Status** column tells us the physical (Layer 1) status of the interface. The following are a list of statuses:

  a) Up: The interface is active and is receiving an incoming electrical signal on the interface.

  b) Down: The network cable is missing or the interface is not receiving an incoming electrical signal.

  c) Administratively down: The device administrator has manually turned off this interface.

- The **Protocol** column determines the Layer 2 status of the interface. There are two status types: *up* and *down*. The *up* status tells us that everything is working fine at Layer 2. The *down* status tells us there is an encapsulation issue on the link.

In the field of networking, you will encounter various types of physical interfaces on devices. The following is a brief description of various interfaces found on Cisco devices:

- Ethernet: Operates up to `10` Mbps

- FastEthernet: Operates up to `100` Mbps

- GigabitEthernet: Operates up to `1000` Mbps

To configure the IP addresses on the router, use the following configurations:

### R1

```
R1#configure terminal
R1(config)#interface GigabitEthernet0/0
R1(config-if)#description Connected to LAN 1 - 192.168.1.0/24
network
R1(config-if)#ip address 192.168.1.1 255.255.255.0
R1(config-if)#no shutdown
R1(config-if)#exit
R1(config)#
```

Various interface modes are accessible from **global config**. Notice that we use the `interface` command, followed by the interface type and number. The Command Prompt changed to `R1(config-if)#`, which indicates any commands we enter here will only affect this specific interface.

Next, using the `description` command is useful as it will allow you to identify the purpose of an interface. Additionally, all interface statuses are set to **administratively down** by default. Using the `no shutdown` command in interface mode will turn up the interface.

Typing `exit` will return you to the previous mode, **global config**. Typing `exit` one more time will carry you back into Privilege mode.

Let's use the `show ip interface brief` command to verify that the IP address has been assigned to the interface and that the interface status is Up/Up. The following screenshot shows the expected results:

```
R1#show ip interface brief
Interface              IP-Address      OK? Method Status                Protocol
GigabitEthernet0/0     192.168.1.1     YES manual up                    up
GigabitEthernet0/1     unassigned      YES NVRAM  administratively down down
GigabitEthernet0/2     unassigned      YES NVRAM  administratively down down
Vlan1                  unassigned      YES NVRAM  administratively down down
R1#
```

Figure 2.38 – show ip interface brief command output

Now that you are familiar with configuring an IP address and a subnet mask on a router's interface, let's configure the interface connected to the 192.168.2.0/24 network. The following is a list of commands that you'll need to complete this task:

```
R1#configure terminal
R1(config)#interface GigabitEthernet0/1
R1(config-if)#description Connected to LAN 2 - 192.168.2.0/24
network
R1(config-if)#ip address 192.168.2.1 255.255.255.0
R1(config-if)#no shutdown
R1(config-if)#exit
R1(config)#
```

Once completed, let's verify the status of our interfaces. The following screenshot shows that we now have both GigabitEthernet 0/0 and GigabitEthernet 0/1. Each has an IP address on their corresponding network, and both are in the Up/Up status:

```
R1#show ip interface brief
Interface              IP-Address      OK? Method Status                Protocol
GigabitEthernet0/0     192.168.1.1     YES manual up                    up
GigabitEthernet0/1     192.168.2.1     YES manual up                    up
GigabitEthernet0/2     unassigned      YES NVRAM  administratively down down
Vlan1                  unassigned      YES NVRAM  administratively down down
R1#
```

Figure 2.39 – Verification of second interface status

Furthermore, using the `show ip interface interface-ID` command will provide you with more IP-related details, as shown here:

```
R1#show ip interface gigabitEthernet 0/0
GigabitEthernet0/0 is up, line protocol is up (connected)
  Internet address is 192.168.1.1/24
  Broadcast address is 255.255.255.255
  Address determined by setup command
  MTU is 1500 bytes
  Helper address is not set
  Directed broadcast forwarding is disabled
  Outgoing access list is not set
  Inbound  access list is not set
```

Figure 2.40 – Output of the show ip interface command

In the preceding screenshot, you can verify the IP address, the subnet mask, interface physical status, and whether any **Access Control Lists** (**ACLs**) have been placed on the interface.

If you prefer to get more statistical information about an interface, use the show interfaces interface-ID command. The output will provide you with the interface status, IP address and subnet mask, interface description, duplex and speed operating modes, and packet flow statistics, as shown here:

```
R1#show interfaces gigabitEthernet 0/0
GigabitEthernet0/0 is up, line protocol is up (connected)
  Hardware is CN Gigabit Ethernet, address is 00d0.588a.0e01 (bia 00d0.588a.0e01)
  Description: Connected to LAN 1 - 192.168.1.0/24 network
  Internet address is 192.168.1.1/24
  MTU 1500 bytes, BW 1000000 Kbit, DLY 10 usec,
     reliability 255/255, txload 1/255, rxload 1/255
  Encapsulation ARPA, loopback not set
  Keepalive set (10 sec)
  Full-duplex, 100Mb/s, media type is RJ45
  output flow-control is unsupported, input flow-control is unsupported
```

Figure 2.41 – Output of the show interfaces command

Lastly, you can use the show running-config command to view the current configurations of the device. By expanding the output, you will see the configurations that are executed under each interface, as shown here:

```
!
interface GigabitEthernet0/0
 description Connected to LAN 1 - 192.168.1.0/24 network
 ip address 192.168.1.1 255.255.255.0
 duplex auto
 speed auto
!
interface GigabitEthernet0/1
 description Connected to LAN 2 - 192.168.2.0/24 network
 ip address 192.168.2.1 255.255.255.0
 duplex auto
 speed auto
!
```

Figure 2.42 – The running-config output

## Task 4 – Configuring the Switch Virtual Interface (SVI)

Cisco IOS Layer 2 switches do not allow you to place an IP address on their physical interfaces. So, how does a user remotely manage or access a switch across a network? Within the Cisco IOS of the Layer 2 switch, you can create a special logical interface that allows you to set an IP address on the switch for remote management. This logical interface is known as a **Switch Virtual Interface (SVI)**.

To create an SVI, use the `interface vlan <vlan-ID>` command. This will both create the SVI and change the command mode to interface mode. For our topology, we need to set an IP address on each of our switches.

To complete this exercise, use the following commands to achieve this task:

**SW1**

```
SW1(config)#interface vlan 1
SW1(config-if)#ip address 192.168.1.10 255.255.255.0
SW1(config-if)#no shutdown
SW1(config-if)#exit
SW1(config)#
```

Let's not forget to configure the SVI switch 2 with the following commands:

**SW2**

```
SW2(config)#interface vlan 1
SW2(config-if)#ip address 192.168.2.10 255.255.255.0
SW2(config-if)#no shutdown
SW2(config-if)#exit
SW2(config)#
```

Now that you have learned how to create an SVI on a Cisco IOS Layer 2 switch, let's take a look at securing administrative access on all devices.

## Task 5 – Securing administrative access

By default, anyone can use a console cable to access the User Exec mode within the Cisco IOS via the console port. If the person is familiar with Cisco IOS syntax, this may be a security concern. This means that anyone who has a console cable and physical access to the device will be able to access various modes and make unauthorized changes to the device's configurations.

To solve this security challenge, the Cisco IOS has security features that allow the device administrator to gain secure access to the console port, **Virtual Terminal (VTY)** lines (remote access), and **Privilege Exec** mode.

To secure access to the console port on all devices, use the following instructions:

1.  Access Global Configuration mode by using the `configure terminal` command.

2.  To access the console line, use the `line console 0` command and hit *Enter*.

3.  Use the `password actual-password` command to set a password under the console port.

4.  Use the `login` command to enable the authentication feature. Without using `login`, a person can still access the console without being prompted for a password.

    The following screenshot shows how the commands should be executed:

```
R1(config)#line console 0
R1(config-line)#password cisco123
R1(config-line)#login
R1(config-line)#exit
R1(config)#
```

Figure 2.43 – Securing the console

The effect of the configurations we made in the preceding screenshot will prompt the user to enter a valid password to access **User Exec** mode via the console port. The password we have configured is `cisco123`.

> **Important note**
>
> In a real-world network, ensure you use more complex passwords. When typing a password within the Cisco IOS, it's usually invisible as a security feature to prevent anyone with prying eyes.

Now that we have secured console access to each device, let's secure access to **Privilege Exec** mode on all devices.

To secure administrative access on all devices, use the following instructions:

1.  Access Global Configuration mode by using the `configure terminal` command.

2.  Enter the `enable password` `actual-password` syntax and hit *Enter*.

3.   If you go back to **User Exec** and try to enter **Privilege Exec**, the Cisco IOS will prompt you for a password. Once you enter the password, which you set using the `enable password` command, the Cisco will grant you access.

The following snippet shows how the commands should be executed:

```
R1(config)#enable password cisco456
R1(config)#exit
R1#
%SYS-5-CONFIG_I: Configured from console by console

R1#disable
R1>enable
Password:          ◄———  Prompt asking for password
R1#
```

Figure 2.44 – Using the enable password command

However, using the `enable password` command is an unsecure method that's used to secure administrative access on the Cisco IOS. Let's see why this is an unsecure method. In **Privilege Exec** mode, use the `show running-config` command to view the current configurations on the device.

The following snippet shows that the `enable password` command sets an unencrypted password:

```
R1#show running-config
Building configuration...

Current configuration : 883 bytes
!
version 15.1
no service timestamps log datetime msec
no service timestamps debug datetime msec
no service password-encryption
!
hostname R1
!                          ┌──────────────────────────┐
!                          │ The password is unencrypted │
!                          └──────────────────────────┘
enable password cisco456
!
```

Figure 2.45 – Unencrypted password shown in the running-config file

It's not recommended to use `enable password` due to this security vulnerability. However, Cisco has implemented a more secure method to restrict access to **Privilege Exec** mode. This method uses the `enable secret` command.

To configure the `enable secret` command on the Cisco IOS for all devices, use the following commands:

```
R1(config)#enable secret cisco789
```

Let's verify our configurations by viewing `running-config` on the device:

```
!
enable secret 5 $1$mERr$B7IJJrJxq2fFyOs8ZEeVD1
enable password cisco456
!
```

Figure 2.46 – running-config containing encrypted and unencrypted passwords

You may be wondering which of these passwords will work when moving from User Exec mode to Privilege Exec mode. Would either password work or just one? The answer is simple: `enable secret` takes precedence in this situation, and therefore `enable password` is obsolete on the device.

It's good practice to always use `enable secret` when securing administrative access. However, in a situation where there are both `enable secret` and `enable password`, such as is the case here, it's recommended to remove the less secure configurations from `running-config`.

> **Important Note**
>
> To remove a command from `running-config`, use the negated form of the command, such as using `no`, followed by the remainder of the command.

To remove `enable password` from `running-config`, use the following command:

```
R1(config)#no enable password
```

If you check `running-config`, you'll notice `enable password` has been removed. Ensure you have secured administrative access to each device before moving on to the next task.

## Task 6 – Setting a banner

Having a legal notification such as a warning banner that's displayed whenever anyone administratively connects to your network devices is recommended. Such legal notifications can be used as an official legal warning for anyone who is attempting or gaining unauthorized access to a device on a corporate network.

To set a legal notification, we can use the `banner motd` command, followed by the legal notice. To set a banner to be displayed whenever anyone establishes a connection to the device via any access methods, use `banner motd`, as shown here:

```
R1(config)#banner motd %Only Authorized Access is permitted!!!%
```

When using the `banner` command, you need to insert both opening and closing delimiters, such as special characters (@, #, $, %, ^, &), before and after the actual banner message, which are used to indicate everything between the delimiters is the actual banner message to be displayed on a logon screen.

The following snippet indicates that the banner is displayed when establishing a new console connection:

```
Only Authorized Access is permitted!!!

User Access Verification

Password:
```

Figure 2.47 – Warning banner

Now that you have learned how to configure a warning disclaimer (banner) on a Cisco IOS device, let's take a look at setting up remote access.

## Task 7 – Setting up secure remote access

After performing your initial configurations on your device, it's time to place it on your network. When a device is on the network, it may not always be convenient to manage the device via the console port. At times, as a networking professional, you may not be close to your device; perhaps the device is located in another country. Remote access allows the administrator to remotely connect and manage the device while being at another location.

There are two main methods to remotely access a Cisco IOS device:

- Telnet
- **Secure Shell (SSH)**

Both Telnet and SSH allow you to remotely access a device via a Terminal, allowing you to gain shell access. However, Telnet is an unsecure method used to remotely access and manage a device as traffic can be seen in plaintext (unencrypted). SSH is the recommended method for remote access as all SSH traffic is encrypted by default. If a hacker is intercepting SSH traffic over a network, they will not be able see the actual contents of the traffic flowing between the SSH client and the SSH server (device).

## Setting up Telnet

To configure Telnet access on the VTY lines, use the following commands:

```
R1#configure terminal
R1(config)#line vty 0 15
R1(config-line)#password class123
R1(config-line)#login
R1(config-line)#exit
R1(config)#
```

The line vty 0 15 command specifies that we configure all 16 **virtual terminal (VTY)** lines on the device, where the first line is VTY 0. Then, we set the Telnet password as class123 and use the login command to enable authentication whenever a user attempts to log in.

Next, ensure each PC is using the following IP configurations:

**PC1**:

- IP address: 192.168.1.20
- Subnet mask: 255.255.255.0
- Default gateway: 192.168.1.1

**PC2**:

- IP address: 192.168.2.20
- Subnet mask: 255.255.255.0
- Default gateway: 192.168.2.1

To test the Telnet connection within Cisco Packet Tracer, use the following instructions:

1. Click on **PC1** and select the **Desktop** tab.

2. Open the Command Prompt and use the ping command to test end-to-end connectivity between **PC1** and the router. Then, use the ping 192.168.1.1 command.

   You should get the following response from the router:

```
C:\>ping 192.168.1.1
Pinging 192.168.1.1 with 32 bytes of data:
Reply from 192.168.1.1 - bytes=32 time<1ms TTL=255
```

```
Reply from 192.168.1.1 - bytes=32 time=3ms TTL=255
Reply from 192.168.1.1 - bytes=32 time<1ms TTL=255
Reply from 192.168.1.1 - bytes=32 time<1ms TTL=255

Ping statistics for 192.168.1.1 -
Packets: Sent = 4, Received = 4, Lost = 0 (0% loss),
Approximate round trip times in milli-seconds:
Minimum = 0ms, Maximum = 3ms, Average = 0ms
```

Once you are able to get a successful reply from the target device (192.168.1.1), you have connectivity.

3.  Close the Command Prompt and open the Telnet/SSH client on **PC1**.

4.  Change the connection type to **Telnet**, enter the IP address of the router (192.168.1.1), and click on **Connect**.

You should see the banner message from *Task 6* with an authentication prompt requesting the VTY Telnet password.

## Configuring Secure Shell (SSH)

As mentioned previously, we should always use SSH when it's available. In the following steps, I will demonstrate how to disable Telnet, enable SSH, and create a local user account:

1.  Change the default hostname on the Cisco IOS device.

2.  Join a local domain by using the ip domain-name <domain> command in **global config** mode:

```
R1(config)#ip domain-name ccna.local
```

3.  Generate encryption keys for the SSH sessions using the following commands:

```
R1(config)#crypto key generate rsa
```

The interactive menu will ask for a modulus key size. The minimum is 512, but it's recommended to use 1024 or higher. The larger the key size, the stronger the encryption. However, a very large key size can use a lot of CPU resources on the network device when performing encryption and decryption tasks.

4.  Create a local user account with a secret password using the following commands:

```
R1(config)#username Admin secret class456
```

5. Configure the VTY lines to only allow SSH connections (disabling Telnet), remove the Telnet password, and use the local user account as the login credentials. To complete this step, use the following commands:

```
R1(config)#line vty 0 15
R1(config-line)#transport input ssh
R1(config-line)#no password
R1(config-line)#login local
R1(config-line)#exit
R1(config)#
```

The `transport input` command can be used with `all`, `none`, `ssh`, or `telnet` to specify the type of incoming traffic on the VTY lines.

The following is an additional command that's required when configuring remote access (Telnet and SSH) on Cisco switches. Switches require a default gateway that enables them to have bi-directional communication over different networks. According to our lab topology, a device on the `192.168.1.0/24` network will not be able to remote access **SW2** and vice versa.

To set the default gateway on the switches in our topology, use the following commands:

**SW1**

```
SW1(config)#ip default-gateway 192.168.1.1
```

**SW2**

```
SW2(config)#ip default-gateway 192.168.2.1
```

## Task 8 – Configuring the console to use the local user accounts

In the previous task, you learned how to create a user account and enable the VTY lines to query it during the login process. Additionally, the same can be done to the console line by using the following commands:

```
R1(config)#line console 0
R1(config-line)#no password
R1(config-line)#login local
R1(config-line)#exit
```

## Task 9 – Disabling domain lookup and encrypting all plaintext passwords

At times, when you enter a *name* or *word* within the Cisco IOS, it attempts to perform a domain name lookup. To abort the translation, use the *Ctrl + Shift + ^* key combination on your keyboard. Additionally, you should disable the domain lookup feature within the Cisco IOS by executing the following command:

```
R1(config)#no ip domain-lookup
```

When setting passwords on the Cisco IOS, you may not have the option to use the secret command to create an encrypted form of the actual password. This means you may have to resort to setting a plaintext password. To add an additional layer of security, use the following command to encrypt all current and future plaintext passwords automatically:

```
R1(config)#service password-encryption
```

## Task 10 – Checking IOS version and saving configurations

As a Cisco networking professional, it's important to determine the current version of your operating system. To check the device's operating system version, use the show version command, as shown here:

```
R1#show version
Cisco IOS Software, C2900 Software (C2900-UNIVERSALK9-M),
Version 15.1(4)M4, RELEASE SOFTWARE (fc2)
Technical Support: http://www.cisco.com/techsupport
Copyright (c) 1986-2012 by Cisco Systems, Inc.
Compiled Thurs 5-Jan-12 15 -41 by pt_team
ROM: System Bootstrap, Version 15.1(4)M4, RELEASE SOFTWARE
(fc1)
cisco2911 uptime is 5 hours, 23 minutes, 55 seconds
System returned to ROM by power-on
System image file is "flash0 -c2900-universalk9-mz.SPA.151-1.
M4.bin"
--More--
```

As shown in the preceding output, the device is using a Cisco IOS version 15.1(4) of the operating system. This information is useful if you are planning on upgrading to a newer version of the IOS. The `show version` command provides us with the **uptime** of the device since it has been powered on.

Lastly, remember that all the configuration changes that are made to each device are stored in `running-config`. If any device should lose power or reboot, all the configurations will be lost. To save `running-config` in `startup-config`, use the following commands:

```
R1#copy running-config startup-config
Destination filename [startup-config]?
Building configuration...
[OK]
R1#show startup-config
```

Hit *Enter* when it asks for the destination filename. The default filename is shown in brackets (`[startup-config]`); there's no need to type a new filename. Once the configurations have been saved, use the `show startup-config` command to view its contents. Additionally, you can use the `reload` command in Privilege Exec mode to reboot the device and see that `startup-config` retains the configurations.

# Performing troubleshooting procedures

After performing configurations on a device, it's good practice to execute the relevant `show` command to verify what you have done is correct and is working as expected. Throughout this book, we will learn about additional methods for designing and optimizing a network using Cisco devices, where you will learn about new configurations and troubleshooting commands to help you along the way.

There are two main tools that help us troubleshoot a network from the client side (PC):

- Ping
- Traceroute

Ping is simply used to test end-to-end connectivity between the devices on a network. This tool uses the `ping ip address of target` syntax. The following is an example of a successful connectivity test:

```
C:\>ping 8.8.8.8

Pinging 8.8.8.8 with 32 bytes of data:
Reply from 8.8.8.8: bytes=32 time=65ms TTL=50
Reply from 8.8.8.8: bytes=32 time=63ms TTL=50
Reply from 8.8.8.8: bytes=32 time=65ms TTL=50
Reply from 8.8.8.8: bytes=32 time=65ms TTL=50

Ping statistics for 8.8.8.8:
    Packets: Sent = 4, Received = 4, Lost = 0 (0% loss),
Approximate round trip times in milli-seconds:
    Minimum = 63ms, Maximum = 65ms, Average = 64ms
```

Figure 2.48 – Ping test on a Windows Command Prompt

However, the Cisco IOS does not provide an output similar to the one shown in the preceding output. The following are the symbols and their descriptions:

- `!`: Successful

- `.`: Request timeout

- `U`: Destination unreachable

The following is an example where a connectivity test was done from R1 to PC1 in the lab topology:

```
R1>ping 192.168.1.10

Type escape sequence to abort.
Sending 5, 100-byte ICMP Echos to 192.168.1.10, timeout is 2 seconds:
!!!!!
Success rate is 100 percent (5/5), round-trip min/avg/max = 0/0/3 ms
```

Figure 2.49 – Ping test using the Cisco IOS

You now have the essential skills to implement Cisco networking solutions for a small network.

# Summary

Having completed this chapter, you have learned some amazing skills and got to build your very own Cisco lab environment. Most importantly, you got hands on with Cisco switches and routers. There are many ways you can get the practical experience you desire, by either purchasing physical equipment or even building a fully virtualized lab environment. Keep in mind that Cisco Packet Tracer is updated quite often and new features are always being added, along with many improvements.

My personal advice is that you shouldn't be afraid of trying new things in your lab environment. If you *break* or misconfigure something, try to figure out what went wrong and how to resolve the issue. Network engineering is a continuous process of designing, configuring, and troubleshooting, but most importantly, it's about problem solving and critical thinking. So, don't be afraid – use the help (?) command, and even try to emulate your home or office network in your Cisco lab.

I hope this chapter has been informative for you and is helpful in your journey toward learning how to implement and administrate Cisco solutions and prepare for the CCNA 200-301 certification. In the next chapter, *IP Addressing and Subnetting*, we will learn all about IP addressing, subnetting, and understanding **Variable-Length Subnet Masks (VLSMs)**.

# Questions

The following are a short list of review questions to help reinforce your learning and help you identify areas that require some improvement:

1.  If you are currently in line console mode, which shortcut will carry you back to **Privilege Exec** mode?

    A. *CTRL + C*

    B. *CTRL + X*

    C. *CTRL + V*

    D. *CTRL + Z*

2.  Which mode allows you to execute the `enable secret` command?

    A. **Privilege Exec**

    B. **User Exec**

    C. **Global config**

    D. **Line**

3.  An interface is showing as administratively down. How do you activate the interface?

    A. No shutdown

    B. Up

    C. Start

    D. None of the above

4.  You are tasked with setting up remote access on various networking devices. Which of the following methods is best suited?

    A. Console

    B. SSH

    C. Telnet

    D. VTY

5.  Which of the following commands will display the banner message "keep out"?

    A. `banner #keep out#`

    B. `banner motd keep out`

    C. `banner motd #keep out%`

    D. `banner motd &keep out&`

6.  Which of the following commands will set a secure password on the Cisco IOS?

    A. `enable password`

    B. `enable`

    C. `enable secret`

    D. `secret`

# Further reading

The following links are recommended for additional reading:

*   Initial device configuration: `https://www.cisco.com/c/en/us/td/docs/routers/access/800/hardware/installation/guide/800HIG/initalconfig.html`

*   Basic router configuration: `https://www.cisco.com/c/en/us/td/docs/routers/access/800M/software/800MSCG/routconf.html`

# 3
# IP Addressing and Subnetting

The internet acts as an enormous digital world, and it's continuously expanding with new users and internet-connected devices coming online every day. Every device on a network requires some type of address to be able to communicate and exchange messages. To meet this need, **Internet Protocol** (**IP**) addresses are commonly used.

Throughout this chapter, you will learn about the characteristics of both IPv4 and IPv6 addressing schemes, while discovering the various types of transmissions that occur on a network, as well as the importance of subnet masks and the role they play in a network.

In this chapter, we will cover the following topics:

- The need for IP addressing
- Characteristics of IPv4
- Classes of IPv4 addresses
- Special IPv4 addresses
- Subnet mask

- Subnetting

- IPv6

- Lab – Configuring IPv6 addresses on a Cisco device

- Lab – Configuring IPv6 addresses on a Windows computer

- Testing end-to-end connectivity

# Technical requirements

To follow along with the exercises in this chapter, please ensure that you meet the following hardware and software requirements:

- Cisco Packet Tracer

- GNS3

- GNS3 VM

- Configuration files: `https://github.com/PacktPublishing/Implementing-and-Administering-Cisco-Solutions/tree/master/Chapter%2003`

Check out the following video to see the Code in Action: `https://bit.ly/3iQDXZT`

# The need for IP addressing

A computer network is a bit like a neighborhood or community. Communities consist of many people, houses, schools, and businesses. Each of these houses and buildings has a postal (mailing) address that allows others to send letters and packages via a courier service to the recipients. Without a mailing or postal address, it's a bit challenging for others to send a physical letter or package to you. Similarly, on a computer network, each device has a unique address that is used for sending and receiving messages (signals) between them. These addresses are known as Internet Protocol addresses and are most commonly referred to as IP addresses.

How do we know which IP addresses can be used on the internet and on private networks? There is a special organization that manages both IPv4 and IPv6 addresses. This organization is known as the **Internet Assigned Numbers Authority (IANA)**. The IANA is also responsible for governing the usage of the **Domain Name System (DNS)** root directories and services via the **Internet Corporation for Assigned Names and Numbers (ICANN)**.

Sometime around 1983, the IPv4 scheme was made available for usage on computer networks and the internet. Most of the internet today is dominated by the IPv4 addressing schemes as the preferred method of communication. On many private networks (such as home networks), IPv4 is still very much commonly used to this day.

When it comes to IP addresses, IANA has created two address spaces for IPv4. These are the **public** and **private** address spaces. The public space is designed to be used on the internet and on all devices that are directly connected to the internet. On the internet, each IP address must always be unique to ensure messages (packets) are delivered to the correct recipient as expected. Imagine if two devices on the internet shared a single public IPv4 address; some messages may be delivered to one device while the other messages may be sent to the second device. This would cause many problems. To help prevent these problems, there are **Regional Internet Registries (RIRs)** around the world.

> **Important note**
>
> To further understand the assignment of IPv4 network blocks, you can refer to the official IANA documentation at the following URL: `https://www.iana.org/assignments/ipv4-address-space/ipv4-address-space.xhtml`.

The IANA does not directly distribute IP network blocks to any organization who wants internet connectivity. Instead, there are currently five RIRs in the world, and each RIR responsible for distributing IP network blocks to **Internet Service Providers (ISPs)**. The following is a list of each RIR and their geolocational responsibility:

- AFRINIC: Supports the continent of Africa

- APNIC: Supports the regions of Asia and the Pacific

- ARIN: Supports the regions of Canada, USA, and part of the Caribbean

- LACNIC: Supports Latin America and part of the Caribbean

- RIPE NCC: Supports Europe, the Middle East, and Central Asia

The following diagram illustrates how IP addresses are distributed across the internet:

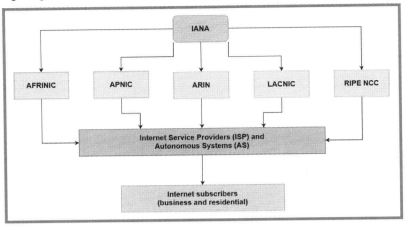

Figure 3.1 – Delegation of IP network blocks

An **Autonomous System** (**AS**) is a very large collection of internet routing network prefixes that are managed by a single organization, known as an operator. An ISP is an example of an AS. Each ISP has a unique **AS number** (**ASN**) that is used to interconnect one AS to another. This allows each Autonomous System to use **Border Gateway Protocol** (**BGP**) to exchange routing updates, as well as network with one another over the internet.

> **Important note**
> To view the **ASNs** for each country, use the following URL:
> `https://ipinfo.io/countries`.

The following diagram shows a representation of multiple ASNs interconnected via BGP:

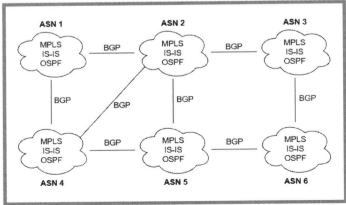

Figure 3.2 – Network representation of Autonomous Systems using BGP

Each Autonomous System exchanges routing updates and shares their public (internet) networks with their directly connected neighbors. As more devices and Autonomous Systems connect to the backbone of the internet, the internet itself continues to grow.

> **Important note**
>
> To view the submarine cables that connect us to the internet, please visit `www.submarinecablemap.com`. Checking out a cable within the map will provide you with the necessary ISPs and names of organizations that own/lease it.

Now that we have covered the global architecture of the IP addressing landscape computer network and the internet, as well as understood the two types of IP addresses, let's take a more detailed look at the characteristics of the first type: IPv4.

# Characteristics of IPv4

Learning about computer networking is always a fascinating topic as it also introduces you to how computing devices interpret data and present information. Using a computer or smart device, we usually see a very well-polished **graphical user interface** (**GUI**). In Microsoft Windows, for example, there is Windows Explorer, which helps us navigate the various areas (locations) of a computer easily. When opening files, such as pictures, the photo viewer application presents us with a picture our minds can interpret. However, by default, computers and networking devices are unable to interpret the objects within a picture.

When data is written onto a **hard disk drive** (**HDD**), there's an actuator arm that contains a read/write head (pin), which is used to magnetize and de-magnetize areas on the platters to represent data. This means that what we see as a picture of a car on the computer screen is, to the device, a portion of the HDD being magnetized and de-magnetized, representing a bunch of 1s and 0s.

> **Important note**
>
> Nowadays, many applications use **machine learning** (**ML**) to actually detect objects within a picture. One such ML algorithm is YOLO – Real Time Objection Detection.

Remember that when a device is sending a message on a network, a series of electrical signals are sent across the wire. The recipient interprets the incoming signals and presents them as data. A high electrical signal (voltage) is commonly represented as a 1, while a low voltage is represented as a 0. Similarly, when data is being written to an HDD, electrical signals are used to magnetize and de-magnetize the surface areas of the platters. When data is read, the read/write head interprets the magnetized and de-magnetized areas that represent data, and thus the device (such as a computer) presents information to us humans.

You are probably wondering what the 1s and 0s have to do with computer networking. Just like everything in the computing world, IP addresses are written in binary notation (1s and 0s). However, we humans usually write IP addresses in decimal format using base 10, with numbers in the range 0-9.

As outlined by IANA, an IPv4 address is 32 bits in length, comprised of 1s and 0s. There is a total of four octets per IPv4 address. Each octet is made up of 8 bits and is separated by a period or dot ( . ). This results in *8 bits per octet x 4 octets = 32 bits in total*.

The need to understand IP addressing and subnetting plays a vital role in network engineering. Incorrectly assigning an IP address and/or a subnet mask will result in no connectivity between devices. In the next section, we will dive into understanding the composition of an IPv4 packet and the purpose of each field.

## Composition of an IPv4 packet

Becoming a networking engineer or advancing your skills within the networking field isn't only about learning how to configure devices to move traffic between networks more efficiently; understanding the composition and the characteristics of an IPv4 packet will also be very beneficial in the troubleshooting phases of your career.

The following diagram shows all the fields within an IPv4 packet:

| Version | Internet Header Length | Differentiated Services (DS) | | Total Length | |
|---------|------------------------|-----------|-----|--------------|------------------|
| | | DSCP | ECN | | |
| Identification | | | | Flag | Fragment Offset |
| Time-to-Live (TTL) | | Protocol | | Header Checksum | |
| Source IP Address | | | | | |
| Destination IP Address | | | | | |
| Options | | | | | |

Figure 3.3 – IPv4 packet

Each field within the IPv4 packet plays an important role during the transmission of a message from one device to another. The following are the names of each field, along with descriptions of their purpose:

- **Version**: This field is generally used to identify the version of the **Internet Protocol (IP)**, such as IPv4 and IPv6. The size of this field is 4 bits.

- **Internet Header Length (IHL)**: This field indicates where the header ends and the data begins within the IPv4 packet. This field is 4 bits.

- **Differentiated Services or DiffServ (DS)**: This field plays an important role when using **Quality of Service (QoS)** tools on a network. This field was formerly known as **Type of Service (ToS)**. The length of this field is 8 bits.

- **Total Length**: This field ensures the entire datagram is no more than 65,535 bytes. This field is 16 bits.

- **Identification**: As we mentioned in *Chapter 1, Introduction to Networking*, before a device sends a datagram to the network, the device creates smaller fragments called bits. Each bit contains the same addressing details within the header, but the payload (data) is made into smaller pieces. This field is used to assign a value to each bit as they are sent to the physical network. The value is used to assist in placing a sequence number to each bit leaving the sender. This allows the recipient to use the sequence number during the process for reassembling the datagram. This field is 16 bits.

- **Flags**: Flags are used for various options within an IPv4 packet. These options may include whether a packet is a **SYN**, **ACK**, **FIN**, or **RST** packet. This field is 3 bits.

- **Fragment Offset**: This field is used to identify the position of a fragmented datagram. This field is 13 bits.

- **Time To Live (TTL)**: This field is found only in packets. Devices sending packets on a network use this field to set the lifespan of the message as it travels across a network. As the packet passes a hop (a Layer 3 device) along a path, the TTL value decreases by 1. If a device renders a packet's TTL value to 0, that device discards the packet. The TTL field is 8 bits in length.

A simple exercise to illustrate how the TTL value affects a message is to send a message to a public IP address, while using the -i parameter to set a TTL value for the **Internet Control Message Protocol (ICMP)** message. In this case, we'll use Google's public DNS server (8.8.8.8), as shown here:

```
C:\>ping -i 2 8.8.8.8

Pinging 8.8.8.8 with 32 bytes of data:
Reply from 172.16.16.1: TTL expired in transit.
Reply from 172.16.16.1: TTL expired in transit.
Reply from 172.16.16.1: TTL expired in transit.
Reply from 172.16.16.1: TTL expired in transit.

Ping statistics for 8.8.8.8:
    Packets: Sent = 4, Received = 4, Lost = 0 (0% loss),

C:\>
```

Figure 3.4 – TTL value expired in ICMP packets

As shown in the preceding snippet, none of the ICMP packets were able to reach the destination; that is, 8.8.8.8. This is because the TTL values of each ICMP packet were set to 2, so each packet expired and was discarded before they were able to reach the intended destination.

- **Protocol**: This 8-bit field is used to identify the network protocol that a datagram belongs to at the destination host.

- **Header Checksum** : This field contains the hash value (checksum) of the header and is 16 bits in length.

- **Source IP address**: This 32-bit field contains the sender's IPv4 address.

- **Destination IP address**: This 32-bit field contains the destination's IPv4 address.

- **Options**: This field ranges between 0 – 40 bytes in length and is used for many purposes, such as record routing and source routing details.

Having completed this section, you are now able to identify and describe each field within an IPv4 packet.

In the next section, you will learn the essential skills involved for understanding IP assignment and subnetting, by first learning how to perform conversions between binary and decimal format.

# Converting binary into decimal

Let's start by taking a look at an IPv4 address in its binary format. We already learned that an IPv4 address is made up of 32 bits, consisting of 1s and 0s. Let's look at an example of one written in binary:

```
11000000.10101000.00000001.10000001
```

All binary numbers are written in `Base 2` with a **radix** of 2. A radix is a unique number used in a positioning system, where the first position's value is 0. I know this may sound a bit confusing, but over the next few paragraphs, you'll find the concept a bit clearer as we'll be providing examples.

In mathematics, we learn that $A^0 = 1$, where A represents the radix or base. Let's use the radix of 2 as part of a positioning system, starting with 0 as the first position:

- $2^0 = 1$
- $2^1 = 2 \times 1 = 2$
- $2^2 = 2 \times 2 = 4$
- $2^3 = 2 \times 2 \times 2 = 8$
- $2^4 = 2 \times 2 \times 2 \times 2 = 16$
- $2^5 = 2 \times 2 \times 2 \times 2 \times 2 = 32$
- $2^6 = 2 \times 2 \times 2 \times 2 \times 2 \times 2 = 64$
- $2^7 = 2 \times 2 \times 2 \times 2 \times 2 \times 2 \times 2 = 128$

When it comes to understanding binary and decimal conversions in the field of networking, we convert only one octet at a time, not the entire 32-bit IPv4 address. This is the reason our positioning system stopped at the eighth position in the sequence, $2^7$. To further understand the position system using binary, the following table shows the calculation for each bit within an octet:

| Radix | $2^7$ | $2^6$ | $2^5$ | $2^4$ | $2^3$ | $2^2$ | $2^1$ | $2^0$ |
|---|---|---|---|---|---|---|---|---|
| Decimal | 128 | 64 | 32 | 16 | 8 | 4 | 2 | 1 |

Figure 3.5 – Base 2 table

When performing conversions, always remember that the first position is always $2^0$ and that the eighth position is $2^7$. The full binary format of each position can be expressed further, as follows:

- $2^0 = 00000001 = 1$
- $2^1 = 00000010 = 2$
- $2^2 = 00000100 = 4$
- $2^3 = 00001000 = 8$
- $2^4 = 00010000 = 16$
- $2^5 = 00100000 = 32$
- $2^6 = 01000000 = 64$
- $2^7 = 10000000 = 128$

Now, let's use our IPv4 address of `11000000.10101000.00000001.10000001` and convert it into a decimal number. To perform this exercise, use the following instructions:

1. Place the values of the first octet, `11000000`, within the table, as shown here:

| Radix | $2^7$ | $2^6$ | $2^5$ | $2^4$ | $2^3$ | $2^2$ | $2^1$ | $2^0$ |
|---|---|---|---|---|---|---|---|---|
| Decimal | 128 | 64 | 32 | 16 | 8 | 4 | 2 | 1 |
| Binary | 1 | 1 | 0 | 0 | 0 | 0 | 0 | 0 |

Figure 3.6 – Conversion – binary to decimal (first octet)

Wherever there's a binary value that = `1` in the preceding table, the radix value is ON. In our table, $2^7$ and $2^6$ are ON. This will provide us with the following results:

```
2⁷ + 2⁶ = 128 + 64 = 192
```

2. Let's repeat the same procedure for the second octet, `10101000`, to determine its decimal value:

| Radix | $2^7$ | $2^6$ | $2^5$ | $2^4$ | $2^3$ | $2^2$ | $2^1$ | $2^0$ |
|---|---|---|---|---|---|---|---|---|
| Decimal | 128 | 64 | 32 | 16 | 8 | 4 | 2 | 1 |
| Binary | 1 | 0 | 1 | 0 | 1 | 0 | 0 | 0 |

Figure 3.7 – Conversion – binary to decimal (second octet)

Using the same principle of 1 = ON and 0 = OFF for the radix, we get the following results:

$$2^7 + 2^5 + 2^3 = 128 + 32 + 8 = 168$$

3. Let's convert the third octet, 00000001, into decimal format by placing it into the following table:

| Radix | $2^7$ | $2^6$ | $2^5$ | $2^4$ | $2^3$ | $2^2$ | $2^1$ | $2^0$ |
|---|---|---|---|---|---|---|---|---|
| Decimal | 128 | 64 | 32 | 16 | 8 | 4 | 2 | 1 |
| Binary | 0 | 0 | 0 | 0 | 0 | 0 | 0 | 1 |

Figure 3.8 – Conversion – binary to decimal (third octet)

Converting 00000001 into decimal, we get the following result:

$$2^0 = 1$$

4. Now, convert the fourth octet by placing 10000001 into the following table:

| Radix | $2^7$ | $2^6$ | $2^5$ | $2^4$ | $2^3$ | $2^2$ | $2^1$ | $2^0$ |
|---|---|---|---|---|---|---|---|---|
| Decimal | 128 | 64 | 32 | 16 | 8 | 4 | 2 | 1 |
| Binary | 1 | 0 | 0 | 0 | 0 | 0 | 0 | 1 |

Figure 3.9 – Conversion – binary to decimal (fourth octet)

We will get the following results:

$$2^7 + 2^0 = 128 + 1 = 129$$

5. The last stage is simply placing all the decimal values together, as shown here:

11000000.10101000.00000001.10000001 = 192.168.1.129

If all eight bits were 1s within an octet, what would be the decimal equivalent? We'd need to add all the powers of 2 ranging from 20 to 27, as shown here:

$$2^7 + 2^6 + 2^5 + 2^4 + 2^3 + 2^2 + 2^1 + 2^0$$

To provide a further breakdown, we get the following value when we add all the powers of 2:

$$128 + 64 + 32 + 16 + 8 + 4 + 2 + 1 = 255$$

This means that an octet has a range of 0 – 255. There is no IPv4 address whose value is greater than 255 in any of its four octets. Now that you have learned how to convert binary into decimal, let's take a look at converting decimal into binary.

# Converting decimal into binary

Let's get started by converting the IP address 172.19.43.67 into binary. We are going to use a simple eight-step method that will guarantee the accuracy of the final result. In the previous section, *Converting binary into decimal*, we used various *radix* values ranging from 20 to 27, and within our eight-step process, we will be leveraging these values once again, but using a slightly different approach: the method of subtraction.

To ensure the results are accurate, please adhere to the following rules:

- Convert only one octet at a time.
- Start by subtracting the decimal value from the highest power of 2 ($2^7$) while working your way down to $2^0$.
- If you can subtract a decimal value from a Radix value, place a 1 to represent yes.
- If you are unable to subtract a decimal value from a Radix value, place a 0 to represent yes.
- If you get a 0, attempt to subtract the decimal value from the next (lower) Radix value.

Let's begin by converting the first octet, 172, into binary format:

1. Can we carry out 172 – 128 ($2^7$)? Yes, giving us a remainder of 44. Therefore, we get a 1.
2. Is it possible to carry out 44 – 64 ($2^6$)? No; therefore, we carry 44 forward to be subtracted from the next power of 2 ($2^5$). Therefore, we get a 0.
3. Can we carry out 44 - 32 ($2^5$)? Yes, giving us a remainder of 12. Therefore, we get a 1.
4. Could 12 – 16 ($2^4$)? No; therefore, carry 44 forward to be subtracted from the next power of 2 ($2^3$). Therefore, we get a 0.
5. Is it possible for 12 – 8 ($2^3$)? Yes, giving us a remainder of 4. Therefore, we get a 1.
6. Could 4 – 4 ($2^2$)? Yes, giving us a remainder of 0. Therefore, we get a 1.
7. It is possible for 0 – 2 ($2^1$)? No; therefore, we get a 0.
8. Could 0 – 1 ($2^0$)? No; therefore, our last value is 0 since this is the last power of 2 in the sequence.

The final answer in binary is taking all the 1s and 0s starting from *step 1* and placing them in sequential order from *step 1 to 8*. Therefore, the binary value of 172 is 10101100.

The following is a visual representation of all 8 steps demonstrating the process we use to convert the decimal value 172 into binary:

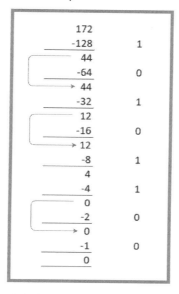

Figure 3.10 – Calculation for decimal value 172 into binary

Let's convert our second octet, 19, into binary using the same procedure:

1. Could 19 – 128 ($2^7$)? No; therefore, we carry 19 forward to be subtracted from the next power of 2 ($2^6$). Therefore, we get a 0.

2. Is it possible for 19 – 64 ($2^6$)? No; therefore, we carry 19 forward to be subtracted from the next power of 2 ($2^5$). Therefore, we get a 0.

3. Could 19 – 32 ($2^5$)? No; therefore, we carry 19 forward to be subtracted from the next power of 2 ($2^4$). Therefore, we get a 0.

4. Could 19 – 16 ($2^4$)? Yes, giving us a remainder of 3. Therefore, we get a 1.

5. Is it possible for 3 – 8 ($2^3$)? No; therefore, we carry 3 forward to be subtracted from the next power of 2 ($2^2$). Therefore, we get a 0.

6. Could 3 – 4 ($2^2$)? No; therefore, we carry 3 forward to be subtracted from the next power of 2 ($2^1$). Therefore, we get a 0.

7. It is possible for 3 – 2 ($2^1$)? Yes, giving us a remainder of 1. Therefore, we get a 1.

8. Could 1 – 1 ($2^0$)? Yes, with a remainder of 0. Therefore, we get a 1 to conclude our process.

The final answer in binary is taking all the 1s and 0s starting from *step 1* and placing them in sequential order from *step 1 to 8*. Therefore, the binary value of 19 is 00010011.

The following is a visual representation of all eight steps demonstrating the process we use to convert the decimal value 19 into binary:

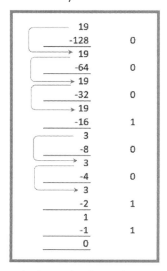

Figure 3.11 – Calculation for decimal value 19 into binary

Let's convert our third octet, 43, into binary using the same procedure:

1. Could 43 – 128 ($2^7$)? No; therefore, we carry 43 forward to be subtracted from the next power of 2 ($2^6$). Therefore, we get a 0.

2. Is it possible for 43 – 64 ($2^6$)? No; therefore, we carry 43 forward to be subtracted from the next power of 2 ($2^5$). Therefore, we get a 0.

3. Could 43 – 32 ($2^5$)? Yes, giving us a remainder of 11. Therefore, we get a 1.

4. Could 11 – 16 ($2^4$)? No; therefore, we carry 11 forward to be subtracted from the next power of 2 ($2^2$). Therefore, we get a 0.

5. Is it possible for 11 – 8 ($2^3$)? Yes, giving us a remainder of 3. Therefore, we get a 1.

6. Could 3 – 4 ($2^2$)? No; therefore, we carry 3 forward to be subtracted from the next power of 2 ($2^1$). Therefore, we get a 0.

7. It is possible for 3 – 2 ($2^1$)? Yes, giving us a remainder of 1. Therefore, we get a 1.

8. Could 1 – 1 ($2^0$)? Yes, with a remainder of 1. Therefore, we get a 1 to conclude our process.

The final answer in binary is taking all the 1s and 0s starting from *step 1* and placing them in sequential order from *step 1 to 8*. Therefore, the binary value of 43 is 00101011.

The following is a visual representation of all eight steps demonstrating the process we use to convert the decimal value 43 into binary:

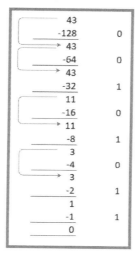

Figure 3.12 – Calculation for decimal value 43 into binary

For our last octet, let's convert 67 into binary using the same procedure:

1.  Could $67 - 128$ ($2^7$)? No; therefore, we carry 67 forward to be subtracted from the next power of 2 ($2^6$). Therefore, we get a 0.

2.  Is it possible for $67 - 64$ ($2^6$)? No; therefore, we carry 3 forward to be subtracted from the next power of 2 ($2^5$). Therefore, we get a 0.

3.  Could $3 - 32$ ($2^5$)? No; therefore, we carry 3 forward to be subtracted from the next power of 2 (25). Therefore, we get a 0.

4.  Could $3 - 16$ ($2^4$)? No; therefore, we carry 3 forward to be subtracted from the next power of 2 ($2^2$). Therefore, we get a 0.

5.  Is it possible for $3 - 8$ ($2^3$)? No; therefore, we carry 3 forward to be subtracted from the next power of 2 ($2^5$). Therefore, we get a 0.

6.  Could $3 - 4$ ($2^2$)? No; therefore, we carry 3 forward to be subtracted from the next power of 2 ($2^1$). Therefore, we get a 0.

7.  It is possible for $3 - 2$ ($2^1$)? Yes, giving us a remainder of 1. Therefore, we get a 1.

8.  Could $1 - 1$ ($2^0$)? Yes, with a remainder of 0. Therefore, we get a 1 to conclude our process.

The final answer in binary is taking all the 1s and 0s starting from *step 1* and placing them in sequential order from *step 1 to 8*. Therefore, the binary value of 43 is 01000011.

The following is a visual representation of all eight steps demonstrating the process we use to convert the decimal value 67 into binary:

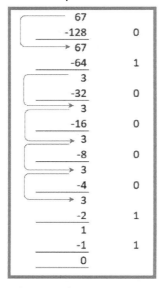

Figure 3.13 – Calculation for decimal value 67 into binary

Having converted each octet, let's put everything together to see the binary numbers:

| 172 | 19 | 43 | 67 |
|---|---|---|---|
| 10101100 | 00010011 | 00101011 | 01000011 |

Figure 3.14 – Binary and decimal equivalents

We can conclude that 172.19.43.67 has a binary value of 10101100.00010011.00 101011.01000011.

> **Important Note**
> The conversion methods used within this chapter can only be applied to values ranging between 0 – 255.

Learning to perform decimal to binary conversions is an essential skill when learning CCNA as it plays a very important role in the later sections of this chapter. Now that you have learned about the essentials of performing binary and decimal conversions, let's take a dive into learning about the various transmission types on an IPv4 network.

# Transmission types

When learning about IP addressing, there are many types of IPv4 and IPv6 addresses to know about. In this section, we will discuss the various types of IPv4 network transmissions and look at how they are applied to computer networks.

## Unicast

Imagine you are standing within a crowd of people prior to the start of a business conference. You meet a fellow colleague and you start a conversation with them. This is a unicast type of communication as it's only between yourself and your colleague (not the entire crowd or multiple people). Similarly, on a computer network, this type of transmission occurs where one device is exchanging messages (packets) with only one other device.

On a network, a PC may be sending data to a local network printer or even uploading/downloading files from the local network storage server. This is a *one-to-one* transmission, commonly referred to as a unicast transmission.

The following diagram shows a graphical representation of a unicast transmission:

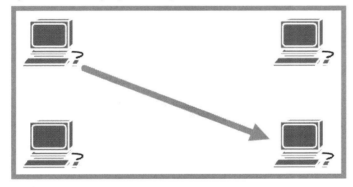

Figure 3.15 – Unicast transmission

## Multicast

Using the same analogy, imagine that, while standing with your colleague and having a mutual discussion, three other people join the conversation. Now, you are speaking with five people in total from the entire crowd present at the business conference. At this point, you are having a multicast type of transmission as you are sending data to selected persons (your colleague and three others) from the entire crowd of people. In this analogy, we can see that when one person speaks to another, it is defined as a transmission. The concept of a transmission is also applied to a computer network where one device may communicate with one or more devices at the same time.

This type of communication is an example of a *one-to-many* transmission (multicast). The following is a graphical representation of a multicast transmission on a PC network:

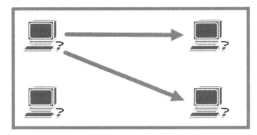

Figure 3.16 – Multicast transmission

Multicast IPv4 addresses range from 224.0.0.0 – 239.255.255.255. These addresses are typically used by network applications over a network. For example, the **Open Shortest Path First (OSPF)** version 2 routing protocol uses addresses 224.0.0.6 and 224.0.0.5 when exchanging OSPF packets between OSPF-enabled routers on a network.

## Broadcast

Continuing with our analogy, the conference is about to start, and the attendees are being seated. However, you are one of the speakers during the conference. When it's your turn to speak, you head on over to the podium to address the audience. While speaking, the microphone and speakers are used to ensure your voice is audible across a wide space to ensure everyone can hear you at the same time. In this type of communication, you are speaking once, and your message is being sent to all the attendees within the conference room.

This is known as broadcast on a computer network, whereby a device sends a message to all other devices on the same IP network.

This type of communication is a *one-to-all* type of transmission. The following diagram shows a graphical representation of a broadcast transmission:

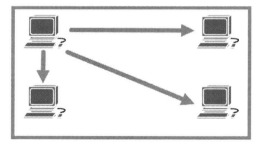

Figure 3.17 – Broadcast transmission

Applications and devices take advantage of using broadcast transmissions to easily send signals (messages) to all other devices on the same network. However, this can be problematic for network performance if there is a high volume of broadcast messages propagating the network.

Additionally, *traffic storms* or *broadcast storms* can occur on a network. This is when a high volume of broadcast messages are being sent the Layer 2 broadcast MAC address, FF:FF:FF:FF:FF:FF, either from a single device or multiple devices.

During my time as an engineer within a regional Telco, I've seen both small and large organizations generate enormous amounts of unexpected broadcast traffic. Investigations show these storms arise due to many different reasons, from malicious applications running on their end devices, to faulty NICs creating corrupted frames and packets.

To configure broadcast storm controls on a Cisco IOS device, use the following commands:

```
Router# configure terminal
Router(config)# interface gigabitethernet 1/0
Router(config-if)# storm-control broadcast level 1.0
Router(config-if)# storm-control action shutdown
Router(config-if)# exit
```

The configurations are placed within **interface** mode and `level` ranges between `0.0 - 100.0` as a percentage value. Therefore, `1.0` means 1% of the interface's bandwidth so that when the threshold is reached, the interface is shut down.

In the preceding configurations, 1% of the `GigabitEthernet` bandwidth is `1000MB x 1% = 10MB`. Additionally, using the `storm-control action shutdown` command changes the device's interface to **error-disable** when the traffic storm threshold (1% bandwidth) is reached.

> **Important Note**
>
> **Error-disable (err-disabled)** means a violation has occurred on the interface and that IOS has logically shut down the port. This state is not administratively down. Administratively shutdown means an interface has been manually disabled or turned off.

To configure multicast storm controls on a Cisco IOS switch, use the following commands:

```
Router# configure terminal
Router(config)# interface gigabitethernet 0/1
Router(config-if)# storm-control multicast level 1.0
Router(config-if)# storm-control action shutdown
Router(config-if)# exit
```

Having covered the most common types of transmissions in IPv4, let's take a look at the only one that is unique to IPv6: *Anycast*.

## Anycast

Anycast is an IPv6 technology that functions as a *one-to-closest* type of transmission. Anycast allows multiple servers (or devices) to share the same IPv6 address. These servers can be physically located at different geographical locations around the world. This allows a client (user) to access the closest server using the Anycast address.

To understand how this works, let's use a real-world scenario. The **Domain Name System** (**DNS**) is an important service on the internet as its purpose is to resolve hostnames for IP addresses. Google has public DNS servers for both IPv4 and IPv6. The IPv6 primary address for Google's DNS server is 2001:4860:4860::8888. This is a single address but is accessible to any device connected to the internet. However, 2001:4860:4860::8888 is not only set on a single device on the internet; rather, it is shared between multiple DNS servers around the world that are owned by Google. As a user, when your device sends a message to the IPv6 address 2001:4860:4860::8888, the routing protocols and technologies of the internet will send your traffic to the closet Google DNS server that has the destination IPv6 address. Hence, Anycast is a one-to-closest transmission.

Now that we have covered the essentials of the four types of transmissions within an IP network, let's take a look at the various IPv4 address classes and spaces.

# Classes of IPv4 addresses

Who determines which IPv4 address can be assigned to our internal devices, and those that are directly connected to, or facing, the internet? When the **Internet Assigned Numbers Authority** (**IANA**) became entrusted with the management of IP addresses, a portion of IPv4 addresses were made to be used on the internet and on the devices that are directly connected to the internet. Meanwhile, another portion was assigned to be strictly usable only on internal networks, such as a home network or within an organization.

In IPv4, there are two address spaces. These are as follows:

- Public IPv4 address space
- Private IPv4 address space

In the following sections, we will discuss each address spaces in further detail, describing the characteristics and uses of both public and private IP addresses.

# Public IPv4 address space

We will first discuss the characteristics of the public IPv4 space. IANA has divided IP addresses into five classes. Each class of addresses can be assigned to a Layer 3 device, such as a router, modem, or any device that is directly connected to the internet, including a firewall appliance.

The following table shows each class and their IPv4 address ranges for the public space:

| Class A | 1.0.0.0 - 9.255.255.255 and 11.0.0.0 - 126.255.255.255 |
| --- | --- |
| Class B | 128.0.0.0 - 171.15.255.255 and 172.32.0.0 - 191.255.255.255 |
| Class C | 192.0.0.0 - 192.167.255.255 and 192.169.0.0 - 223.255.255.255 |
| Class D | 224.0.0.0 - 239.255.255.255 |
| Class E | 240.0.0.0 - 255.255.255.255 |

Figure 3.18 – IPv4 public address space

Classes **A**, **B**, and **C** can be assigned to any device that is directly connected to the internet, while **Class D** is reserved for multicast communications. **Class E** is reversed for experimental usage.

> **Important note**
> Further information on the IPv4 address space can be found at `https://www.iana.org/assignments/ipv4-address-space/ipv4-address-space.xhtml`.

Additionally, within the **Class A**, **B**, and **C** network ranges, there are certain network blocks missing. These missing network blocks from the public space are reserved for the private address space.

> **Important note**
> IPv4 **Class D** and **Class E** addresses can't be assigned to any devices.

Each device on the internet must have a unique IPv4 public address. This address is provided by the local ISP and the customer is responsible for assigning it to their company's router or firewall appliance.

The following diagram shows an organization that has a router to interconnect their private, internal network to the internet – the public network:

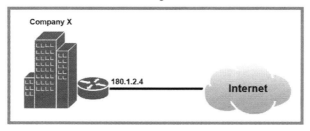

Figure 3.19 – Internet connectivity

As you can see, the public IP address is assigned to the public/internet-facing interface. In a real-world scenario, the public IP address is provided by the ISP to the customer. In the preceding diagram, **Company X** is the customer. The ISP usually provides the organization with a **default gateway**. This is an IP address within the ISP network that allows **Company X** to forward all their traffic destined for the internet via the ISP. However, residential customers (home users) are usually provided with a modem that is already pre-configured to receive a public IP address from the ISP and the default gateway configurations automatically.

These public addresses are usually said to be `routable on the internet` compared to private IP addresses. In the next section, we will discuss the usage of private IPv4 addresses.

## Private IPv4 address space

There are approximately four billion public IPv4 addresses in the world. To be exact, this is $2^{32}$ the number of addresses that exist in the public space. Four billion probably seems like a lot, but in today's world, this number of public IPv4 addresses has almost completely been exhausted. At the time of writing of this book, almost all RIRs have exhausted their public IPv4 address blocks.

Over the past decade, there has been a huge rise in manufacturing smart technologies such as mobile devices and internet-connected sensors. Each of these devices requires an IP to communicate over the internet. Furthermore, cloud computing has been skyrocketing, allowing organizations and individuals to deploy virtual machines on the cloud easily. These virtual machines require a unique IP address as well.

So, four billion isn't a huge amount of public IPv4 addresses considering that there are so many devices. Additionally, if each device on a private network (computers, servers, printers, and so on) were assigned a unique public IPv4 address, each RIR would have exhausted their IPv4 pools long before 2013.

If devices within a private network such as a home or within an organization are not using a public IPv4 address, what type of address are they using to communicate on the internet? RFC 1918 defines three classes of IPv4 addresses that are designated to be assigned only within a private network.

The following are the private IPv4 address spaces:

| Class | Network Address Block | Address Range |
|-------|----------------------|---------------|
| A | 10.0.0.0/8 | 10.0.0.0 - 10.255.255.255 |
| B | 172.16.0.0/12 | 172.16.0.0 - 172.31.255.255 |
| C | 192.168.0.0/24 | 192.168.0.0 - 192.168.255.255 |

Figure 3.20 – Private IPv4 address space

Private IPv4 addresses, as defined in RFC 1918, are non-routable on the internet. This means any device that is directly connected to the internet can only use a public IP address. ISPs usually place a filter on the link between the ISP network and their customer to filter any IP address that is non-routable on the internet, which are those outlined in RFC 1918.

> **Important note**
> Further details on RFC 1918 can be found at https://tools.ietf.org/html/rfc1918.

Typically, when a residential or business customer subscribes to internet services for their homes or organizations, the ISP usually assigns a single public IPv4 address to the customer. For residential customers, a pre-configured fiber modem is usually provided that is automatically assigned a public IPv4 address from the ISP network. On the other hand, for business customers, the ISP sometimes provide the customer with the public IPv4 settings that are to be placed on the public-facing interface of the customer's router.

If private IPv4 addresses are non-routable on the internet, how are internal devices able to communicate on the internet? There is an IP service that allows the router or modem to translate a private IPv4 address into a public IPv4 address. This service is known as **Network Address Translation (NAT)**.

The following diagram shows a NAT-enabled router interconnecting both a private and public network:

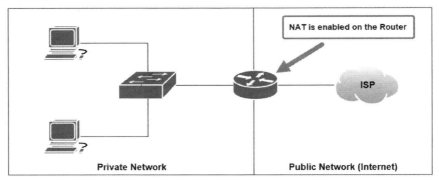

Figure 3.21 – Network segmentation of private and public IP address spaces

In *Chapter 9, Configuring Network Address Translation (NAT)*, we will discuss the functionality of various types of NAT in more detail, as well as how to implement each variation on a Cisco IOS router.

Having completed this section, you are now able to identify IPv4 addresses that belong to both the public and private address spaces. In the next section, we are going to discuss the importance of the subnet mask and how it helps us in the world of computer networking.

# Special IPv4 addresses

In the IPv4 address space, there are three special network blocks that are reserved for special usage. These special IPv4 addresses are as follows:

- Loopback address
- Test-Net
- Link Local

In this section, we will look at each of their characteristics and use cases.

# Loopback address

The loopback range of an address is built into the TCP/IP protocol suite. This range of addresses allows an application running on a host machine to communicate with an application on the same machine. To put it more simply, loopback addresses allow a host operating system to send network traffic to itself.

The network block is reserved for loopback and has the range `127.0.0.1/8` to `127.255.255.254/8`. Therefore, to test the functionality of the TCP/IP protocol suite, you ping any address from the loopback range. Most commonly, network professionals **ping** the `127.0.0.1` address.

# Test-Net

According to `RFC 3330`, the block of addresses `192.0.2.0/24` to `192.0.2.255/24` are created for usage within protocol and vendor documentation. As such, these addresses should not be used on the internet via any device. The Test-Net network block is designed for educational purposes.

# Link Local

Most commonly, whenever you connect a device such a smartphone or computer to a network, the device seeks out a **Dynamic Host Configuration Protocol (DHCP)**, which provides automatic assignment of IP configurations to the device. Without an IP address, a subnet mask, and a default gateway, your device will not be able to communicate on the local network, and without a default gateway, there is no connectivity to the internet.

In the event that a device connects to a network where there is no active DHCP server to provide automatic IP configurations, the device will automatically assign itself a special address. This is known as the **Automatic Private IP Addressing (APIPA)** scheme. It has a network block of `169.254.0.0/16`, and the APIPA network has the range of `169.254.0.1/16` to `169.254.255.254/16`.

The purpose of APIPA is to enable devices within the same LAN to establish at least a basic form of communication between themselves until an active DHCP server is made available.

Having completed this section and learned about the various types of IPv4 addresses, let's take a look at understanding the purpose of the subnet mask.

# Subnet mask

An IP address is not complete without being associated with a subnet (work) mask. The subnet mask has the following characteristics and responsibilities on a network:

- IPv4 subnet masks are 32 bits in length, while IPv6 subnet masks are 128 bits.

- A subnet mask is used to identify both the network and host portions of an IP address.

- A subnet mask is used to assist us and network devices in determining the total number of networks, as well as the total usable IP addresses that exist on an IP subnet.

- The subnet mask is used to help a host device determine whether a packet should be sent to the default gateway if the intended destination is beyond the local network.

As we have learned in the previous sections, there are typically three classes (**A**, **B**, and **C**) of assignable IP addresses for both public and private address spaces. Similarly, there are three default subnet masks for each class of IPv4 address.

The following are the three default subnet masks for class:

- **Class A**: 255.0.0.0
- **Class B**: 255.255.0.0
- **Class C**: 255.255.255.0

If you are using an IP address from a Class A network such as 10.1.2.3, the associated default subnet mask will be 255.0.0.0. A Class B IPv4 address such as 172.15.5.6 will be associated with the Class B subnet mask 255.255.0.0, and so on for a Class C address as well. However, in a lot of situations, the custom subnet masks are assigned IP addresses. In the next section, *Subnetting*, we will cover the topics of subnetting and VLSM, where you will learn about custom subnet masks.

# Network prefix

Prior to starting your journey in gaining your CCNA certification, you may have seen an IP address such as 10.10.1.2/8 and wondered what the /8 part was all about. This is known as the **network prefix**. The network prefix is another format that is commonly used within the computer networking world to represent a subnet mask in a simplified form.

You are probably wondering how /8 is equal to 255.0.0.0. To answer this question, let's take a look at the binary format of the subnet mask:

- Decimal format: 255.0.0.0
- Binary format: 11111111.00000000.00000000.00000000

When writing a subnet mask in binary, it's always written with a continuous length of 1s. There are no 0s between any 1s within a subnet mask; the 0s are placed after the stream of 1s has ended. Looking at the previous example, there are eight 1s within the 255.0.0.0 subnet mask.

Therefore, the network prefix can be written as /8 to represent a default **Class A** subnet mask.

Let's determine the network prefix for a **Class B** subnet mask:

- Decimal format: 255.255.0.0
- Binary format: 11111111.11111111.00000000.00000000

In this example, there are a total of 16 1s within the subnet mask. Therefore, the network prefix can be denoted as /16.

Lastly, in calculating the network prefix for the default **Class C** subnet mask, we get the following:

- Decimal format: 255.255.255.0
- Binary format: 11111111.11111111.11111111.00000000

As expected, there are 24 1s within the default Class C subnet mask, so we get a /24 network prefix.

When attempting to determine the network prefix of a custom subnet mask, we convert each octet of the custom subnet mask into binary. Your results should provide you with a continuous stream of 1s. Calculating the total number of 1s will give you the /x value, where x is the number of 1s in the subnet mask.

Let's imagine you have to determine the network prefix for the following:

- IP address: 192.1.2.3
- Subnet: 255.255.224.0

Perform the following steps to quickly gain our answer:

1.  Convert the first octet into binary. We will get `255 = 11111111`.

2.  Convert the second octet into binary. We will also get `255 = 11111111`.

3.  Converting the third octet, we get `224 = 11100000`.

4.  For the last octet, `0 = 00000000`.

5.  Putting the entire binary subnet together, we get `11111111.11111111.11100 000.00000000`. There are 19 1s in the subnet mask `255.255.224.0`, so we can simply denote the network prefix as `/19` and the IP address as `192.1.2.3/19`.

Now that you have the skills to calculate the network prefix, let's take a deeper look at identifying the Network ID.

## Identifying the Network ID

Configuring IP addresses and subnet masks to devices is a simple task. However, if either an IP address or subnet mask is incorrectly assigned to a device on the network, the device will not be able to communicate with others. To illustrate this theory, the following diagram shows a computer that is unable to communicate with the router:

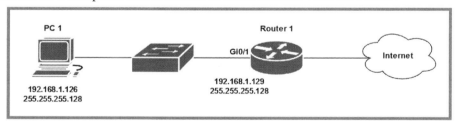

Figure 3.22 – Small network

Considering all the devices are powered on and the right cables are being used to connect each device to another, what could be the issue? As we can see, the IP addresses and subnet mask seem to be correct as they are just a few IP address apart, but is this really accurate? Let's determine if the PC and router both exist on the same logical network. Visually, both devices exist on the same physical network, but in the field of networks, we can logically segment a physical network into multiple logical IP networks.

In this scenario, let's perform some calculations to determine if the PC is on the same logical network as the router, thus determining the Network ID for each device. The Network ID is simply the community address, similar to a neighborhood where each home shares the same community address with differing house or mailbox numbers.

To determine the Network ID, you need to perform a logical operation known as **ANDing** between the IP address and subnet mask of a device.

The following are the laws of AND:

```
0 AND 0 = 0
0 AND 1 = 0
1 AND 0 = 0
1 AND 1 = 1
```

We can determine whether two devices are on the same logical network as follows:

1. Convert the computer's IP address and subnet mask into binary format using the Laws of AND. When the IP address is AND against the subnet mask, the result is known as the Network ID.

   The following snippet shows the ANDing process for **PC1**:

   | | |
   |---|---|
   | IP address | 11000000.10101000.00000001.01111110 |
   | Subnet mask | 11111111.11111111.11111111.10000000 |
   | Network ID | 11000000.10101000.00000001.00000000 |

   Figure 3.23 – Network ID for PC1

2. Convert PC1's Network ID into decimal, which determines that **PC1** belongs to the 192.168.1.0/25 network.

3. Let's perform the ANDing operating on the router's IP address and subnet mask.

   The following snippet shows the ANDing process for the router:

   | | |
   |---|---|
   | IP address | 11000000.10101000.00000001.10000001 |
   | Subnet mask | 11111111.11111111.11111111.10000000 |
   | Network ID | 11000000.10101000.00000001.10000000 |

   Figure 3.24 – Network ID for the router

4. Converting router's Network ID into decimal, we can determine that the router belongs to the 192.168.1.128/25 network.

In conclusion, even though the preceding diagram shows that the devices are physically interconnected, this does not mean that each device has end-to-end connectivity with the others. In our calculation, we have proved that both the computer and the router were on different logical networks, hence they won't be able to intercommunicate. To solve such issues, it's a matter of assigning the PC an IP address from the router's network or vice versa.

Now that you have the skills to determine Network IDs and help solve interconnectivity issues on a network, let's learn how to perform subnetting.

# Subnetting

Hearing the word **subnetting** can be a bit intimidating when learning a networking-related certification. However, learning subnetting is unavoidable on your journey to becoming an awesome network engineer. You may be wondering, what is subnetting and why do we need to learn how to perform this task as a networking professional? To get a better understanding of the answer to this question, let's use a simple analogy. Let's imagine you are the network administrator at a company that has 6 networks, and each of these networks has no more than 50 devices that require an IP address.

It would be easy to simply take a **Class C** network block such as `192.168.1.0/24` and assign it to the network, then choose another **Class C** address block to assign to the next network, and so on. The following is a typical workable solution for assigning network blocks to the 6 networks:

- Network 1: `192.168.1.0/24`

- Network 2: `192.168.2.0/24`

- Network 3: `192.168.3.0/24`

- Network 4: `192.168.4.0/24`

- Network 5: `192.168.5.0/24`

- Network 6: `192.168.6.0/24`

Using such an addressing scheme is workable but it is definitely not efficient. Let's take a look at why. In our scenario, each network has 50 devices or less. To determine why this isn't a suitable solution, let's first determine the number of usable IP addresses per **Class C** network block using the following formula:

`Usable IP addresses = ` $2^H$ ` - 2`

> **Important Note**
> On an IPv4 network, both the **Network-ID** and **Broadcast** IP addresses can't be assigned to any device. Therefore, we subtract 2 from the total number of IP addresses to get the usable amount on a network.

Since there are eight host bits in any of the **Class C** networks, we get the following results:

```
Usable IP addresses = 2ᴴ - 2
                    = 2⁸ - 2
                    = 256 - 2
                    = 254 usable IP addresses per Class C network
```

In effect, each network will have a wastage of approximately 204 IP addresses (254 - 50 hosts). Imagine if everyone assigned huge network blocks to their network infrastructure without being concerned about the wastage of addresses. On a larger scale, if ISPs distributed large network blocks to organizations who do not require more than just a few IP addresses, the public IPv4 network blocks would have been exhausted decades ago.

This bring us back to understanding the reasons why we need to subnet. The process of subnetting has the following benefits:

- To efficiently distribute IP addresses with the least wastage
- To create more networks with smaller broadcast domains

Why is having a large broadcast domain a bad thing? Imagine that a network has approximately 300 devices, and a few hosts are generating unnecessary broadcast packets. All the other devices will receive the broadcast message and process it. A large broadcast domain with many host devices can, in effect, slow network operations if there is a significant amount of network traffic, such as broadcast storms. To put this simply, it's like rush-hour in the morning or evening, where there are too many vehicles on the road. This results in traffic congestion and commuters taking longer to reach their destination.

By creating subnets, you can reduce the size of a broadcast domain. Using a Layer 3 switch or a router, these subnets can be interconnected, thus allowing users and devices to communicate. Subnets can be determined by the location of branches and departments within a building, such as **Human Resources**, **Accounting**, **Sales**, **Administration**, and so on.

To further help you understand subnetting, let's take a dive into some hands-on exercises. To get started, let's create a simple scenario. Imagine you are the network administrator for **Company X**, a fictional-based company with four office locations. Each branch has their own LAN, and each branch is connected to the HQ location.

The following diagram shows a visual representation of the network topology:

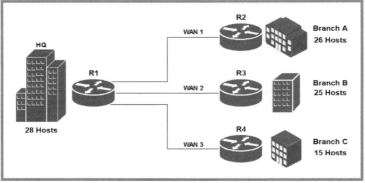

Figure 3.25 – Network diagram

Your objective is to design an IP scheme to ensure the least wastage and that each branch location has their own subnet. To get started with this assignment, the following sections will guide you through how to create an efficient design for the network topology.

# Step 1 – Determining the appropriate IP address

To begin, let's determine which class of IP addressing is most suitable for our network topology. As you may recall, there are three address classes: **A**, **B**, and **C**. Each class has a unique number of available IP addresses based on their default subnet masks.

To help us figure out which is the best class, let's use the following formula to determine the total number of IP addresses of each class:

```
Total number of IP addresses = 2^H
```

Here, *H* represents the number of host bits in a network ID, which is 4.

In this step, we are using the subnet mask to help us determine the number of IP address available in a network. The 1s in the subnet masks identify the *network portion* of an IP address, while the 0s identify the *host portion* of an IP address.

The following table illustrates the default subnets for each class and their binary equivalent:

| Class A - 255.0.0.0 | 11111111 | 00000000 | 00000000 | 00000000 |
| Class B - 255.255.0.0 | 11111111 | 11111111 | 00000000 | 00000000 |
| Class C - 255.255.255.0 | 11111111 | 11111111 | 11111111 | 00000000 |

Figure 3.26 – Subnet masks

Let' use our formula, adjust to $2^H$, to determine the total number of IPv4 addresses per class:

- Class A = adjust to $2^{24}$ = 16,777,216 total IP addresses
- Class B = adjust to $2^{16}$ = 65,536 total IP addresses
- Class C = adjust to $2^8$ = 256 total IP addresses

Furthermore, when assigning IPv4 addresses on a network, there are two addresses that can't be assigned. These are the Network ID and broadcast addresses. Therefore, to determine the number of usable IP addresses, you need to subtract two addresses from the total number of IP addresses for a network block or subnet.

To calculate the number of usable IP addresses, use the following formula:

```
Number of Usable IP addresses = adjust to 2ᴴ - 2
```

The following are the number of usable (assignable) IPv4 addresses for the following class:

- Class A = Adjust to $2^{24} - 2$ = 16,777,214 usable IP addresses
- Class B = Adjust to $2^{16} - 2$ = 65,534 usable IP addresses
- Class C = Adjust to $2^8 - 2$ = 254 usable IP addresses

Next, we need to identify the total number of networks within the topology and the size of each network. We have the following seven networks:

- HQ LAN: 28 hosts
- Branch A LAN: 26 hosts
- Branch B LAN: 25 hosts
- Branch C LAN: 15 hosts
- WAN 1 (R1-R2): 2 IPs are needed
- WAN 2 (R2-R3): 2 IPs are needed
- WAN 3 (R3-R4): 2 IPs are needed

Using a **Class A** is not suitable as there will be over 16 million IP addresses being wasted. Using a **Class B** will result in appropriately 65,000 addresses being wasted. This leaves us with using a **Class C** network block (as it's the smallest network block available), with 254 usable IP addresses.

> **Important Note**
>
> Keep in mind that when creating subnets, each newly created subnetwork must be able to fit the largest network in your topology.

Over the following steps, we will be using the subnet mask to help us determine what portion of the network ID or IP address is the network portion, and what part is the host portion.

# Step 2 – Creating new subnets (subnetworks)

When creating subnetworks (subnets), we need to convert the bits on the host portion of the address into new network bits. This process allows us to create new networks (subnets) while reducing the number of IPs per network.

To get started, let's use the **Class C** network block `192.168.1.0/24`. When we convert both the IP address and subnet mask, the following results will be obtained:

| Network block | 11000000.10101000.00000001.**00000000** |
|---|---|
| Subnet mask | 11111111.11111111.11111111.**00000000** |

Figure 3.27 – Network ID and default subnet mask

The 1s in the subnet mask tells us the portion of the IP address that belongs to the network, while the 0s in the subnet mask indicate the host portion of the IP address. As you can see, the network portion of the address is the first 24 bits, while the last 8 bits represent the host portion. Remember, all the hosts on a subnet will have the same network portion for their IP address, while each host will have a unique value in the host portion.

We can use the following formula to determine the number of networks:

```
Number of subnets = Adjust to 2ᴺ
```

N represents the number of hosts we are going to convert into new network bits.

In the previous image, where the 1s stop in the subnet mask, we can begin taking hosts to convert. Let's take two hosts and substitute in our formula to determine the number of networks we can create:

| Network block | 11000000.10101000.00000001.00**000000** |
|---|---|
| Subnet mask | 11111111.11111111.11111111.11**000000** |

Figure 3.28 – Using two host bits

When we take bits of the host portion of the address, the subnet bits are changed to 1s to represent the network portion of the address.

To calculate the number of subnets, use the following formula:

**Number of subnets = Adjust to $2^N$**

```
adjust to 2² = 2 x 2 = 4 subnets
```

Using 2 bits isn't sufficient as it only gives us 4 subnets. However, our goal is to create 7 subnets, with each subnet having the capacity to support our largest network of 28 hosts. Let's take an additional host bit and perform our calculations one more time:

| Network block | 11000000.10101000.00000001.000**00000** |
|---------------|------------------------------------------|
| Subnet mask   | 11111111.11111111.11111111.111**00000** |

Figure 3.29 – Using three host bits

We do this using our formula, where $N = 3$:

**Number of subnets = Adjust to $2^N$**

```
Adjust to 2³ = 2 x 2 x 2 = 8 subnets
```

Using the 3 bits, we get 8 subnets. Keep in mind that we really need 7 subnets but using 2 bits from the host portion was not sufficient. Therefore, we need to use the 3 bits and make them into network bits. The additional eighth network can be reserved for further usage.

Having established that 3 bits are being taken from the host portion of the address, we are left with 5 host bits. We need to ensure this host's bits are sufficient to create enough IP addresses to fit our largest network in the topology. Therefore, we can use the following formula to determine the total number of IP addresses per network:

**Total number of IP address = adjust to $2^H$**

```
adjust to 2⁵ = 2 x 2 x 2 x 2 x 2 = 32 total IP address
```

These 5 host bits gives us a total of 32 IP addresses per subnet. However, we cannot assign two specific IPv4 addresses to any device: the Network ID address and the broadcast IP address. Therefore, we can use the following formula to calculate the number of usable IP addresses:

**Number of usable IP address = Adjust to $2^N - 2$**

```
adjust to 2⁵ - 2 = 32 - 2 = 30 usable IP addresses
```

This means that, based on our calculations, we will be able to take three hosts from the address and create a total of 8 subnets. Each of these eight subnetworks will have 30 usable IP addresses. We now have a workable solution. Lastly, when taking bits from the host portion, the subnet bits must also be changed from 0s to 1s. The 1s represent the network portion of the address. Since we took 3 host bits, we have a new subnet mask for each of the new subnets we are about to create. Therefore, our new subnet for each of the 8 networks is 255.255.255.224, with a network prefix of /27.

> **Important note**
> Keep in mind that each time we perform a subnetting process, the original network is broken down and each new network we create is smaller than the original. However, each subnetwork that's created is of equal size.

Before we begin to create the actual subnetworks, please be sure to use the following guidelines:

- Do not modify the original network portion of the IP address (the first 24 bits).
- Do not modify the new host portion of the IP address (the last 5 host bits).
- Only modify the new network bits (the 3 host bits that we are converting into network bits).

When modifying the new network bits, we simply change the 0s into 1s to create all the different possibilities. The following are the calculations used to create the 8 new subnets:

| Subnet 1 | 11000000.10101000.00000001.00000000 | 192.168.1.0/27 |
|----------|-------------------------------------|----------------|
| Subnet 2 | 11000000.10101000.00000001.00100000 | 192.168.1.32/27 |
| Subnet 3 | 11000000.10101000.00000001.01000000 | 192.168.1.64/27 |
| Subnet 4 | 11000000.10101000.00000001.01100000 | 192.168.1.96/27 |
| Subnet 5 | 11000000.10101000.00000001.10000000 | 192.168.1.128/27 |
| Subnet 6 | 11000000.10101000.00000001.10100000 | 192.168.1.160/27 |
| Subnet 7 | 11000000.10101000.00000001.11000000 | 192.168.1.192/27 |
| Subnet 8 | 11000000.10101000.00000001.11100000 | 192.168.1.224/27 |

Figure 3.30 – Creating eight subnets

Always remember to start with the original Network ID when performing subnetting. In our calculations, the first subnet is the `192.168.1.0/27` network. Each of our subnets is an increment of `32`, and this value is derived from our formula, which is used to calculate the number of total IP addresses.

> **Tip**
>
> At times, calculating the binary may be challenging. However, each subnet is equal in size. This means using the formula `2x` (*x represents the number of bits*) will provide you with the incremental value for each Network ID. This technique will help you in calculating the new Network IDs (subnets) quickly. Additionally, the last subnet (Network ID) in your calculation always ends with the last part of the new subnet mask.

Now that we have calculated all our Network IDs (subnets), in the next step, you will learn how to calculate the network range for a subnet.

# Step 3 – Assigning subnets to each network

In this step, we are going to perform a few tasks, such as calculating the network ranges (such as the first and last usable IP address with the broadcast IP for each network). To perform your calculations efficiently, use the following guidelines:

- Calculate all subnets (Network IDs) as your first task.

- To calculate the first usable IP address, use the `Network ID + 1` formula. In binary, the first bit from the right is set to `1`.

- To calculate the broadcast IP address, use the `Next Network ID - 1` formula. In binary, all host bits are changed to 1s.

- To calculate the last usable IP address, use the `Broadcast IP address - 1` formula. In binary, all host bits are 1s except for the last bit in the address.

Now, let's apply our guidelines, calculate the first subnet range, and assign it to the **HQ LAN** network:

| Subnet 1 | 11000000.10101000.00000001.00**00000** | 192.168.1.0/27 |
|---|---|---|
| First usable IP | 11000000.10101000.00000001.00**00001** | 192.168.1.1/27 |
| Last usable IP | 11000000.10101000.00000001.00**011110** | 192.168.1.30/27 |
| Broadcast | 11000000.10101000.00000001.00**011111** | 192.168.1.31/27 |

Figure 3.31 – Subnet 1 range

Next, let's calculate the second subnet and assign it to the **Branch A LAN**:

| Subnet 2 | 11000000.10101000.00000001.00100000 | 192.168.1.32/27 |
|---|---|---|
| First usable IP | 11000000.10101000.00000001.00100001 | 192.168.1.33/27 |
| Last usable IP | 11000000.10101000.00000001.00111110 | 192.168.1.62/27 |
| Broadcast | 11000000.10101000.00000001.00111111 | 192.168.1.63/27 |

Figure 3.32 – Subnet 2 range

Next, let's calculate the third subnet and assign it to the **Branch B LAN**:

| Subnet 3 | 11000000.10101000.00000001.01000000 | 192.168.1.64/27 |
|---|---|---|
| First usable IP | 11000000.10101000.00000001.01000001 | 192.168.1.65/27 |
| Last usable IP | 11000000.10101000.00000001.01011110 | 192.168.1.94/27 |
| Broadcast | 11000000.10101000.00000001.01011111 | 192.168.1.95/27 |

Figure 3.33 – Subnet 3 range

Next, let's calculate the fourth subnet and assign it to the **Branch C LAN**:

| Subnet 4 | 11000000.10101000.00000001.01100000 | 192.168.1.96/27 |
|---|---|---|
| First usable IP | 11000000.10101000.00000001.01100001 | 192.168.1.97/27 |
| Last usable IP | 11000000.10101000.00000001.01111110 | 192.168.1.126/27 |
| Broadcast | 11000000.10101000.00000001.01111111 | 192.168.1.127/27 |

Figure 3.34 – Subnet 4 range

We can successfully assign the first 4 subnets to each of the **LANs** in each respective location. However, we still need to assign subnets to the **WAN** links that are interconnecting each branch to the head office network. There are four subnets remaining. We can take any three of the remaining subnets and assign them to each of the WAN links, but this will not be efficient as each of the WAN links in the topology only requires two IP addresses on the router's interfaces, as follows:

- **WAN 1 (R1-R2)**: 2 IPs are needed.
- **WAN 2 (R2-R3)**: 2 IPs are needed.
- **WAN 3 (R3-R4)**: 2 IPs are needed.

Taking any one of the subnets to assign to any of the WAN links will result in the following wastage:

```
Usable IP address per subnet = Adjust to 2^H - 2
```

```
Adjust to 2^5 - 2 = 32 - 2 = 30 usable IP address
```

The following is what we get when using only two IPs from a subnet:

```
30 - 2 = 28 IP address will be wasted
```

We can use a slightly more advanced technique known as **Variable-Length Subnet Masking** (**VLSM**) to break a subnet down into small subnetworks. Since we have four remaining subnets from our original calculations, let's reserve the following subnet for future usage:

| Subnet 5 | 11000000.10101000.00000001.10000000 | 192.168.1.128/27 |
|----------|-------------------------------------|------------------|
| Subnet 6 | 11000000.10101000.00000001.10100000 | 192.168.1.160/27 |
| Subnet 7 | 11000000.10101000.00000001.11000000 | 192.168.1.192/27 |

Figure 3.35 – Reserve subnets

In the next step, we will cover how to use VLSM to break the eighth subnet, `192.168.1.224/27`, down into smaller networks to fit our WAN links.

# Step 4 – Performing Variable-Length Subnet Masking (VLSM)

Performing VLSM calculations is simply subnetting a subnet. For each of our WAN links, we only require two usable IP addresses on each link. To determine the number of host bits required to give us two usable IP addresses, use the following formula:

```
Number of usable IP addresses = Adjust to 2^H - 2
```

Here, H is the number of host bits taken from the right.

For a better visual, let's convert the eighth subnet into binary:

| Network ID  | 11000000.10101000.00000001.11100000 | 192.168.1.224   |
|-------------|-------------------------------------|-----------------|
| Subnet mask | 11111111.11111111.11111111.11100000 | 255.255.255.224 |

Figure 3.36 – Binary

If we use the 32nd bit (1 bit) on the network ID, `192.168.1.224/27`, within our formula – Adjust to $2^H$ – 2, – the result is 0 usable IP addresses. Therefore, 1 host bit is not sufficient. Let's use an additional host bit; that is, adjust to $2^2$ – 2 = 2 usable IP addresses. Now that we have a workable solution, we simply need to permanently make the last 2 bits (`00`) from the Network ID `192.168.1.224` the only host bits, while the remaining hosts are converted into network bits. This is a little bit of reverse engineering where we start calculating the host IP address first, followed by the number of networks.

Furthermore, we will have three new network bits, which provide us the following formula:

**Number of subnets = Adjust to $2^N$**

Adjust to $2^3$ = 2 x 2 x 2 = 8 subnets

Additionally, we can flip the new network bits in the subnet mask, as shown here:

| Network ID | 11000000.10101000.00000001.11100000 | 192.168.1.224 |
|---|---|---|
| Subnet | 11111111.11111111.11111111.11111100 | 255.255.255.252 |

Figure 3.37 – New subnet mask

Hence, each of the 8 newly created subnets will have a subnet mask of `255.255.255.252`, or a network prefix of `/30`.

Let's calculate the total number of IP addresses per subnet and our network incremental value:

**Total number of IP address = Adjust to $2^H$**

Adjust to $2^2$ = 4 total IP addresses

Here, each number will have only two usable IP addresses, adjust to $2^H$ – 2 = 4 – 2 = 2.

Before we begin to create the new subnetworks from the `192.168.1.224/27` network block, please be sure to use the following guidelines:

- Do not modify the original network portion of the IP address (the first 27 bits).
- Do not modify the new host portion of the IP address (the last 2 host bits).
- Only modify the new network bits (the 3 host bits that we are converting into network bits).

When modifying the new network bits, we simply change the 0s into 1s to create all the different possibilities. The following are the calculations to create the 8 new subnets:

| Subnet 1 | 11000000.10101000.00000001.11100000 | 192.168.1.224/30 |
|---|---|---|
| Subnet 2 | 11000000.10101000.00000001.11100100 | 192.168.1.228/30 |
| Subnet 3 | 11000000.10101000.00000001.11101000 | 192.168.1.232/30 |
| Subnet 4 | 11000000.10101000.00000001.11101100 | 192.168.1.236/30 |
| Subnet 5 | 11000000.10101000.00000001.11110000 | 192.168.1.240/30 |
| Subnet 6 | 11000000.10101000.00000001.11110100 | 192.168.1.244/30 |
| Subnet 7 | 11000000.10101000.00000001.11111000 | 192.168.1.248/30 |
| Subnet 8 | 11000000.10101000.00000001.11111100 | 192.168.1.252/30 |

Figure 3.38 – Networks created via the VLSM network

Now, we have 8 new networks that can be used for point-to-point WAN links. Let's calculate and assign the subnets accordingly.

Let's calculate the first subnet and assign it to **WAN 1 (R1-R2)**:

| Subnet 1 | 11000000.10101000.00000001.11100000 | 192.168.1.224/30 |
|---|---|---|
| First usable IP | 11000000.10101000.00000001.11100001 | 192.168.1.225/30 |
| Last usable IP | 11000000.10101000.00000001.11100010 | 192.168.1.226/30 |
| Broadcast | 11000000.10101000.00000001.11100011 | 192.168.1.227/30 |

Figure 3.39 – WAN 1 allocation

Next, let's calculate the second subnet and assign it to **WAN 2 (R2-R3)**:

| Subnet 2 | 11000000.10101000.00000001.11100100 | 192.168.1.228/30 |
|---|---|---|
| First usable IP | 11000000.10101000.00000001.11100101 | 192.168.1.229/30 |
| Last usable IP | 11000000.10101000.00000001.11100110 | 192.168.1.230/30 |
| Broadcast | 11000000.10101000.00000001.11100111 | 192.168.1.231/30 |

Figure 3.40 – WAN 2 allocation

Next, let's calculate the third subnet and assign it to **WAN 3 (R3-R4)**:

| Subnet 3 | 11000000.10101000.00000001.11101000 | 192.168.1.232/30 |
|---|---|---|
| First usable IP | 11000000.10101000.00000001.11101001 | 192.168.1.233/30 |
| Last usable IP | 11000000.10101000.00000001.11101010 | 192.168.1.234/30 |
| Broadcast | 11000000.10101000.00000001.11101011 | 192.168.1.235/30 |

Figure 3.41 – WAN 3 allocation

Having allocated the first three subnets of the /30 networks, we are left with five additional networks, as shown here:

| Subnet 4 | 11000000.10101000.00000001.11101100 | 192.168.1.236/30 |
|---|---|---|
| Subnet 5 | 11000000.10101000.00000001.11110000 | 192.168.1.240/30 |
| Subnet 6 | 11000000.10101000.00000001.11110100 | 192.168.1.244/30 |
| Subnet 7 | 11000000.10101000.00000001.11111000 | 192.168.1.248/30 |
| Subnet 8 | 11000000.10101000.00000001.11111100 | 192.168.1.252/30 |

Figure 3.42 – Additional WAN subnets

These remaining subnets can be reserved for future uses in the event the organization decides to create further branches that require additional WAN links. In *Chapter 5, Implementing VLANs, Layer 2 Discovery Protocols, and EtherChannels*, you will learn about **Virtual Local Area Networks** (**VLANs**) and will see the importance of having multiple subnetworks within an organization. This helps improve network performance and security.

Having completed this section, you have learned how to use subnetting to create smaller IP subnetworks. Additionally, you have learned how to use VLSM to break a subnet down even further by subnetting a subnet. In the next section, we will learn about the functions of IPv6.

# IPv6

The need for IPv6 is ever-demanding on the internet today, with the creation of new smart and **Internet of Things** (**IoT**) technologies causing an exhaustion of the public IPv4 address space quicker than expected. Nowadays, a typical person may have more than one smart device in their household, from internet-connected appliances to home security systems. The need for internet connectivity is an ever-increasing demand, hence the creation of a new address space.

The following is a brief summary of IPv4 exhaustion statistics:

- APNIC: Exhausted in April 2011
- RIPE NCC: Exhausted in September 2012
- LACNIC: Exhausted in June 2014
- ARIN: Exhausted in July 2015
- AfriNIC: Expected to be exhausted in 2019

This is where **IP** version 6 comes in. Back in December 1995 (circa), the **IANA** was entrusted to manage the IPv6 addressing scheme (RFC 1881). This means that IPv6 was developed and ready for distribution a long time ago. IANA, RIRs, and **AS** were waiting for the last set of public IPv4 addresses to be exhausted before distributing and assigning IPv6 addresses to customers and internet-connected devices.

Unlike IPv4 – which is 32 bits in length with approximately four billion public IPv4 addresses – an IPv6 address is 128 bits in length, which provides approximately one undecillion ($10^{36}$) addresses. Each IPv6 address has eight hextets, each of which are made up of 16 bits. This means 8 hextets x 16 bits per hextet = 128 bits.

Additionally, IPv6 is written using hexadecimal values and not decimal, as with IPv4. Hexadecimal values have the following range:

```
0 1 2 3 4 5 6 7 8 9 A B C D E F
```

Each hextet has the range 0000 – FFFF.

To get a better idea of IPv6 addressing, let's take a look at the following address:

```
2001:0DB8:0000:1111:0000:0000:0000:0200
```

Notice each hextet is separated with a colon (:).

The cool thing about writing an IPv6 address is that the alphabetical characters (A - F) are not case-sensitive. This means that regardless of whether you use a lowercase or uppercase character within the address, the device will accept it.

Additionally, we write the preceding IPv6 address in a shortened format. The leading zeros (0s) in a hextet can be removed as they have no value. Therefore, if an IPv6 address has a hextet of 0000, we can use a single 0 to represent the entire hextet, as shown here:

```
2001:DB8:0:1111:0:0:0:200
```

Additionally, when there are two (2) or more hextets with a continuous stream of zeros, you can substitute two or more hextets with a double colon (::), as shown here:

```
2001:DB8:0:1111::200
```

This is the shortest form of the original IPv6 address. Lastly, the double colon (::) can be used only once within an IPv6 address.

> **Important Note**
>
> The default subnet mask of an IPv6 address is /64. This means that the first half of an IPv6 address is known as the prefix, while the second half is referred to as the Interface-ID. In comparison to IPv4, **Prefix** is the network address while Interface-ID is the host address.

Natively, devices assigned IPv4 addresses won't be able to exchange messages with a device that has an IPv6 address. To allow intercommunication between these two versions of IP, the following methods are used:

- Dual stacking
- NAT64
- Tunneling: 6to4 and 4to6

Dual stacking allows a single **Network Interface Card** (**NIC**) to be configured with both IPv4 and IPv6 addresses. This allows the device to use the IPv4 address to communicate with devices on an IPv4 network, while the IPv6 address is used to communicate with devices on an IPv6 network.

This is possible because the internet layer of TCP/IP is responsible for encapsulating the datagram in the appropriate IP version before passing it down to the lower layer of the TCP/IP.

> **Important Note**
>
> Further information about IPv6 address management can be found at https://www.iana.org/assignments/ipv6-address-space/ipv6-address-space.xhtml.

The following diagram shows each field within an IPv6 packet:

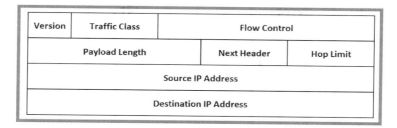

Figure 3.43 – Composition of an IPv6 packet

Each field within the IPv6 packet plays an important role when transmitting a message from one device to another. The following are the names and descriptions of each field:

- **Version**: This field is generally used to identify the version of the IP, such as IPv4 and IPv6.

- **Traffic Control**: This field plays an important role when using **Quality of Service (QoS)** tools on a network and has the same functionality as the **Differentiated Services (DS)** field of an IPv4 packet.

- **Flow Control**: This field is used to instruct a receiving router to process all packets that have the same flow label in the same exact way.

- **Payload Length**: This field contains the size of the data portion.

- **Next Header**: This field identifies the network protocol that the datagram belongs to on the destination host.

- **Hop Limit**: This field is equivalent to the TTL field within an IPv4 packet.

- **Source IPv6 Address**: Specifies the sender's IPv6 address.

- **Destination IPv6 Address**: Specifies the destination's IPv6 address.

Next, let's take a look at various types of IPv6 address.

## Types of IPv6 addresses

Similar to IPv4, there are various types of IPv6 addresses with unique purposes on an IPv6 network. In this section, we will look at the following types of IPv6 address:

- Global unicast

- Loopback

- Link-Local

- Unique local

- Anycast
- Multicast
- Modified EUI 64

In this section, we will understand the characteristics, functionality, and purpose of each type of IPv6 address.

## Global unicast

Similar to using term "public" to describe an internet assignable IPv4 address, in the IPv6 world, the public address is referred to as a global unicast address and belongs to the `2000::/3` network block of addresses.

## Loopback

There is also a lookback address in the IPv6 address space, which is known as `::1/128`. The loopback IPv6 address has the same functionality as the IPv4 version, as mentioned in the previous, *Special IPv4 address* section in this chapter. However, the loopback address in IPv6 is a single address only, unlike IPv4, which has a network block.

## Link-Local

Within an IPv6 network, an interface usually has two IPv6 addresses: a global unicast address and a Link-Local address. The global unicast address is used when communicating beyond the local network. However, when a device wants to exchange messages with another device on the same local network, the Link-Local IPv6 address take effect.

> **Important note**
>
> On a LAN, when devices want to exchange messages, they use source and destination MAC addresses because switches are only able to read Layer 2 header information such as source and destination MAC addresses. Therefore, when a device wants to send a message beyond the LAN, the sender device will set the destination MAC address of the default gateway on the message, and use the destination IP address as the actual destination device, such as the web server.

The IPv6 Link-Local address plays the same role for LAN communication between devices that are logically connected to the same network segment. The IPv6 link-local address belongs to the `FE80::/10` network block. Keep in mind that the link-local address is used for local communication only.

## Unique local

The unique local address functions similarly to private IPv4 addresses, which only allow communication on a local (private) network. The unique local address block is `FC00::/7`.

## Anycast

As mentioned in the *Transmission types* section, Anycast is an IPv6 technology that functions as a one-to-closest type of transmission. Anycast allows multiple servers (or devices) to share the same IPv6 address.

## Multicast

This type of communication can be seen as a one-to-many type of transmission. The following are the associated network blocks for IPv6 multicast addresses:

- Assigned: `FF0s::/8`
- Solicited node: `FF02::1:FF00:0000/104`

## Modified EUI 64

There may be a time when the network is using an IPv6 technology known as **Stateless Address Autoconfiguration** (**SLAAC**) to provide IPv6 global unicast addresses without the use of a **DHCPv6** server. SLAAC is a stateless service, which means there is no server (such as a DHCP server) to maintain network addressing details. In other services, when a DHCP server provides IP addressing details to a client, the server keeps a record of the transactions and allocations of IP addresses. However, with SLAAC, there isn't such a functionality.

Therefore, only the prefix portion of the IPv6 address is provided to a client. The Interface-ID uses the `EUI-64` process to create a 64-bit address from the 48-bit MAC address of the client's physical interface.

To get a better idea of this operation, let's take the MAC address `FC-99-47-75-CE-E0` and run it through the `EUI-64` process:

1. Split the MAC address in half by separating the OUI portion from the device portion and convert it into binary:

| FC | 99 | 47 | 75 | CE | E0 |
|----------|----------|----------|----------|----------|----------|
| 11111100 | 10011001 | 01000111 | 01110101 | 11001110 | 11100000 |

Figure 3.44 – MAC into binary

2.  Insert `FFFE` in-between the OUI and device portion:

| FC | 99 | 47 | **FF** | **FE** | 75 | CE | E0 |
|---|---|---|---|---|---|---|---|
| 11111100 | 10011001 | 01000111 | **11111111** | **11111110** | 01110101 | 11001110 | 11100000 |

Figure 3.45 – FFFE inserted between the MAC address

3.  Flip the Universally/Locally (U/L) bit. If the bit is 0, change it to 1 and vice versa. The U/L bit is the seventh bit in this exercise:

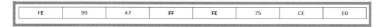

| 11111110 | 10011001 | 01000111 | **11111111** | **11111110** | 01110101 | 11001110 | 11100000 |
|---|---|---|---|---|---|---|---|

Figure 3.46 – Flipping the U/L bit

4.  Convert the binary back into hexadecimal to get the EUI-64 address:

| FE | 99 | 47 | **FF** | **FE** | 75 | CE | E0 |
|---|---|---|---|---|---|---|---|

Figure 3.47 – EUI-64 address

Therefore, all `EUI-64` generated addresses will always have **FFFE** in the middle section of the Interface-ID of an IPv6 address. Please note that the `EUI-64` address is automatically generated by the device when IPv6 routing is enabled.

> **Important note**
>
> On Cisco devices, use the `ipv6 unicast-routing` command in global configuration mode to enable IPv6 routing.

Having completed this section, you are now able to describe the characteristics of IPv6 addressing. In the next section, we'll take a look at how to configure interfaces on a Cisco IOS router so that they work with IPv6 configurations.

# Lab – Configuring IPv6 on a Cisco IOS router

To get started, we are going to use the following topology:

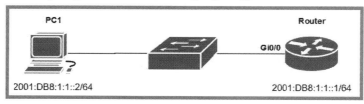

Fig 3.48 – Lab topology

To configure IPv6 address on a Cisco IOS router, use the following steps:

1.  Enable IPv6 routing using the following command:

    ```
    R1(config)#ipv6 unicast-routing
    ```

2.  Enter interface mode for the desired interface:

    ```
    R1(config)#interface GigabitEthernet0/0
    ```

3.  Use the `ipv6 address` command, followed by the IPv6 address with the network prefix:

    ```
    R1(config-if)#ipv6 address 2001:DB8:1:1::1/64
    ```

4.  (Optional) To manually configure a Link-Local IPv6 address on the interface, use the `link-local` command after the IPv6 address, as shown here:

    ```
    R1(config-if)#ipv6 address FE80::1 link-local
    ```

5.  Enable the interface using the `no shutdown` command:

    ```
    R1(config-if)#no shutdown
    ```

Now that you have learned how to configure IPv6 global and Link-Local addresses, let's take a look at how to verify our configurations using Cisco IOS commands.

Using the `show ipv6 interface brief` command, we can view a summary of our IPv6 interfaces, along with their assigned IPv6 addresses, as shown here:

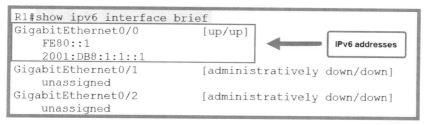

Figure 3.49 - Output of the show ipv6 interface brief command

Another command we can use to verify the status of an interface is the `show ipv6 interface <interface-ID>` command. The following snippet shows the expected output:

```
R1#show ipv6 interface GigabitEthernet 0/0
GigabitEthernet0/0 is up, line protocol is up
  IPv6 is enabled, link-local address is FE80::1
  No Virtual link-local address(es):
  Global unicast address(es):
    2001:DB8:1:1::1, subnet is 2001:DB8:1:1::/64
```

Figure 3.50 - Output of the show ipv6 interface command

Furthermore, we can verify the configurations under each interface by using the `show running-config` command, but using the pipe (|) parameter followed by the `section` command and the section's name, as shown here:

```
R1#show running-config | section interface
interface GigabitEthernet0/0
 no ip address
 duplex auto
 speed auto
 ipv6 address FE80::1 link-local
 ipv6 address 2001:DB8:1:1::1/64
```

Figure 3.51 – Output of the show running-config command

Having completed this section, you are now able to perform verification on Cisco IOS devices to determine IPv6 configurations. In the next section, you will learn how to assign a static IPv6 address to a Microsoft Windows computer.

# Lab – Configuring IPv6 on a Windows computer

Now that you have learned how to manually configure an IPv6 address on a Cisco router, let's take a look at how to manually configure an IPv6 address on a Microsoft Windows computer.

To get started with this task, use the following steps:

1.  Open the Windows **Control Panel** and go to **Network and Sharing Center**.

2.  On the left, click on **Change adapter settings**.

3.  Right-click on your corresponding network adapter and select **Properties**.

4.  Click on **Internet Protocol version 6 (TCP/IPv6)** and then click on **Properties**:

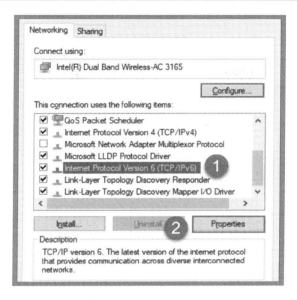

Figure 3.52 – Network adapter properties

5.   Use the following setting to assign the IPv6 address, network prefix, and default gateway configurations to the PC:

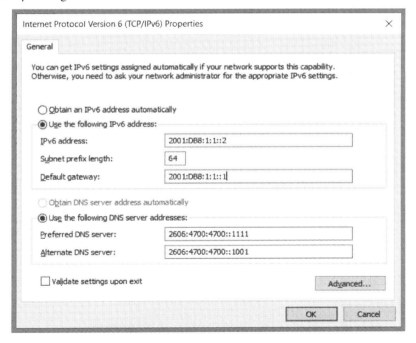

Figure 3.53 – IPv6 settings on PC

The DNS server settings can be adjusted to your preference. I am using a Cloudflare IPv6 DNS server as my DNS server.

6.  Click **OK** to save your settings.

7.  To check your configurations, open the Command Prompt and use the `ipconfig` and `ipconfig /all` commands to verify your IP settings on your network adapters.

# Testing end-to-end connectivity

After configuring and verifying your IPv6 configurations, the last thing a professional must always do is test end-to-end network connectivity between devices.

On our router, let's test the connection between the router and the computer on our topology using the `ping` command:

```
R1>ping 2001:DB8:1:1::2

Type escape sequence to abort.
Sending 5, 100-byte ICMP Echos to 2001:DB8:1:1::2, timeout is 2 seconds:
!!!!!
Success rate is 100 percent (5/5), round-trip min/avg/max = 0/0/2 ms
```

Figure 3.54 – Ping results on Cisco IOS

As you can see, we got five exclamation marks (!). This means we have successful replies from the PC. Receiving a dot (.) means **Request Timeout**, while U means **destination unreachable** on the Cisco IOS. If you are not getting a successful connection, double-check your configurations and ensure the cables are connected to the configured interfaces on each device.

# Summary

Throughout this chapter, we have covered the essentials for understanding both the IPv4 and IPv6 address spaces, demonstrated how to convert an IP address into binary, determined the Network ID of devices, and learned about the various types of network transmissions.

You also learned how to identify each class of IP address, how to perform subnetting, how to describe the characteristics of both IPv4 and IPv6, and how to configure and verify interfaces on a Cisco device.

I hope this chapter has been informative for you and has been helpful in your journey toward learning how to implement and administer Cisco solutions, in preparation for the CCNA 200-301 certification. In the next chapter, *Wireless Architectures and Virtualization*, we will learn about Cisco wireless architectures and virtualization technologies.

# Further reading

The following links are recommended for additional reading:

- IP addressing and subnetting: `https://www.cisco.com/c/en/us/support/docs/ip/routing-information-protocol-rip/13788-3.html`

- Configuring IPv4: `https://www.cisco.com/c/en/us/td/docs/ios-xml/ios/ipaddr_ipv4/configuration/xe-3s/ipv4-xe-3s-book/configuring_ipv4_addresses.html`

- IPv6 addressing and connectivity: `https://www.cisco.com/c/en/us/td/docs/ios-xml/ios/ipv6_basic/configuration/xe-3s/ip6b-xe-3s-book/ip6-add-basic-conn-xe.html`

- Implementing IPv6 addressing: `https://www.cisco.com/c/en/us/td/docs/ios-xml/ios/ipv6/configuration/15-2mt/ipv6-15-2mt-book/ip6-addrg-bsc-con.html`

# 4
# Detecting Physical Issues, Wireless Architectures, and Virtualization

Computer networking has evolved tremendously over the past decade. Today, in order for networking to adapt to the ever-changing landscape of the internet, companies such as Cisco not only produce physical network devices and security appliances but also work with virtualization and cloud technologies.

We live in an age where smart technologies allow people to be more connected digitally than ever. Wireless networks need to be able to support the vast number of connected wireless devices and, most importantly, be able to efficiently transport data between a wired network and a wireless one, and vice versa.

Throughout this chapter, you will learn about physical issues on a network, principles of wireless technologies, and how to transmit messages between devices. Additionally, you will learn how to access and deploy a Cisco **Wireless LAN Controller (WLC)** on a network and implement basic configurations. Lastly, you will be able to describe virtualization and cloud computing technologies.

Here is a breakdown of the topics we will cover in this chapter:

- Understanding network switch functions and physical issues
- Wireless principles
- Cisco wireless architectures
- Access point modes
- Wireless components and management
- Virtualization fundamentals
- Cloud computing

# Technical requirements

To follow along with the exercises in this chapter, please ensure that you have met the following hardware and software requirements:

- Cisco Packet Tracer: `https://www.netacad.com`
- Wi-Fi Analyzer: `https://www.microsoft.com/en-us/p/wifi-analyzer/9nblggh33n0n`

# Understanding network switch functions

With network engineering comes great responsibility and critical thinking. Not only do you have to perform device configurations, but a lot of your time may go into problem-solving and performing extensive troubleshooting techniques. On a network, at times you may encounter users reporting they are experiencing poor network performance such as high latency. Such issues may be caused by interface misconfigurations or a physical issue.

As you have learned, switches play a vital role in almost all networks of any size; from the **small-office home office (SOHO)** to a large enterprise network with hundreds of connected devices, they are the main network intermediary devices that physically connect everything together. In this section, we are going to discuss various network-related issues that can affect the performance of a network and how to resolve them.

In an ideal environment, we should connect only one end device to a single physical interface on a switch. Each physical interface on a switch is known as a **collision domain**. A collision domain is the area or segment in which a device can generate a signal and is heard by all other devices on the same area or segment. A simple example is all devices connected to a hub; if one device sends a signal to the hub, it is broadcasted out of all other ports. Therefore, all devices connected to the hub make up a single collision domain. Layer 2 switches are smart devices and are designed to overcome such issues. Switches are able to isolate the signals on their individual ports, therefore each physical interface represents a unique collision domain.

> **Important note**
> Each interface on a switch is a collision domain, and each interface on a router is also a collision domain. If a switch is connected a router, the shared link is recognized as a collision domain.

To ensure there are no accidents or collisions, there should be only one device connected to a switch's physical port. Therefore, when an end device such as a PC generates a signal, only the switch's interface will be the recipient of that signal.

The following diagram shows the ideal physical setup when connecting end devices to a switch:

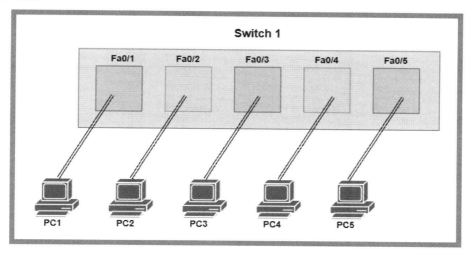

Figure 4.1 – Switch interfaces

In the preceding diagram, there are a total of five collision domains. If **PC1** generates a signal, it is isolated by interface **Fa0/1** on the switch. When the frame enters **Fa0/1**, it analyzes the destination MAC address and forwards it only its destination.

# Detecting physical issues

You're probably thinking that if switches are able to isolate a collision domain to an interface level, then can collisions occur on a network? The simple answer is collisions can still occur, and Cisco IOS switches and routers are able to gather network statistics, which helps us identify whether there's an issue in the physical layer.

What are physical errors and why do we need to identify them? To help you understand the importance of finding and eliminating a collisions network, we'll use a simple analogy. Let's imagine each day, there are hundreds of commuters within a city. Some are traveling using public services, while others are driving a vehicle. Apart from commuters, there are also others who are transporting items such as building materials to a work site. To ensure people do not drive dangerously on the roadways, there are laws, driving regulations, and various traffic signs and lights along each street. There are times when an unfortunate event may occur, such as two or more vehicles colliding, causing an accident on the street. This collision does not only affect the people within the collision but also the other people who have to use that route to reach their destination. Sometimes, within a vehicular collision the vehicle is beyond repair and the owner has to discard it. A similar series of events takes place on a computer network.

To determine whether there are any physical errors on a collision domain, such as on a switch or a router's interface, use the `show interfaces interface-ID` command. The output will provide you with details of both incoming and outgoing traffic. You'll be able to see the types of errors that are occurring on the physical interface, the transmitting and receiving load on the interface (`txload` and `rxload`), the encapsulation type, and other traffic counters.

> **Important note**
>
> Both `txload` (transmitting) and `rxload` (receiving) values are given in `x/255` format. A high `x` value in `txload` simply indicates the percentage of the interface's bandwidth that is currently being used to send traffic in real time. For `rxload`, the percentage indicates the amount of traffic being received on the interface. If `txload` and `rxload` are `255/255`, this means the interface has 100% saturation for both inbound and outbound traffic.

The following snippet shows the output of the `show interfaces` commands on a Cisco 2960 switch:

```
SW1#show interfaces FastEthernet 0/1
FastEthernet0/1 is up, line protocol is up (connected)
  Hardware is Lance, address is 00d0.ff55.dc01 (bia 00d0.ff55.dc01)
  BW 100000 Kbit, DLY 1000 usec,
      reliability 255/255, txload 1/255, rxload 1/255
  Encapsulation ARPA, loopback not set
  Keepalive set (10 sec)
  Full-duplex, 100Mb/s
  input flow-control is off, output flow-control is off
  ARP type: ARPA, ARP Timeout 04:00:00
  Last input 00:00:08, output 00:00:05, output hang never
  Last clearing of "show interface" counters never
  Input queue: 0/75/0/0 (size/max/drops/flushes); Total output drops: 0
  Queueing strategy: fifo
  Output queue :0/40 (size/max)
```

Figure 4.2 – show interfaces output

As a nascent network professional, it is important to understand the information provided in the preceding figure. We are able to determine the following details and status of `FastEthernet 0/1`:

- Both Layer 1 and Layer 2 (protocol) statuses are up, and the cable is connected to the physical interface.

- The **burned-in address** (**BIA**) or MAC address of the interface is `00d0.ff55.dc01`.

- You are able to see the **bandwidth** (**BW**), **delay** (**DLY**), reliability, current **transmitting load** (**txload**), and **receiving load** (**rxload**) on the interface.

- Both **speed** and **duplex** modes.

- Input and output flow control.

The lower section in the output is the area that provides us with specific details about the traffic entering and leaving the physical interface. It is here that you'll be able to determine whether there are any errors, collisions, or issues on the physical layer.

Common misconfigurations that create issues on a network segment are the match settings of **speed** and **duplex**. Speed defines the maximum bandwidth supported on an interface. Additionally, speed is used to indicate how quickly a device is able to exchange messages with another device. Think of it as speaking with a friend: if the person speaks too quickly, you may not quite understand each word. If the person speaks more slowly (in terms of words per second), you will be able to understand the conversation properly.

In very old devices, the interfaces were regular Ethernet, which operated at 10 MB/s. In more recent devices, there are FastEthernet interfaces, such a Cisco 2960 switch that operated at 100 MB/s and in newer and current devices, we have GigabitEthernet, which operates at 1,000 MB/s.

> **Important note**
>
> In device specification sheets, you may see the description of interfaces as 10/100/1000. This format indicates the different Ethernet standards that are supported on the physical interface of the device. Therefore, if an interface speed is 10/100/1000, the maximum support bandwidth is 1,000 MB/s.

How does speed affect the network performance? If there's a mismatch in speed between two devices, this will create the effect of one device sending a message faster than the recipient is able to process. Additionally, when connecting two devices (A and B) using a cable (copper or fiber), their **network interface cards** (**NICs**) need to negotiate common speed exchange messages between each other. The Cisco IOS allows you to configure one of four available settings on the interface. These are as follows:

- 10: Force 10 Mbps operation.
- 100: Force 100 Mbps operation.
- 1000: Force 1,000 Mbps operation.
- auto: Enable auto speed configuration.

By default, each interface is set to auto. This allows the interface to detect the signals incoming from the device on the other end of the cable and adjust the local interface with a suitable speed. However, there are many times when the auto-negotiation mechanism does not set the speed correctly. Let's take a look at the following diagram, where **SW1** is using auto and **SW2** is manually configured as 1000:

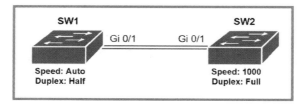

Figure 4.3 – Speed settings

The expected result is **SW1** will auto-negotiate and adjust its interface to 1,000 MB/s, but this does not always happen. Sometimes, it sets to 10 MB/s or 100 Mb/s. Therefore it's highly recommended to manually set the speed on all interfaces on your Cisco devices to prevent a mismatch.

To configure an interface to operate at a particular speed, use the following instructions:

1. Enter interface mode:

```
SW1(config)#interface GigabitEthernet0/1
```

2. Use the shutdown command to administratively shut down the interface before making adjustments to the speed.

3. Use the speed command followed by the actual speed value (10, 100, 1000, or auto):

```
SW1(config-if)#description Connected to SW2
SW1(config-if)#speed ?
  10      Force 10 Mbps operation
  100     Force 100 Mbps operation
  1000    Force 100 Mbps operation
  auto    Enable AUTO speed configuration
```

Let's say you want to manually set the speed to 100 MB/s, use the speed 100 command, as shown here:

```
SW1(config-if)#speed 1000
```

4. Then use the no shutdown command to enable the interface.

5. To verify the speed on an interface, use the show interfaces status command to verify the speed settings on the interface, as shown here:

```
SW1#show interface status

Port     Name              Status      Vlan    Duplex  Speed Type
Gi0/0                      notconnect  1       a-full   auto RJ45
Gi0/1    Connected to SW2  connected   1       a-full   1000 RJ45
Gi0/2                      notconnect  1       a-full   auto RJ45
Gi0/3                      notconnect  1       a-full   auto RJ45
Gi1/0                      notconnect  1       a-full   auto RJ45
```

Figure 4.4 – Interface status on SW1

Notice the speed is hard set to 1000, compared to all other interfaces, which are using the default setting, auto.

6. Additionally, let's take a look at the current operating status of **SW2**:

```
SW2#show interfaces status

Port        Name               Status        Vlan      Duplex Speed Type
Gi0/0                          notconnect    1         a-full  auto RJ45
Gi0/1       Connected to SW1   connected     1         a-full  auto RJ45
Gi0/2                          notconnect    1         a-full  auto RJ45
Gi0/3                          notconnect    1         a-full  auto RJ45
```

Figure 4.5 – Interface status on SW2

As expected, **SW2** is using all the default configurations on each of its interfaces. This is indicated with the auto keyword as seen in the **Speed** column. Another useful troubleshooting command that provides the current operating status of an interface is the show interfaces command:

```
SW1#show interfaces GigabitEthernet 0/1
GigabitEthernet0/1 is up, line protocol is up (connected)
  Hardware is iGbE, address is 0cdb.5070.d301 (bia 0cdb.5070.d301)
  Description: Connected to SW2
  MTU 1500 bytes, BW 1000000 Kbit/sec, DLY 10 usec,
     reliability 255/255, txload 1/255, rxload 1/255
  Encapsulation ARPA, loopback not set
  Keepalive set (10 sec)
  Auto Duplex, 1000Mbps, link type is force-up, media type is RJ45
  output flow-control is unsupported, input flow-control is unsupported
```

Figure 4.6 – show interfaces output

Coupling the show interfaces command with an interface type and identifier will provide specific results to the interface only. In the preceding output, notice the current operating speed is 1000 Mbps on the link. Lastly, using the show running-config command will provide you with the configurations made for each interface. To view the configurations for a specific interface, you can use the commands shown in the following snippet:

```
SW1#show running-config interface gigabitEthernet 0/1
Building configuration...

Current configuration : 99 bytes
!
interface GigabitEthernet0/1
 description Connected to SW2
 speed 1000
 no negotiation auto
end

SW1#
```

Figure 4.7 – show running-config output for the interface

Another common issue is a mismatch in duplex settings between devices. What is duplex? Duplex is a common method by which two devices exchange messages. In the field of digital communication, there are three forms of duplex. These are Simplex, Half-duplex, and Full-duplex. Simplex is simply a one-way method of communication, such as tuning in to a radio station on your daily commute.

Half-duplex is where only one device is able to communicate at a time over a network. An example of half-duplex communication is using walkie-talkies, which only allow one person to speak at a time. Another example is on a computer network where end devices are connected to a hub. Once again, only one device is able to use the medium to exchange messages.

> **Important note**
>
> Please refer to *Chapter 1, Introduction to Networking*, where we discussed **Carrier-Sense Multiple Access with Collision Detection (CSMA/CD)** in further detail.

Full-duplex is the preferred method that devices should use to operate and exchange messages with each other. Full-duplex allows two devices to simultaneously exchange messages, unlike half-duplex.

The interfaces on Cisco devices such as switches and routers have the following duplex modes:

- `Auto`: Enables auto duplex negotiation.
- `Full`: Forces full-duplex mode.
- `Half`: Forces half-duplex mode.

By default, the interfaces on Cisco devices are set to use the `auto` duplex mode. The idea of using `auto` is to allow two devices to negotiate how they want to exchange messages between each other (half-duplex or full-duplex). Ideally, if you connect two devices together with default configurations, they are supposed to negotiate their interfaces to both being full-duplex. There are times when the negotiation process does not work properly. For example, one device's interface may be operating at half-duplex and the other device is set to full-duplex. Additionally, if there are misconfigurations on the interface that do not allow both devices to operate using the same duplex mode, this will result in latency issues and collisions of packets on the network.

The following diagram shows two switches with a mismatch in duplex settings:

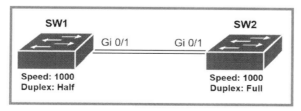

Figure 4.8 – Duplex mismatch

As a network professional, it is highly recommended to statically configure the interfaces on your Cisco devices to operate in full-duplex mode. However, half-duplex is recommended when connecting to a hub.

To configure an interface to operate in a specific duplex mode, use the following instructions:

1. Enter interface mode and administratively shut down the interface:

```
SW1(config)#interface gigabitEthernet 0/1
SW1(config-if)#shutdown
```

2. Use the `duplex` command followed by the duplex mode (`auto`, `full`, or `half`):

```
SW1(config-if)#duplex ?
  auto  Enable AUTO duplex configuration
  full  Force full duplex operation
  half  Force half-duplex operation
```

Let's say you want to manually set the duplex to full, use the `duplex full` command as shown here:

```
SW1(config-if)#duplex full
```

3. Then use the `no shutdown` command to enable the interface and exit interface mode:

```
SW1(config-if)#no shutdown
SW1(config-if)#exit
```

4. To verify the duplex operation mode on an interface, use the `show interfaces status` to verify the duplex settings on the interface, as shown here:

```
SW1#show interfaces status

Port      Name               Status       Vlan      Duplex  Speed Type
Gi0/0                        connected    1         a-full   auto RJ45
Gi0/1     Connected to SW2   connected    1           full   1000 RJ45
Gi0/2                        notconnect   1         a-full   auto RJ45
Gi0/3                        notconnect   1         a-full   auto RJ45
Gi1/0                        notconnect   1         a-full   auto RJ45
```

Figure 4.9 – Duplex mode on physical interface

If you look carefully, you should see that the duplex mode is set to `full`, as per our configurations. The other interfaces are using the default configurations, as indicated by the `a-full` status shown in the output. `a-full` indicates the interface is auto-negotiated as full-duplex.

> **Important note**
>
> The `show interfaces` command allows you to also verify the duplex mode on an interface.

5. Additionally, using the `show running-config interface GigabitEthernet 0/1` command allows us to view the configurations applied to specifically the `GigiabitEthernet 0/1` interface of the switch, as shown here:

```
SW1#show running-config interface GigabitEthernet 0/1
Building configuration...

Current configuration : 112 bytes
!
interface GigabitEthernet0/1
 description Connected to SW2
 speed 1000
 duplex full
 no negotiation auto
end

SW1#
```

Figure 4.10 – Configurations made on the GigabitEthernet 0/1 interface

Let's imagine a user reports that they are experiencing latency issues such as slow loading times with their computer and the local application server. The Cisco IOS provides some very nice and detailed statistics of all the errors and collisions that an interface is experiencing.

Using the `show interfaces` command, you will be able to see whether an interface is encountering any errors, collisions, or physical issues. The following snippet shows the second half of the `show interface` command for a physical interface:

```
5 minute input rate 0 bits/sec, 0 packets/sec
5 minute output rate 0 bits/sec, 0 packets/sec
   956 packets input, 193351 bytes, 0 no buffer
   Received 956 broadcasts, 0 runts, 0 giants, 0 throttles
   0 input errors, 0 CRC, 0 frame, 0 overrun, 0 ignored, 0 abort
   0 watchdog, 0 multicast, 0 pause input
   0 input packets with dribble condition detected
   2357 packets output, 263570 bytes, 0 underruns
   0 output errors, 0 collisions, 10 interface resets
   0 babbles, 0 late collision, 0 deferred
   0 lost carrier, 0 no carrier
   0 output buffer failures, 0 output buffers swapped out
```

Figure 4.11 – Checking for physical errors

The following is a brief description of each type of counter on an interface:

- **Input errors**: This counter provides the **total number of faulty packets** that has entered the interface of the Cisco device. The value is the sum of **runts, giants, no buffer, CRC, frame, overrun**, and ignored counts on the interface.

- **Runts**: These packets are discarded because they are less than 64 bytes in size and are smaller than the minimum packet size.

- **Giants**: These packets are discarded because they exceed the maximum packet size. They are usually greater than 1,518 bytes in size.

- **CRC**: **Cyclic redundancy check** (**CRC**) errors occur when the checksum within the frame trailer does not match the checksum received. The CRC value is stored within the **File Check Sequence** (**FCS**).

- **Output errors**: These are a sum of the total errors that have prevented the transmission of a message from leaving the interface.

- **Collisions**: These are the number of messages that have been retransmitted due to a collision on the network.

- **Late collisions**: These collisions occur after 512 bits or 64 bytes of a frame have been transmitted.

If these counters are increasing, it's a sign that interface errors or network collisions are occurring. To resolve these issues, use the following as a guide:

- Check the duplex and speed settings on both devices that are sending and receiving messages.

- If the duplex and speed configurations are good, change the network cable and check whether the counters are still increasing.

- If changing the cable does not resolve the issue, connect the network to another interface on the device and check the counters again.

At times, a faulty network cable or **network interface card** (**NIC**) can generate a lot of errors and collisions, which then results in poor network performance, such as high latency and packet loss.

Having completed this section, you have acquired the skills required to identify errors and collisions in the physical layer of the OSI reference model. Additionally, you have learned how to use troubleshooting techniques to resolve errors and collisions on a network. In the next section, we will discuss enterprise wireless architectures and deployment models.

# Wireless principles

Nowadays, almost anywhere you visit, whether it's the mall or the local coffee shop, there are wireless networks everywhere. Many organizations have invested a great deal in implementing a robust wireless infrastructure to ensure employees, customers, and guests have the best experience at their establishment.

A great deal of work goes into ensuring a wireless network is able to support all users and their traffic load at any time. This involves various technologies and components, as well as complicated plans and designs, configurations, and troubleshooting. Throughout this section, you will learn about the backend technologies used to create a wireless network and how to efficiently configure our components to provide optimal performance for an enterprise organization.

So, what exactly is a wireless network connection? In a typical **local area network** (**LAN**), we usually interconnect computers, IP phones, servers, and printers using a copper cable such as **Cat 5**, **Cat 5e**, or even **Cat 6** to the rest of the network. Having a wired connection is advantageous because the outer coating of those copper cables provides a protective shield around the actual wires. However, using physical wires has its limitations as it does not allow a user to roam between rooms or office spaces. This is where wireless networking provides us with the convenience of mobility.

As we learned in *Chapter 1, Introduction to Networking*, we use wireless **access points** (**APs**), which connect to a wired network to provide us with a wireless signal. For a home network, you simply have to connect a wireless router or AP to your modem with some basic configurations, such as the wireless network's name, and some security measures. In an organization, however, it is not as simple. Connecting multiple APs randomly without considering any physical constraints, such as signal levels, channel assignments, security, and central management, can create an inefficient wireless network topology.

# Wireless technologies

We know that a copper or fiber cables use electrical or light signals to exchange messages across a network. Wireless networks operate differently, however. Wireless network components, such as an AP, take the electrical signal (1s and 0s) received on the **Ethernet NIC** and convert it into a radio signal, which compatible devices such as laptops and smart devices are able to understand. The wireless signal is still the same 1s and 0s that are transmitted across a wired network, but it's simply encapsulated into another format.

With a wireless signal, the signal is not directly protected like it is with a copper or fiber cable. There are limitations to wireless signals, such as security risks, signal strength, and the operating frequencies.

We need to understand the characteristics of a wireless signal. There are a lot of wireless signals operating at different frequencies all around us. Whether it's radio stations, walkie-talkies, household wireless routers, or the signals generated by wireless networks, each type of wireless technology uses a different radio frequency.

> **Important note**
>
> The **Federal Communications Commission** (**FCC**) is responsible for regulating the usage of various radio frequencies for communication.

The FCC allocated many unlicensed radio frequency bands, allowing people and organizations to use a certain radio frequency without needing to register it. As such, the FCC allocated two radio frequency bands for Wi-Fi: the 2.4 GHz and 5.0 GHz bands. We can use either of these two frequencies, or both. One of the first questions to ask yourself as a nascent network engineer is, which frequency should I use and why?

Each frequency operates at different signal strengths, sometimes referred to as **amplitude**. The amplitude determines how powerful or weak a signal might be as it travels away from a device such as an AP. Using a signal that has a low amplitude will provide a degraded network performance between the AP and the associated clients. Using a signal that provides a very high amplitude may not always be good for a wireless network as it can be too noisy on the airwave, thus creating distortion.

However, the **Receive Signal Strength Indicator** (**RSSI**) can be used to help us determine a suitable amplitude for our wireless networks. The RSSI is like the signal bars shown in the corner of our smartphone screens, but on a computer or network device. The RSSI is represented using a value in dBm, the unit used to measure the power ratio in decibels (dBm) to one milliwatt.

Using the **Wi-Fi Analyzer** app from Microsoft, you will be able to see the RSSI value for your wireless network, as shown here:

Figure 4.12 – RSSI value

The RSSI value is always given as a negative value. When the value is close to zero the signal strength is good, but as you move further away from an AP the RSSI value will decrease, which is bad for transmitting data as some messages may be dropped due to signal loss.

## 2.4 GHz versus 5 GHz

At this point, we know there are two frequencies to choose from: 2 . 4 GHz and 5 GHz. We need to decide which of these two frequencies is the best choice to implement in an enterprise network. To get a better understanding of them, let's dissect them both to further understand their characteristics.

When radio frequencies are transmitting, there are waves in the form of **peaks** and **valleys** moving in a continuous stream. The 5 GHz frequency has a shorter wavelength and operates at a higher frequency than the 2 . 4 GHz frequency. This means that using the 5 GHz frequency on a wireless network will provide much greater bandwidth capacity; however, due to the short wavelengths, the signal cannot travel very far.

**Important note**

Wireless frequencies such as 2.4 GHz and 5 GHz are susceptible to deterioration when passing through objects such as walls and metal. In other words, having a lot of walls between an AP and a client's device will drastically reduce the wireless signal and, as a result, the wireless network's performance.

The following diagram is a visual representation of the 5 GHz frequency:

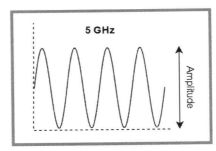

Figure 4.13 – 5.0 GHz wavelength

Compared to the 5 GHz frequency, the 2.4 GHz frequency has a much longer wavelength between **peaks,** thus allowing the signal to travel a greater distance from the AP. However, one major downside of using the 2.4 GHz frequency is its shorter amplitude, meaning it supports a much lower bandwidth capacity.

The following diagram is a visual representation of the 2.4 GHz frequency:

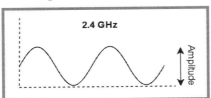

Figure 4.14 – 2.4 GHz wavelength

So, the longer wavelength is one of the benefits of using the 2.4 GHz frequency; however, it is also a disadvantage in the wireless networking world. Let's imagine you have just set up your home wireless network and are ready to connect to the Wi-Fi. When you check the available wireless networks, you're seeing your neighbors' wireless networks as well. This is where the issue lies with the 2.4 GHz frequency; it is very powerful and will give you a great signal reach, but when there are other nearby wireless APs operating on the same 2.4 GHz frequency it creates interference with other wireless networks.

The following diagram shows the signals of two wireless networks:

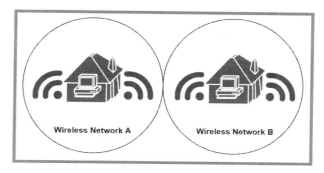

Figure 4.15 – Wireless signals overlapping

To help prevent signal overlap on a wireless network, channels allow us to set a range on either the 2.4 GHz or 5 GHz frequencies.

> **Important note**
> The coverage area of a wireless signal is known as the **Basic Service Area (BSA)**.

Therefore, our AP can use a frequency and a specific channel for operation. In the 2.4 GHz world, there are 14 channels to choose from, but most of the channels overlap each other. However, if you choose channels 1, 6, and 11, they will not overlap with each other.

> **Important note**
> Each channel is between 20–22 MHz wide. Channel 1 in the 2.4 GHz frequency is 2.412 GHz, channel 2 is 2.417 GHz, and channel 3 is 2.422 GHz, and so on.

The non-overlapping channels in the 2.4 GHz frequency are channels 1, 6, and 11 as shown here:

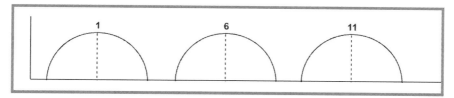

Figure 4.16 – Non-overlapping 2.4 GHz channels

Due to the high number of APs online and within close proximity to each other, there is high possibility a neighbor may be using the same channel as you are for your organization or home wireless network.

The 5 GHz frequency introduced far more channels than the older 2.4 GHz frequency. Additionally, the 5 GHz frequency has the technology to perform **channel bonding**, which allows 2 or more 5 GHz channels to have a large channel capacity. The following points further break down how channel bonding works:

- Each channel is 20 MHz in size.

- Using **channel bonding**, we can combine two 20 MHz channels to form a 40 MHz channel.

- Using channel bonding again, we can combine two 40 MHz channels to form an 80 MHz channel.

- Finally, we can combine two 80 MHz channels using channel bonding to form a 160 MHz channel.

The benefit of using channel bonding is that it provides a greater bandwidth capacity in **gigabits per second** (**Gbps**) on a wireless network. This is why it is more efficient to use the 5 GHz frequency within an organization where a large number of wireless clients need to be supported.

When designing your wireless network infrastructure, ensure there are almost zero overlapping frequencies (channels) between the APs in your organization. Additionally, between each AP, ensure there is a little overlap between signals to ensure there are no dead zones in your wireless network. Dead zones are places where clients will not be able to detect a signal and will be dropped from the wireless network.

## Wireless bands

So far, we have discussed the need to use an appropriate wireless frequency when implementing a wireless network and the choices involved. Now we need to address some other questions: who manages the standard of wireless network communication, and what standards are available?

The **Institute of Electrical and Electronics Engineers** (**IEEE**) introduced the IEEE 802.11 standard in 1997. This allows vendors to develop **wireless interface cards** (**WICs**) on devices such as APs, wireless routers, laptops, and mobile devices. However, the IEEE has created multiple variations of the 802.11 standard over the years with many improvements.

The following chart is a summary of the various Wi-Fi standards over the years:

| IEEE Standard | Frequency | Maximum Bandwidth | Backward Compatibility |
|---|---|---|---|
| 802.11b | 2.4 GHz | 11 Mbps | n/a |
| 802.11a | 5 GHz | 54 Mbps | n/a |
| 802.11g | 2.4 GHz | 54 Mbps | 802.11b |
| 802.11n | 2.4 GHz and 5 GHz | 300 Mbps | 802.11a/b/g |
| 802.11ac | 5 GHz | 7 Gbps | 802.11a/n |
| 802.11ax (Wi-Fi 6) | 2.4 GHz and 5 GHz | 4.8 Gbps | 802.11b/g/n/ac |

Figure 4.17 – Wi-Fi standards

The most recent is IEEE 802.11ax, sometimes referred to as **Wi-Fi 6**. With the other versions of IEEE 802.11, the AP is only able to transmit messages to one device at a time. This means if there are 50 laptops all connected to and communicating with a single AP, the AP can only send traffic to one device at a time while trying to distribute messages quickly to everyone. Think of it as a mail courier driver who has multiple packages for people across the city; they can only drop off packages to one person at time. This is similar to how Wi-Fi networks operate; however, IEEE 802.11ax fixes this issue.

> **Important note**
>
> Further information about Wi-Fi 6 can be found at `https://www.cisco.com/c/en/us/products/wireless/what-is-wi-fi-6.html`.

IEEE 802.11ax allows an AP to allocate a dedicated channel to each client device, therefore improving network performance between the wireless clients and the AP.

## SSID, BSSID, and ESS

Whether you're setting up an AP for your home or an enterprise network, typically the first thing to do is to change the default network name to something users will be familiar with. The name of the network is known as the **Service Set Identifier** (**SSID**).

When an AP boots up, it begins to send **beacons** at predefined intervals. The beacons are a type of advertisement message from an AP that contains the SSID and other parameters. When a client such as a laptop or smart device enables their wireless settings, they are able to see the details from these beacons, such as the SSID. If there are multiple nearby APs advertising their SSID, they will all appear in the wireless network settings on a client device.

When a client connects to a wireless network, this is known as an **association**. Most commonly, when we connect our smart devices or computers to a wireless network, the settings are saved automatically. This allows us to reconnect to the saved wireless network in the future without having to re-enter network configurations such as a password. However, when a client device boots up, it begins to send **probes**. The probes are designed to search and establish an **association** with a saved wireless network that may be within range of the client device.

The following diagram shows the probe and beacon advertisements:

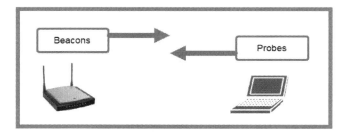

Figure 4.18 – Probes and beacons

When a client is associated with an AP, it accepts and becomes part of everything the AP is providing. This is known as the **Basic Service Set (BSS)**. Using a real-world example, if your local coffee shop only has one AP providing wireless network coverage for their customers and a person connects their device to the network, their device now becomes part of the BSS.

In many organizations, there are multiple APs connected to the same wired network, where each AP is using the same SSID and is providing wireless signal allowing users to connect. This type of infrastructure is referred to as an **Extended Service Set (ESS)**. On the client's side, the device does not see individual SSIDs with the same name, they see only one SSID.

To further understand how an ESS works let's imagine that, within a building, there are five APs and they are all connected to the same wired network, forming an ESS for a small organization. Each AP is broadcasting the SSID as Company_X. All Wi-Fi-enabled clients are seeing a single SSID, Company_X, instead of seeing the same SSID listed five times. When a client connects to the wireless network, Company_X, it is associated to an AP. The client knows which AP it is associated with by recording the **Basic Service Set Identifer (BSSID)** of the AP.

> **Important note**
> The BSSID is the MAC address of an AP.

In the following snippet, the BSSID is shown for the associated wireless network on a Windows machine:

```
C:\>netsh wlan show interface

There is 1 interface on the system:

    Name                   : Wi-Fi
    Description            : Intel(R) Dual Band Wireless-AC 3165
    GUID                   : d7aaa22a-
    Physical address       : ee:80:
    State                  : connected
    SSID                   : !|>_<|!
    BSSID                  : 9c:3d:
    Network type           : Infrastructure
    Radio type             : 802.11ac
    Authentication         : WPA2-Personal
    Cipher                 : CCMP
    Connection mode        : Auto Connect
    Channel                : 161
    Receive rate (Mbps)    : 433.3
    Transmit rate (Mbps)   : 433.3
    Signal                 : 99%
    Profile                : !|>_<|!

    Hosted network status  : Not available
```

Figure 4.19 – BSSID for a wireless network

The client has the choice to associate itself to a specific AP by using the BSSID information. Lastly, when a client device is moving between APs within an **ESS**, the client device will disassociate from an AP that has a weaker signal and attempt to associate with a nearby AP that has a stronger signal. This is known as **roaming**.

During the disassociation and re-association process, there's a tiny drop in network connectivity as the client device has to re-exchange networking and security information with the AP.

Having completed this section, you have acquired the necessary knowledge to understand and describe how devices on a wireless network operate. In the next section, we will move on to learning about various Cisco wireless architecture models.

# Cisco wireless architectures

When designing a wireless network, one of the main objectives is to ensure the network is designed to perform at optimal capacity for all users. Acquiring APs is as simple as purchasing them from a local retailer. However, when it comes to implementing the APs in a network, there are a few Cisco wireless architectures we need to understand, as each one has different usage scenarios, advantages, and disadvantages.

In the following sections, we will cover the essentials of the following wireless architectures:

- Autonomous
- Cloud-based
- Split-MAC

Let's get started!

## Autonomous

In an autonomous architecture, each AP is statically assigned a management IP address, which allows the network administrator to log in and configure the device across the network. This deployment model is good if you have a couple of APs to manage.

However, in this type of architecture, each AP is independently managed. This means if you have to make a universal change to the configurations of the wireless network, you'll need to log in to each device independently to make the changes.

The following diagram shows the typical deployment model for the autonomous architecture:

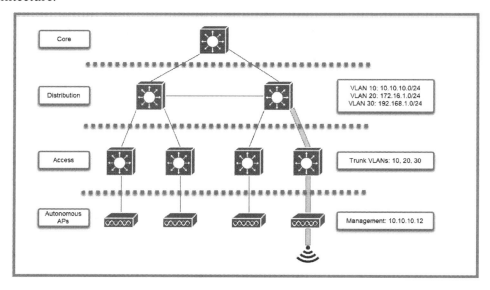

Figure 4.20 – Cisco autonomous wireless architecture

In the next section, we will learn about Cisco's cloud-based wireless network architecture.

# Cloud-based

As more APs are deployed on an enterprise network, the management task becomes a bit challenging. Let's imagine you are the network administrator at a company with a large wireless network containing about 50 APs. One day, you have to make an adjustment to the wireless network configurations; logging on to each AP individually is time-consuming and inefficient.

In a cloud-based architecture, a **WLC** such as Cisco Meraki is deployed in the cloud. This model allows each AP to receive a management IP address, similarly to the autonomous architecture. However, the Cisco Meraki cloud model allows the WLC to gather network and Wi-Fi statistics, detect rogue devices, find **radio frequency** (**RF**) interference, and generate reports easily. In addition, this model provides a single dashboard that allows you to centrally management all APs.

The following diagram shows the typical deployment model for the cloud-based architecture:

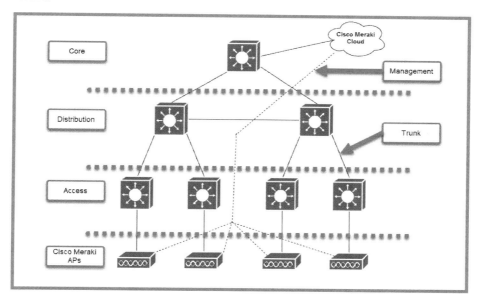

Figure 4.21 – Cisco cloud-based wireless architecture

In the next section, we will cover the essentials of the Split-MAC wireless network architecture.

## Split-MAC

In this architecture, both a local WLC and **Light-weight Access Points (LAPs)** are implemented. The link between a WLC and a LAP is known as a **Control and Provisioning of Wireless Access Points (CAPWAP)** tunnel. The CAPWAP tunnel handles the encapsulation of data between devices.

The CAPWAP tunnel allows an AP and a WLC to be separated geographically and logically, allowing different **virtual LAN (VLAN)** traffic to be delivered to a specific AP without the need to create a trunk port on the switch. The WLC handles the RF management, client authentication, security management, **quality of service (QoS)**, and association and roaming management of each LAP on the enterprise network. Additionally, each LAP manages the RF transmission, MAC management, and data encryption.

The following diagram shows a representation of the CAPWAP tunnel between a WLC and a LAP:

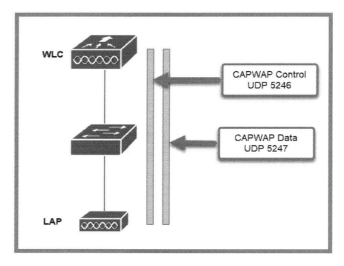

Figure 4.22 – CAPWAP tunnel

The CAPWAP tunnel requires two network ports. These are UDP port 5246, which allows the WLC to manage each LAP, and the UDP port 5247, which is used for encapsulating data between the controller and the AP.

In the next section, we will cover the various modes of operating for a Cisco AP.

# AP modes

Cisco APs are designed to operate in either autonomous (independent) or lightweight (centrally managed) mode. Using a WLC, you can configure a LAP to operate in the following modes:

- **Local**: This is the default mode for a LAP, which allows the AP to provide one or more **BSS** using a specific channel. When the AP is not transmitting, it will scan other wireless channels to determine the level of noise and interference and detect any nearby rogue APs.

- **Monitor**: In monitor mode, the AP does not transmit any traffic at all; however, it is able to receive incoming transmissions from nearby wireless-enabled devices such as other APs and client devices (laptops, smartphones, and so on). This mode allows the AP to function as a dedicated sensor for checking **intrusion detection system** (**IDS**) security events, such as rogue APs, and determining the positions of stations (clients) using location-based services.

- **FlexConnect**: In FlexConnect mode, the AP has the capability to switch traffic between an SSID and a VLAN if the CAPWAP tunnel is down. However, the AP needs to be configured to do so.

- **Sniffer**: In sniffer mode, the AP dedicates its radios to capture IEEE 802.11 traffic from nearby sources and forwards it to a computer running a protocol analyzer software such as Wireshark for offline packet analysis.

- **Rogue detector**: Rogue detector mode allows the AP to detect rogue devices by correlating MAC addresses found on the wired IEEE 802.3 network with those found on the wireless IEEE 802.11 airways.

- **Bridge**: In bridge mode, the AP can be configured to operate as a bridge between two networks. In this configuration, two or more APs must be used in bridge mode to link (bridge) multiple locations together.

- **Flex+Bridge**: Cisco APs can be configured to operate in a mesh network. In a mesh, each device is connected to all other devices. The benefit of using a mesh network is the fact that it has full redundancy. However, the downside is that because the mesh grows as more devices are added, it becomes challenging to manage and troubleshoot. The Flex-Bridge mode allows the APs to operate in this method.

- **SE-Connect**: The AP dedicates its radios to enable spectrum analysis on all wireless channels. The data is sent to a computer running spectrum analysis such as **MetaGeek Chanalyzer** or **Cisco Spectrum Expert** to discover the sources of interference.

In the next section, we will discuss wireless components and management techniques.

# Wireless components and management

As mentioned in the previous section, *Cisco wireless architectures*, autonomous deployment is good enough if there are just a few APs on the network, but as the wireless network grows and more APs are added, management becomes more challenging. This is where LAPs come in to help us as network professionals.

LAPs are designed to be managed by a WLC. In a large network, a single WLC is usually physically connected to a network switch, which allows the LAPs to reach the WLC on the network. Keep in mind, though, the LAPs do not have any configurations when connected to the physical (wired) network, thus they are made available to the WLC for management.

> **Important note**
> A LAP can support multiple VLANs by using the CAPWAP tunnel between the WLC and the LAP. This means the AP only requires an access link to connect to the network infrastructure.

For your CCNA certification, it is important to understand the various interfaces supported by the Cisco WLC device. These interfaces are virtual interfaces that exist within the operating system of the device. However, these virtual interfaces are usually mapped to a physical port on the WLC.

There are several different types of controller ports that can be connected to your network:

- **Service port**: This port is used for out-of-band management to the device, system recovery, and initial boot functions. Furthermore, this port is connected to an access port on a switch.

- **Distribution system port**: This port is used for all normal AP and management traffic and is connected to an IEEE 802.1Q trunk port on a switch. This port is usually referred to as a **Link Aggregation Group** (**LAG**) interface. LAG allows you to configure multiple distribution system ports into a single logical group, such as an **EtherChannel** or **port-group** on a switch. LAG provides resilience such that if one distribution system port fails, the traffic can be redirected to the remaining working ports.

- **Console port**: This port is used for out-of-band management to the device, system recovery, and initial boot functions. A console cable is required.

- **Redundancy port**: This port is used when configuring another controller to establish **high availability** (**HA**).

- **Management interface**: This interface is used for management traffic such as traffic between the AAA server (RADIUS or TACACS+), WLC-to-WLC communications, and SSH and SNMP connections.

In the next section, we will walk through the process of accessing a Cisco WLC.

# Lab – accessing a Cisco WLC GUI

In this section, you will learn how to set up a Cisco WLC for the first time and access its **graphical user interface** (**GUI**). To complete this exercise, use Cisco Packet Tracer to build the following topology:

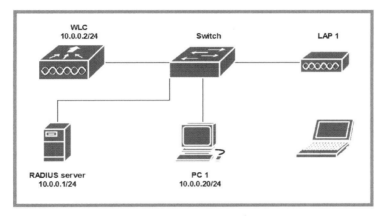

Figure 4.23 – WLC topology

To configure a Cisco WLC, use the following steps:

1.  Using a console cable, connect the PC to the WLC (WLC 2504) and power on the device.

2.  Using PuTTY or another terminal application, establish a terminal session with the WLC.

3.  If there are existing configurations on the WLC, enter 5 – Clear Configurations to clear the memory. The device will reboot automatically after the contents are cleared.

4.  After the device is rebooted, the interactive wizard will ask whether you want to terminate autoinstall. Type yes and hit *Enter*.

5. Type a hostname for the device and hit *Enter*.

6. Next, set an Administrative user name and hit *Enter*.

7. Next, set an Administrative password and hit *Enter*.

8. Next, set a Management interface IP address and hit Enter. This IP address will allow you to remotely connect to the device via Telnet, SSH, and HTTPS. Use 10.0.0.2/24 as the IP address and subnet mask for the device, as shown the topology.

9. Next, set the Interface netmask (subnet mask) and hit *Enter*.

10. Next, set the Interface default router (gateway) IP address and hit *Enter*.

11. If there is a VLAN assigned to the switch port, set it at this stage. If there are no VLANs, simply hit Enter to leave the defaults and continue.

12. Next, the wizard will ask which of the physical ports on the WLC should assume the role of the management interface. Choose the port that is connected to the switch.

13. Next, the wizard may ask for a DHCP server IP address. If there is a DHCP server available on the network, insert the server's IP address here.

14. Next, the WLC will ask you to set an AP manager IP address. This IP address is used by the WLC to manage the APs. This address should be different from the management interface IP address.

15. The Virtual gateway IP address should be set to 192.0.2.1, as recommended by Cisco.

16. Next, set a Mobility/RF group name. This is used to allow you to move between APs on the network.

17. The wizard will then ask to you set an SSID, DHCP mode, static IP address for clients, RADIUS server, country code, IEEE 802.11 standards, NTP server, and so on.

18. The final step will ask whether the configurations are correct. Type yes to save and reboot. Additionally, you can use show sysinfo to verify the configurations on the Cisco WLC device.

After the Cisco WLC has rebooted, it's now accessible via the browser on a PC attached on the network, thus providing its GUI. In the next section, we will cover how to configure a Cisco WLC with LAPs on a network.

# Lab – configuring a wireless network using a Cisco WLC

In this section, you will learn how to create WLANs, implement secure features, configure interfaces, and adjust the **QoS** features on a Cisco WLC.

> **Tip**
>
> The WLC topology can be built within the Cisco Packet Tracer application. However, you'll need to enable the DHCP service on the server to provide automatic IP address configurations to the APs. Assigned static IP addresses are shown in the topology.

To get started setting up the WLC with the LAP, use the following instructions:

1.  On **PC1**, open your web browser and go to the URL of the WLC, `https://10.0.0.2` or `http://10.0.0.2`.

2.  Log in with the username and password set in the previous exercise. On the main dashboard, you will see a similar view showing the physical ports that are currently in use by the WLC:

Figure 4.24 – Cisco WLC dashboard

3.  If you scroll down a bit, you'll notice the WLC has auto-detected any available LAPs on the network:

**Access Point Summary**

|  | Total | Up | Down |  |
| --- | --- | --- | --- | --- |
| 802.11a/n/ac Radios | 1 | ● 1 | ● 0 | Detail |
| 802.11b/g/n Radios | 1 | ● 1 | ● 0 | Detail |
| Dual-Band Radios | 0 | ● 0 | ● 0 | Detail |
| All APs | 1 | ● 1 | ● 0 | Detail |

Figure 4.25 – Access Point Summary

4.  Furthermore, if you click the **WIRELESS** tab at the top, you'll be able to get more details about each associated LAP.

5.  To configure **interfaces** on the Cisco WLC, click on **CONTROLLER | Interfaces | New** as follows:

Figure 4.26 – Creating interfaces on a Cisco WLC

6.  When you click on **New**, you'll have the option to set a name for the interface and assign a VLAN ID, as shown here:

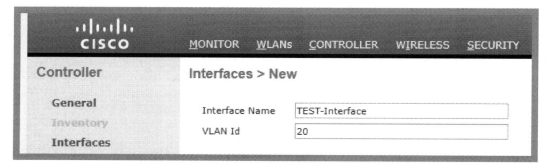

Figure 4.27 – Naming an interface on a Cisco WLC

7. After clicking on **Apply** to create the interface, the wizard will present a new screen allowing you to configure the **VLAN Identifier**, **IP address**, **Netmask**, **Gateway**, **Primary**, and **Secondary DHCP server**, as shown here:

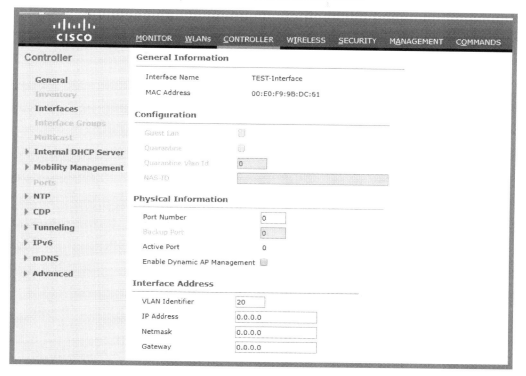

Figure 4.28 – Interface options

8. Click **Apply** to finish setting up the virtual interface on the Cisco WLC.

9. To create a wireless network, go to the **WLANs** tab, set the option to **Create New**, and click on **Go** as follows:

Figure 4.29 – Creating a WLAN

10. Next, set **Profile Name** and the **SSID** to your preference, as shown here:

Figure 4.30 – Setting the SSID name

11. Click **Apply** to continue.

12. Next, you'll be presented with the profile menu for the SSID. On the **General** tab, enable the SSID, as shown here:

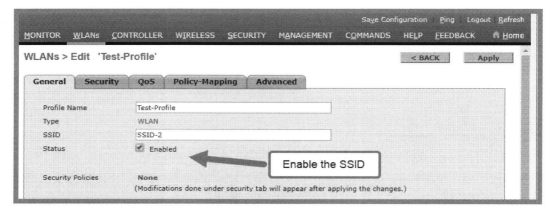

Figure 4.31 – General tab

13. Click on the **Security** tab to adjust the security configurations for the wireless network, as shown here:

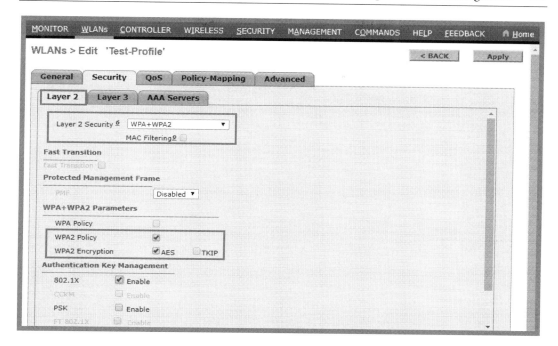

Figure 4.32 – Security tab

Here, you can configure layer security options and enable 802.1X authentication if there is a RADIUS server on the network.

> **Important note**
>
> The RADIUS server handles the authentication, authorization, and accounting services of network devices and users. On this server, user accounts are created and centrally managed. Additionally, the RADIUS server removes the need to create user accounts directly on the APs on the network as the APs will query the RADIUS server when a user is attempting to log on to the network.

14. To add a RADIUS server within the Cisco WLC, go to **SECURITY | AAA | RADIUS | Authentication** and click on **New**. A new page will open, and you can simply set the IP address of the RADIUS server and a secret key for authentication:

Figure 4.33 – Adding a RADIUS server

15. If there's a RADIUS server on the network, click on the **AAA Servers** tab to set a RADIUS server, as shown here:

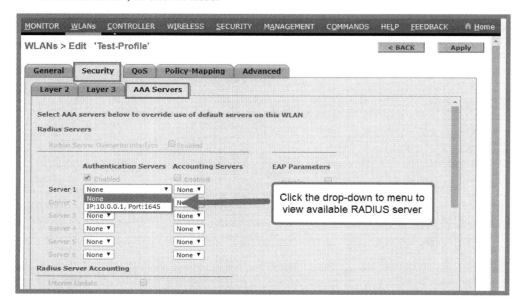

Figure 4.34 – RADIUS settings

16. To adjust the **QoS** configurations on the WLAN, click on the **QoS** tab. You'll be able to choose **Platinum**, **Gold**, **Silver**, or **Bronze**.

17. Click **Apply** to save the settings for the newly created WLAN network.

Having completed this section, you now have the skills required to configure various Cisco wireless architectures and implement a Cisco WLC on a network. In the next section, we will cover the fundamentals of virtualization technologies.

# Virtualization fundamentals

To begin this section, we will start with a simple analogy to help you understand the important role and benefits of implementing virtualization technologies. Let's imagine you have a single computer running Microsoft Windows 10. Upon learning more about IT-related topics, you have realized that having some Linux skills may be important to your career, but you have only one computer. One option is to create a partition on the local disk drive and install the Linux operating system on the new partition, creating a dual-boot system. The downside to this is that only one operating system will be able to boot.

It would be highly advantageous if you could have multiple operating systems running simultaneously on a single system, such as your Microsoft Windows 10 and Linux, as this would allow you to work between different operating systems quickly and efficiently. The technology to make this a reality is known as **virtualization**.

Virtualization allows you to **emulate** the hardware requirements to run an operating system. Think of it as creating a container and placing Linux inside. The virtualization application, known as a **hypervisor**, is the key component to create the necessary virtual hardware requirements such as CPU, RAM, disk drives, I/O, and other components to emulate a physical computer. The hypervisor allows you to install supported operating systems onto the virtual environment. These operating systems are referred to as virtual machines or guest operating systems.

> **Important note**
> A **guest operating system** is installed on a hypervisor application, while a **host operating system** is installed directly on the physical device.

There are two types of hypervisor:

- Type 1 hypervisor
- Type 2 hypervisor

We will discuss them in the following subsections.

## Type 1 hypervisor

A **Type 1 hypervisor** is most commonly referred to as a *bare-metal hypervisor* simply because it's installed directly onto the hardware. You might be wondering, "What do you mean, *directly on the hardware*?". To a get a better idea, let's imagine you are going to build a desktop computer, so you buy the essential components such as CPU, RAM, motherboard, HDD/SSD, NIC, case, and so on, and you assemble all the components together to create a computer. Now you need an operating system to control all of the components. Instead of installing Windows or Linux on the hardware (HDD/SDD), you install a Type 1 hypervisor as the operating system, which will still allow you to communicate with all the physical hardware components.

The following diagram shows a visual representation of a **Type 1 hypervisor** and its virtual machines:

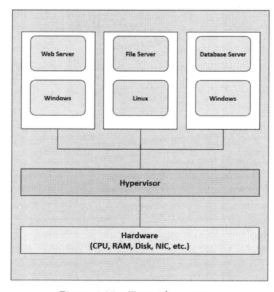

Figure 4.35 – Type 1 hypervisor

The benefit of using a Type 1 hypervisor is that each virtual machine has direct access to the hardware resources on the physical system.

The following is a list of Type 1 hypervisor applications:

- VMware ESXi (free)
- Proxmox (free)
- XCP-ng (free)

Now that you have read about the Type 1 hypervisor, let's take a look at the functionality of the Type 2 hypervisor.

## Type 2 hypervisor

The **Type 2 hypervisor** is installed on top of a host operating system. This type of hypervisor provides all the same essential functions and capabilities as a Type 1 hypervisor, but it is installed on your existing operating system. The virtual machines installed on a Type 2 hypervisor do not have direct access to all the available hardware resources, in contrast with Type 1 hypervisors.

The following diagram shows a visual representation of a Type 2 hypervisor and its virtual machines:

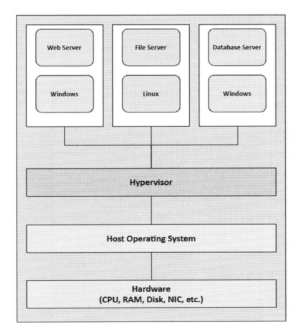

Figure 4.36 – Type 2 hypervisor

The host operating system has full access to the physical hardware resources, while some of the resources are shared with the virtual machines via the hypervisor application. This type of hypervisor is beneficial if you have a single computer and would like to create virtual machines on it.

The following is a list of Type 2 hypervisor applications:

- Oracle VM VirtualBox (free)
- VMware Player (free)
- VMware Workstation Pro (commercial)
- VMware Fusion (commercial)
- Parallels Desktop for Mac (commercial)

Imagine a system such as Microsoft Windows Server 2019 on a physical rack server with a 12-core CPU, 128 GB of RAM, and 12 TB of storage, and the role of the server is to provide **Active Directory** (**AD**) and DHCP services. Those server roles combined will not use more than half of the available computing power. Thus, where a single operating system is installed on a physical device and the operating system is not maximizing the full potential of the available hardware resources, the CPU and RAM are hugely underutilized. This is known as server sprawl and is a major issue in the computing industry. Using virtualization technologies helps solve this problem.

The following screenshot is an example of a machine experiencing server sprawl:

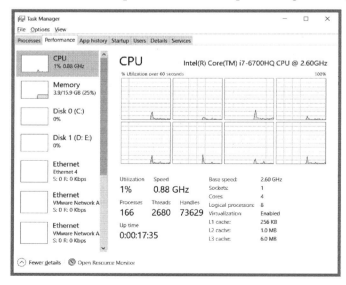

Figure 4.37 – Underutilized hardware on a Windows machine

The hypervisor application allows us to allocate virtual resources to each virtual machine as we see fit. Therefore, we can assign various amounts of RAM to different virtual machines, and likewise for CPU cores and other virtual hardware components.

The following screenshot shows a virtual machine settings window in VMware Workstation Pro:

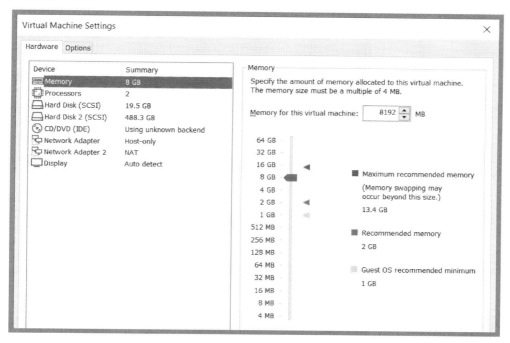

Figure 4.38 – Virtual Machine Settings

As you can see in the preceding screenshot, the hypervisor application allows you to customize the entire virtual environment, allowing you to add, modify, and remove virtual hardware components on a virtual machine.

Virtualization technology has been around in the computing industry for over a decade. Within the last 10 years, there has been a growing need for professionals who can implement and support data center environments to create cloud computing technologies. In the next section, we will explore various cloud computing architectures.

# Cloud computing

What is cloud computing? Cloud computing allows us to use computing resources that are located in someone else's data center via the internet. In today's world, the need to have physical servers in an organization is slowly disappearing.

Having physical servers within an organization has the following downsides:

- An IT team is required to always be available to manage the servers.

- Servers require physical storage space in a building.

- They use a lot of power (electricity).

- They generate a lot of heat because the devices are always powered on.

- If a hardware failure occurs on a server, this may cause a disruption in network services.

With cloud computing, an organization can eliminate the need for physical servers and simply pay for only the resources it uses from a cloud computing service provider such as Microsoft Azure, Amazon's AWS, or Google's GCP. On the backend of cloud providers, they use a lot of virtualization and automation technologies to quickly **spin up** resources for their customers within a matter of minutes. Each application and server deployed on a cloud platform is a virtual machine on the provider's backend.

One such example is the email services provided by Microsoft and Google. Microsoft offers Office 365 and Google offers G Suite; each provider has a plan that costs about USD 5-6 per user per month. This allows an organization to simply pay for the number of employees that require an email. If an employee requires additional services or storage, the plan allows the organization to simply pay for the additional service or features for that user. This provides greater flexibility for employers and organizations.

The following are benefits of using cloud computing technologies:

- Cloud computing service providers usually guarantee over 99% uptime annually.

- Cloud computing services are accessible anywhere and anytime.

- It reduces the number of physical services within an organization.

- Cloud computing providers are responsible for all hardware maintenance on the virtual servers and services.

- Organizations only pay for what they use from a service provider.

- Service providers allow the customer to scale their platform or services.

Though there are many benefits to using cloud computing, there are also some disadvantages:

- When using a cloud computing platform, you do not have full control of the backend platform as it is managed by the service provider.

- You need to secure your cloud platform just as you would have to secure local servers in your organization.

- An internet connection is required from the user's end to access resources online.

Over the years, Cisco has adapted to cloud computing technologies. Most of the time when we think of a Cisco router, switch, or even a firewall, we think of a physical device. However, there are many virtual appliances sold by Cisco that enable you to deploy a hypervisor within your organization, your personal cloud platform, or on a reputable cloud service provider infrastructure.

> **Tip**
> Check out the Cisco DevNet website to learn more about their cloud technologies at `https://developer.cisco.com/`.

In the next section, you will learn about the various cloud computing service architectures and delivery models.

# Cloud services

A cloud computing provider has many services, all of which usually belong to one of three parent categories:

- **Software-as-a-Service (SaaS)**
- **Platform-as-a-Service (PaaS)**
- **Infrastructure-as-a-Service (IaaS)**

In the following sections, we will describe each of these in further detail.

# SaaS

In a SaaS model, the user is only provided with the application's user interface on the frontend. An example of a SaaS service is Office 365 or the G Suite applications, where the user accesses the applications they use such as their email inbox – SharePoint, Google Docs, or Microsoft Office 365 – using a web browser. The application is not installed on the user's device.

In a SaaS environment, the user does not have to be concerned with the hardware or the underlying infrastructure required to deliver the application. The cloud service provider is responsible for all the technical requirements, such as application updates and patching and hardware resources, which ensure the application is working properly for the user.

## PaaS

The PaaS model is designed to allow the user access to any underlying applications such as programming frameworks and application development environments. With this model, the user has a bit more control over the working environment than they do with SaaS. Some examples of PaaS are AWS Elastic Beanstalk, Google App Engine, and Microsoft Azure. With PaaS, the service provider supplies the user or developer with software tools.

## IaaS

IaaS provides the user with more control over the physical hardware and software resources on the cloud platform, allowing the user to modify storage containers, networking configurations, and so on. Additionally, the user is able to deploy virtual appliances such as virtual firewalls, routers, switches, and other appliances on the cloud provider's platform. Examples of IaaS providers are Microsoft Azure, AWS, and GCP.

In the next section, we will take a look at cloud delivery models.

## Cloud delivery models

In the world of cloud computing, there are four main types of deployment models for a cloud infrastructure. These are private, public, hybrid, and community cloud models. In this section, we will take a look at each of them to understand how a user or organization is able to access resources across a network and the internet.

### Private cloud

In a private cloud, the organization owns the data center and the infrastructure that is used to manage it. A lot of companies build their own local/internal host data center, running all their critical applications for their employees and users. In this type of cloud, the organization is responsible for the maintenance and support of their cloud platform.

## Public cloud

In a public cloud, the cloud infrastructure is owned by another organization, who rents part of or an entire data center to other organizations or individuals. Examples of general clouds are Microsoft Azure and Amazon's AWS. If you want to create a virtual Microsoft Windows Server 2019 on the cloud, it's as simple as accessing the Azure platform, choosing the right hardware configurations for the virtual machine (CPU, RAM, SSD/HDD), and paying for only the resources you use. Some cloud providers charge you by the minute, while some charge per hour.

## Hybrid cloud

The hybrid cloud model consists of a private and public cloud. Organizations usually have a private cloud hosting their applications and data. The private cloud provides faster data transfer rates between the users within the organization as it is locally hosted. However, the organization also pays for a public cloud service. This allows them to ensure they continuously replicate the private cloud onto the public cloud for redundancy and availability.

## Community cloud

The community cloud model is a type of deployment that allows several organizations to share resources on a single cloud provider. This can be a group or partnership of companies simply sharing resources with each other.

Having completed this section, you now have the skills to describe and identify various types of cloud technology.

# Summary

Throughout the course of this chapter, we have discussed the importance of discovering physical issues that may cause errors and collisions on a network. Having learned about speed and duplex configurations and how they affect traffic flow, you now have the essential skills to perform troubleshooting at layer 1 of the OSI reference model.

Additionally, we have covered the essential principles of wireless communication on an IEEE 802.11 network. We have looked in depth at how channels and frequencies all work together to deliver messages between devices. Additionally, we have discussed various Cisco wireless architectures and seen the benefits of using one deployment model over another based on the size of the wireless network. We have also covered the steps required to access and deploy a Cisco **WLC** on a network.

Now that you have completed this chapter, you should be able to describe various wireless principles such as the operation of channels, **RFs**, and **SSIDs**. You also now have the skills to implement a Cisco WLC on a network and configure WLANs, security, and QoS features. Lastly, you have learned about the importance of virtualization and the role it plays in cloud computing.

I hope this chapter has been informative for you and helps you in your journey toward learning how to implement and administer Cisco solutions and prepare for the CCNA 200-301 certification. In the next chapter, *Chapter 5, Implementing VLANs, Layer 2 Discovery Protocols, and EtherChannels,* we will learn how to segment your network to improve performance and security, and implement link aggregation technologies and discovery protocols.

# Questions

The following are a short list of review questions to help reinforce your learning and help you identify areas that require some improvement:

1.  What is the standard used to define a wireless network?

    A. IEEE 802.3

    B. IEEE 802.15

    C. IEEE 802.11

    D. IEEE 802.16

2.  On a wireless network, what measurement is used to determine signal strength?

    A. Amps

    B. Gbps

    C. dBm

    D. RSSI

3.  Which of the following frequencies does an AP uses?

    A. 5 GHz

    B. 6 GHz

    C. 2 GHz

    D. 4 GHz

4. The _____ is known as the coverage area of wireless signal.

   A. SSID

   B. BSA

   C. ESSID

   D. BSSID

5. Which of the following is used by a wireless client to identify an AP?

   A. SSID

   B. BSA

   C. ESSID

   D. BSSID

6. Which Cisco wireless architecture allows an AP to be independently managed?

   A. Autonomous

   B. Meraki

   C. Split-MAC

   D. Flex+Connect

7. What ports are used in a CAPWAP tunnel?

   A. TCP 5246

   B. UDP 5246

   C. TCP 5247

   D. UDP 5248

8. Which mode does the AP use to capture traffic?

   A. Flex+Connect

   B. Monitor

   C. Sniffer

   D. SE-Connect

9.  A _____ is required to emulate a virtual environment.

    A. Linux

    B. Microsoft Windows Server

    C. CPU

    D. Hypervisor

10. Which cloud service provides only the application user interface?

    A. IaaS

    B. SaaS

    C. PaaS

    D. Private cloud

11. Which command allows you to see the physical issues on an interface?

    A. `show version`

    B. `show ip interface`

    C. `show interface`

    D. `show interface fa0/1 switchport`

12. What is the default operating speed of an interface?

    A. `1000`

    B. Auto

    C. `100`

    D. `10`

13. Which commands quickly allow you to check the duplex mode on an interface? (Choose two)

    A. `show interface status`

    B. `show ip interface brief`

    C. `show interface trunk`

    D. `show interfaces`

14. Which of the following describes a frame with less than 64 bytes in size?

    A. Giant

    B. CRC

    C. Runt

    D. Collision

# Further reading

The following links are recommended for additional reading:

- The Road to Wi-Fi 6: `https://www.cisco.com/c/en/us/products/collateral/wireless/e-nb-06-preparing-for-wifi-6-ebook-cte-en.html`

- Cisco WLC configuration guide: `https://www.cisco.com/c/en/us/support/wireless/wireless-lan-controller-software/products-installation-and-configuration-guides-list.html`

- Cisco Wireless Architecture: `https://www.cisco.com/c/en/us/td/docs/solutions/Enterprise/Mobility/emob41dg/emob41dg-wrapper/ch2_Arch.html`

# Section 2: Network Access

This section teaches you how to logically segment a network by implementing **Virtual Local Area Network (VLAN)** practices, allowing multiple VLANs to exchange data, and designing an enterprise switched network using the **Spanning-Tree Protocol (STP)**.

This section contains the following chapters:

- *Chapter 5, Implementing VLANs, Layer 2 Discovery Protocols, and EtherChannels*
- *Chapter 6, Understanding and Configuring Spanning-Tree*

# 5
# Implementing VLANs, Layer 2 Discovery Protocols, and EtherChannels

As you're building your network, you will be learning a lot about configurations and techniques to ensure you have an optimally performing network. However, let's not forget about the actual engineering aspect of computer networking. There are many technologies at all layers of the OSI reference model, and a TCP/IP protocol suite that helps us to create an efficient network.

Throughout this chapter, you will learn about the importance of segmenting a *flat* physical network into smaller broadcast domains to improve both network security and the efficiency of network performance, using a layer 2 technology known as **Virtual Local Area Network** (**VLAN**). You will also learn about the various types of VLANs and useable ranges within an organization, and how to implement and establish end-to-end connectivity between devices and different VLANs on a network.

Additionally, you'll discover how to map a network topology by utilizing various layer 2 discovery protocols, such as **Cisco Discovery Protocol** (**CDP**) and **Link-Layer Discovery Protocol** (**LLDP**). Lastly, you'll learn how to bundle multiple physical ports on a switch to act as a single logical interface to provide high-bandwidth links between switches.

In this chapter, we will cover the following topics:

- Understanding VLANs
- Types of VLANs
- Configuring VLANs and trunks
- Implementing inter-VLAN routing
- Enabling discovery protocols
- Understanding and configuring EtherChannels

# Technical requirements

To follow along with the exercises in this chapter, please ensure that you have met the following hardware and software requirement:

- Cisco Packet Tracer: `https://www.netacad.com`

The code files for this chapter are available at `https://github.com/PacktPublishing/Implementing-and-Administering-Cisco-Solutions/tree/master/Chapter%2005`.

Check out the following video to see the Code in Action:
`https://bit.ly/33WlzIG`

# Understanding VLANs

In a small LAN operating at optimal performance, there are typically a few devices exchanging messages simultaneously. As an organization grows to support more business services, so does a network to support more connected users and network applications. Physically, expanding a network seems simple, but we also need to consider the logical traffic flow and its capacity between devices. For us humans, we don't see the actual traffic flowing across a network without using tools such as **Wireshark**.

> **Important note**
> Wireshark is a network protocol analyzer that has the ability to display the raw details within a packet.

Let's imagine that within an organization, there are hundreds of devices all connected to the same physical network. If one device sends a broadcast (shouts on the network), all other connected devices will receive and process each broadcast message. What if a lot more devices are generating broadcast messages simultaneously? The high amount of broadcast messages will begin to flood the network, causing network traffic congestion.

Additionally, with the high level of broadcast messages propagating the network, all other devices will be using unnecessary computing resources to constantly process each broadcast message a device receives. Having too much unnecessary traffic on a network can cause deterioration in the network performance and adversely affect the user experience. Think of the network as a nation's roadways – during certain times of the day/night, there are fewer vehicles, allowing you to reach your destination quickly. During peak times, on the other hand, such as after-work hours, there is more traffic, and it takes longer to arrive at your destination.

The following are some important concerns for an organization:

- How do we reduce the amount of unnecessary messages (traffic) on a network?

- How do we improve the network performance?

- There is voice, video, and data traffic that needs to be separated. How can this be done without spending money on new equipment?

- How can we create a separate network for devices and users with similar job roles?

The answer to all these questions is **VLAN**. What do we mean by VLAN? How can a physical network be virtual and still support all connected users and devices? This is where we begin our journey of learning how to move from a flat layer 2 network into a more structured and hierarchical network using Cisco IOS switches.

A VLAN is a virtual layer 2 network that provides the ability to reduce the size of a **broadcast domain**. Imagine an enterprise network with over 100 devices all interconnected using switches. When an end device sends a broadcast message, all other devices receive and process it. This is referred to as a layer 2 **broadcast domain**. It is simply a logical segment that allows all connected devices to reach others via the data link layer. To get a better understanding of how to identify broadcast domains, let's take a look at the following topology:

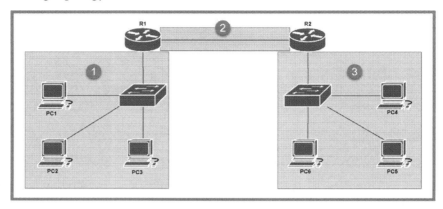

Figure 5.1 – Broadcast domains

When an end device sends a broadcast message, the switch that receives the message checks the destination MAC address within the frame to make a forwarding decision. In a layer 2 broadcast message, the destination MAC address is FF-FF-FF-FF-FF-FF. Therefore, the switch will send the frame out all other ports, and if there are other switches on the same network, they too will do the same. A layer 2 broadcast is stopped by a layer 3 device, such as a router.

Reviewing the previous diagram, if **PC1** sends a layer 2 broadcast message, only **PC2**, **PC3**, and the router's connected interface will receive it. Therefore, this is one broadcast domain. If **R1** sends a broadcast message over the link, connecting both **R1** and **R2**, only **R2** will receive the broadcast message, hence this is another broadcast domain. Lastly, if **PC4** sends a broadcast, only **PC5**, **PC6**, and the **R2** LAN interface will receive it, meaning another broadcast domain. Overall, the topology has a total of three broadcast domains.

> **Tip**
> Each port on a switch can be identified as a collision domain. Additionally, each port on a router can be identified as both a collision domain and a broadcast domain.

Rather than using multiple routers on a network to create physical segmentation, VLANs allows us to perform logical segmentation through the Cisco IOS switches via software.

The following diagram shows a single physical network where all devices are on the same broadcast domain:

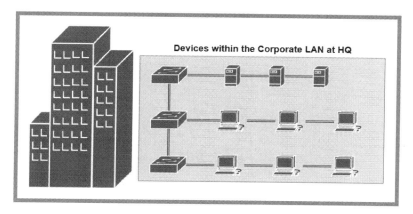

Figure 5.2 – Physical network in a building

Let's say the organization has three departments (**Sales**, **HR**, and **IT**) where a computer/device of each department resides at each floor of the building. We can configure our switches with VLANs to provide the following:

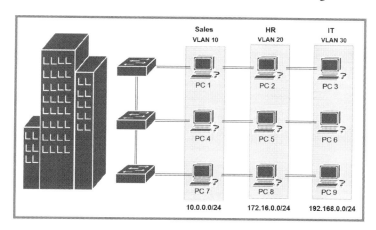

Figure 5.3 – Network with VLANs

Apart from implementing VLANs using switches, we also need to assign each VLAN a unique subnet, as in the preceding diagram. Remember, a VLAN is a logical network and therefore, each device on a VLAN will need an IP address to communicate with other devices.

If there are multiple VLANs on a physical network, how does the traffic remain logically separated from other VLAN traffic transferring on the same switches? Firstly, VLANs are assigned on the switch's interface and any traffic (frame) that enters a switch's interface becomes *tagged* with an IEEE 802.1Q tag, containing the VLAN ID. These interfaces are known as **access ports**. Only one VLAN is allowed to be assigned to an access port; the only exception for having two VLANs on the same access port is when one VLAN is a **data VLAN** and the other is a **voice VLAN**. To get a better understanding of how the switch isolates traffic, let's take a look at the following diagram:

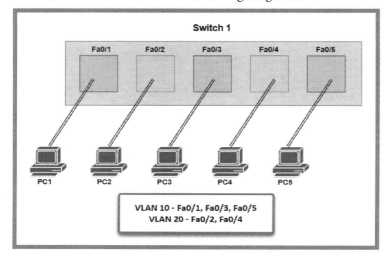

Figure 5.4 – VLAN assignment per interface

If **PC1** sends traffic to **Fa 0/1**, the switch will insert an IEEE 802.1Q tag that contains **VLAN 10** on all traffic entering that interface. Similarly, any traffic entering **Fa 0/2** will be *tagged* with **VLAN 20**.

The following diagram is a representation of an 802.1Q tag within a frame:

Figure 5.5 – Tagged frame

While there is different VLAN traffic moving within and between switches on a physical network, the switches will keep each VLAN traffic separated from other VLANs, hence the term *virtual local area network*. Before traffic exits an access port, the switch removes the IEEE 802.1Q tagging from the frame because the end device is not concerned about the VLAN ID, but rather the data stored in the frame itself.

To create a VLAN on a Cisco IOS switch, use the following commands:

```
SW1(config)#vlan 10
SW1(config-vlan)#name Sales
SW1(config-vlan)#exit
```

To delete a VLAN, use the following command:

```
SW1(config)#no vlan 10
```

Always remember to remove a configuration from `running-config`; use the negated form of the original configuration, such as `no` followed by the remaining portions of the command.

> **Important note**
> VLANs are not able to communicate with one another by default. This means devices on VLAN 10 are not able to communicate with those that are on VLAN 20 or another VLAN. A router can be used to perform a technique called **inter-VLAN routing** to move traffic between VLANs on an enterprise network.

Not only do VLANs allow you to create smaller broadcast domains while improving network performance, but there are also additional benefits, such as the following:

- Reduced costs
- Improved security
- Both improved IT efficiency and management

How do VLANs reduce costs on a network? Let's imagine that the organization has a **Voice-over-IP (VoIP)** network, containing all their IP-based phones and a unified communication server. All voice (and video) traffic uses UDP as the preferred transport layer protocol for its low overhead in a network. It's a good idea to ensure all voice traffic remains separate from data traffic. This is because data traffic usually uses TCP, which is connection-oriented; therefore, the routers and switches will prioritize TCP over UDP by default, and additionally, UDP traffic has a high chance of being discarded over TCP if there is any congestion on a segment along a network. Rather than implementing a physically separate network for a different traffic type, a good strategy is to implement a VLAN for all voice traffic. As a result, all voice-related devices, such as IP phones, will be on the voice VLAN and the voice traffic will be separate from all data traffic types.

How do VLANs improve security on a network? Let's think of a network without VLANs. All devices connected to any of the layer 2 switches will be able to exchange messages with all other connected devices as well. From a networking point of view, this a good thing, right? But from a security point of view, this is bad as there is no segmentation of traffic and devices. Thus, a malicious user can insert their device into the network and reach all other devices easily. VLANs help us to create logically separated networks and allow us to apply a layer 3 technology on the Cisco IOS routers known as **Access Control Lists** (**ACLs**) to filter traffic between VLANs.

How can IT efficiency and management be improved by adding VLANs to a network? Let's imagine that recently some organizational changes took place where users were relocated to other areas within a building. Without having to physically move a computer from one area of a network to another, the network administrator/engineer can simply reassign the VLAN ID on the switch's physical interface. Reconfiguring a VLAN ID takes a few seconds, and the connected device will be on an entirely different network once the reconfiguration is done.

## VLAN ranges

VLANs are identified by a numerical value within their configurations and the frame. However, as network professionals, there are two different ranges of VLANs that are available to us. These are as follows:

- Normal range
- Extended range

The following are the characteristics for the normal range of VLANs:

- These are VLAN IDs that range from 1–1005.
- VLANs 1002 to 1005 are reserved for various layer 2 technologies, such as token ring and **Fiber Distributed Data Interface** (**FDDI**) technologies.
- VLANs 1 and 1002–1005 are automatically created on Cisco IOS switches and cannot be deleted.
- VLANs are stored in a special database file known as vlan.dat in flash memory.
- If you use the show flash: command in privilege mode on a Cisco IOS switch, you will see the vlan.dat file. If you are factory restoring a switch, be sure to use the delete vlan.dat command to delete the VLAN database file.

The following are the characteristics of the extended range of VLANs:

- These VLANs range from `1006` to `4094`.
- The configurations are not stored in the `vlan.dat` file as compared to the normal range.
- The configurations are stored in the `running-config` file by default.
- There are fewer VLAN features in the extended ranges compared to the normal range.

Let's now have a look at the types of VLANs.

## Types of VLANs

There are five main types of VLANs that exist within switches. In this section, we will learn about each of these types of VLANs and how they are used within an enterprise network.

**Default**: When you buy a new Cisco IOS switch, it works straight out of the box. This means if you plug any device with a suitable IP scheme into physical interfaces, they are able to exchange messages by default without any configurations on the switch. Cisco IOS switches contain default configurations, but most importantly, all ports are assigned to the default VLAN. Hence, all connected devices are able to exchange messages.

The following are the characteristics of the default VLAN:

- The default VLAN is VLAN `1`.
- All ports on a Cisco IOS switch are assigned to VLAN `1` by default.
- The management VLAN is VLAN `1` by default.
- The native VLAN is VLAN `1` by default.
- VLAN `1` cannot be renamed.

Since VLAN `1` is the default VLAN, it should not be used at all on a network for security reasons.

**Data**: When you create a VLAN on a Cisco IOS switch, it can be used for any purpose you choose. These VLANs are assigned to a physical interface on the switch; these interfaces are known as **access ports**. The switch tags all inbound traffic entering the switch and it remains tagged until it exits an access port. Data VLANs allow all types of frames to transverse to the network. Only one data VLAN can be assigned to a switch interface.

To assign a VLAN to interface, use the following command within `interface` mode:

```
SW1(config)#interface FastEthernet 0/1
SW1(config-if)#switchport mode access
SW1(config-if)#switchport access vlan vlan-ID
SW1(config-if)#no shutdown
SW1(config-if)#exit
```

The `switchport mode access` command statically sets the interface as an **access port** and the `switchport access vlan vlan-ID` command assigns a VLAN to the interface.

Additionally, to reset the interface to its default settings, use the following commands:

```
SW1(config)#interface FastEthernet 0/1
SW1(config-if)#no switchport mode access
SW1(config-if)#no switchport access vlan
SW1(config-if)#exit
```

Once again, we have used the negated form of the original configurations to reset the interface to its original state.

**Voice**: The voice VLAN is self-explanatory. It is used to transport voice messages while keeping them separate from other VLANs on the network. Ensuring the *voice* network is logically separated from the *data* network will result in a significant improvement for VoIP.

To assign a voice VLAN on an interface, use the following command within `interface` mode:

```
Switch(config)#interface FastEthernet 0/1
Switch(config-if)#switchport mode access
Switch(config-if)#switchport voice vlan vlan-ID
```

By default, there can only be one VLAN on an interface. However, the exception for having two VLANs assigned on a single interface is where one is a data VLAN and the other is a voice VLAN.

**Management**: The management VLAN is used to remotely access the switch over a network for management purposes. To put it simply, it is the **Switch Virtual Interface (SVI)**, which is configured with an IP address and subnet mask. A network administrator can use HTTP, HTTPS, Telnet, or SSH to remotely connect to and manage the device.

To create a management VLAN or SVI, use the following configurations:

```
Switch#configure terminal
Switch(config)#vlan 99
Switch(config)#name Management
Switch(config-vlan)#exit
Switch(config)#interface vlan 99
Switch(config-if)#ip address 10.0.0.2 255.255.255.0
Switch(config-if)#no shutdown
Switch(config-if)#exit
```

Please keep in mind that the management VLAN should be on a separate IP subnet from the remainder of the network. This will help improve security and access management to devices. *Do not* combine the management VLAN with another VLAN on the network; it is bad practice to do so.

**Native**: The native VLAN is used to transport *untagged* traffic across an `IEEE 802.1Q` `trunk` link. Whenever an end device such as a computer sends traffic into a switch, the receiving switch port inserts `IEEE 802.1Q tag` (VLAN ID) into the frame; this is known as tagged traffic. However, untagged traffic does not originate from a switch port, so where does it come from? An example of untagged traffic is simply traffic that is generated by switches and routers themselves, such as CDP messages.

To assign a native VLAN to a trunk interface, use the following configurations:

```
SW1(config)#interface FastEthernet 0/24
SW1(config-if)#switchport mode trunk
SW1(config-if)#switchport trunk native vlan native-vlan-ID
```

Ensure you statically set the interface into trunk mode using the `switchport mode trunk` command, then use the `switchport trunk native vlan` command to change the native VLAN from its default settings.

> **Important note**
> The native VLAN must match between trunk interfaces. If the native VLAN does not match, you will experience connectivity issues on the trunk link.

In the next section, we will describe how switches allow multiple VLANs to span across the entire local area network using trunks.

# Trunk interfaces

Implementing trunks helps us solve major issues when spanning VLANs across multiple switches on a network. Trunks allow us to transport VLAN traffic simultaneously between switches as opposed to using an access port, which only allows a single VLAN. To get a better understanding, let's take a look at the following diagram where an access link is configured between the switches:

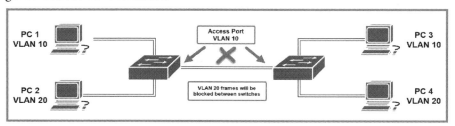

Figure 5.6 – Access link between switches

In the preceding topology, an access link is configured between both switches. However, **VLAN ID 10** is assigned on both physical interfaces. This means **PC 1** is able to exchange messages with **PC 3**, as they are both on **VLAN 10**, but none of the **VLAN 20** traffic is allowed between the switches. This is because the access ports are configured between the switches, which allows only one VLAN.

> **Important note**
> The link between a switch to another switch is known as a trunk and the link between a switch to the router is also known as a trunk.

Trunks allow switches to carry multiple VLAN traffic between them. The following diagram shows the effect of converting the link between two switches into a trunk:

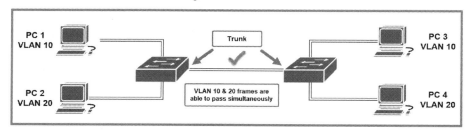

Figure 5.7 – Trunk link between switches

As expected, both **VLAN 10** and **VLAN 20** traffic is allowed to flow bi-directionally, therefore allowing devices **PC 2** to exchange messages with **PC 4**.

To create a trunk interface, use the following commands:

```
Switch(config)#interface FastEthernet 0/1
Switch(config-if)#switchport mode trunk
Switch(config-if)#switchport trunk allowed vlan 10,20,30
Switch(config-if)#switchport trunk native vlan vlan-ID
Switch(config-if)#no shutdown
Switch(config-if)#exit
```

The following is a breakdown of the configurations used to create a trunk:

1.  (Optional) In older Cisco switches, you may need to execute the `switchport trunk encapsulation dot1q` command before setting the mode to **Trunk** on the interface. Older Cisco switches support 802.1Q and **Inter-Switch Link** (**ISL**). Cisco ISL is an older Cisco proprietary encapsulation protocol that is no longer being used on newer devices; therefore, you would need to choose the encapsulation type before enabling trunking.

2.  The `switchport mode trunk` command is used to static-set the interface into **Trunk** mode.

3.  The `switchport trunk allowed vlan` command is used to set which VLANs are allowed across the trunk link.

4.  Lastly, using the `switchport trunk native vlan` command sets the native VLAN onto the trunk interface.

5.  To remove the allowed list of VLANs on a trunk interface, use the `no switchport trunk allowed vlan` command.

6.  To reset the native VLAN to its default, use the `no switchport trunk native vlan` command.

Now that you have completed this section, you will learn about an auto-negotiation feature on Cisco IOS switch interfaces, the **Dynamic Trunking Protocol** (**DTP**).

## Dynamic Trunking Protocol

So far, we have learned that switch ports can be either an access port or a trunk port. However, a switch port has a few other modes that allow it to negotiate whether to establish an access or trunk link between two switches. This protocol is known as DTP.

> **Important note**
> By default, DTP is enabled on Cisco IOS switches while applying the default mode: **dynamic auto**.

The following are the various DTP modes on a switch interface:

- **switchport mode access**: Puts the interface (access port) into a permanent non-trunking mode and converts the link into a non-trunk link.

- **switchport mode dynamic auto**: Makes the interface able to convert the link to a trunk link. This is the default mode set on Cisco switches.

- **switchport mode dynamic desirable**: The interface actively attempts to convert the link to a trunk link.

- **switchport mode trunk**: Puts the interface into permanent trunking mode and converts the neighboring link into a trunk link.

Additionally, applying the `switchport nonegotiate` command prevents the interface from generating DTP frames. Without DTP messages being sent out, the interface will turn-up faster, as it does not have to negotiate its status. You can use this command only when the interface is statically configured as an access port or trunk interface. Furthermore, you must manually configure the neighboring interface as a trunk interface in order to establish a trunk link between the switches.

> **Important note**
> The `show dtp interface interface-id` command can be used to determine the current DTP mode on a switch port. Alternatively, you can use the `show interface interface-id switchport` command to validate both the administrative and operational modes of the interface, as well as DTP mode.

The following chart provides all the possible outcomes when two switch interfaces are configured with a DTP mode:

|  | Dynamic Auto | Dynamic Desirable | Trunk | Access |
|---|---|---|---|---|
| **Dynamic Auto** | Access | Trunk | Trunk | Access |
| **Dynamic Desirable** | Trunk | Trunk | Trunk | Access |
| **Trunk** | Trunk | Trunk | Trunk | Limited Connectivity |
| **Access** | Access | Access | Limited Connectivity | Access |

Figure 5.8 – DTP negotiation chart

To get a better understanding of this, let's imagine two switches, **A** and **B**, are interconnected using a cable. If both switches have default configurations, what is the type of link formed between them? Since the default interface mode on a Cisco IOS switch is `switchport mode dynamic auto`, according to the chart, their ports will negotiate into being access ports. However, if switch **A** is configured as `switchport mode dynamic desirable` and switch **B** is using its default configuration, the result will be a trunk link between **A** and **B**.

Now that you have completed this section, let's learn how a device on one VLAN is able to exchange messages with another located on a separate VLAN.

## Inter-VLAN routing

**Inter-VLAN routing** is the method used to allow devices on one VLAN to communicate with other devices on another VLAN. To make this happen, you will need a single Cisco IOS router with an available physical interface. Nowadays, we use a technique known as **router-on-a-stick**, which allows us to create multiple sub-interfaces on a single physical interface on a router.

Typically, each port on a router is usually connected to a unique network or subnet. Let's imagine there are five VLANs on a network, and each VLAN is also a unique IP subnet. This means that for each subnet to communicate outside its own network, a default gateway is required. Most commonly, network professionals configure the default gateway's IP address on the router's interface, but in a situation where there are five VLANs, we need 5 interfaces on the router.

When you purchase a physical Cisco IOS router, it usually comes with 2 – 4 built-in interfaces. If you require additional ports on the same router, you'll need to purchase modules with 4 network ports that can be installed in available slots on the router. Overall, this method will cost you money. How can we connect multiple VLANs onto a single router?

Rather than connecting each VLAN from a switch to a unique physical interface (the router), we can create sub-interfaces within a router's physical port. Each sub-interface will be configured to carry specific VLAN traffic and assigned the default gateway IP address.

The following diagram is a representation of sub-interfaces on a router:

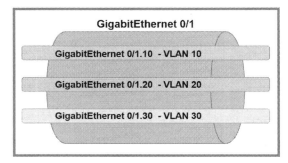

Figure 5.9 – Sub-interfaces on a router

To have a better understanding of traffic flows between VLANs, let's examine the following topology:

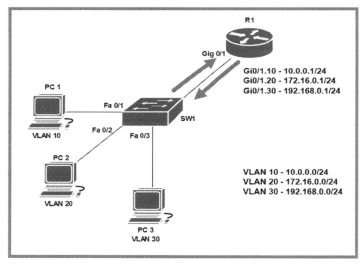

Figure 5.10 – Inter-VLAN routing

In the topology, each computer is on a different VLAN (Layer 2) and on a different IP subnet (Layer 3). If **PC 1** sends a message to **PC 2**, the following actions take place:

1.  **PC 1** will determine the destination of (**PC 2**) on a different IP subnet. Therefore, **PC 1** sends the message to its default gateway, `10.0.0.1`.

2.  The switch receives the incoming message from **PC 1** on **FastEthernet 0/1** and inserts an `IEEE 802.1Q` tag with **VLAN 10**.

3.  The switch checks the destination MAC address and forwards the frame out of its trunk interface to the router.

4.  The router receives the incoming message with **VLAN ID 10** in its **GigabitEthernet 0/1.10** sub-interface.

5.  The router checks the destination's IP address within the inbound packet and for a suitable route in its routing table. The router notices the destination network is connected to its **GigabitEthernet 0/1.20** sub-interface.

6.  The router forwards the message out of the sub-interface, **GigabitEthernet 0/1.20**, and the switch will receive it on its trunk.

7.  The switch checks the destination MAC address and forwards a message out of the **FastEthernet 0/2** interface with `IEEE 802.1Q` removed.

This technique allows us to create many sub-interfaces to support each VLAN within an enterprise network.

To configure a sub-interface on a router, use the following steps:

1.  Create a sub-interface using the following commands:

```
R1(config)#interface GigabitEthernet 0/1.10
```

2.  Associate the VLAN for this sub-interface:

```
R1(config-subif)#encapsulation dot1Q 10
```

3.  Assign the default gateway IP address onto the sub-interface:

```
R1(config-subif)#ip address 10.0.0.1 255.255.255.0
```

4.  Exit the sub-interface mode using the `exit` command.

5.  To enable all sub-interfaces within a physical port on the router, use the following commands:

```
R1(config)#interface GigabitEthernet 0/1
R1(config-if)#no shutdown
R1(config-if)#exit
```

When you apply `no shutdown` to a physical interface, all sub-interfaces are enabled automatically.

Now that you have completed this section, let's take a hands-on approach and start implementing VLANs.

# Lab – implementing VLANs

It's time to get our hands dirty with some hands-on experience of implementing VLANs on a network. To get started, we'll be using the Cisco Packet Tracer application, which allows us to simulate a Cisco environment. Within the application, please design the following network topology:

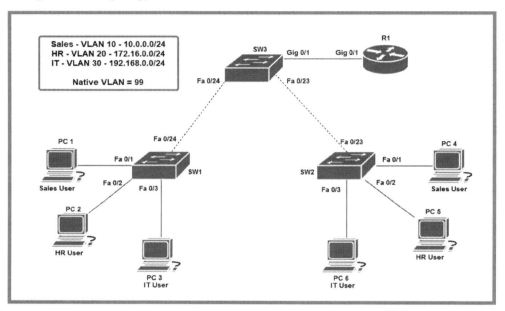

Figure – 5.11 Network topology

Be sure to use the following recommended devices and components:

- 3 Cisco 2960 switches.

- 1 Cisco 2911 router.

- 6 PCs.

- Use crossover copper cables between switches.

- Use a straight-through copper cable to connect different devices together – for example, PC to switch and router to switch.

- Use the `logging synchronous` command under **line console 0** to prevent any syslog messages from breaking into your CLI while entering configurations.

Once you're finished building the topology, use the following instructions to both create and configure VLANs on a Cisco IOS switch:

1. On **SW1**, use the following commands to create each VLAN and assign a name:

```
SW1(config)#vlan 10
SW1(config-vlan)#name Sales
SW1(config-vlan)#exit
SW1(config)#vlan 20
SW1(config-vlan)#name HR
SW1(config-vlan)#exit
SW1(config)#vlan 30
SW1(config-vlan)#name IT
SW1(config-vlan)#exit
SW1(config)#vlan 99
SW1(config-vlan)#name Native
SW1(config-vlan)#exit
```

2. Ensure you create the same VLANs on all other switches within the topology. If a VLAN does not exist on a switch, that VLAN traffic will not be allowed to pass. To perform this task, use the following configurations:

## SW2 Configurations

```
SW2(config)#vlan 10
SW2(config-vlan)#name Sales
SW2(config-vlan)#exit
SW2(config)#vlan 20
SW2(config-vlan)#name HR
SW2(config-vlan)#exit
SW2(config)#vlan 30
SW2(config-vlan)#name IT
SW2(config-vlan)#exit
SW2(config)#vlan 99
SW2(config-vlan)#name Native
SW2(config-vlan)#exit
```

## SW3 Configurations

```
SW3(config)#vlan 10
SW3(config-vlan)#name Sales
SW3(config-vlan)#exit
SW3(config)#vlan 20
SW3(config-vlan)#name HR
SW3(config-vlan)#exit
SW3(config)#vlan 30
SW3(config-vlan)#name IT
SW3(config-vlan)#exit
SW3(config)#vlan 99
SW3(config-vlan)#name Native
SW3(config-vlan)#exit
```

3.  Next, use the `show vlan brief` command to verify that the VLANs are created and named properly, as shown:

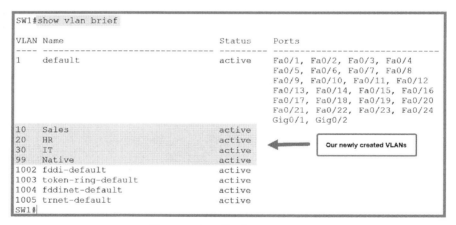

Figure 5.12 – Verifying VLANs

In the preceding snippet, all the ports are assigned to VLAN 1 by default. In our later configuration, we'll reassign ports as shown in our network topology.

4. Let's assign each VLAN to their respective interfaces using the following configurations:

## SW1 VLAN Assignment Configurations

```
SW1(config)#interface FastEthernet 0/1
SW1(config-if)#switchport mode access
SW1(config-if)#switchport access vlan 10
SW1(config-if)#switchport nonegotiate
SW1(config-if)#no shutdown
SW1(config-if)#exit
SW1(config)#interface FastEthernet 0/2
SW1(config-if)#switchport mode access
SW1(config-if)#switchport access vlan 20
SW1(config-if)#switchport nonegotiate
SW1(config-if)#no shutdown
SW1(config-if)#exit
SW1(config)#interface FastEthernet 0/3
SW1(config-if)#switchport mode access
SW1(config-if)#switchport access vlan 30
SW1(config-if)#switchport nonegotiate
SW1(config-if)#no shutdown
SW1(config-if)#exit
```

## SW2 VLAN Assignment Configurations

```
SW2(config)#interface FastEthernet 0/1
SW2(config-if)#switchport mode access
SW2(config-if)#switchport access vlan 10
SW2(config-if)#switchport nonegotiate
SW2(config-if)#no shutdown
SW2(config-if)#exit
SW2(config)#interface FastEthernet 0/2
SW2(config-if)#switchport mode access
SW2(config-if)#switchport access vlan 20
SW2(config-if)#switchport nonegotiate
SW2(config-if)#no shutdown
```

```
SW2(config-if)#exit
SW2(config)#interface FastEthernet 0/3
SW2(config-if)#switchport mode access
SW2(config-if)#switchport access vlan 30
SW2(config-if)#switchport nonegotiate
SW2(config-if)#no shutdown
SW2(config-if)#exit
```

Since there are no end devices connected to **SW3**, we do not have to create access ports.

5. Use the `show vlan brief` command to verify that the interfaces have been reassigned on both **SW1** and **SW2**. The following snippet shows the results on **SW1**:

```
SW1#show vlan brief

VLAN Name                             Status    Ports
---- -------------------------------- --------- -------------------------------
1    default                          active    Fa0/4, Fa0/5, Fa0/6, Fa0/7
                                                Fa0/8, Fa0/9, Fa0/10, Fa0/11
                                                Fa0/12, Fa0/13, Fa0/14, Fa0/15
                                                Fa0/16, Fa0/17, Fa0/18, Fa0/19
                                                Fa0/20, Fa0/21, Fa0/22, Fa0/23
                                                Fa0/24, Gig0/1, Gig0/2
10   Sales                            active    Fa0/1
20   HR                               active    Fa0/2
30   IT                               active    Fa0/3
99   Native                           active
1002 fddi-default                     active
1003 token-ring-default               active
1004 fddinet-default                  active
1005 trnet-default                    active
SW1#
```

Figure 5.13 – Interface assignments

Additionally, you can use the following commands to gain specific information about a VLAN:

--Use `show vlan id vlan-ID` to view details about a VLAN if you know the VLAN ID.

--Use `show vlan name vlan-name` to view details about a VLAN if you know the name of the VLAN.

--The `show vlan summary` command provides a quick summary of all the VLANs on the switch.

6.  Use the `show interface interface-id switchport` command to view the administrative and operational status and the VLAN assignments on a specific interface, as shown:

```
SW1#show interfaces FastEthernet 0/1 switchport
Name: Fa0/1
Switchport: Enabled
Administrative Mode: static access
Operational Mode: static access
Administrative Trunking Encapsulation:
Operational Trunking Encapsulation: native
Negotiation of Trunking: Off
Access Mode VLAN: 10 (Sales)
Trunking Native Mode VLAN: 1 (default)
Voice VLAN: none
Administrative private-vlan host-association: none
Administrative private-vlan mapping: none
Administrative private-vlan trunk native VLAN: none
Administrative private-vlan trunk encapsulation: dot1q
Administrative private-vlan trunk normal VLANs: none
Administrative private-vlan trunk private VLANs: none
Operational private-vlan: none
Trunking VLANs Enabled: All
Pruning VLANs Enabled: 2-1001
Capture Mode Disabled
Capture VLANs Allowed: ALL
```

Figure 5.14 – Verifying the interface status

Additionally, `show running-config` will provide you with the configurations listed under each interface.

Now that we have implemented VLANs on all switches and made our assignments to the interface accordingly, let's now make the **trunk** interfaces carry **VLAN 10**, **20**, **30**, and **99** traffic between the switches in our topology.

# Lab – creating trunk interfaces

In this section, we will be using the same topology from the previous section and simply continuing the configurations. To give you an idea of our objective, we'll be configuring the links shown in the following diagram as trunks:

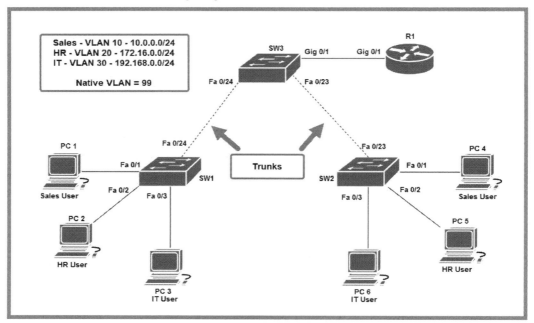

Figure 5.15 – Trunk interfaces

To start creating and configuring trunk interfaces, use the following configurations:

1. Configure the trunk interface on **SW1** using the following configurations:

**SW1 Trunk Interface Configurations**

```
SW1(config)#interface FastEthernet 0/24
SW1(config-if)#switchport mode trunk
SW1(config-if)#switchport trunk allowed vlan 10,20,30
SW1(config-if)#switchport trunk native vlan 99
SW1(config-if)#switchport nonegotiate
SW1(config-if)#no shutdown
SW1(config-if)#exit
```

After changing the default native VLAN setting from 1 to 99, you will see a Syslog message, as follows:

```
%CDP-4-NATIVE_VLAN_MISMATCH: Native VLAN mismatch
discovered on FastEthernet0/24 (1), with SW3
FastEthernet0/24 (99)
```

This message is generated because the native VLANs must match between switches that are sharing a trunk. Currently, we have the native VLAN set to 99 on **SW1** but the native VLAN remains as 1 (default) on **SW3** as it hasn't been adjusted yet. The logging synchronous command will prevent this message from breaking into your command line while you work.

2.  Configure the trunk interface on **SW2** using the following configurations:

### SW2 Trunk Interface Configurations

```
SW2(config)#interface FastEthernet 0/23
SW2(config-if)#switchport mode trunk
SW2(config-if)#switchport trunk allowed vlan 10,20,30
SW2(config-if)#switchport trunk native vlan 99
SW2(config-if)#switchport nonegotiate
SW2(config-if)#no shutdown
SW2(config-if)#exit
```

3.  Configure the trunk interfaces on **SW3** to share VLANs with both **SW1** and **SW2**, respectively, using the following configurations:

### SW3 Configuration – Interface connecting SW1

```
SW3(config)#interface FastEthernet 0/24
SW3(config-if)#switchport mode trunk
SW3(config-if)#switchport trunk allowed vlan 10,20,30
SW3(config-if)#switchport trunk native vlan 99
SW3(config-if)#switchport nonegotiate
SW3(config-if)#no shutdown
SW3(config-if)#exit
```

## SW3 Configuration – Interface connecting SW2

```
SW3(config)#interface FastEthernet 0/23
SW3(config-if)#switchport mode trunk
SW3(config-if)#switchport trunk allowed vlan 10,20,30
SW3(config-if)#switchport trunk native vlan 99
SW3(config-if)#switchport nonegotiate
SW3(config-if)#no shutdown
SW3(config-if)#exit
```

The native VLAN mismatch log messages should stop as all trunk interfaces are now using native **VLAN ID 99**.

4.  Use the `show interfaces trunk` command on each switch to verify that each trunk has the same allowed list of VLANs and native VLANs as the following:

```
SW3#show interfaces trunk
Port          Mode          Encapsulation  Status        Native vlan
Fa0/23        on            802.1q         trunking      99
Fa0/24        on            802.1q         trunking      99

Port          Vlans allowed on trunk
Fa0/23        10,20,30
Fa0/24        10,20,30

Port          Vlans allowed and active in management domain
Fa0/23        10,20,30
Fa0/24        10,20,30

Port          Vlans in spanning tree forwarding state and not pruned
Fa0/23        10,20,30
Fa0/24        10,20,30
```

Figure 5.16 – Verifying the trunk interfaces

Ensure that the `switchport trunk allowed vlan` command contains all the VLANs that are required to allow inter-switch connectivity. If VLAN traffic is not able to go across to other switches, check the following:

- Check whether the VLAN has been created on all switches using the `show vlan brief` command.

- Check whether the VLAN is allowed on the trunk interfaces on all switches using the `show interfaces trunk` command.

- Check the administrative and operational status of interfaces using the `show interfaces interface-ID switchport` command.

- Check the physical connections between devices on the topology.

Additionally, use the `show running-config` command to check the configurations applied to each interface, as shown:

```
!
interface FastEthernet0/23
 switchport trunk native vlan 99
 switchport trunk allowed vlan 10,20,30
 switchport mode trunk
 switchport nonegotiate
!
interface FastEthernet0/24
 switchport trunk native vlan 99
 switchport trunk allowed vlan 10,20,30
 switchport mode trunk
 switchport nonegotiate
!
```

Figure 5.17 – Configurations on trunk interfaces

To complete the lab, use the following IP configurations for each PC on the topology:

|  |  | IP Address | Subnet Mask | Default Gateway |
|---|---|---|---|---|
| VLAN 10 - Sales | PC 1 | 10.0.0.10 | 255.255.255.0 | 10.0.0.1 |
| VLAN 20 - HR | PC 2 | 172.16.0.10 | 255.255.255.0 | 172.16.0.1 |
| VLAN 30 - IT | PC 3 | 192.168.0.10 | 255.255.255.0 | 192.168.0.1 |
| VLAN 10 - Sales | PC 4 | 10.0.0.11 | 255.255.255.0 | 10.0.0.1 |
| VLAN 20 - HR | PC 5 | 172.16.0.11 | 255.255.255.0 | 172.16.0.1 |
| VLAN 30 - IT | PC 6 | 192.168.0.11 | 255.255.255.0 | 192.168.0.1 |

Figure 5.18 – IP addressing scheme for PCs on the topology

Once you're finished assigning the IP addresses, open the Command Prompt on each PC and attempt to test connectivity to another device on the same VLAN.

The following shows **PC1** has connectivity to **PC4**:

```
C:\>ping 10.0.0.11

Pinging 10.0.0.11 with 32 bytes of data:

Reply from 10.0.0.11: bytes=32 time<1ms TTL=128
Reply from 10.0.0.11: bytes=32 time<1ms TTL=128
Reply from 10.0.0.11: bytes=32 time<1ms TTL=128
Reply from 10.0.0.11: bytes=32 time=1ms TTL=128

Ping statistics for 10.0.0.11:
    Packets: Sent = 4, Received = 4, Lost = 0 (0% loss),
Approximate round trip times in milli-seconds:
    Minimum = 0ms, Maximum = 1ms, Average = 0ms
```

Figure 5.19 – Ping results between PC1 and PC4

If you recall, you can only communicate with devices on the same VLAN as your device; therefore, **PC1** will not be able to reach devices on **VLAN 20** and **30**. To enable two or more VLANs to exchange messages, we will need the help of a router. In the next section, you will learn how to configure the Cisco IOS router to perform **inter-VLAN routing**.

# Lab – configuring inter-VLAN routing

To perform inter-VLAN routing between VLANs, we simply need one router and only one of its interfaces; this physical layout is known as *router-on-a-stick*:

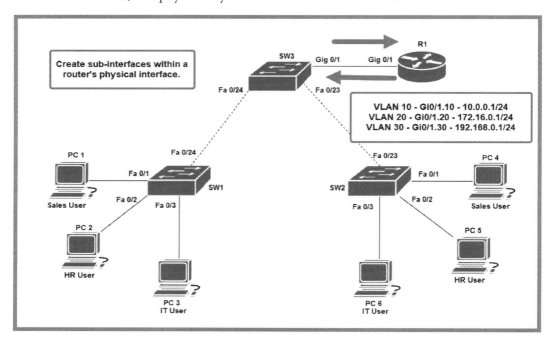

Figure 5.20 – Inter-VLAN routing topology

To get started with configuring inter-VLAN routing, use the following steps:

1.  Create a trunk interface on the SW3 that is connected to the router:

```
SW3(config)#interface GigabitEthernet 0/1
SW3(config-if)#switchport mode trunk
SW3(config-if)#no shutdown
SW3(config-if)#exit
```

For this trunk configuration on the switch, you are not required to use either the `switchport trunk allowed vlan` or `switchport trunk native vlan` commands on the interface. Using only the `switchport mode trunk` command will allow all VLANs on the interface by default.

2.  Create a sub-interface on the router to carry traffic to and from VLAN 10:

```
R1(config)#interface GigabitEthernet 0/1.10
R1(config-subif)#encapsulation dot1Q 10
R1(config-subif)#ip address 10.0.0.1 255.255.255.0
R1(config-subif)#exit
```

3.  Create a sub-interface on the router to carry traffic to and from VLAN 20:

```
R1(config)#interface GigabitEthernet 0/1.20
R1(config-subif)#encapsulation dot1Q 20
R1(config-subif)#ip address 172.16.0.1 255.255.255.0
R1(config-subif)#exit
```

4.  Create a sub-interface on the router to carry traffic to and from VLAN 30:

```
R1(config)#interface GigabitEthernet 0/1.30
R1(config-subif)#encapsulation dot1Q 30
R1(config-subif)#ip address 192.168.0.1 255.255.255.0
R1(config-subif)#exit
```

5.  Turn up the physical interface to enable all sub-interfaces:

```
R1(config)#interface GigabitEthernet 0/1
R1(config-if)#no shutdown
R1(config-if)#exit
```

When configuring a sub-interface to transport specific VLAN traffic, ensure that the `encapsulation dot1Q` VLAN ID is set correctly. If not, the sub-interface may not accept or transmit tagged traffic properly.

Now that our lab is fully configured and ready, let's test connectivity between VLANs. Try to ping between VLANs from one PC to another.

The following snippet proves connectivity between **PC 1** (**VLAN 10**) and **PC 2** ( **VLAN 20**):

```
C:\>ping 172.16.0.10

Pinging 172.16.0.10 with 32 bytes of data:

Reply from 172.16.0.10: bytes=32 time<1ms TTL=127
Reply from 172.16.0.10: bytes=32 time=13ms TTL=127
Reply from 172.16.0.10: bytes=32 time<1ms TTL=127
Reply from 172.16.0.10: bytes=32 time=3ms TTL=127

Ping statistics for 172.16.0.10:
    Packets: Sent = 4, Received = 4, Lost = 0 (0% loss),
Approximate round trip times in milli-seconds:
    Minimum = 0ms, Maximum = 13ms, Average = 4ms
```

Figure 5.21 – Connectivity between PC 1 and PC 2

Additionally, we can perform a traceroute between **PC 1** and **PC 2** to see the path that the packet is using:

```
C:\>tracert 172.16.0.10

Tracing route to 172.16.0.10 over a maximum of 30 hops:

  1    0 ms      3 ms      1 ms      10.0.0.1
  2    0 ms     12 ms     11 ms      172.16.0.10

Trace complete.
```

Figure 5.22 – Traceroute between PC 1 and PC 2

As you can see, **PC 1** sends its packet to its default gateway, `10.0.0.1`, which is a sub-interface – `GigabitEthernet 0/1.10` – on the router. Then, the router forwards the packet to the intended destination, **PC 2** – `172.16.0.10`.

Lastly, use the following points as guidelines for troubleshooting both VLANs and trunk interfaces:

- Check the IP addressing on all devices.
- Verify the VLAN assignment on the switch ports.
- Check for native VLAN mismatch.
- Check for allowed VLANs on the trunk interface.
- Check for trunk mode mismatch.
- Use the `show ip interface brief` command to verify the IP addresses on each sub-interface.
- Use the `show interface trunk` command to verify the port, mode, and allowed and native VLANs.

- Use the `show interface interface-ID switchport` command to check the administrative and operating mode of an interface.

- Use the `show interface sub-interface-ID` command on the router to verify the encapsulation mode and VLAN ID on the sub-interface.

- Use the `show running-config` command to verify configurations applied to interfaces.

Having completed this section, you've learned all about VLANs, trunking, inter-VLAN routing, and much more. In the next section, we will learn how to discover connected devices using various layer 2 discovery protocols.

# Layer 2 Discovery Protocols

In this section, we will discuss two popular layer 2 protocols that help us as networking professionals to map a network topology without seeing a network diagram. At the end of this topic, you'll be able to determine the roles, local interfaces, model numbers, and even IP addresses of directly connected neighbor devices while having a clear idea of the actual network topology.

The following exercises are executed in our existing VLAN topology lab.

## Cisco Discovery Protocol (CDP)

**CDP** is a Cisco proprietary protocol that operates at layer 2, the data link layer. CDP is used to assist Cisco devices to learn about their directly connected neighbors, such as other switches and routers. CDP is enabled by default on Cisco switches and routers.

> **Important note**
> Devices exchange advertisements (messages) using a multicast address, `01:00:0C:CC:CC:CC`.

A CDP message contains the following:

- The IOS version
- The device model and type
- Connected interfaces for both local and remote devices
- Hostnames

This helps other devices on the network to have an idea of what type of devices they are directly connected to.

To enable CDP **globally** on a Cisco IOS switch, use the following command:

```
SW1(config)#cdp run
```

To turn off CDP globally on the entire switch, simply execute the `no cdp run` command in global configuration mode.

Additionally, CDP can be enabled on an individual **interface** using the following commands:

```
SW1(config)#interface fastEthernet 0/1
SW1(config-if)#cdp enable
```

Since CDP messages contain important and identifiable information regarding devices on a network, this is a security issue. If a malicious user is able to capture those CDP messages, they'll be able to determine the various roles and functions of network components. Therefore, it is recommended to disable CDP messages from existing interfaces that are connected to the end device. CDP messages should only be exchanged between switches and routers that are authorized on the network.

Using the `show cdp neighbors` command will provide you with the characteristics and roles of directly connected devices. The following snippet shows various devices connected to **SW3**:

```
SW3#show cdp neighbors
Capability Codes: R - Router, T - Trans Bridge, B - Source Route Bridge
                  S - Switch, H - Host, I - IGMP, r - Repeater, P - Phone
Device ID    Local Intrfce   Holdtme   Capability   Platform   Port ID
R1           Gig 0/1         157            R        C2900      Gig 0/1
SW1          Fas 0/24        157            S        2960       Fas 0/24
SW2          Fas 0/23        157            S        2960       Fas 0/23
R1           Gig 0/1         157            R        C2900      Gig 0/1.10
R1           Gig 0/1         157            R        C2900      Gig 0/1.20
R1           Gig 0/1         157            R        C2900      Gig 0/1.30
SW3#
```

Figure 5.23 – CDP neighbors

The preceding snippet shows us a few switches and routers that are connected, their functions, platform or model number, and the local and remote ports that are being used. Such information is useful when you are remotely accessing a device via IP address and are not too sure about the network topology. Additionally, this information helps you map a network without seeing a network diagram.

Using the `show cdp neighbors detail` command provides you with more information about directly connected devices and their IP addresses, as shown in the following snippet:

```
Device ID: R1
Entry address(es):
  IP address : 10.0.0.1
Platform: cisco C2900, Capabilities: Router
Interface: GigabitEthernet0/1, Port ID (outgoing port): GigabitEthernet0/1.10
Holdtime: 167

Version :
Cisco IOS Software, C2900 Software (C2900-UNIVERSALK9-M), Version 15.1(4)M4, RELEASE
(fc2)
Technical Support: http://www.cisco.com/techsupport
Copyright (c) 1986-2012 by Cisco Systems, Inc.
Compiled Thurs 5-Jan-12 15:41 by pt_team

advertisement version: 2
Duplex: full
```

Figure 5.24 – CDP provides the IP address of the connected device

The following are additional characteristics of CDP:

- CDP messages are sent every 60 seconds.

- The default hold-down timer is 180 seconds. If a CDP message is not received within this time, the neighbor device is removed from the CDP cache/database.

- The `show cdp interface` *interface-ID* command is used to determine the CDP timers on an interface.

The challenge that network professionals face when using CDP, is the fact that it only works on Cisco devices. In a lot of enterprise networks, we get a mix of vendor equipment and this is a major shortcoming of CDP. In the next section, we will take a look at using an industry standard to help us discover network devices: LLDP.

# Link-Layer Discovery Protocol (LLDP)

**LLDP** is another discovery protocol that operates over layer 2. LLDP is supported on both Cisco and non-Cisco devices, thus surpassing the shortcomings of being a proprietary protocol as is the case with CDP. For this reason, LLDP is the standard used for discovery protocols on enterprise networks.

> **Important note**
> LLDP is defined by `IEEE 802.1AB`, which makes it inter-operable on other vendor devices. LLDP is not turned on by default on Cisco devices.

To configure LLDP on a Cisco IOS device, use the following steps:

1.  To turn on LLDP globally, execute the `lldp run` command in global configuration mode, as shown:

```
SW1>enable
SW1#configure terminal
SW1(config)#lldp run
```

2.  Configure the interfaces you want to use with LLDP:

```
SW1(config)#interface FastEthernet 0/24
SW1(config-if)#lldp receive
SW1(config-if)#lldp transmit
```

3.  To verify the LLDP status on a device, use the `show lldp` command, as shown:

```
SW3#show lldp

Global LLDP Information:
    Status: ACTIVE
    LLDP advertisements are sent every 30 seconds
    LLDP hold time advertised is 120 seconds
    LLDP interface reinitialisation delay is 2 seconds
SW3#
```

Figure 5.25 – LLDP status output

4.  To view all connected devices, use the `show lldp neighbors` command:

```
SW3#show lldp neighbors
Capability codes:
    (R) Router, (B) Bridge, (T) Telephone, (C) DOCSIS Cable Device
    (W) WLAN Access Point, (P) Repeater, (S) Station, (O) Other
Device ID           Local Intf     Hold-time  Capability      Port ID
SW1                 Fa0/24         120        B               Fa0/24
R1                  Gig0/1         120        R               Gig

Total entries displayed: 2
```

Figure 5.26 – LLDP connected neighbors

5.  To get further details and the IP addresses of connected LLDP neighbors, use the show lldp neighbors detail command, as shown:

```
SW3#show lldp neighbors detail
-------------------------------------------------
Chassis id: 0003.E411.4818
Port id: Fa0/24
Port Description: FastEthernet0/24
System Name: SW1
System Description:
Cisco IOS Software, C2960 Software (C2960-LANBASE-M),
SOFTWARE (fc1)
Copyright (c) 1986-2005 by Cisco Systems, Inc.
Compiled Wed 12-Oct-05 22:05 by pt_team
Time remaining: 90 seconds
System Capabilities: B
Enabled Capabilities: B
Management Addresses - not advertised
Auto Negotiation - supported, enabled
Physical media capabilities:
    100baseT(FD)
    100baseT(HD)
    1000baseT(HD)
Media Attachment Unit type: 10
Vlan ID: 1
```

Figure 5.27 – LLDP neighbor with IP address

Gathering the information from either the CDP or LLDP output, you are now able to build an up-to-date network diagram easily. In the next section, we'll learn how to combine multiple physical interfaces on a switch to operate as a single logical interface, an EtherChannel.

# Understanding and configuring EtherChannels

Let's imagine you are connecting two switches using their GigabitEthernet interfaces; your objective is to combine the bandwidth of the two physical interfaces to get a total of 2 GB/s between the switches. Making the physical connections between both switches does not simply combine the bandwidth automatically. The following diagram shows a visual representation of the connection:

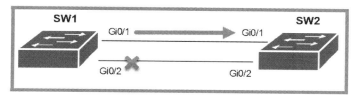

Figure 5.28 – Two switches connected together

Why is one link blocked between the switches? By default, Cisco switches have a layer 2 loop prevention protocol known as **Spanning-Tree Protocol** (**STP**). Therefore, physically interconnecting switches, as shown in the previous diagram, will cause STP to automatically block one of the interfaces.

This is where **EtherChannels** come in to save us once more. An **EtherChannel** allows us to combine multiple physical ports on a switch to create a single logical interface. Therefore, the EtherChannel will carry the total bandwidth of all the physical ports combined.

> **Important note**
> In the Cisco world, physical link aggregation is known as **EtherChannel**. With other vendors, this technology is known as **Link Aggregation Group** (**LAG**).

EtherChannel provides the following benefits in an enterprise network:

- Rather than configuring individual interfaces, the configurations can be done directly on the EtherChannel interface, rather than the physical ports.

- Implementing EtherChannels on a network can assist with load balancing and the link aggregation of traffic between switches.

- EtherChannels use the existing physical interfaces on a switch; therefore, you do not need to install additional modules.

The following criteria are required when creating an EtherChannel between switches:

- The interface type must match between switches. If switch **A** is using GigabitEthernet interfaces, then switch **B** must use the same.

- Use the same number of physical interfaces on both devices. If switch **A** is using 4 physical interfaces, then switch **B** must use 4 physical interfaces as well.

- Both duplex and speed must match on all physical interfaces that are being used to create the EtherChannel.

- The VLANs and native VLANs must match on the interfaces.

- To put it simply, everything must match in order to create the EtherChannel.

The following diagram shows the result when two switches attempt to form an EtherChannel when all configurations match:

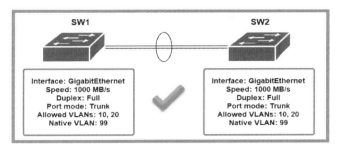

Figure 5.29 – EtherChannel

However, if there are any configurations off on either of the switches, the Etherchannel will not be formed. The following diagram shows a misconfiguration on one device that prevents the formation of the EtherChannel:

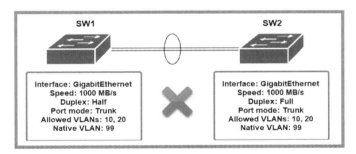

Figure 5.30 – Misconfiguration preventing the formation of the EtherChannel

On Cisco IOS devices, there are two layer 2 protocols that allow us to form an EtherChannel:

- **Port Aggregation Protocol (PAGP)**
- **Link Aggregation Control Protocol (LACP)**

PAGP is a Cisco proprietary protocol that is used to form an EtherChannel. PAGP uses the following modes to help two switches negotiate whether to form an EtherChannel:

- **On**: Sets the interface to become an EtherChannel without negotiating
- **Desirable**: Actively seeks whether the other device wants to form an EtherChannel
- **Auto**: Passively waits for the other device to negotiate in creating an EtherChannel

When using PAGP, an EtherChannel will only be formed when using the following conditions:

| SW1 | SW2 | Status |
|---|---|---|
| On | On | Yes |
| Auto/Desirable | Desirable | Yes |
| On/Auto/Desirable | No Configuration | No |
| On | Desirable | No |
| On/Auto | Auto | No |

Figure 5.31 – PAGP conditions

LACP, on the other hand, is an open source protocol defined by IEEE 802.3ad that allows any vendor of switches to form EtherChannels. LACP has become the standard when creating EtherChannels. LACP has the following modes:

- **On**: Sets the interface to become an EtherChannel without negotiating

- **Active**: Actively seeks whether the other device wants to form an EtherChannel

- **Passive**: Passively waits for the other device to negotiate in creating an EtherChannel

When using LACP, an EtherChannel will only be formed when using the following conditions:

| SW1 | SW2 | Status |
|---|---|---|
| On | On | Yes |
| Active/Passive | Active | Yes |
| On/Active/Passive | No Configuration | No |
| On | Active | No |
| On/Passive | Passive | No |

Figure 5.32 – LACP conditions

Now that you have an idea of the purpose and functionality of an EtherChannel, let's gain some hands-on experience of using LACP to create an EtherChannel.

# Lab – implementing EtherChannels

To get started, we'll be using the Cisco Packet Tracer application, which allows us to simulate a Cisco environment. Within the application, design the following network topology using Cisco 2960 switches. Make sure you're using crossover cables between the switches:

Figure 5.33 – EtherChannel lab topology

To create an EtherChannel, use the following instructions:

1. On **SW1** and **SW2**, administratively shut down the physical interfaces that you are planning to use to form the EtherChannel. In **SW1** and **SW2**, apply the shutdown command on both interfaces: **Gi0/1** and **Gi0/2**. This will prevent any layer 2 loops from forming, meaning the interfaces go into an err-disable state.

> **Important note**
>
> To restore an interface from err-disabled to connected, firstly you must administratively shut down the interface using the shutdown command, wait for a few seconds, then apply the no shutdown command to restore the affected interfaces.

2. On **SW1**, use the following commands to activate LACP on both the **Gi0/1** and **Gi0/2** interfaces:

```
SW1(config)#interface range GigabitEthernet 0/1 -
GigabitEthernet 0/2
SW1(config-if-range)#channel-group 1 mode active
SW1(config-if-range)#no shutdown
SW1(config-if-range)#exit
```

3. On **SW1**, access the newly created channel-group (EtherChannel) and configure it on the trunk:

```
SW1(config)#interface port-channel 1
SW1(config-if)#switchport mode trunk
SW1(config-if)#exit
```

4. On **SW2**, use the following commands to activate LACP on both the **Gi0/1** and **Gi0/2** interfaces:

```
SW2(config)#interface range GigabitEthernet 0/1 -
GigabitEthernet 0/2
SW2(config-if-range)#channel-group 1 mode active
SW2(config-if-range)#no shutdown
SW2(config-if-range)#exit
```

5. On **SW2**, access the newly created channel-group (EtherChannel) and configure it to the trunk:

```
SW2(config)#interface port-channel 1
SW2(config-if)#switchport mode trunk
SW2(config-if)#exit
```

6. To verify EtherChannels on your devices, use the show etherchannel summary command, as shown:

```
SW1#show etherchannel summary
Flags:  D - down         P - in port-channel
        I - stand-alone  s - suspended
        H - Hot-standby (LACP only)
        R - Layer3       S - Layer2
        U - in use       f - failed to allocate aggregator
        u - unsuitable for bundling
        w - waiting to be aggregated
        d - default port


Number of channel-groups in use: 1
Number of aggregators:           1

Group  Port-channel  Protocol    Ports
------+-------------+-----------
+---------------------------------------------

1      Po1(SU)              LACP   Gig0/1(P) Gig0/2(P)
SW1#
```

Figure 5.34 – The show etherchannel summary output

The output shows that there's one EtherChannel on **SW1** using LACP. Additionally, the codes on the port-channel tell us that both **Gi0/1** and **Gi0/2** are layer 2 port-channels in use.

7. Lastly, using the `show etherchannel port-channel` command provides us with more details about the EtherChannels on the switch:

```
SW1#show etherchannel port-channel
                  Channel-group listing:
                  ----------------------

Group: 1
----------
                  Port-channels in the group:
                  ---------------------------

Port-channel: Po1    (Primary Aggregator)
------------

Age of the Port-channel   = 00d:00h:04m:39s
Logical slot/port   = 2/1    Number of ports = 2
GC                  = 0x00000000      HotStandBy port = null
Port state          = Port-channel
Protocol            =   LACP
Port Security       = Disabled

Ports in the Port-channel:

Index   Load   Port    EC state          No of bits
------+------+------+------------------+-----------
  0     00     Gig0/1   Active              0
  0     00     Gig0/2   Active              0
Time since last port bundled:      00d:00h:03m:09s     Gig0/2
```

Figure 5.35 – The show etherchannel port-channel output

In this section, you have gained the skills to implement and troubleshoot EtherChannel technologies in a Cisco environment.

# Summary

In this chapter, you have learned the importance of segmenting a network using VLANs to improve both network performance and security. You also now have the hands-on experience to create and assign VLANs, configure both access and trunk ports, and perform inter-VLAN routing on a Cisco network. You have gained the skills needed to implement and perform network discovery using the LLDP layer 2 protocol. Lastly, you have gained the knowledge and hands-on experience of merging physical interfaces into a single logical interface known as an EtherChannel.

I hope this chapter has been informative and helps you in your journey toward implementing and administrating Cisco solutions and preparing for the CCNA 200-301 certification. In the next chapter, *Chapter 6, Understanding and Configuring Spanning-Tree*, you will learn how to segment your network to improve performance and security and implement link aggregation technologies and discovery protocols.

# Questions

The following is a short list of review questions to reinforce your learning and help you identify the areas you need to revisit:

1. Which VLANs are not usable on a Cisco IOS switch?

    A. 945

    B. 1002

    C. 1001

    D. 1

2. When creating VLANs, where does the switch store the VLANs?

    A. running-config

    B. startup-config

    C. vlan.bin

    D. vlan.dat

3. Which mode allows a switch interface to carry multiple VLANs?

    A. Access

    B. Up

    C. Trunk

    D. Administratively up

4. Which standard defines tagged traffic?

    A. IEEE 802.1Q

    B. IEEE 802.3ab

    C. IEEE 802.1X

    D. IEEE 802.11

5. Which command disables DTP on an interface?

    A. switchport trunk encapulation dot1q

    B. switchport nonegotiate

    C. switchport access no vlan

    D. switchport no dtp

6.  Which port states will create a trunk?

    A. Switch A – Dynamic Auto and Switch B – Dynamic Auto

    B. Switch A – Dynamic Auto and Switch B – Dynamic Desirable

    C. Switch A – Dynamic Auto and Switch B – Access

    D. Switch A – Access and Switch B – Dynamic Trunk

7.  When configuring a sub-interface, which command needs to be executed before assigning an IP address?

    A. `switchport traffic encapsulation dot1Q`

    B. `switchport trunk dot1Q 10`

    C. `encapsulation trunk dot1Q`

    D. `encapsulation dot1Q 10`

8.  Which layer 2 discovery protocol is able to work on all vendor devices?

    A. CDP

    B. ISL

    C. LLDP

    D. DSL

9.  What is another name for EtherChannels?

    A. LAG

    B. LACP

    C. PAGP

    D. Port-channel

10. Which LACP mode actively seeks to determine whether the other device wants to form an EtherChannel?

    A. On

    B. Desirable

    C. Auto

    D. Active

# Further reading

The following links are recommended for additional reading:

- Configuring EtherChannels: `https://www.cisco.com/c/en/us/td/docs/switches/lan/catalyst3750x_3560x/software/release/12-2_55_se/configuration/guide/3750xscg/swethchl.html`

- Configuring access and trunk interfaces: `https://www.cisco.com/c/en/us/td/docs/switches/datacenter/nexus5000/sw/configuration/guide/cli/CLIConfigurationGuide/AccessTrunk.html`

- Configuring inter-VLAN routing: `https://www.cisco.com/c/en/us/support/docs/lan-switching/inter-vlan-routing/41860-howto-L3-intervlanrouting.html`

- Configuring LLDP: `https://www.cisco.com/c/en/us/td/docs/switches/lan/catalyst4500/12-2/46sg/configuration/guide/Wrapper-46SG/swlldp.html`

# 6
# Understanding and Configuring Spanning-Tree

When extending your Layer 2 network and ensuring all devices are connected, it is important to implement physical redundancy. This is to ensure that there are multiple paths available in the event where a network switch or link goes down. In this chapter, you will learn how redundancy can create a broadcast storm and deteriorate network stability. You'll also learn how to configure Layer 2 loop prevention protocols to ensure that there are no loops on your switch network.

In this chapter, we will cover the following topics:

- What is Spanning-Tree Protocol?
- Spanning-Tree standards
- Port roles and states
- Determining the root bridge
- Configuring and troubleshooting Spanning-Tree Protocol labs

# Technical requirements

To follow along with the exercises in this chapter, please ensure that you have met the following software requirement:

- Cisco Packet Tracer: `https://www.netacad.com`.

The code files for this chapter can be found at `https://github.com/PacktPublishing/Implementing-and-Administering-Cisco-Solutions/tree/master/Chapter%2006`.

Check out the following video to see the Code in Action: `https://bit.ly/2RQY8uS`

# What is Spanning-Tree Protocol?

One of the major topics in the CCNA certification is understanding how the **Spanning-Tree Protocol** (**STP**) works on a Layer 2 switch network. In networks of all sizes, from small businesses to large enterprises and multiple branch sites, there are many interconnected switches that provide connectivity to end devices. In *Chapter 1, Introduction to Networking*, we spoke about the Cisco hierarchical three-tier design, which contains the core, distribution, and access layers.

To recap, the following is a diagram showing the Cisco three-tier switch model:

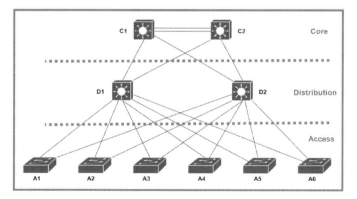

Figure 6.1 – Cisco three-tier model

Cisco recommends that this model should be implemented in any sized network as it provides the following benefits:

- Allows scalability
- Allows EtherChannels between devices
- Provides redundancy

Scalability allows us to simply add more **access** switches and connect the newly added switches to the **distribution** layer to support growth, as an organization may be expanding its physical infrastructure. Additionally, as you learned in the previous chapter, EtherChannels play a vital role in our networks as they are used to combine physical interfaces into a single logical interface and therefore carry more bandwidth between switches. Lastly, redundancy is very important on a network of any size. Without redundancy, should a switch or link go down, an area of the network will be unavailable without any alternative paths.

Let's focus a little more on how redundancy is both a good and bad thing in a network. It's a bit like a double-edged sword, where one side is used to attack an enemy while the other side can hurt you. We all know that redundancy is fundamentally a very good thing on a network, but how can redundancy be a bad thing in a network environment? To get a better understanding of how redundancy can cripple a network, take a look at the following diagram:

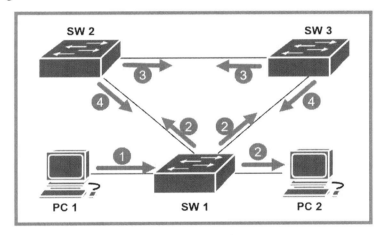

Figure 6.2 – Layer 2 loops

If **PC 1** sends a broadcast message on the network, the following is the effect without spanning-tree:

1.  **PC 1** sends a broadcast message with a destination MAC address of FF-FF-FF-FF-FF-FF to **SW 1**.

2.  **SW 1** will see that the destination MAC address of the frame is a broadcast, and forward it out of all other ports. This means the message is sent to **SW 2**, **SW 3**, and **PC 2**. When **PC 2** receives the message, it will process it.

3.  When **SW 2** receives the broadcast from **SW 1**, it will forward it to **SW 3**. Additionally, **SW 3** will receive the broadcast from **SW 1** and forward it to **SW 2**.

4.  When **SW 2** receives the broadcast from **SW 3**, it will forward it to **SW 1**. Furthermore, when **SW 3** receives the broadcast from **SW 2**, it will also forward it to **SW 1**.

5.  This creates a never-ending Layer 2 loop on the network where the broadcast messages are being regenerated constantly.

The overall effect of **PC 1** generating a single broadcast message will result in never-ending regenerating broadcast messages between the switches that are continuously being created and looping between devices. This will cause a **broadcast storm** on the network, and therefore will eventually cripple the Layer 2 network infrastructure.

**STP** is a **Layer 2 loop prevention** protocol that is defined by `IEEE 802.1D`. STP is automatically created by one logical active path between all devices on a Layer 2 network while logically blocking a redundancy path to prevent loops from occurring on the network.

The following diagram shows spanning-tree blocking a redundant path to ensure there are no loops:

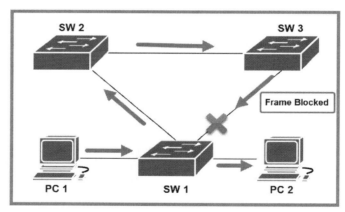

Figure 6.3 – Redundant path blocked

In the preceding diagram, if **PC 1** sends a broadcast message, STP has already placed its blocking mechanism to prevent the regeneration of the broadcast message from propagating across the network. Each switch will automatically send **Bridge Protocol Data Units** (**BPDUs**) every 2 seconds; these BPDUs help STP to determine redundant paths.

If the active path goes down, what will STP do? Spanning-tree will automatically detect the failure on the network within a few seconds and automatically convert a logically blocked path into an active state to allow devices to reach each other while ensuring there are no loops.

# Bridge Protocol Data Unit

How does Spanning-Tree know when a path is down? By default, spanning-tree is enabled and every 2 seconds, each Cisco switch exchanges a special frame known as a BPDU.

The following diagram shows a graphical representation of a BPDU frame:

| Bridge Priority | Extended System ID | MAC Address |
|---|---|---|
| 4 Bits | 12 Bits | 48 Bits |

Figure 6.4 – BPDU frame

The following points outline the composition of each BPDU frame sent by a Cisco IOS switch:

- **Bridge ID**: Each switch contains a priority value that is used to elect a root bridge. The default bridge ID on all Cisco switches is set to 32768. This value can be modified to increments of 4096 and supports a range from 0 to 61440. The benefit of adjusting the priority means that the lower the value, the more likely the switch is to be elected as the root bridge on the network.

- **Extended system ID**: This value is the same as the **VLAN ID** for the spanning-tree instance. On a Cisco IOS switch, there is a separate spanning-tree instance for each VLAN existing on the device. This means if there are six VLANs on the network, then there are six instances of spanning-tree.

- **MAC address**: Each switch has its own unique MAC address that it uses for communication with other devices on the network. To view the MAC address of a switch, use the show version command, as shown:

```
63488K bytes of flash-simulated non-volatile configuration memory.
Base ethernet MAC Address       : 000A.4123.B2A7
Motherboard assembly number     : 73-9832-06
Power supply part number        : 341-0097-02
Motherboard serial number       : FOC103248MJ
Power supply serial number      : DCA102133JA              Device's MAC Address
Model revision number           : B0
Motherboard revision number     : C0
Model number                    : WS-C2960-24TT
System serial number            : FOC1033Z1EY
Top Assembly Part Number        : 800-26671-02
Top Assembly Revision Number    : B0
Version ID                      : V02
CLEI Code Number                : COM3K00BRA
Hardware Board Revision Number  : 0x01
```

Figure 6.5 – MAC address of a Cisco IOS switch

The information contained with the BPDU message helps the switches to determine (elect) a root bridge on the network. Now that you've learned the fundamentals of spanning-tree, let's take a deeper dive into learning how spanning-tree makes its choices on a network in the following section.

## Root bridge and secondary root bridge

In many organizations, there are managers for almost all types of employees. The purpose of the manager is to guide and support the employees in their daily duties. The organization usually hires a manager to ensure their department is able to meet the business objectives and goals on a daily basis.

Similarly, on a network, a special switch has to be elected to inform all other switches which paths to leave as active to ensure there is only one logical path between any devices on the network, while all other paths are logically blocked to prevent any Layer 2 loops. This special switch is known as the root bridge.

The root bridge is determined by the switch with the *lowest priority* on the network. All Cisco IOS switches have a *default priority* of 32768. In the situation where all switches have the same priority value, then the switch with the *lowest MAC address* is elected as the root bridge on the network. Once the root bridge has been elected, all other switches on the network will now point toward the root bridge, as it serves as the *central reference point* for all traffic.

Using the show spanning-tree command, we can view the STP details and operations on a switch:

```
D2#show spanning-tree
VLAN0001
  Spanning tree enabled protocol ieee
  Root ID    Priority    4097
             Address     00D0.FFA3.AC10
             Cost        19
             Port        7(FastEthernet0/7)
             Hello Time  2 sec  Max Age 20 sec  Forward Delay 15 sec

  Bridge ID  Priority    32769  (priority 32768 sys-id-ext 1)
             Address     0001.9671.BEDE
             Hello Time  2 sec  Max Age 20 sec  Forward Delay 15 sec
             Aging Time  20

Interface         Role Sts Cost      Prio.Nbr Type
---------------- ---- --- --------- -------- --------------------------
Fa0/2             Desg FWD 19        128.2    P2p
Fa0/5             Desg FWD 19        128.5    P2p
Fa0/7             Root FWD 19        128.7    P2p
Fa0/6             Desg FWD 19        128.6    P2p
```

Figure 6.6 – Spanning-tree operation

On each switch, you will always see both the root bridge information, as seen in the upper section of the preceding screenshot, and the local switch's information, which is shown in the **Bridge ID** section in the middle portion of the screenshot. Each switch on the network will always point toward the root bridge and have the root ID details in their spanning-tree instance for the VLAN.

From the preceding snippet, we can determine the following about the root bridge:

- The spanning-tree instance is for VLAN 1.
- This switch is running the default spanning-tree mode, **Per-VLAN Spanning-Tree+ (PVST+)**. This is indicated by the ieee protocol.
- The root ID for the root bridge is 4097.
- The root bridge MAC address is 00D0.FFA3.AC10.
- The cost is 19, therefore the local switch is using a Fast Ethernet interface as the root port.

> **Important note**
> Each type of interface on a Cisco IOS switch has a cost value associated with it. An Ethernet interface supports a speed of 10 Mbps = 100, FastEthernet interfaces are 100 Mbps = 19, GigabitEthernet interfaces are 1 Gbps = 4, and 10 GigabitEthernet interfaces are 10 Gbps = 2.

- The Hello Timer is 2 seconds (default).

Additionally, we can determine the following about the local switch (D2):

- The Priority value of D2 is 32768 (default value).
- The extended system ID (VLAN) is 1.
- *Bridge ID = Priority + Ext. Sys. ID* = 32768 + 1 = 32769. Keep in mind that the bridge ID is not the priority value only.
- The MAC address of D2 is 0001.9671.BEDE.

Spanning-tree also uses the sum of the cost between a local switch and the root bridge in choosing the closest path.

Spanning-tree will automatically elect a switch to the root bridge, which is not a good thing. In a bad situation, spanning-tree will elect the oldest switch on the network and this switch may be on the access layer where there are no redundancy power supplies. Since access layer switches are used to connect end devices to the network, these can be regularly moved (disconnected). Therefore, it's recommended that a switch in the core layer be configured as the root bridge.

One major concern is if the root bridge goes down, spanning-tree will automatically elect another switch to take up the role of being the new root bridge on the network. As a network professional, it's not recommended to allow the auto-election process to select a root bridge for us, but rather we manually configure a specific switch to be the *secondary root bridge* in the event that the primary root bridge goes offline.

A secondary root bridge can be created by simply assigning a priority value higher than the root bridge. The priority value can only be in increments of 4096. If the root bridge fails, the secondary root bridge will step in and take the role as the new root bridge on the network.

Additionally, if there are multiple VLANs on the network, there must be a root bridge for each VLAN. At times, you may think it's wise that one core switch is the root bridge for all the VLANs, but in reality, it should not. If a single core switch is the root bridge for all VLANs, that's extra load and resources that the core switch has to exert in performance. What if we load-balance the VLANs between multiple core switches?

The following diagram shows two core switches load balancing the root bridge function between multiple VLANs on a network:

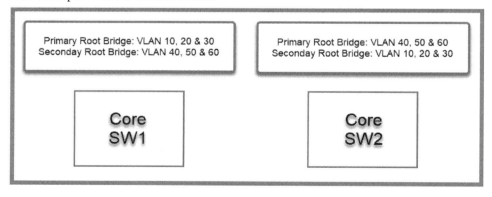

Figure 6.7 – Spanning-tree load balancing

Should core **SW1** go down, **SW2** will take the role of the root bridge for **VLAN 10, 20, and 30** in addition to **VLAN 40, 50, and 60**, and vice versa if **SW2** goes down as well.

# Spanning-tree standards

The STP is an open source Layer 2 loop prevention mechanism that is enabled on switches by default. STP is defined by `IEEE 802.1D`. However, Cisco does not implement the `IEEE 802.1D` version of spanning-tree on their devices.

## Port roles and states

In this section, you will learn about the various port roles and states involved when an interface transitions into forwarding or blocking traffic.

The following are the port roles used in spanning-tree:

- **Root ports**: These are the ports that are closest to the root bridge. If you recall, each switch always points toward the root bridge at the end of the election process. This means that each switch has a root port that points back to the root bridge on the network. Root ports are never on the root bridge itself.

- **Designated ports**: These are what are known as non-root ports, which are still always able to forward traffic between devices on the network.

- **Alternate or backup ports**: These are interfaces that are in a *logically blocked* state that is caused by the STP to prevent any Layer 2 loops on redundant paths.

To view the port roles and state of each interface on a Cisco IOS switch, use the `show spanning-tree` command. The following snippet shows both the roles and states of each interface:

```
Interface          Role Sts Cost        Prio.Nbr Type
---------------    ---- --- ---------   -------- ------
Fa0/1              Desg LRN 19          128.1    P2p
Fa0/2              Desg FWD 19          128.2    P2p
Fa0/3              Root FWD 19          128.3    P2p
Fa0/4              Desg FWD 19          128.4    P2p
Fa0/5              Desg FWD 19          128.5    P2p
Fa0/6              Desg LRN 19          128.6    P2p
Fa0/7              Desg FWD 19          128.7    P2p
Fa0/8              Desg FWD 19          128.8    P2p
```

Figure 6.8 – Ports' roles and states

When a switch boots up, its interfaces do not go directly to a forwarding state to allow traffic to flow immediately, but go through a few phases. The following is the order in which an interface transitions from the time a switch boots up:

1. `Blocking`: In this state, user data is not passed onto the network; however, BPDUs are still received on the port.

2. `Listening`: This state processes BPDUs but neither forwards user data nor frames onto the network.

3. `Learning`: This state processes BPDUs and learns the MAC addresses but does not forward frames.

4. `Forwarding`: This is the normal operating state of a switch's interface. It is able to send and receive users' data and process BPDUs.

5. `Disabled`: This state is administratively shut down by the device administrator.

Now that you have learned about the various port roles and states, in the next sub-section, you will learn how to use a systematic approach to identify the root bridge and port roles in a network topology.

## Determining the root bridge and port roles

An important skill for any upcoming network professional is the ability to look at a spanning-tree topology and identify the root bridge and all the port roles. In this section, I will guide you through the process of how easily this can be done by using the information from the previous sections and a few additional guidelines.

The following is my personal *rule of thumb* to help identify the roles of each port in spanning-tree:

1. Identify the root bridge.
2. Identify the root ports.
3. Identify the designated ports.
4. Identify the alternate ports.

To get started, let's study the following network topology with spanning-tree:

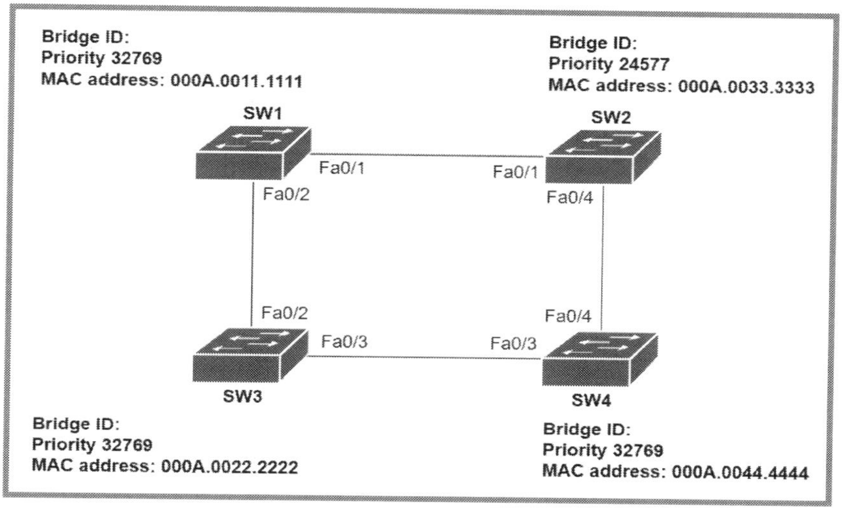

Figure 6.9 – Spanning-tree topology

Using all you have learned so far, including the guidelines and the network topology, let's determine all the port roles and understand why each port has a specific role. The following steps show how to determine what is taking place in the spanning-tree topology:

1.  Firstly, identify the *root bridge*. From the topology, we can see that **SW2** has the *lowest bridge ID* and therefore will take the role of the root bridge in the network.

2.  Identify all the *root ports* on the network. Root ports are those that are *closest* to the root bridge. From the topology, the **SW1** FastEthernet 0/1 and **SW4** FastEthernet 0/4 interfaces are closest and directly connected to the root bridge. Therefore, these are root ports.

3.  Does **SW3** have any root ports? Yes, it does. There are two paths from **SW3** to the root bridge. These are **SW3** to **SW1** and **SW3** to **SW4**. These paths are of equal cost (interface value). Therefore, we need to take a look at which device has a lower **bridge ID** between **SW1** and **SW4**. Looking closely, we can see that both adjacent switches, **SW1** and **SW4**, have the same **bridge ID** value. Therefore, the switch with the lowest **MAC address** breaks the tie on determining the preferred path. This means the preferred path from **SW3** to the root bridge is via **SW1**. Therefore, **SW3** FastEthernet 0/2 will also be a root port.

4.  Now that we have labeled all our root ports, let's assign designated ports. All ports on the root bridge are always *designation ports*.

5.  Since the preferred path from **SW3** to the root bridge is via **SW1**, FastEthernet 0/2 on **SW1** will also be *designated port*.

6.  Lastly, one of the interfaces between **SW3** and **SW4** has to be an *alternate port* to prevent a Layer 2 loop on the network. The question is how to determine which interface should be an alternate port and which should be a designated port. To help us, let's take a look at their bridge IDs. Since **SW3** has the same bridge ID but a different MAC address than **SW4**, **SW3** FastEthernet 0/3 will be a designated port and **SW4** FastEthernet 0/3 will be the alternate port.

The following diagram shows the complete port labels of each switch in our network topology:

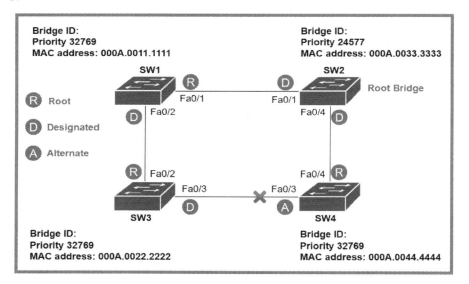

Figure 6.10 – Port labels

You may be wondering, since **SW3** FastEthernet 0/3 is a designated port (the Forwarding state) and **SW4** FastEthernet 0/3 is an alternate port (the Blocking state), how does **SW3** forward traffic to **SW4** and vice versa? Each switch will only forward traffic using the available path created by STP. **SW3** will take the path to **SW1** – **SW2** – **SW4** and **SW4** will use the reverse path to send traffic back to **SW3**.

Identifying and understanding how spanning-tree works is important in networks as it also has an important part to play in your CCNA examination. Having completed this section, you have gained the skills to identify the roles and functions of each port in a spanning-tree topology. In the next section, you will learn about Cisco's proprietary implementation of spanning-tree, PVST+.

# PVST+

Cisco has taken the open source IEEE 802.1D standard and has created their improved proprietary version known as PVST+, which is enabled on all Cisco IOS switches by default. Unlike STP (IEEE 802.1D), Cisco PVST+ creates a unique instance for each VLAN existing on the network, hence the name *Per VLAN Spanning Tree+*.

Both STP and PVST+ have the following port states:

- Blocking: During this state, the interface does not forward frames or learn about MAC addresses. It simply sends and receives BPDUs.

- Listening: The interface listens for BPDUs to determine the path to the root bridge and send BPDUs. It does not forward data frames or learn MAC addresses.

- Learning: MAC addresses are learned and populate the **Content Addressable Memory (CAM)** table.

- Forwarding: The interface continues to send and receive BPDUs and learn MAC addresses. The interface begins to forward data frames to other devices on the network.

- Disabled: The interface is administratively down.

> **Important note**
> Cisco allows its PVST+ to inter-operate with other venders that are running the IEEE 802.1D STP.

Networks that are running STP and PVST+ usually take around 30-50 seconds to converge and allow traffic to flow on the network. Sometimes, after devices are booted up from a power outage or modifications are being made on the network, 50 seconds may be a lot of time to get traffic flowing.

> **Important note**
> **Multiple Spanning-Tree Protocol (MSTP)**, defined by IEEE 802.1s, is an open source protocol that is designed to use a single instance of spanning-tree to manage all the VLANs on a network.

In the next section, you will learn how to use the **Command-Line Interface (CLI)** to find the root bridge and identify various port roles and states on a Cisco environment.

## Lab – discovering the root bridge

It's time to get our hands on some practical experience and learn how to discover the root bridge on a Cisco switch network. To get started, we'll be using the Cisco Packet Tracer application, which allows us to simulate a Cisco environment. Within the application, please design the following network topology:

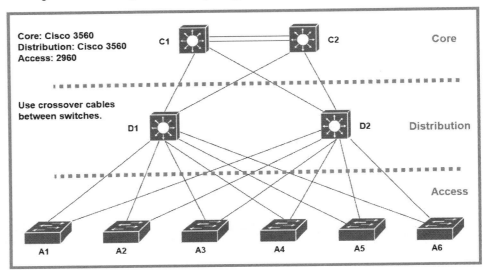

Figure 6.11 – Discovering the root bridge on a Cisco network

Please ensure to use the following guidelines to make sure you get the same results:

- Use the crossover cable to interconnect all the switches.
- Use only FastEthernet interfaces when attaching the cables to each device. The interface ID is not needed as it's a simple lab.
- Use the Cisco 2960 switches at the **access** layer.
- Use the Cisco 3560 switches at both the **distribution** and **core** layers.
- Assign the hostnames to each device as shown in the topology.
- Do not create any EtherChannels between C1 and C2 in the core layer.
- Start by placing the access layer switches on the Cisco Packet Tracer interface, then the distribution, and lastly the core switches. Cabling should be applied in the same sequence as well. This is to create a specific outcome.

One of the first tasks you may have as a network professional is to discover which switch within your network has the role of being the root bridge. To ensure you can successfully perform this task, use the following instructions:

1.  In an enterprise network, it's recommended that the core switch becomes the root bridge, but this isn't always the expected result in many networks. Use the `show spanning-tree` command, as shown, to verify the status:

```
C1#show spanning-tree
VLAN0001
  Spanning tree enabled protocol ieee
  Root ID    Priority    32769
             Address     0001.4293.B109
             Cost        38
             Port        2(FastEthernet0/2)              Switch is running PVST+
             Hello Time  2 sec  Max Age 20 sec  Forward Delay 15 sec

  Bridge ID  Priority    32769  (priority 32768 sys-id-ext 1)
             Address     00D0.FFA3.AC10
             Hello Time  2 sec  Max Age 20 sec  Forward Delay 15 sec
             Aging Time  20

Interface        Role Sts Cost      Prio.Nbr Type
---------------- ---- --- --------- -------- --------------------------------
Fa0/1            Altn BLK 19        128.1    P2p
Fa0/2            Root FWD 19        128.2    P2p
Fa0/3            Altn BLK 19        128.3    P2p
Fa0/4            Altn BLK 19        128.4    P2p
```

Figure 6.12 – Spanning-Tree status on C1

The output shows the Spanning-Tree instance for VLAN 1. Here, we are able to see that C1 is running **PVST+** by default as highlighted in the snippet. Additionally, you are able to see the root ID information about the root bridge and C1's Bridge ID information. Notice that the root ID details do not match that of C1's bridge information. This indicates that C1 is not the root bridge. Remember, the *root ports* are always closest to the root bridge. Notice that C1 has a root port, FastEthernet 0/2. We can use this information to help to find the root bridge.

2.  Let's use the `show cdp neighbors` command to identify the type of device that is connected to C1 on its FastEthernet 0/2 interface:

```
C1#show cdp neighbors
Capability Codes: R - Router, T - Trans Bridge, B - Source Route Bridge
                  S - Switch, H - Host, I - IGMP, r - Repeater, P - Phone
Device ID    Local Intrfce    Holdtme    Capability    Platform    Port ID
C2           Fas 0/3          179                      3560        Fas 0/3
C2           Fas 0/4          179                      3560        Fas 0/4
D1           Fas 0/1          131                      3560        Fas 0/7
D2           Fas 0/2          145                      3560        Fas 0/7
C1#
```

Figure 6.13 – Discovering connected devices on C1

We can see that there's another switch (3560 model) connected on C1's FastEthernet 0/2 interface. We can now log on to D2 and check whether it's the *root bridge*.

> **Tip**
>
> If you do not get the same results are outlined in this lab exercise, that's OK. Please use the same concepts on identifying the root bridge and port states. Use the show spanning-tree and show cdp neighbors commands to help you trace the path to the root bridge on your network topology.

3. On D2, let's execute the show spanning-tree command to verify whether it's the root bridge:

```
D2#show spanning-tree
VLAN0001
  Spanning tree enabled protocol ieee
  Root ID    Priority    32769
             Address     0001.4293.B109
             Cost        19
             Port        3(FastEthernet0/3)
             Hello Time  2 sec  Max Age 20 sec  Forward Delay 15 sec

  Bridge ID  Priority    32769  (priority 32768 sys-id-ext 1)
             Address     0001.9671.BEDE
             Hello Time  2 sec  Max Age 20 sec  Forward Delay 15 sec
             Aging Time  20

Interface        Role Sts Cost      Prio.Nbr Type
---------------- ---- --- --------- -------- --------------------
Fa0/7            Desg FWD 19        128.7    P2p
Fa0/1            Desg FWD 19        128.1    P2p
Fa0/2            Desg FWD 19        128.2    P2p
Fa0/3            Root FWD 19        128.3    P2p
Fa0/4            Desg FWD 19        128.4    P2p
```

Figure 6.14 – Spanning-Tree status on D2

The results indicate that D2 isn't the root bridge but it also has a root port, FastEthernet 0/3, which points to the root bridge.

4. Once again, let's use the show cdp neighbors command to help us identify what is connected to D2's FastEthernet 0/3 interface:

```
D2#show cdp neighbors
Capability Codes: R - Router, T - Trans Bridge, B - Source Route Bridge
                  S - Switch, H - Host, I - IGMP, r - Repeater, P - Phone
Device ID    Local Intrfce   Holdtme   Capability  Platform   Port ID
A2           Fas 0/2         146                S  2960       Fas 0/2
C2           Fas 0/8         146                   3560       Fas 0/2
A1           Fas 0/1         146                S  2960       Fas 0/2
A3           Fas 0/3         146                S  2960       Fas 0/2
A4           Fas 0/4         146                S  2960       Fas 0/2
```

Figure 6.15 – Discovering connected devices on D2

We can see that there's another switch (2960 model) connected on D2's `FastEthernet 0/3` interface. We can now log on to A3 and check whether it's the root bridge.

5.   On A3, let's execute the `show spanning-tree` command once more to verify whether it's the root bridge:

```
A3#show spanning-tree
VLAN0001
  Spanning tree enabled protocol ieee
  Root ID    Priority    32769
             Address     0001.4293.B109
             This bridge is the root
             Hello Time  2 sec  Max Age 20 sec  Forward Delay 15 sec

  Bridge ID  Priority    32769  (priority 32768 sys-id-ext 1)
             Address     0001.4293.B109
             Hello Time  2 sec  Max Age 20 sec  Forward Delay 15 sec
             Aging Time  20

Interface          Role Sts Cost      Prio.Nbr Type
----------------   ---- --- --------- -------- ----------------------------
Fa0/1              Desg FWD 19        128.1    P2p
Fa0/2              Desg FWD 19        128.2    P2p
```

Figure 6.16 – Spanning-Tree status on A3

We have hit a pot of gold here by finding the root bridge in our topology. The first thing that tells us we have found the root bridge is the sentence that says `This bridge is the root`. If you cross-reference each `show spanning-tree` output from all other switches in the topology, you'll see they all have the root ID that matches that of A3's bridge ID details.

> **Important note**
> Furthermore, all ports on the root bridge always have the role of being **designated ports** with their operating statuses as `Forwarding`.

Throughout this lab exercise, you have seen how each switch on the topology has been using its default configurations with the exception of its hostname. Each switch has a **bridge priority** of 32768 and an **extended system ID** of 1 (for VLAN 1).

The following diagram shows the highlight links being those that are made active by the root bridge, while others are logically blocked to prevent any Layer 2 loops on the network:

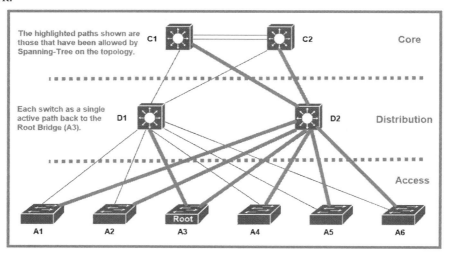

Figure 6.17 – Active paths

Additionally, if you recall, the root bridge is the *central reference point* for all traffic on the switch network. As we have discovered, the root bridge in our network is at the access layer. The access layer switches are not as robust and resilient as the core switches in a network with their redundant power supplies and support for hot-swappable components. Therefore, as an upcoming networking professional, it's recommended to configure one of the core switches as the root bridge, as shown in the next exercise.

The learning outcome of this exercise was to provide you with the hands-on experience of discovering the root bridge on a network using one of the most important spanning-tree commands, the show spanning-tree command. The show cdp neighbors command has also been very helpful in the process. Lastly, to demonstrate an enterprise environment that isn't configured properly, the root bridge may not always be the switch we expect.

In the next section, you will learn about a faster converging version of PVST+, Rapid-PVST+.

## Rapid-PVST+

There's a much faster version of STP, known as **Rapid STP (RSTP)**. It is defined by IEEE 802.1w and has the ability to converge an entire network in approximately 2 seconds, compared to the other IEEE 802.1D standard. Cisco took the improved RSTP (IEEE 802.1w) standard and made a proprietary version known as **Rapid-PVST+**.

To enable Rapid-PVST+ on a Cisco network, use the following command in global configuration mode on all Cisco IOS switches:

```
spanning-tree mode rapid-pvst
```

Rapid-PVST+ supports the following port states:

- `Discarding`: This state is similar to `Blocking`. It does not forward frames or learn about MAC addresses. It simply sends and receives BPDUs.

- `Learning`: MAC addresses are learned and populate the **Content Addressable Memory** (**CAM**) table.

- `Forwarding`: The interface continues to send and receive BPDUs and learn MAC addresses. The interface begins to forward data frames to other devices on the network.

Keep in mind when using Rapid-PVST+ that there are no `Blocking` and `Listening` states simply because RSTP and Rapid-PVST+ do not need to have a listening state to learn MAC addresses and populate the CAM table.

> **Important note**
> `PortFast`, `BPDUguard`, `BPDUfilter`, root guard, and `loopguard` are applicable in Rapid-PVST+.

## PortFast

This feature allows the port to go directly into a `Forwarding` state without having to move through the `Learning` and `Listening` states. `PortFast` should be configured on *edge ports* only.

> **Important note**
> Edge ports are those that are not connected to another switch.

Edge ports (`PortFast`) should not receive BPDUs on their interfaces. The `BPDUguard` feature should be used with `PortFast` to prevent BPDUs from entering an edge port. If a BPDU is received on an edge port with `BPDUguard` enabled, the port will switch into an `err-disabled` state (logically shuts down).

> **Important note**
> BPDUguard is also implemented for security reasons; it will not allow a rogue switch to automatically connect to the port with BPDU Guard enabled due to PortFast, which will create L2 looping issues.

In the following lab, you will learn how to efficiently configure Rapid-PVST+ on a Cisco network.

# Lab – implementing Rapid-PVST+ on a Cisco network

Having completed the previous exercise, the spanning-tree election process has automatically selected an access layer (A3) switch to be the root bridge. To configure the root bridge on our topology, use the following instructions:

1. By default, the Cisco IOS switch is running **Per-VLAN Spanning Tree+** (**PVST+**). Let's first configure Rapid-PVST+ to ensure convergence on our network. Execute the spanning-tree mode rapid-pvst command in global configuration mode on *all switches* on the network. The following is a demonstration of one of the core switches:

```
C1(config)#spanning-tree mode rapid-pvst
```

2. After enabling Rapid-PVST+ on all switches, use the show spanning-tree command on each device to verify whether the new operating standard has been changed to Rapid-PVST+. The following snippet shows how to identify that Rapid-PVST+ is enabled:

```
C1#show spanning-tree
VLAN0001
  Spanning tree enabled protocol rstp
  Root ID    Priority    32769
             Address     0001.4293.B109
             Cost        38                    Rapid-PVST+ is enabled
             Port        2(FastEthernet0/2)
             Hello Time  2 sec   Max Age 20 sec   Forward Delay 15 sec

  Bridge ID  Priority    32769   (priority 32768 sys-id-ext 1)
             Address     00D0.FFA3.AC10
             Hello Time  2 sec   Max Age 20 sec   Forward Delay 15 sec
             Aging Time  20
```

Figure 6.18 – Rapid-PVST+ status

The Cisco IOS has a very unusual way of telling you that Rapid-PVST+ is running; on the output, it says **RSTP** (**Rapid Spanning Tree Protocol**), but in reality, it is actually Rapid-PVST+ that is running on the device, as shown in the preceding screenshot, because Cisco runs only its proprietary version of IEEE 802.1w.

3.  To make C1 the root bridge on the network, we have to adjust its *bridge priority* to be lower than all the other switches on the topology. The bridge priority ranges from 0 – 61440 in increments of 4096. We can use the following command to set a bridge priority of 4096 for VLAN 1 on our C1 switch:

```
C1(config)#spanning-tree vlan 1 priority 4096
```

4.  Let's use the show spanning-tree command to verify that C1 is the root bridge on the network:

```
C1#show spanning-tree
VLAN0001
  Spanning tree enabled protocol rstp
  Root ID    Priority    4097
             Address     00D0.FFA3.AC10
             This bridge is the root
             Hello Time   2 sec  Max Age 20 sec   Forward Delay 15 sec

  Bridge ID  Priority    4097   (priority 4096 sys-id-ext 1)
             Address     00D0.FFA3.AC10
             Hello Time   2 sec  Max Age 20 sec   Forward Delay 15 sec
             Aging Time   20

Interface         Role Sts Cost      Prio.Nbr Type
---------------- ---- --- --------- -------- --------------------------------
Fa0/3            Desg FWD 19         128.3    P2p
Fa0/1            Desg FWD 19         128.1    P2p
Fa0/2            Desg FWD 19         128.2    P2p
Fa0/4            Desg FWD 19         128.4    P2p
```

Figure 6.19 – Root bridge status on C1

As expected, C1 has now become the root bridge for VLAN 1 on the network and is running Rapid-PVST+.

5.  Additionally, we can create a secondary root bridge such that in the event C1 goes offline, the secondary root bridge can take the role of being the primary root bridge for VLAN 1. To set C2 as the secondary root bridge, use the following command:

```
C2(config)#spanning-tree vlan 1 priority 8192
```

To create the secondary root bridge, ensure that the priority value is one increment of 4096 higher than the primary root bridge priority value.

> **Important note**
> The Cisco IOS will not allow you to set any value that is not an increment of 4096.

6.  Lastly, let's check switch A3 to verify that the change has also taken place:

```
A3#show spanning-tree
VLAN0001
  Spanning tree enabled protocol rstp
  Root ID    Priority    4097
             Address     00D0.FFA3.AC10              C1 Details
             Cost        38
             Port        1(FastEthernet0/1)
             Hello Time  2 sec  Max Age 20 sec  Forward Delay 15 sec

  Bridge ID  Priority    32769  (priority 32768 sys-id-ext 1)
             Address     0001.4293.B109
             Hello Time  2 sec  Max Age 20 sec  Forward Delay 15 sec
             Aging Time  20

Interface         Role Sts Cost      Prio.Nbr Type
----------------- ---- --- --------- -------- ----------------------------
Fa0/1             Root FWD 19        128.1    P2p
Fa0/2             Desg FWD 19        128.2    P2p
```

Figure 6.20 – Switch A3 points to C1 as the new root bridge

As expected, switch A3 contains the details of the new root bridge, C1, within its spanning-tree of VLAN 1 and has a root port that points toward C1 on the topology.

The highlighted links in the following diagram are those that are made active by the new root bridge on the network, while others are logically blocked to prevent any Layer 2 loops on the network:

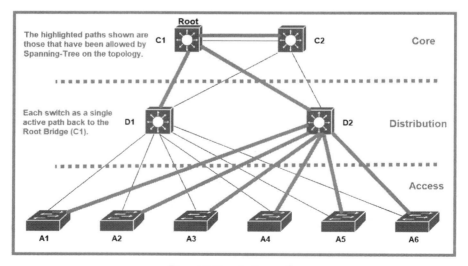

Figure 6.21 – Active paths

As you can see, the entire logical topology has changed with the configuration of the new root bridge and there is only one logical path, therefore preventing any Layer 2 loops on the network.

Both the *primary root bridge* and the *secondary root bridge* can be configured to automatically adjust their bridge priority value to be the lowest on the network at all times. Using an alternative command of each switch provides this option for us.

To configure the primary root bridge, use the following command:

```
C1(config)#spanning-tree vlan 1 root primary
```

To configure the secondary root bridge, use the following command:

```
C2(config)#spanning-tree vlan 1 root secondary
```

Having completed this exercise, you have gained the skills to configure and implement Rapid-PVST+ on a Cisco network. In the next lab, we will continue using this existing topology where you will gain hands-on experience of configuring PortFast and BPDUguard on a Cisco switch.

# Lab – configuring PortFast and BPDUguard

As we learned earlier, PortFast is a feature that allows an interface to transition into a Forwarding state without going through both the Learning and Listening states. It is a feature used when running Rapid-PVST+ on a Cisco switch. In this lab, you will learn how to configure an interface with PortFast and implement BPDUguard to prevent any unwanted BPDU messages from entering the interface.

> **Important note**
> These configurations should only be applied to edge ports. Edge ports are ports that are not connected to another switch, such as end devices, routers, firewalls, printers, and so on.

To get started with this exercise, please use the following instructions:

1. Let's imagine a PC is connected to switch A1 on FastEthernet 0/3. We can implement PortFast by ensuring the interface is an access port:

```
A1(config)#interface FastEthernet 0/3
A1(config-if)#switchport mode access
A1(config-if)#switchport nonegotiate
```

2. To enable the PortFast feature on the interface, use the following command:

```
A1(config-if)#spanning-tree portfast
```

3. Once PortFast has been enabled, enable BPDUguard to prevent BPDUs from entering the port:

```
A1(config-if)#spanning-tree bpduguard enable
```

The following snippet shows the expected sequence and outcomes of completing the previous steps:

```
A1(config)#interface FastEthernet 0/3
A1(config-if)#switchport mode access
A1(config-if)#switchport nonegotiate
A1(config-if)#spanning-tree portfast
%Warning: portfast should only be enabled on ports connected to a single
host. Connecting hubs, concentrators, switches, bridges, etc... to this
interface  when portfast is enabled, can cause temporary bridging loops.
Use with CAUTION

%Portfast has been configured on FastEthernet0/3 but will only
have effect when the interface is in a non-trunking mode.
A1(config-if)#spanning-tree bpduguard enable
A1(config-if)#exit
```

Figure 6.22 – Configuring PortFast and BPDUguard

4. Lastly, we can use the show running-config command to verify the configuration under the interface, as shown:

```
A1#show running-config
Building configuration...

Current configuration : 1186 bytes
!
version 12.2
no service timestamps log datetime msec
no service timestamps debug datetime msec
no service password-encryption
!
hostname A1
!
spanning-tree mode rapid-pvst
spanning-tree extend system-id
!
interface FastEthernet0/3
 switchport mode access
 switchport nonegotiate
 spanning-tree portfast
 spanning-tree bpduguard enable
!
```

Figure 6.23 – The running-config file

Additionally, the `show spanning-tree interface fastEthernet 0/3 portfast` command can be used to verify whether `PortFast` has been enabled on an interface.

Having completed this exercise, you have acquired the skills to implement the `PortFast` and `BPDUguard` features on all edge ports within a Cisco environment.

# Summary

We took a deep dive into learning how redundancy can be a good but also a bad thing, as it may create a Layer 2 loop in our switch network. Most importantly, we covered the importance of understanding spanning-tree and how it works to help prevent physical redundancy from taking down our enterprise network. Having completed this chapter, you have gained the skills to determine port roles in a spanning-tree topology, configure both primary and secondary root bridges, and lastly, implement `PortFast` with `BPDUguard`.

I hope this chapter has been informative to you and is helpful in your journey toward learning how to implement Cisco solutions and prepare for the CCNA 200-301 certification. In the next chapter, *Chapter 7, Interpreting Routing Components*, you will learn about the importance of routing and how routers determine the best path to a destination network.

# Questions

The following are a short list of review questions to help reinforce your learning and help you identify areas you might need to work on:

1.  Which command allows you to see the MAC address of a switch?

    A. `show version`

    B. `show ip interface brief`

    C. `show running-config`

    D. `show startup-config`

2.  Which of the standards prevents Layer 2 loops on a network?

    A. `IEEE 802.1X`

    B. `IEEE 802.3`

    C. `IEEE 802.11`

    D. `IEEE 802.1D`

3.  What is the priority value of a switch that has been factory restored?

    A. 0

    B. 32768

    C. 32769

    D. 4096

4.  Which is the default spanning-tree operating mode on Cisco IOS switches?

    A. PVST+

    B. STP

    C. Rapid-PVST+

    D. RSTP

5.  Which port is not included in Rapid-PVST+?

    A. Discarding

    B. Forwarding

    C. Listening

    D. Learning

6.  Which port is closest to the root bridge?

    A. Backup port

    B. Alternate port

    C. Designated port

    D. Root port

# Further reading

The following links are recommended for additional reading:

- Understanding Spanning-Tree: `https://www.cisco.com/c/en/us/support/docs/lan-switching/spanning-tree-protocol/5234-5.html`

- Configuring Rapid PVST+: `https://www.cisco.com/c/en/us/td/docs/switches/datacenter/nexus5000/sw/configuration/guide/cli/CLIConfigurationGuide/RPVSpanningTree.html`

- Configuring PortFast and BPDU Guard: `https://www.cisco.com/c/en/us/td/docs/switches/lan/catalyst4000/8-2glx/configuration/guide/stp_enha.html`

# Section 3:
# IP Connectivity

This section begins by introducing you to how routers are used to interconnect remote networks and how routers make their forwarding decisions to send a packet to its intended destination. Next, you will learn about both static and dynamic routing protocols, their advantages, and use cases. Then, you will learn how to implement and troubleshoot both static and dynamic routing on a network to ensure connectivity.

This section contains the following chapters:

- *Chapter 7, Interpreting Routing Components*
- *Chapter 8, Understanding First Hop Redundancy, Static and Dynamic Routing*

# 7
# Interpreting Routing Components

All network professionals must have an understanding of the concepts of routing. In embarking upon this new domain on IP connectivity, you will be introduced to the topics of routers and how they help us connect to remote networks. Routers helps us reach the internet, access resources online, and share information with each other. Therefore, if you are unable to configure routers to send packets between remote networks and to enable them to automatically exchange routes, you will have great difficulty working in networking.

Upon completing this chapter, you will have learned the process Cisco IOS routers use to make their forwarding decisions. Additionally, you will have gained the ability to identify and describe each component within the **routing table** of a router and will be able to predict the forwarding decision of each device in a Cisco environment.

In this chapter, we will cover the following topics:

- Understanding IP routing
- Components of the routing table
- Routing protocol codes

- Prefix and network mask
- Next hop
- Administrative distance
- Routing metrics

# Technical requirements

To follow along with the exercises in this chapter, please ensure that you have met the following software requirement:

- Cisco Packet Tracer: `https://www.netacad.com`

The code files for this chapter are available at: `https://github.com/PacktPublishing/Implementing-and-Administering-Cisco-Solutions/tree/master/Chapter%2007.`

# Understanding IP routing

Routers play an important role in how networks operate day to day. Without them, we wouldn't be able to connect to other networks or the internet. In this section, we will learn how Cisco routers connect remote and foreign networks, allowing us to access devices and applications located within a data center or even another location somewhere on the internet. We will consider the question *How does a router make the decision to forward traffic to the right network?*

In the previous chapters, we have spent a lot of time learning how to build an optimal local area network using a lot of technologies with Cisco IOS switches. One of the key things you may have noticed regarding Cisco IOS switches is that a new Cisco switch with default configurations will still allow you to connect end devices onto its physical interfaces and will forward traffic (frames) without you inserting any additional configurations on the device. However, this is not the case with a Cisco IOS router.

The Cisco IOS router, which has default configurations or factory settings, does not do things such as forward traffic (packets) between its interfaces. To make a router operational, the network professional such as yourself has to tell the router how traffic should flow between its interfaces. In other words, without configuring the Cisco router, it will simply do nothing on a network when it's powered on.

A router has the capability to read the Layer 3 header of an IP packet and make a decision on how to proceed in forwarding the packet. When a packet enters an interface on a router, it is de-encapsulated by removing the Layer 2 header information, such as the source and destination MAC addresses. However, the router takes a look at the destination IPv4 or IPv6 address and checks its routing table for a suitable route.

The routing table is dynamically updated when a local interface on the router is assigned an IP address and is enabled. In addition, the router has the capability of running dynamic routing protocols that allow other routers on the network to exchange **routes**. A route is simply a path to reach a destination network; without any routes, a router won't be able to forward packets to their destinations.

Let's take a look at the following topology to gain a better understanding of how routers work:

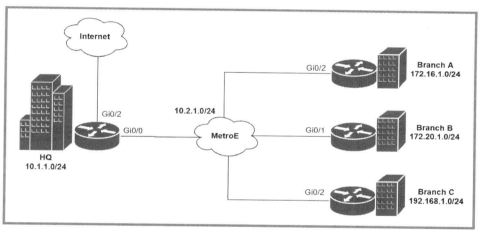

Figure 7.1 – Simple network topology

The topology illustrates an organization's network, consisting of the headquarters and three remote branches/offices. The organization uses a **Metro Ethernet (MetroE)** WAN to interconnect their branches to the headquarters. The WAN service is managed by a local **Internet Service Provider (ISP)**.

> **Important note**
> A Metropolitan-area Ethernet or MetroE connection is a type Layer 2 WAN service that is commonly provided by an ISP using Ethernet standards.

Let's imagine that a PC on the Branch A network (172.16.1.0/24) has to send traffic to a server in HQ that is located on the 10.1.1.0/24 network. What will be the path or route the traffic will take? To answer this question and fully understand what takes places, let's look at a low-level view of the topology:

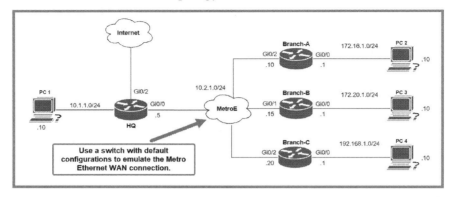

Figure 7.2 – Low-level topology

I would recommend taking some time to build this topology using Cisco Packet Tracer as you will be able to perform the same validation checks that I will be using for the remainder of this chapter and the next. When building the topology, use the following guidelines:

- Use only Cisco 2911 routers.

- Ensure you configure the IP address on each device as shown in the diagram.

- Ensure each PC is able to ping its default gateway.

- Ensure each router can ping all other routers on the network.

Let's see whether **PC 2** on the Branch A network is able to ping **PC 1** on the **HQ** network. First, let's verify the IP address on **PC 2** by using the ipconfig command:

```
C:\>ipconfig

FastEthernet0 Connection:(default port)

    Link-local IPv6 Address.........: FE80::202:4AFF:FE61:7DD5
    IP Address......................: 172.16.1.10
    Subnet Mask.....................: 255.255.255.0
    Default Gateway.................: 172.16.1.1
```

Figure 7.3 – PC 2 IP addressing

You need to check network connectivity between **PC 2** and its default gateway, the **Branch-A** router:

```
C:\>ping 172.16.1.1

Pinging 172.16.1.1 with 32 bytes of data:

Reply from 172.16.1.1: bytes=32 time=1ms TTL=255
Reply from 172.16.1.1: bytes=32 time<1ms TTL=255
Reply from 172.16.1.1: bytes=32 time<1ms TTL=255
Reply from 172.16.1.1: bytes=32 time<1ms TTL=255

Ping statistics for 172.16.1.1:
    Packets: Sent = 4, Received = 4, Lost = 0 (0% loss),
Approximate round trip times in milli-seconds:
    Minimum = 0ms, Maximum = 1ms, Average = 0ms
```

Figure 7.4 – Connectivity test to the Branch A router

From the preceding snippet, we can determine that four **Internet Control Message Protocol (ICMP)** *Echo Request* messages were sent from **PC 2** to the **Branch-A** router. The router has responded to each message with an ICMP Echo **Reply**. This means that **PC 2** has connectivity to its default gateway, the **Branch-A** router.

The next step is to check whether **PC 2** has connectivity to **PC 1**. Let's ping **PC 1** from **PC 2**:

```
C:\>ping 10.1.1.10

Pinging 10.1.1.10 with 32 bytes of data:

Reply from 172.16.1.1: Destination host unreachable.
Reply from 172.16.1.1: Destination host unreachable.
Reply from 172.16.1.1: Destination host unreachable.
Reply from 172.16.1.1: Destination host unreachable.

Ping statistics for 10.1.1.10:
    Packets: Sent = 4, Received = 0, Lost = 4 (100% loss),
```

Figure 7.5 – Connectivity failure between PC 2 and PC 1

This time, we did not get the expected results. Whenever the response is *Destination host (or network) is unreachable*, this means that the device you are testing connectivity from does not know how to reach the destination host or network. In our previous step, **PC 2** is able to reach its default gateway. Let's attempt to perform some basic troubleshooting to further investigate and learn why there's no end-to-end connectivity. We can use the **traceroute** tool in Microsoft Windows to check the path the packet will take from **PC 2** to **PC 1**. On Microsoft Windows, the `tracert` command is used:

```
C:\>tracert 10.1.1.10

Tracing route to 10.1.1.10 over a maximum of 30 hops:

  1    1 ms      1 ms      0 ms      172.16.1.1
  2    0 ms      *         0 ms      172.16.1.1
  3    *         0 ms      *         Request timed out.
```

Figure 7.6 – Performing a traceroute

The traceroute utility uses the ICMP to send *ICMP Echo Requests* to a destination host device while adjusting the **Time To Live (TTL)** value of each packet it sends to the destination. The purpose of this tool is to check the path a packet will take between two devices and also check for latency issues between hops. A **hop** refers to each Layer 3 device the packet has to pass in order to reach its destination. The latency is simply a measurement of the time it takes a device to respond to a message such as a request. Higher latency means a device takes a longer time to respond. As a network engineer, we want to ensure that our network has latency to ensure faster response times.

> **Important note**
>
> On Microsoft Windows systems, the `tracert` command is used within the command prompt, while Linux and Cisco devices use the `traceroute` command.

The traceroute results show that at `172.16.1.1` (the **Branch-A** router), there are *request timed out* messages. It's at this point that we can begin troubleshooting to understand why we are experiencing a problem.

Let's head over to the **Branch-A** router and check its routing table using the `show ip route` command:

```
Gateway of last resort is not set

      10.0.0.0/8 is variably subnetted, 2 subnets, 2 masks
C        10.2.1.0/24 is directly connected, GigabitEthernet0/2
L        10.2.1.10/32 is directly connected, GigabitEthernet0/2
      172.16.0.0/16 is variably subnetted, 2 subnets, 2 masks
C        172.16.1.0/24 is directly connected, GigabitEthernet0/0
L        172.16.1.1/32 is directly connected, GigabitEthernet0/0
```

Figure 7.7 – Routing table of the Branch-A router

The Cisco IOS router will only contain destination routes within its routing table. In the preceding snippet, there is no destination network of 10.1.1.0/24 in any of the rows (entries). If a route is not present here, it simply means the router does not know how to forward the packet to the 10.1.1.0/24 network and will send an ICMP message back to **PC 2** indicating it does not have a valid route to the destination, hence the response was *Destination host is unreachable.*

> **Tip**
> If you would like to learn more about the different ICMP message types, please refer to my article at https://hub.packtpub.com/understanding-network-port-numbers-tcp-udp-and-icmp-on-an-operating-system/.

Furthermore, we can see in *Figure 7.7* that the **Branch-A** router only knows about two unique networks; the 10.2.1.0/24 network that is used for the MetroE WAN connection on the GigabitEthernet 0/2 interface, and the 172.16.1.0/24 network that is connected on GigabitEthernet 0/0 for the LAN interface. However, the **Branch-A** router does not know about the other three LANs: **Branch-B**, **Branch-C**, and **HQ** locations.

If the **Branch-A** router had known about all networks within the topology, the expected route would be pointing toward the **HQ** router at the IP address 10.2.1.5. Routers are not concerned with the entire path a packet will take to reach its destination host or network. All a router is concerned with is handing-off the packet to a next hop; in other words, another router that will forward the packet toward its destination. Keep in mind that this process is repeated until the packet is delivered.

> **Important note**
> Cisco routers read their routing table from top to bottom each time they have to check for a suitable or available route.

The following outlines the process of actions taken by a router when it receives an IP packet:

1. When a router receives an IP packet on one of its interfaces, it checks the destination IP address with the Layer 3 header of the packet.

2. It then uses the destination IP address and checks its routing table for an available route (path).

3. If a suitable route is found, it sends the packet to the next hop via the exit interface.

4. If a route is not found, the router checks for a gateway of last resort to forward the packet.

5. If neither route is found, the router replies to the sender with a *Destination host (network) not found* message.

Now that you have completed this section, you have learned how Cisco IOS routers determine a suitable path to forward a packet. In the next section, we will discuss each component within the routing table.

# Components of the routing table

To further understand how routers make their decisions when it comes to forwarding packets between networks, it's important to understand each component of the routing table within a Cisco IOS router. In this section, we will cover all the essential components that are part of the routing table, including:

- Routing protocol codes
- Prefix
- Network mask
- Next hop
- **Administrative distance** (**AD**)
- Metric
- Gateway of last resort

Let's start with routing protocol codes.

## Routing protocol codes

When you execute the `show ip route` command on a Cisco router, the very first thing you will see is a concise list of codes. These codes are formally referred to as *routing protocol codes*. Each code is used to help you identify how a route has been learned and added to the routing table.

The following snippet shows the routing protocol codes of a Cisco IOS router:

```
Branch-A#show ip route
Codes: L - local, C - connected, S - static, R - RIP, M - mobile, B - BGP
       D - EIGRP, EX - EIGRP external, O - OSPF, IA - OSPF inter area
       N1 - OSPF NSSA external type 1, N2 - OSPF NSSA external type 2
       E1 - OSPF external type 1, E2 - OSPF external type 2, E - EGP
       i - IS-IS, L1 - IS-IS level-1, L2 - IS-IS level-2, ia - IS-IS inter area
       * - candidate default, U - per-user static route, o - ODR
       P - periodic downloaded static route
```

Figure 7.8 – Routing protocol codes

The following is a brief description of the essential codes you need to know as a CCNA student:

- C: This code indicates that the route is *directly connected* to the router. Put simply, when you configure an IP address on a router's interface and it's made active, the router automatically inserts a directly connected route to that network within its routing table.

- L: This code indicates the route is a *local route.* A local route is one that points not to a network like the others, but to a specific host device on a network. Local routes are commonly inserted into the routing table by default when you configure an IP address on an active interface on a router. If you look closely at the routing table, you will notice that the IP address on a local route is the same as the address on the interface itself. Additionally, you can configure a local route that points to a device on a remote network.

- S: This code indicates the route has been manually configured and inserted into the routing table; this is known as a *static route.*

- R: This routing code indicates that the router has learned about a remote network via a dynamic routing protocol known as **Routing Information Protocol** (**RIP**). RIP is an old routing protocol that allows routers to simultaneously exchange routing information and update their routing tables automatically. RIP is used within an internal or private network.

- B: This code indicates that the router has learned about a remote network via the **Border Gateway Routing Protocol** (**BGP**). BGP is known as an **Exterior Gateway Protocol** (**EGP**) and is commonly used on the internet between ISPs to exchange public networks.

- D: This routing code indicates that the route has been learned by the **Enhanced Interior Gateway Routing Protocol** (**EIGRP**).

- EX: This code indicates that an external route, such as the route to the internet, has been learned via the EIGRP.

- O: This code indicates that the route has been learned by the **Open Shortest Path First (OSPF)** routing protocol.

- *: This code indicates the route is a *default route* that usually points to the internet. This code is commonly coupled with other routing codes, as you will discover in the next chapter.

The following snippet shows the current route of the Branch-A router:

```
Gateway of last resort is not set

     10.0.0.0/8 is variably subnetted, 2 subnets, 2 masks
C        10.2.1.0/24 is directly connected, GigabitEthernet0/2
L        10.2.1.10/32 is directly c            tEthernet0/2
     172.16.0.0/16 is variably subn    Parent Route   , 2 masks
C        172.16.1.0/24 is directly co            tEthernet0/0
L        172.16.1.1/32 is directly connected, GigabitEthernet0/0
```

Figure 7.9 – Parent route

Within the routing table, you will commonly see routes installed without an actual path to reach the destination network. The highlighted route is known as a *parent* route. The parent route is usually indicated by a classful network ID. In the preceding snippet, the parent route contains a destination network of 10.0.0.0./8 with two child routes: 10.2.1.0/24 and 10.2.1.10/32.

Let's take a look at the following snippet, which shows examples of child routes on the Branch-A router:

```
Gateway of last resort is not set

     10.0.0.0/8 is variably subnetted, 2 subnets, 2 masks
C        10.2.1.0/24 is directly connected, GigabitEthernet0/2
L        10.2.1.10/32 is directly connected, GigabitEthernet0/2
     172.16.0.0/16 is variably subnetted, 2 subnets, 2 masks
C        172.16.1.0/24 is directly connected, GigabitEthernet0/0
L        172.16.1.1/32 is directly connected, GigabitEthernet0/0
```

Figure 7.10 – Child routes

Looking closely at the highlighted areas in the preceding snippet, you should notice that only child routes contain the routing protocol codes; the parent routes do not. A nice feature of the Cisco IOS is that it places each route in numerical order within the routing table, which makes it easy for both us and the router to perform route lookups.

The following snippet shows an example of routes learned via the OSPF routing protocol:

```
Branch-A#show ip route
Gateway of last resort is 10.2.1.5 to network 0.0.0.0

      2.0.0.0/8 is variably subnetted, 2 subnets, 2 masks
C        2.2.2.0/24 is directly connected, Loopback0
L        2.2.2.2/32 is directly connected, Loopback0
      10.0.0.0/8 is variably subnetted, 3 subnets, 2 masks
O        10.1.1.0/24 [110/2] via 10.2.1.5, 00:01:21, GigabitEthernet0/2
C        10.2.1.0/24 is directly connected, GigabitEthernet0/2
L        10.2.1.10/32 is directly connected, GigabitEthernet0/2
      172.16.0.0/16 is variabl                        2 masks
C        172.16.1.0/24 is dir     Dynamically learnt routes    hernet0/0
L        172.16.1.1/32 is d                           thernet0/0
      172.20.0.0/24 is subnetted, 1 subnets
O        172.20.1.0/24 [110/2] via 10.2.1.15, 00:01:21, GigabitEthernet0/2
O        192.168.1.0/24 [110/2] via 10.2.1.20, 00:01:11, GigabitEthernet0/2
O*E2 0.0.0.0/0 [110/1] via 10.2.1.5, 00:01:21, GigabitEthernet0/2
```

Figure 7.11 – Dynamically learned routes

A dynamically learned route always contains extra parameters within the route compared to both local and directly connected routes. In the next few sections, we will take a look at these additional components and their functions.

## Prefix and network mask

Another important component of the routing table, and specifically part of a route, is the prefix. The prefix is identified as the destination network ID. When the router is looking for a suitable route, it checks the prefix of each installed route in its routing table for a suitable match.

The following snippet shows the prefix within the routing table:

```
Gateway of last resort is 10.2.1.5 to network 0.0.0.0

      2.0.0.0/8 is variably subnetted, 2 subnets, 2 masks
C        2.2.2.0/24 is directly connected, Loopback0
L        2.2.2.2/32 is d              ed, Loopback0
      10.0.0.0/8 is var      Prefix       3 subnets, 2 masks
O        10.1.1.0/24                .5, 00:05:16, GigabitEthernet0/2
C        10.2.1.0/24 is directly connected, GigabitEthernet0/2
L        10.2.1.10/32 is directly connected, GigabitEthernet0/2
      172.16.0.0/16 is variably subnetted, 2 subnets, 2 masks
C        172.16.1.0/24 is directly connected, GigabitEthernet0/0
L        172.16.1.1/32 is directly connected, GigabitEthernet0/0
      172.20.0.0/24 is subnetted, 1 subnets
O        172.20.1.0/24 [110/2] via 10.2.1.15, 00:05:16, GigabitEthernet0/2
O*E2 0.0.0.0/0 [110/1] via 10.2.1.5, 00:05:16, GigabitEthernet0/2
```

Figure 7.12 – Prefix

For every prefix within the routing table, there's an associated network mask in the form of /x format. The following snippet shows that the highlighted area within each route has a prefix and network mask:

```
Gateway of last resort is 10.2.1.5 to network 0.0.0.0

      2.0.0.0/8 is variably subnetted, 2 subnets, 2 masks
C        2.2.2.0/24 is directl_____oopback0
L        2.2.2.2/32 is direct [ Network Mask ] opback0
      10.0.0.0/8 is variabl_____nets, 2 masks
O        10.1.1.0/24 [110_____00:05:16, GigabitEthernet0/2
C        10.2.1.0/24 is directly connected, GigabitEthernet0/2
L        10.2.1.10/32 is directly connected, GigabitEthernet0/2
      172.16.0.0/16 is variably subnetted, 2 subnets, 2 masks
C        172.16.1.0/24 is directly connected, GigabitEthernet0/0
L        172.16.1.1/32 is directly connected, GigabitEthernet0/0
      172.20.0.0/24 is subnetted, 1 subnets
O        172.20.1.0/24 [110/2] via 10.2.1.15, 00:05:16, GigabitEthernet0/2
O*E2 0.0.0.0/0 [110/1] via 10.2.1.5, 00:05:16, GigabitEthernet0/2
```

Figure 7.13 – Network mask

The network mask in the routing table represents the subnet mask for each prefix (network ID). If you recall, in *Chapter 3*, *IP Addressing and Subnetting*, we learned that the value represents the number of ones within the subnet mask of each network. For example, a network mask of /24 simply means there are 24 ones within the subnet mask; when converting the mask from binary to decimal, the result will be 255.255.255.0.

# Next hop

When a remote route is inserted into the routing table, a next hop is usually associated with reaching the destination network. To gain a better understanding of this, let's take a look at the following snippet:

```
Gateway of last resort is 10.2.1.5 to network 0.0.0.0

      2.0.0.0/8 is variably subnetted, 2 subnets, 2 masks
C        2.2.2.0/24 is directly connected, Loopback0
L        2.2.2.2/32 is directly connected, Loopback0
      10.0.0.0/8 is variably subnetted, 3 subnets, 2 masks
O        10.1.1.0/24 [110/2] via 10.2.1.5, 00:07:45, GigabitEthernet0/2
C        10.2.1.0/24 is directly connected, GigabitEthernet0/2
L        10.2.1.10/32 is directly connected, Gi_____/2
      172.16.0.0/16 is variably subnetted, 2 su[ Next-Hop ]0
C        172.16.1.0/24 is directly connected,_____0
L        172.16.1.1/32 is directly connecte____GigabitEthernet0/0
      172.20.0.0/24 is subnetted, 1 subnets
O        172.20.1.0/24 [110/2] via 10.2.1.15, 00:07:45, GigabitEthernet0/2
O        192.168.1.0/24 [110/2] via 10.2.1.20, 00:07:45, GigabitEthernet0/2
O*E2 0.0.0.0/0 [110/1] via 10.2.1.5, 00:07:45, GigabitEthernet0/2
```

Figure 7.14 – Next hop

In the preceding snippet, we can identify a total of four remote networks learned via the OSPF routing protocol. Let's take a look at the route for the 10.1.1.0/24 network. From our topology, we can see that this network is located on the HQ LAN and the only way a branch router is able to forward a packet to that network is via the packet being sent to the HQ router on the 10.2.1.5 address.

Let's break down the route and the topology a bit further. Once again, let's dissect the following route:

```
O        10.1.1.0/24 [110/2] via 10.2.1.5, 00:07:45,
GigabitEthernet0/2
```

We can determine the following:

- The route was learned via the OSPF routing protocol.
- The destination network is 10.1.1.0/24.
- The only way to reach the destination network (10.1.1.0/24) is through 10.2.1.5, which is known as the next hop in the routing table.
- The timer indicates how long the route has been in the routing table.
- The interface (GigiabitEthernet 0/2) represents the exit interface. The exit interface is simply the exit door from the Branch-A router that leads toward 10.2.1.5.

In the next chapter, we will explore routing in more detail. We will need to address the fact that not all configured routes have a next hop since some routers may be configured to use only an exit interface, while others use a next hop and exit interface at the same time.

## Administrative Distance

**Administrative Distance** (**AD**) is simply the *trustworthiness* of a route or path. A Cisco IOS router can support multiple routing protocols running at one time. Each routing protocol has its own unique algorithm that is used to choose a best path or route to install within the routing table. The best route will be used when forwarding packets to a destination.

Let's take a look at the following topology:

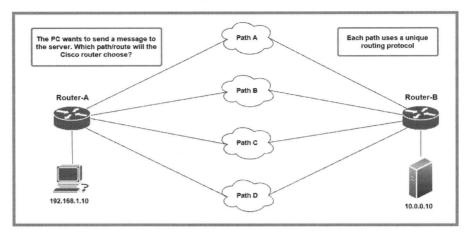

Figure 7.15 – Administrative Distance topology

In the preceding diagram, let's imagine the **PC** wants to send a message to the server. The following are the steps taken by the **PC** and the router when forwarding a packet:

1.  The **PC** will check the destination's IP address and determine whether 10.0.0.10 belongs on the same IP network as the **PC**. Since it's a different network, the **PC** will proceed to send the message to its default gateway. Additionally, the **PC** will set the destination MAC address as that of the default gateway, **Router-A**. This is how end devices, such as **PCs** and servers, send messages to their default gateway that is intended to leave the network.

> **Important note**
> The default gateway is a device such as a router that has a path to the internet or a foreign network that does not belong to the organization. This is also a node that packets are forwarded to when no other specific routes are found in the routing table to the destination.

2.  When the router receives the incoming packet from the **PC**, it will de-encapsulate it and check the destination IP address. In this scenario, the destination IP address is 10.0.0.10.

3.  The router will then check its routing table for a suitable route (path) to forward the packet.

At this point, the router is connected to four routes to reach the server. These are **Path A**, **Path B**, **Path C**, and **Path D**. Let's assume each path has a unique routing protocol:

*   RIP – configured on **Path A**

*   OSPF – configured on **Path B**

*   EIGRP – configured on **Path C**

*   Static route – configured on **Path D**

What would the router do? Cisco has set the default administrative distance for each routing protocol within their Cisco IOS for all their devices. The following table contains the administrative distances for each routing protocol:

| Routing Protocol | Administrative Distance |
| --- | --- |
| Connected | 0 |
| Static | 1 |
| eBGP | 20 |
| EIGRP | 90 |
| OSPF | 110 |
| RIP | 120 |
| iBGP | 200 |

Figure 7.16 – Administrative Distance table

Back to our scenario. Looking at the preceding table, the route with the lowest administrative distance will be the preferred route to the destination network. So, the preferred route would be the static route via **Path D** because it has an AD of 1, which is the lowest out of all the other routing protocols and paths.

Another important question we must consider is: *How can you determine the administrative distance of a route?* The simplest method would be to learn the table provided. Additionally, for each route installed in its routing table, the router inserts the AD after the prefix and network mask, as shown in the following snippet:

```
Gateway of last resort is 10.2.1.5 to network 0.0.0.0

     2.0.0.0/8 is variably subne  Administrative   2 masks
C       2.2.2.0/24 is directly        Distance     ck0
L       2.2.2.2/32 is direct                        ack0
     10.0.0.0/8 is variably subnetted, 3 subnets, 2 masks
O       10.1.1.0/24 [110/2] via 10.2.1.5, 00:05:16, GigabitEthernet0/2
C       10.2.1.0/24 is directly connected, GigabitEthernet0/2
L       10.2.1.10/32 is directly connected, GigabitEthernet0/2
     172.16.0.0/16 is variably subnetted, 2 subnets, 2 masks
C       172.16.1.0/24 is directly connected, GigabitEthernet0/0
L       172.16.1.1/32 is directly connected, GigabitEthernet0/0
     172.20.0.0/24 is subnetted, 1 subnets
O       172.20.1.0/24 [110/2] via 10.2.1.15, 00:05:16, GigabitEthernet0/2
O*E2 0.0.0.0/0 [110/1] via 10.2.1.5, 00:05:16, GigabitEthernet0/2
```

Figure 7.17 – Administrative Distance in the routing table

Let's imagine the routing table does not contain any routing protocol codes. Simply by looking at the AD value next to each prefix and cross-referencing the table, you can quickly determine the routing protocol, and vice versa if there isn't any administrative distance value but only routing protocols.

If you look closely at the preceding routing table, you see that directly connected (C) routes do not contain any administrative distances. It is simply implied that the AD value is 0, since 0 is the most trustworthy route given that it is physically connected to the router.

# Routing metrics

In the previous section, we spoke about a router that was running multiple routing protocols and had to choose the most trustworthy route to install in its routing table. So, what if the router is using only one routing protocol such as OSPF and there are multiple paths to the same destination network. What will the router do then? In this situation, the router will check the metric value for each possible route and will only install the route that has the lowest metric.

> **Important note**
> The metric is also referred to as the cost of a route. Each routing protocol uses its own algorithm, which is used to calculate the best possible path to a destination network, and assigns a numerical value (metric) to each available path.

The following snippet shows a routing table containing various routes and their metric values:

```
Gateway of last resort is 10.2.1.5 to network 0.0.0.0

      2.0.0.0/8 is variably subnet            , 2 masks
C        2.2.2.0/24 is directly c    Metric        ack0
L        2.2.2.2/32 is directly                  pback0
      10.0.0.0/8 is variably subnetted, 3 subnets, 2 masks
O        10.1.1.0/24 [110/2] via 10.2.1.5, 00:05:16, GigabitEthernet0/2
C        10.2.1.0/24 is directly connected, GigabitEthernet0/2
L        10.2.1.10/32 is directly connected, GigabitEthernet0/2
      172.16.0.0/16 is variably subnetted, 2 subnets, 2 masks
C        172.16.1.0/24 is directly connected, GigabitEthernet0/0
L        172.16.1.1/32 is directly connected, GigabitEthernet0/0
      172.20.0.0/24 is subnetted, 1 subnets
O        172.20.1.0/24 [110/2] via 10.2.1.15, 00:05:16, GigabitEthernet0/2
O*E2 0.0.0.0/0 [110/1] via 10.2.1.5, 00:05:16, GigabitEthernet0/2
```

Figure 7.18 – Metric

As mentioned, each routing protocol uses a different method of calculating the metric (cost) to reach a destination network. Here, we will take a brief look at the metrics used by each **Interior Gateway Protocol** (**IGP**).

The following is a brief list of dynamic routing protocols.

## Routing Information Protocol

RIP is one of the first-generation routing protocols that allowed routers to automatically learn about new networks and update the routing table if a change was made on the network topology. The downside of RIP is that it uses a metric of **hop count** and only supports a maximum hop count of 15. This means, between a sender and a destination network, there must exist 15 or fewer routers. If there are more than 15 hops between the sender and the destination, the 15th hop router will discard the packet and the sender of the message will receive a *Destination host unreachable* response from the router.

If you recall, in the *Understanding IP routing* section, we noted that an IP packet contains a **Time To Live** (**TTL**) field, which contains a numerical value that decreases as it passes each hop (router or Layer 3 device) on the way to its destination. This is a loop prevention mechanism to ensure that a packet does not live forever on a computer network.

> **Important note**
> RIP is a distance-vector routing protocol. However, since RIP is no longer a part of the CCNA 200-301 examination objectives, we will not be discussing RIP further.

RIP uses the **Bellman Ford** algorithm, which calculates the hop count between a local router and the destination networks. It will use the route with the lowest number of hops (metric) and install it within the routing table.

## Open Shortest Path First

The OSPF routing protocol uses the **Shortest Path First** (**SPF**) algorithm, which was created by Edsger Dijkstra. This algorithm was designed to use the *cumulative bandwidth* to calculate the metrics for a route (path) to a destination network. With OSPF, the number of hops a packet has to pass before reaching its destination does not matter; rather it is the fastest route to reach there that is important.

## Enhanced Interior Gateway Routing Protocol

EIGRP was a Cisco proprietary protocol until 2013. It uses the **Diffusing Update Algorithm** (**DUAL**) to calculate the best and most cost-effective path. Unlike the other dynamic routing protocols, EIGRP is considered to be a hybrid routing protocol as it does not only calculate the best loop-free path to a destination network, but also a backup, loop-free path. Thus, in the event the main path goes down, EIGRP can almost immediately place the backup loop-free path into the routing table.

> **Important note**
> EIGRP is no longer part of the CCNA 200-301 examination objectives.

DUAL uses the following to calculate the metric for network routes:

- Bandwidth
- Delay
- TX Load
- RX Load
- Reliability

These are known as EIGRP metric weights and are represented by a K value. By default, EIGRP only uses the bandwidth and delay values during its metric calculations.

# Gateway of last resort

The last component of the routing table, and one that is of great importance, is the gateway of last resort. This is the default gateway that is inserted within the routing table of a Cisco router. Cisco routers also need to be configured with a default gateway that points to the internet. Without a gateway of last resort, Cisco routers will not be able to forward traffic from the internal **Local Area Networks** (**LANs**) to the internet.

The gateway of last resort is either statically configured by a network professional on the Cisco router or distributed via a dynamic routing protocol such as OSPF.

The following snippet shows a Cisco router that has a gateway of last resort within its routing table:

```
Gateway of last resort is 10.2.1.5 to network 0.0.0.0

      2.0.0.0/8 is variably subnetted, 2 subnets, 2 masks
C        2.2.2.0/24 is directly con
L        2.2.2.2/32 is directly connec    Default Gateway
     10.0.0.0/8 is variably subnetted,    for the Router
O        10.1.1.0/24 [110/2] via 10.2.1.            abitEthernet0/2
C        10.2.1.0/24 is directly connected, GigabitEthernet0/2
L        10.2.1.10/32 is directly connected, GigabitEthernet0/2
     172.16.0.0/16 is variably subnetted, 2 subnets, 2 masks
C        172.16.1.0/24 is directly connected, GigabitEthernet0/0
L        172.16.1.1/32 is directly connected, GigabitEthernet0/0
     172.20.0.0/24 is subnetted, 1 subnets
O        172.20.1.0/24 [110/2] via 10.2.1.15, 00:05:16, GigabitEthernet0/2
O*E2 0.0.0.0/0 [110/1] via 10.2.1.5, 00:05:16, GigabitEthernet0/2
```

Figure 7.19 – Gateway of last resort

In the preceding snippet, the gateway of last resort is `10.2.1.5`. Additionally, the last route in the routing table contains a default route that is learned via OSPF and that also has a next hop of `10.2.1.5`. In best practice, default routes are always placed at the bottom of the routing table.

> **Important note**
> A default route is only configured to point toward any network that does not exist within a routing table. Cisco routers do not contain every network that exists on the internet and, if they did, the routing table would be huge. The default route is designed to send traffic to a device that leads to the internet; this device is known as the gateway of last resort.

The reason for this placement is that, when a router performs a lookup, it always starts at the top of the list and works its way down. If there are no available routes to forward the packet, the default route is used to forward the packet. However, if a router does not have an available route or a default route, the router sends a *Destination unreachable* message back to the sender.

Having completed this section, you have gained the essential knowledge to predict the decisions of a Cisco router. Furthermore, you have learned how routers make their decisions on populating routes within their routing table and how they make forwarding decisions to ensure that the packets always take the most trusted and cost-efficient paths to their destinations.

## Summary

During the course of this chapter, we have discussed the strategies that Cisco IOS routers use to forward packets to their intended destinations. We looked at the routing table and broke down each component to give you a greater understanding of each component's purpose and responsibility on the router. You have learned how to predict the forwarding decision of a Cisco router in the following situations: when there are multiple routing protocols giving a route to the same destination network, when the same routing protocol has multiple paths to the same network, and when there are multiple paths with the same cost (metric).

I hope that this chapter has been informative and helps you on your journey toward learning how to implement and administrate Cisco solutions and prepare for the CCNA 200-301 certification. In the next chapter, *Understanding Static and Dynamic Routing*, we will learn how to set up static and dynamic routing protocols to ensure IP connectivity between multiple networks in a Cisco environment.

## Questions

The following is a short list of review questions to help reinforce your learning and help you identify which areas require improvement.

1.  What is the administrative distance of a directly connected route?

    A. 0

    B. 1

    C. 5

    D. 110

2.  A router has RIP, EIGRP, and OSPF running at the same time. Each protocol has a path to the network `192.168.1.0/27`. Which path will be installed in the routing table?

    A. EIGRP

    B. RIP

    C. OSPF

    D. All of the above

3.  Which of the following routing protocol codes is used to represent a default route in the routing table?

    A. D

    B. *

    C. S

    D. O

4.  Which of the following statements is true regarding administrative distance?

    A. Administrative distance is the cost between a source and destination network.

    B. Administrative distance represents the actual distance between the source and destination network

    C. Administrative distance is calculated by the router

    D. Administrative distance is used to represent the trustworthiness of a route

5.  A router is using only the OSPF routing protocol to learn remote networks. If there are three paths to the same destination network, what will the router do?

    A. The router will install the path with the highest metric.

    B. The router will install the path with the lowest metric.

    C. The router will install all paths that have the same metrics.

    D. The router will install all paths regardless of their metrics.

6.  A router uses the parent routes when forwarding packets to a destination. True or false?

    A. True

    B. False

7. The network mask of a parent route is the same as the child routes. True or false?

    A. True

    B. False

8. What is the purpose of the timer within the routing table?

    A. It indicates the current time on the router.

    B. It indicates how long the router has been powered-on.

    C. It indicates how long the routing table is available for.

    D. It indicates how long the route has been installed in the routing table.

9. Which of the following statements is not true?

    A. The routing table is stored in the running config.

    B. The routing table is stored in Flash.

    C. The routing table is stored in NVRAM.

    D. All of the above.

10. Which of the following protocol codes represents EIGRP in the routing table?

    A. O

    B. E

    C. D

    D. R

# Further reading

The following links are recommended for additional reading:

- Route selection: https://www.cisco.com/c/en/us/support/docs/ip/enhanced-interior-gateway-routing-protocol-eigrp/8651-21.html

- Understanding the routing table: https://www.ciscopress.com/articles/article.asp?p=2180210&seqNum=12

# 8
# Understanding First Hop Redundancy, Static and Dynamic Routing

Routers are computers too. They help us interconnect different IP networks. Without them, we can't communicate or exchange messages with a device or user on another network in a different location. These devices are super smart and help forward packets to their intended destinations. Routers determine the best path to forward packets to their destinations, rather than us having to make a decision each time a device wants to exchange a message across a network.

In this chapter, you will learn the essential details of static routing. We'll talk about the types of static routes that can be implemented on a network and their use cases. Furthermore, you will learn how dynamic routing protocols automatically learn remote networks and update routing tables. Lastly, you will learn how to implement static routes and configure the OSPF routing protocol on a Cisco environment.

In this chapter, we will cover the following topics:

- Understanding static routing
- Configuring static routing
- Understanding dynamic routing
- Configuring the dynamic routing protocol
- Understanding first hop redundancy

# Technical requirements

To follow along with the exercises in this chapter, please ensure that you have met the following hardware and software requirements:

- Cisco Packet Tracer: `https://www.netacad.com`
- Cisco IOSv
- GNS3
- Cisco 2911 routers

The code files for this chapter are available here: `https://github.com/PacktPublishing/Implementing-and-Administering-Cisco-Solutions/tree/master/Chapter%2008`.

Check out the following video to see the Code in Action: `https://bit.ly/33QUbvL`

# Understanding static routing

Why don't Cisco routers automatically forward traffic like Cisco IOS switches? Each interface on a Cisco router must be on a unique IP network. Without configuring an IP address on a router's interface, the router will not know what to do with incoming messages without an IP assignment. To put this simply, when you unbox a new Cisco IOS router and insert it into your network, it does not do anything. That's right – it does absolutely nothing by default.

When you configure an IP address on a Cisco IOS router's interface, the router inserts two routes within its routing table. Let's take a look at the following topology to get a better understanding of this:

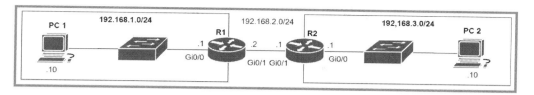

Figure 8.1 – Simple network topology

Within the network topology, there are a total of three networks: 192.168.1.0/24, 192.168.2.0/24, and 192.168.3.0/24. We would assume the routers automatically know about all the networks and update the routing table, but this does not happen.

Let's take a look at **R1**'s routing table after configuring the IP addresses on both its GigabitEthernet 0/0 and GigabitEthernet 0/1 interfaces:

```
R1#show ip route

Gateway of last resort is not set

      192.168.1.0/24 is variably subnetted, 2 subnets, 2 masks
C        192.168.1.0/24 is directly connected, GigabitEthernet0/0
L        192.168.1.1/32 is directly connected, GigabitEthernet0/0
      192.168.2.0/24 is variably subnetted, 2 subnets, 2 masks
C        192.168.2.0/24 is directly connected, GigabitEthernet0/1
L        192.168.2.2/32 is directly connected, GigabitEthernet0/1

R1#
```

Figure 8.2 – Routing table

**R1** only knows about its directly connected networks: 192.168.1.0/24 and 192.168.2.0/24. Therefore, if **PC 1** tries to send a message to the 192.168.3.0/24 network, **R1** will respond with a *destination host unreachable* message. By default, routers only know about directly connected networks. All other networks are considered to be remote networks. Static routing allows us to manually implement a static route that tells **R1** how to reach the 192.168.3.0/24 network.

How do we create a static route? A static route is the path to a remote network that may or may not be directly connected to the router. Firstly, looking at the topology, we must ask ourselves: if a packet is currently on **R1**, how does it reach the 192.168.3.0/24 network? It definitely has to be sent to **R2**. More specifically, it has to be sent to **R2**'s GigabitEthernet 0/1 interface via the 192.168.2.1 IP address. If we were to write a statement, we would get the following:

*"Traffic whose destination is 192.168.3.0 that has a subnet mask of 255.255.255.0 should be forwarded to 192.168.2.1 as the next hop."*

When we create a static route on **R1** from the preceding statement, we get the following command:

```
ip route 192.168.3.0 255.255.255.0 192.168.2.1
```

Whenever you're creating a static route, start with the destination network (192.18.3.0), then its subnet mask (255.255.255.0), and lastly, specify the next hop IP address (192.168.2.1). Additionally, instead of specifying the next hop, you can specify the exit-interface of **R1**, GigabitEthernet 0/1. Keep in mind that **R2** will also need a route to return traffic back to the 192.168.1.0/24 network.

Implementing static routes has both its pros and cons. In the next section, we will take a look at the benefits and downsides of using static routing in an enterprise network.

## Do we need static routing?

As a network grows, additional static routes are created. Therefore, the number of static routes increases as the network topology grows. If there is a change on the network topology, whether a new network is created, removed, or modified, the network engineer has to manually adjust the static route configurations on each device to support the change on the network. Static routes are good enough for small and simple network topologies but for a large enterprise topology that has many IP subnets with remote sites (offices/networks), static routing can become complex.

However, there are advantages to using static routing on a network. When a network administrator installs a static route within the routing table of a router, it is manually configured and inserted. This provides improved security, compared to using dynamic routing protocols, which have the ability to modify the routing table automatically. Let's imagine a hacker injects unsolicited dynamic routes to an enterprise routing domain and causes all the organization's routers to forward traffic destined for the internet through the hacker's computer. With static routes, the routes have to be manually adjusted.

With dynamic routing protocols, their algorithms have to calculate the best path by using various metrics. With static routing, there's no algorithm. The router simply checks the routing table for a best-match route. Once a suitable route is found, the router simply stops searching and executes the static route.

When it comes to predicting the next hop, this is easy with static routing as the path does not change. With dynamic routing protocols, if there is a change on the network topology, the next hop address may change based on the dynamic routing protocol algorithm's choice when selecting the best path and the next hop to forward packets.

The following are the best situations when static routes should be used in your network environment:

- To create a static route to a specific network in order to, for example, ensure the path to a specific network does not change
- To create a default route to forward packets to the internet
- To create a backup route

In the following sections, we'll learn about various types of static routes and how to apply them to the Cisco IOS router.

# Types of static routes

There are many types of static routes, and each is used within a certain scenario on a network. In this section, we will learn about the characteristics of each type of static route and how to implement them on a Cisco network.

## Network routes

Static network routes are those that are commonly used when configuring static routing. These routes are created to tell the router how to forward packets that are destined for a remote network.

To configure an IPv4 static route, use the following syntax:

```
Router(config)# ip route destination-network-address subnet-mask [next-hop-IP-address | exit-interface]
```

To configure an IPv6 static route, use the following syntax:

```
Router(config)# ipv6 unicast-routing
Router(config)# ipv6 route ipv6-prefix/ipv6-mask [next-hop-ipv6-address | exit-interface]
```

In the next section, we will take a look at next hop static routes.

## Next hop static routes

Next hop static routes do the same as the previously described *network route*, but this time we will use the next hop to specify which IP address the local router should forward the packet to.

To configure an IPv4 next hop static route, use the following syntax:

```
Router(config)# ip route destination-network-address subnet-
mask next-hop-IP-address
```

The following is an example of an IPv4 static route using a next hop:

```
Branch-A(config)#ip route 10.1.1.0 255.255.255.0 10.2.1.5
```

To configure an IPv6 next hop static route, use the following syntax:

```
Router(config)# ipv6 unicast-routing
```
```
Router(config)# ipv6 route ipv6-prefix/ipv6-mask next-hop ipv6
address
```

The following is an example of an IPv6 next hop static route:

```
HQ(config)# ipv6 unicast-routing
```
```
HQ(config)#ipv6 route 2001:ABCD:1234:2::/64
2001:ABCD:1234:5::10
```

The benefit of using a next hop is that the route specifies an IP address. Remember that static routes do not change without user intervention. Therefore, the router will always use the next hop IP address.

In the next section, we'll take a look at using directly connected static routes.

## Directly connected static routes

A directly connected static route has the same functionality as the network route but rather than specifying a next hop, we use the exit-interface of the local router when configuring this route.

To configure an IPv4 directly connected static route, use the following syntax:

```
Router(config)# ip route destination-network-address subnet-
mask exit-interface
```

The following is an example of an IPv4 directly connected static route:

```
Branch-A(config)#ip route 10.1.1.0 255.255.255.0
gigabitethernet 0/2
```

To configure an IPv6 directly connected static route, use the following syntax:

```
Router(config)# ipv6 unicast-routing
Router(config)# ipv6 route ipv6-prefix/ipv6-mask exit-interface
```

The following is an example of an IPv6 directly connected static route:

```
HQ(config)# ipv6 unicast-routing
HQ(config)#ipv6 route 2001:ABCD:1234:2::/64 gigabitethernet 0/1
```

The exit-interface acts as the doorway to leave the local router. When using this type of static route, the router is not concerned about the device on the other end catching this packet. It simply shoots the packet out a doorway (exit-interface).

In the next section, we'll take a look at configuring a fully specified static route.

## Fully specified static routes

A fully specified static route is created by simply specifying both the exit-interface of the local router and the next hop IP address of the next router.

To configure an IPv4 fully specified static route, use the following syntax:

```
Router(config)# ip route destination-network-address subnet-
mask exit-interface next-hop IP address
```

The following is an example of an IPv4 fully specified static route:

```
Branch-A(config)#ip route 10.1.1.0 255.255.255.0
gigabitethernet 0/2 192.168.2.1
```

To configure an IPv6 fully specified static route, use the following syntax:

```
Router(config)# ipv6 unicast-routing
Router(config)# ipv6 route ipv6-prefix/ipv6-mask exit-interface
next-hop Link-Local-IPv6 address
```

The following is an example of an IPv6 fully specified static route:

```
HQ(config)# ipv6 unicast-routing
HQ(config)#ipv6 route 2001:ABCD:1234:2::/64 gigabitethernet 0/1
FE80::2
```

The fully specified static route ensures all parameters are manually configured on the local router. In the next section, we'll take a look at the purpose of a default route.

## Default route

What if the router receives a packet that has a destination address located on the internet? What will the router do? As you will have realized by now, if a router does not have a route within its routing table, it will reply to the sender with either a *destination host unreachable* or *destination network unreachable* message. On the internet, there are hundreds of thousands of public networks, so it would be very inefficient to install all those public networks within the routing table of your router. It's a major issue if your router doesn't know how to reach or forward packets to the internet.

To solve this problem, we can use a special type of static route known as a **default** route. The default route is used to forward traffic to another router that may know what to do with a packet. Practically speaking, we use default routes to forward traffic to the internet.

To configure an IPv4 default route, use the following syntax:

```
Router(config)# ip route 0.0.0.0 0.0.0.0 <next-hop-IP-address |
exit-interface>
```

Notice that in the preceding syntax, the destination network ID and subnet mask are all zeros (0s). This implies any network that does not exist within the routing table uses this route.

The following is an example of an IPv4 default route that is using 10.2.1.5 as the next hop:

```
Branch-A(config)#ip route 0.0.0.0 0.0.0.0 10.2.1.5
```

To configure an IPv6 default route, use the following syntax:

```
Router(config)# ipv6 unicast-routing
Router(config)# ipv6 route ::/0 <next-hop-IPv6-address | exit-
interface>
```

The following is an example of an IPv6 default route:

```
Branch-A(config)# ipv6 unicast-routing
Branch-A(config)#ipv6 route ::/0 2001:ABCD:1234:5::5
```

Why use ::/0 as the IPv6 destination network? As you may recall from *Chapter 3, IP Addressing and Subnetting*, the double-colon (::) represents that two or more hextets are zeros (0s). In this instance, the double-colon (::) represents that all hextets are 0s with a subnet mask of 0 as well.

In the next section, we'll take a look at how host routes are used within a network.

## Host routes

Host routes are either in the form of IPv4 or IPv6 addresses in the routing table. They can be installed automatically in the routing table, configured as static host routes, or obtained automatically through other methods. Host routes are used to route traffic to a specific host.

The following snippet shows some host routes that were automatically installed in the routing table:

```
R3#show ip route
Codes: L - local, C - connected, S - static, R - RIP, M - mobile, B - BGP
       D - EIGRP, EX - EIGRP external, O - OSPF, IA - OSPF inter area
       N1 - OSPF NSSA external type 1, N2 - OSPF NSSA external type 2
       E1 - OSPF external type 1, E2 - OSPF external type 2, E - EGP
       i - IS-IS, L1 - IS-IS level-1, L2 - IS-IS level-2, ia - IS-IS inter area
       * - candidate default, U - per-user static route, o - ODR
       P - periodic downloaded static route

Gateway of last resort is not [Host Route]

      172.31.0.0/16 is vari               ets, 5 masks
S        172.31.0.0/24 i     ectly connected, Serial0/0/1
S        172.31.1.0/25       directly connected, Serial0/0/1
C        172.31.1.128/26 is directly connected, GigabitEthernet0/0
L        172.31.1.129/32 is directly connected, GigabitEthernet0/0
S        172.31.1.192/30 is directly connected, Serial0/0/1
C        172.31.1.196/30 is directly connected, Serial0/0/1
L        172.31.1.198/32 is directly connected, Serial0/0/1
```

Figure 8.3 – Host routes

A host route is a static route that simply specifies a host rather than a network. This type of static route allows you to create individual static routes that specify how to reach a specific host on a network.

To configure an IPv4 host route, use the following syntax:

```
Router(config)# ip route destination-ipv4-address
255.255.255.255 <next-hop-IP-address | exit-interface>
```

The following is an example of an IPv4 host route:

```
Router(config)# ip route 192.168.1.14 255.255.255.255
gigabitethernet 0/2
```

To configure an IPv6 host route, use the following syntax:

```
Router(config)# ipv6 unicast-routing
```
```
Router(config)# ipv6 route destination-ipv6-global-unicat-
address/128 <next-hop-IP-address | exit-interface>
```

The following is an example of an IPv6 host route:

```
Router(config)# ipv6 unicast-routing
Router(config)# ipv6 route 2001::201/128 gigabitethernet 0/3
```

When configuring a host route, ensure all bits are 1s within the subnet mask to imply all the bits at the destination IPv4 addresses match. For an IPv4 host route, the subnet mask is 255.255.255.255; for IPv6, it's /128.

In the next section, we'll take a look at how to create a backup route using floating routes.

## Floating route

Let's imagine your organization is using two internet service providers: **ISP A** and **ISP B** for internet connectivity redundancy. **ISP A** serves as the primary link while **ISP B** is the backup in the event the connection to **ISP A** goes down.

The following diagram shows a simple network topology:

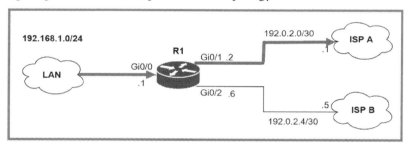

Figure 8.4 – Redundant internet connections

All traffic from the internal LAN will use **ISP A** as the preferred route. The following is the configuration used on **R1** to ensure packets are sent to **ISP A**:

```
R1config)# ip route 0.0.0.0 0.0.0.0 192.0.2.1
```

A floating static route can be created by simply specifying an **Administrative Distance (AD)** as higher than a static route or a dynamic routing protocol. As an example, to create a floating static route, the floating static route should be configured with an AD greater than 1. Floating static routes are very useful on a router, as they can action a backup route to the primary route.

To create a floating route on **R1** with an **AD** value of 2, we can use the following commands:

```
R1config)# ip route 0.0.0.0 0.0.0.0 192.0.2.1 2
```

Notice that, at the end of the next hop, there is a numerical value. Cisco IOS allows us to specify an AD value for the route. This allows us to create backup routes for dynamic routes that are no longer available.

The following snippet shows the path the packets it will take if **ISP A** goes down:

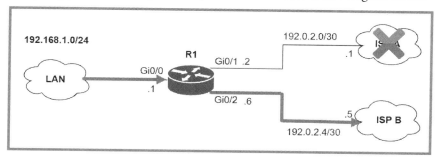

Figure 8.5 – Backup route

The original route will be removed from the routing table and the floating route will be installed and will become the primary route/path to reach the internet.

To configure an IPv4 floating route, use the following syntax:

```
Router(config)# ip route destination-network-address subnet-
mask [next-hop IP address | exit-interface] administrative-
distance-value
```

To configure an IPv6 floating route, use the following syntax:

```
Router(config)# ipv6 unicast-routing
```

```
Router(config)# ipv6 route ipv6-prefix/ipv6-mask [next-hop ip
address | exit-interface] administrative-distance-value
```

> **Important Note**
> Floating static routes are created as backups for the default route or a dynamic route on the router. Keep in mind that static routes are persistent in the routing table.

Having completed this section, you have learned about the various types of static routes and how to implement them. The following sections will take you through a few hands-on labs, which will help you develop your static routing skills as a professional.

# Lab – configuring static routing using IPv4

It's time to get some practical experience in implementing static routes to gain connectivity between remote networks. To get started, we'll be using the Cisco Packet Tracer application, which allows us to simulate a Cisco environment. Within the application, please design the following network topology:

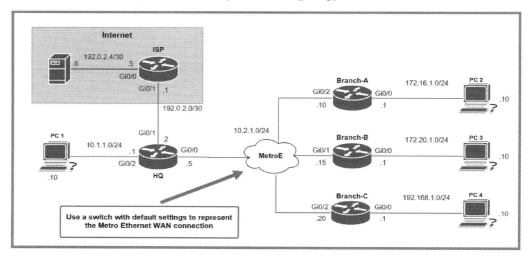

Figure 8.6 – IPv4 static routing lab topology

Use the following guidelines to create this lab to ensure you get the same results:

- Each PC is configured correctly with its appropriate IP addressing schemes, as shown in the topology diagram.

- Ensure each PC can ping only its default gateway. For example, **PC 2** should be able to ping the **Branch-A** router via its 172.16.1.1 IP address.

- The routers should be able to ping each other via their interfaces on the 10.2.1.0/24 network only.

- Use only Cisco 2911 routers.

Having built the network topology, use the following instructions to implement static routes:

1.  Firstly, as a good network professional, it is wise to verify your IP configurations on your devices. On each PC, open the **Command Prompt** program and execute the ipconfig command to verify that the correct IP address, subnet mask, and default gateway have been assigned.

> **Important Note**
>
> If you are using a physical lab with a Linux operating system, use the `ifconfig` command to validate your IP address configurations.

2. On each router, use the `show ip interface brief` command to verify that the appropriate IP address is assigned on the correct interfaces and that the interfaces are in an Up/Up status.

3. Let's test the connectivity between each PC and its default gateway. On **PC 1**, let's ping the **HQ** router, as shown in the following snippet:

```
C:\>ping 10.1.1.1

Pinging 10.1.1.1 with 32 bytes of data:

Reply from 10.1.1.1: bytes=32 time<1ms TTL=255
Reply from 10.1.1.1: bytes=32 time<1ms TTL=255
Reply from 10.1.1.1: bytes=32 time<1ms TTL=255
Reply from 10.1.1.1: bytes=32 time<1ms TTL=255

Ping statistics for 10.1.1.1:
    Packets: Sent = 4, Received = 4, Lost = 0 (0% loss),
Approximate round trip times in milli-seconds:
    Minimum = 0ms, Maximum = 0ms, Average = 0ms
```

Figure 8.7 – Default gateway connectivity test

The **HQ** router responds by sending the ICMP messages back to **PC 1**. This response verifies connectivity between **PC 1** and its default gateway.

4. Next, let's attempt to test connectivity between remote networks between **PC 1** and **PC 2**. On **PC 1**, use the `ping 172.16.1.10` command, as shown in the following snippet:

```
C:\>ping 172.16.1.10

Pinging 172.16.1.10 with 32 bytes of data:

Reply from 10.1.1.1: Destination host unreachable.
Reply from 10.1.1.1: Destination host unreachable.
Reply from 10.1.1.1: Destination host unreachable.
Reply from 10.1.1.1: Destination host unreachable.

Ping statistics for 172.16.1.10:
    Packets: Sent = 4, Received = 0, Lost = 4 (100% loss),
```

Figure 8.8 – Connectivity test from PC 1 to PC 2

The default gateway, which is the **HQ** router, has responded with a *destination host unreachable* message. This indicates it does not have a route to reach host `172.16.1.10` in its routing table.

5.  We can use the `show ip route` command on each router to determine which networks they have within their routing table. The following snippet shows the routing table on the **HQ** router:

```
Gateway of last resort is not set

      10.0.0.0/8 is variably subnetted, 4 subnets, 2 masks
C        10.1.1.0/24 is directly connected, GigabitEthernet0/2
L        10.1.1.1/32 is directly connected, GigabitEthernet0/2
C        10.2.1.0/24 is directly connected, GigabitEthernet0/0
L        10.2.1.5/32 is directly connected, GigabitEthernet0/0
```

Figure 8.9 – Routing table of the HQ router

You'll notice that each router only knows about its directly connected networks. Our job is to ensure each router knows how to reach all other networks. We will configure the default routes in the next lab.

6.  Let's begin by configuring the **HQ** router with static routes to reach **Branch B**, **Branch C**, and the **HQ** networks. Ensure you enter the following commands in *global configuration* mode:

```
HQ(config)#ip route 172.16.1.0 255.255.255.0 10.2.1.10
HQ(config)#ip route 172.20.1.0 255.255.255.0 10.2.1.15
HQ(config)#ip route 192.168.1.0 255.255.255.0 10.2.1.20
```

The preceding configurations will install a static route for each branch network in the topology.

> **Important Note**
>
> To remove a static route, use the `no` command, followed by the entire static route, such as `no ip route 172.16.1.0 255.255.255.0 10.2.1.10`.

We can use the `show ip route` command to verify that the routing table has been updated:

```
      10.0.0.0/8 is variably subnetted, 4 subnets, 2 masks
C        10.1.1.0/24 is directly connected, GigabitEthernet0/2
L        10.1.1.1/32 is directly connected, GigabitEthernet0/2
C        10.2.1.0/24 is directly connected, GigabitEthernet0/0
L        10.2.1.5/32 is directly connected, GigabitEthernet0/0
      172.16.0.0/24 is subnetted, 1 subnets
S        172.16.1.0/24 [1/0] via 10.2.1.10
      172.20.0.0/24 is subnetted, 1 subnets
S        172.20.1.0/24 [1/0] via 10.2.1.15
S     192.168.1.0/24 [1/0] via 10.2.1.20
```

Figure 8.10 – Updated routing table on the HQ router

Now, there are static routes that have been installed on the **HQ** routing table for each remote branch network.

7. Let's attempt to ping between **PC 1** and **PC 2** again to verify whether we have end-to-end connectivity:

```
C:\>ping 172.16.1.10

Pinging 172.16.1.10 with 32 bytes of data:

Request timed out.
Request timed out.              PC is not receiving any
Request timed out.          ◄─  ICMP Echo Replies
Request timed out.

Ping statistics for 172.16.1.10:
    Packets: Sent = 4, Received = 0, Lost = 4 (100% loss),
```

Figure 8.11 – Request timed out messages

As you can see, the responses have changed. Now, we're getting *Request timed out* responses. What does this mean? These responses are provided when the target device (**PC 2**) has disabled ICMP responses, a firewall or security appliance is blocking ICMP messages, or the target does not have a route back to the sender (**PC 1**). In this situation, there isn't a firewall or ICMP being blocked anywhere, so it's the third reason.

8. Let's check the routing table on the **Branch-A** router to verify whether it has a route back to the **HQ** network:

```
Gateway of last resort is not set

      10.0.0.0/8 is variably subnetted, 2 subnets, 2 masks
C        10.2.1.0/24 is directly connected, GigabitEthernet0/2
L        10.2.1.10/32 is directly connected, GigabitEthernet0/2
     172.16.0.0/16 is variably subnetted, 2 subnets, 2 masks
C        172.16.1.0/24 is directly connected, GigabitEthernet0/0
L        172.16.1.1/32 is directly connected, GigabitEthernet0/0
```

Figure 8.12 – Routing table of the Branch-A router

As suspected, the **Branch-A** router does not have a router back to the 10.1.1.0/24 network, nor the other remote networks.

9. Using the following commands, we will configure the **Branch-A** router with static routes to all other remote branch networks within the topology:

```
Branch-A(config)#ip route 10.1.1.0 255.255.255.0 10.2.1.5
```
```
Branch-A(config)#ip route 172.20.1.0 255.255.255.0
10.2.1.15
```
```
Branch-A(config)#ip route 192.168.1.0 255.255.255.0
10.2.1.20
```

Check the routing table of the **Branch-A** router. This way, we can verify that the new routes are in place:

```
      10.0.0.0/8 is variably subnetted, 3 subnets, 2 masks
S        10.1.1.0/24 [1/0] via 10.2.1.5
C        10.2.1.0/24 is directly connected, GigabitEthernet0/2
L        10.2.1.10/32 is directly connected, GigabitEthernet0/2
      172.16.0.0/16 is variably subnetted, 2 subnets, 2 masks
C        172.16.1.0/24 is directly connected, GigabitEthernet0/0
L        172.16.1.1/32 is directly connected, GigabitEthernet0/0
      172.20.0.0/24 is subnetted, 1 subnets
S        172.20.1.0/24 [1/0] via 10.2.1.15
S     192.168.1.0/24 [1/0] via 10.2.1.20
```

Figure 8.13 – Static routes on the Branch-A router

Now that the **Branch-A** router has a route (path) back to the **HQ** network (`10.1.1.0/24`) via `10.2.1.5`, let's test end-to-end connectivity once more.

10. Test connectivity from **PC 1** to **PC 2** to verify routing is working properly between the **HQ** and **Branch-A** routers:

```
C:\>ping 172.16.1.10

Pinging 172.16.1.10 with 32 bytes of data:

Reply from 172.16.1.10: bytes=32 time<1ms TTL=126
Reply from 172.16.1.10: bytes=32 time<1ms TTL=126
Reply from 172.16.1.10: bytes=32 time=1ms TTL=126
Reply from 172.16.1.10: bytes=32 time=4ms TTL=126

Ping statistics for 172.16.1.10:
    Packets: Sent = 4, Received = 4, Lost = 0 (0% loss),
Approximate round trip times in milli-seconds:
    Minimum = 0ms, Maximum = 4ms, Average = 1ms
```

Figure 8.14 – Connectivity test

Additionally, we can perform a traceroute to validate the path the packet takes between **PC 1** and **PC 2**:

```
C:\>tracert 172.16.1.10

Tracing route to 172.16.1.10 over a maximum of 30 hops:

  1    0 ms      0 ms      0 ms      10.1.1.1
  2    0 ms      1 ms      0 ms      10.2.1.10
  3    0 ms      0 ms      0 ms      172.16.1.10

Trace complete.
```

Figure 8.15 – Traceroute showing path

The first hop is the default gateway for **PC 1**, while the second hop is the next hop for the address for the `172.16.1.0/24` network, as seen within the routing table of the **HQ** router. The third hop is the actual destination host.

11. Let's not forget to configure the static routes on the **Branch-B** router. Use the following commands:

```
Branch-B(config)#ip route 10.1.1.0 255.255.255.0 10.2.1.5
Branch-B(config)#ip route 172.16.1.0 255.255.255.0
10.2.1.10
Branch-B(config)#ip route 192.168.1.0 255.255.255.0
10.2.1.20
```

12. To configure the static routes on the **Branch-C** router, use the following commands:

```
Branch-C(config)#ip route 10.1.1.0 255.255.255.0 10.2.1.5
Branch-C(config)#ip route 172.16.1.0 255.255.255.0
10.2.1.10
Branch-C(config)#ip route 172.20.1.0 255.255.255.0
10.2.1.15
```

13. Lastly, use `ping` to validate end-to-end connectivity between all the devices on the topology.

Having completed this lab, you have gained the hands-on skills to implement static routing and perform troubleshooting techniques in a Cisco environment.

# Lab – configuring an IPv4 default route

In this lab, you will learn how to implement a default route that points to the internet. Please keep in mind that this lab is simply an extension of the previous lab. As you may recall, a default route is a route that points to a foreign network that does not belong to your organization. It's simply your path (route) to the internet.

To get started with configuring a default route, use the following instructions:

1. On the **Branch-A** router, use the following command to create a default route that points to the **HQ** router, as that's where the internet link is located:

```
Branch-A(config)#ip route 0.0.0.0 0.0.0.0 10.2.1.5
```

2. Check the routing table of the **Branch-A** router to validate that the default route has been installed and that the last resort gateway has been set:

```
Branch-A#show ip route

Gateway of last resort is 10.2.1.5 to network 0.0.0.0

      10.0.0.0/8 is variably subnetted, 3 subnets, 2 masks
S         10.1.1.0/24 [1/0] via 10.2.1.5
C         10.2.1.0/24 is directly connected, GigabitEthernet0/2
L         10.2.1.10/32 is directly connected, GigabitEthernet0/2
      172.16.0.0/16 is variably subnetted, 2 subnets, 2 masks
C         172.16.1.0/24 is directly connected, GigabitEthernet0/0
L         172.16.1.1/32 is directly connected, GigabitEthernet0/0
      172.20.0.0/24 is subnetted, 1 subnets
S         172.20.1.0/24 [1/0] via 10.2.1.15
S     192.168.1.0/24 [1/0] via 10.2.1.20
S*    0.0.0.0/0 [1/0] via 10.2.1.5
```

Figure 8.16 – Default route

Configuring the default route on **Branch-A** will create the following effect: if any packets are destined for a network that does not exist within the routing table of the **Branch-A** router, the default route (gateway of last resort) will be used. The router will forward the packet to `10.2.1.5`.

Furthermore, since the default route does not have an exit-interface, the router will perform a **recursive lookup** within the routing table to determine which network `10.2.1.5` belongs to. This is done to determine which exit-interface the router should use when forwarding the packet. According to the routing table, the router will forward the packet out of interface `GigabitEthernet 0/2` since `10.2.1.5` belongs to the `10.2.1.0/24` subnet.

3. Repeat both *steps 1* and *2* on the **Branch-B** and **Branch-C** routers to configure a default route.

4. Let's configure the **HQ** router as the stub router that has the actual internet connection. On the **HQ** router, we will configure a default route that points to the `192.0.2.1` internet gateway address on the ISP router:

```
HQ(config)#ip route 0.0.0.0 0.0.0.0 192.0.2.1
```

> **Important Note**
> In a real environment, the ISP will provide you with the public IP address you need to configure on your stub router's interface, as well as the internet gateway address.

At this point, all the routers have a default route that points toward the internet or ISP network. To *kick it up a notch*, ensure the ISP router and the server have been configured with the IP scheme, as shown in the topology. Ensure the server can ping the ISP router and vice versa.

5.  Configure a default route on the **ISP** router that points toward the **HQ** router:

```
ISP(config)#ip route 0.0.0.0 0.0.0.0 192.0.2.2
```

The purpose of this step to allow the PCs to reach the public server on the *internet* within our lab.

6.  Let's test the connectivity from any PC to the server, which is on the *internet*. The following screenshot shows the results from **PC 2** on our network:

```
C:\>ping 192.0.2.6

Pinging 192.0.2.6 with 32 bytes of data:

Reply from 192.0.2.6: bytes=32 time<1ms TTL=125
Reply from 192.0.2.6: bytes=32 time=11ms TTL=125
Reply from 192.0.2.6: bytes=32 time=12ms TTL=125
Reply from 192.0.2.6: bytes=32 time=12ms TTL=125

Ping statistics for 192.0.2.6:
    Packets: Sent = 4, Received = 4, Lost = 0 (0% loss),
Approximate round trip times in milli-seconds:
    Minimum = 0ms, Maximum = 12ms, Average = 8ms
```

Figure 8.17 – Connectivity test to the server

7.  Next, let's perform a traceroute to the server:

```
C:\>tracert 192.0.2.6

Tracing route to 192.0.2.6 over a maximum of 30 hops:

  1    0 ms       0 ms       0 ms       172.16.1.1
  2    0 ms       1 ms       0 ms       10.2.1.5
  3    0 ms       0 ms      11 ms       192.0.2.1
  4   11 ms       0 ms      14 ms       192.0.2.6

Trace complete.
```

Figure 8.18 – Traceroute test

As you can see, the traceroute shows the path the packet took from **PC 2** to the server.

8. Furthermore, looking at the routing table, we can see that `192.0.2.4/30` does not exist:

```
Branch-A#show ip route
Gateway of last resort is 10.2.1.5 to network 0.0.0.0

      10.0.0.0/8 is variably subnetted, 3 subnets, 2 masks
S        10.1.1.0/24 [1/0] via 10.2.1.5
C        10.2.1.0/24 is directly connected, GigabitEthernet0/2
L        10.2.1.10/32 is directly connected, GigabitEthernet0/2
      172.16.0.0/16 is variably subnetted, 2 subnets, 2 masks
C        172.16.1.0/24 is directly connected, GigabitEthernet0/0
L        172.16.1.1/32 is directly connected, GigabitEthernet0/0
      172.20.0.0/24 is subnetted, 1 subnets
S        172.20.1.0/24 [1/0] via 10.2.1.15
S     192.168.1.0/24 [1/0] via 10.2.1.20
S*    0.0.0.0/0 [1/0] via 10.2.1.5
```

Figure 8.19 – Routing table of the Branch-A router

The **Branch-A** router used the default route gateway as a last resort to forward the packet to another device, which may have a path or route to the destination host.

> **Tip**
>
> For each branch router, rather than installing a static route for each remote network, you can simply install a single default route to the main office, such as the HQ router. This will ensure the routing table is within reach and that the remote branch router is kept small and concise. Additionally, the HQ router should contain static routes to each remote branch network. To put this simply, whenever a branch officer has to send a message to another branch or remote network, the message will always be sent to the HQ router. In the next lab exercise, we will apply this method and learn how to perform this task.

Having completed this lab, you have gained the hands-on skills and experience you need to configure and implement a default route on an IPv4 network.

# Lab – configuring static routing using IPv6

In this lab, you will learn how to configure both IPv6 static and default routes in a Cisco environment. You are not required to rebuild a new topology for this exercise; IPv6 supports *dual stacking*, which allows you to configure both IPv4 and IPv6 addresses on the same interfaces. Therefore, you can simply continue working from the previous lab.

The following is the IPv6 topology we'll be using to complete this hands-on exercise:

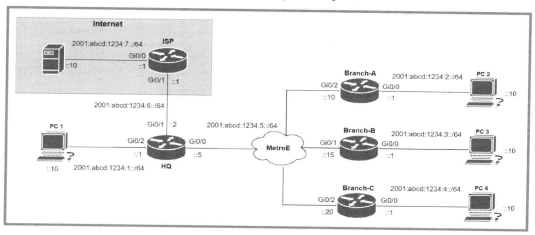

Figure 8.20 – IPv6 routing lab topology

Before you begin, ensure you have configured the devices with both the global unicast and link-local IPv6 addressing schemes, as shown in the following table:

| Device | Interface | IPv6 Address |
|---|---|---|
| ISP | Gi 0/0 | 2001:abcd:1234:7::5/64 |
| | | FE80::1 |
| | Gi 0/1 | 2001:abcd:1234:6::1/64 |
| | | FE80::1 |
| HQ | Gi 0/0 | 2001:abcd:1234:5::5/64 |
| | | FE80::1 |
| | Gi 0/1 | 2001:abcd:1234:6::2/64 |
| | | FE80::2 |
| | Gi 0/2 | 2001:abcd:1234:1::1/64 |
| | | FE80::1 |

Figure 8.21 – ISP and HQ device IPv6 addressing schemes

The following table provides the IPv6 addressing schemes for each branch router:

| Device | Interface | IPv6 Address |
|---|---|---|
| Branch-A | Gi 0/0 | 2001:abcd:1234:2::1/64 |
| | | FE80::1 |
| | Gi 0/2 | 2001:abcd:1234:5::10/64 |
| | | FE80::2 |
| Branch-B | Gi 0/0 | 2001:abcd:1234:3::1/64 |
| | | FE80::1 |
| | Gi 0/1 | 2001:abcd:1234:5::15/64 |
| | | FE80::3 |
| Branch-C | Gi 0/0 | 2001:abcd:1234:4::1/64 |
| | | FE80::1 |
| | Gi 0/2 | 2001:abcd:1234:5::20/64 |
| | | FE80::4 |

Figure 8.22 – Branch routers' IPv6 addressing scheme

Lastly, each end device, such as the PCs and the server, also require IPv6 addresses:

| Device | Interface | IPv6 Address | Default Gateway |
|---|---|---|---|
| PC 1 | Fa 0 | 2001:ABCD:1234:1::10/64 | 2001:ABCD:1234:1::1 |
| | | FE80::2 | |
| PC 2 | Fa 0 | 2001:ABCD:1234:2::10/64 | 2001:ABCD:1234:2::1 |
| | | FE80::2 | |
| PC 3 | Fa 0 | 2001:ABCD:1234:3::10/64 | 2001:ABCD:1234:3::1 |
| | | FE80::2 | |
| PC 4 | Fa 0 | 2001:ABCD:1234:4::10/64 | 2001:ABCD:1234:4::1 |
| | | FE80::2 | |
| Server | Fa 0 | 2001:ABCD:1234:7::10/64 | 2001:ABCD:1234:7::1 |
| | | FE80::2 | |

Figure 8.23 – End device IPv6 addressing scheme

Once each device has been fully configured with its IPv6 addresses, ensure there is end-to-end connectivity:

- Ping between each PC and its default gateway using both the global unicast and link-local IPv6 addresses.

- Ping from one branch router to another.

- Ping from the **HQ** router to the **ISP** router.

To get started with implementing IPv6 static routes, use the following instructions:

1.  Enter *global configuration mode* on each router and execute the `ipv6 unicast-routing` command to allow IPv6 routing.

2.  Firstly, install IPv6 static routers for each branch network on the **HQ** router, as follows:

```
HQ(config)#ipv6 route 2001:ABCD:1234:2::/64
2001:ABCD:1234:5::10
```

```
HQ(config)#ipv6 route 2001:ABCD:1234:3::/64
2001:ABCD:1234:5::15
```

```
HQ(config)#ipv6 route 2001:ABCD:1234:4::/64
2001:ABCD:1234:5::20
```

3.  On each branch router, install only an IPv6 default route that points to **HQ** as its IPv6 gateway of last resort. Use the following commands to achieve this task:

```
Branch-A(config)#ipv6 route ::/0 2001:ABCD:1234:5::5
Branch-B(config)#ipv6 route ::/0 2001:ABCD:1234:5::5
Branch-C(config)#ipv6 route ::/0 2001:ABCD:1234:5::5
```

At this point, each PC can reach another PC on a remote network and all traffic passes through the **HQ** router.

4.  Let's install a **default route** on the **HQ** router to point toward the internet:

```
HQ(config)#ipv6 route ::/0 2001:abcd:1234:6::1
```

To ensure we can simulate the *internet* within our lab environment, we also need to install a default route on the **ISP** router that points back to the **HQ** router using the following command:

```
ISP(config)#ipv6 route ::/0 2001:abcd:1234:6::2
```

5. Verify end-to-end connectivity from one PC to another. The following snippet shows the ping results between **PC 2** and **PC 4**:

```
C:\>ping 2001:abcd:1234:4::10

Pinging 2001:abcd:1234:4::10 with 32 bytes of data:

Reply from 2001:ABCD:1234:4::10: bytes=32 time<1ms TTL=125
Reply from 2001:ABCD:1234:4::10: bytes=32 time=10ms TTL=125
Reply from 2001:ABCD:1234:4::10: bytes=32 time=10ms TTL=125
Reply from 2001:ABCD:1234:4::10: bytes=32 time=11ms TTL=125

Ping statistics for 2001:ABCD:1234:4::10:
    Packets: Sent = 4, Received = 4, Lost = 0 (0% loss),
Approximate round trip times in milli-seconds:
    Minimum = 0ms, Maximum = 11ms, Average = 7ms
```

Figure 8.24 – Connectivity between PC 2 and PC 4

The following snippet shows the path the packet took from **PC 2** and **PC 4**:

```
C:\>tracert 2001:abcd:1234:4::10

Tracing route to 2001:abcd:1234:4::10 over a maximum of 30 hops:

  1    0 ms     0 ms     0 ms     2001:ABCD:1234:2::1
  2    0 ms     0 ms     0 ms     2001:ABCD:1234:5::5
  3    0 ms    10 ms    10 ms     2001:ABCD:1234:5::20
  4   12 ms    12 ms    10 ms     2001:ABCD:1234:4::10

Trace complete.
```

Figure 8.25 – Traceroute between PC 2 and PC 4

As expected, all traffic passes through the **HQ** router since we have configured it using the default route on each branch router.

6. Using the `show ipv6 route` command, we can validate the IPv6 routing table of each router. The following snippet shows the routing table of the **Branch-A** router:

```
Branch-A#show ipv6 route
IPv6 Routing Table - 6 entries
Codes: C - Connected, L - Local, S - Static, R - RIP, B - BGP
       U - Per-user Static route, M - MIPv6
       I1 - ISIS L1, I2 - ISIS L2, IA - ISIS interarea, IS - ISIS summary
       O - OSPF intra, OI - OSPF inter, OE1 - OSPF ext 1, OE2 - OSPF ext 2
       ON1 - OSPF NSSA ext 1, ON2 - OSPF NSSA ext 2
       D - EIGRP, EX - EIGRP external
S   ::/0 [1/0]
     via 2001:ABCD:1234:5::5
C   2001:ABCD:1234:2::/64 [0/0]
     via GigabitEthernet0/0, directly connected
L   2001:ABCD:1234:2::1/128 [0/0]
     via GigabitEthernet0/0, receive
C   2001:ABCD:1234:5::/64 [0/0]
     via GigabitEthernet0/2, directly connected
L   2001:ABCD:1234:5::10/128 [0/0]
     via GigabitEthernet0/2, receive
L   FF00::/8 [0/0]
     via Null0, receive
```

Figure 8.26 – Branch-A IPv6 routing table

7. Lastly, we can use the `show ipv6 interface brief` command to verify the IPv6 addresses on each router's interface. The following snippet shows both the IPv6 link-local and global unicast addresses on the **HQ** router:

```
HQ#show ipv6 interface brief
GigabitEthernet0/0              [up/up]
     FE80::1
     2001:ABCD:1234:5::5
GigabitEthernet0/1              [up/up]
     FE80::2
     2001:ABCD:1234:6::2
GigabitEthernet0/2              [up/up]
     FE80::1
     2001:ABCD:1234:1::1
Vlan1                           [administratively down/down]
     unassigned
```

Figure 8.27 – IPv6 interfaces on the HQ router

With this, you will be able to test connectivity between each branch network and the simulated internet with the server.

Having completed this lab, you have gained the hands-on skills to implement IPv6 static routes within a Cisco networking environment. In the next section, we will learn how to configure our Cisco routers to automatically learn routes and update their routing table using the dynamic routing protocol.

# Understanding dynamic routing

Let's imagine you're the network engineer for a very large organization that has a lot of subnets spanning across multiple remote offices, which are all interconnected by routers. Manually implementing static routes to each network can be a very daunting task. Imagine that there is a failure on the network; routers will not automatically discover a new path and re-route network traffic. Furthermore, as the network engineer, your job gets tougher when there are issues on the network as static routing becomes more difficult to troubleshoot as the network expands.

To save the day, there are dynamic routing protocols. What exactly are dynamic routing protocols? The answer to this question is quite simple: they are layer 3 routing protocols that can be configured on a router to automatically discover remote networks, maintain and update routing tables, and calculate the best path to a destination network. In the event a route or path is no longer available, dynamic routing protocols can find a new path and install it in the routing table automatically.

There are various types of dynamic routing protocols. The following figure provide a breakdown of them:

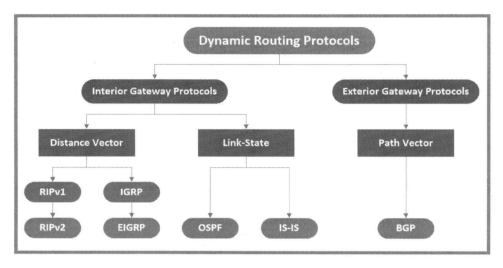

Figure 8.28 – Dynamic routing protocols

There are various categories and sub-categories of dynamic routing protocols that are grouped based on their characteristics and how they function. Let's take a look at them.

## Types of dynamic routing protocols

There are two main categories of dynamic routing protocols: **Interior Gateway Protocols** (**IGPs**) and **exterior gateway protocols** (**EGPs**). The difference between these two is quite simple. IGPs are used within a private network owned by an organization. If IGPs are used on private networks, where do you think EGPs are used? They are mostly used on the internet, which is a public network.

There is currently one EGP and it's called the **border gateway protocol** (**BGP**). BGP is used to exchange routing information between **Autonomous Systems** (**ASes**) on the internet. An AS is defined as an organization that manages a lot of public networks. A simple example of this is an ISP. Imagine ISP_A has to inform other ISPs around the world about the networks ISP_A owns and how to reach them. Each ISP shares routing information via the BGP routing protocol on the internet.

Each ISP has a unique **Autonomous System Number** (**ASN**), which allows it to establish a BGP adjacency with another ASN to exchange BGP routes. BGP is unlike the other routing protocols as it chooses the best route based on its path.

The following diagram shows a simple representation of BGP interconnecting via ASNs:

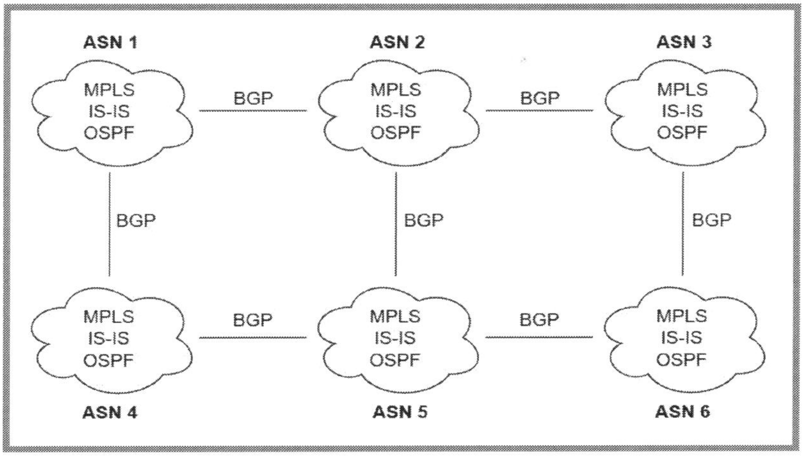

Figure 8.29 – BGP being used between various ASNs

BGP is a very slow converging dynamic routing protocol, which is why it is mostly used on the internet rather than on private networks. When we speak about BGP, we usually mean **external BGP (eBGP)**, which is used on the internet and between ASes. However, there's another version known as **internal BGP (iBGP)** that exchanges routing information within a single Autonomous System.

> **Important Note**
> BGP is no longer covered in the CCNA 200-301 exam objectives and has moved to the **Cisco Certified Network Professional (CCNP)** Enterprise certification level. However, it's worth mentioning in this section.

The following is the BGP routing table of a public BGP router:

```
route-views>show bgp
BGP table version is          , local router ID is
Status codes: s suppressed, d damped, h history, * valid, > best, i - internal,
              r RIB-failure, S Stale, m multipath, b backup-path, f RT-Filter,
              x best-external, a additional-path, c RIB-compressed,
Origin codes: i - IGP, e - EGP, ? - incomplete
RPKI validation codes: V valid, I invalid, N Not found

     Network          Next Hop            Metric LocPrf Weight Path
Nr>  0.0.0.0          162.251.163.2                     0 53767 3257 i
V*   1.0.0.0/24       202.93.8.242                       0 24441 13335 i
V*                    212.66.96.126                      0 20912 13335 i
V*                    91.218.184.60                      0 49788 13335 i
V*                    37.139.139.17            0         0 57866 13335 i
V*                    140.192.8.16                       0 54728 20130 6939 13335 i
V*                    194.85.40.15             0         0 3267 13335 i
```

Figure 8.30 – BGP routing table

The preceding snippet shows the destination networks on the left, their next hop, and path. The path provides the ASN values. Therefore, for each of the 1.0.0.0/24 networks, the packet has to be sent to AS 24441 via 202.93.8.242, then to AS 13335, and so on.

> **Tip**
>
> The *BGP Lookup Glass project* is created among ISPs around the world; it allows anyone to Telnet into their BGP-enabled routers to learn more about the BGP routing protocol. Simply use the search term bgp looking glass within your web browser to find publicly accessible BGP routers.

One of the oldest IGP dynamic routing protocols is the **routing information protocol** (**RIP**). RIP is defined as a distance vector routing protocol. A distance vector routing protocol is only concerned about the distance and direction of the destination network. RIP uses the **Bellman-Ford** algorithm, which uses **hop count** as its **metric** to calculate the distance between the router and the destination network.

> **Important Note**
>
> RIP has a maximum hop count of 15. For a network that has more than 15 hops, RIP will not be suitable. Additionally, RIP does not support VLSM.

The path with the least number of hops (routers) will be elected as the best route and will be installed in the routing table. Furthermore, being a distance vector protocol, RIP will forward the packet to the next hop (neighbor) along the path until the packet is delivered.

> **Important Note**
>
> RIP was covered in the previous versions of CCNA. It is no longer part of the CCNA 200-301 examination objectives and is beyond the scope of this book.

The **enhanced interior gateway routing protocol** (**EIGRP**) is another distance vector routing protocol and was a Cisco-proprietary routing protocol until March 2013, when Cisco announced that it's open to the network community and vendors in regard to its implementation. EIGRP uses the **diffusing update algorithm** (**DUAL**) to calculate the best path to a destination network.

DUAL uses the following factors when calculating a suitable route:

- Bandwidth

- Delay

- **Transmitting Load (txload)**

- **Receiving Load (rxload)**

- Reliability

However, EIGRP uses bandwidth and delay by default. The other factors are off by default. The following snippet shows the values used by DUAL for its calculation:

```
Branch-A#show interfaces gigabitEthernet 0/2
GigabitEthernet0/2 is up, line protocol is up (connected)
  Hardware is CN Gigabit Ethernet, address is 0000.0c41.b003
  Description: WAN interface to HQ
  Internet address is 10.2.1.10/24
  MTU 1500 bytes, BW 1000000 Kbit, DLY 100 usec,
     reliability 255/255, txload 1/255, rxload 1/255
  Encapsulation ARPA, loopback not set
  Keepalive set (10 sec)
  Full-duplex, 100Mb/s, media type is RJ45
```

Figure 8.31 – Interface details

The advantage EIGRP has over other dynamic routing protocols is its ability to calculate a backup loop-free path at the same time it is calculating a primary route to a destination network.

> **Important Note**
> EIGRP is no longer covered in the CCNA 200-301 exam objectives and has moved to the **Cisco Certified Network Professional** (**CCNP**) Enterprise certification level. However, it's worth mentioning in this section.

A loop-free path is one that does not have a layer 3 routing loop on a network. This is very useful in the event a route is unavailable as EIGRP can almost immediately insert the backup loop-free path within the routing table to ensure connectivity.

# Open Shortest Path First

One of the most popular link-state routing protocols is **Open Shortest Path First version 2** (**OSPFv2**). Defined by RFC 1247, OSPFv2 was introduced to the networking industry back in 1991 and since then, it has been widely adopted and implemented in many organizations.

The following are the benefits of using OSPF:

- **Open source**: Being open source allows an organization with mixed vendor equipment to implement OSPF to exchange routing information between the various manufacturers of routers.

- **Scalability**: OSPF can be implemented in a network of any size. Additionally, OSPF can be configured in a hierarchical system where OSPF-enabled routers can be grouped into areas.

- **Secure**: The OSPF routing protocol supports both **Message Digest 5** (**MD5**) and **Secure Hashing Algorithm** (**SHA**) for authentication. This allows two OSPF-enabled routers to authenticate with each other before exchanging OSPF routing details such as network information.

- **Efficiency**: Unlike older dynamic routing protocols, OSPF will only send an update if a change occurs on a network rather than sending periodic updates at specific intervals.

- **Classless**: The OSPF routing protocol supports the use of custom subnet masks and VLSM.

The OSPF routing protocol is made up of various components. These enable the protocol to have a clear idea of the entire network topology when it has to tell the router how to forward a packet.

The following are the OSPF components:

- **Adjacency table**: Before OSPF exchanges routing information with a neighbor router on the network, they both need to establish an OSPF *adjacency* with each other. This adjacency is simply like a mutual handshake indicating that both are willing to share network routes. This adjacency table contains a list of all the *neighbor* routers that have established an adjacency with a local router. This table is sometimes referred to as the *neighbor table*. The `show ip ospf neighbor` command allows you to view the adjacency table.

- **Link-state database**: The **Link-State Database** (**LSDB**) simply contains a list of information about all the OSPF-enabled routers on the network. The LSDB is also used to create the network topology table that OSPF uses to determine the cost of the best path or route to a destination network. The `show ip ospf database` command will allow you to view the contents of the LSDB.

- **Forwarding database**: This is simply the routing table. After the OSPF algorithm, **Shortest Path First** (**SPF**) calculates all the paths to all the destination networks. It will install the best path (route) within the router's routing table. By using the `show ip route` command, you can view the forwarding database.

In the following section, we will take a much deeper dive to further understand the operations of OSPF as a link-state routing protocol.

## OSPF operations

OSPF-enabled routers ensure they all maintain up-to-date information about the entire network topology; this enables OSPF to choose the best path at all times. However, to ensure everything works smoothly, OSPF uses the following sequence of operations between all enabled routers on the network:

1.  OSPF will attempt to establish *neighbor adjacencies* with other OSPF-enabled routers on the network. When OSPF is enabled on a router's interface, it sends a *Hello Packet* every *10 seconds* like a pulse out of its interface. The Hello Packet is simply a way to let a neighbor router know it wants to establish adjacency.

2.  After establishing OSPF adjacencies, the routers will begin to exchange **Link-State Advertisements** (**LSAs**) with their neighbors on the network. These LSAs are simply special OSPF packets that contain information about the cost and state of the directly connected networks on each neighbor router. When an OSPF-enabled router receives an LSA, it will then forward that same LSA to all other directly connected neighbors. This process is repeated until all the routers within the network receive all the LSAs.

3.  Next, all OSPF-enabled routers will use the information contained within the LSAs to build the LSDB. This allows OSPF to virtually see the entire network topology, their interface costs, and their states.

4.  After the LSDB has been built, OSPF executes its SPF algorithm to calculate the best path between networks.

5.  The SPF algorithm then installs the best path to each network within the forwarding database, also known as the routing table.

> **Important Note**
> Keep in mind that if there is a route with a lower AD than OSPF that already exists within the routing table, the OSPF route will not be installed since AD takes priority.

The OSPFv2 routing protocol uses the following layer 2 and layer 3 addresses to exchange information:

- Destination multicast MAC address: `01-00-5E-00-00-05` or `01-00-5E-00-00-06`

- IPv4 multicast address: `224.0.0.5` or `224.0.0.6`

In the next section, we will discuss the various types of OSPF messages that are exchanged between routers on a network.

## OSPF messages

Enabling the OSPF routing protocol on a router's interface is quite simple. As a network professional, you need to understand the technical details that occur in the background in OSPF. The OSPF protocol uses various OSPF packet types to send information to a neighbor router. The following are the OSPF packet types and their descriptions:

- **Type 1**: These are the OSPF Hello Packets that are used to create and maintain the neighbor adjacencies.

- **Type 2**: These are known as **Database Description** (**DBD**) packets. These packets are used to ensure each OSPF-enabled router's LSDB is exactly the same.

- **Type 3**: This type of packet is known as a **Link-State Request** (**LSR**) packet. OSPF-enabled routers use this packet to request further information about any entry in the DBD by simply sending an LSR.

- **Type 4**: This packet is known as the **Link-State Update** (**LSU**). These packets are used by OSPF to respond to LSRs and new routing information.

- **Type 5**: This type of packet is the **Link-State Acknowledgement** (**LSA**). These are sent when an LSU is received from another router.

In the next section, we will learn about the importance of the OSPF Hello Packet.

## OSPF Hello Packet and dead timers

To create and maintain an OSPF adjacency with a neighbor router, Hello Packets are sent every `10` seconds by default to the IPv4 multicast address of `224.0.0.5` and the IPv6 address of `FF02::5`. Sending a Hello Packet constantly creates a pulse that tells a router its neighbor is alive. This does not remove any network from the routing table that belongs to the neighbor router. However, on slower networks, such as those that are defined as non-broadcast multiple access networks, OSPF uses a default Hello timer of `30` seconds.

What would happen if an OSPF-enabled router does not receive a Hello Packet from one of its neighbors within 10 seconds? The neighbor router will be considered down and will be removed from the routing table, its directly connected networks, and its associated routes. However, OSPF has a **Dead timer**, which is 40 seconds by default and 120 seconds for non-broadcast multiple access networks. The Dead timer is simply the time for which an OSPF-enabled router will wait to receive a Hello Packet from its neighbor before declaring the neighbor device is down.

The Hello timer must match between neighbors for an OSPF adjacency to be formed. The following diagram shows two routers. **R1** is using the default OSPF Hello Timer of 10 seconds on its GigabitEthernet 0/1 interface and **R2** is using 11 seconds:

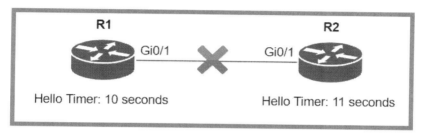

Figure 8.32 – Hello Timer mismatch

Using the show ip ospf interface command, we can verify the Hello and Dead timers on the interface:

```
R2#show ip ospf interface gigabitEthernet 0/1

GigabitEthernet0/1 is up, line protocol is up
  Internet address is 192.168.1.1/30, Area 0
  Process ID 1, Router ID 192.168.1.1, Network Type BROADCAST, Cost: 1
  Transmit Delay is 1 sec, State WAITING, Priority 1
  No designated router on this network
  No backup designated router on this network
  Timer intervals configured, Hello 11, Dead 40, Wait 40, Retransmit 5
    Hello due in 00:00:08
  Index 1/1, flood queue length 0
  Next 0x0(0)/0x0(0)
```

Figure 8.33 – Checking interface timers

The preceding snippet shows that the OSPF Hello Timer has been adjusted to 11 seconds on the interface. OSPF allows us to modify the Hello and Dead timers on each interface on a router. To adjust the Hello Timer and Dead timers, use the following commands:

```
R2(config)#interface gigabitEthernet 0/1
R2(config-if)#ip ospf hello-interval time-in-seconds
R2(config-if)#ip ospf dead-interval time-in-seconds
```

> **Important Note**
> Keep in mind that the de facto standard for the Dead timer is 4 times what it is for the Hello Timer.

In the next section, we will take a look at the various OSPF interface states and their descriptions.

## OSPF interface states

Before OSPF establishes an adjacency with a neighbor, the OSPF-enabled interface on a router has to transition between various operational states. These states are used when creating neighbor adjacencies, exchanging routing details, calculating the best path to a destination network, and ensuring all routers converge.

The following is the sequence of an interface as it reaches convergence:

1. Down: At this state, the router sends Hello Packets but hasn't received any Hello Packets from any neighbor routers.

2. Init: Hello Packets are received from a neighbor router.

3. Two-way: This state indicates there is a two-way communication between two routers.

4. ExStart: This state indicates that the link is a point-to-point network and the router negotiates which interface will send the DBD.

5. Exchange: This state is where routers exchange DBD packets on the network.

6. Loading: Within this state, LSR and LSU packets are exchanged between routers to gain more information about routes. The SPF algorithm processes all the routes to calculate the best path to destination networks.

7. Full: This state indicates that all the routers have converged and know about all the networks, interface costs, and routers.

To verify the OSPF interface states, use the `show ip ospf neighbor` command, as shown in the following snippet:

```
Branch-C#show ip ospf neighbor

Neighbor ID    Pri   State          Dead Time   Address      Interface
3.3.3.3        1     2WAY/DROTHER   00:00:35    10.2.1.15    GigabitEthernet0/2
2.2.2.2        1     FULL/BDR       00:00:35    10.2.1.10    GigabitEthernet0/2
4.4.4.4        1     FULL/DR        00:00:35    10.2.1.5     GigabitEthernet0/2
Branch-C#
```

Figure 8.34 – Verifying OSPF interface states

In the next section, we will learn how OSPF uses interface bandwidth to choose its best path.

## OSPF interface cost

OSPF is a link-state routing protocol, which means it uses cumulative bandwidth as its metric to determine the most cost-efficient path to a destination network. OSPF uses the following formula to calculate its path cost:

```
Cost = reference bandwidth / interface bandwidth
```

Firstly, you'll need to determine the default reference bandwidth on a router. This can be done by using the `show ip ospf` command, as shown in the following snippet:

```
Number of areas transit capable is 0
External flood list length 0
IETF NSF helper support enabled
Cisco NSF helper support enabled
Reference bandwidth unit is 100 mbps          ◄──────
    Area BACKBONE(0)
        Number of interfaces in this area is 2
        Area has no authentication
        SPF algorithm last executed 00:00:42.221 ago
        SPF algorithm executed 3 times
        Area ranges are
        Number of LSA 3. Checksum Sum 0x018A6A
        Number of opaque link LSA 0. Checksum Sum 0x000000
        Number of DCbitless LSA 0
        Number of indication LSA 0
        Number of DoNotAge LSA 0
        Flood list length 0
```

Figure 8.35 – Reference bandwidth

As shown in the preceding snippet, the default reference bandwidth is set to `100`. Next, we can use the `show interfaces` command to obtain the bandwidth value on an interface, as shown in the following snippet:

```
Branch-A#show interfaces GigabitEthernet 0/2
GigabitEthernet0/2 is up, line protocol is up
  Hardware is iGbE, address is 0ce5.e030.2302 (bia 0ce5.e030.2302)
  Description: Connected to WAN
  Internet address is 10.2.1.10/24     ◄──────
  MTU 1500 bytes, BW 1000000 Kbit/sec, DLY 10 usec,
     reliability 255/255, txload 1/255, rxload 1/255
  Encapsulation ARPA, loopback not set
```

Figure 8.36 – Interface bandwidth

Now, we can substitute our values in our formula:

```
Cost = 100 / 1000000
```

The result rounds to 1. We can verify the cost of an OSPF-enabled interface like so:

```
Branch-A#show ip ospf interface GigabitEthernet 0/2
GigabitEthernet0/2 is up, line protocol is up
  Internet Address 10.2.1.10/24, Area 0, Attached via Network Statement
  Process ID 1, Router ID 2.2.2.2, Network Type BROADCAST, Cost: 1
  Topology-MTID    Cost    Disabled    Shutdown    Topology Name
       0            1         no          no           Base
  Transmit Delay is 1 sec, State BDR, Priority 1
  Designated Router (ID) 4.4.4.4, Interface address 10.2.1.5
  Backup Designated router (ID) 2.2.2.2, Interface address 10.2.1.10
  Timer intervals configured, Hello 10, Dead 40, Wait 40, Retransmit 5
```

Figure 8.37 – OSPF cost

As expected, the OSPF cost on this interface is 1. OSPF calculates the cost of each interface on all the routers between all networks, then uses the path that has the overall least cost as the best path to a destination network.

Interface costs can be manually adjusted simply by using the following commands:

```
R2(config)#interface gigabitEthernet 0/1
R2(config-if)#ip ospf cost value-in-kilobits
```

In the next section, we will cover the concepts of the **Designated Router (DR)** and **Backup Designated Router (BDR)**.

## Designated router

As mentioned previously, each OSPF-enabled router has established an adjacency with its neighbors before they can share network routes. Once the adjacencies have been established, Hello Packets are continuously exchanged between neighbors. But what if a router has multiple adjacencies on the same interface?

Let's take a look at the following diagram, where each router has an adjacency to every other router:

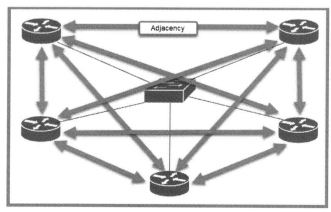

Figure 8.38 – OSPF adjacencies

In the preceding diagram, all the routers share a single multi-access network via the switch. In such situations, each router will be sending Hello Packets to all other routers. If there's a topology change, the routers will flood updates to all routers as well.

> **Tip**
> To calculate the number of adjacencies on a multi-access network, use the formula $N(N - 1)/2$, where $N$ is the number of routers.

Having so many adjacencies causes extensive flooding of LSAs across the network, thus creating an unnecessarily high number of OSPF adjacencies. To help solve this issue, OSPF assigns a DR and a BDR on the network.

All other routers that are not a DR or BDR become a **DROTHER**. Each DROTHER will create an adjacency to the DR and the BDR only. Each router will send its Hello Packet to both the DR and BDR. When the DR receives the packet from another router, the DR sends the packet to all other routers that require the message. Therefore, a DROTHER will have two adjacencies only: one adjacency to the DR and another to the BDR. This concept reduces the number of unnecessary adjacencies and flooding of link-state messages across the network.

## Router ID

A Router ID is required by each router to participate in an OSPF domain. Router IDs can be assigned manually or automatically by the router. The Router ID is used to uniquely identify a router and participate in the DR and BDR election process.

The Router ID is taken in the following order of precedence:

1. The Router ID is manually configured via the `router ospf` mode.

2. An IPv4 loopback interface is configured and the IPv4 address of this interface is then used as the Router ID.

3. As the last resort, OSPF will use the highest active configured IPv4 address on the router's interfaces.

The following snippet shows how to configure the Router ID using the loopback interface on the router and how to manually configure it within the router `ospf` mode:

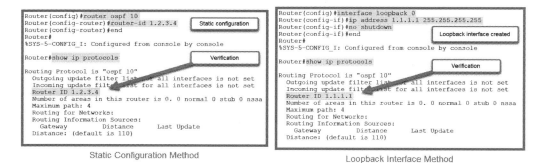

Static Configuration Method          Loopback Interface Method

Figure 8.39 – Router ID configuration

To reset the Router ID, use the `clear ip ospf process` command within privileged mode.

The Router ID plays a key role during the DR and BDR election process. In the next section, we will take a look at how OSPF makes its choice in electing a DR on the network.

## DR and BDR election process

In this section, we will cover the OSPF **DR** and **BDR** election process thoroughly. Let's imagine there are five OSPF-enabled routers all sharing a single broadcast network. Each router has been manually configured with a unique 32-bit Router ID, as shown in the following diagram:

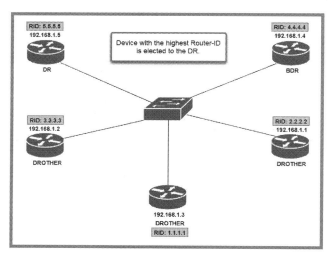

Figure 8.40 – DR and BRD election process – part 1

By default, the router with the highest Router ID is elected as the DR, while the router with the second highest router ID is elected **BDR**. All other routers will take the role of being **DROTHER**.

Let's imagine the **DR** goes down. The BDR will take the role of becoming the new **DR** within the network, while the **DROTHER** with the highest router ID will now become the new **BDR**, as shown in the following diagram:

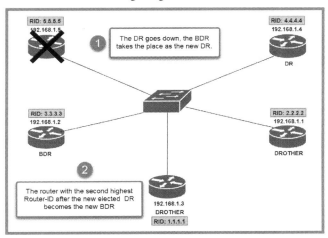

Figure 8.41 – DR and BRD election process – part 2

What if the original **DR** comes back online? Does it regain the role of **DR** on the network? The answer is no – it becomes a **DROTHER** simply because the election process has ended. The following diagram shows the effect of this situation:

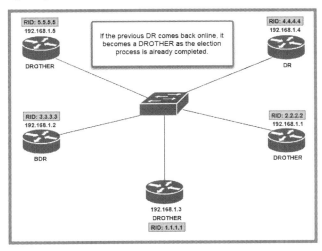

Figure 8.42 – DR and BRD election process – part 3

In another situation, what if a new router with a higher Router ID than the **DR** is inserted into the network? Would the new router with the higher router ID become the new **DR**? As with the previous scenario, since the election process has ended, the new router will be a **DROTHER**, as shown in the following diagram:

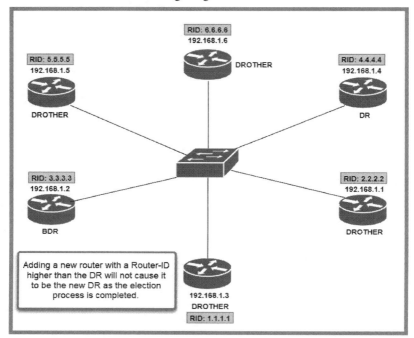

Figure 8.43 – DR and BRD election process – part 4

Having completed this section, you have gained the essential skills to predict the election of a **DR** and a **BDR** on a multiaccess network. In the next section, we'll discuss how to configure OSPFv2 on a Cisco IOS router.

## OSPFv2 commands

Let's imagine we have to enable the OSPF routing protocol to share routing information on the following network topology:

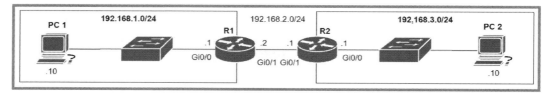

Figure 8.44 – Simple network

We can begin by enabling OSPF on **R1**. First, you'll need to access `router ospf` mode by using the following syntax:

```
R1(config)#router ospf process-id
```

`process-id` is a numerical value that ranges from `1-65535` and does not have to be the same on other OSPF-enabled routers on the network.

When configuring a dynamic routing protocol, you only advertise your directly connected networks. On **R1**, there are two directly connected networks: `192.168.1.0/24` and `192.168.2.0/24`. To advertise these two networks, we can use the following syntax:

```
R1(config-router)#network network-ID wildcard-mask area area-id
```

> **Important Note**
> OSPF-enabled routers have the functionality to be segmented into multiple areas to ensure their routing table is kept small, as well as to reduce the amount of LSAs that are being exchanged on a network. This functionality is referred to as **Multi-Area OSPF**. Area 0 is defined as the backbone area and you should always start with `Area 0` on your network. Cisco recommends that all other OSFP areas should be directly connected to `Area 0`. However, Multi-Area OSPF is beyond the scope of the CCNA 200-301 exam objectives.

When using the `network` command to advertise a network, OSPF does not allow you to specify a subnet mask; instead, it uses a wildcard mask. A wildcard mask is simply the inverse of a subnet mask. Let's say we have to represent the `255.255.255.0` as subnet mask a wildcard. Here, we use the following calculations:

| | | | | |
|---|---|---|---|---|
| Broadcast Address | 255 | 255 | 255 | 255 |
| Subnet Mask | − 255 | 255 | 255 | 0 |
| Wildcard Mask | 0 | 0 | 0 | 255 |

Figure 8.45 – Wildcard mask calculations

The broadcast IP address, which is `255.255.255.255` here, is used at all times with the subnet mask of the network ID. As shown in the preceding snippet, the subnet mask is subtracted from the broadcast IP address and the result is the wildcard mask.

To advertise the directly connected networks on **R1**, we use the following command:

```
R1(config-router)#network 192.168.1.0 0.0.0.255 area 0
R1(config-router)#network 192.168.2.0 0.0.0.255 area 0
```

Additionally, you can choose to enable OSPF on a specific interface. To do this, use the following commands:

```
R1(config-router)#network 192.168.1.1 0.0.0.0 area 0
```

```
R1(config-router)#network 192.168.2.2 0.0.0.0 area 0
```

Each zero (0) within an octet on the wildcard simply tells the router to match the corresponding octet within the Network ID. Therefore, the preceding sets of commands imply that OSPF will only be enabled on interfaces that match/assigned the IP addresses; that is, 192.168.1.1 and 192.168.2.2. Therefore, OSPF will not be enabled on an interface with an IP address of 192.168.1.129/25.

Once OSPF has been enabled on a router interface, it is recommended to prevent OSPF messages from entering and leaving interfaces that are not connected to another OSPF neighbor router. Such interfaces include those that are connected to the internet and the LAN interfaces that have switches and end users.

To prevent OSPF messages from entering and leaving an interface, use the following command:

```
R1(config-router)#passive-interface GigabitEthernet 0/0
```

Please keep in mind that this command also prevents OSPF Hello Packets from being sent and received on the interface, and therefore prevents OSPF adjacency from forming on this interface.

To manually configure the Router ID on **R1**, use the router-id command, as follows:

```
R1(config-router)#router-id 1.1.1.1
```

To adjust the global reference bandwidth on OSPF, use the following syntax:

```
R1(config-router)#auto-cost reference-bandwidth ?
  <1-4294967>  The reference bandwidth in terms of Mbits per
second
```

On Cisco 2911 routers, this is set to 100 Mbps. To change the default to 1 Gbps, use the following command in router ospf mode:

```
R1(config-router)#auto-cost reference-bandwidth 1000
```

This configuration must be applied to all other OSPF-enabled routers on the network to ensure OSPF makes accurate calculations to determine the best path and routes.

Now that you have learned about the essential commands needed to implement OSPF on a network, we will get hands-on with some labs.

# Lab – configuring OSPFv2

In this hands-on lab, you will learn how to implement the OSPF routing protocol to automatically populate the routing table on each Cisco router, as well as calculate the best path to each remote network. The following topology is the same one we used in the previous labs in this chapter:

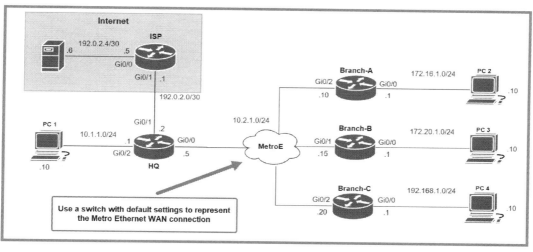

Figure 8.46 – IPv4 OSPF routing lab topology

Feel free to create a new copy of the lab file, but ensure you have removed any static routes from the routing table of each router. If there are static routes while we are configuring the OSPF routing protocol, the OSPF routes will not be installed in the routing table of any route since static routes have an Administrative Distance of 1, whereas OSPF has a value of 110.

To get started with configuring OSPF in our topology, use the following instructions:

1.  First, we will begin by configuring the **HQ** router so that it uses OSPF to automatically learn remote networks. To begin, enter the router's OSPF mode using a process-ID of 1:

```
HQ(config)#router ospf 1
```

2. Manually set the `router-id` value to 4.4.4.4:

```
HQ(config-router)#router-id 4.4.4.4
```

3. As a security measure, disable LSAs or OSPF packets from going out of all the interfaces:

```
HQ(config-router)#passive-interface default
```

4. Use the `network` command to advertise the networks that are directly connected to **HQ** and use the default area value of 0:

```
HQ(config-router)#network 10.1.1.0 0.0.0.255 area 0
HQ(config-router)#network 10.2.1.0 0.0.0.255 area 0
```

5. Allow OSPF packets/LSAs to only be sent out of interfaces that have another OSPF-enabled router:

```
HQ(config-router)#no passive-interface GigabitEthernet
0/0
HQ(config-router)#exit
```

If the `passive-interface` command is applied to the WAN interface, it will not be able to form an adjacency with the other OSPF-enabled routers. This is because this prevents Hello Packets from entering and leaving the interface. Now that you have configured OSPF on the HQ router, we will do the same for the other branch routers.

6. Next, use the following commands on the **Branch-A** router to enable the OSPF routing protocol:

```
Branch-A(config)#router ospf 1
Branch-A(config-router)#router-id 2.2.2.2
Branch-A(config-router)#passive-interface default
Branch-A(config-router)#network 172.16.1.0 0.0.0.255 area
0
Branch-A(config-router)#network 10.2.1.0 0.0.0.255 area 0
Branch-A(config-router)#no passive-interface
GigabitEthernet 0/2
Branch-A(config-router)#exit
```

7.  To configure the **Branch-B** router, use the following configurations:

```
Branch-B(config)#router ospf 1
Branch-B(config-router)#router-id 3.3.3.3
Branch-B(config-router)#passive-interface default
Branch-B(config-router)#network 172.20.1.0 0.0.0.255 area
0
Branch-B(config-router)#network 10.2.1.0 0.0.0.255 area 0
Branch-B(config-router)#no passive-interface
GigabitEthernet 0/1
Branch-B(config-router)#exit
```

8.  Let's not forget about the **Branch-C** router! Use the following configurations to enable OSPF:

```
Branch-C(config)#router ospf 1
Branch-C(config-router)#router-id 1.1.1.1
Branch-C(config-router)#passive-interface default
Branch-C(config-router)#network 192.168.1.0 0.0.0.255
area 0
Branch-C(config-router)#network 10.2.1.0 0.0.0.255 area 0
Branch-C(config-router)#no passive-interface
GigabitEthernet 0/2
Branch-C(config-router)#exit
```

At this point, each branch network can intercommunicate. However, we cannot forget about setting up a default route to the internet.

9.  To configure a default route on **HQ** that points toward the internet, use the following commands:

```
HQ(config)#ip route 0.0.0.0 0.0.0.0 192.0.2.1
```

10. Let's use OSPF to automatically propagate the default route to all other OSPF-enabled routers from **HQ**:

```
HQ(config)#router ospf 1
HQ(config-router)#default-information originate
HQ(config-router)#exit
```

By using the `default-information originate` command, the default route will be automatically distributed to all other OSPF-enabled routers. This saves you time that would be spent manually configuring a default route on each router within your topology and network.

11. Lastly, to simulate our internet connection properly, let's create a default route from the **ISP** router back to **HQ**:

```
ISP(config)#ip route 0.0.0.0 0.0.0.0 192.0.2.2
```

Having completed this lab, you have gained the hands-on skills you need to deploy the OSPF routing protocol in a real-world network environment using Cisco routers. In the next section, we will learn how to perform troubleshooting when using the OSPF routing protocol.

## Validating OSPF configurations

As a network professional, we always need to verify our configurations on our devices. We can start by taking a look at the routing table and ensuring each router has routes to all remote networks, as well as a route that points to the internet.

The following snippet shows the routing table of the **Branch-A** router:

```
Branch-A#show ip route
Gateway of last resort is 10.2.1.5 to network 0.0.0.0

     10.0.0.0/8 is variably subnetted, 3 subnets, 2 masks
O       10.1.1.0/24 [110/2] via 10.2.1.5, 00:37:01, GigabitEthernet0/2
C       10.2.1.0/24 is directly connected, GigabitEthernet0/2
L       10.2.1.10/32 is directly connected, GigabitEthernet0/2
     172.16.0.0/16 is variably subnetted, 2 subnets, 2 masks
C       172.16.1.0/24 is directly connected, GigabitEthernet0/0
L       172.16.1.1/32 is directly connected, GigabitEthernet0/0
     172.20.0.0/24 is subnetted, 1 subnets
O       172.20.1.0/24 [110/2] via 10.2.1.15, 00:33:19, GigabitEthernet0/2
O    192.168.1.0/24 [110/2] via 10.2.1.20, 00:32:11, GigabitEthernet0/2
O*E2 0.0.0.0/0 [110/1] via 10.2.1.5, 00:30:01, GigabitEthernet0/2
```

Figure 8.47 – The Branch-A routing table

In the preceding snippet, we can see that all the remote networks are learned and populated within the routing table via the OSPF routing protocol. Furthermore, the last route is the default route from the **HQ** router that we propagate using the `default-information originate` command. This is why our **Branch-A** router has a gateway of last resort that has been set automatically via OSPF.

Another important troubleshooting command you must know about is the `show ip protocols` command. Whenever we are using a dynamic routing protocol such as OSPF, EIGRP, or RIP, the `show ip protocols` command will always present details about the protocols running on the local router.

Let's take a look at the following snippet:

```
Branch-A#show ip protocols
                                        process-id
Routing Protocol is "ospf 1"
  Outgoing update filter list for all interfaces is not set
  Incoming update filter list for all interfaces is not set
  Router ID 2.2.2.2
  Number of areas in this router is 1. 1 normal 0 stub 0 nssa
  Maximum path: 4
  Routing for Networks:
    172.16.1.0 0.0.0.255 area 0
    10.2.1.0 0.0.0.255 area 0
```

Figure 8.48 – OSPF process-id

From the output, we can determine the following about the routing protocol:

- The OSPF routing protocol is currently enabled on the **Branch-A** router.

- OSPF is currently using the `process-id` value of 1. Please note that the `process-id` value does not need to match between OSPF-enabled routers.

- `router-id` was manually configured as 2.2.2.2.

- If there are multiple routes to the same network that have the same cost value (metric), OSPF will load-balance up to a total of four paths.

- The **Branch-A** router is advertising that it has two networks: 10.2.1.0/24 and 172.16.1.0/24.

Let's take a look at the remaining portions of the `show ip protocols` output:

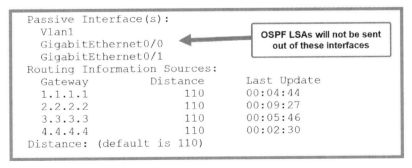

```
Passive Interface(s):
  Vlan1                           OSPF LSAs will not be sent
  GigabitEthernet0/0              out of these interfaces
  GigabitEthernet0/1
Routing Information Sources:
  Gateway          Distance      Last Update
  1.1.1.1               110      00:04:44
  2.2.2.2               110      00:09:27
  3.3.3.3               110      00:05:46
  4.4.4.4               110      00:02:30
Distance: (default is 110)
```

Figure 8.49 – Analyzing the routing protocol

We can determine the following based on the preceding snippet:

- The interfaces listed under **Passive Interface(s)** will not send or receive any OSPF messages.

- The local router is sharing routes with additional OSPF-enabled routers, their AD, and their last update timer.

The `show ip ospf neighbor` command provides us with details about OSPF-enabled neighbor devices:

```
Branch-A#show ip ospf neighbor


Neighbor ID     Pri    State            Dead Time    Address       Interface
4.4.4.4          1     FULL/DR          00:00:34     10.2.1.5      GigabitEthernet0/2
3.3.3.3          1     FULL/BDR         00:00:38     10.2.1.15     GigabitEthernet0/2
1.1.1.1          1     2WAY/DROTHER     00:00:31     10.2.1.20     GigabitEthernet0/2
Branch-A#
```

Figure 8.50 – OSPF neighbors

The following is a breakdown of each column from the `show ip ospf neighbor` output:

- The **Neighbor ID** column contains a list of OSPF neighbors that have an adjacency with the local router. This value is the Router ID.

- The **Pri** column contains the priority value for each neighbor adjacency.

- The **State** column contains the link status for each OSPF neighbor adjacency.

- The Dead timer is used to indicate when a Hello Packet was last received from each neighbor. This timer always counts down and refreshes whenever the local router receives a Hello Packet.

- The **Address** column contains the actual IP address assigned on the neighbor's interface.

- The **Interface** column displays the local interface used to create an adjacency with the neighbor router.

The `show ip ospf interface` command can be used to verify the following details about OSPF:

- The OSPF `process-id` associated with the OSPF-enabled interface on the router
- The OSPF `router-id` value
- The DR and its IP address

- The BDR and its IP address

- The OSPF Hello and Dead timers values on the interface

- The number of OSPF adjacencies that exists on this interface

The following snippet shows the output of using the `show ip ospf interface` command on **Branch-A**:

```
Branch-A#show ip ospf interface GigabitEthernet 0/2

GigabitEthernet0/2 is up, line protocol is up
  Internet address is 10.2.1.10/24, Area 0
  Process ID 1, Router ID 2.2.2.2, Network Type BROADCAST, Cost: 1
  Transmit Delay is 1 sec, State DROTHER, Priority 1
  Designated Router (ID) 4.4.4.4, Interface address 10.2.1.5
  Backup Designated Router (ID) 3.3.3.3, Interface address 10.2.1.15
  Timer intervals configured, Hello 10, Dead 40, Wait 40, Retransmit 5
    Hello due in 00:00:09
  Index 2/2, flood queue length 0
  Next 0x0(0)/0x0(0)
  Last flood scan length is 1, maximum is 1
  Last flood scan time is 0 msec, maximum is 0 msec
  Neighbor Count is 3, Adjacent neighbor count is 2
    Adjacent with neighbor 4.4.4.4  (Designated Router)
    Adjacent with neighbor 3.3.3.3  (Backup Designated Router)
  Suppress hello for 0 neighbor(s)
Branch-A#
```

Figure 8.51 – Verifying OSPF interface details

Another useful command to check whether the interface on a router is participating in OSPF is the `show ip ospf interface brief` command. This command only works on the actual Cisco IOS devices and not on Cisco Packet Tracer. The link will provide you with details about an interface. Let's take a look at the following snippet, which was taken from the **Branch-A** router:

```
Branch-A#show ip ospf interface brief
Interface    PID   Area        IP Address/Mask       Cost  State  Nbrs F/C
Gi0/2        1     0           10.2.1.10/24          1     BDR    3/3
Gi0/0        1     0           172.16.1.1/24         1     DR     0/0
Branch-A#
```

Figure 8.52 – OSPF interfaces

The first row indicates that `GigabitEthernet 0/2` is participating in the OSPF instance, which has a Process ID of 1 and states that the interface belongs to OSPF `Area 0`, which is the backbone area. Additionally, the IP address and subnet mask are provided, as well as the OSPF cost on the interface and the OSPF state on the interface.

Lastly, we must not forget to test end-to-end connectivity on our lab network. The following snippet shows a ping test from the **Branch-A** LAN interface (172.16.1.1) to the server at 192.0.2.6. The following command will work only on the actual Cisco IOS and not on Cisco Packet Tracer:

```
Branch-A#ping 192.0.2.6 source 172.16.1.1
Type escape sequence to abort.
Sending 5, 100-byte ICMP Echos to 192.0.2.6, timeout is 2 seconds:
Packet sent with a source address of 172.16.1.1
!!!!!
Success rate is 100 percent (5/5), round-trip min/avg/max = 9/14/23 ms
Branch-A#
```

Figure 8.53 – Connectivity test

This allows you to specify a source IP address, so that you can use the source IP address from an interface on the router that is attempting to establish connectivity between remote networks.

Now that you have completed this section, you have the knowledge and hands-on skills to describe, configure, troubleshoot, and validate OSPF and its configurations on a Cisco environment.

# Understanding first hop redundancy

Let's imagine that, within your organization, each device is configured to use a specific IP address as its default gateway to the internet. What if that IP address or device goes offline? How will your client devices reach the internet?

The following diagram shows the default gateway going down, thus preventing clients from reaching the internet:

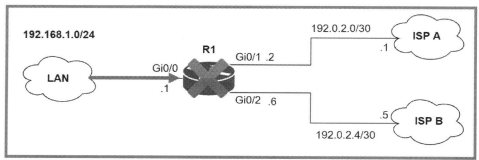

Figure 8.54 – Default gateway goes offline

You may be thinking, we can replace the router with another and apply the same configurations to it and our internet connectivity will be restored. This is a workable solution, but it's not too efficient because it's a reactive solution and requires too many interventions.

What if we could implement redundancy on the default gateway to ensure that, if the main router goes down, there's another device that will act as the new default gateway, without us having to change the default gateway's IP address on any of the clients? This is definitely possible with a Cisco IOS router.

The technology known as **First Hop Redundancy Protocol (FHRP)** allows us to use two Cisco IOS routers to create a single virtual router that has a virtual IP address and virtual MAC address. The virtual IP address and virtual MAC address will be shared between the two physical routers. Additionally, the virtual IP address will act as the default gateway for clients. Therefore, one physical router will have a role as the active router, which will route traffic back and forth to the internet, and the other physical router will be the standby router in the event the Active router goes offline, taking up the role as the new active router with the virtual IP address.

The following diagram shows **R1** as the Active router:

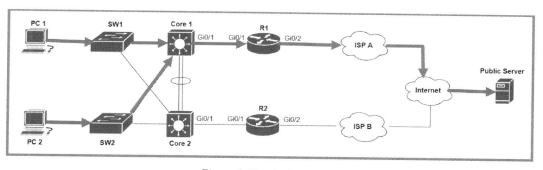

Figure 8.55 – Active router

In the event **R1** goes down in the network topology, the Standby router will take up the role as the Active router on the network. This causes very little service interruption as the failover happens. The following diagram shows the traffic flow when **R2** becomes the new Active router on the network:

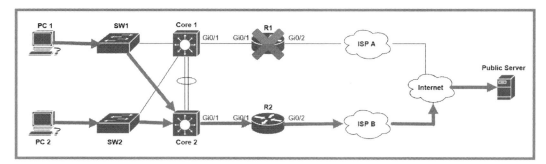

Figure 8.56 – New Active router

Using an FHRP is a better solution as it's proactive and does not require a network professional's intervention. There are a few FHRPs that exist in the industry. We'll look at their characteristics in the next section.

# Various FHRPs

The following sub-section will briefly outline the characteristics of each FHRP that can be implemented in a network to ensure that internal host devices are always able to reach their default gateway.

## Hot Standby Router Protocol

The **Hot Standby Router Protocol** (**HSRP**) is a Cisco-proprietary FHRP that allows a number of Cisco IOS routers to be grouped into a cluster to create a virtual router. The virtual router will have a virtual IP address that will be shared between all physical routers that are part of the HSRP group.

The following are the two states of an HSRP router:

- Active
- Standby

The Active router is one that is actively forwarding the packet as the default gateway. In the event that the Active router goes offline, the Standby router will assume the role of being the new Active router and traffic will be routed through the new Active router.

The following table outlines the differences between HSRP version 1 and version 2:

| Version 1 | Version 2 |
|---|---|
| Enabled by default on Cisco IOS 15 | Not enabled by default |
| Supports group numbers between 0 to 255 | Support group numbers between 0 to 4095 |
| Uses multicast address of 224.0.0.2 | Uses multicast address of 224.0.0.102 |
| Uses virtual MAC address range 0000.0C07.AC00 to 0000.0C07.ACFF | Uses virtual MAC address range from 0000.0C9F.F000 to 0000.0C9F.FFFF for IPv4 and 0005.73A0.0000 through 0005.73A0.0FFF for IPv6 addresses |
| Does not support authentication | Uses MD5 for authentication |

Figure 8.57 – HSRP versions

When configuring HSRP, the router with the highest IPv4 address will be selected as the Active router within the group, while all others will be Standby routers. The default HSRP priority is 100 on all routers; the router with the highest HSRP priority value will be elected as the Active router. The preempt command enables preemption and forces an HSRP re-election process. This should be done to ensure a specific router becomes the Active router.

> **Important Note**
> By default, preemption is disabled in HSRP.

Since preemption is disabled, the router that boots up first will take the role of being the Active router. HSRP uses Hello Packets that are sent every 3 seconds by default. If a Standby router does not receive a Hello Packet from the Active router after 10 seconds, it will assume that the Active router is down and take up the role of being the new Active router. Furthermore, there is HSRP for IPv6 networks. This version of HSRP has the same functionality as its IPv4 version.

## Lab – implementing HSRP

In this hands-on lab, you will learn how to implement HSRP as the preferred FHRP on a Cisco environment, ensuring the default gateway is always available. The following topology can be built within the Cisco Packet Tracer application:

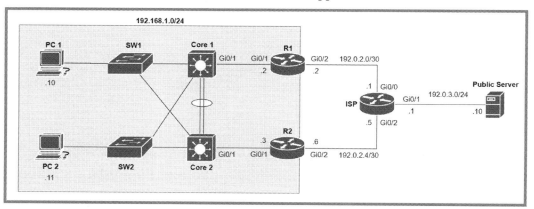

Figure 8.58 – HSRP lab topology

Please ensure you use the following guidelines when running this lab to ensure you get the same results:

- Assign the IP addresses shown in the topology to each device accordingly.
- Each router interface must be configured as shown in the topology.
- Configure the default gateway on both PCs as 192.168.1.1.
- Ensure the default gateway on the **Public Server** is set to 192.0.3.1.
- Create an EtherChannel using LACP between **Core 1** and **Core 2** using ports FastEthernet 0/23 and 0/24 on both switches.

Now that your lab is ready, use the following instructions to create a virtual router using HSRP:

1.  Ensure **R1** and **R2** have the following default routes within their routing tables:

```
R1(config)#ip route 0.0.0.0 0.0.0.0 192.0.2.1
R2(config)#ip route 0.0.0.0 0.0.0.0 192.0.2.5
```

2.  On **R1**, enable HSRP version 2 on the LAN interface on the router using the following commands:

```
R1(config)#interface GigabitEthernet 0/1
R1(config-if)#standby version 2
```

3.  Next, create the virtual IP address that will be used as the default gateway for clients on the network:

```
R1(config-if)#standby 1 ip 192.168.1.1
```

4.  Set the HSRP priority number to be greater than 100 to ensure this router becomes the Active (desired) router by using the following command:

```
R1(config-if)#standby 1 priority 150
```

5.  Configure this router to preempt the standby router:

```
R1(config-if)#standby 1 preempt
R1(config-if)#exit
```

Now that you have configured **R1** as the active router, let's head on over to **R2** as it requires some configuration in order to become the Standby router within the HSRP group. The Standby router will take the place of the Active router in the event **R1** goes down or offline. To configure **R2** as the Standby router, use the following instructions:

1.  On the R2 LAN interface, enable HSRP version 2:

```
R2(config)#interface GigabitEthernet 0/1
R2(config-if)#standby version 2
```

2.  Next, configure the virtual IP address of the default gateway:

```
R2(config-if)#standby 1 ip 192.168.1.1
R2(config-if)#exit
```

3.  Lastly, to ensure the internet side portion of our lab is working, configure the following default routes on the **ISP** router:

```
ISP(config)#ip route 0.0.0.0 0.0.0.0 192.0.2.2
ISP(config)#ip route 0.0.0.0 0.0.0.0 192.0.2.6 2
```

Now that you have finished the configuration aspect of this lab, let's take a look at validating and troubleshooting the configurations on our lab environment.

One of the most important troubleshooting commands for HSRP is the `show standby` command. The output of this command provides us with vital information about the HSRP status on the local router, such as the following:

- The HSRP router's state, whether it's Active or Standby
- The virtual IP address and MAC address for the virtual router
- The Hello and Hold down timers on the interface
- Whether preempt has been configured on the interface or not
- Whether the local router is the Active or Standby router
- The IP address of the Standby router
- The HSRP priority value

The following snippet shows the output of the `show standby` command on **R1** in our lab:

```
R1#show standby
GigabitEthernet0/1 - Group 1 (version 2)
  State is Active
    15 state changes, last state change 00:21:43
  Virtual IP address is 192.168.1.1
  Active virtual MAC address is 0000.0C9F.F001
    Local virtual MAC address is 0000.0C9F.F001 (v2 default)
  Hello time 3 sec, hold time 10 sec
    Next hello sent in 0.638 secs
  Preemption enabled
  Active router is local
  Standby router is 192.168.1.3, priority 100 (expires in 9 sec)
  Priority 150 (configured 150)
  Group name is hsrp-Gig0/1-1 (default)
R1#
```

Figure 8.59 – HSRP status on R1

Let's take a look at the `show standby` command's output on **R2**. You'll notice that the state of **R2** is set to `Standby` and that the Active router in the group is `192.168.1.1`, which is **R1**'s IP address:

```
R2#show standby
GigabitEthernet0/1 - Group 1 (version 2)
  State is Standby
    13 state changes, last state change 00:22:03
  Virtual IP address is 192.168.1.1
  Active virtual MAC address is 0000.0C9F.F001
    Local virtual MAC address is 0000.0C9F.F001 (v2 default)
  Hello time 3 sec, hold time 10 sec
    Next hello sent in 1.031 secs
  Preemption disabled
  Active router is 192.168.1.2, priority 150 (expires in 8 sec)
    MAC address is 0000.0C9F.F001
  Standby router is local
  Priority 100 (default 100)
  Group name is hsrp-Gig0/1-1 (default)
R2#
```

Figure 8.60 – HSRP status on R2

Furthermore, to see a summary HSRP status on either router, use the `show standby brief` command:

```
R1#show standby brief
                 P indicates configured to preempt.
                 |
Interface   Grp  Pri P State     Active          Standby         Virtual IP
Gig0/1      1    150 P Active    local           192.168.1.3     192.168.1.1
R1#
```

Figure 8.61 – HSRP status summary

The `show standby brief` command's output provides us with the local interface that's been configured with HSRP, the HSRP group number, the HSRP priority value, the interface state, the HRSP router state, the standby router, and the virtual IP address of the virtual router.

For our final connectivity test, let's perform a traceroute from **PC 1** (`192.168.1.10`) to the Public Server at `192.0.3.10`:

```
C:\>tracert 192.0.3.10

Tracing route to 192.0.3.10 over a maximum of 30 hops:

  1    1 ms      0 ms      0 ms      192.168.1.2
  2    0 ms      0 ms      1 ms      192.0.2.1
  3    1 ms      0 ms      0 ms      192.0.3.10

Trace complete.
```

Figure 8.62 – Traceroute connectivity test

According to the output shown in the preceding snippet, the packet took the path via **R1** as the Active router within the HSRP group, as expected.

Let's create a network failure by shutting down `GigabitEthernet 0/1` and `GigabitEthernet 0/2` on **R1** only. This will create the effect of **R1** going offline on the network. After a few seconds, perform another traceroute test from **PC 1** to the server once more.

The following are the new traceroute results when **R1** has gone offline:

```
C:\>tracert 192.0.3.10

Tracing route to 192.0.3.10 over a maximum of 30 hops:

  1    1 ms      0 ms      0 ms      192.168.1.3
  2    0 ms      0 ms      0 ms      192.0.2.5
  3    0 ms      0 ms      1 ms      192.0.3.10

Trace complete.
```

Figure 8.63 – New traceroute results

**R2** has assumed the role of being the Active router within the HSRP group, and the packets are now taking a new path via **R2** (192.168.1.3) to reach the **Public Server**. The default gateway configured on the client devices remains as 192.168.1.1.

Having completed this section, you have gained hands-on experience with configuring first hop redundancy using HSRP. You created a virtual router to ensure the internal devices on the corporate LAN can access the internet. In the next section, we will configure VRRP to provide redundancy for our default gateway.

## Virtual Router Redundancy Protocol

The **Virtual Router Redundancy Protocol** (**VRRP**), currently at version 2, is a vendor-neutral FHRP that also supports grouping together two or more physical routers to create a virtual router on an IPv4 network. VRRPv2 allows multiple routers to join the VRRP group and share the same virtual IP address to provide default gateway redundancy on an enterprise network.

> **Important Note**
> Preemption is enabled by default in VRRP.

VRRP uses the following two router states:

- Master
- Backup

The Master router is the one that currently has the responsibility of acting as the default gateway and forwarding packets back and forth between networks. The Backup router takes the role of Master only in the event of the actual Master router going offline.

Additionally, VRRPv3 supports first hop redundancy on an IPv6 network environment and is a bit more scalable compared to VRRPv2.

## Lab – implementing VRRP

In this hands-on lab, you will learn how to implement VRRP on a Cisco environment to ensure the default gateway is always available. The following topology is the same as we have used in the previous labs in this chapter. However, you will need either physical Cisco routers or Cisco IOSv images to complete this lab:

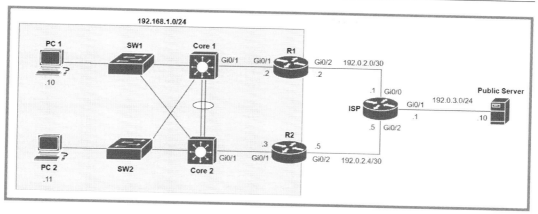

Figure 8.64 – VRRP lab

Follow the same guidelines that you followed for the lab for HSRP when running this lab to ensure you get the same results.

Now that your lab is ready, use the following instructions to create a virtual router using VRRP:

1.  Ensure **R1** and **R2** have the following default routes within their routing tables:

    ```
    R1(config)#ip route 0.0.0.0 0.0.0.0 192.0.2.1
    R2(config)#ip route 0.0.0.0 0.0.0.0 192.0.2.5
    ```

2.  On **R1**, enter interface mode and use the following command to create the VRRP group and virtual IP:

    ```
    R1(config)#interface GigabitEthernet 0/1
    R1(config-if)#vrrp 1 ip 192.168.1.1
    ```

    > **Important Note**
    > The VRRP commands are very similar to those of HSRP.

3.  On **R2**, enter interface mode, set the VRRP group to 1, and configure the virtual router IP address:

    ```
    R2(config)#interface GigabitEthernet 0/1
    R2(config-if)#vrrp 1 ip 192.168.1.1
    ```

4. To ensure the internet side portion of our lab is working, configure the following default routes on the **ISP** router:

```
ISP(config)#ip route 0.0.0.0 0.0.0.0 192.0.2.2
ISP(config)#ip route 0.0.0.0 0.0.0.0 192.0.2.6 2
```

Now that you have finished with the configuration aspect of this lab, let's take a look at validating and troubleshooting our configurations on our lab environment.

5. Next, using the show vrrp command on **R1**, we can verify that **R1** is the *Backup* router:

```
R1#show vrrp
GigabitEthernet0/1 - Group 1
  State is Backup
  Virtual IP address is 192.168.1.1
  Virtual MAC address is 0000.5e00.0101
  Advertisement interval is 1.000 sec
  Preemption enabled
  Priority is 100
  Master Router is 192.168.1.3, priority is 100
  Master Advertisement interval is 1.000 sec
  Master Down interval is 3.609 sec (expires in 2.774 sec)
```

Figure 8.65 – Verifying VRRP

**R1** has the lower IPv4 address, 192.168.1.2, configured on the VRRP LAN interface, whereas **R2** has the higher IPv4 address of 192.168.1.3. **R2** was elected to be the Master router and **R1** became the Backup router. Furthermore, you can see the virtual IPv4 and MAC addresses that the clients will be using as the default gateway.

6. Let's use the show vrrp brief command to verify additional VRRP details:

```
R1#show vrrp brief
Interface      Grp Pri Time  Own Pre State    Master addr    Group addr
Gi0/1          1   100 3609      Y   Backup   192.168.1.3    192.168.1.1
R1#
```

Figure 8.66 – The show vrrp brief command's output

The show vrrp brief command provides us with the interface that is using VRRP, the VRRP group number, the VRRP interface priority value, the VRRP router state, the Master IP address, and the virtual group IP address.

7.   Lastly, the following snippet shows the output of `show vrrp` on **R2**:

```
R2#show vrrp
GigabitEthernet0/1 - Group 1
  State is Master
  Virtual IP address is 192.168.1.1
  Virtual MAC address is 0000.5e00.0101
  Advertisement interval is 1.000 sec
  Preemption enabled
  Priority is 100
  Master Router is 192.168.1.3 (local), priority is 100
  Master Advertisement interval is 1.000 sec
  Master Down interval is 3.609 sec
```

Figure 8.67 – VRRP output on R2

The output shows that **R2** is definitely the Master router within the VRRP group and has the same virtual IP and MAC addresses. Furthermore, we can verify that preemption is indeed enabled by default on VRRP-enabled routers and has a default priority of `100`.

Having completed this lab, you have gained hands-on experience with implementing VRRP as an FHRP on a Cisco environment. In the next section, you will learn how to implement and configure GLBP for load balancing.

## Gateway Load Balancing Protocol

The **Gateway Load Balancing Protocol** (**GLBP**) is a bit different from the aforementioned FHRPs. GLBP allows load balancing between the routers that are part of the GLBP group. To put this simply, if you have two physical routers within a GLBP group, traffic that is sent to the default gateway IP address will be load-balanced between all the routers using a round-robin technique.

> **Important Note**
> GLBP is another Cisco-proprietary FHRP. Preemption is disabled by default on GLBP.

GLBP ensures that one router does not handle all the load and constraints of being the default gateway; it allows the other routers to share the load as well. GLBP uses the following router statuses:

- Active
- Standby

Similarly to HSRP, the Active router is the one that has the current role as the default gateway, while the Standby router provides failover in the event that the Active router goes down. GLBP for IPv6 supports this implementation within an IPv6 environment.

## Lab – implementing GLBP

In this hands-on lab, you will learn how to implement GLBP on a Cisco environment to ensure the default gateway is always available. The following topology is the same one that we used in the previous labs in this chapter. However, you will need either physical Cisco routers or Cisco IOSv images to complete this lab:

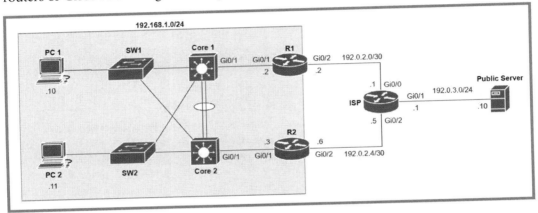

Figure 8.68 – GLBP lab

Please follow the same guidelines that you did in the HSRP lab when running this lab to ensure you get the same results.

Now that your lab is ready, use the following instructions to create a virtual router using GLBP:

1.  Ensure **R1** and **R2** have the following default routes within their routing tables:

    ```
    R1(config)#ip route 0.0.0.0 0.0.0.0 192.0.2.1
    R2(config)#ip route 0.0.0.0 0.0.0.0 192.0.2.5
    ```

2.  On **R1**, enter interface mode and use the following command to create the GLBP group and set the virtual router IP address:

    ```
    R1(config)#interface GigabitEthernet 0/1
    R1(config-if)#glbp 1 ip 192.168.1.1
    ```

3. On **R2**, enter interface mode, set the GLBP group to 1, and configure the virtual router IP address:

```
R2(config)#interface GigabitEthernet 0/1
R2(config-if)#glbp 1 ip 192.168.1.1
```

4. Lastly, to ensure the internet side of our lab is working, configure the following default routes on the **ISP** router:

```
ISP(config)#ip route 0.0.0.0 0.0.0.0 192.0.2.2
ISP(config)#ip route 0.0.0.0 0.0.0.0 192.0.2.6 2
```

Now that you have finished the configuration part of this lab, let's take a look at validating and troubleshooting the configurations on our lab environment, as shown in the following steps:

1. Use the show glbp command to verify the GLBP state, as shown in the following snippet:

```
R1#show glbp
GigabitEthernet0/1 - Group 1
  State is Active
    1 state change, last state change 00:01:08
  Virtual IP address is 192.168.1.1
  Hello time 3 sec, hold time 10 sec
    Next hello sent in 1.696 secs
  Redirect time 600 sec, forwarder timeout 14400 sec
  Preemption disabled
  Active is local
  Standby is 192.168.1.3, priority 100 (expires in 7.808 sec)
  Priority 100 (default)
  Weighting 100 (default 100), thresholds: lower 1, upper 100
  Load balancing: round-robin
  Group members:
    0c32.2d2f.c901 (192.168.1.2) local
    0c32.2dd8.7301 (192.168.1.3)
  There are 2 forwarders (1 active)
```

Figure 8.69 – GLBP output

From the preceding snippet, we can determine **R1** is the Active router within the GLBP group, the default GLBP priority is 100, and that preemption is disabled by default.

2. Let's use the show glbp brief command to verify the status of the local interfaces on **R1**:

```
R1#show glbp brief
Interface  Grp  Fwd Pri State   Address         Active router  Standby router
Gi0/1      1    -   100 Active  192.168.1.1     local          192.168.1.3
Gi0/1      1    1   -   Active  0007.b400.0101  local          -
Gi0/1      1    2   -   Listen  0007.b400.0102  192.168.1.3    -
R1#
```

Figure 8.70 – The show glbp brief command's output

The output provides us with various GLBP details, such as the interfaces that are participating in GLBP group 1, the virtual IP router's IP address, and which devices are the Active and Standby routers.

Having completed this lab, you have gained the essential skills required to implement GLBP within a Cisco environment.

# Summary

In this chapter, we've discussed and demonstrated how to establish IP connectivity between remote networks using Cisco routers. Having completed this chapter on IP connectivity, you have gained the skills to set up both static and dynamic routing on an enterprise network to ensure end-to-end connectivity. Furthermore, you've learned how to propagate a default router through a Cisco environment, which allows users to reach the internet from their client device.

I hope this chapter has been informative for you and is helpful in your journey toward learning how to implement and administrate Cisco solutions and prepare for the CCNA 200-301 certification. In the next chapter, *Chapter 9, Configuring Network Address Translation (NAT)*, we will learn how to implement various types of network address translation on a Cisco router.

# Questions

The following is a short list of review questions to help reinforce your learning and help you identify areas you might need to work on:

1. What is the default Administrative Distance of a static route?

    A. `0`

    B. `1`

    C. `2`

    D. `90`

2. Which of the following commands will allow you to configure a static route?

    A. `network`

    B. `route`

    C. `ip`

    D. `ip route`

3.  Which command will allow a router to perform IPv6 routing?

    A. `enable ipv6 routing`

    B. `ipv6 router`

    C. `ipv6 unicast-routing`

    D. `ipv6 enable`

4.  Which IPv4 address represents a default route?

    A. `0.0.0.0 255.255.255.255`

    B. `0.0.0.0 0.0.0.0`

    C. `255.255.255.255 255.255.255.255`

    D. `255.255.255.255 0.0.0.0`

5.  What is the Administrative Distance of the OSPF?

    A. `110`

    B. `120`

    C. `90`

    D. `170`

6.  Which routing protocol is used between ISPs?

    A. IS-IS

    B. OSPF

    C. BGP

    D. MPLS

7.  Which command allows you to view the forwarding database in OSPF?

    A. `shows ip ospf interface brief`

    B. `show ip ospf interface`

    C. `show ip ospf database`

    D. `show ip route`

8.  What is the default Hello Timer in OSPF?

    A. `30`

    B. `10`

    C. 5

    D. 15

9.  Which command allows you to verify the HSRP status on a router?

    A. `show hsrp`

    B. `show router standby`

    C. `show running-config`

    D. `show standby`

10. Which FHRP is open source?

    A. VRRP

    B. HSRP

    C. GLBP

    D. ICMP

# Further reading

The following links are recommended for additional reading:

- Understanding static routing: `https://www.cisco.com/c/en/us/td/docs/switches/datacenter/sw/5_x/nx-os/unicast/configuration/guide/l3_cli_nxos/l3_route.html`

- RIP routing: `https://www.cisco.com/c/en/us/td/docs/ios-xml/ios/iproute_rip/configuration/15-mt/irr-15-mt-book/irr-cfg-info-prot.html`

- EIGRP routing: `https://www.cisco.com/c/en/us/td/docs/ios-xml/ios/iproute_eigrp/configuration/15-mt/ire-15-mt-book/ire-enhanced-igrp.html`

- OSPF routing: `https://www.cisco.com/c/en/us/td/docs/ios-xml/ios/iproute_ospf/configuration/xe-16/iro-xe-16-book/iro-cfg.html`

- Understanding HSRP: `https://www.cisco.com/c/en/us/td/docs/switches/lan/catalyst3750x_3560x/software/release/12-2_55_se/configuration/guide/3750xscg/swhsrp.html`

# Section 4:
# IP Services

This section teaches you the importance of various network services that are critical to daily operations. You will then learn how to implement various services using industry best practices on networks. Furthermore, you will learn how to troubleshoot each service as you are taken through each section and chapter.

This section contains the following chapters:

- *Chapter 9, Configuring Network Address Translation (NAT)*
- *Chapter 10, Implementing Network Services and IP Operations*

# 9
# Configuring Network Address Translation (NAT)

How do devices on private networks access the internet? **Network address translation (NAT)** is what connects the magic between the private and public networks. In this chapter, you will learn about the various types of NAT and how to implement static NAT, dynamic NAT, and **port address translation (PAT)** on a Cisco network. You will also learn how to implement NAT to ensure that you have internet connectivity on an enterprise network.

In this chapter, we will cover the following topics:

- The challenge of using IPv4 on the internet
- Understanding NAT
- Types of NAT
- Configuring PAT
- Configuring static NAT with port forwarding
- Implementing dynamic NAT

# Technical requirements

To follow along with the exercises in this chapter, please ensure that you have met the following hardware and software requirement:

- Cisco Packet Tracer: `https://www.netacad.com`

The code files for this chapter are available at `https://github.com/PacktPublishing/Implementing-and-Administering-Cisco-Solutions/tree/master/Chapter%2009`.

Check out the following video to see the Code in Action: `https://bit.ly/3clR4Qr`

# The challenge of using IPv4 on the internet

One of the many issues we face is that there aren't enough public IPv4 addresses to assign to each unique device on the internet. As you learned in *Chapter 3, IP Addressing and Subnetting*, each device that is directly connected to the internet must be assigned a unique IP address. Furthermore, there are 232 public IPv4 addresses, which means that there are approximately 4,294,967,296 public IPv4 addresses that are routable on the internet. This number seems huge, but the reality is that most internet-connected devices have already been assigned a public IPv4 address and the rest of the public IPv4 pool is reserved by various organizations for special use.

In the world today, there are more than 4 billion devices connected to the internet. How is it possible to have more devices online than the number of available public IPv4 addresses? RFC 1918 defines three classes of IPv4 addresses that are assignable on private networks and are not routable on the internet.

The following table shows the private IPv4 address classes:

| Class | Network Address Block | Address Range |
|-------|----------------------|---------------|
| A | 10.0.0.0/8 | 10.0.0.0 - 10.255.255.255 |
| B | 172.16.0.0/12 | 172.16.0.0 - 172.31.255.255 |
| C | 192.168.0.0/24 | 192.168.0.0 - 192.168.255.255 |

Figure 9.1 – Private IPv4 address classes

Each class of private IPv4 address needs to be unique between organizations and private networks. Each organization can use whichever class of private IPv4 address they see fit. Each class of private IPv4 address provides a range of usable IPv4 addresses per network, ranging from 254 to over 16 million usable addresses.

RFC 1918 addresses allow an organization of any size to assign one of these addresses to a unique device without needing to assign a public IPv4 address to each device. Therefore, these addresses are strictly for use on private computer networks only.

The **Internet Assigned Numbers Authority (IANA)** has designated these specific IPv4 classes as private and nonroutable on the internet. **Internet Service Providers (ISPs)** have implemented security mechanisms, such as **access-control lists (ACLs)**, to prevent RFC 1918 addresses from entering the ISP network and the internet.

Another important concern is how, since RFC 1918 addresses are nonroutable on the internet, does a device with a private IPv4 address communicate and access resources on the internet? In the next section, we will discuss how devices that are on private networks are able to communicate on the internet.

# Understanding NAT

A device that is assigned a private IPv4 address is not able to simply communicate with devices on the internet on its own—it needs some assistance. For example, your computer or smart device is mostly likely assigned a private IPv4 address on your network, but it's able to connect to devices on the internet. This is because of something called NAT. NAT makes our lives in networking that bit easier as it allows a router to *translate* a private address into a public address. Let's take a look at the following diagram to get a clear idea of how NAT really works:

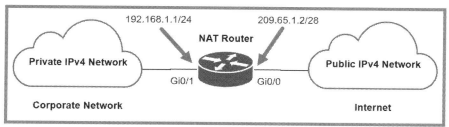

Figure 9.2 – NAT topology

In the preceding figure, there are two networks—a corporate network and the internet—and in between both is a **NAT router**. Let's imagine that there is a device on the corporate network, **PC 1**, with an IP address of 192.168.1.10. **PC 1** wants to send a message to a device on the internet, let's say a Cisco web server at 23.10.104.199. The following are the actions taken by the router:

1. **PC 1** sends the message to its default gateway, the router in our topology.

2. When the packet is received by the router, the Layer 3 header is inspected to determine the destination IP address.

3. Since the destination address is a public IP address, the router will translate the source IP address from 192.168.1.10 to the router's public IP address of 209.65.1.2. This process is known as NAT.

4. After the NAT process is completed, the router forwards the packet to its destination, 23.10.104.199.

If another device on the corporate network wishes to communicate with another device on the internet, then the process is repeated. Devices on the internet do not see the corporate, private network. They only see the internet IP address of 209.65.1.2. Therefore, the returning traffic will be sent to the 209.65.1.2 address and the router will reverse the translation process and forward the message back to **PC 1**.

A feature such as NAT allows us to conserve the IPv4 public address space, allowing us to assign a single public IPv4 address per organization or private network owner. A simple example is your home modem, which has a single public IPv4 address assigned to its internet-facing interface (port) and on the internal side of your home network; you're using a private address scheme with many devices being NATed through that single public IP address. The same concept applies to organizations with hundreds of devices on their private network; they all have a single public IPv4 address via NAT on their internet router or modem.

> **Important note**
> The primary benefit of using NAT is to conserve the public IPv4 address space.

There are many advantages of using NAT on a network. The following are the key benefits of using NAT:

- The primary benefit is the conservation of the public IPv4 address space.

- NAT allows the flexibility of using pools of addresses, such as public IPv4 addresses for load-balancing traffic to the internet. This feature ensures the reliability of connections to public networks such as the internet.

- NAT hides users and devices that are using RFC 1918 addressing schemes. In other words, NAT prevents users and devices that are located on the internet from seeing into your private network—instead, they will only see your public IP address.

- NAT allows the network administrators to maintain consistency for their internal network addressing standards. This allows all internal devices to use RFC 1918 addresses without having to be assigned a public IPv4 address to access the internet. The NAT router handles the translations of addresses between the internal and public networks.

While there are clear advantages to using NAT, we must also understand that NAT has some disadvantages on a network, such as the following:

- One of the major disadvantages of using NAT is related to the degradation of network performance on various types of network traffic, such as **voice over IP (VoIP)**. As traffic passes through a NAT-enabled router, there is some delay as the router has to perform the address translation process. As each packet enters the router, the router has to inspect the Layer 3 header of each packet to determine whether to perform NAT before forwarding the packet to its destination.

- Another important disadvantage to note is that end-to-end addressing is lost with NAT. As a packet passes through NAT-enabled routers, the source IP address of the packet is changed, and this makes it harder to trace the actual source or sender of a packet.

- **Virtual private network (VPN)** technologies, such as **IP security (IPSec)**, do not work well with NAT. Since NAT modifies the Layer 3 header of packets, it causes a major problem for IPSec VPNs trying to establish a secure tunnel between remote branches.

Now that we have understood the basics of NAT, let's look at its operation and terminology.

## Understanding NAT operation and terminology

In the world of Cisco and NAT, there are a few terms that are used to help us identify whether an IPv4 address is on the private network or the public network. In this section, you will learn about the NAT terminology.

Let's inspect the following figure to better understand NAT operations:

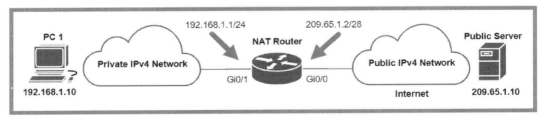

Figure 9.3 – Simple NAT operations

In the preceding network topology, there are two types of networks: the private network, which is typically the corporate network owned by an organization, and the public network known as the internet. By default, the Cisco IOS router does not know which type of network **PC 1** or the server belongs to. All the router knows is that there are two different IPv4 networks and its job is to forward packets between them. However, when we as humans look at the topology here, we can simply say that **PC 1** is on the private network with a private IPv4 address class that is nonroutable on the internet, while the public server has a public IPv4 address and is on the internet.

The main question now, when the router has to perform NAT operations by translating the private IPv4 address into a public address, is how does the router know which side of the network each IP address belongs to? To understand this, we must first identify the **inside address** and the **outside address**.

The inside address is the IP address that is to be translated by the router. In the previous topology, we can identify the inside address as any address on the private or internal network. The outside address is simply the address of the destination device. So, if the PC is attempting to communicate with the server, then the outside address is 209.65.1.10; however, as simple as it seems, the router does not see this as plainly as we do. Furthermore, NAT uses the local and global parameters to tell the router additional details about the addresses that are to be translated. The local address is any IP address that is on the inside network while the global address is any address on the public side of the network.

To explore this further, let's take a look at the following figure:

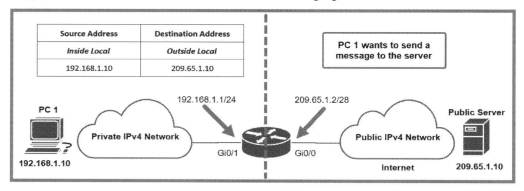

Figure 9.4 – NAT process part 1

In the preceding diagram, **PC 1** has created a message for the **public server**. When NAT is enabled on the Cisco IOS router, it sees the **inside local** address as 192.168.1.10 and the **outside local** address as the destination device, which is 209.65.1.10. The address as shown in the preceding figure is prior to the NAT process.

The following figure shows the results after the address has been translated by NAT:

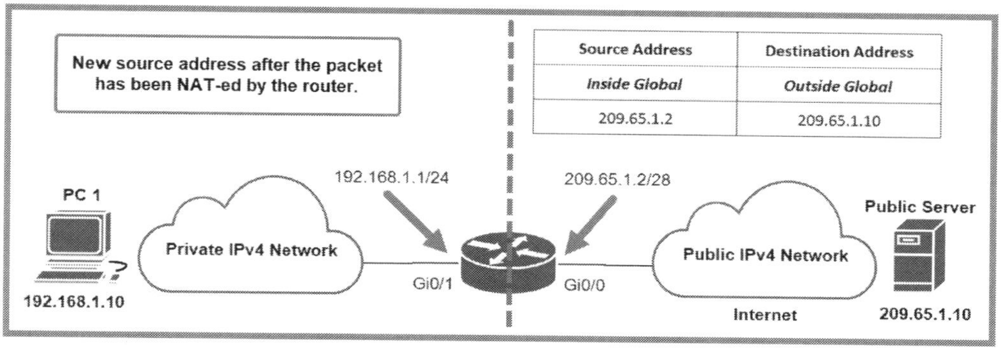

Figure 9.5 – NAT process part 2

When the packet enters the router, the process of NAT takes place. The router takes a look at the source and destination address. If the destination address belongs to the global network, then the router performs NAT on the **inside local** address, converting it to the **inside global** address. In other words, NAT translates the private IPv4 address of the PC to the public IPv4 address on the router's interface.

> **Important note**
> The **outside local** and **outside global** addresses are usually the same IP address. These addresses are those that belong to the destination device.

In the next section, we will discuss the various types of NAT, their uses, and how to configure each one on a Cisco IOS router.

# Types of NAT

There are many types of NAT translations. Each type has its own advantages, disadvantages, and real-world use. In this section, you will learn about their characteristics and operations, and how to configure each type of NAT on a Cisco IOS router.

## Static NAT

Static NAT uses a *one-to-one* mapping of the inside local address with the inside global address. This type of NAT mapping does not change—as the name implies, the mapping remains constant. This type of NAT is very useful when you want to allow external users on the internet to access a device such as a web server that sits on your internal private network in your organization.

Let's imagine that your organization has a web server located on a private network and you are tasked to allow users from the internet access to the server. To complete this task, you can create a one-to-one static mapping between the web server's private IP address (inside local) and the public IP address on the router (inside global). This will allow anyone on the internet to simply enter the public IP address (inside global) on their web browser and, when the router receives traffic, it will simply forward it to the inside local address, which is the server.

The following figure shows how **PC 2** is able to access the internal web server via static NAT:

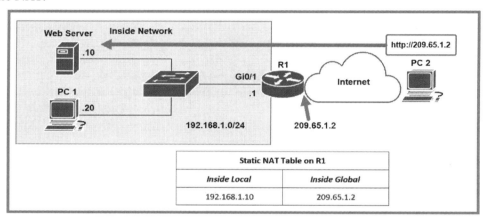

Figure 9.6 – Static NAT

The devices that are on the internet, such as **PC 2**, will not see the **inside local** address of the server—they will only see the **inside global** address. Additionally, devices on the internet will not be aware that the router is performing NAT in the background.

To configure static NAT on a Cisco IOS router, go through the following instructions:

1.  Configure the inside interface on the router. This interface is connected to the inside network:

    ```
    Router(config)#interface interface-ID
    Router(config-if)#ip nat inside
    Router(config-if)#exit
    ```

2.  Configure the outside interface. This interface is connected to the outside network:

    ```
    Router(config)#interface interface-ID
    Router(config-if)#ip nat outside
    Router(config-if)#exit
    ```

3.  Create the map between the **inside local** address and the **inside global** address:

```
Router(config)#ip nat inside source static inside-local-ip inside-
global-ip
```

Now, let's see how dynamic NAT works.

# Dynamic NAT

Dynamic NAT uses a pool of inside global addresses that are automatically translated on a first-come first-served basis by the NAT-enabled router. Unlike static NAT, which manually creates a static mapping between an inside local address and an inside global address, dynamic NAT allows you to allocate a range of available addresses via a NAT pool.

Let's say that your company has a range of public IPv4 addresses allocated to your organization by the local ISP, and you want to allow a small IP subnet of end devices to use any address with the allocated range when communicating with the outside network. Dynamic NAT simply allows you to create an ACL to specify which IP subnets are allowed to use the range (pool) of public IP addresses.

The following figure shows a router that is configured with a range of public IPv4 addresses:

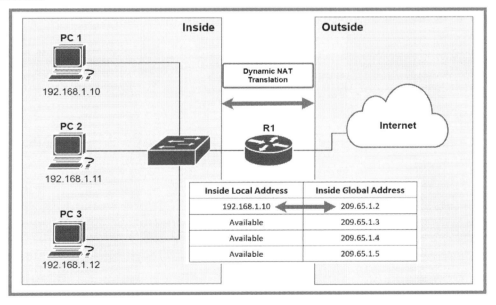

Figure 9.7 – Dynamic NAT

The outside interface of the router is configured with a NAT pool of addresses ranging from 209.65.1.2–209.65.1.5. These addresses are allocated for use by the inside network. When **PC 1** communicates on the outside network, the router checks the NAT pool for an available IPv4 address and translates the inside local address to an available **inside global** address. In this situation, the **inside local** address is 192.168.1.10, which will then be translated to 209.65.1.2. If another device, such as **PC 2** (192.168.1.11), wants to communicate over the internet (outside network), then the process is repeated, and this time the router will use the next available address from the pool, 209.65.1.3.

The disadvantage of dynamic NAT is that since each address in the pool can be mapped to only one inside local address, the number of addresses in the pool is limited. Therefore, if more devices on the inside network are attempting to simultaneously communicate on the outside network, the pool of available addresses will become exhausted.

When dynamic mapping occurs, it is only temporary for the duration of the session between the inside device and the destination device. The router monitors for inactivity in dynamic NAT. When it detects that dynamic NAT translation is no longer being used, it will make the inside global address available for future translations.

> **Important note**
> The clear ip nat translation * command will allow you to clear all NAT translation on the router.

Keep in mind that if you are implementing dynamic NAT within your network, you should ensure that there are enough public IP addresses to satisfy the number of simultaneous sessions that will be generated by the inside network.

To configure Dynamic NAT on a Cisco IOS router, use the following instructions:

1. Configure the inside interface on the router. This interface is connected to the inside network:

```
Router(config)#interface interface-ID
Router(config-if)#ip nat inside
Router(config-if)#exit
```

2. Configure the outside interface. This interface is connected to the outside network:

```
Router(config)#interface interface-ID
Router(config-if)#ip nat outside
Router(config-if)#exit
```

3. Create a pool of *global inside* addresses to use with dynamic NAT:

```
Router(config)#ip nat pool pool-name start-ip end-ip [netmask
subnet-mask | prefix-length prefix-length]
```

4. Create an ACL to allow the addresses that are to be translated:

```
Router(config)#ip access-list standard access-list-name
Router(config-std-nacl)#permit network-ID wildcard-mask
Router(config-std-nacl)#exit
```

Additionally, you can use the `access-list <acl-number> permit <network-ID> <wildcard-mask>` command to create a numbered standard ACL.

5. Merge the dynamic NAT pool of addresses with the ACL of the address to be translated:

```
Router(config)#ip nat inside source list access-list-name pool
pool-name
```

Next, let's learn about PAT.

## Configuring PAT

PAT, also known as **NAT overload**, differs from both static and dynamic NAT translations. PAT allows a router to translate multiple private IPv4 addresses into a single public address. This type of NAT is commonly used within home networks. The ISP usually assigns a single public IP address to the internet modem/router. The modem is configured with PAT (NAT overload), which translates any number of private addresses on the inside network to the single public address assigned on the modem/router interface on the outside network.

If you recall from previous chapters, when a device wants to initiate a connection with another device, the sender generates either a TCP or UDP source port and destination port, based on the application layer protocol/service. PAT takes advantage of this and keeps track of the port numbers being used for each session and IP address. Within each session, the sender always generates a unique source port with its source IP address; this ensures that the IP-to-port combination is always unique, and thus PAT can track these unique sessions to identify specific NAT translations.

> **Important note**
> PAT also ensures that devices always use unique TCP ports for sessions with web servers on the internet.

To get a better understanding of how PAT works, let's take a look at the following figure. There are two devices on the inside network—**PC 1** and **PC 2**—that want to communicate with the web servers on the internet:

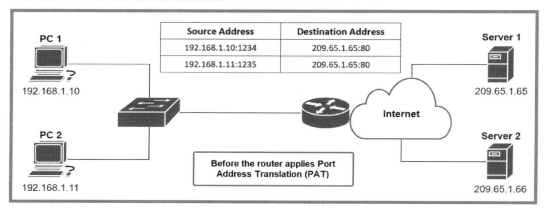

| Source Address | Destination Address |
| --- | --- |
| 192.168.1.10:1234 | 209.65.1.65:80 |
| 192.168.1.11:1235 | 209.65.1.65:80 |

Figure 9.8 – PAT operations

Each device on the inside network sends its message containing the source IP address, source port, destination IP address, and destination port to the router. When the router receives messages on its **inside** interface, it will inspect the destination IP address in the Layer 3 header. Since the destination devices are located on the **outside** network, the router performs PAT. The router translates the **inside local** address to the **inside global** address while keeping track of the port number, as shown in the following figure:

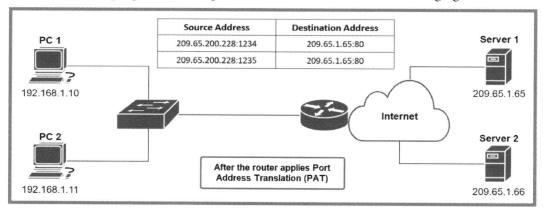

| Source Address | Destination Address |
| --- | --- |
| 209.65.200.228:1234 | 209.65.1.65:80 |
| 209.65.200.228:1235 | 209.65.1.65:80 |

Figure 9.9 – PAT operations

When the message leaves the router's outside interface, it will contain the new source IP address of `209.65.200.228`. Devices on the internet such as the web servers in the preceding figure will see `209.65.200.228` as the sender and not the devices on the inside network (**PC 1** and **PC 2**).

During sessions between the inside and outside network, PAT tries to maintain the original port numbers that are being used; however, if a source port number is already being used by another **inside** device, PAT will attempt to use the next available port number and keep track of the session and translation mapping.

There are two methods to configure PAT (NAT overload) on a Cisco IOS router. The first method configures PAT to use a pool of **inside global** addresses. This method is useful in situations where all port numbers are being used by a single public IP address. PAT then moves on to the next available public IP address within the pool and begins allocating port numbers.

To configure PAT with a pool of addresses, use the following instructions:

1.  Configure the inside interface on the router. This interface is connected to the inside network:

    ```
    Router(config)#interface interface-ID
    Router(config-if)#ip nat inside
    Router(config-if)#exit
    ```

2.  Configure the outside interface. This interface is connected to the outside network:

    ```
    Router(config)#interface interface-ID
    Router(config-if)#ip nat outside
    Router(config-if)#exit
    ```

3.  Create a pool of *global inside* addresses to use with NAT overload:

    ```
    Router(config)#ip nat pool pool-name start-ip end-ip [netmask
    subnet-mask | prefix-length prefix-length]
    ```

4.  Create an ACL to allow the addresses that are to be translated:

    ```
    Router(config)#ip access-list standard access-list-name
    Router(config-std-nacl)#permit network-ID wildcard-mask
    Router(config-std-nacl)#exit
    ```

5.  Merge the dynamic NAT pool of addresses with the ACL of the address for translation using the `overload` keyword:

    ```
    Router(config)#ip nat inside source list access-list-name
    pool pool-name overload
    ```

Additionally, you can also use a numbered standard ACL rather than using a named ACL.

The second method of configuring PAT allows you to translate all inside addresses to a single public IP address. This method is useful when you have only one single public IP address and multiple *inside* devices that require connectivity to the internet.

To configure PAT to use a single inside global address, use the following instructions:

1. Configure the inside interface on the router. This interface is connected to the inside network:

```
Router(config)#interface interface-ID
Router(config-if)#ip nat inside
Router(config-if)#exit
```

2. Configure the outside interface. This interface is connected to the outside network:

```
Router(config)#interface interface-ID
Router(config-if)#ip nat outside
Router(config-if)#exit
```

3. Create a pool of *global inside* addresses to use with NAT overload:

```
Router(config)#ip nat pool pool-name start-ip end-ip [netmask
subnet-mask | prefix-length prefix-length]
```

4. Create an ACL to allow the addresses that are to be translated:

```
Router(config)#ip access-list standard access-list-name
Router(config-std-nacl)#permit network-ID wildcard-mask
Router(config-std-nacl)#exit
```

5. Merge the Dynamic NAT pool of addresses with the interface on the router that has the inside global address:

```
Router(config)#ip nat inside source list access-list-name
interface interface-ID overload
```

Lastly, we can use NAT to perform port forwarding on a Cisco router.

To configure port forwarding on a Cisco IOS router, use the following instructions:

1.  Configure the inside interface on the router. This interface is connected to the inside network:

    ```
    Router(config)#interface interface-ID
    Router(config-if)#ip nat inside
    Router(config-if)#exit
    ```

2.  Configure the outside interface. This interface is connected to the outside network:

    ```
    Router(config)#interface interface-ID
    Router(config-if)#ip nat outside
    Router(config-if)#exit
    ```

3.  Create the map between the *inside local* address and the *inside global* address:

    ```
    Router(config)#ip nat inside source static inside-local-ip local-
    port inside-global-ip global-port
    ```

Having completed this section, you have learned how to configure various types of NAT translations on a Cisco IOS router. In the next section, you will gain hands-on experience of implementing each type of NAT on a Cisco environment.

# Lab – implementing NAT overload (PAT)

In this hands-on lab, you will learn how to implement PAT. The following network topology shows an organization's network to the left of the ISP that is connected to the internet. For this lab, we'll be using Cisco Packet Tracer to build our lab and complete the exercise:

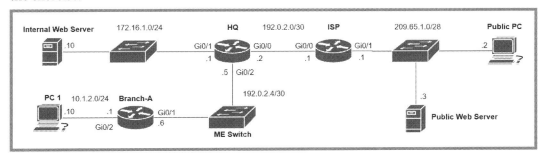

Figure 9.10 – NAT overload topology

The objective of this lab is to configure the HQ router with NAT overload to all devices on the corporate network, such as the **PC 1** private IP address (10.1.2.10/24), to be translated to a public IP address when it's attempting to connect to the **Public Web Server** (209.65.1.3/28).

Please use the following guidelines when creating this lab:

- Assign the IP addresses to each device accordingly, as shown in *Figure 9.10*.

- Use only Cisco 2911 models. Ensure that each interface is configured as shown in the topology.

- Configure each end device with the corresponding IP address, subnet mask, and default gateway, as shown in the topology.

- Configure a default route on HQ to point to the ISP router at 192.0.2.1.

- Configure a default router on the ISP router that points to **HQ** at 192.0.2.2. This is to simulate the internet on the network.

- Enable OSPFv2 on the private network, which is between the **HQ** and **Branch-A** networks. Use OSPF to propagate the default route to the **Branch-A** router.

Now that your lab environment is ready, use the following instructions to configure NAT overload:

1. Configure the *inside* interfaces on the **HQ** router for NAT:

   ```
   HQ(config)#interface GigabitEthernet 0/1
   HQ(config-if)#ip nat inside
   HQ(config-if)#exit
   HQ(config)#interface GigabitEthernet 0/2
   HQ(config-if)#ip nat inside
   HQ(config-if)#exit
   ```

2. Configure the *outside* interface on the **HQ** router for NAT:

   ```
   HQ(config)#interface GigabitEthernet 0/0
   HQ(config-if)#ip nat outside
   HQ(config-if)#exit
   ```

3. Create an ACL with a wildcard mask on the HQ router to only allow the private addresses to be translated via NAT:

```
HQ(config)#ip access-list standard NAT-LIST
HQ(config-std-nacl)#permit 172.16.1.0 0.0.0.255
HQ(config-std-nacl)#permit 10.1.2.0 0.0.0.255
HQ(config-std-nacl)#exit
```

We've used a named ACL called NAT-LIST to help us understand the purpose of the access list on the router.

4. Merge the NAT-LIST ACL to the interface with the public IP address (192.0.2.2):

```
HQ(config)#ip nat inside source list NAT-LIST interface
gigabitEthernet 0/0 ove orload
```

5. On **PC 1**, open the web browser, enter the IP address of the **Public Web Server**, and hit *Enter*:

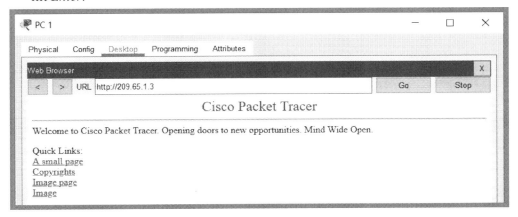

Figure 9.11 – Web page

This is a good indicator of whether **PC 1** has connectivity to the **Public Web Server**.

6. On **HQ**, use the show ip nat translations command to validate the private IP addresses that are being translated to the public IP address using NAT overload or PAT:

```
HQ#show ip nat translations
Pro   Inside global      Inside local       Outside local       Outside global
tcp 192.0.2.2:1025     10.1.2.10:1025     209.65.1.3:80       209.65.1.3:80
```

Figure 9.12 – PAT translations

The translation is using `tcp` as expected, since we access the default web page on the server via HTTP. The **inside global** address is the public IPv4 address on the **outside** interface on **HQ**: `192.0.2.2` with a source port of `1025`. The **inside local** address is the private IPv4 address of **PC 1**: `10.1.2.10` with a source port of `1025`. Both the **outside local** and **outside global** addresses belong to the **Public Web Server**: `209.65.1.3` with a destination port of `80`.

7.  On **HQ**, use the `show ip nat statistics` command to verify the NAT interfaces and pool:

```
HQ#show ip nat statistics
Total translations: 1 (0 static, 1 dynamic, 1 extended)
Outside Interfaces: GigabitEthernet0/0
Inside Interfaces: GigabitEthernet0/1 , GigabitEthernet0/2
Hits: 9  Misses: 1
Expired translations: 0
Dynamic mappings:
```

Figure 9.13 – NAT statistics

The output provides us with information about which interfaces are used as *inside* and *outside* interfaces on the router for NAT, the number of translations that have occurred, and whether there are any dynamic mappings. Since the lab is translating private IPv4 addresses to a single public IPv4 address via the `GigabitEthernet 0/0` interface, there are no dynamic mappings in the output. Additionally, `Total translations` indicates whether the router is using static NAT, dynamic NAT, or extended (NAT overload (or PAT)).

Having completed this lab, you have acquired the skills needed to implement and validate NAT overload (PAT) configurations on a Cisco environment. In the next lab, you will learn how to configure static NAT to perform port forwarding to an internal web server within a private corporate network.

# Lab – implementing static NAT with port forwarding

In this lab, you will learn how to implement static NAT on an organization router to forward traffic that is originating from the internet to an internal private server. This exercise is an extension of the previous lab. We'll be using the following topology and the same guidelines as before:

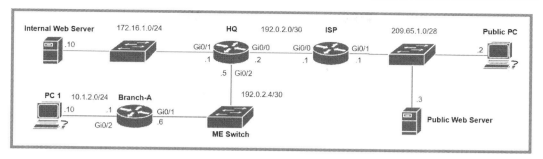

Figure 9.14 – Static NAT with port

The objective of this lab is to allow users (**Public PC**) on the internet to access the internal web server on the private corporate network via NAT. Therefore, when the **Public PC** enters the public IP address into the web browser, the HQ router will translate and forward the traffic to only the internal web server.

To implement static NAT with port forwarding, use the following instructions:

1.  Configure the *inside* interface on the **HQ** router that points to the **internal web server**:

    ```
    HQ(config)#interface GigabitEthernet 0/1
    HQ(config-if)#ip nat inside
    HQ(config-if)#exit
    ```

2.  Configure the *outside* interface on the **HQ** router for NAT:

    ```
    HQ(config)#interface GigabitEthernet 0/0
    HQ(config-if)#ip nat outside
    HQ(config-if)#exit
    ```

3.  Configure a static translation between the *inside global* address and the *inside local* address of the internal web server using the following command. Since it's a web server, use the default service 80:

    ```
    HQ(config)#ip nat inside source static tcp 172.16.1.10 80
    190.0.2.2 80
    ```

    This static mapping will allow any device that is on the internet side of the topology to access the **internal web server** by simply using the public IP address of the **HQ** router: 192.0.2.2 with a destination port of 80.

4.  On **HQ**, use the `show ip nat translations` command to verify the static
    NAT map:

```
HQ#show ip nat translations
Pro  Inside global      Inside local       Outside local      Outside global
tcp 190.0.2.2:80        172.16.1.10:80     ---                ---
```

Figure 9.15 – Static NAT mapping

Whenever you create a static NAT map on a Cisco IOS router, both the inside
global and inside local map are shown within the `show ip nat translations`
output. Keep in mind that if the port numbers were not specified during the
previous step, they won't appear in the preceding snippet.

5.  On **PC 2** (**Public PC**), open the web browser and enter the public IP address of the
    **HQ** router and hit *Enter* to verify that you have connectivity:

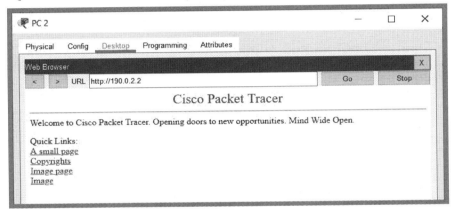

Figure 9.16 – Connectivity test via web browser

The preceding snippet validates that there is connectivity to the internal web server
on the private corporate network from the internet side of the topology.

6.  On **HQ**, use the `show ip nat translations` command to show that the static
    NAT translation is working with port forwarding:

```
HQ#show ip nat translations
Pro  Inside global      Inside local       Outside local      Outside global
tcp 190.0.2.2:80        172.16.1.10:80     ---                ---
tcp 190.0.2.2:80        172.16.1.10:80     209.65.1.2:1029    209.65.1.2:1029
```

Figure 9.17 – Static NAT translations on HQ

As shown in the preceding snippet, NAT is working as expected. The traffic is originating from **PC 2** (**Public PC**) with IP address 209.65.1.2 and the **HQ** router is performing a static NAT translation with port forwarding to the internal web server at 172.16.1.10:80. The public PC is seeing the **internal web server** as 190.0.2.2, but **HQ** translates and forwards the traffic to the private IP address 172.16.1.10.

7.  On **HQ**, use the show ip nat statistics command as shown in the following figure:

```
HQ#show ip nat statistics
Total translations: 2 (1 static, 1 dynamic, 2 extended)
Outside Interfaces: GigabitEthernet0/0
Inside Interfaces: GigabitEthernet0/1 , GigabitEthernet0/2
Hits: 57  Misses: 175
Expired translations: 10
Dynamic mappings:
HQ#
```

Figure 9.18 – NAT statistics

From the output, we can determine that there is a static NAT map on the **HQ** router with two port translations having taken place. Furthermore, the NAT *outside* and *inside* interfaces are displayed as this information helps us determine whether any misconfigurations exist on a NATed interface.

Having completed this lab, you will have learned how to configure a Cisco IOS router to perform static NAT with port forwarding. This exercise also demonstrates how to allow users on the internet to access internal servers on a corporate network, specifically via a service port such as port 80 for the HTTP server, as in our lab. In the next lab, you will learn how to implement dynamic NAT on a Cisco environment.

# Lab – implementing dynamic NAT

In this lab, you will learn how to implement dynamic NAT with a pool of IP addresses. The following network topology shows an organization network (left) that is connected to the internet via the ISP router:

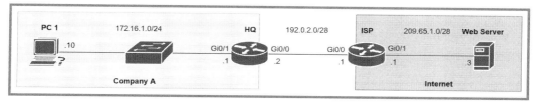

Figure 9.19 – Dynamic NAT topology

The objective of this lab is to allow the IP addresses of devices in the company attempting to communicate on the internet to be translated to an available public IP address, via dynamic NAT, on the **HQ** router.

Please be sure to use the following guidelines when creating this lab to ensure that you get the correct results:

- Assign the IP addresses as shown in the preceding figure to each device accordingly.

- Each router (Cisco 2911 model) interface must be configured as shown in the topology.

- Configure each end device with the corresponding IP address, subnet mask, and default gateway, as shown in the topology.

- Configure a default route on **HQ** to point to the ISP router at 192.0.2.1.

- Configure a default router on the **ISP** router that points to **HQ** at 192.0.2.2. This is to simulate the internet on the network.

To configure Dynamic NAT on a Cisco IOS router, use the following instructions:

1. Configure the inside interfaces on the HQ router for NAT:

```
HQ(config)#interface GigabitEthernet 0/1
HQ(config-if)#ip nat inside
HQ(config-if)#exit
```

2. Configure the outside interface on the HQ router for NAT:

```
HQ(config)#interface GigabitEthernet 0/0
HQ(config-if)#ip nat outside
HQ(config-if)#exit
```

3. Create a NAT pool to specify the range of usable public IP addresses. Begin with the starting IP address of 190.0.2.2 and the ending IP address of 192.0.2.5, and a network mask of 255.255.255.240:

```
HQ(config)#ip nat pool NAT-IPAdd 192.0.2.2 192.0.2.5
netmask 255.255.255.240
```

4. Create an ACL with a wildcard mask on the **HQ** router to only allow the private addresses to be translated via NAT. Use the ACL name `NAT-List`:

```
HQ(config)#ip access-list standard NAT-List
HQ(config-std-nacl)#permit 172.16.1.0 0.0.0.255
HQ(config-std-nacl)#exit
```

5. Merge the ACL list (`NAT-List`) with the NAT IP pool (`NAT-IPAdd`) to create the dynamic mapping:

```
HQ(config)#ip nat inside source list NAT-List pool
NAT-IPAdd
```

6. On **PC 1**, open the web browser, enter the IP address of the **web server**, and hit *Enter*:

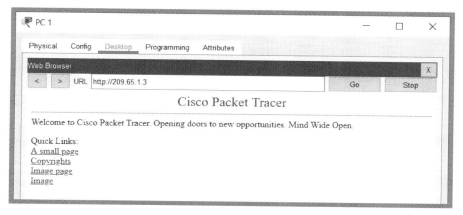

Figure 9.20 – Web server

7. On **HQ**, use `show ip nat translations` to verify whether dynamic NAT is working:

```
HQ#show ip nat translations
Pro  Inside global    Inside local      Outside local     Outside global
tcp 192.0.2.2:1026    172.16.1.10:1026  209.65.1.3:80     209.65.1.3:80
tcp 192.0.2.2:1027    172.16.1.10:1027  209.65.1.3:80     209.65.1.3:80
tcp 192.0.2.2:1028    172.16.1.10:1028  209.65.1.3:80     209.65.1.3:80
tcp 192.0.2.2:1029    172.16.1.10:1029  209.65.1.3:80     209.65.1.3:80
```

Figure 9.21 – Dynamic NAT translations

The output proves that dynamic NAT is working as expected. If another client device on the company side of the network establishes a connection to the web server, then another public IP address will be used from the NAT pool and this will reflect in the translation window.

8.  On **HQ**, use the `show ip nat statistics` command to validate dynamic NAT configurations:

```
HQ#show ip nat statistics
Total translations: 4 (0 static, 4 dynamic, 4 extended)
Outside Interfaces: GigabitEthernet0/0
Inside Interfaces: GigabitEthernet0/1
Hits: 28  Misses: 4
Expired translations: 0
Dynamic mappings:
-- Inside Source
access-list NAT-List pool NAT-IPAdd refCount 4
 pool NAT-IPAdd: netmask 255.255.255.240
        start 192.0.2.2 end 192.0.2.5
        type generic, total addresses 4 , allocated 1 (25%), misses 0
```

Figure 9.22 – Dynamic NAT statistics

The output shows the name of the dynamic NAT pool, the IP ranges and subnet mask, the number of IP addresses that are being used at that point in time (allocated), and the **inside** and **outside** NAT interfaces.

Having completed this lab, you have gained the essential skills needed to configure dynamic NAT in a Cisco environment.

# Summary

In this chapter, we have discussed the important role that **NAT** plays in almost all private networks of all sizes. We explored the characteristics and functions of each type of NAT and in which situations they would be used. By completing this chapter, you have gained both a theoretical understanding of the operations of NAT on an enterprise network, and the hands-on skills to implement static NAT, dynamic NAT, and **PAT** on a Cisco network.

I hope that this chapter has been informative and helps you in your journey toward learning how to implement and administrate Cisco solutions and prepare for the CCNA 200-301 certification. In the next *Chapter 10, Implementing Network Services and IP Operations*, we will learn how to implement the **Network Time Protocol (NTP)**, **Dynamic Host Configuration Protocol** (**DHCP**), and other IP services on a Cisco environment.

# Questions

The following is a short list of review questions to help reinforce your learning and help you identify which areas of your knowledge require some improvement:

1.  Which of the following network addresses are nonroutable on the internet?

    A. `192.167.68.200`

    B. `192.169.87.23`

    C. `172.31.1.5`

    D. `172.32.1.6`

2.  Which of the following is a benefit of using NAT?

    A. Hides users behind a single public IP address

    B. Allows VoIP communication over the internet

    C. Ensures end-to-end connectivity between internal and external devices

    D. Supports IPSec

3.  In terms of NAT, what is defined as the inside address?

    A. The public IP address

    B. The MAC address

    C. The address that is visible on the internet

    D. The address to be translated

4.  How would you describe the address of the destination device?

    A. Inside local

    B. Outside local

    C. Inside global

    D. Outside global

5.  Which type of NAT is recommended for forwarding all traffic to an internal server if a user on the internet knows the public IP address?

    A. Port forwarding

    B. PAT

    C. Dynamic NAT

    D. Static NAT

6.   When configuring NAT, which keyword must be used to tell the router to perform port address translation?

   A. `ip nat`

   B. `overload`

   C. `source`

   D. `static`

7.   Which command tells the router that an interface belongs on the inside network?

   A. `ip nat inside`

   B. `ip nat`

   C. `ip nat internal`

   D. `ip nat enable`

8.   What is another name for **port address translation** (**PAT**)?

   A. NAT port address translation

   B. NAT port

   C. NAT overload

   D. NAT overwork

9.   Which command allows you to see the pool of NAT addresses?

   A. `show nat`

   B. `show ip nat statistics`

   C. `show nat statistics`

   D. `show statistics`

10.  How many inside local addresses can be mapped when using dynamic NAT?

   A. `65,535`

   B. `0`

   C. `1`

   D. None of the options presented here

# Further reading

The following links are recommended for additional reading:

- Network address translation: `https://www.cisco.com/c/en/us/support/docs/ip/network-address-translation-nat/13772-12.html`

- Configuring NAT: `https://www.cisco.com/c/en/us/td/docs/ios-xml/ios/ipaddr_nat/configuration/15-mt/nat-15-mt-book/iadnat-addr-consv.html`

# 10
# Implementing Network Services and IP Operations

The Cisco IOS operating system is filled with many features that we are yet to explore. The operating system contains a wide variety of network services that are designed to provide scalability and flexibility on a network; these features are commonly referred to as IP services. IP services are the essential services each network needs, such as the **Dynamic Host Configuration Protocol** (**DHCP**) to assist with the automatic assignment of IP addresses to client devices, the **Domain Name System** (**DNS**) to resolve hostnames to IP addresses, and even network monitoring and management protocols to provide accountability and visibility on a network.

During the course of this chapter, you will learn how to implement the **Network Time Protocol** (**NTP**) to ensure all devices' clocks are synchronized and that proper timekeeping is maintained on a network. You'll learn how to implement DHCP on a Cisco system to distribute IP configurations to end devices to allow network connectivity, understand the importance of DNS on a network and the vital role it plays on the internet, and configure **Simple Network Management Protocol** (**SNMP**) and Syslog to assist in network management. Lastly, you will learn about the importance of using **Quality of Service** (**QoS**) to improve network performance.

In this chapter, we will cover the following topics:

- Understanding NTP
- Understanding DHCP
- DNS
- Understanding the benefits of using Syslog
- SNMP
- QoS traffic classification

# Technical requirements

To follow along with the exercises in this chapter, please ensure that you have met the following software requirement:

- Cisco Packet Tracer: `https://www.netacad.com`

The code files for this chapter are available at `https://github.com/PacktPublishing/Implementing-and-Administering-Cisco-Solutions/tree/master/Chapter%2010`.

Check out the following video to see the Code in Action: `https://bit.ly/3mKumGp`

# Understanding NTP

Time...what an important role it plays in our daily lives. From helping us measure how long it takes us to arrive at a destination or event to calculating how quickly athletes perform at the Olympic games. Time is simply the measurement between past, present, and future events.

Time is used to help us take account of an event. Timestamps are used on electronic devices, surveillance systems, and computer and networking devices to provide an account of when certain actions and events occur. On an enterprise network, it is critical to ensure proper timekeeping is maintained throughout the organization.

Why is timekeeping a critical factor on a network? Ensuring all devices are configured with accurate time is important for log and event management on an enterprise network. Events occur frequently on networks; in all the labs you've completed thus far, when you make a change on a Cisco device, a Syslog message is generated and presented on the console window. The message usually contains information and specific details about the event that occurred, which is known as a **Syslog** message.

Log messages are generated all the time for various purposes, such as indicating that an interface status may have changed, checking security-related events, and troubleshooting network issues. Time helps us coordinate and gain a better picture of the sequences that occur on a network. Therefore, it is important to ensure all devices' system clocks are accurately configured within the organization. Cisco IOS devices have an internal clock known as the system clock that the device uses as its primary source of timekeeping. The system clock begins ticking when the device boots up.

> **Important note**
>
> By default, the system clock on Cisco IOS does not automatically assume the current time and date as expected, simply because Cisco starts its devices' clocks at UTC Monday, March 1, 1993.

There are two methods by which we can configure timekeeping on a Cisco IOS device:

- Manually
- Using the NTP

With the manual method, we use the `clock set` command followed by the time and date in privilege mode. The following is an example of the syntax for configuring the time manually:

```
clock set hh:mm:ss month day year
```

The issue we face when configuring time manually on a network is it's a very time-consuming process and, most importantly, the time may not be synchronous with other devices on the network. As mentioned previously, accurate timekeeping is very important on a network, as timestamps are inserted within event logs such as Syslog messages generated by your devices. If the time is not accurate, when tracking the sequence of log messages for an event, there may be inconsistencies. These inconsistencies will result in inaccurate log events between devices.

To view the system clock on a Cisco IOS device, use the `show clock` command as shown in the following snippet:

```
R1#show clock
*15:03:22.694 UTC Tue Apr 28 2020
R1#
```

Figure 10.1 – System clock on a Cisco router

As a network grows, it becomes even harder to maintain accurate timekeeping on devices. Using the NTP helps us easily synchronize time throughout an entire network of any size. Cisco IOS devices, such as routers and switches, can synchronize their system clocks with NTP servers as their source of time, thus enabling the routers and switches to become NTP clients on a network.

> **Important note**
> NTP uses UDP port 123 by default.

NTP uses a hierarchical system to manage the time sources through your network and the internet. Each level within the hierarchy is referred to as a **Stratum**. A Stratum level is used to measure the distance between an authoritative source and the NTP clients.

> **Important note**
> An authoritative source is the device that is manually configured to provide time and has the most accurate time on the network. The authoritative source is at the top of the hierarchy at all times.

The following diagram shows the NTP Stratum hierarchical structure:

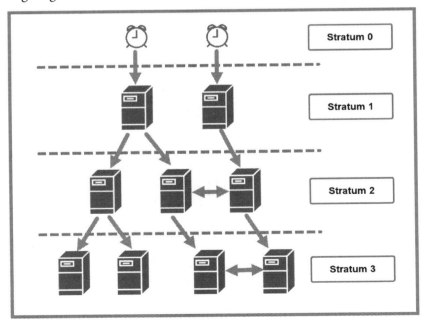

Figure 10.2 – Stratum hierarchy

The *authoritative sources* are the devices with the most accurate time and are located within the **Stratum 0** layer. **Stratum 0** devices are very precise at timekeeping and it is assumed that there are no delays or inaccuracies in their time management. **Stratum 1** devices are those that are associated with **Stratum 0**. **Stratum 2** are those that are associated with the upper layer, and so on. When a device has a lower Stratum number, it's an indication the NTP client is closer to the authoritative source of time, while a higher Stratum number indicates the NTP client is further away. However, the maximum number of hops within NTP is 15.

> **Important note**
> Stratum levels range from 0 – 15.

Any device that exists in a Stratum 16 layer is considered to be unsynchronized with the network time protocol. In the next section, you will learn how to configure Cisco devices as both an NTP server and NTP clients.

# Lab – configuring NTP

In this hands-on lab, you will learn how to implement NTP throughout a Cisco environment to ensure time is synchronized between the Cisco switches and routers. For this lab, we will be using the following network topology:

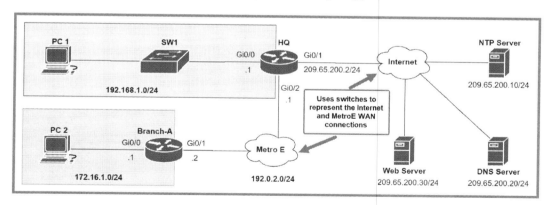

Figure 10.3 – IP service lab topology

Please ensure you use the following guidelines when creating this lab to ensure you get the same results:

- Use switches to represent the Metro Ethernet WAN and the internet connections.

- Use Cisco 2911 routers and Cisco 2960 switches.

- Configure a static route on the **HQ** router to reach the `172.16.1.0/24` network via the **Branch-A** router using the `ip route 172.16.1.0 255.255.255.0 192.0.2.2` command. You also have the option to use dynamic routing between the **HQ** LAN and **Branch-A** LAN.

- Configure a default route on the **Branch-A** router that points to **HQ** via `192.0.2.1` using the `ip route 0.0.0.0 0.0.0.0 192.0.2.1` command.

- Configure all the IP addresses on all the interfaces on the routers and servers.

- Ensure you configure the default gateway on each server to `209.65.200.2`.

- This lab topology will be used to configure NTP, DHCP, DHCP relay, and DNS.

Now that your Cisco lab is ready, use the following instructions to implement NTP:

1. Firstly, let's configure the NTP server with the current time. Click on **NTP Server**, choose the **Services** tab, and click on **NTP**, as in the following screenshot:

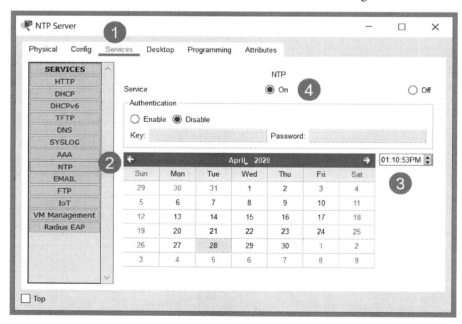

Figure 10.4 – NTP Server configurations

Ensure the NTP service is on and the time is accurately configured. The NTP server will operate as a **Stratum 0** device within the topology.

2. Configure the **HQ** router to be an NTP client and synchronize it with the NTP server by using the following commands in **global config** mode:

```
HQ(config)#ntp server 209.65.200.10
```

The preceding command is used to inform the **HQ** router to use 209.65.200.10 as its NTP server for its time source. After a few minutes, the router's system clock will be in sync with the time on the NTP server. Sometimes there is a long delay for an NTP client to synchronize with an NTP server.

3. Use the show ntp status command to validate that the NTP client and server have been synchronized:

```
HQ#show ntp status
Clock is synchronized, stratum 2, reference is 209.65.200.10
nominal freq is 250.0000 Hz, actual freq is 249.9990 Hz, precision is 2**24
reference time is E22B2084.000003CA (13:26:28.970 UTC Tue Apr 28 2020)
clock offset is 0.00 msec, root delay is 0.00  msec
root dispersion is 10.89 msec, peer dispersion is 0.12 msec.
loopfilter state is 'CTRL' (Normal Controlled Loop), drift is - 0.000001193
s/s system poll interval is 4, last update was 13 sec ago.
HQ#
```

Figure 10.5 – NTP synchronization

The output validates that the **HQ** router (NTP client) is synchronized with the NTP server, 209.65.200.10, and the router is operating as a **Stratum 2** device. This indicates that the NTP server is a **Stratum 1** device.

4. Use the show ntp associations command to validate any NTP associations on the **HQ** router:

```
HQ#show ntp associations

address          ref clock      st   when   poll   reach  delay        offset
*~209.65.200.10 127.127.1.1     1    13     16     377    0.00         0.00
  * sys.peer, # selected, + candidate, - outlyer, x falseticker, ~ configured
HQ#
```

Figure 10.6 – NTP associations

The output verifies that the **HQ** router is configured and paired with the device 209.65.200.10 as a **Stratum 1** NTP server. Sometimes the sys.peer (*) code takes a bit of time to appear next to the IP address.

5.  Use the show clock command to verify that the time is now accurate and is the same as the NTP server:

```
HQ#show clock
13:29:12.19 UTC Tue Apr 28 2020
HQ#
```

Figure 10.7 – System clock

6.  Let's make the **HQ** router an NTP server for the **HQ** LAN and **Branch-A** LAN networks. To perform this task, use the ntp master <stratum-number> command, or we can simply use the ntp master command and the router will automatically increment the Stratum number by 1 from the NTP server:

```
HQ(config)#ntp master
```

7.  Use the show ntp associations command once more to validate that the **HQ** router is now an NTP server:

```
HQ#show ntp associations

address          ref clock      st   when    poll    reach  delay      offset
*~209.65.200.10 127.127.1.1     1    4       16      377    0.00       0.00
 ~127.127.1.1   .LOCL.          7    8       64      377    0.00       0.00
 * sys.peer, # selected, + candidate, - outlyer, x falseticker, ~ configured
HQ#
```

Figure 10.8 – NTP associations

The second line indicates that the **HQ** router is operating as an NTP server because it is represented by a loopback IP address (link-local) and the reference clock is set to local.

8.  Next, configure the **Branch-A** router as an NTP client and use **HQ** for time synchronization:

```
Branch-A(config)#ntp server 192.0.2.1
```

The show ntp associations command verifies that the **Branch-A** router is synchronized with **HQ** as the NTP server:

```
Branch-A#show ntp associations

address          ref clock      st   when    poll    reach  delay          offset
*~192.0.2.1      209.65.200.10  2    13      32      377    0.00           0.00
 * sys.peer, # selected, + candidate, - outlyer, x falseticker, ~ configured
Branch-A#
```

Figure 10.9 – NTP associations on the Branch-A router

9.  Next, before we can configure the switch within the **HQ** LAN as an NTP client, we need to configure a **Switch Virtual Interface (SVI)** by using the following commands:

```
SW1(config)#interface vlan 1
SW1(config-if)#ip address 192.168.1.2 255.255.255.0
SW1(config-if)#no shutdown
SW1(config-if)#exit
```

The concept of using SVIs was covered in *Chapter 2, Getting Started with Cisco IOS Devices.*

10. Configure the default gateway on the switch using the following command:

```
SW1(config)#ip default-gateway 192.168.1.1
```

11. Use the ntp server command to configure the switch as an NTP client:

```
SW1(config)#ntp server 192.168.1.1
```

12. Lastly, use the show ntp associations command to validate that the switch is associated with **HQ**:

```
SW1#show ntp associations

address          ref clock      st   when    poll    reach  delay          offset
*~192.168.1.1    209.65.200.10  2    32      32      377    0.00           0.00
 * sys.peer, # selected, + candidate, - outlyer, x falseticker, ~ configured
SW1#
```

Figure 10.10 – NTP association on the switch

By completing this lab, you have gained the hands-on skills you need to implement both NTP clients and NTP servers on a Cisco network. In the next section, you will learn about the importance of DHCP as an IP service on an enterprise network.

# Understanding DHCP

On any computer network, there are many end devices, network intermediary devices, and even servers. Each device requires an IP address to exchange messages and share resources with each other. A network administrator usually assigns static IP addresses to devices that provide a service or resource to the network – devices such as switches, routers, firewalls, and servers. When a device is assigned a static IP address, it allows network administrators to remotely access and manage the device, as the address will never change.

Since a network is mostly made up of a computer and other end devices that often change physical locations, it's not wise to always assign static IP addresses to such devices. When a device with a static IP address is moved to another location, whether physical or logical, the IP scheme at the new location may not be the same as the IP configurations on the device itself. Therefore, the network administrator will be required to reconfigure the device with the appropriate IP configurations to match the addressing scheme at the new location on the network.

As a network grows, it becomes challenging and a bit time consuming to manually configure static IP addresses on new devices as users move between locations. Additionally, static IP address configuration is also vulnerable to human error. For example, the administrator might misconfigure a device with a duplicate IP address that is assigned to another machine or even an incorrect subnet mask.

The DHCP server can be implemented on a local network to automatically provide IP configurations, such as an IP address, subnet mask, default gateway, and DNS server settings. Having a DHCP server on a network simplifies and automates the task of assigning IP configurations to end devices efficiently.

A Cisco IOS router has many network services; a network administrator can configure a Cisco IOS router to provide DHCP services on a network. The DHCP server feature within Cisco IOS allows the router to also provide DHCP services to clients on a network. This feature is useful for small offices, as a dedicated DHCP server is not required. The Cisco IOS router is capable of providing the DHCP services to the local network.

# DHCP operations

Whenever a client is connected to a network, whether it's a wired or wireless connection, most clients automatically search for an active DHCP server, which will assign or lease an IP address and other IP configurations to the client. The IP addresses that are provided by the DHCP server are always leased for a period of time.

To get a better idea of DHCP operations, let's take a look at the following DHCP process:

1.  When a client is connected to a network, it starts looking for a local DHCP server. It creates a DHCP **Discover** message and sends it as a broadcast on the network, as shown:

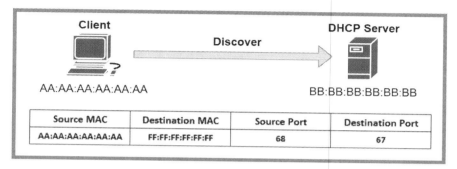

Figure 10.11 – DHCP Discover

The DHCP **Discover** packet contains the source MAC address as the DHCP client, with a source port of 68, a destination MAC address of FF:FF:FF:FF:FF:FF, and a destination port of 67. The DHCP client uses UDP port 68, while the DHCP server uses UDP port 67. The source IP address is left as blank, while the destination IP address is 255.255.255.255.

2.  When the DHCP server receives the DHCP **Discover** message, it will respond with a DHCP **Offer**. At this phase, the DHCP server uses the source MAC address from the DHCP **Discover** message to create a lease for an available IP address for the client. The DHCP server will send the information in the DHCP **Offer** message back to the client, as shown:

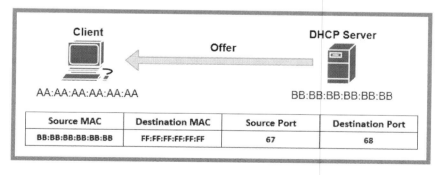

Figure 10.12 – DHCP offer

The DHCP server responds with a broadcast and sets the destination MAC address as the layer 2 broadcast, FF:FF:FF:FF:FF:FF.

3.  When the client receives the DHCP offer from the server, a DHCP **Request** message is sent back to the DHCP server as a form of acceptance for the IP configurations the client has received, as shown in the following diagram:

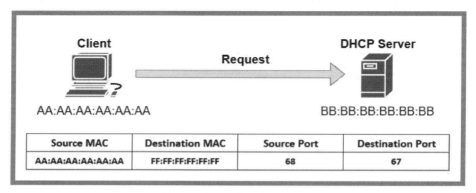

Figure 10.13 – DHCP request

The DHCP **Request** message is sent as a broadcast to the server.

4.  When the DHCP server receives the DHCP request from the client, the server verifies that the lease information is not being used already by sending an ICMP ping message to the IP address it has assigned to the new client. The DHCP server responds with a DHCP **Acknowledgement** to complete the DHCP process, as shown:

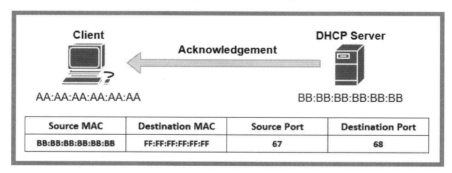

Figure 10.14 – DHCP acknowledgement

The DHCP **Acknowledgement** message is also sent as a broadcast to the client on the network.

The lease provided to the DHCP client is valid for a period of time. If a client wants to continue using the IP address assigned by the DHCP sever, the client sends a DHCP **Request** (unicast) message to the DHCP server requesting the lease be renewed.

> **Important note**
>
> For the renewal of leases, both DHCP **Request** and DHCP **Acknowledgment** messages are sent as unicast messages.

The DHCP server will verify that the lease information is available and return a DHCP **Acknowledgment** (unicast) message. The client will continue using the current IP address once it's available. Keep in mind that the client does not wait until a lease has expired to request a renewal; it does this renewal process prior to the expiration.

# Cisco's DHCP configurations

Configuring the DHCP service on a Cisco IOS device is quite simple. Use the following steps as a guideline when configuring DHCP on a Cisco router.

## Excluding addresses

When creating a DHCP pool of addresses, the Cisco IOS router begins distributing IP addresses automatically. It's recommended to create an exclusion pool or range of addresses that you do not want the DHCP server to distribute on the network. These addresses may include those that are statically assigned to devices and any reservations:

- To exclude a single address, use the `ip dhcp excluded-address ip-address` command.

- To exclude a range of addresses, use the `ip dhcp excluded-address start-address end-address` command.

Next, you'll learn how to create a DHCP pool on a Cisco IOS router.

## Creating the DHCP pool

The DHCP pool contains all the IP configurations that will be sent to DHCP clients on the network, such as the IP address, subnet mask, default gateway, DNS server, and so on. Take the following steps when creating a DHCP pool on a Cisco IOS router:

1. To create a DHCP pool, use the `ip dhcp pool pool-name` command. Once you've created a pool, you will enter the DHCP configuration mode for the pool.

2. Use the `network network-ID subnet-mask` command to define the address pool.

3. The `default-router ip-address` command is used to specify the default gateway address.

4.  The `dns-server ip-address` command is used to define the DNS servers.

5.  The `domain-name domain` command is used to define the domain name on the network.

> **Important note**
>
> To disable DHCP services on a Cisco IOS router, use the `no service dhcp` command in global configuration mode. To enable DHCP services, use the `service dhcp` command.

Multiple pools can be created on the same DHCP server or Cisco IOS device to facilitate an organization with multiple networks and a single DHCP server.

> **Tip**
>
> A Cisco device interface can be configured as a DHCP client by using the `ip address dhcp` command.

In the next section, we will learn about the concepts and benefits of using DHCP relay on a Cisco network.

## DHCP relay

In many organizations with large and complex networks, the servers are usually logically located within a data center or a different subnet. These servers usually provide network services and host applications for the entire organization's users and devices. These services include DHCP, DNS, file hosting services, and so on. When a client wants to access these network services, the client device sends a broadcast message in the hope of locating the relevant server.

Let's imagine a client is connected to a network. It broadcasts a DHCP **Discover** message to locate a DHCP server because it needs an IP address. If the DHCP server is not on the same subnet as the DHCP client, the router will prevent the DHCP **Discover** message from propagating below the local subnet. This causes an issue because the client will not receive an IP address and other IP configurations to communicate with other devices on the network.

The following diagram shows a DHCP server is located on another subnet:

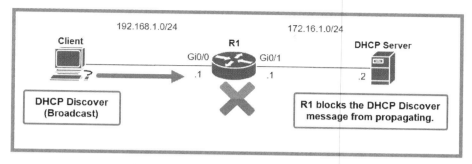

Figure 10.15 – The router does not forward broadcast messages

A DHCP **Discover** message is sent as a broadcast, and routers (layer 3 devices) block any broadcast messages from propagating by default. However, Cisco IOS has a solution to allow the forwarding of DHCP **Discover** and DHCP **Request** messages to a DHCP server on a different subnet.

The `ip helper-address` command can be applied to the interface of the router that receives DHCP **Discover** and DHCP **Request** messages. Therefore, we can use the following commands to configure the router to forward DHCP broadcast messages:

```
R1(config)#interface GigabitEthernet 0/0
R1(config-if)#ip helper-address 172.16.1.2
R1(config-if)#exit
```

The following diagram shows the effect of applying the `ip helper-address` command:

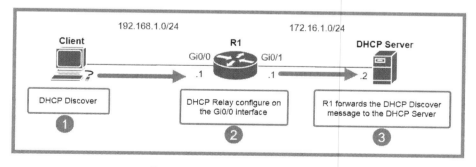

Figure 10.16 – DHCP propagation

`ip helper-address` should always be applied to the interface that is connected to or facing the DHCP clients on the network. In the next section, you will learn how to configure DHCP services and DHCP relay on a Cisco IOS router.

# Lab – configuring DHCP and DHCP relay

In this lab, you will learn how to configure DHCP services in a Cisco environment. Please keep in mind that this lab is simply an extension of the previous lab on NTP services, so we will be using the same network topology as shown in the following screenshot:

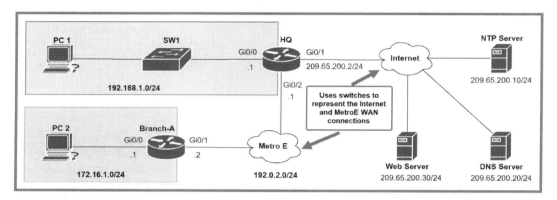

Figure 10.17 – DHCP lab

To get started, use the following instructions to implement DHCP on the topology:

1.  Exclude addresses that you do not want to be assigned to client devices by the DHCP server:

    ```
    HQ(config)#ip dhcp excluded-address 192.168.1.1
    192.168.1.10
    ```

    ```
    HQ(config)#ip dhcp excluded-address 172.16.1.1
    172.16.1.10
    ```

    We have excluded the first 10 addresses of each private network: 192.168.1.0/24 and 172.16.1.0/24. This is an example to demonstrate how to use the DHCP exclusion command.

2.  Create a DHCP pool for the **HQ** LAN network on the **HQ** router:

    ```
    HQ(config)#ip dhcp pool HQ-LAN
    HQ(dhcp-config)#network 192.168.1.0 255.255.255.0
    HQ(dhcp-config)#default-router 192.168.1.1
    HQ(dhcp-config)#dns-server 209.65.200.20
    HQ(dhcp-config)#exit
    ```

For each DHCP pool, configure the range of addresses to be distributed via the server by using the network command. The default-router command is used to specify the default gateway for DHCP clients. (The DNS server information will be used in the next lab.)

3.  Create another DHCP pool for the **Branch-A** LAN network on the **HQ** router:

```
HQ(config)#ip dhcp pool Branch-A-LAN
HQ(dhcp-config)#network 172.16.1.0 255.255.255.0
HQ(dhcp-config)#default-router 172.16.1.1
HQ(dhcp-config)#dns-server 209.65.200.20
HQ(dhcp-config)#exit
```

4.  Configure the **Branch-A** router as a DHCP **relay** to the **HQ** router:

```
Branch-A(config)#interface GigabitEthernet 0/0
Branch-A(config-if)#ip helper-address 192.0.2.1
Branch-A(config-if)#exit
```

ip helper-address is always configured on the LAN side of the router with the IP address of the DHCP server.

5.  On the **Branch-A** router, use the show ip interface command to validate that the DHCP helper address is configured:

```
Branch-A#show ip interface gigabitEthernet 0/0
GigabitEthernet0/0 is up, line protocol is up (connected)
  Internet address is 172.16.1.1/24
  Broadcast address is 255.255.255.255
  Address determined by setup command
  MTU is 1500 bytes
  Helper address is 192.0.2.1
  Directed broadcast forwarding is disabled
```

Figure 10.18 – Helper address

6.   Click on **PC 1** and **PC 2**, select the **Desktop** tab, then click on **IP Configuration** and set it to **DHCP**, as shown:

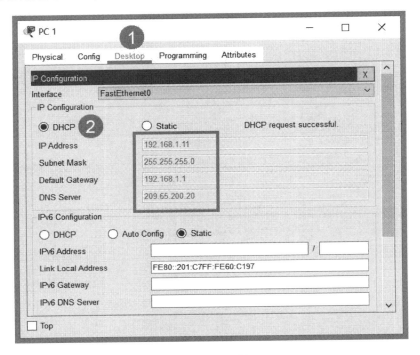

Figure 10.19 – IP addressing

After a while, each DHCP client – **PC 1** and **PC 2** – will receive its IP configurations from the DHCP server, the **HQ** router.

7.   On the **HQ** router, the `show ip dhcp binding` command shows the number of client devices that are using an IP address from the DHCP server, the client's MAC address, the lease time, and the type:

```
HQ#show ip dhcp binding
IP address          Client-ID/          Lease expiration      Type
                    Hardware address
192.168.1.11        0001.C760.C197      --                    Automatic
172.16.1.11         00E0.B0E8.1A13      --                    Automatic
HQ#
```

Figure 10.20 – DHCP binding table

Since a DHCP pool has a finite number of available IP addresses, a lease is used to set the duration of how long a client can use an IP address. When the lease expires, the IP address on the client machine is returned to the DHCP server. However, clients can renew the lease prior to expiration to keep the IP address in use. The Type column simply defines how a client was assigned an IP address from the DHCP server.

8. Lastly, the show ip dhcp pool command provides details about statistics within each DHCP pool on the Cisco IOS router:

```
HQ#show ip dhcp pool

Pool HQ-LAN :
 Utilization mark (high/low)    : 100 / 0
 Subnet size (first/next)       : 0 / 0
 Total addresses                : 254
 Leased addresses               : 1
 Excluded addresses             : 2
 Pending event                  : none

 1 subnet is currently in the pool
 Current index          IP address range                    Leased/Excluded/Total
 192.168.1.1            192.168.1.1     - 192.168.1.254       1    / 2     / 254
```

Figure 10.21 – DHCP pool

Having completed this lab, you have gained the hands-on skills to use a Cisco IOS router as a DHCP server and a DHCP relay on a network. In the next section, we will take a look at DNS as a network service.

# Domain Name System

Let's imagine you want to research additional information about the **Cisco Certified Network Associate (CCNA)** certification. The best place to start researching would be Cisco's website at www.cisco.com. Open your favorite web browser and simply enter the URL into the address bar and hit *Enter*. After a few seconds, the Cisco website appears and you can continue your research. Everything seems to work like magic, but have you ever wondered how your computer determines the IP address for the web server that is hosting Cisco's website?

As mentioned in *Chapter 3, IP Addressing and Subnetting*, each device that is connected and exchanging messages on a computer-based network must be assigned a unique IPv4 or IPv6 address. The same is also applied to all devices on the internet, such as web and mail exchange servers. If a web server is identified by its IP address, why does it have a website URL address such as www.cisco.com?

To help you understand the situation a bit better, imagine having to remember all the IP addresses of each website you want to visit on the internet. That would be very challenging as IP addresses may change or be reassigned to another device on a network and even the internet. You cannot connect to a server or device on the internet if you do not have knowledge of the IPv4 or IPv6 address.

To solve this issue, the DNS network service protocol was created with the primary purpose of resolving the hostname to the IP address. In reality, it's a lot easier to remember a **Uniform Resource Locator** (**URL**) or domain name of a website. With the benefit and convenience of using DNS, IT professionals can easily purchase a domain name and point it to a web server or device. This allows anyone who knows the domain name, such as www.cisco.com, to easily visit the Cisco website using a computer or smart device with a standard web browser.

Before the days of DNS, each computer had a file known as the hosts file. The hosts file would contain the hostname for IP address mapping. Whenever a user wants to visit a website, they enter the hostname, and the computer then queries the local hosts file in search of an available map that informs the computer of the IP address to reach the hostname. However, if the hosts file does not have an available entry for the hostname, the computer will not know how to reach the server. Users have to ensure that the hosts file is frequently updated to contain the most up-to-date records.

To view the hosts file on a Windows operating system, go to C:\Windows\System32\drivers\etc\hosts. The following is the contents within the hosts file on a Windows 10 operation system:

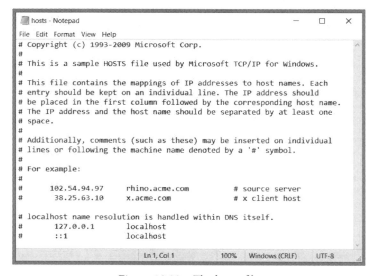

Figure 10.22 – The hosts file

Frequently updating the hosts file is not a good strategy as the internet is continuously growing, and new devices are coming online with new and unique hostnames. The creation of DNS servers came about, with each server being the root for its domain and containing all the DNS records for a specific **Top-Level Domain (TLD)**. A TLD is a domain that has the root ( . ) and ends with a name such as .com, .net, .org, .xyz, and so on. A domain name is a domain that contains a name with a TLD, such as cisco.com. A **Fully Qualified Domain Name (FQDN)** contains an additional extension, a hostname, and a domain such as www.cisco.com. The FQDN specified the exact location or device. For example, cisco.com is simply a domain name that may contain many devices, but specifying an FQDN such as www.cisco.com simply says we are trying to connect to the device with the hostname www that belongs within the cisco.com domain.

## DNS root servers

As mentioned, there are various root DNS servers that contain the DNS records for each object that belongs to the parent domain. As shown in the following diagram, the .com root server contains all the DNS records for cisco.com and its sub-domains, such as community.cisco.com:

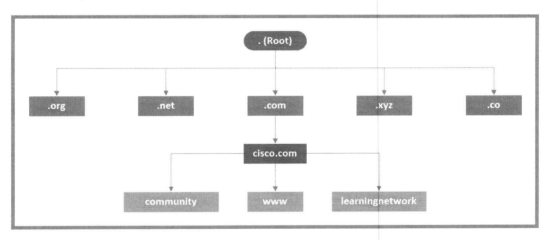

Figure 10.23 – DNS hierarchy

Whenever a device wants to look up the IP address for a hostname, it will send a DNS query to its configured DNS server. Once the record is found, the DNS server will send a DNS reply with the IP address for the hostname back to the computer. The computer will use the IP address to reach the hostname or device.

The following diagram shows the DNS process when a user enters a URL within the web browser:

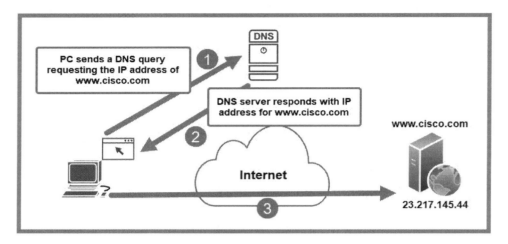

Figure 10.24 – DNS process

There are many free public and reliable DNS servers on the internet; the following are some of my personal recommendations as they provide speed and security:

- Cloudflare DNS: `https://1.1.1.1/`

- Cisco OpenDNS: `https://www.opendns.com/`

- Google DNS: `https://developers.google.com/speed/public-dns`

What if your DNS server does not have the record of a specific hostname or domain name? What will it do? DNS servers often exchange information with each other to ensure their records are always up to date. If a DNS server does not have a record, it can respond by informing the client it does not have one or by simply asking another DNS server for the information and then relaying the response back to the client.

## DNS record types

There are many DNS record types that are used on a DNS server:

- `A`: Resolves the hostname to an IPv4 address

- `AAAA`: Resolves the hostname to an IPv6 address

- `MX`: Maps the domain to mail exchange (email) servers

- NS: Points to the domain's name servers
- CNAME: Allows you to create an alias name for the domain
- SOA: Used to specify the authority for the domain
- SVR: Specifies the service records
- PTR: Maps an IP address to a hostname
- RP: Specifies the responsible person for a domain
- HINFO: Specifies host information
- TXT: Allows you to add text as a DNS record

Therefore, if a computer wants to determine the IPv4 address for Cisco's website, www. cisco.com, the computer will need to send a DNS query requesting the A record from the DNS server. The nslookup utility on both Microsoft Windows and Linux operating systems are used to troubleshoot DNS issues on the client side of the network.

# Lab – configuring DNS

In this lab, you will learn how to configure DNS services in a Cisco environment. Please keep in mind that this lab is simply an extension of the previous lab on NTP and DHCP services and we will be using the same network topology as shown in the following diagram:

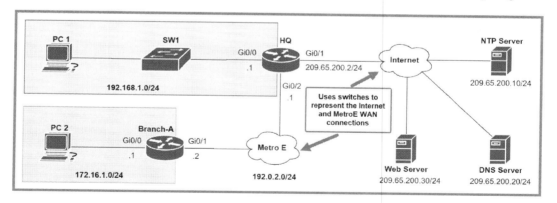

Figure 10.25 – DNS lab

To get started, use the following instructions to implement DNS on the topology:

1.  Firstly, we need to create and configure our DNS server within Cisco Packet Tracer. Click on **DNS Server**, select the **Services** tab, and then select **DNS**, as in the following screenshot:

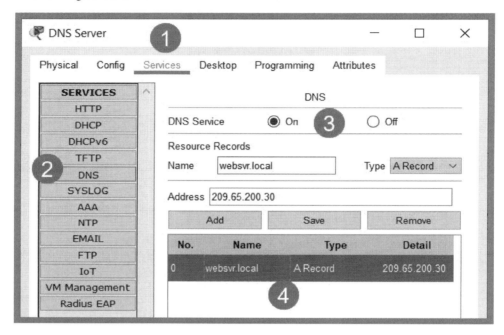

Figure 10.26 – DNS Server

Ensure the DNS services are **On**. Create a new resource record, setting **Name** to websvr.local, **Type** to A Record, and the IP address as the web server on the network – 209.65.200.30 – and click on **Add** to save the DNS record.

2.  Since we have already configured each client to use the DNS server as 209.65.200.20 via DHCP, we can move on to the next step.

3.  On **PC 1** and **PC 2**, click on **Desktop** and open the **Web Browser** application. Enter the web address of the web server, http://websvr.local, and click on **Go**:

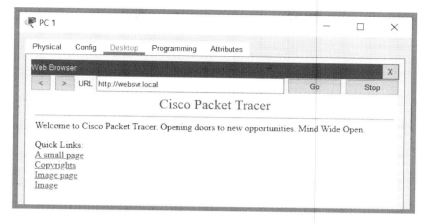

Figure 10.27 – Web page

The output shows **PC 1** is able to reach the web server via the hostname, websvr.local. This is validation that the DNS server is able to resolve the websvr.local hostname to its IP address in the background.

4.  On **PC 1**, open the **Command Prompt** application. Use the nslookup utility to verify the DNS configurations on the local machine:

Figure 10.28 – DNS validation

After entering the nslookup command, the system provides us with the DNS settings it is currently using – 209.65.200.20 – as its DNS server. Next, by entering the hostname, websvr.local, the system queries the DNS server (209.65.200.20) to retrieve the DNS A Record to the hostname. The DNS server (209.65.200.20) was able to resolve the websvr.local hostname to the IP address 209.65.200.30. Additionally, if you attempt to ping the domain name, websvr.local, the DNS server will resolve the IP address and will respond.

Having completed this lab, you have gained the essential skills needed to configure and understand DNS concepts on a Cisco enterprise network.

# Understanding the benefits of using Syslog

When events occur on a network, networking devices, such as routers, switches, and firewalls, generate a log message to notify the administrator with details about the event. These log messages can contain details about critical or non-critical events. Network professionals use a wide range of tools and options for managing these log messages, such as storing, displaying, interpreting, and normalizing. This helps network professionals to focus on the more critical log messages and determine the timeline of an event that has occurred.

Syslog is both a protocol and standard for accessing, creating, and managing log messages on a computer and network device. Syslog defines the method of how system messages, such as logs, are generated, formatted, and accessed.

> **Important note**
> The Syslog log uses UDP port 514 to send event messages across a network to a centralized Syslog server for management.

Implementing proper log management on a network has several benefits, such as the following:

- Having proper log management within a network helps network professionals to improve both monitoring and troubleshooting.

- You can configure devices to send log messages of a certain severity level to the centralized Syslog server on the network.

- As a network professional, you can specify the destination of your Syslog message, such as a server.

By default, Cisco devices log their system messages to the console line. However, a device can be configured to log its messages to an internal buffer within the device itself, on a **Terminal line (VTY)**, and even to a Syslog server on the network. It's recommended to set up a centralized log server on the network to capture log messages from all network devices; this strategy will allow you to view all the correlated logs in sequential order. This allows you to see a timeline of events throughout the network through a single dashboard interface on the server.

# Syslog severity levels

Each Syslog message contains a severity level and a facility. The following table shows all the severity levels in descending order and their description:

| Severity Name | Severity Level | Description |
|---|---|---|
| Emergency | 0 | System is unusable |
| Alert | 1 | Immediate action is needed |
| Critical | 2 | Critical condition |
| Error | 3 | Error condition |
| Warning | 4 | Warning condition |
| Notification | 5 | Normal but significant condition |
| Informational | 6 | Informational message |
| Debugging | 7 | Debugging message |

Figure 10.29 – Syslog severity levels

Here's a simple way to remember the Syslog severity levels – take each initial letter from each level and create a phrase. I found the following phrase on the internet and thought it was a bit goofy but an awesome way to remember each severity level: *Every Awesome Cisco Engineer Will Need Ice-cream Daily.*

The following is the default Syslog message format on Cisco IOS devices:

```
seq no: timestamp: %facility-severity-MNEMONIC: description
```

The following is a breakdown of each part of the Syslog format message:

- `seq no` represents the sequence number assigned to each log message. To enable the sequence number, use the `service sequence-numbers` command on the global configuration mode.
- The `timestamp` area includes the date and time of the event. To enable a timestamp, use the `service timestamps` command on the global configuration mode.
- `facility` represents what the log message is referring to, such as a protocol, module, or the source of the problem.

- severity provides a severity code in the range 0-7, which describes how critical the alarm is.
- MNEMONIC is simply text that is used to uniquely describe the alarm.
- description simply contains a brief description of the event or alarm.

The following is an example of a Syslog message generated by a Cisco IOS router:

```
*Apr 28, 15:53:58.5353: %LINEPROTO-5-UPDOWN: Line protocol on
Interface GigabitEthernet0/1, changed state to up
```

We can see that the timestamp is Apr 28 with the time as 15:53:58.5353, facility is LINEPROTO, the severity level is 5, MNEMONIC is UPDOWN and the description is Line protocol on Interface GigabitEthernet0/1, changed state to up.

The following is an example of a Syslog message containing a sequence number:

```
000019: %SYS-5-CONFIG_I: Configured from console by vty2
```

The sequence number in the example is 000019.

> **Important note**
> To force the log messages to display a date and time, use the service timestamps log datetime command in the global configuration mode. By default, Syslog messages are generated without dates and this can be a problem when we need to track issues by date.

When it comes to acquiring a logging server, there are many free and commercial products from reputed vendors that allow you to simply download and install them on your operating system. For example, **Solarwinds** has its Kiwi Syslog Server (www.kiwisyslog.com) as a commercial product, while **PRTG** (www.paessler.com) is able to function as a free Syslog server.

In the next section, you will learn how to implement Syslog on a Cisco network.

# Lab – configuring Syslog

In this lab, you will learn how to configure Cisco IOS devices to use Syslog and forward log messages to a centralized log management server on the network. The following diagram is the topology we'll be using for this exercise; please note it's the same as the one we used in previous labs with the addition of a Syslog server on the `192.168.1.0/24` network with a static IP address of `192.168.1.5`:

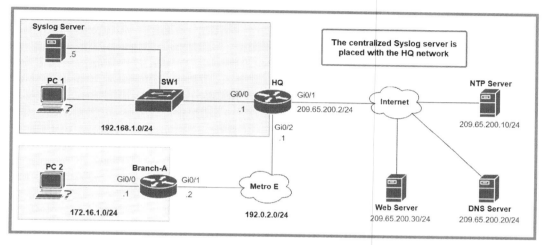

Figure 10.30 – Syslog topology

Please ensure you use the following guidelines when creating this lab to ensure you get the same results:

- As mentioned previously, the only addition to the topology is the Syslog server.

- Configure the Syslog server with the IP address and subnet mask as shown in the diagram.

- Ensure the Syslog server is configured with a default gateway address of `192.168.1.1`.

Now that you're lab-ready, use the following instructions to configure Syslog on your network topology:

1.  Firstly, we will configure the new server to accept Syslog messages. Click on the new server (192.168.1.5), select the **Services** tab, then click on **SYSLOG**, as in the following screenshot:

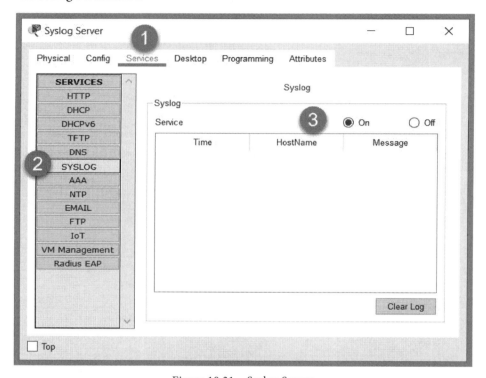

Figure 10.31 – Syslog Server

Ensure the Syslog service is set to **On**, as in the preceding screenshot.

2.  Configure the **Branch-A** router to send Syslog messages to the Syslog server:

```
Branch-A(config)#logging 192.168.1.5
```

3.  Configure the **Branch-A** router to send all Syslog message to the Syslog server by specifying the severity level as 7, debugging:

```
Branch-A(config)#logging trap debugging
```

When you specify a severity level, the router will send all severity level messages that range from severity level 0 to the severity level you specify. By specifying `debugging`, the router will send all Syslog severity messages from level 0-7, as debugging is severity level 7.

4. To enable the service timestamp with milliseconds on log messages, use the following commands:

```
Branch-A(config)#service timestamps log datetime msec
```

5. On the **Branch-A** router, either disconnect and reconnect the LAN cable or administratively shut down the LAN interface to generate some Syslog messages on the device.

6. Configure the **HQ** router to send Syslog messages to the Syslog server.

7. Head on over to the Syslog server and check the Syslog service:

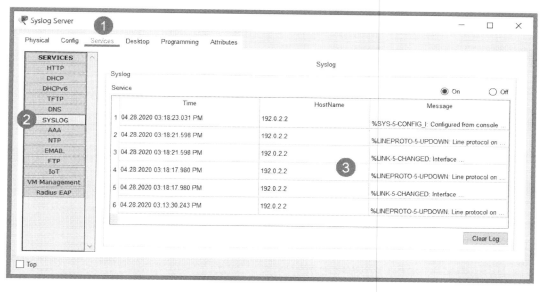

Figure 10.32 – Syslog messages

The Syslog messages that appear here are those that are generated by the **Branch-A** router.

8.  Use the `show logging` command to verify the default logging service settings on the router:

```
Branch-A#show logging
Syslog logging: enabled (0 messages dropped, 0 messages rate-limited,
          0 flushes, 0 overruns, xml disabled, filtering disabled)

No Active Message Discriminator.


No Inactive Message Discriminator.


   Console logging: level debugging, 10 messages logged, xml disabled,
         filtering disabled
   Monitor logging: level debugging, 10 messages logged, xml disabled,
         filtering disabled
   Buffer logging:  disabled, xml disabled,
         filtering disabled
```

Figure 10.33 – Logging service

We can determine that the local router logs to the console and includes all message types, from `Emergency` to `Debugging`. 10 messages have been logged so far.

Having completed this lab, you have gained the hands-on skills to implement Syslog on Cisco IOS devices. In the next section, we will discover how to monitor and manage your network using SNMP.

# Simple Network Management Protocol

SNMP was designed to enable IT administrators to manage network and end devices, such as workstations, servers, switches, routers, and security appliances, easily on an IP-based network. SNMP provides the functionality to allow device administrators to monitor, manage, and troubleshoot network performance.

SNMP is made up of the following three components:

- SNMP manager
- SNMP agent
- **Management Information Base (MIB)**

These three components all work together to create a **Network Management System (NMS)**. The *SNMP manager* is the application that is installed and running on the administrator's computer. The SNMP manager is responsible for collecting the information from the SNMP agents using SNMP `GET` messages. The manager is able to make modifications to the network device's configuration by using SNMP `SET` messages.

The *SNMP agent* and *MIB* exist on the actual networking device, such as a switch or router. The SNMP agent is the component that communicates with the SNMP manager across the network. The user interacts with the SNMP manager, which then relays the information to the SNMP agent. The SNMP agent either gathers information and sends it back to the SNMP manager or executes a set of instructions.

The MIB is like a database that contains data on the network device and its operational state. This information is available only to users who are authenticated via SNMP on the local device. Put simply, the SNMP agent must be configured on a network device, then the user opens an SNMP manager application on their computer and simply specifies the IP address of the target device and user credentials, such as a community string. If the credentials are valid, the SNMP manager will authenticate the SNMP agent on the network device, allowing the user to interact with the device and gather information and make adjustments on it.

> **Important note**
>
> SNMP operates on UDP port 161. However, SNMP agents send SNMP trap messages to the SNMP manager on UDP port 162.

The following diagram shows the overall flow of messages on the NMS:

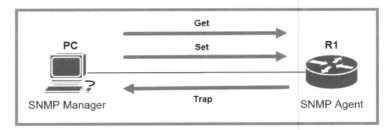

Figure 10.34 – SNMP messages

The SNMP GET request is used to gather or query the device for information and the SNMP SET request is used to modify the configuration on the device via the SNMP agent. Trap messages are like notifications that are generated and sent by an SNMP agent to alert the SNMP manager about an event on the network device.

The following figure shows an SNMP manager interface:

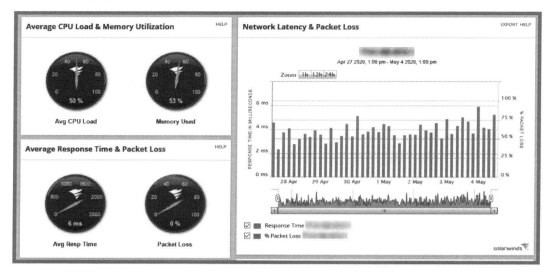

Figure 10.35 – SNMP manager

The preceding screenshot shows some information about a switch on an enterprise network. To gather this information, the SNMP manager (Solarwinds) has sent an SNMP GET message to retrieve the information for us. Once the information is gathered, it is presented on the SNMP manager GUI. The SNMP protocol was able to gather details such as the CPU and memory load, latency, and packet loss statistics. Without using the command line, the SNMP manager is able to show us the days and times when network latency was higher than others. This information can be used to generate reports, create network baselines, and assess any network performance issues.

The SNMP traps are continuously exchanged between the SNMP manager and the SNMP agent to gather information about the network device. The downside of the SNMP polling mechanism is the delay between an event occurring on a network device and the SNMP manager taking notice of it. Some organizations configure their SNMP polling intervals to 10 minutes, which allows the NMS to detect an event/issue within 10 minutes of occurrence. However, this interval may be too long when it comes to detecting a failure on a critical network, so polling intervals can be adjusted to fit the organization's response time to meet network issues. Keep in mind that too many polling messages may flood the available bandwidth on the network.

# SNMP versions

There are several versions of SNMP. These are as follows:

- SNMPv1
- SNMPv2c
- SNMPv3

SNMPv1 does not provide any form of authentication, privileges, or encryption between the SNMP manager and the SNMP agent. SNMPv2c uses community strings – `public` and `private` – for administrative tasks. The `public` string is used for *read-only* tasks, while the `private` string is used for *read-write* actions. However, SNMPv2c does not provide any authentication or encryption. SNMPv3 comes with improved security to provide authentication for users and user groups. SNMPv3 uses **Message Digest 5 (MD5)** or **Secure Hashing Algorithm (SHA)** during its authentication phase, and **Data Encryption Standard (DES)** or **Advanced Encryption Standard (AES)** for data encryption.

SNMPv1 and SNMPv2c both use community strings to access MIB on a network or computer device. The following are two types of community strings used in SNMP:

- **Read-only** (`ro`): This string allows you to access the MIB on the network device but does not allow you to make modifications on the device, hence read-only.
- **Read-write** (`rw`): Allows you to both read and write to all objects within the MIB on the device.

Next, you will discover the purpose of the MIB and the key roles it plays in SNMP.

# Management information base

The MIB is a database that contains all the **Object IDs (OIDs)** for each component on the network device. To put it simply, for the SNMP manager to interact with an interface of a router, to gather network statistics from the interface, for example, an OID must exist for that specific task on the router.

OIDs are represented as variables within the MIB. The MIB is designed as a hierarchical tree structure containing many child sub-sections known as branches. The following diagram shows the MIB OIDs used by Cisco devices:

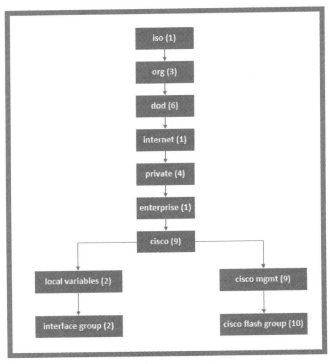

Figure 10.36 – MIB

The SNMP manager uses the OID values from the MIB to gather information or make changes to objects on the SNMP agent device. The hierarchical structure defines where an SNMP manager can find specific information about a device.

> **Tip**
> The **Cisco SNMP Object Navigator** tool is a free online tool to help you translate OIDs into their respective object names and details.

In the following exercise, you will learn how to configure SNMP on Cisco devices.

# Lab – configuring SNMP

In this lab, you will learn how to configure the SNMP service in a Cisco environment. Please keep in mind that this lab is simply an extension of the previous lab on DNS services and we will be using the same network topology as shown in the following diagram:

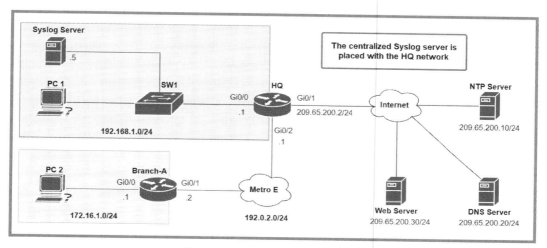

Figure 10.37 – SNMP lab topology

The objective of this lab is to enable SNMP on both the **HQ** and **Branch-A** routers. Once SNMP is enabled, we'll use **PC 1** as the SNMP manager to retrieve device information and make configurations to the running-config file on the router.

To configure SNMP on the Cisco IOS router, use the following instructions:

1. On the **Branch-A** router, configure the community string (public) and the access level for read-only (ro) using the following commands:

```
Branch-A(config)#snmp-server community public ro
```

2. Next, configure a community string (private) with access level for read-write (rw) on the **Branch-A** router:

```
Branch-A(config)#snmp-server community private rw
```

Read-write will allow the SNMP manager to use the private community string to make modifications to the configurations of the device.

3. Apply *steps 1* and *2* on the **HQ** router:

```
HQ(config)#snmp-server community public ro
HQ(config)#snmp-server community private rw
```

4. Head on over to **PC 2**, open the **Desktop** tab, and select **MIB Browser**, as in the following screenshot:

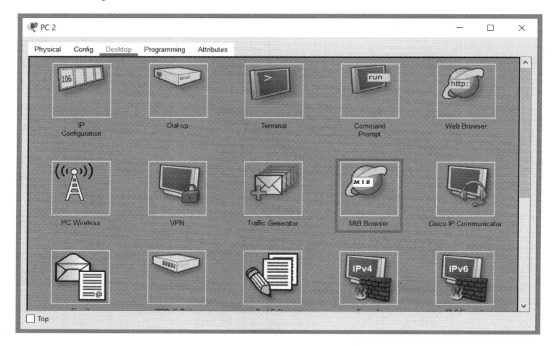

Figure 10.38 – PC 2 Desktop interface

5. Click the **Advanced…** button, as in the following screenshot:

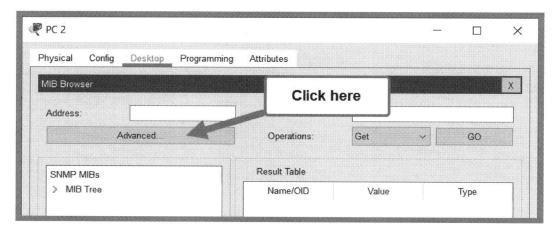

Figure 10.39 – MIB Browser

6.   A new window will appear. Set the **Read Community** value as `public`, **Write Community** as `private`, and **SNMP Version** as `v3` and click **OK**:

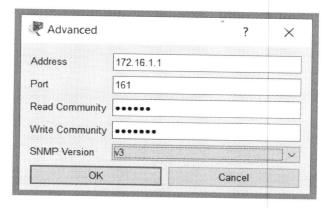

Figure 10.40 – SNMP browser settings

7.   In the left panel, expand the MIB tree structure to `ios > org > dod > internet > mgmt > mib-2 > system > sysUpTime`, set **Operations** as **Get**, and click on **GO**:

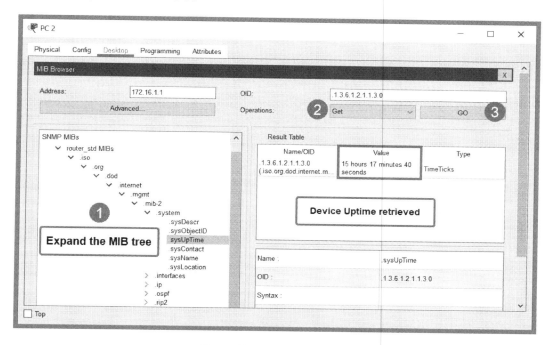

Figure 10.41 – Device uptime

The SNMP manager on **PC 2** was able to retrieve (GET) the device's uptime from the SNMP agent on the router.

8.  To make a modification to the device's configuration, we can use the SNMP SET operation. To change the device's hostname to Branch-A-RTR, navigate to the sysName branch, use the SET operation, and set **Data Type** to OctetString and **Value** to Branch-A-RTR, as shown in the following screenshot:

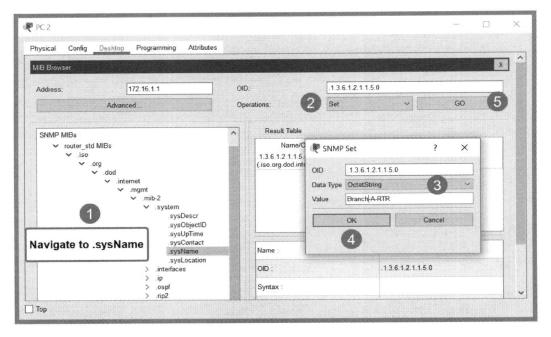

Figure 10.42 – The SNMP SET operation

Once you click on **GO**, the MIB manager will use the SNMP SET message to inform the SNMP agent on the router to make the adjustment on the device.

Having completed this lab, you have learned how to enable SNMP on a Cisco IOS device and saw the operations of SNMP on a Cisco network. In the next section, we will take a look at understanding the key role QoS plays in an enterprise network.

# QoS traffic classification

Let's imagine the roadways of a city do not widen automatically and if there are too many vehicles using the medium (roadways) and they are not exiting quickly enough, traffic starts accumulating and results in congestion. Therefore, each person may take a much longer time to reach their destination.

In a production environment, you're the network engineer for a very large organization with a lot of users and many network applications. Each day, users are simultaneously accessing both internal resources on the network, such as locally hosted applications, and external resources; there are tons of various traffic types that are traveling along the network each day. What would you do if users began experiencing an unacceptable user experience on the corporate network, such as very slow response times?

Each day, there are thousands and even millions of packets being generated by devices and they are sent with messages to another device as a form of digital communication. Sometimes, when there is too much traffic on the network that exceeds the bandwidth between a sender and destination, network congestion occurs.

On a network, some of these traffic types include voice and video transmission for online and virtual collaboration with other members of staff, while other traffic types may be using **User Datagram Protocol (UDP)** as their transport layer protocol, which does not guarantee the delivery of a message. Using QoS tools on a network, professionals can classify and prioritize network traffic types, such as voice and video, over non-time-sensitive traffic, such as web browsing and email.

While devices such as computers, servers, and IP phones are sending traffic to the network switch and routers, they are not considering whether the networking devices are able to transmit messages as fast as it's being received. Switches and routers are used to connect devices and networks; they sit at the core of all exchange points on an enterprise network. This means they accept thousands of packets per minute on their physical interfaces and have to process each incoming message and forward it through an outgoing interface toward its destination. All networking devices have a buffer of limited size that temporarily stores incoming messages (in a queue) until the device is able to process and forward them. When a device, such as a router, receives too many incoming messages and the buffer is full, new incoming messages may be discarded until the router is able to process the existing messages and free the buffer memory.

> **Important note**
> The queuing of traffic increases the delay on a network. Hence, network congestion causes delays.

This is not good for a network that has critical applications that generate time-sensitive traffic, such as voice and video. Imagine your organization has a **Voice over IP (VoIP)** solution and during each phone call with another employee or external party, for the duration of the call, the other person and yourself have an unacceptable experience, such as not hearing each word the other person is saying, hearing static, and even experiencing delays. Voice and video traffic use UDP as their preferred transport layer protocol because UDP creates a lot less overhead on the network and it's much faster than **Transmission Control Protocol (TCP)**. However, the disadvantage of using UDP, especially for voice and video traffic types, is that UDP is a connectionless protocol and there is no guarantee of delivery for any messages. Therefore, voice and video traffic has a much higher possibility of being discarded or dropped on a network if congestion occurs along the path. Using QoS tools, a network engineer can configure network devices to prioritize certain traffic types over others to ensure users have an acceptable experience on the network.

> **Important note**
> A network device will only implement QoS when it is experiencing some form of congestion.

# QoS terminologies

Throughout your journey in the field of networking, you will encounter many technologies and terminologies. In this section, you will learn about the terminologies that are used to describe certain characteristics of a network and how they help us to define network transmission quality.

**Bandwidth**: Bandwidth refers to the amount of bits that can be transmitted in a second. This is commonly measured as **bits per second (bps)**. On newer network devices, there are higher capacity interfaces, such as Gigabit Ethernet ports, which can support up to one gigabit per second of traffic.

**Congestion**: As mentioned earlier, congestion causes delays on a network. Congestion occurs when there is a lot more traffic on a network than it can handle. The buffer within network devices becomes overwhelmed when there is a lot of incoming traffic filling up the buffer memory faster than the network device can process it and forward it to an outgoing interface. Network devices are usually located at the congestion points on a network, which is where QoS should be applied.

**Delay**: Delay is also referred to as latency. This is the time it takes a packet to travel between a source and a destination. A network with high latency will result in users experiencing slower response times to network-based applications that are hosted on a local server. The objective is to ensure a network has a very low response time between any sender and destination.

**Jitter**: Jitter is the variation of the delay of incoming packets. On a stable network, the latency of a continuous stream of packets received from a single source will be the same. However, network congestion, improper queuing, and interface errors (collisions) affect the latency between each packet being received on a device.

**Packet loss**: Once the buffer is full, new incoming packets will be discarded or dropped from the network. This results in packet loss. Having too much packet loss on a network makes it difficult to transmit a message between a source and destination. If the message is using TCP, the sender will re-transmit the dropped packet until the destination sends an **acknowledgement**, unlike UDP, where the sender will not re-transmit the message.

# Traffic type characteristics

More users are moving their business applications to the cloud, employees are working remotely at home, and academic institutions are using the internet and technologies to deliver their classes to a global audience. The increase in voice and video traffic over the years has been rapid, and it is continuing to surpass data traffic on an enterprise network.

Voice traffic is quite predictable and smooth flowing. However, it is very susceptible to packet loss and delays over a network. Since voice traffic uses UDP, if a packet is lost, the sender does not re-transmit the message. Therefore, voice traffic should be configured with a higher priority over all other traffic on the network. Voice traffic can tolerate some levels of packet loss, latency (delay), and jitter before it becomes noticeable by the receiver.

Voice traffic should use the following recommendations:

- The delay or latency should not exceed more than 150 milliseconds (ms).
- Jitter should not exceed more than 30 milliseconds (ms).
- Packet loss should not exceed more than 1%.
- Voice traffic requires a minimum of 30 kbps of bandwidth.

Unlike voice traffic, video traffic uses a lot of extra bandwidth and without any QoS mechanism to prioritize the traffic type, the quality of the video stream degrades. From a user point of view, the video will begin to appear blurry and jagged and the audio may not be synchronous with the picture. Compared to voice traffic, video traffic is known to be inconsistent, unpredictable, and less resilient. With video traffic, packets may be received at 20-millisecond time intervals, which then changes randomly to 40-millisecond intervals, then back again to 20 milliseconds. Additionally, each video packet is not always the same size in bytes; this causes inconsistency when transporting small and large video packets along a network.

To put it simply, video traffic uses UDP as its transport layer protocol, which is very vulnerable to packet loss and delays on a network. Video traffic also uses a lot of network bandwidth and the message size varies from packet to packet.

Video traffic should use the following recommendations:

- Latency should not exceed over 400 milliseconds (ms).
- Jitter should not exceed more than 50 milliseconds (ms).
- Packet loss should not be more than 1%.
- Video traffic requires a minimum of 384 kbps of bandwidth.

Another traffic type is data. There are many applications and network resources that do not have tolerance for packet loss during transmission, so they use TCP as the transport layer protocol. During a TCP stream, if any packet is lost during the transmission, the sender will re-transmit the message to the destination. There are certain traffic types, such as web browsing, that use **Hypertext Transfer Protocol** (**HTTP**) and **HTTP Secure** (**HTTPS**); these protocols sometimes occupy a lot of bandwidth on a network and do not leave room for other time-sensitive protocols. If TCP traffic takes up all the bandwidth on a network, the UDP traffic will have a higher chance of being discarded or dropped.

Although some data traffic types may be mission-critical to the organization to improve the **Quality of Experience** (**QoE**), a network administrator can simply configure the QoS tools to prioritize certain data traffic types on the network.

# QoS queuing algorithms

One method a Cisco device uses to queue incoming traffic is called **First-In, First-Out (FIFO)**. This technique is quite simple; it operates like the phrase *first come, first serve*. When packets enter the interface of a network device, they are placed in a queue while the device processes each message one at a time, then forwards the message out of an exit interface to its destination. With FIFO, the packets are processed in the order they arrive. No packet is prioritized over the other, as there is only a single queue and all packets are treated equally. Packets will be processed and sent out in the same order as they arrive on the device, hence the name FIFO.

The following are additional QoS queuing algorithms:

- Another algorithm is **Weighted Fair Queuing (WFQ)**. WFQ ensures fair bandwidth allocation is given to all traffic on the network. This algorithm uses the concept of applying weights (*priority*) to identify and classify network traffic into what it calls conversations or flows. Once the traffic has been classified, WFQ then automatically determines the amount of bandwidth that should be allocated to each flow.

> **Important note**
> The **Type of Service (ToS)** field within an IP packet can be used to classify traffic types. TOS is where DSCP (layer 3 marking) is located in the IP packet field.

  The downside of using WFQ is it does not support encryption tunneling simply because these security features modify the packet content information that is required by WFQ for its classification mechanism.

- The **Class-Based Weighted Fair Queuing (CBWFQ)** algorithm is simply an extension of WFQ. With CBWFQ, traffic classes can be defined based on various matching criteria, such as network protocols, **Access-Control Lists (ACLs)**, and even the input interfaces on network devices. Once a match is found, a FIFO queue is reserved for each class and the traffic that belongs to a class is then sent to the queue. For each class of traffic, you can assign various characteristics, such as bandwidth, maximum packet limit, and even weights. During times of congestion, the allocated bandwidth is delivered to the class.

- The **Low-Latency Queuing** (**LLQ**) algorithm adds very strict priority queuing to CBWFQ. Priority queuing enables traffic types such as voice traffic to be sent before packets that are in other queues. With LLQ, there is jitter reduction on voice conversations on a network. With LLQ, traffic types that are vulnerable to delay are sent first before all other packets in other queues.

Next, we will discuss various QoS policy models.

## QoS policy models

When it comes to choosing the appropriate QoS policy for a network, we must first understand the following three QoS policy models:

- **Best effort**
- **Integrated services** (**IntServ**)
- **Differentiated services** (**DiffServ**)

Using best effort as a policy model simply provides no guarantee or reassurance of the delivery of a message on a network. A simple analogy to help explain this model is the local postal service. When you send a letter using the standard postal service, your letter is treated the same as all other letters within the postal company. There is no prioritization. When the letter is delivered to the intended recipient, there isn't any notification that the letter has been delivered successfully. On both private and public networks, best effort is the predominant method used on the internet today and will continue to be used for most general purposes by application and protocol vendors.

The best effort model has the following advantages:

- It is very scalable.
- No QoS mechanisms are required.
- It is very simple and available to deploy on a network.

The following are the disadvantages of using the best effort model:

- It does not provide any guarantee of message delivery.
- Packets may arrive out of order and not all at once.
- There is no prioritization applied to mission-critical applications or time-sensitive traffic types.

Since best effort is not an implementation of QoS, it's not configured by the network administrator. However, it is still used by QoS on the network even though it is not required. Keep in mind that when using this model, all messages are treated exactly the same as all other messages that are traveling across the network. This means voice traffic will be treated the same as web browsing traffic; no prioritization is applied.

Another QoS model is IntServ. IntServ supports real-time traffic types, such as remote video, online conferencing, and virtual reality applications. This model was designed to support multiple QoS requirements. It has the capability to provide end-to-end QoS between a source and destination, unlike the other models. Such a feature is usually required by real-time applications to manage packet streams of traffic; this is known as *microflow*.

IntServ uses a connection-oriented technique, which allows each unique or individual connection between a source and destination to specify requested resources on the network. These resources may include bandwidth, delay, and even packet loss metrics to ensure the delivery of each *microflow*. To ensure each network device between the source and destination is made aware of the required resources, IntServ uses the **Resource Reservation Protocol (RSVP)**. However, if the resources are not available on the path, the sending application does not forward any data along the path.

The following are the advantages of using IntServ:

- It provides end-to-end admission control of resources.
- Individual connections between a source and destination have their own per-request policy admission controls along the network.

The following are the disadvantages of IntServ:

- IntServ is very resource-intensive.
- The flow-based approach is not scalable in large networks.

The third policy model is known as DiffServ. DiffServ uses a simple and scalable mechanism to classify and manage traffic types using QoS. This model is able to provide *low-latency* for mission-critical and time-sensitive traffic types, such as voice and video, while using best effort for non-critical traffic types, such as web browsing and email. One major advantage DiffServ has over IntServ is that it can provide an *almost guaranteed* QoS to packet streams while remaining scalable.

DiffServ does not provide the end-to-end QoS feature. However, being scalable on large implementations has its advantages. When a sender forwards its traffic to a router, the router will classify the traffic flow in a class and provide the appropriate QoS policy for the class.

# QoS implementation methods

In this section, you will discover how QoS mechanisms are applied to traffic types.

## Classification

QoS tools are applied to a device's interface. This enables the router or switch to match the fields in a packet (*message*) to make a choice on taking or applying some QoS action. After the device has classified packets, they are placed in a waiting queue for the outgoing interface. The queuing tool will then schedule which packet should be taken from the waiting queue to forward. The schedule is based on the priority placed on a packet (*message*).

The following diagram shows the classification process:

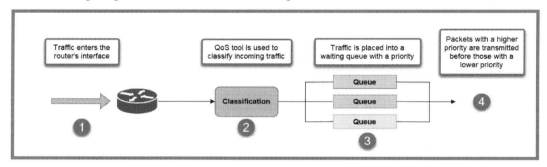

Figure 10.43 – Traffic type classification

Next, let's learn about marking.

## Marking

Marking is the process where the QoS tool changes one or more header fields in a packet, setting a value in the header. Within an IP packet, there are certain header fields that are designed for the purpose of marking by a QoS tool. When the marked packet is passed along to other networking devices, it makes classification much easier.

> **Important note**
> The **Differentiated Services Code Point** (**DSCP**) field is a 6-bit field within an IP packet, which is used for QoS marking. **Class of Service** (**COS**) is layer 2 marking in QoS.

The following diagram shows the DSCP field within an IP packet using Wireshark:

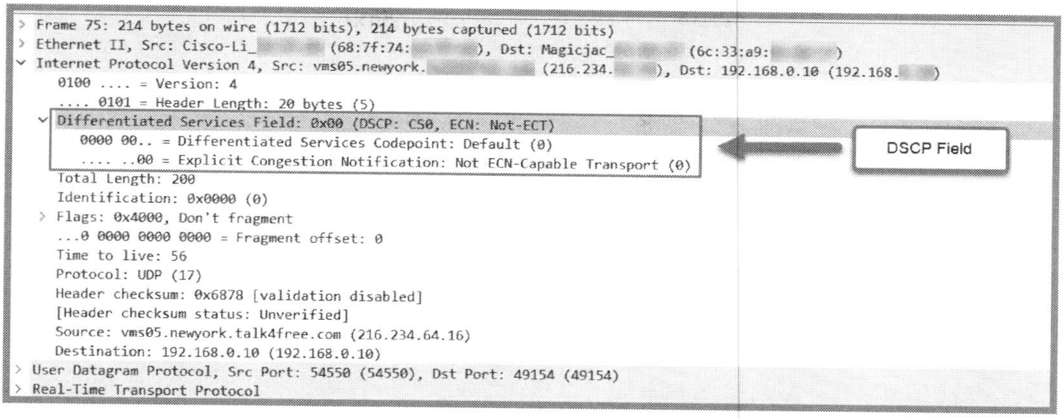

```
> Frame 75: 214 bytes on wire (1712 bits), 214 bytes captured (1712 bits)
> Ethernet II, Src: Cisco-Li_        (68:7f:74:         ), Dst: Magicjac          (6c:33:a9:         )
v Internet Protocol Version 4, Src: vms05.newyork.          (216.234.       ), Dst: 192.168.0.10 (192.168.    )
    0100 .... = Version: 4
    .... 0101 = Header Length: 20 bytes (5)
  v Differentiated Services Field: 0x00 (DSCP: CS0, ECN: Not-ECT)
      0000 00.. = Differentiated Services Codepoint: Default (0)
      .... ..00 = Explicit Congestion Notification: Not ECN-Capable Transport (0)
    Total Length: 200
    Identification: 0x0000 (0)
  > Flags: 0x4000, Don't fragment
    ...0 0000 0000 0000 = Fragment offset: 0
    Time to live: 56
    Protocol: UDP (17)
    Header checksum: 0x6878 [validation disabled]
    [Header checksum status: Unverified]
    Source: vms05.newyork.talk4free.com (216.234.64.16)
    Destination: 192.168.0.10 (192.168.0.10)
> User Datagram Protocol, Src Port: 54550 (54550), Dst Port: 49154 (49154)
> Real-Time Transport Protocol
```

DSCP Field

Figure 10.44 – DSCP field

Cisco has created a tool called **Network-Based Application Recognition (NBAR)**, which is used to match packets (traffic) for classification.

## Queuing

Queuing refers to the QoS tools for managing the queues that hold packets while they wait for their turn to exit an interface on a network device, such as a switch or router. All network devices place packets in a queue while they make a decision on whether to forward the packet out of an exit interface to its destination.

When using a queuing system, the traffic must first be classified so that it can be placed in an appropriate queue (if there are multiple queues present). Additionally, a scheduler is used to determine which packet is to be sent when the interface of the device becomes available.

Cisco devices use a scheduler algorithm known as **round-robin**. This algorithm cycles through each queue, taking either one message or a number of bytes from each queue. In other words, the algorithm takes a few messages from the first queue, then a few from the second queue, and so on, then starts back at queue 1 until the algorithm acquires enough messages to create a total number of bytes to send to an exit interface.

The router uses the CBWFQ tool to ensure a minimum amount of bandwidth is needed for each class of traffic. The network engineer will configure the weights as a percentage – the percentage of bandwidth needed per traffic class.

## Policing and shaping

These QoS tools are typically used on the WAN edge of a typical enterprise network. Both of these tools note each packet as it passes and measures the number of bits per second over time. The policer tool is responsible for discarding packets, while the shaper tool is responsible for holding/keeping packets in the queue. These tools are designed to keep the bit rate below a certain speed.

## Congestion avoidance

Congestion avoidance is used to reduce the overall packet loss by preemptively discarding some packets in a TCP connection.

Having completed this section, you have gained essential knowledge of the operations of QoS and its importance on a network.

# Summary

In this chapter, we covered a wide array of IP services that are crucial for improving the efficiency of an enterprise network. You learned about the importance of proper timekeeping and how to implement NTP to ensure devices' system clocks are synchronized. Furthermore, you saw the benefits of implementing DHCP on a network to automatically distribute IP addresses to end devices and DNS to help resolve hostnames to IP addresses easily.

Next, you saw how network management protocols such as SNMP can be used to help network engineers to easily monitor and manage network devices, and Syslog can be used to improve log management using a centralized logging server. Lastly, you gained an insight into the difference that QoS can make on a network.

I hope this chapter has been informative for you and is helpful in your journey toward learning how to implement Cisco solutions and prepare for the CCNA 200-301 certification. In the next chapter, *Chapter 11*, *Exploring Network Security*, you will learn the essentials of protecting your network from cyber threats and improving your organization's security.

# Questions

The following is a short list of review questions to help reinforce your learning and identify areas that require some improvement:

1. What is the default port for NTP?

   A. 143

   B. 110

   C. 123

   D. 1234

2. Which command allows you to configure the system clock on a device?

   A. `ntp server`

   B. `ntp master 1`

   C. `ntp master`

   D. `clock set`

3. Which Stratum level has the most accurate time on a network?

   A. 0

   B. 4

   C. 1

   D. All

4. DHCP has which of the following open ports?

   A. 68

   B. 67

   C. 69

   D. 53

5. After a DHCP server receives a DHCP **request** message, what message will the server send to the client?

   A. None

   B. Discover

   C. Acknowledgement

   D. Offer

6.  Which DNS record is used to resolve an IP address to a hostname?

    A. SOA

    B. MX

    C. A

    D. PTR

7.  Syslog uses which of the following ports?

    A. 123

    B. 161

    C. 512

    D. 514

8.  Which port does SNMP use?

    A. TCP 123

    B. UDP 161

    C. TCP 161

    D. UDP 514

9.  Which SNMP message is used to modify a device's configuration?

    A. Set

    B. Trap

    C. Get

    D. Create

10. Which of the following is the default QoS method for forwarding traffic?

    A. CBWFQ

    B. Best effort

    C. LLQ

    D. DiffServ

# Further reading

The following links are recommended for additional reading:

- Configuring NTP: `https://www.cisco.com/c/en/us/td/docs/switches/datacenter/sw/5_x/nx-os/system_management/configuration/guide/sm_nx_os_cg/sm_3ntp.html`

- Configuring DHCP: `https://www.cisco.com/c/en/us/td/docs/ios-xml/ios/ipaddr_dhcp/configuration/xe-3se/3850/dhcp-xe-3se-3850-book/config-dhcp-server.html`

- Configuring DNS: `https://www.cisco.com/c/en/us/support/docs/ip/domain-name-system-dns/24182-reversedns.html`

- Configuring Syslog: `https://www.cisco.com/c/en/us/td/docs/routers/access/wireless/software/guide/SysMsgLogging.html`

- Configuring SNMP: `https://www.cisco.com/c/en/us/td/docs/ios-xml/ios/snmp/configuration/xe-16/snmp-xe-16-book/nm-snmp-cfg-snmp-support.html`

- Configuring QoS: `https://www.cisco.com/c/en/us/td/docs/routers/access/800M/software/800MSCG/QoS.html`

# Section 5:
# Security
# Fundamentals

This section begins by introducing you to the essentials of cyber threats and how they can impact a network. Then, you will learn how to use various tools to discover security vulnerabilities and implement security controls to help mitigate and prevent both internal and external cyber threats in an enterprise network.

This section contains the following chapters:

- *Chapter 11, Exploring Network Security*
- *Chapter 12, Configuring Device Access Control and VPNs*
- *Chapter 13, Implementing Access Control Lists*
- *Chapter 14, Implementing Layer 2 and Wireless Security*

# 11
# Exploring Network Security

Designing and implementing a network without security in mind is like leaving all of the windows and doors open at home when you go out. An unauthorized visitor can simply access your personal space and remove your valuables, simply because all points of entry are open. The same concepts should be applied to a network; security is one of the most important factors a network engineer should always remember when designing any network.

During the course of this chapter, we'll look at how to identify various threat actions and attacks, understand the need for network security on an enterprise network, and understand how to develop a security program to improve user awareness and training.

In this chapter, we will cover the following topics:

- Security concepts (threats, vulnerabilities, and exploits)
- Password management
- Vulnerability assessment tools
- **Authentication**, **Authorization**, and **Accounting** (**AAA**)
- Wireshark 101 elements of a security program

# Technical requirements

To follow along with the exercises in this chapter, please ensure that you meet the following hardware and software requirements:

- Cisco Packet Tracer: `https://www.netacad.com`
- Wireshark: `https://www.wireshark.org`
- Nessus Essentials: `https://www.tenable.com/products/nessus/nessus-essentials`

The code files for this chapter are available at `https://github.com/PacktPublishing/Implementing-and-Administering-Cisco-Solutions/tree/master/Chapter%2011`.

Check out the following video to see the Code in Action: `https://bit.ly/361vb7B`

# Security concepts

As a network professional, our primary responsibility is to ensure all devices have end-to-end connectivity. However, with the rise of cyber-crime, organizations must ensure their assets are well protected from cybercriminals trying to compromise systems and networks.

When designing a security network, it's important to first identify all assets within the organization. An **asset** is simply anything that is valuable to an organization. Assets are usually broken down into the following categories:

- Tangible
- Intangible
- People

Tangible assets are items that are physically within the organization such as furniture, computers, servers, network devices, and components. These assets usually store data about the organization and sometimes contain system logs that are useful during an incident. Intangible assets are items that are non-physical—these include intellectual property, procedures, data, and anything digital that is worth value to the organization. Another type of asset that some businesses do not focus on is people. "People" refers to employees, customers, and even suppliers. An organization also needs to protect its human resources from cyber-attacks and threats.

Many organizations in various industries usually sell a product or service to their customers, so they'll keep records of customer information such as names, locations, and contact details. This type of data is referred to as **Personally Identifiable Information (PII)**. Such data must be secured at all times and kept away from hackers.

Nowadays hackers aren't just launching disruptive attacks to prevent users from accessing a resource— they are creating more sophisticated attacks to steal money and other financial assets such as cryptocurrency (for example, Bitcoin). Hackers have realized they can make money by simply stealing your data and selling it on the dark web or holding it hostage and encouraging you to pay a ransom to retrieve it.

The need for information security is always rising, and so is the need for security professionals in all industries to help organizations to protect their assets from hackers and other threats. The foundations of information security start with three main pillars: **Confidentiality**, **Integrity**, and **Availability**. These three pillars form what is commonly referred to as the **CIA triad** within the field of information security.

# The CIA triad

As mentioned previously, data is the most important asset to an organization. The way data is managed is crucial to its security. Data itself exists in three states:

- Data at rest
- Data in use
- Data in motion

*Data at rest* refers to any data that is stored on a medium or device. This can be data that is currently stored on a **Hard Disk Drive** (**HDD**), in online storage such as AWS S3 buckets, or even at an off-site location. Data at rest is simply data that is not currently being used by an application or a user. *Data in motion* is simply data that is traveling along a network or being accessed remotely by an application or a user. An example of data in motion can be a user copying a file from the local/remote file server onto their local computer. *Data in use* is defined as any data that is currently being accessed/used by an application or a user. A simple example of *data in use* is opening a PDF file on your hard disk and reading its contents—while the application is currently accessing the PDF file, the state changes from *data at rest* to *data in use*. As a security professional, our task is to protect all forms and states of data within an organization. Applying **Confidentiality**, **Integrity,** and **Availability (CIA)** will help us to achieve information security.

## Confidentiality

Confidentiality ensures that only authorized persons have access to view a system or data. We can apply cryptography, such as encryption, to any data to keep it private. During the encryption process, an encryption algorithm and secret key are used to perform the encryption process. A secret key is used to encrypt and decrypt the message. The secret key should always be kept private and safe at all times; if the key is lost or stolen, the data is compromised.

Confidentiality plays an important role in ensuring hackers and other threat actors do not gain access to an organization's data. The Microsoft Windows 10 operating system contains a data encryption application known as BitLocker. This application allows a user to create an encrypted storage container to store *data at rest*. If a hacker is able to access the Windows 10 system, the hacker will not be able to access the contents of the BitLocker container as long as it's locked and the secret key is safe. However, if the attacker has the secret key and access to the BitLocker contain, he/she can retrieve the contents and therefore the data is compromised.

> **Tip**
>
> To get more information about BitLocker on Windows 10, please visit the following link: `https://docs.microsoft.com/en-us/windows/security/information-protection/bitlocker/bitlocker-overview`.

## Integrity

Integrity plays the role of ensuring data isn't modified between source and destination. In the digital world, when a device receives a message, it needs to validate whether that message was modified during transmission from the source to the destination. Hackers and other malicious threats can intercept messages as they are passing along a network and modify the message before sending it off to the destination. Hackers use this technique for various purposes, such as spoofing, pretending to be someone or something else on a network, and attempting to trick an unsuspecting person into falling victim to a cyber-attack.

> **Important note**
>
> The Data Link layer of the **Transmission Control Protocol/internet Protocol (TCP/IP)** inserted a **Cyclic Redundancy Check (CRC)** value into each message before sending it on a network. This CRC value is a cryptographic hash value used to determine whether the message was modified or not.

Integrity plays an important part in information security, ensuring a receiver is able to detect whether a message was compromised.

## Availability

The role of availability is a simple but challenging one—to ensure a system or resource is always available to those who have access to it. During a cyber-attack, an organization's resources, data, applications, network devices, and even system may become unreachable and unusable. Once a system or resource is unusable by legitimately authorized persons, an organization may not be able to continue working at optimal performance.

An example of availability being disrupted is a **Denial of Service (DoS)** attack. A DoS attack is designed to exhaust all of the available computing power of a target system, hence making it unavailable to legitimate users. Such an attack can be applied to a scenario with an online web server; if an attacker launches a DoS attack on the web server, the web application will process all of the incoming `HTTP/HTTPS` web request messages and eventually become overwhelmed with the high volume of messages originating from the attacker. Therefore, when legitimate users on the internet are attempting to retrieve the web pages from the server, the server may not respond to them. Hence, availability has been compromised.

## Putting the three pillars of CIA together

One of the objectives of information security is to ensure all three pillars are applied equally within an organization. Maintaining this balance is somewhat difficult as some organizations focus more on confidentiality; this means the ball (representing an organization's focus) in the following diagram would be placed closer to the confidentiality pillar, moving away from integrity and availability. This means data will be more secure (*confidentiality*), but access to the data will be more difficult (*availability*) and checking any modification of data will also be more difficult (*integrity*).

The following diagram shows the CIA Triad in a triangular format:

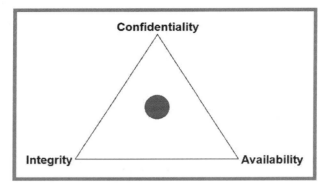

Figure 11.1 – CIA Triad

If an organization makes its data and resources very easy to access and focus on availability more than the other pillars, there will be fewer security controls in place to ensure the data is kept private to only authorized persons only (confidentiality) and the checking of any unauthorized changes on the data.

As a security professional, it's important to understand what threats, exploits, vulnerabilities, and attacks stand to compromise the assets of an organization. In the following sections, these terms will be covered in greater detail.

# Threats

In the world of information technology, as more devices are moving online and people are connecting to the internet, we find ourselves facing security threats each day. *A threat is defined as anything with the motivation to cause harm or damage to a person, system, or network.* As more devices are going online and persons are connecting to the internet, there is also a high increase in cyber threats. In today's world, many organizations are going online to expand their customer reach and support for their products and services. There are many companies that are no longer are considered traditional *brick and mortar* companies, but instead, use the internet as a tool to support their organization. One such organization is Amazon, which sells many items, including books. Amazon is not a traditional walk-in book store but, rather, an online book store that allows potential buyers to read the outline, descriptions, and reviews of books and even get a preview before making the choice to purchase one.

Almost all modern-day businesses have an internet connection. This creates a huge risk—an attacker or malware can access the organization's internal network. Throughout my career, I've seen many organizations from various industries who invest in scalable network infrastructure, which is resilient and has redundancy to ensure all devices have end-to-end connectivity. However, security is such an important factor that isn't always acknowledged. Designing a network to perform at optimal capacity is great but without security, your entire network infrastructure is left vulnerable to both internal and external threats.

Threats exist in many forms; a hacker may attempt to retrieve a victim's username and password for their online accounts, gain unauthorized access into a system by exploiting a security vulnerability on a computer, or even crack the passphrase for the wireless network in your organization.

## Assets

As a security professional, it's important to secure the organization's assets. An asset is anything of value to an organization.

Tangible assets are physical objects such as computers, servers, and furniture. This type of asset needs to be protected just as equally as everything else. Tangible assets are vulnerable to physical damage and even theft. Imagine a small business that has a customer service outlet that allows customers to walk in and conduct transactions on a daily basis. Let's say each customer service representative was assigned a laptop at their desk to perform their duties and complete tasks. If each laptop was not physically secured using a Kensington Cable, a *customer* with bad intent may simply pick up a laptop while the employee is not looking and walk away. Some companies may look at the incident as physical theft, but a cybersecurity professional will determine it as both physical and data theft; the laptop has storage media such as an HDD, upon which important and confidential data may be stored. A malicious user can simply retrieve the data from the HDD and sell it on the dark web.

The most valuable asset to any organization is data. Hackers are continuously developing new strategies and techniques to gain access to systems and networks to steal data. Our job as network professionals is not only to create an efficient network but also to create a secure network design to prevent various cyber threats. Creating a secure network design extends to all areas where an organization stores its data; these will include the local area network and even the cloud.

The cloud is an important location many professionals do not consider to be vulnerable. With cloud computing becoming cheaper as time passes, more organizations are migrating their physical infrastructure to a cloud service provider. There are many companies that have almost all of their data and other assets such as servers and applications on the cloud. However, the cloud is just as vulnerable as a physical network. Equal attention must be given to the security of your cloud platform as you would for your physical network.

## Threat actors

Threat actors are usually someone or something that is responsible for a security event or incident. Threat actors can be categorized by their characteristics and their motivations.

The following are various types of threat actors in the cybersecurity world:

- One type of threat actor is known as **script kiddies**. A script kiddie isn't necessarily a child or young person, but rather someone who is a novice within the cybersecurity realm who uses instructions and tutorials provided by the real, malicious hackers to guide his/her actions. This type of hacker does not fully understand the technical details of the actual cyber-attack or the tools being used. However, by simply following instructions and launching the same type of attack, they have the ability to compromise a system or network.

- The **hacktivist** is another type of hacker who is between an activist and a hacker. This person uses their technical skills to serve a social or political agenda. Some hacktivist actions include defacing political and government websites, coordinating DoS attacks against an organization's network resources, and leaking confidential data such as documents to various online sites.

- Hackers often work in groups using the most elite tools and resources money can buy; this is referred to as **organized crime**. Within this group, each hacker is an expert within their own field and is assigned a unique role and function, so that one person may be responsible for developing an exploit kit while another is performing extensive reconnaissance on the target. This type of hacking group is well-funded and has the best hacking tools; their motivation is to steal currency from their victims.

- Each nation usually has its own team of hackers and these are referred to as **state-sponsored** hackers. This group of hackers are well-funded and are provided with the best tools and resources the government can buy. These types of hackers are usually hired to protect the security of their country and even perform cyber-attacks on other nations. There are many movies that explain this type of hacking group, one of which was *Snowden (2016)*, which explains how various nations are preparing for cyber warfare.

> **Tip**
>
> To learn more about cyber warfare, check out the book *Cyber Warfare – Truth, Tactics, and Strategies* by *Dr. Chase Cunningham* published by *Packt Publishing* at `https://www.packtpub.com/security/cyber-warfare-truth-tactics-and-strategies`.

- Some people think all cyber threats originate from the internet. Sometimes an **insider** threat can occur and remain undetected because the organization is busy looking at the internet and neglecting its own corporate network for internal threats and attacks. An insider is simply someone who has gained employment with a target organization under the guise of being a trusted person who can fill a role within the company. However, this person has other intentions; once within the organization, he/she will learn the ins-and-outs of the network and infiltrate the organization from within.

- With the rise in cyber-attacks, organizations are investing in cybersecurity solutions and people to help to safeguard their network and assets. In every network and system, there are vulnerabilities that are known and those that haven't been discovered yet. Organizations hire a special type of hacker known as a **white hat hacker**—these are commonly referred to as *ethical* hackers. These are the good guys who use their skill set to help organizations to discover vulnerabilities within their own infrastructure before the bad guys find and exploit them. White hat hackers obtain legal permission before their engagement in a penetration test exercise; this is a real-world simulation attack on the systems and network, to see how a malicious hacker might be able to exploit vulnerabilities and gain access into the network.

- A **black hat hacker** uses their skill set to perform malicious and unethical actions on computers and networks for personal gain. These are the type of hackers that your organization and assets need to be well protected and fortified against. A **gray hat hacker** simply sits between a white hat and black hat hacker. This type of hacker could commit crimes and perform malicious actions. However, they can use their skill set for both good and bad things.

Now, let's look at vulnerabilities.

# Vulnerabilities

One question students frequently ask at the beginning of their cybersecurity journey is: how are hackers able to break into a system or network? The simple answer is hackers and other threat actors look for vulnerabilities on a target system. A vulnerability is a security weakness or flaw in a system that could be exploited by a threat. The competition between security researchers and hackers has been an ongoing one—a race to discover security flaws first. Security researchers are always looking for new vulnerabilities to help software and product vendors to fix and close security weaknesses while hackers are looking to exploit and gain access to their victims' systems.

> **Tip**
>
> **Nessus** is one of the most popular vulnerability assessment tools within the cybersecurity industry. Further information on Nessus can be found at `https://www.tenable.com/products/nessus`.

A vulnerability can exist in the form of a weakness or flaw in a configuration, security policy, or even something technological in nature. Let's look at an example. A network device such as a router is configured to use Telnet and not SSH as the preferred method for remote access management. Telnet is an unsecured protocol that transfers data in plaintext whereas SSH encrypts all traffic. As you have learned so far, TCP/IP is the language all devices speak when connected to an Ethernet network, so you may think the TCP/IP protocol suite is designed with good security but in reality, it's not.

Many vulnerabilities exist in the various protocols within TCP/IP. These protocols include **Internet Protocol (IP)**, **Internet Control Message Protocol (ICMP)**, **Hypertext Transfer Protocol (HTTP)**, and even **Simple Network Management Protocol (SNMP)**. If the IP was not designed with good security, an attacker can simply spoof the IP address of another device on the network. SNMPv1 does not support user authentication, so this means an attacker is able to remotely connect to an SNMP enabled-device and gather sensitive information. Attackers can take advantage of various weaknesses within these protocols and capture sensitive information while network traffic is traveling along a network.

Hackers are always looking for a way inside your network and devices, and your network components provide an easy way in if they are not updated and secured properly.

The following screenshot shows the NMap tool has found the `EternalBlue` vulnerability on a Windows system:

```
Host script results:
| smb-vuln-ms17-010:
|   VULNERABLE:
|   Remote Code Execution vulnerability in Microsoft SMBv1 servers (ms17-010)
|     State: VULNERABLE
|     IDs:  CVE:CVE-2017-0143
|     Risk factor: HIGH
|       A critical remote code execution vulnerability exists in Microsoft SMBv1
|       servers (ms17-010).
|
|     Disclosure date: 2017-03-14
|     References:
|       https://technet.microsoft.com/en-us/library/security/ms17-010.aspx
|       https://blogs.technet.microsoft.com/msrc/2017/05/12/customer-guidance-for-wannacrypt-attacks/
|_      https://cve.mitre.org/cgi-bin/cvename.cgi?name=CVE-2017-0143
```

Figure 11.2 – EternalBlue

In the preceding screenshot, NMap reported that the target system is vulnerable to the `EternalBlue` exploit, which will allow an attacker to exploit the vulnerability in **Server Message Block (SMB)** version 1 and execute remote code. Furthermore, NMap reports the risk is high on the target and provides reference URLs for additional research.

Also, some enterprise network devices such as routers and switches support network security functions to help to prevent various malicious threats and attacks on your network. Sometimes, a misconfiguration on a router can give an attacker remote access into the management pane of the device.

Each device requires a firmware or an operating system in order to work and perform functions. Operating system vendors are always researching for vulnerabilities within their product to quickly release updates and security patches to fix any issues for their customers. Many organizations do not update their computers' operating systems for many months, and this increases the risk of it being compromised. Imagine if a new threat came about and the operating system vendor releases a security patch to fix the issues but the organization ignores the updates and patches by the vendor; their systems will be vulnerable to the threat until security patching occurs on their network. Remember, each day hackers are always looking for ways into your systems, so operating system vendors release updates very frequently to help to protect you.

Many configuration vulnerabilities exist on a network. This type of security weakness exists within user account management, misconfigured network services, and default configurations on devices. When logging in to a system, your user credentials may be sent across the network via an unsecured protocol.

The following screenshot shows a Windows user credential was captured as it was sent to the Active Directory server on the network:

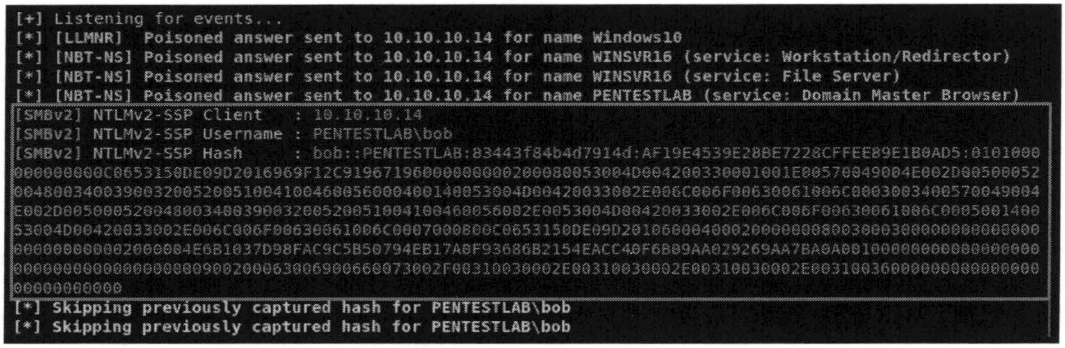

Figure 11.3 – User account details

In the preceding screenshot, we can see the user, Bob, enters his username and password on a Windows 10 system to authenticate himself on the network. However, in this scenario, the Active Directory server (Windows Server) is using the default directory query protocol, **Lightweight Directory Access Protocol** (**LDAP**). LDAP does not encrypt the user information by default; only the user's password is hashed using NTLMv2 and sent across the network. In the preceding screenshot, the hash was captured, allowing the attacker to perform offline decryption of the hash to retrieve Bob's password. This is an example of an unsecured user account and insecure protocols on a network.

Configuration vulnerabilities also exist when an administrator configures weak or insecure passwords for user accounts. Such vulnerability enables a hacker to easily compromise user accounts on a system and quickly gain access. Another vulnerability occurs if default configurations are used on a system or network device. Default configurations are applied on a device at the point it leaves the manufacturer; they allow us to easily get the device up and working quickly without having to spend too much time trying to figure out how to get it working. Default configurations often contain many configuration weaknesses such as security features are absent and remote access is enabled for all. It's important to ensure default configurations are never used on systems and devices on a production network.

## Human vulnerabilities

One major vulnerability we often overlook when designing a secure network is the human factor. Humans are also vulnerable to various online and offline cyber-attacks, such as being a victim of social engineering attacks. Social engineering is simply when an attacker is able to manipulate a person to reveal sensitive information or perform a certain task.

> **Important note**
>
> Social engineering is usually a non-technical in nature. This means a computer is not required to perform various types of social engineering attacks on a victim. The attack usually exploits the trust and social behavior of the victim.

The following are various types of cyber-attacks that target human vulnerabilities:

- **Phishing** is a form of social engineering that is done using a computer; the attacker creates and sends a fake email to a potential victim. The email is crafted to look and sound as if it came from a legitimate source, such as a financial institution. The message usually contains some instructions and a malicious link embedded within the message. The instructions might say, *Your user account has been hacked and click the following link to reset it*. If the user follows these instructions, they'll end up downloading malware and infecting the system, visiting a site that allows the attacker is able to capture the victim's username and password.

- Another type of social engineering is spear phishing. In a **spear phishing** attack, the attacker makes a fake message or email look more legitimate and believable. This type of attack is usually focused on a specific group of people. An example would be an attacker who crafts an email that looks like it originates from *Bank X* and sends it to everyone associated with that bank. People who have an account with *Bank X* will be more susceptible to the scam, click any malicious links, or follow any instructions with the message whereas a person who does not have an account with *Bank X* will simply block, delete, or ignore the message.

- **Whaling** is a type of phishing attack that focuses on the high profile persons within an organization such as a CEO or even a director. The objective of the attack is to compromise a high profile person's account and use the account to conduct transactions. Imagine if a CEO's email account is compromised, the attacker could send emails to the accounting department requesting confidential financial details about the organization. People within the accounting department will see the email originating from the CEO and trust it's the actual CEO requesting the information. In such an attack, trust is being exploited between the employee and the CEO.

- Social engineering attacks can be done over a telephone conversation—this is known as **vishing**. In vishing, the attacker calls the potential victim while pretending to be someone with authority or a person the victim may trust. During the conversation, the attacker may also try to build or improve the trust between the victim and the attacker and take advantage of that trust. In vishing attacks, the attacker may pretend to be calling from the victim's bank and request the victim's online banking user credentials or perhaps request their credit card number and pin.

- Social engineering can also be done using **Short Message Service** (**SMS**), a form of attack known as **smishing**. This is when an attacker attempts to perform social engineering using the text messaging service on mobile phones.

- Sometimes an attacker may take a more aggressive approach to get victims to visit a compromised website. Hackers are able to compromise vulnerable **Domain Name System** (**DNS**) servers and can modify the DNS records, for example, by changing the DNS A record for a hostname to point to a compromised website rather than the legitimate IP address. This means any device requesting the IP address of a certain website will be redirected to a malicious website. This type of social engineering is known as **pharming**.

- It's important to build a fortress around and within your organization to protect it from both internal and external cyber-attacks and threats. Sometimes, when an attacker realizes he/she is unable to compromise the target's network, the attacker may attempt to perform a waterhole attack. In a **waterhole attack**, the attacker will attempt to compromise a site or location the employees of the target organization commonly visit, such as a local coffee shop. By compromising the coffee shop Wi-Fi network, any device connected to that network will download a payload and the mobile device will be infected. When an employee connects their infected mobile device to the corporate network, it will compromise the organization. However, anyone who connects to the Wi-Fi network, or the waterhole, will be infected, not just the target users who belong to the organization.

Next, let's go ahead and learn about password vulnerabilities and management.

## Password vulnerabilities and management

To prove our identity to a system, we must provide a valid user name and password. Many people often create simple and easy-to-remember passwords for their online accounts. While it's simple for the user to remember, it's a security vulnerability as a hacker can easily gain access to the victim's account. Creating a secure and complex password is important and prevents hackers and other threat actors from compromising a user account and gaining access to sensitive information.

When creating secure and complex passwords, use the following guidelines:

- Passwords should at least 8 characters in length.

- Ensure the password includes a combination of uppercase and lowercase letters, numbers, special characters, and symbols.

- Ensure the password is not being used on another account you may own.

- Passwords should not be regular words you'd find in the dictionary.

- Passwords should not contain any personal details such as birthdays or relative names.

- Passwords should be changed frequently.

- Passwords should not be written down anywhere around your workplace.

Using a password manager can help you to create, store, and manage secure passwords. There are many free password managers available on the internet.

The following screenshot shows a secure password generated by the **LastPass** password manager:

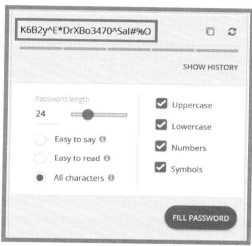

Figure 11.4 – Secure password

Passwords are still breakable by a hacker who has a lot of time and computing power. Using **Multifactor Authentication (MFA)** adds an extra layer of security to our user accounts; therefore, the user has to provide multiple sets of information to prove his/her identity.

Sometimes, after a username and password combination has been validated by a system, it requests a second form of authentication to validate your identity. This is sometimes referred to as **2-Factor Authentication (2FA)**. Authenticator apps on your smartphone can be associated with a supported website. Cisco is an example of this as its user accounts support 2FA, which allows you to add a third-party authenticator, such as Google Authenticator, on your Cisco user account. Each time you attempt to log in to the Cisco website, a unique code is required from the authenticator app. This code changes approximately every 30 seconds, making it difficult for a hacker to guess the sequence of codes being generated each time.

Rather than using passwords, you can use biometrics. Biometrics allows you to use a part of your body to authenticate to a system. Most new smartphones support biometric authentication, which allows a person to unlock their smartphone using their fingerprint. On Microsoft Windows 10, **Windows Hello** uses facial recognition technology.

> **Important note**
> Other forms of biometrics are voice, iris, and retina scans.

Digital certificates are an alternative method to authenticate to a system. Digital certificates are granted by a **Certificates Authority** (**CA**), which verifies the identity and authenticity of the requester. The CA functions as a trusted third party who can verify the holder of the certificate is who they claim to be.

## Lab – Using Nessus to perform a vulnerability assessment

In this lab, you will learn how to perform a vulnerability assessment on a target system using **Nessus Essentials**.

To get started, use the following instructions:

1.  Go to `https://www.tenable.com/products/nessus/nessus-essentials` and register for an **Activation Code**:

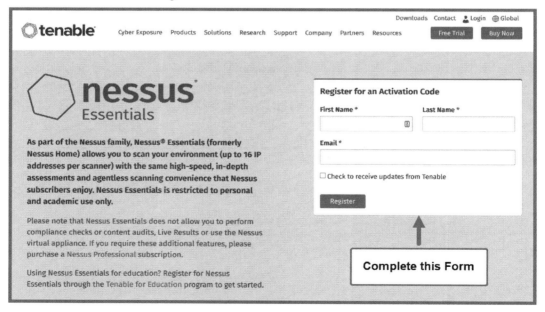

Figure 11.5 – Nessus Essentials home page

2. You will be redirected to a *Thank You* page containing a **Download** button—click it:

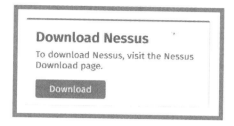

Figure 11.6 – Download button

3. Choose the latest version of Nessus Essentials that is available for your operating system:

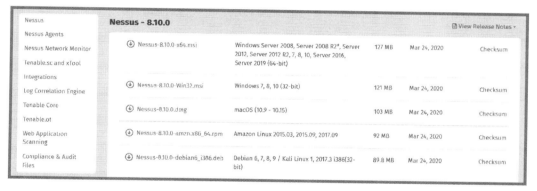

Figure 11.7 – Nessus Essentials download page

4. Once the file has been downloaded onto your computer, install it using all of the default settings.

5. After installation, your web browser will open the following URL:
   `http://localhost:8834/WelcomeToNessus-Install/welcome.`

6.  Click on **Connect via SSL** to ensure your connection is secure:

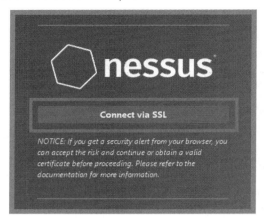

Figure 11.8 – Ensure SSL

If your web browser gives a security warning, add an exception. This warning is created because Nessus is using a self-signed digital certificate.

7.  Choose the **deployment type**: **Nessus Essentials** and click **Continue**.

8.  An **Activation Code Request** page will appear. Simply click **Skip** as we have already completed this task in *step 1*:

Figure 11.9 – Skip registration

9. Check your inbox for a confirmation email with your *Nessus Essentials License Key*.

10. Insert the **Activation Code** in the field as shown in the following screenshot and click **Continue**:

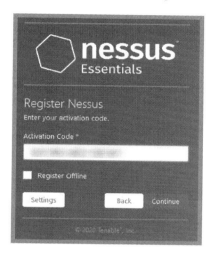

Figure 11.10 – Activation window

11. Create a local user account for the Nessus Essentials application and click **Submit**.

12. After the setup process, Nessus Essentials will initialize on your computer.

13. If the Nessus Plugins fail to download during the initialization phase, open Command Prompt with Administrator privileges and execute the command shown in the following screenshot:

```
Microsoft Windows [Version 10.0.18363.836]
(c) 2019 Microsoft Corporation. All rights reserved.

C:\WINDOWS\system32>cd C:\Program Files\Tenable\Nessus

C:\Program Files\Tenable\Nessus>nessuscli update
Refreshing Nessus license information... complete; continuing with updates.


----- Fetching the newest updates from nessus.org -----

Nessus Plugins: Downloading (0%)
Nessus Plugins: Downloading (1%)
Nessus Plugins: Downloading (3%)
Nessus Plugins: Downloading (4%)
```

Figure 11.11 – Reinitializing the Nessus Plugins download phase

14. Once the process is complete, go to `https://localhost:8834/#/` and log in using your user credentials.

15. Once you're logged in, click **New Scan**. You'll see the following scan templates to choose:

Figure 11.12 – Nessus pre-configuration templates

You can choose any scan template and even customize it to fit your needs.

16. Click on **Basic Network Scan**.

17. Complete the basic information within the fields, as shown in the following screenshot:

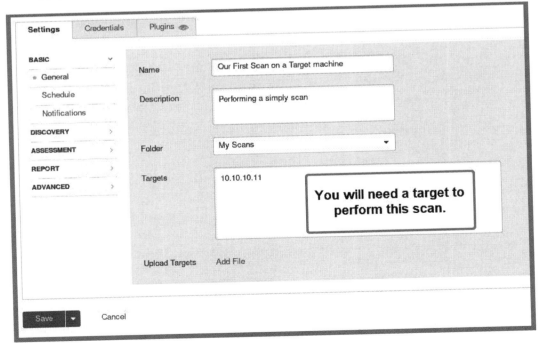

Figure 11.13 – Configuring a basic scan on Nessus

> **Important note**
>
> For legal purposes, do not scan any devices or networks that you have not been legally authorized to. For this exercise, I am performing a vulnerability scan on a personal machine within my own network.

18. Click **Save**.

19. Once the scan has been saved, click the **Play/Launch** icon on the furthest right column to launch the scan.

20. Once the scan is finished, click on it to access the details. You will see an overview of all of the vulnerabilities found with a severity level.

21. Click on **Vulnerabilities** to see all of the security weaknesses found on the target machine:

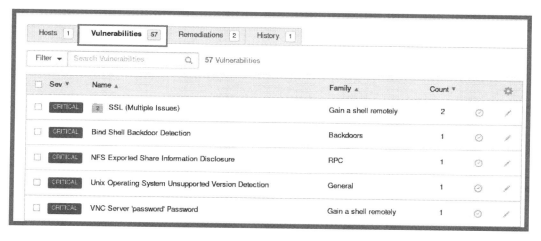

Figure 11.14 – Vulnerabilities

As shown in the preceding screenshot, Nessus provides a list of all of the vulnerabilities found on the target system and sorts the list from Critical to Informational.

22. Selecting a vulnerability will provide you with a description and solution on how to fix the security flaw, as shown in the following screenshot:

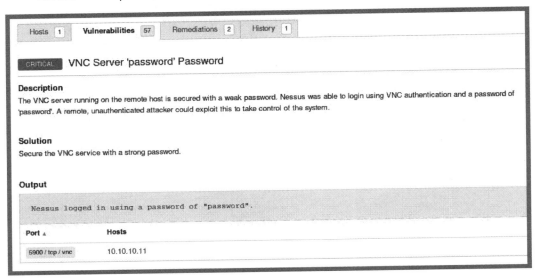

Figure 11.15 – Security flaw in VNC Server

23. Also, you can click the **Export/Report** button in the top-right corner to export a report of the assessment in PDF, CSV, or HTML format. Nessus can generate an **Executive Summary** or a **Custom** report.

The Executive Summary will contain a summary list of all of the vulnerabilities found, the severity levels, and their **Common Vulnerability Scoring System** (**CVSS**) score. The Custom report contains specific details such as the description, solutions, references, and even risk factors for each vulnerability.

Having completed this lab, you have gained the skills to perform a basic vulnerability scan and create reports using the Nessus vulnerability scanner. In the next section, you will learn about exploits.

# Exploits

Exploits are the malicious code or actions an attacker uses to take advantage of a vulnerability on a system. Within each operating system, application, and device, there are known and unknown vulnerabilities. Once a hacker has discovered a vulnerability on his/her target system, the next step is to acquire an exploit that will leverage the security flaw. One popular website to find exploits is **Exploit Database** (`www.exploit-db.com`). This website is maintained by Offensive Security, the creators of the popular penetration testing Linux distro, Kali Linux. The purpose of such a website is information sharing for other cybersecurity professionals such as penetration testers who require exploits during their jobs.

> **Tip**
>
> To understand how threats, vulnerabilities, and exploits all fit together, consider the following sentence: a *threat* uses an *exploit* to take advantage of a *vulnerability* on a *system*.

One such vulnerability is known as **EternalBlue** (MS17-010); this vulnerability is a weakness found in Microsoft Windows operating systems with **Microsoft Server Message Block 1.0 (SMBv1)**. An attacker with an exploit for `EternalBlue` will be able to perform remote code execution on a vulnerable machine.

> **Important note**
>
> Further information about the MS17-010 security bulletin can be found at `https://docs.microsoft.com/en-us/security-updates/securitybulletins/2017/ms17-010`.

The following are the search results for the `EternalBlue` (MS17-010) vulnerability on Exploit Database:

| Date | D | A | V | Title | Type | Platform |
|------|---|---|---|-------|------|----------|
| 2018-02-05 | ⬇ | | ✓ | Microsoft Windows - 'EternalRomance'/'EternalSynergy'/'EternalChampion' SMB Remote Code Execution (Metasploit) (MS17-010) | Remote | Windows |
| 2017-07-11 | ⬇ | | ✓ | Microsoft Windows 7/8.1/2008 R2/2012 R2/2016 R2 - 'EternalBlue' SMB Remote Code Execution (MS17-010) | Remote | Windows |
| 2017-05-17 | ⬇ | | ✓ | Microsoft Windows 7/2008 R2 - 'EternalBlue' SMB Remote Code Execution (MS17-010) | Remote | Windows |
| 2017-05-17 | ⬇ | | ✓ | Microsoft Windows 8/8.1/2012 R2 (x64) - 'EternalBlue' SMB Remote Code Execution (MS17-010) | Remote | Windows_x86-64 |
| 2017-05-10 | ⬇ | | ✗ | Microsoft Windows Server 2008 R2 (x64) - 'SrvOs2FeaToNt' SMB Remote Code Execution (MS17-010) | Remote | Windows_x86-64 |
| 2017-04-17 | ⬇ | | ✓ | Microsoft Windows - SMB Remote Code Execution Scanner (MS17-010) (Metasploit) | DoS | Windows |

Figure 11.16 – Search Results for EternalBlue

Additionally, the attacker or the penetration tester can use an exploitation development framework such as **Metasploit** to create a custom payload and deliver it on to the target. Metasploit allows a cybersecurity professional to build custom payloads to leverage the weaknesses found in applications and operating systems; however, an attacker can do this as well.

> **Tip**
>
> If you want to learn more about Metasploit, please see the following link: `https://www.offensive-security.com/metasploit-unleashed/`.

Once an attacker has gained access to a system, he/she is able to escalate their user privileges on the victim's system and even pivot the attack through the compromised system to all other internal devices on the network.

# Attacks

In this section, you will learn about various types of cyber-attacks and how they can cause harm to systems and networks.

## Malware

Malware is code that is designed to perform malicious actions on a system. The term malware is taken from the words malicious software, which has the capability to exfiltrate data, make a system unusable, or even delete important files on its local disk. There are many types of malware on the internet and each day security researchers and cybersecurity professionals are discovering these new threats.

The following are descriptions of the most commonly known types of malware:

- One type of malware we all know is the **virus**. A computer virus is similar to a human virus; once a system is infected, the virus begins to unleash its payload and cause more harm. Computer viruses are malicious code that is designed to reproduce themselves on an infected system and cause additional damage. Computer viruses are not self-executable; this means a user has to download a virus on their system and manually execute it, then the payload is unleashed on the victim's system.

> **Important note**
>
> There are other types of viruses such as boot sector virus, program virus, macro virus, and even firmware viruses.

- Another type of malware is the **worm**. A worm is self-replicating and automatically propagates in a network. Once a system is infected with a worm, it automatically attempts to spread to other vulnerable systems on the network. A worm is designed to exhaust the computing resources on a system, which will make the infected system work very slowly or render it unusable.

- Hackers are creating **crypto-malware** and **ransomware**. These types of malware are designed to infect a system, encrypt all of the victim's data, and request a ransom be paid to release the hostage (data). Once a system is infected with ransomware, all data is encrypted except the operating system files. Hackers want to ensure your operating system is still working so they can present you with an on-screen banner asking you to pay the ransom by providing your credit card number, Bitcoin, or another cryptocurrency. It's never recommended to pay the ransom as there is no guarantee or assurance the hackers will keep their word and provide you with the decryption key. It's important to regularly backup your data so that in the event systems are not recoverable, the systems can be wiped and data can be restored.

- The **Trojan Horse** is a type of malware that disguises itself to look like a legitimate program or application but contains a malicious payload. Once an unsuspecting user executes the Trojan Horse, the malicious payload executes in the background and the system is compromised. This type of malware is typically used to trick a user into installing it and the payload opens a *backdoor* to on the victim's system. Once a backdoor is opened on the victim's system, the hacker can gain access. Trojan Horses are sometimes in the form of fake anti-virus software, games, and even applications. The **Remote Administration Trojan** (**RAT**) is another type of Trojan Horse. A RAT simply allows the hacker to gain remote access and control over the victim's system. The attacker is able to modify configurations, enable microphones to record audio, enable webcams to record video, perform actions, and exfiltrate data.

- There's a type of malware that infects the kernel of an operating system. This is known as a **rootkit**. Once a rootkit infects the kernel, is gains *root* level access on the system. The rootkit is taken from the Linux world, the highest level user account on a Linux system is the *root* account. The root account is able to perform unrestricted tasks and actions on a system. Similarly, a rootkit can control the kernel and therefore can perform administrative actions on a compromised system. Since rootkits infect the kernel, this area in the operating system is usually inaccessible by anti-virus programs, however, some anti-virus programs allow you to perform a *boot system scan*, which is done before an operating system is loaded in memory; this type of scan is able to detect rootkits.

- **Adware** is a type of malware that displays advertisements in the form of popups on your desktop and within your browser. Adware is usually distributed by software from the internet. During the installation of software, adware may be installed in the background and will only appear after the installation process is complete.

- **Spyware** is a type of malware that spies on the victim's activities without consent. This information is sent back to the hacker. A user's activity may seem a bit harmless in the cybersecurity industry but it's actually worth a lot of money to various organizations on the dark web and even companies that perform data analytics on human behavior for targeted advertisements.

Now, let's read about reconnaissance.

## Reconnaissance

The first phase in hacking is information gathering or reconnaissance. During this phase, the attacker attempts to gather as much information as possible about the target prior to exploiting any weaknesses. The attacker usually attempts to discover any operating systems, open ports on systems, vulnerabilities, and even running services on the target. Such information can be gathered using **Open Source Intelligence** (**OSINT**) techniques such as performing various online searches using Google Hacking techniques and checking the target's website, databases, and even **Domain Name System** (**DNS**) records.

> Tip
>
> **Nmap** is one of the best network scanners to detect open ports, profile operating systems, service versions, and much more.

Furthermore, an attacker uses vulnerability scanners to detect open ports and vulnerabilities within an operating system and applications. Some well-known vulnerability scanners in the industry are Nessus, Saint, and Core Impact.

> Tip
>
> To learn more about how to perform ethical hacking and penetration testing techniques, check out my book *Learn Kali Linux 2019* by *Glen D. Singh* published by *Packt Publishing* at `https://www.packtpub.com/networking-and-servers/learn-kali-linux-2018`.

Once vulnerabilities are found, the attacker can then use exploitation tools such as Metasploit, SQLmap, Core Impact, and even **Social Engineer Toolkit** (**SET**) to gain access to a vulnerable system.

## Spoofing

Spoofing is the technique an attacker uses to fake his/her identity on a network. In technical terms, when a device such as a computer is sending a message to another device, the sender inserts its source IP address within the Layer 3 header of the packet. This information is needed to identify the source and sender of the message. Attackers are able to spoof both their MAC address and IP address, simply to fake their identity when launching any attack.

The following diagram shows an attacker sending a message to a target with a spoof IP address:

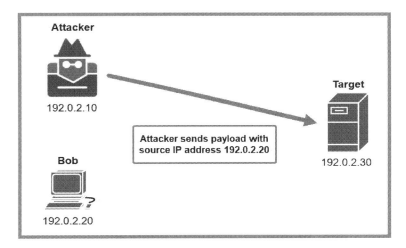

Figure 11.17 – Spoofing attack

As you can see in the preceding diagram, the attack uses Bob's IP address as the source IP address. Therefore, when the victim checks the source of the traffic, it shows the attack came from Bob's computer.

## Denial of Service

Sometimes gaining access or stealing data from a victim's system isn't the goal; some hackers simply want to disrupt service and prevent legitimate users from accessing resources. This type of attack is known as a DoS. A DoS attack is typically launched from a single source against a target such as a web server; the attacker sends a continuous stream (flood) of unsolicited messages to the target. The target device has to process all of the messages it is receiving from both the attacker and legit users on the network. Since the DoS attack is sending hundreds and even thousands of messages per minute, the target will eventually become overwhelmed by processing each message.

The following diagram shows an attacker is launching a TCP SYN flood attack to a server:

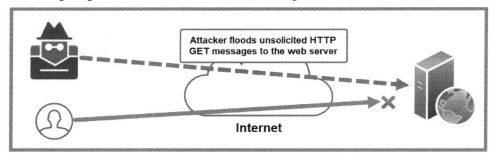

Figure 11.18 – HTTP DoS attack

When the target is overwhelmed, it won't be able to respond to legitimate users' requests and hence create the effect of denying the legitimate users access to the resources/ services. Since a DoS attack is usually from a single source, it's easy to block the attack as it happens. When a denial of service attack is launched from multiple geographic locations, the attack is amplified and more difficult to block as there are multiple sources of the attack. This is known as a **Distributed Denial of Service (DDoS)**.

## Amplification and reflection

Another type of DoS attack is a reflective attack. In a reflective attack, the attacker spoofs the IP address of the target device. The attacker then sends a flood of unsolicited request messages to a server on the network or internet. The server will respond to each request and the responses will be sent to the actual target and not the attacker.

The following diagram shows an example of a reflective attack:

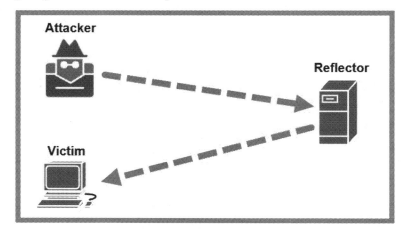

Figure 11.19 – DoS reflective attack

On the target system, the logs will indicate the attack is originating from the server and not the attacker's machine.

In an amplification attack, the attacker sends spoofed request messages to multiple servers on the internet; each server will then respond to each message. Therefore, the victim's machine will receive a flood of messages from multiple servers.

The following diagram shows an example of an amplification attack:

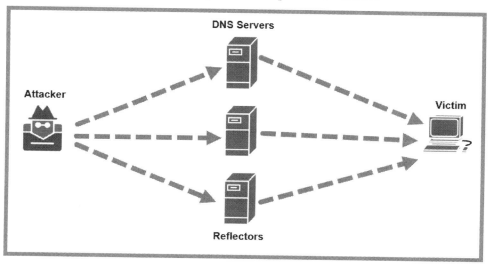

Figure 11.20 – Amplification attack

The attacker spoofs the victim's IP address and sends request messages to multiple servers (reflectors). When each server receives a request, they will process and send a reply. However, the reply message is sent to the victim instead.

## Man-in-the-Middle

In a **Man-in-the-Middle** (**MiTM**) attack, the attacker sits between the source and destination of network traffic. This allows an attacker to intercept and capture all data that is flowing between a victim's machine and its destination. This type of attack is usually done on an internet network within an organization to capture any sensitive data and user credentials that are passing along the network.

For this attack to work properly, the attacker's machine must be connected to the local area network. It learns both the IP address and MAC addresses associated with the victim machines and the default gateway. The attacker then sends gratuitous ARP messages to the victim machine, informing it that the attacker machine is the default gateway. Therefore, any traffic with a destination to the internet will now be sent to the attacker's machine. The attacker machine also sends gratuitous ARP messages to the default gateway, tricking the router into believing the attacker machine is the victim's device.

The following diagram shows the effect of a MiTM attack on a network:

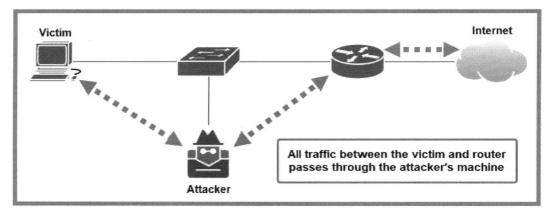

Figure 11.21 – MiTM attack

All traffic between the victim machines and the internet will flow through the attacker machine. This type of attack takes advantage of a vulnerability within the **Address Resolution Protocol** (**ARP**). ARP was not designed with the security to prevent such types of attacks. However, Cisco IOS switches do support many security features to prevent these attacks. In later chapters, we will cover how to implement Layer 2 security on an enterprise network.

## Buffer overflow

Operating systems and software developers can create a special area in memory to temporarily store data while an application is running; this area is known as a buffer. A buffer is limited to the amount of data an application can store at any time, software developers continually test their software or application to ensure data is being processed accurately and efficiently.

There are times when application/software developers do not properly test their applications, and sometimes a buffer overflow vulnerability may exist. In a buffer overflow, surplus data that cannot be stored in the buffer spills over onto reserved areas of memory that are not allocated for code execution. If an attacker is able to determine that an application is vulnerable to such security weakness, malicious code can be injected into the buffer, causing it to overflow. The spilled code/data is the malicious code sent by the attacker; this code will then be executed in the reserved area of memory.

Attackers can create custom payloads to create backdoors on a victim's system and even set up a reverse shell/connection from the victim's machine back to the attacker.

In this section, you have learned about cyber-attacks and their characteristics. In the next section, we will cover the importance of implementing **Authentication**, **Authorization**, and **Accounting** (**AAA**) on a network.

# Authentication, Authorization, and Accounting

Implementing AAA within a network is very important to ensure authorized persons can access a system or network. The appropriate privileges or user rights are granted to the user, and each action performed by the user is accounted for. Let's imagine your organization has multiple network devices such as switches, routers, and firewalls at various remote branches and at headquarters locations. Your team of IT professionals is responsible for ensuring the IT infrastructure of the organization is well maintained and operating efficiently. Since each IT professional may be required to log in to various network devices, a user account containing the appropriate privileges is required for each user.

Creating individual user accounts for each user for each device is a tedious and redundant task. Imagine a user has to change their password; this means the password for the user account has to be manually changed on each individual device the user can access. What if a user makes an unauthorized change on a device's configuration and causes a network outage? How can we determine when the change was made? Who made the change? On which device(s) was the change made? Using AAA can help us to better manage user accounts and their privileges and log all actions performed by a user for accountability and record keeping.

The issue with a system such as a computer or a device is it cannot recognize a trusted user the same way as humans can. As a simple example, you can identify a family member such as a sibling by simply looking at their face. Once you recognize the person, trust is established. However, a system is unable to do this. Therefore, computers identify a human user by simply checking their user accounts details—a username (identity) and password combination. To log in to a computer, you must provide a valid user name and password. If the computer determines the user credentials are valid, the user is authenticated to the system and access is granted. **Authentication** is the process of verifying an account holder is able to use the account. Without authentication, anyone could access a system and perform any task, good or bad.

To authenticate yourself to a system, a user will need credentials to prove their identity. The following are examples of user credentials:

- Something the user knows: This is a password, a PIN, or even a passphrase.

- Something the user has: This can be a physical security token or a smart card.

- Something you are: This is something such as your fingerprint, iris, or retina, or patterns on your body.

After a user has been authenticated on a system, the user is now able to perform any tasks or actions until the authorization phase is complete. **Authorization** is the process by which an authenticated user is granted or assigned privileges to access and modify resources on the system or network. To put it simply, authorization simply determines what a user can and cannot do on a system. Within an organization, there are many groups of users with various roles and responsibilities. Each person may not have the same role and tasks, therefore, each person should be granted only the privileges to complete the tasks based on their job description and nothing more.

Once a user has been granted the necessary privileges, logs are generated as a record for all of the actions performed by the user while he/she is logged in to the system. This is known as **Accounting**. Having logs for each user's actions on a network can help to determine who performed an action, which device was affected, and the time and date the action was completed.

Within an enterprise organization, an AAA server is usually deployed at a centralized location on the network. This server is used to centrally manage all user accounts, assign privileges, and log all user actions.

The following diagram shows an AAA server on a network:

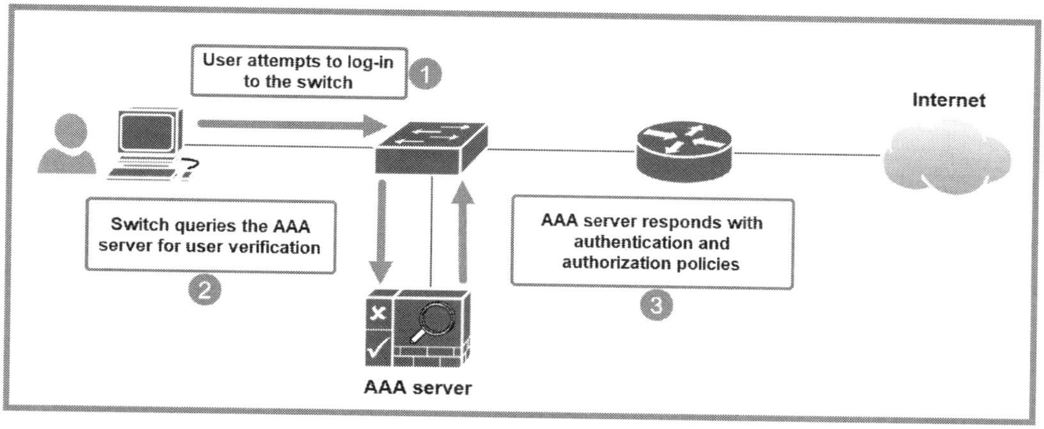

Figure 11.22 – AAA server

In the preceding diagram, the network administrator wants to log in to the switch to make a configuration change. The switch prompts the user to provide a user name and password. The user credentials are then sent to the AAA server to verify the identity of the user. The AAA server confirms the user's identity and applies user privileges. The information is sent back to the switch and the user is granted access. While the user is logged in, all actions are being logged on the AAA server for accountability.

There are currently two AAA servers:

- **Remote Authentication Dial-in User Service (RADIUS)**: RADIUS is an AAA service that supports a multi-vendor environment and uses UDP port 1812 for authentication and UDP port 1813 for accounting. However, the communication between an AAA client and a RADIUS server is not completely encrypted. RADIUS encrypts only the password that is exchanged between the client and the server.

- **Terminal Access Controller Access-Control System + (TACACS+)**: TACACS+ is a Cisco-proprietary AAA service that is similar to RADIUS but provides more flexibility. TACACS+ separates each AAA function into its own secure, encrypted communication between a AAA client and a TACACS+ server over TCP port 49.

> **Important note**
> In the Cisco world, the Cisco **Identity Services Engine** (**ISE**) security appliance is used as an AAA server.

In the next section, you will learn how to implement AAA in a Cisco environment to provide authentication for an administrator to remotely connect and manage a network device.

# Lab – Implementing AAA

In this lab, you'll learn how to implement AAA within a Cisco environment between a Cisco 2911 router and an AAA server using the TACACS+ protocol. For this lab, we will be using the following topology within Cisco Packet Tracer:

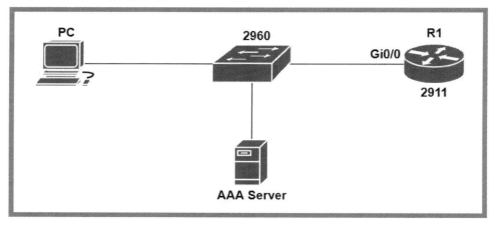

Figure 11.23 – AAA lab topology

Configure the following IP scheme on each device within the topology:

| Device | IP Address | Subnet Mask | Gateway |
|---|---|---|---|
| PC | 192.168.1.10 | 255.255.255.0 | 192.168.1.1 |
| Router | 192.168.1.1 | 255.255.255.0 | |
| Server | 192.168.1.5 | 255.255.255.0 | 192.168.1.1 |

Figure 11.24 – IP scheme

Now that your lab is ready, use the following instructions to implement AAA:

1.  On the server, enable the AAA **Service**, configure the client information (**Client Name: R1**, **Client IP**: 192.168.1.1, **Secret**: aaa-secret, and **ServerType**: Tacacs), and configure a user account for remote access from the PC to the router:

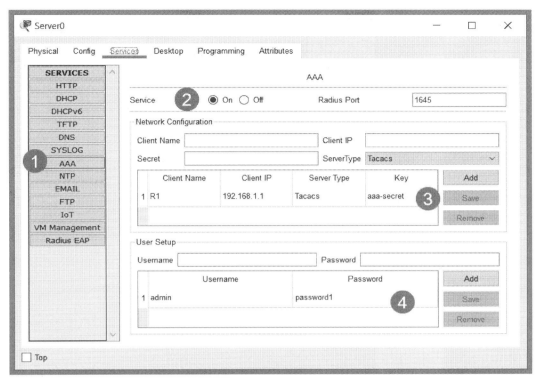

Figure 11.25 – AAA server configurations

2.  Next, enable the new AAA features on the router using the following commands:

```
R1(config)#aaa new-model
```

3.  Specify the TACACS server and the secret key on the router:

```
R1(config)#tacacs-server host 192.168.1.5 key aaa-secret
```

4.  Create an AAA method list (*AAA-Login*) for authentication (`login`) using the server group (`group`) using TACACS+:

```
R1(config)#aaa authentication login AAA-Login group
tacacs+
```

5.  Apply the method list (*AAA-Login*) to the **Virtual Terminal** (**VTY**) lines on the router:

```
R1(config)#line vty 0 15
R1(config-line)#login authentication AAA-Login
R1(config-line)#exit
```

6.  On the PC, click the **Desktop** tab, open the **Telnet/SSH Client**, and connect to the router using **Telnet**:

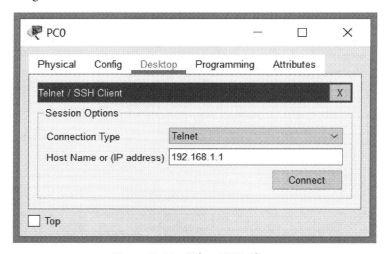

Figure 11.26 – Telnet/SSH Client

7.  Once you're logged in, enter the user credentials to test the AAA service between the router and the AAA server:

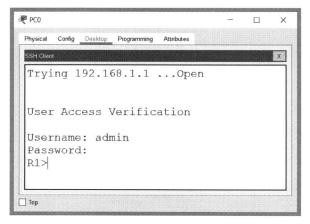

Figure 11.27 – AAA service

As shown in the preceding screenshot, the AAA service works between the router and the AAA server. Having completed this lab you have gained the essential skills in deploying AAA on a Cisco network for authentication using Telnet.

# Elements of a security program

Often when designing a security network, we forget to train all users within the organization on cybersecurity awareness. Not all corporate users are able to identify threats and attacks or perhaps understand what procedures should be taken if their computer gets infected with a virus. Therefore, it's important to design a proper security program to train all users within the organization.

**User awareness** is a key factor of any security program. This element teaches a user about the importance of confidentiality to keep data safe and secure it from unauthorized persons. Users should be taught about potential threats and attacks and procedures on how to report a security incident within the organization.

Continual **user training** is important to make sure each user is made aware of any updates to the security training program and ensuring they are familiar with the security policies and procedures within the organization.

**Physical access control** should be made mandatory in restricted areas of the organization, such as access to data centers, network closets, and any other areas unauthorized persons are not allowed.

# Wireshark 101

Wireshark is one of the most popular network protocol analyzers and sniffers within the networking and cybersecurity industry. This tool allows a network engineer to dissect each message and determine whether it's a frame or packet as it passes through a network, hence allowing network engineers and cybersecurity professionals to perform various tasks such as packet analysis and network forensics.

> **Tip**
> To download Wireshark, please visit the URL:
> `https://www.wireshark.org/`.

Furthermore, Wireshark allows you to see all the details contained within a message, such as source and destination IP addresses, MAC addresses, and Transport layer information such as ports and protocols. Such information is very useful whether you're troubleshooting an issue on the network or looking for any abnormal behavior on network traffic.

The following is a brief list of *how to's* with Wireshark:

- To capture network packets between your computer and their destination, simply open Wireshark and double-click on the interface on which you wish to capture network packets:

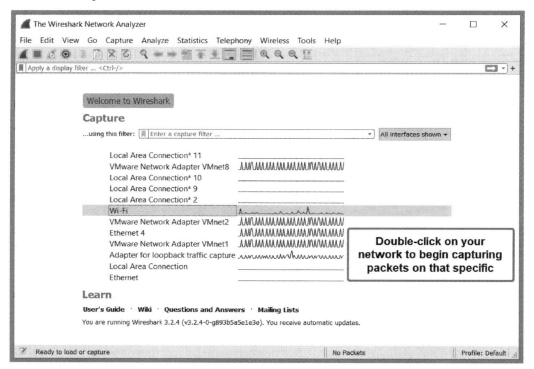

Figure 11.28 – Wireshark interfaces

Each interface will show an active flow of traffic to indicate which interfaces are sending and receiving data. After double-clicking an interface, Wireshark will begin populating its user interface with real-time traffic details.

- By default, Wireshark will display IP addresses and port numbers in its numerical format. To allow Wireshark to resolve public IP addresses to hostnames and port numbers to a service network, click **Edit | Preferences** and enable the options shown in the following screenshot:

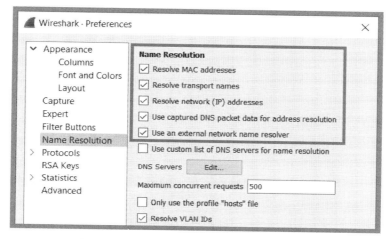

Figure 11.29 – Name resolution in Wireshark

- To display traffic from a specific source, use the `ip.src == <ip address>` display filter, as shown in the following screenshot:

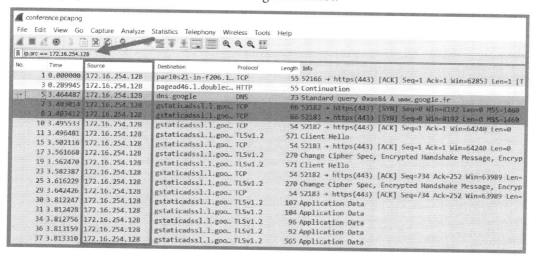

Figure 11.30 – Source IP address display filter

Additionally, you can right-click on a source IP address on the **Source** column, then choose **Apply as Filter | Selected** to automatically create a display filter, as shown in the following screenshot:

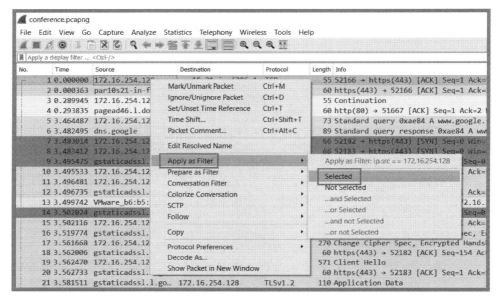

Figure 11.31 – Automatic display filters

- To display traffic between a specific source and destination, use the (ip.src == <ip address>) && (ip.dst == <ip address>) display filter shown in the following screenshot:

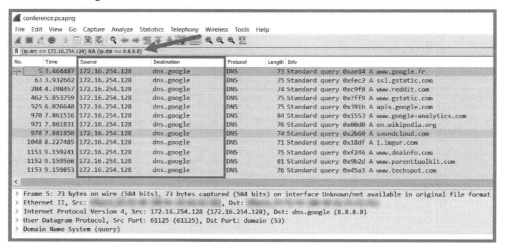

Figure 11.32 – Source and Destination display filter

> **Tip**
>
> To learn more about Wireshark display filters, please see the URL:
> `https://wiki.wireshark.org/DisplayFilters`.

- To view a summary of all network conversations between all devices, click **Statistics | Conversations**, as shown in the following screenshot:

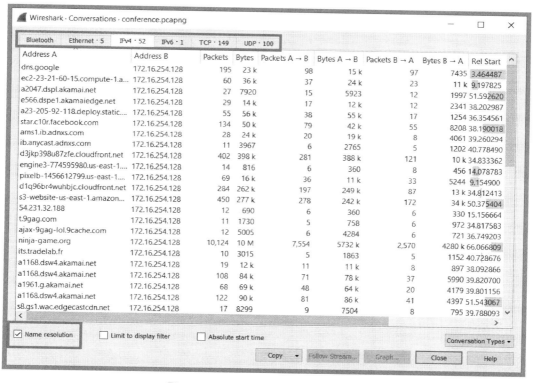

Figure 11.33 – Network conversations

This window will provide you with various tabs such as Ethernet, IPv4, IPv6, TCP, and UDP, which will allow you to view specific types of traffic based on Layer 2, Layer 3, or Layer 4 details.

> **Important note**
>
> To discover the full potential of Wireshark, be sure to check out the book *Learn Wireshark*, by *Lisa Bock* published by *Packt Publishing* at the URL: `https://www.packtpub.com/networking-and-servers/learn-wireshark-fundamentals-wireshark`.

In the next section, you will learn how to use Wireshark to export objects from a packet capture.

# Lab – Analyzing packets

In the lab, you will learn the fundamentals of getting started with Wireshark.

To begin, use the following instructions:

1.  Go to `https://www.wireshark.org/`, and download and install Wireshark on your computer.

2.  Go to `https://wiki.wireshark.org/SampleCaptures`, download the `http_with_jpegs.cap.gz` file, and open with Wireshark. Once the capture is loaded, you can see each packet and its details.

3.  Double-click on the first packet to view the contents:

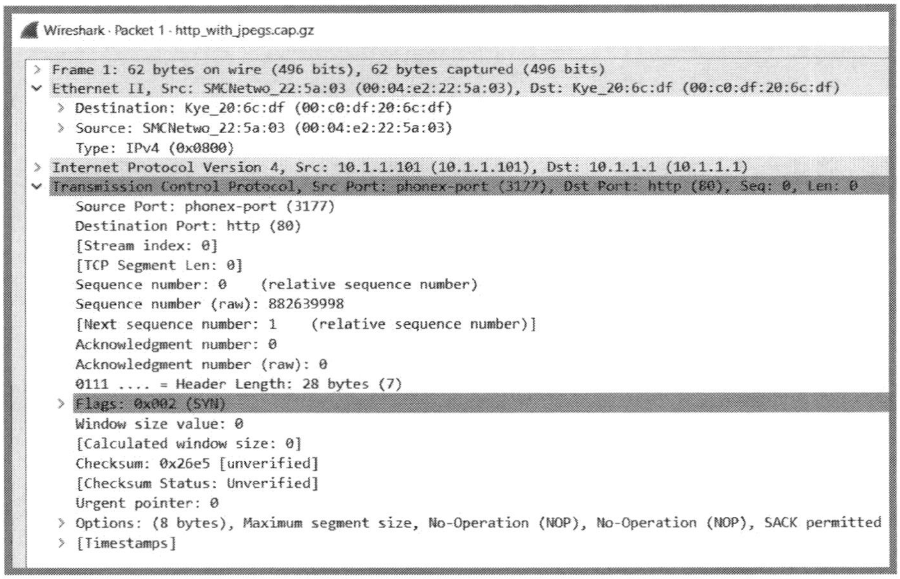

Figure 11.34 – Packet details

Here, you can see all of the specific details about this packet such as the source and destination MAC addresses, source and destination IP addresses, and the transport layer protocol and port numbers being used.

4.  To see a list of all of the conversations that happened during this capture, click on **Statistics | Conversations**:

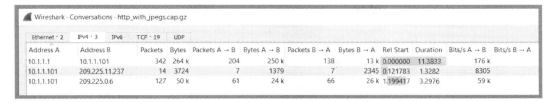

Figure 11.35 – Network conversations

Each tab will provide you with details about the transactions between all devices via their MAC addresses (Ethernet), IPv4 and IPv6 addresses, and TCP and UDP port numbers.

5.  During a capture, Wireshark is also capturing all files and data being sent across the network. To see a list of all files that were either uploaded or downloaded during the capture, click on **File | Export Objects | HTTP**:

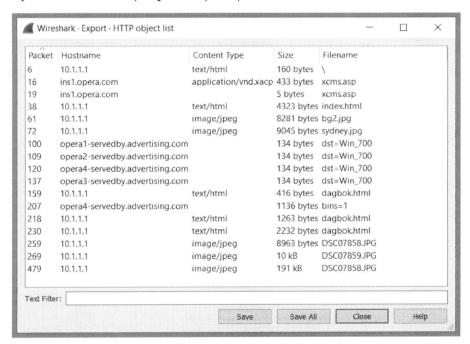

Figure 11.36 – Viewing files with Wireshark

The preceding snippet shows a list of files, their source of origin, file type, size, and filename.

6.  To export a file onto your desktop, click on a file (packet 72) and click **Save**. Once the file has been saved, you can view it locally on your system. Additionally, the **Save All** option will automatically export all files on your local computer.

Having completed this section, you have learned how to view all conversations on a network, export files that were transmitted between a source and destination, and see full details within a packet.

# Summary

In this chapter, you have learned about the importance of information security and the need to protect all assets within an organization. We have covered the various types of threats, vulnerabilities, and attacks. Furthermore, we've discussed the importance of implementing AAA within an organization to help manage user access on a corporate network.

I hope this chapter has been informative for you and is helpful in your journey toward learning how to implement and administrate Cisco solutions and prepare for the CCNA 200-301 certification. In the next chapter, *Configuring Device Access Controls and VPNs*, you will learn how to secure your network devices and learn about **Virtual Private Networks (VPNs)**.

# Questions

The following is a short list of review questions to help to reinforce your learning and identify which areas you might need to work on:

1.  Which of the following is an example of an intangible asset?

    A. Computer

    B. Operation procedures

    C. Customer

    D. Employee

2.  Ensuring a message is not altered during transmission between a source and destination is referred to as which of the following?

    A. Hashing

    B. Confidentiality

    C. Integrity

    D. Availability

3. Which of the following best describes a person who doesn't fully understand how to perform hacking techniques but follows the instructions given by real hackers?

    A. Hobbyist

    B. Disgruntled employee

    C. Insider threat

    D. Script kiddie

4. A hacker is attempting to trick people into clicking a malicious link with a text message. What type of attack is this?

    A. Smishing

    B. Vishing

    C. Phishing

    D. Spear phishing

5. An attacker decided to compromise a DNS server to redirect all users to a malicious domain in the hope the unsuspecting user enters their user credentials on the fake website. What is the name of this attack?

    A. Whaling

    B. Spear phishing

    C. Pharming

    D. Hoax

6. Which type of malware encrypts all the data on your local drive and asks for money?

    A. Worm

    B. Trojan Horse

    C. RAT

    D. Ransomware

7. An attacker is attempting to prevent users from accessing a website on the internet. Which type of attack will the attacker mostly likely use?

   A. Virus

   B. DoS

   C. RAT

   D. Worm

8. Which AAA protocol works on all vendor equipment?

   A. RADIUS

   B. TACACS+

   C. `aaa new-model`

   D. Kerberos

9. Which command enables the new AAA features on a Cisco device?

   A. `aaa-new features`

   B. `aaa-new model`

   C. `aaa new-model`

   D. `new-model aaa`

10. How can a user improve the management of their passwords?

   A. Use the same password on all user accounts.

   B. Use easy-to-remember passwords.

   C. Write the passwords on paper notes and store them away.

   D. User a password manager.

# Further reading

The following links are recommended for additional reading:

- Types of malware: `https://www.cisco.com/c/en/us/products/security/advanced-malware-protection/what-is-malware.html`

- Configuring AAA: `https://www.cisco.com/c/en/us/td/docs/routers/connectedgrid/cgr1000/1_0/software/configuration/guide/security/security_Book/sec_aaa_cgr1000.html`

- Wireshark user's guide: `https://www.wireshark.org/docs/wsug_html/`

# 12
# Configuring Device Access Control and VPNs

A key topic within the field of **Information Technology (IT)** is ensuring secure configurations are always applied to our devices. Secure configurations help to ensure unauthorized persons are not granted access to a device due to a device's misconfiguration. Quite often, hackers can gain access to companies' perimeter devices such as routers and firewalls simply by guessing the required password, and at times, device administrators use default configurations and default user accounts. Sometimes, administrative access is not securely configured, and attackers are able to access devices and perform malicious actions. Ensuring secure access to networking devices should be a top priority for all IT professionals.

In this chapter, you will learn how to secure your networking devices to prevent unauthorized access by implementing secure configuration best practices. Furthermore, you will discover and learn about the importance of using **Virtual Private Networks (VPNs)** to establish secure communication between remote offices and remote workers.

In this chapter, we will cover the following topics:

- Device access control
- VPNs

# Technical requirements

To follow along with the exercises in this chapter, please ensure you have the Cisco Packet Tracer application installed on your computer.

Check out the following video to see the Code in Action: `https://bit.ly/2RSWn0m`

# Device access control

We are always excited to configure our networking devices so that we can forward traffic efficiently either on a local network or between subnets. It's always a fascinating experience to design an efficient and robust network for your organization or customer. However, our networking devices have important and confidential information being stored on them, such as the device's configurations, routing protocol, and network routers; MAC addresses; and even Syslog information. If an attacker or unauthorized person is able to successfully access your network devices, that person can perform a lot of malicious actions, such as reconfiguring your network routes to forward traffic to another path, erasing the Cisco IOS image and device's configurations, adjusting Spanning-Tree paths, and so on.

In this section, we will focus on securing physical, remote, and administrative access to your Cisco devices.

## Securing console access

When you acquire a new Cisco IOS device, a console cable is usually provided in the box. This cable allows you to connect your computer to the console port of a Cisco device for the purpose of device management. By default, no security is applied to this interface. Anyone who has physical access to your network devices and a console cable on hand will be able to access your Cisco switches, routers, firewalls, and even the **Access Points** (**APs**), allowing the person to make unauthorized changes to these components. Securing the console port on all Cisco devices is mandatory to ensure an unauthorized person is not able to physically access the device.

## Lab – Securing the console port

In this hands-on lab, you will learn how to secure and enable authenticated access to the console port of a Cisco IOS router. For this lab, we will be using the following network topology within Cisco Packet Tracer:

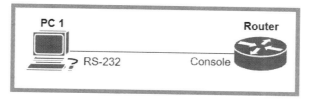

Figure 12.1 – Console lab topology

Please ensure you follow these guidelines when creating this lab to ensure you get the same results:

- Use a Cisco 2911 router on this topology.

- Use a console cable between **PC 1** and the router.

- Ensure the console cable is connected to the **RS-232** interface on **PC 1** and that the other end is connected to the **console port** on the router.

Now that your Cisco lab is ready, use the following instructions to understand the default configurations on the console port and how to secure physical access to it:

1.  Click on **PC 1**, select the **Desktop** tab, and click on **Terminal**:

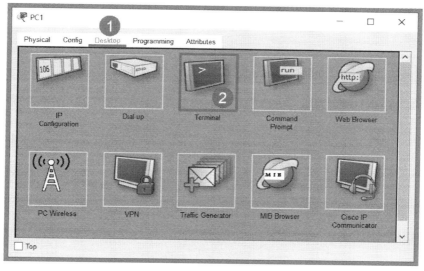

Figure 12.2 – Accessing the Terminal on Cisco Packet Tracer

In a production environment, you will need to use a Terminal emulation application such as Putty, SecureCRT, or Tera Term to interface with a Cisco device over a console connection.

2.  Ensure the following parameters are set on the Terminal application and click **OK** to establish a session:

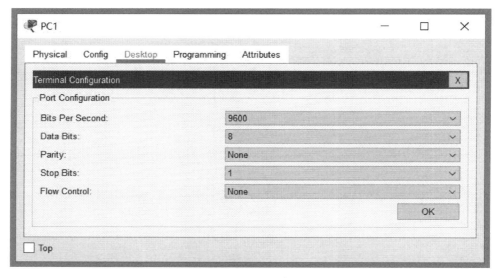

Figure 12.3 – Terminal settings

The settings shown in the preceding screenshot are used to ensure the PC's serial interface matches the settings on the console port of the Cisco device.

3.  The initial system configuration dialog will appear. Type no and hit *Enter* twice:

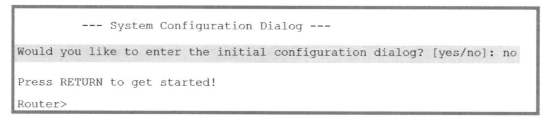

Figure 12.4 – Terminal connection

Notice that you have gained access to the **User Exec** mode on the router without any prompt to authenticate yourself to the device. This is the default setting on the console port; there is no authentication.

4.  Use the `show users` command to verify the method you are currently using to access the router:

```
Router>show users
    Line        User        Host(s)              Idle        Location
*   0 con 0                 idle                 00:00:00

    Interface   User                    Mode        Idle    Peer Address
Router>
```

Figure 12.5 – Verifying access

The asterisk (*) indicates the current method you are using to access the device. To put it simply, we are currently accessing the router via its console interface.

5.  In `User Exec` mode, the user has the least privileges and can perform the least actions. Use the `show privilege` command to verify the privilege levels:

```
Router>show privilege
Current privilege level is 1
Router>
```

Figure 12.6 – Checking user privilege in User Exec mode

Privilege levels range from `1-15`. A user with privilege level `1` access is not able to perform or execute many actions compared to a user with privilege level `15` access, who has full administrative rights to perform any action on the device.

> **Important Note**
>
> Additional information on the Cisco IOS privilege levels can be found at `https://www.cisco.com/c/en/us/td/docs/ios/sec_user_services/configuration/guide/12_4/sec_securing_user_services_12-4_book/sec_cfg_sec_4cli.html#wp1054522.`

6.  Access **Privilege Exec** mode using the `enable` command, then use the `show running-config` command to verify the configurations on the console line:

```
!
line con 0
!
line aux 0
!
line vty 0 4
 login
!
```

Figure 12.7 – Checking the configurations

As shown here, there are no configurations on the console port. Therefore, anyone is able to access the device via this interface.

7.  Let's apply a password and enable authentication on the console port:

```
Router#configure terminal
Enter configuration commands, one per line.  End with CNTL/Z.
Router(config)#line console 0
Router(config-line)#password consolepass
Router(config-line)#login
Router(config-line)#exit
```

Figure 12.8 – Securing the console port

The line console 0 command was used to access the console line mode, the password command was used to set the password, and the login command was used to enable user authentication on the console port. Without the login command, any unauthenticated user can access the device.

8.  Upon re-establishing a console connection between PC 1 and the router, the Cisco IOS will provide an authentication prompt, as follows. The password that's been configured under the console line is consolepass:

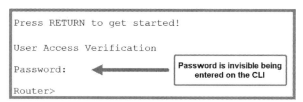

Figure 12.9 – Verifying console authentication

9.  Lastly, we can use the show running-config command to verify that the configuration has been updated on the console port:

```
Router#show running-config | section line
line con 0
 password consolepass
 login
```

Figure 12.10 – Verifying console configurations

In this lab, you have gained the skills to both secure and verify physical access to a Cisco IOS device via its console port.

# Securing an AUX line

On older, legacy Cisco devices, you would find an **auxiliary (AUX)** port. This interface was used to connect a modem that allows a user to remotely access a Cisco router over a **command-line interface (CLI)** session. By default, the AUX port is not secure and allows unauthenticated access.

## Lab – Securing the AUX port

In this hands-on lab, you will learn how to secure and enable authenticated access to the AUX port of a Cisco IOS router. For this lab, we will be using the following network topology within Cisco Packet Tracer:

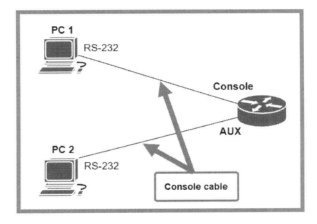

Figure 12.11 – AUX line topology

Please ensure you use the following guidelines when creating this lab to ensure you get the same results:

- This topology is an extension of the previous lab exercise; that is, *Securing the console port*.
- Simply add an additional **PC 2** to the topology.
- Use a console cable between **PC 2** and the AUX port on the router.

Now that your Cisco lab is ready, use the following instructions to understand the default configurations on the AUX port and how to secure physical access to it:

1.  On **PC 2**, open a **Terminal** connection to the router via its AUX port. Press *Enter* a couple of times to see the CLI prompt.

2.  Use the `show users` command to verify the method and interface being used to access the router:

```
Router>show users
    Line       User        Host(s)              Idle         Location
    0 con 0                idle                 00:00:12
*   1 aux 0                idle                 00:00:00

  Interface    User                    Mode         Idle     Peer Address
Router>
```

Figure 12.12 – AUX connection

As shown here, the router indicates that the current connection is being made via the AUX port. Additionally, you gain unauthenticated access to `User Exec` mode. This means no security is applied to the AUX port by default.

3.  Let's use the `enable` command to go into `Privilege Exec` mode to verify the configurations under the AUX line:

```
Router>enable
% No password set.
Router>
```

Figure 12.13 – Access restricted to Privilege Exec mode

By default, access is restricted to **Privilege Exec** mode via the **AUX port**, but only if no password has been configured for **Privilege Exec** mode.

4.  To secure the AUX port, open a **Terminal** on **PC 1** to the router via the `console` port.

5.  Use the following commands to access the AUX port, configure a password, and enable authentication:

```
Router(config)#line aux 0
Router(config-line)#password auxpass
Router(config-line)#login
Router(config-line)#exit
```

6.  Upon re-establishing an AUX session between PC 2 and the router, a user authentication prompt will be presented:

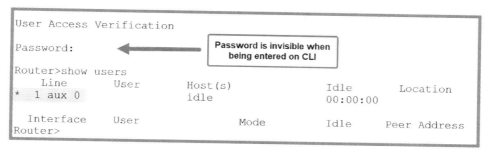

Figure 12.14 – Verifying AUX authentication

7.  Lastly, use the `show running-config` command to verify that the configurations are present under the `aux` line, as shown here:

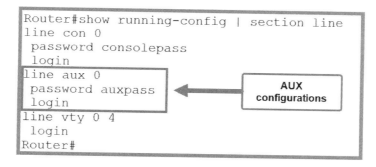

Figure 12.15 – AUX configurations

In this lab, you have gained the skills to both secure and verify access to a Cisco IOS device via its AUX interface.

## VTY line access

On a Cisco IOS router or switch, there are `16` **virtual terminal** (**VTY**) lines ranging from `0 – 15`. These VTY lines allow a network engineer to remotely connect to the device for management. As a network engineer, you don't always have physical access to the network components, as they may be deployed at a remote location such as another branch office or at a customer's site. Furthermore, these VTY lines also support outgoing connections to other Cisco devices. VTY lines allow both inbound and outbound Telnet and SSH sessions.

Telnet is a network protocol that allows you to establish a remote terminal session between a client and a server. On a Cisco device, there's a built-in Telnet server that allows network engineers to remotely connect to and perform remote administration on the device. However, Telnet is an unsecured protocol and transfers all data in plaintext. Due to this security vulnerability within the protocol, it's highly recommended to not use Telnet for anything as an attacker could capture the data between the client and server.

> **Important Note**
> Telnet operates on port 23 by default.

Since Telnet contains this vulnerability, **Secure Shell (SSH)** is the preferred protocol for remote terminal access on a network. SSH provides data encryption for all the messages between the client and the server. Additionally, a user must provide their identity details, such as a username and password, to be authenticated to the SSH server. This feature adds improved security compared to Telnet.

> **Important Note**
> SSH operates on port 22 by default.

## Lab – Configuring Telnet on a Cisco router

In this hands-on lab, you will learn how to configure Telnet access on a Cisco IOS router. For this lab, we will be using the following network topology:

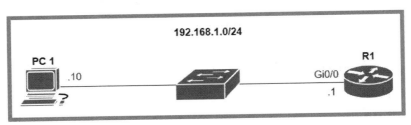

Figure 12.16 – Telnet lab topology

Please ensure you use the following guidelines when creating this lab to ensure you get the same results:

- Use a Cisco 2911 router and a Cisco 2960 switch.
- Ensure you configure the IP addresses and subnet mask accordingly.
- Ensure **PC 1** can ping the router.

Now that your Cisco lab is ready, use the following instructions to configure Telnet for remote access from the PC to the router:

1.  Access the `console` aspect of the router and use the `show running-config` command to verify the Telnet settings on the VTY lines:

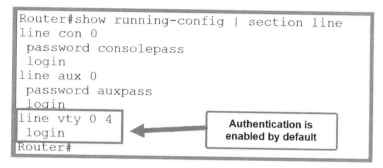

Figure 12.17 – VTY default configuration

On VTY lines 0-4, Telnet is enabled by default and authentication is also enabled. However, if we try to access the router remotely using Telnet, the connection will automatically terminate simply because no password has been set on the VTY lines.

2.  To configure Telnet on all 16 VTY lines on the router, use the following configurations:

```
Router(config)#line vty 0 15
Router(config-line)#password telnetpass
Router(config-line)#login
Router(config-line)#exit
```

The `login` command is not required in this instance as it's already there from the default configurations; however, it's good practice to still enable authentication on the VTY lines.

3.  Use the `show running-config` command once more to verify the configurations are present under the VTY lines:

```
Router#show running-config | section line
line vty 0 4
 password telnetpass
 login
line vty 5 15
 password telnetpass
 login
Router#
```

Figure 12.18 – Verifying Telnet configurations

4.  To test the Telnet connection, open **Telnet / SSH Client** on the **Desktop** tab on **PC1**:

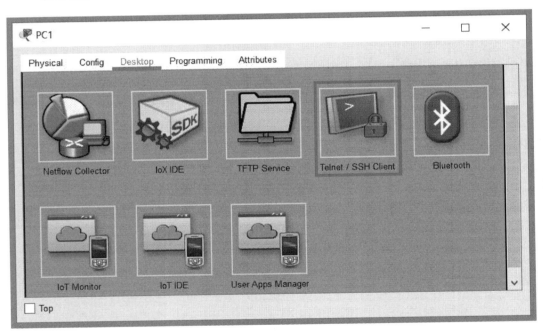

Figure 12.19 – Telnet client

5.  Change **Connection Type** to `Telnet`, set the router's IP address, and click **Connect**:

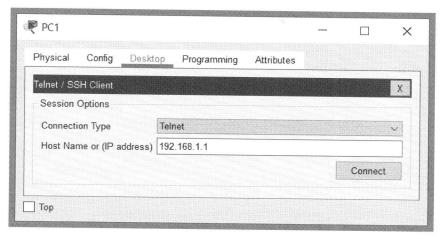

Figure 12.20 – Telnet client settings

6.  You'll be prompted for a password. Use the Telnet password (`telnetpass`) we have assigned under the VTY lines:

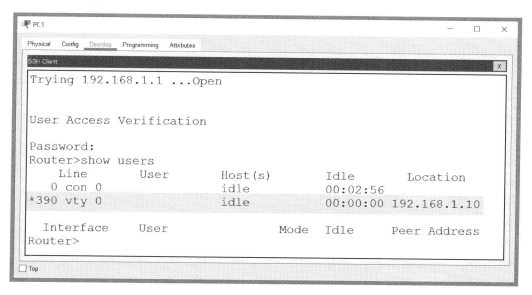

Figure 12.21 – Telnet connection

Since the authentication prompt was present, this is an indication that Telnet was enabled on the router. Additionally, the `show users` command verifies that the current connection to the router is via the VTY line from `192.168.1.10` (**PC 1**).

Having completed this lab, you have gained hands-on experience with enabling Telnet on a Cisco IOS device. In the next lab, you will learn how to configure SSH for remote access.

## Lab – Enabling SSH on a Cisco IOS device

In this hands-on lab, you will learn how to configure SSH access on a Cisco IOS router. For this lab, we will be using the following network topology:

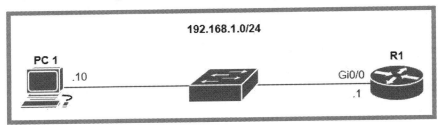

Figure 12.22 – SSH lab topology

Please note that this lab is simply an extension of the previous exercise; you do not need to rebuild the network. Now that your Cisco lab is ready, use the following instructions to configure SSH for remote access from the PC to the router:

1.  Change the default hostname on the router:

    ```
    Router(config)#hostname R1
    ```

2.  Join the device to a domain:

    ```
    R1(config)#ip domain-name ccnalab.local
    ```

3.  Create a local user account for the SSH user:

    ```
    R1(config)#username user1 secret sshpass
    ```

4.  Generate RSA encryption keys and set the key size to `1024`:

    ```
    R1(config)#crypto key generate rsa general-keys modulus
    1024
    ```

5.  Enable SSH version 2 to improve security:

    ```
    R1(config)#ip ssh version 2
    ```

    By default, SSHv1 is enabled.

6.  Configure VTY lines 0-15 so that they only accept SSH connections (this disables Telnet):

```
R1(config)#line vty 0 15
R1(config-line)#transport input ssh
```

7.  Configure the VTY lines to query the local user database for authentication:

```
R1(config-line)#login local
```

8.  Since Telnet is disabled and the local database will be used for user authentication, remove the password under the VTY lines:

```
R1(config-line)#no password
```

9.  Configure an inactivity timeout for idle sessions on the VTY lines. Let's use 2 minutes:

```
R1(config-line)# exec-timeout 2
```

10. To test SSH, head on over to **PC 1** and open **Telnet/SSH Client**.

11. Set **Connection Type** to SSH, specify the IP address of the router, and use the username from the user account, as shown here:

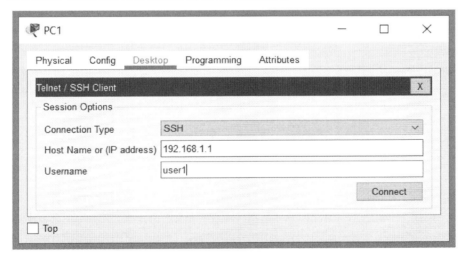

Figure 12.23 – SSH client configurations

12. You will receive an authentication prompt asking for a password (the username was already specified on the SSH client). Simply enter the password for the account and hit *Enter*:

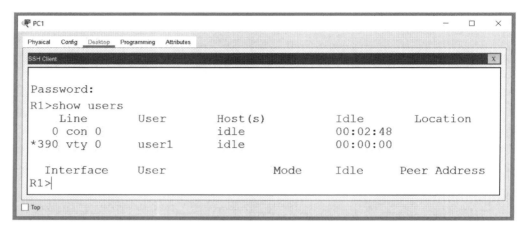

Figure 12.24 – SSH session

As shown in the preceding screenshot, we are connected to the router on VTY line 0 with the `user1` account.

13. Additionally, the `show ip ssh` command verifies the SSH version, the authentication time value, and the number of authentication retries, as shown here:

```
R1#show ip ssh
SSH Enabled - version 2.0
Authentication timeout: 120 secs; Authentication retries: 3
R1#
R1#show ssh
Connection    Version Mode Encryption  Hmac State           Username
389           1.99    IN   aes128-cbc  hmac-sha1  Session Started       user1
389           1.99    OUT  aes128-cbc  hmac-sha1  Session Started  user1
%No SSHv1 server connections running.
R1#
```

Figure 12.25 – Verifying SSH details

Furthermore, `show ssh` verifies the current SSH sessions and users. The `ip ssh time-out seconds` command allows you to modify the default SSH timeout values, while the `ip ssh authentication-retries number` command allows you to change the authentication retry value.

> **Important Note**
>
> The `login block-for seconds attempts tries within seconds` command is used to disable user login after a specified number of failed authentication attempts within a specific time interval.

By completing this lab, you have gained hands-on experience with configuring and enabling SSH for remote access on a Cisco IOS router.

# Securing Privilege Exec mode

By now, you may have noticed that once someone is able to access `Privilege Exec` mode, the user is able to gather sensitive and confidential information about the network and the device. Furthermore, a user can escalate their privileges to `Global Config` mode, where the user is able to apply configurations and make modifications to the device. This creates a security risk.

> **Important Note**
>
> The `secure boot-image` command prevents a user from either purposely or accidentally deleting the Cisco IOS image, while the `secure boot-config` command is used to protect the running configurations.

The Cisco IOS has many security features built into it that enable us to prevent unauthorized access. One such feature is preventing unauthorized access specifically to `Privilege Exec` mode. One method is to use the `enable password <mypassword>` command to restrict access to `Privilege Exec` mode.

> **Important Note**
>
> The `auto secure` command is used to initialize the Cisco IOS lockdown feature on the device.

The following is an example of using the `enable password` command with a password of `cisco123`:

```
R1(config)#enable password cisco123
```

Once this configuration is applied, each time a user moves from `User Exec` mode to `Privilege Exec` mode, the Cisco IOS will prompt the user to authenticate before proceeding. The downside of using the `enable password` command is that it does not provide any encryption of the actual password. If a user can access the `running-config` or `startup-config` files, the password is visible in plaintext, as shown here:

```
R1#show running-config
Building configuration...

Current configuration : 998 bytes
!
version 15.1
no service timestamps log datetime msec
no service timestamps debug datetime msec
no service password-encryption
!
hostname R1                    Password is in plaintext
!
!
!
enable password cisco123
!
```

Figure 12.26 – Enabling password in plaintext

Due to this security vulnerability, Cisco has implemented a secure version of the `enable password` command. This improved method uses the `enable secret` command, which encrypts the password by default using the **Message Digest 5 (MD5)** hashing algorithm.

The following is an example of securing access to `Privilege Exec` mode using the `enable secret` command, followed by `cisco456`, which is the password:

```
R1(config)#enable secret cisco456
```

The following snippet shows that the password has been encrypted within the `running-config` file:

```
R1#show running-config
Building configuration...

Current configuration : 1045 bytes
!
hostname R1                          ┌─────────────────────────┐
!                                    │  Password is encrypted  │
!                                    └─────────────────────────┘
!
enable secret 5 $1$mERr$nU5A2OzzVK4SU1SP717zP.
enable password cisco123
!
```

Figure 12.27 – The enable secret command

Cisco uses a numerical value to indicate the type of password stored within `running-config` and `startup-config`. The following are various password types on Cisco IOS devices:

- `enable password`: Plaintext password, encoding `Type 0`.

- `enable secret`: MD5 algorithm used to encrypt the password, encoding `Type 5`.

Since the device has been configured with both `enable password` and `enable secret`, which password will be accepted by the Cisco IOS? The simple answer is that it will always be the stronger password, which is the one that's applied using the `enable secret` command. Since the stronger password will be used by the device, `enable password` is now obsolete and should be removed. Using the `Global Config` command, `no enable password` will remove `enable password` from the device's `running-config` file, as shown here:

```
R1(config)#no enable password
R1(config)#
R1(config)#do show running-config
Building configuration...

Current configuration : 1020 bytes
!
version 15.1
no service password-encryption
!
hostname R1                          ┌─────────────────────────────────┐
!                                    │  The "enable password" removed.  │
!                                    └─────────────────────────────────┘
!
enable secret 5 $1$mERr$nU5A2OzzVK4SU1SP717zP.
!
!
```

Figure 12.28 – Removing enable password

Over the years, security researchers and hackers have been able to compromise the MD5 hashing algorithm. This means an attacker has been able to reverse the MD5 hash value of the password and retrieve the actual password. In light of this security vulnerability, Cisco has implemented a more secure hashing algorithm known as **SCRYPT**.

The following snippet shows the command that's used to create a secure password using SCRYPT on a Cisco IOS device:

```
Router(config)#enable algorithm-type ?                           1
  md5      Encode the password using the MD5 algorithm
  scrypt   Encode the password using the SCRYPT hashing algorithm
  sha256   Encode the password using the PBKDF2 hashing algorithm

Router(config)#enable algorithm-type scrypt ?                    2
  secret   Assign the privileged level secret (MAX of 25 characters)

Router(config)#enable algorithm-type scrypt secret ?            3
  LINE    The UNENCRYPTED (cleartext) 'enable' secret
  level   Set exec level password

Router(config)#enable algorithm-type scrypt secret level9password   4
Router(config)#
```

Figure 12.29 – Enabling SCRYPT on Cisco devices

SCRYPT is more secure than MD5 and therefore uses an encoding of Type 9 with the SHA256 hashing algorithm. The following snippet shows that the SCRYPT hash is a lot longer than the enable secret MD5 hash:

```
Router#show running-config
Building configuration...

Current configuration : 3228 bytes
!
! Last configuration change at 15:27:08 UTC Tue May 26 2020
!
version 15.7
service timestamps debug datetime msec
service timestamps log datetime msec
no service password-encryption
!
hostname Router
!
boot-start-marker
boot-end-marker
!
!
enable secret 9 $9$h5kKO0lYugj8L9$jHWp1AnEkO8zVCPzu2.DOKPI806LRxSxpLCGe01w5EA
!
```

Figure 12.30 – Type 9 encoding

When configuring access to Privilege Exec mode, ensure you use the most secure method available on the device. Some devices may not support SCRYPT. In this situation, enable secret will be the more secure option compared to enable password, which does not provide any encryption.

# Encrypting all plaintext passwords

Within some modes on the Cisco IOS, we are not able to configure secure passwords, such as `line console 0`, `line aux 0`, and even the VTY lines. Within these modes, the only command that allows us to create and set a password is the `password` command. From our discussions in the previous sections of this chapter, you have learned that the `password` command does not encrypt the passwords stored within the device's configuration.

The following snippet shows how passwords are stored when the `password` command is used:

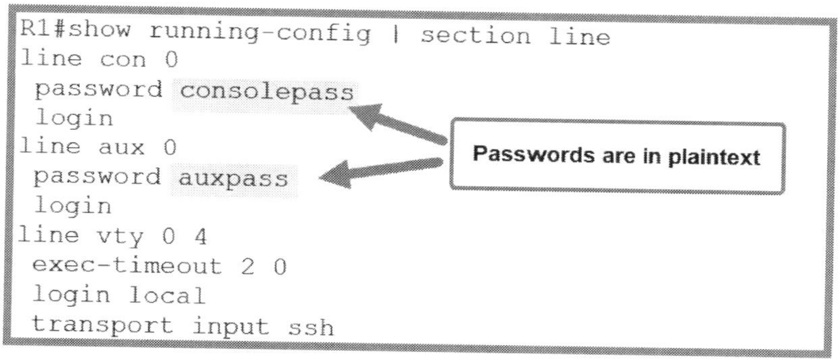

```
R1#show running-config | section line
line con 0
 password consolepass
 login
line aux 0
 password auxpass
 login
line vty 0 4
 exec-timeout 2 0
 login local
 transport input ssh
```

Passwords are in plaintext

Figure 12.31 – Plaintext passwords

Additionally, within the Cisco IOS, there are other modes and configurations that require a password to be configured but only support the `password` command. A simple example is configuring **Point-to-Point (PPP)** using the **Password Authentication Protocol (PAP)** on a **Wide Area Network (WAN)**. The Cisco IOS configurations require a password to be sent across the WAN link to authenticate both routers before establishing the WAN connection. In PAP authentication, the `password` command is available. This means the password is stored in plaintext on the router.

On a Cisco IOS device, the `service password-encryption` command is applied to `Global Config` mode to encrypt all plaintext passwords. Once this command has been applied to a device, all the passwords that have been configured in plaintext will automatically be encrypted. The following is an example of using this command on a Cisco IOS router:

```
R1(config)#service password-encryption
```

The following snippet shows that the passwords under the console (`con`) and auxiliary (`aux`) lines are now encrypted:

```
R1#show running-config | section line
line con 0
 password 7 082243401A160912020A1F17
 login
line aux 0
 password 7 0820595619181604          Passwords are
 login                                    encrypted
R1#
```

Figure 12.32 – The service password-encryption command

Password encoding `Type` 7 is not strong encryption on a device. This type of encryption can easily be broken by an attacker. However, this is the only form of encryption for plaintext passwords on a Cisco IOS device at this time.

# Virtual Private Networks

Let's imagine you've started a business where you provide products and services to your potential customers. You begin by opening a single physical location and hire staff to help run your company and ensure day-to-day transactions are conducted efficiently. After some time, you realize the business needs you require in order to expand and provide more support and services to customers who are located within another country. Due to this, you have decided that another branch office is better suited to meet the demands at the new location. However, one concern is how the employees at the new remote location will access the resources at the main building in your home country.

There are a few solutions to this issue. One method is to replicate the IT infrastructure of the home branch at the new remote branch, but this will be a bit costly as the new branch only requires a few employees and having a dedicated IT team is not necessary. Another solution may be to set up a WAN via your local **Internet Service Provider** (**ISP**) to extend your local area network from your main office, over to the remote branch. Having a dedicated WAN connection will ensure both offices will be able to interconnect and share network resources. However, the downside of having a WAN service is its subscription fees, which are payable to the service provider. The cost of a dedicated WAN service may not be within your budget and perhaps an alternative solution may be required.

Another solution is to create a **Virtual Private Network** (**VPN**) between the two offices. A VPN creates an encrypted tunnel between two or more devices over an unsecured network such as the internet. This means all traffic that is sent through the VPN tunnel will be encrypted and kept confidential from hackers on a network or the internet.

The following are the benefits of using a VPN:

- Using a VPN will save you money as it's free.

- VPNs provide security for all your traffic that is sent across the VPN tunnel.

- A VPN supports scalability, so more remote sites and users can connect to the corporate network securely.

Since many organizations already have a firewall at their network perimeter, most firewalls already have built-in support for VPN capabilities in their operating systems. Therefore, you don't need to purchase additional components or devices. Since a VPN encrypts all traffic sent across its tunnel, you don't have to worry about whether a hacker is intercepting and reading your data. Data encryption provides an extra layer of security as the traffic is passing through the internet. Additionally, VPNs use authentication protocols to ensure your data is protected from unauthorized access while it's being sent to the destination. VPNs allow two or more branch networks and users to establish a secure connection over the internet to the corporate network.

Since VPNs can be used over the internet, this makes it very simple to add new remote workers without having to expand the infrastructure of the service. To put it simply, once a user has access to the internet, they can access the corporate network using a VPN connection.

In the next section, you will learn about a type of VPN that allows you to connect remote branch networks together over the network.

## Site-to-Site VPNs

One challenge many organizations experience is ensuring all their remote branch offices are always connected to their corporate headquarters' location. This is simply because most resources, such as application servers, are centrally stored at the main office. As we mentioned previously, there are many different types of WAN solutions, from various ISPs such as **Metro Ethernet (MetroE)** and **Multiprotocol Label Switching (MPLS)** solutions.

> **Important Note**
>
> To learn about the essentials of MPLS, please see the following URL: `https://www.cisco.com/c/en/us/support/docs/multiprotocol-label-switching-mpls/mpls/4649-mpls-faq-4649.html`.
> To learn more about Metro Ethernet, see the following link: `https://www.cisco.com/c/dam/global/fr_ca/training-events/pdfs/Deploying_Metro_Ethernet.pdf`.

However, these solutions are subscription-based services and a customer may not have the required budget or may be looking for an alternative solution.

> **Important Note**
>
> An Internet Service Provider can use MPLS to create Layer 2 or Layer 3 virtual paths between sites. On a Layer 2 MPLS VPN, the ISP is not responsible for routing the customer's traffic; instead, the ISP implements a **Virtual Private LAN Service** (**VPLS**) to emulate Ethernet over the MPLS network. On a Layer MPLS VPN, the customer and the ISP routers are peered, and the customer's routers are redistributed via the MPLS network to the customer's remote sites.

A simple solution is to create a Site-to-Site VPN between the HQ location and the branch office. Since both locations will already have an internet connection, there is no need to purchase any additional services from your local ISP. However, each location will require a VPN concentrator device for both establishing and terminating the VPN tunnel. A VPN concentrator is a router or firewall with the capabilities of establishing a VPN connection between itself and a VPN client or another VPN concentrator.

The following diagram shows two branch networks interconnected using a Site-to-Site VPN:

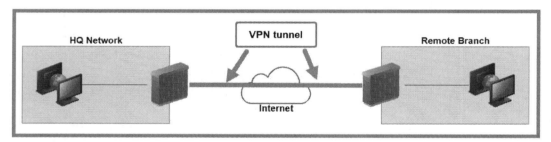

Figure 12.33 – Site-to-Site VPN

As shown in the preceding diagram, the VPN tunnel is established between the two firewalls only. Therefore, traffic between the remote branch and HQ networks will be sent across the VPN tunnel and all data will be encrypted by the firewalls. Keep in mind that all traffic within each LAN will not be encrypted; only the traffic that is passing through the VPN tunnel will.

This type of VPN allows an organization to reduce its expenditure on connecting remote sites and uses its existing infrastructure and devices. Additionally, a Site-to-Site VPN can be used as a redundant connection between branch offices.

# Remote access VPNs

There are many employees who work remotely at home or who are mostly in the field, and away from the office. They may need to access resources on the corporate network, and going into the office to retrieve or access such resources may not be convenient. A simple solution is to deploy a remote access VPN, which allows remote workers to establish a VPN tunnel between their device, such as a computer, and the corporate network through the internet.

The following diagram shows the VPN tunnel between a remote worker's PC and the corporate network:

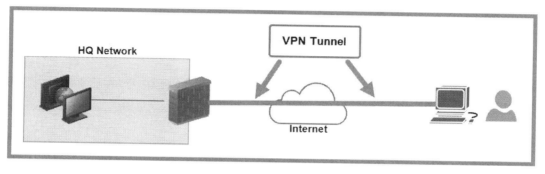

Figure 12.34 – Remote access VPN

With a remote access VPN, a VPN client such as **Cisco AnyConnect Secure Mobility Client** must be installed on the remote worker's device. When the remote worker must access a resource at the HQ network, the VPN client is used to establish a secure tunnel between the device and the VPN concentrator, such as a firewall or router at the corporate site.

The firewall administrator can configure the remote access VPN for users in one of the following modes:

- **Full Tunnel**
- **Split Tunnel**

In **Full Tunnel** mode, all traffic that must go out to the internet from the client's PC will be sent across the VPN tunnel to the VPN concentrator, where it will be sent out to the internet. All returning traffic will take the same path back to the client's PC.

In **Split-Tunnel** mode, only traffic with the corporate network as its destination will be encrypted and sent across the VPN tunnel. Traffic that has the internet as its destination will not be sent via the VPN tunnel but rather directly out to the internet from the user's PC. This mode creates less overhead on the VPN tunnel and reduces the CPU and RAM consumption on the VPN concentrator.

Another type of VPN connection is using a **clientless VPN**. With a clientless VPN, there is no need to install a VPN client on the user's machine. However, the connection is encrypted and secure between a client's web browser using **Secure Sockets Layer (SSL)** or **Transport Layer Security (TLS)** encryption over HTTPS. Keep in mind that traffic between the web browser and the VPN concentrator is encrypted; all other traffic is not.

# IPsec

**Internet Protocol security (IPsec)** is a framework that simply defines how VPNs can be secured over an IP-based network. The following are the benefits of using an IPsec VPN:

- **Confidentiality**: Confidentiality simply ensures all data sent across the IPsec VPN tunnel is encrypted with an encryption algorithm such as the **Data Encryption Standard (DES)**, **Triple DES (3DES)**, or **Advanced Encryption Standard (AES)**. Data encryption prevents eavesdropping while data is being transmitted.

- **Integrity**: Integrity ensures that all data sent across the IPsec VPN tunnel is not altered or modified. On an IPsec VPN, hashing algorithms such as MD5 and SHA are used to detect any alteration of messages over the IPsec tunnel.

- **Origin authentication**: Authentication on an IPsec VPN ensures each user is identified correctly and that the messages are not originating from someone else. In IPsec, the **Internet Key Exchange (IKE)** is used to authenticate users and VPN clients. IKE uses various methods to validate users such as digital certificates such as RSA, a **pre-shared key (PSK)**, or a username and password.

- **Anti-replay**: Anti-replay prevents a user from capturing and attempting to perform a replay attack on the IPsec VPN tunnel.

> **Important Note**
> IPsec contains two protocols: **Authentication Header (AH)** and **Encapsulating Security Payload (ESP)**. The difference between these two protocols is that AH authenticates the Layer 3 packet only, while ESP encrypts the entire Layer 3 packet. Keep in mind that these protocols are not commonly used together.

**Diffie-Hellman (DH)** is defined as an algorithm used to securely distribute public keys over an unsecured network. The public keys are part of a key pair: the private key and a public key are used for data encryption and decryption. There are various DH groups, such as 1, 2, 4, 14, 15, 16, 19, 20, 21, and 24.

In the next section, you will learn how to configure a Site-to-Site VPN using IPsec on a Cisco environment.

# Lab – Configuring a site-to-site VPN

In this hands-on lab, you will learn how to configure and implement a Site-to-Site IPsec VPN using Cisco IOS routers. For this lab, we will be using the following topology within Cisco Packet Tracer:

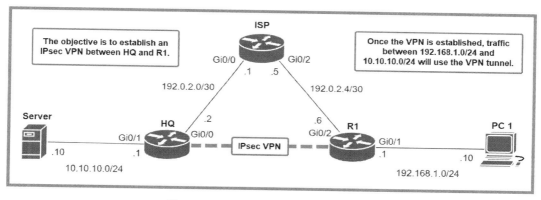

Figure 12.35 – Site-to-site VPN topology

Please use the following guidelines when creating this lab to ensure you get the same results:

- Use Cisco 2911 routers.
- Configure a default route from both the **HQ** and **R1** routers that points to the ISP.
- On the ISP, configure network static routers to the LAN of **HQ** and the LAN of **R1**.

Ensure you assign an IP address to each device, as shown in the following table:

| Device | Interface | IP Address | Subnet Mask | Default Gateway |
|--------|-----------|------------|-------------|-----------------|
| PC 1 | Fa0 | 192.168.1.10 | 255.255.255.0 | 192.168.1.1 |
| Server | Fa0 | 10.10.10.10 | 255.255.255.0 | 10.10.10.1 |
| R1 | Gi0/1 | 192.168.1.1 | 255.255.255.0 | n/a |
| R1 | Gi0/2 | 192.0.2.6 | 255.255.255.252 | n/a |
| HQ | Gi0/1 | 10.10.10.1 | 255.255.255.0 | n/a |
| HQ | Gi0/0 | 192.0.2.2 | 255.255.255.252 | n/a |
| ISP | Gi0/0 | 192.0.2.1 | 255.255.255.252 | n/a |
| ISP | Gi0/2 | 192.0.2.5 | 255.255.255.252 | n/a |

Figure 12.36 – IP scheme

Now that your lab environment is ready, use the following instructions to configure an IPsec Site-to-Site VPN between **R1** and the **HQ** router:

1. Configure the following static routes on each router to simulate the internet:

```
HQ(config)#ip route 0.0.0.0 0.0.0.0 192.0.2.1
R1(config)#ip route 0.0.0.0 0.0.0.0 192.0.2.5
ISP(config)#ip route 10.10.10.0 255.255.255.0 192.0.2.2
ISP(config)#ip route 192.168.1.0 255.255.255.0 192.0.2.6
```

2. Use the following command on both the **HQ** and **R1** routers to boot the securityk9 license. The securityk9 license enables features such as IPsec, SSL, SSH, and other security capabilities on a router. This command enables the VPN capabilities on each device:

```
HQ(config)#license boot module c2900 technology-package
securityk9
```

3. Accept the user agreement by entering yes and hitting *Enter*.

4. Save the device configurations and reboot each for the license to take effect:

```
HQ#copy running-config startup-config
HQ#reload
```

5. Once each device has been rebooted, use the `show version` command to verify that the security technology package has been abled on both the **HQ** and **R1** routers:

```
-------------------------------------------------------------
Technology      Technology-package        Technology-package
                Current      Type         Next reboot
-------------------------------------------------------------
ipbase          ipbasek9     Permanent    ipbasek9
security        securityk9   Evaluation   securityk9
uc              disable      None         None
data            disable      None         None

Configuration register is 0x2102
```

Figure 12.37 – Verifying the security package

6. Create an **Access Control List** (**ACL**) on **HQ** to identify traffic that is allowed between the LAN on **HQ** and the LAN on **R1**. This traffic will be encrypted and sent across the IPsec VPN tunnel between the LANs:

```
HQ(config)#ip access-list extended VPN-Traffic
HQ(config-ext-nacl)#permit ip 10.10.10.0 0.0.0.255
192.168.1.0 0.0.0.255
HQ(config-ext-nacl)#exit
```

7. Configure the **Internet Key Exchange** (**IKE**) Phase 1 ISAKMP policy on the **HQ** router. IKE Phase 1 creates an outer tunnel that both VPN routers/firewalls use to negotiate security parameters before establishing the IKE Phase 2 tunnel for data transfer. The following commands are used to create the IKE Phase 1 ISAHMP policy:

```
HQ(config)#crypto isakmp policy 5
HQ(config-isakmp)#encryption aes 256
HQ(config-isakmp)#authentication pre-share
HQ(config-isakmp)#group 5
HQ(config-isakmp)#exit
HQ(config)#crypto isakmp key myipseckey address 192.0.2.6
```

8.  Configure the IKE Phase 2 IPsec policy on the **HQ** router. IKE Phase 2 is established after the IKE Phase 1 tunnel and is used to transport the actual data between networks or end devices. Create the transform set, name it IPsec-VPN, and use esp-aes and esp-sha-hmac for confidentiality and integrity:

```
HQ(config)#crypto ipsec transform-set IPsec-VPN esp-aes
esp-sha-hmac
```

9.  Create a crypto map on the **HQ** router, which will be used to actually apply security to the traffic that is sent along the VPN tunnel, name it IPsec-Map, and bind it to the VPN-Traffic ACL:

```
HQ(config)#crypto map IPsec-Map 5 ipsec-isakmp
HQ(config-crypto-map)#description IPsec VPN between HQ
and R1
HQ(config-crypto-map)#set peer 192.0.2.6
HQ(config-crypto-map)#set transform-set IPsec-VPN
HQ(config-crypto-map)#match address VPN-Traffic
HQ(config-crypto-map)#exit
```

10. Assign the crypto map to the outbound interface on the **HQ** router:

```
HQ(config)#interface gigabitEthernet 0/0
HQ(config-if)#crypto map IPsec-Map
HQ(config-if)#exit
```

Now, we will start configuring the IPsec Site-to-Site VPN on **R1** using the following instructions:

1.  Create an ACL on **R1** to identify traffic that is allowed between the LAN on **R1** and the LAN on **HQ**. This traffic will be encrypted and sent across the IPsec VPN tunnel between the LANs:

```
R1(config)#ip access-list extended VPN-Traffic
R1(config-ext-nacl)#permit ip 192.168.1.0 0.0.0.255
10.10.10.0 0.0.0.255
R1(config-ext-nacl)#exit
```

2. Configure the IKE Phase 1 ISAKMP policy on the **R1** router:

```
R1(config)#crypto isakmp policy 5
R1(config-isakmp)#encryption aes 256
R1(config-isakmp)#authentication pre-share
R1(config-isakmp)#group 5
R1 (config-isakmp)#exit
R1(config)#crypto isakmp key myipseckey address 192.0.2.2
```

3. Configure the IKE Phase 2 IPsec policy on the **R1** router. Create the transform set, name it IPsec-VPN, and use esp-aes and esp-sha-hmac for confidentiality and integrity:

```
R1(config)#crypto ipsec transform-set IPsec-VPN esp-aes
esp-sha-hmac
```

4. Create a crypto map, name it IPsec-Map, and bind it to the VPN-Traffic APL:

```
R1(config)#crypto map IPsec-Map 5 ipsec-isakmp
R1(config-crypto-map)#description IPsec VPN between R1
and HQ
R1(config-crypto-map)#set peer 192.0.2.2
R1(config-crypto-map)#set transform-set IPsec-VPN
R1(config-crypto-map)#match address VPN-Traffic
R1(config-crypto-map)#exit
```

5. Assign the crypto map to the outbound interface on the **R1** router:

```
R1(config)#interface gigabitEthernet 0/2
R1(config-if)#crypto map IPsec-Map
R1(config-if)#exit
```

6. At this point, both the **R1** and **HQ** routers should establish an IPsec tunnel. On **PC 1**, open Command Prompt and send a ping to the server at 10.10.10.10. A few packets may drop since the IPsec tunnel may still be initializing.

7.  To verify the status of the IPsec tunnel, perform a `traceroute` test between **PC 1** and the server:

```
C:\>tracert 10.10.10.10

Tracing route to 10.10.10.10 over a maximum of 30
hops:

    1    1 ms        0 ms        0 ms        192.168.1.1
    2   11 ms        0 ms       10 ms        192.0.2.2
    3   11 ms       13 ms        0 ms        10.10.10.10

Trace complete.
```

Figure 12.38 – Traceroute between PC 1 and the server

Based on the preceding results, the packet went from **PC 1** to **R1**, then from **R1** to **HQ**, and, lastly, from **HQ** to the server. Notice that the packet did not go to the ISP router but rather straight from **R1** to **HQ**. This is because the packet was encrypted and sent across `IPsec tunnel` on the network.

8.  To view the `IKE Phase 1` tunnel, use the `show crypto isakmp sa` command, as shown here:

```
R1#show crypto isakmp sa
IPv4 Crypto ISAKMP SA
dst              src              state        conn-id slot status
192.0.2.2        192.0.2.6        QM_IDLE         1076      0 ACTIVE
```

Figure 12.39 – IKE Phase 1 tunnel

9.  To view the `IPsec Phase 2` tunnel, which is transporting the users' traffic, use the `show crypto ipsec sa` command, as shown here:

```
R1#show crypto ipsec sa

interface: GigabitEthernet0/2
    Crypto map tag: IPsec-Map, local addr 192.0.2.6

    protected vrf: (none)
    local  ident (addr/mask/prot/port): (192.168.1.0/255.255.255.0/0/0)
    remote ident (addr/mask/prot/port): (10.10.10.0/255.255.255.0/0/0)
    current_peer 192.0.2.2 port 500
     PERMIT, flags={origin_is_acl,}
    #pkts encaps: 17, #pkts encrypt: 17, #pkts digest: 0
    #pkts decaps: 14, #pkts decrypt: 14, #pkts verify: 0
    #pkts compressed: 0, #pkts decompressed: 0
    #pkts not compressed: 0, #pkts compr. failed: 0
    #pkts not decompressed: 0, #pkts decompress failed: 0
    #send errors 1, #recv errors 0
```

Figure 12.40 – IPsec Phase 2 tunnel

10. To view the details about the crypto map on the local router, use the `show crypto map` command:

```
R1#show crypto map
Crypto Map IPsec-Map 5 ipsec-isakmp
        Peer = 192.0.2.2
        Extended IP access list VPN-Traffic
            access-list VPN-Traffic permit ip 192.168.1.0 0.0.0.255 10.10.10.0 0.0.0.255
        Current peer: 192.0.2.2
        Security association lifetime: 4608000 kilobytes/3600 seconds
        PFS (Y/N): N
        Transform sets={
                IPsec-VPN,
        }
        Interfaces using crypto map IPsec-Map:
                GigabitEthernet0/2
```

Figure 12.41 – Crypto map

The details shown in the preceding snippet validate the configurations we have applied to the device. We can see that the VPN peer is **HQ**, the ACL for the permitted traffic on the VPN tunnel, and other details about the IPsec tunnel, such as the active interface.

Having completed this lab, you have gained the hands-on skills to implement an IPsec Site-to-Site VPN in a Cisco environment. In the next lab, you will learn how to configure a Cisco IOS router in order to support a remote access VPN between a client device and a corporate network.

# Lab – Configuring a remote access VPN

In this hands-on lab, you will learn how to configure a Cisco IOS router so that it acts as a VPN gateway to support a remote access VPN. In this lab, we will be using the following topology in Cisco Packet Tracer:

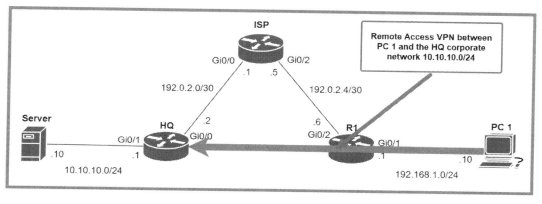

Figure 12.42 – Remote access VPN lab topology

Please use the following guidelines when creating this lab to ensure you get the same results:

- Use Cisco 2911 routers.

- Configure a default route from both the **HQ** and **R1** routers that points to the **ISP**.

- On the **ISP**, configure network static routers to the LAN of **HQ** and the LAN of **R1**.

Ensure you assign an IP address to each device, as shown in the following table:

| Device | Interface | IP Address | Subnet Mask | Default Gateway |
|---|---|---|---|---|
| PC 1 | Fa0 | 192.168.1.10 | 255.255.255.0 | 192.168.1.1 |
| Server | Fa0 | 10.10.10.10 | 255.255.255.0 | 10.10.10.1 |
| R1 | Gi0/1 | 192.168.1.1 | 255.255.255.0 | n/a |
| | Gi0/2 | 192.0.2.6 | 255.255.255.252 | n/a |
| HQ | Gi0/1 | 10.10.10.1 | 255.255.255.0 | n/a |
| | Gi0/0 | 192.0.2.2 | 255.255.255.252 | n/a |
| ISP | Gi0/0 | 192.0.2.1 | 255.255.255.252 | n/a |
| | Gi0/2 | 192.0.2.5 | 255.255.255.252 | n/a |

Figure 12.43 – IP scheme

Now that your lab environment is ready, use the following instructions to configure an IPsec remote access VPN on the **HQ** router:

1. Configure the following static routes on each router to simulate the internet:

```
HQ(config)#ip route 0.0.0.0 0.0.0.0 192.0.2.1
R1(config)#ip route 0.0.0.0 0.0.0.0 192.0.2.5
ISP(config)#ip route 10.10.10.0 255.255.255.0 192.0.2.2
ISP(config)#ip route 192.168.1.0 255.255.255.0 192.0.2.6
```

2. Use the following command on **HQ** to boot the `securityk9` license. This command enables the VPN capabilities on each device:

```
HQ(config)#license boot module c2900 technology-package
securityk9
```

3. Accept the user agreement by entering `yes` and hitting *Enter*.

4.  Save the device configurations and reboot each for the license to take effect:

```
HQ#copy running-config startup-config
HQ#reload
```

5.  Once each device has been rebooted, use the show version command to verify that the security technology package has been abled on the **HQ** router:

```
--------------------------------------------------------------
Technology      Technology-package              Technology-package
                Current         Type            Next reboot
--------------------------------------------------------------
ipbase          ipbasek9        Permanent       ipbasek9
security        securityk9      Evaluation      securityk9
uc              disable         None            None
data            disable         None            None

Configuration register is 0x2102
```

Figure 12.44 – Verifying the security package

6.  Create an IP address pool for remote access users via the VPN; the range is within the **HQ** corporate network:

```
HQ(config)#ip local pool RA-VPN-Pool 10.10.10.100
10.10.10.110
```

7.  Enable the AAA services on the **HQ** router and configure the authentication login method in order to use the local user database:

```
HQ(config)#aaa new-model
HQ(config)#aaa authentication login RA-UserVPN local
```

8.  Configure the AAA authorization for network services on the HQ corporate network in order to use the local user database:

```
HQ(config)#aaa authorization network RA-Group-VPN local
```

9.  Create a username and password for the remote access user:

```
HQ(config)#username user1 secret ciscovpn1
```

10. Configure the IKE Phase 1 ISAKMP policy on the **HQ** router:

```
HQ(config)#crypto isakmp policy 10
HQ(config-isakmp)#encryption aes 256
HQ(config-isakmp)#authentication pre-share
HQ(config-isakmp)#group 5
HQ(config-isakmp)#exit
```

11. Create the remote user client configurations and the password for the group (RA-Group-VPN) on the **HQ** router:

```
HQ(config)#crypto isakmp client configuration group
RA-Group-VPN
HQ(config-isakmp-group)#key remoteaccessvpn
HQ(config-isakmp-group)#pool RA-VPN-Pool
HQ(config-isakmp-group)#exit
```

12. Configure the IKE Phase 2 IPsec policy on the **HQ** router. Create the transform set, name it RA-VPN, and use esp-aes and esp-sha-hmac for confidentiality and integrity:

```
HQ(config)#crypto ipsec transform-set RA-VPN esp-aes
esp-sha-hmac
```

13. Create a dynamic crypto map on the **HQ** router, name it RemoteAccessVPN, and set the sequence number to 100:

```
HQ(config)#crypto dynamic-map RemoteAccessVPN 100
HQ(config-crypto-map)#set transform-set RA-VPN
HQ(config-crypto-map)#reverse-route
HQ(config-crypto-map)#exit
```

14. Create the static crypto map for the client configuration for both authentication and authorization:

```
HQ(config)#crypto map StaticVPNMap client configuration
address respond
HQ(config)#crypto map StaticVPNMap client authentication
list RA-UserVPN
HQ(config)#crypto map StaticVPNMap isakmp authorization
list RA-Group-VPN
```

15. Specify a sequence number to insert the crypto map entry:

```
HQ(config)#crypto map StaticVPNMap 20 ipsec-isakmp
dynamic RemoteAccessVPN
```

16. Configure the internet-facing interface on **HQ** with the crypto map:

```
HQ(config)#interface gigabitEthernet 0/0
HQ(config-if)#crypto map StaticVPNMap
HQ(config-if)#exit
```

17. On **PC1**, open the **Desktop** tab and client on the VPN client, as shown here:

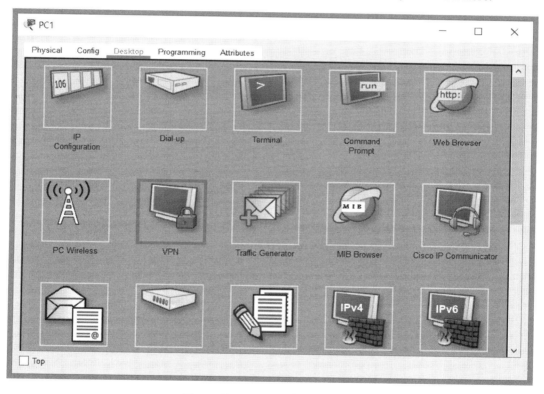

Figure 12.45 – VPN client on PC1

18. Enter the following configurations into the VPN client interface and click **Connect**:

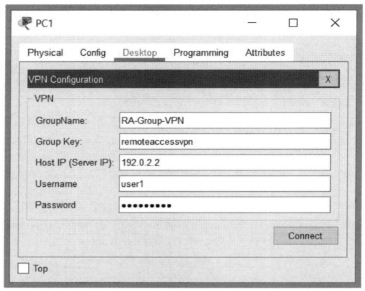

Figure 12.46 – VPN client configurations

This process may take some time to establish the VPN tunnel between the **PC** and **HQ** routers.

19. Once the VPN tunnel has been established, open Command Prompt and use the `ipconfig /all` command to verify that **PC1** has a VPN tunnel interface with an IP address from the **HQ** network:

```
C:\>ipconfig /all

FastEthernet0 Connection:(default port)

   Connection-specific DNS Suffix..:
   Physical Address................: 0010.11AD.54B7
   Link-local IPv6 Address.........: FE80::210:11FF:FEAD:54B7
   IP Address......................: 192.168.1.10
   Subnet Mask.....................: 255.255.255.0
   Default Gateway.................: 192.168.1.1
   DNS Servers.....................: 0.0.0.0
   DHCP Servers....................: 0.0.0.0
   DHCPv6 Client DUID..............: 00-01-00-01-AB-C8-B7-7D-00-10-11-AD-54-B7

   Tunnel Interface IP Address.....: 10.10.10.100
```

Figure 12.47 – VPN tunnel

20. Perform a connectivity test from **PC1** to the server on the **HQ** network using the `ping` command:

```
C:\>ping 10.10.10.10

Pinging 10.10.10.10 with 32 bytes of data:

Reply from 10.10.10.10: bytes=32 time=1ms TTL=127
Reply from 10.10.10.10: bytes=32 time=1ms TTL=127
Reply from 10.10.10.10: bytes=32 time=1ms TTL=127
Reply from 10.10.10.10: bytes=32 time<1ms TTL=127

Ping statistics for 10.10.10.10:
    Packets: Sent = 4, Received = 4, Lost = 0 (0% loss),
Approximate round trip times in milli-seconds:
    Minimum = 0ms, Maximum = 1ms, Average = 0ms
```

Figure 12.48 – Connectivity test

21. To verify that the packets are going through the remote access VPN tunnel, perform a `traceroute` from **PC1** to the server:

```
C:\>tracert 10.10.10.10

Tracing route to 10.10.10.10 over a maximum of 30 hops:

  1    0 ms      0 ms      0 ms      192.0.2.2
  2    0 ms      0 ms      0 ms      10.10.10.10

Trace complete.
```

Figure 12.49 – Checking the VPN tunnel

As shown in the preceding results, the packet was sent from **PC1** to 192.0.2.2, which is the **HQ** router. This is simply because the VPN tunnel was established between **PC1** and the **HQ** router. All packets from **PC1** to the 10.10.10.0/24 network will be encrypted and sent through the remote access VPN tunnel. Hence, the **R1** and **ISP** routers were not shown as any hops along the path.

Having completed this lab, you have gained the hands-on skills to implement a remote access VPN on a Cisco IOS router.

# Summary

During the course of this chapter, you learned how to secure access to the console, AUX ports, and the VTY lines, how to set up secure remote access, and how to lock down administrative access on a Cisco device. Furthermore, you discovered how to establish a secure tunnel between two remote sites, such as Cisco IOS routers, to simply extend the LAN at the HQ corporate office to a remote branch site using a VPN.

I hope this chapter has been informative for you and is helpful in your journey toward learning how to implement and administer Cisco solutions and prepare for the CCNA 200-301 certification. In the next chapter, *Implementing Access Controls Lists (ACLs)*, you will learn how to create and implement Layer 3 security controls on a Cisco IOS router to filter traffic.

# Questions

The following is a short list of review questions to help reinforce your learning and help you identify areas that require some improvement:

1.  Which command is used to enable authentication on the console line?

    A. `enable login`

    B. `login enable`

    C. `login`

    D. `login all`

2.  Which command is used to set a password on the AUX line?

    A. `password`

    B. `password enable`

    C. `enable password`

    D. `password login`

3.  Which show command allows you to verify the method used to connect to a Cisco device?

    A. `show ssh`

    B. `show login`

    C. `show users`

    D. `show ip ssh`

4. Which command is used to disable Telnet on VTY lines?

   A. `no transport`

   B. `transport input ssh`

   C. `transport ssh only`

   D. `transport no telnet`

5. Which command is recommended when creating a secure password to access `Privilege Exec` mode?

   A. `enable password secret`

   B. `enable password`

   C. `enable secure`

   D. `enable secret`

6. Which encoding type is used on the `enable password` command?

   A. `Type 0`

   B. `Type 9`

   C. `Type 2`

   D. `Type 5`

7. Which command can be used to encrypt all existing and future plaintext passwords?

   A. `enable service encryption`

   B. `service password-encryption`

   C. `service encryption`

   D. `service encryption-password`

8. Which of the following is a requirement for a remote access VPN?

   A. Metro E

   B. Wi-Fi

   C. VPN client software

   D. MPLS

9.  Which protocol/standard does IPsec use to securely exchange secrets keys over an unsecured network?

    A. AES

    B. Encapsulating Security Protocol

    C. Authentication Header

    D. Diffie-Hellman

10. Which IPsec protocol encrypts the entire IP packet?

    A. ESP

    B. DH

    C. AH

    D. AES

# Further reading

The following links are recommended for additional reading:

- Cisco Guide to Hardening Cisco IOS Devices: `https://www.cisco.com/c/en/us/support/docs/ip/access-lists/13608-21.html`

- Configuring a Site-to-Site IPsec VPN: `https://www.cisco.com/c/en/us/support/docs/cloud-systems-management/configuration-professional/113337-ccp-vpn-routerA-routerB-config-00.html`

# 13
# Implementing Access Control Lists

Whenever the need arises to interconnect two or more networks, a router is always the preferred choice, simply because the primary function of a router is to forward packets between networks. However, the Cisco IOS router has many more features aside from simply forwarding. One major feature is to filter traffic based on its source and destination. This feature simply enables the Cisco IOS router to perform *packet filtering* in a similar fashion to a firewall appliance on the network.

Throughout this chapter, you will learn how **Access Control Lists** (**ACLs**) can be applied to a Cisco IOS router to filter both inbound and outbound traffic. Furthermore, you will discover the various types of ACLs and how they can be used in various situations to allow or deny traffic between networks.

In this chapter, we will cover the following topics:

- What are ACLs?
- ACL operation
- ACL wildcard masks
- Working with standard ACLs
- Working with extended ACLs

# Technical requirements

To follow along with the exercises in this chapter, please ensure that you have met the following hardware and software requirement:

- Cisco Packet Tracer

The code files for this chapter are available at `https://github.com/PacktPublishing/Implementing-and-Administering-Cisco-Solutions/tree/master/Chapter%2013`.

Check out the following video to see the Code in Action:
`https://bit.ly/3cqh8JX`

# What are ACLs?

As you have learned so far, routers are used to forward traffic between different networks. As a packet enters an inbound interface of a router, the operating system has to read the Layer 3 header information, such as the source and destination IP addresses, and check the *routing table* for a suitable route. Once a route has been found, the router forwards the packet through an outbound interface to its destination. Ensuring that all users are able to send and receive messages is excellent in terms of connectivity, but what do security and the restriction of traffic flow between certain networks mean?

The Cisco IOS router has many amazing features and can perform a variety of roles on a network. One such feature is to perform traffic filtering between networks. This is done using a very special method that firewall appliances use to filter traffic, known as an ACL.

> **Important note**
> Firewall appliances use a variety of methods to filter inbound and outbound traffic. ACLs are simply one of many methods.

ACLs can be applied to the interfaces of a router to filter traffic as it is either entering or leaving the router. ACLs filter traffic based on their source or destination information. ACLs are typically rules created on a router that determine how traffic should be filtered, such as whether it is allowed or denied. Implementing ACLs on a Cisco IOS router does not convert the router into a firewall appliance, nor does it replace the need for a dedicated firewall on your network. ACLs are simply used to filter traffic passing through your router, such as filtering messages between IP subnets and **Virtual Local Area Networks (VLANs)**.

By default, the Cisco IOS router is not configured with any ACLs and traffic is able to flow without any restrictions. However, when an ACL is created, it must be applied to an interface to take effect. ACLs can be used to filter inbound or outbound traffic on a router's interface. When applied to an inbound interface, the router has to perform additional checks on all traffic entering the interface before checking the routing table for a suitable path. Additionally, when an ACL is applied to an outbound interface, the router still has to perform additional checks before allowing the message to leave the router.

There are two types of ACLs. They are as follows:

- **Standard ACLs**
- **Extended ACLs**

A standard ACL is used to filter all traffic types of a source host or network. This type of ACL is very straightforward in terms of application. If you want to deny all traffic originating from a single host or network, a standard ACL is the better choice.

An extended ACL allows you to be more granular when filtering traffic. This type of ACL allows you to filter packets based on the following criteria:

- Protocol type
- Source IP address
- Source port number (TCP or UDP)
- Destination IP address
- Destination port number (TCP or UDP)

Extended ACL is the better choice when filtering specific traffic types between a source and a destination.

# Benefits of using ACLs

There are many benefits associated with using ACLs to filter traffic within an organization. In this section, you'll learn about the various scenarios where ACLs can help improve security and traffic flow on a network.

Imagine within your organization that there are many users who frequently stream online videos during their work schedule. This video traffic can consume a lot of bandwidth simply by increasing the load on the network. By implementing an ACL, you can enforce and restrict video traffic within the organization and increase network performance. Additionally, by implementing ACLs on a corporate network, you can restrict or limit access to various network resources to a specific group of users. This adds a layer of network security by granting access to resources to authorized users only.

ACLs can be used to filter unwanted network services and traffic. Some organizations may have security policies to prevent unsecured communication protocols on their network. One example of an unsecured protocol is Telnet. An ACL can be used to enforce this policy within the organization and restrict all Telnet traffic.

In the previous chapter, you learned how to implement secure remote access to your Cisco devices. Imagine configuring remote access on all your devices and anyone is able to establish an SSH session with your routers and switches. By implementing an ACL, you can restrict remote access to be granted to a specific user group, such as those within the IT department of your organization. The ACL can be applied to the **Virtual Terminal (VTY)** lines to filter inbound traffic.

When applying **Quality of Service (QoS)** to a network, it's important to identify the traffic types correctly for classification and prioritization. ACLs can be used with QoS to identify various traffic types, such as **Voice over IP (VoIP)**, thereby enabling the QoS tools to process the traffic quickly.

Having completed this section, you have learned about the need for ACLs and their benefits to a network. In the next section, you will learn how ACLs operate in permitting or denying traffic between networks.

# ACL operation

ACLs are rules created by a network professional on the router or firewall appliance to filter traffic either entering or leaving the device. ACLs are a list of security rules, with each ACL containing either a `permit` or `deny` statement. Each statement within an ACL is referred to as an **Access Control Entry (ACE)**. These ACEs are the real workers that allow and block packets between networks. When a router receives packets on an interface, the router checks each ACE, starting with the first entry at the top of the list and moving down until a match is found. Once a matching ACE is found, the router stops searching and executes the rule on the ACE, either permitting or denying the traffic. This process is known as packet filtering.

> **Important note**
>
> If no matches are found in the ACLs, the packet is discarded by the router. The last ACE within all ACLs is an `implicit deny` statement. An `implicit deny` statement simply states that if no matches are found in the previous ACEs, the packet should be deined. The `implicit deny` statement is automatically inserted as the last entry within an ACL. It is usually invisible.

With packet filtering, you can configure the Cisco IOS router to analyze traffic and control access between networks. ACLs can be used to filter inbound or outbound traffic or to permit or deny traffic based on its source and destination IP address (Layer 3) and/or by the source and destination port numbers (Layer 4).

> **Important note**
>
> Standard ACLs are designed to filter traffic found at Layer 3 only. Extended ACLs are able to filter traffic at Layer 3 and 4 of the OSI model.

ACLs can be configured on a router to filter inbound traffic or outbound traffic:

- **Inbound ACLs**: With inbound ACLs, packets entering a router are processed before they are forwarded to their destination. The placement of the inbound ACLs allows the router to conserve its resources, such as performing routing lookups, since the inbound ACL can filter packets as they enter the device. If the packet is allowed by the inbound ACL, the router will then perform a route lookup and forward the packet to its destination. It is recommended to use inbound ACLs to perform packet filtering when the source of the traffic is attached or connected to the inbound interface of a router.

- **Outbound ACLs**: Outbound ACLs are placed on the outgoing interface of a router. Outbound ACLs filter packets after they have been processed by the router. The placement of this ACL is useful when filtering traffic that originates from multiple interfaces or sources.

The following diagram shows the concepts of inbound and outbound ACLs on a router:

Figure 13.1 – Inbound and outbound ACLs

To get a better understanding of how ACLs are applied to a router, let's take a look at the following output:

```
HQ#show ip interface GigabitEthernet 0/2
GigabitEthernet0/2 is up, line protocol is up (connected)
  Internet address is 172.16.1.1/24
  Broadcast address is 255.255.255.255
  Address determined by setup command
  MTU is 1500 bytes
  Helper address is not set
  Directed broadcast forwarding is disabled
  Outgoing access list is 10
  Inbound access list is Restrict-FTP
  Proxy ARP is enabled
  Security level is default
```

Figure 13.2 – Verifying ACLs on an interface

The show ip interface command is used to verify whether an ACL is applied to an interface and its direction to filter traffic. As demonstrated in the preceding code snippet, there are 2 ACLs applied to the GigabitEthernet 0/2 interface. A numbered ACL, 10, is applied to filter outbound packets leaving the interface, and a named ACL, Restrict-FTP, is applied to filter inbound packets on the router's interface.

The following snippet shows the ACEs for the outbound ACL on the GigabitEthernet 0/2 interface:

```
HQ#show access-lists 10
Standard IP access list 10
    permit host 192.168.1.10
    permit 10.1.1.0 0.0.0.255

HQ#
```

Figure 13.3 – Verifying ACEs within ACL 10

As shown, ACL 10 contains two ACEs. The first ACE is a permit statement to only allow traffic from the host device with an IP address of 192.168.1.10. The host command is used to specify a single IP address in this statement. Therefore, a *wildcard mask* is not required when the host command is invoked. The wildcard mask is simply an inverse of the subnet mask, which tells the router which bits in the IP address to match and which parts to ignore.

The second ACE is a permit statement to allow all traffic originating from the 10.1.1.0/24 network. When specifying a network range, wildcard masks are used to tell the router which bits to match in the address and which bits to ignore.

Next, let's examine the contents of the inbound ACL on the `GigabitEthernet` `0/2` interface:

```
HQ#show access-lists Restrict-FTP
Extended IP access list Restrict-FTP
    deny tcp host 172.16.1.10 any eq ftp
    permit ip any any
HQ#
```

Figure 13.4 – Verifying ACEs within ACL Restrict-FTP

As shown in the preceding code snippet, there are two ACEs within the inbound ACL. The first ACE is a `deny` statement to prevent any TCP traffic originating from the host IP address, `172.16.1.10`, from reaching any destination network that has a port of `21` open for **File Transfer Protocol** (**FTP**). The second ACE indicates that IP traffic is permitted from any source to any destination.

> **Important note**
>
> The keyword is also used to indicate port `21` within an ACL.

The second ACE is a `permit` statement to allow all IP traffic from any source to any destination. Since neither a source nor destination port was specified within the ACE, all ports are automatically considered. Keep in mind that there are `65,535` logical network ports.

Additionally, in order to view all the ACLs on a router, the `show access-lists` command can be executed without specifying an ACL name or number. The following is a list of all the ACLs present on a Cisco IOS router:

```
HQ#show access-lists
Standard IP access list 10
    10 permit host 192.168.1.10
    20 permit 10.1.1.0 0.0.0.255
Standard IP access list INT_Access
    10 permit 172.16.1.0 0.0.0.255
Standard IP access list Secure-VTY
    10 permit host 172.16.1.10
    20 deny any
Extended IP access list Restrict-FTP
    10 deny tcp host 172.16.1.10 any eq ftp
    20 permit ip any any
HQ#
```

Figure 13.5 – Viewing all ACLs

The output is a bit different as it contains placement values such as 10, 20, and 30. When creating an ACL, it's important that the ACEs are placed in order as you want the router to process each packet. To put it simply, the router reads an ACL from top to bottom each time it has to reference an ACL on an interface. It is recommended to place more specific ACEs at the top of the ACL and less specific ACEs at the bottom. As an example, take a look at the following snippet:

```
HQ#show access-lists
Extended IP access list Restrict-FTP
    10 deny tcp host 172.16.1.10 any eq ftp
    20 permit ip any any
HQ#
```

Figure 13.6 – Analyzing an ACL

As shown, the ACEs are placed according to their numerical value. By default, the router automatically inserts a placement value for new ACEs under an ACL with increments of 10. This allows a network engineer to insert ACEs between each other on an ACL.

## ACL wildcard masks

When creating an ACE, you may need to specify a network ID and the subnet mask. However, within ACLs and ACEs, you cannot use a subnet mask as Cisco IOS on the router was not built or designed to accept subnet masks as part of an ACE. ACLs use a wildcard mask, which is a 32-bit binary string used by the Cisco IOS router to determine which bits within the address to match and which bits to ignore.

As with a subnet mask, ones and zeroes are used to indicate the network and host portions of an IP address. For example, the ones within a subnet mask are used to identify the network portion of an address, while the zeroes are used to identify the host portion. Within a wildcard mask, these bits are used for a different purpose. Here, the ones and zeroes are used to filter either a group of addresses or a single IP address to decide whether to permit or deny access to a network resource.

In a wildcard mask, the zeroes are used to match the corresponding bit value in the address, while the ones are used to ignore the corresponding bit value in the address. You can think of a wildcard mask as the inverse of a subnet mask.

To get a better idea, let's take a look at the following examples of using wildcard masking:

- 00000000: Since all the bits are zeroes, this wildcard indicates to match all corresponding bits in the address.
- 11110000: This indicates to ignore the first four address bits.

ACL wildcard masks    569

- 00001111: This indicates to match the first four address bits.

- 11111111: This ignores all the bits within the octet.

- 11111100: This ignores the first six address bits.

Let's take a look at applying a 0.0.255.255 wildcard mask to a 32-bit address:

| | Decimal | Binary | | | |
|---|---|---|---|---|---|
| IP Address | 192.168.1.0 | 11000000 | 10101000 | 00000001 | 00000000 |
| Wildcard | 0.0.0.255 | 00000000 | 00000000 | 11111111 | 11111111 |
| Result Address | 192.168.0.0 | 11000000 | 10101000 | 00000000 | 00000000 |

Figure 13.7 – Wildcard masking example 1

As shown in the preceding table, a wildcard mask of 0.0.255.255 is used to match the first 16-bits in the address. The zeros within the wildcard mask indicate a match, while the ones indicate that the router should ignore the corresponding bits in the address.

Let's take a look at another example of how to match all the corresponding bits on an address:

| | Decimal | Binary | | | |
|---|---|---|---|---|---|
| IP Address | 172.16.10.1 | 10101100 | 00010000 | 00001010 | 00000001 |
| Wildcard | 0.0.0.0 | 00000000 | 00000000 | 00000000 | 00000000 |
| Result Address | 172.16.10.1 | 10101100 | 00010000 | 00001010 | 00000001 |

Figure 13.8 – Wildcard masking example 2

As shown in the preceding table, a wildcard mask of 0.0.0.0 is used to match all the corresponding bits in the address. This ensures that the exact IP address of 172.16.10.1 must match the ACL. Next, we are going to take a deep look into calculating the wildcard mask for ACLs.

## Calculating the wildcard mask

This is a straightforward technique that will quickly provide you with a wildcard when configuring ACLs. To calculate the wildcard mask, simply subtract the subnet mask from 255.255.255.255.

In our first example, imagine you want to permit access to all users within the `192.168.20.0/24` network. Since the subnet mask is `255.255.255.0`, we can subtract the subnet mask from the `255.255.255.255` address, as shown here:

| | | | | |
|---|---|---|---|---|
| Broadcast Address | 255 | 255 | 255 | 255 |
| Subnet Mask − | 255 | 255 | 255 | 0 |
| Wildcard Mask | 0 | 0 | 0 | 255 |

Figure 13.9 – Calculating a wildcard mask

Our resulting wildcard mask is `0.0.0.255`. This allows us to create the following ACL statement:

```
Router(config)#access-list 10 permit 192.168.20.0 0.0.0.255
```

In our next example, imagine you want to deny traffic from all users within the `172.16.24.64/28` network. The subnet mask is `255.255.255.240`. We can use the same technique as in the previous example:

| | | | | |
|---|---|---|---|---|
| Broadcast Address | 255 | 255 | 255 | 255 |
| Subnet Mask − | 255 | 255 | 255 | 240 |
| Wildcard Mask | 0 | 0 | 0 | 15 |

Figure 13.10 – Calculating a wildcard mask

The resulting wildcard mask is `0.0.0.15`. This allows us to create the following ACL statement:

```
Router(config)#access-list 10 deny 172.16.24.64 0.0.0.15
```

Sometimes, working with wildcard masks can be a bit complex. What if you need to specifically allow a single host device, such as `192.168.1.10`, within an ACL? Rather than using the `0.0.0.0` wildcard mask, you can use the `host` keyword command, as shown here:

```
Router(config)#access-list 20 permit host 192.168.1.10
```

The `host` keyword command simply states that all the bits within the address must match within the ACL.

In another scenario, you may need to create an ACL to ignore the entire IPv4 address or to accept any addresses. To create an ACE to represent any address, we can write the 0.0.0.0 255.255.255.255 statement. However, we can also use the any keyword command as a shortcut to represent the entire statement, as shown here:

```
Router(config)#access-list 30 permit any
```

The preceding ACL simply states that any traffic is permitted from any source address or network. In the next section, we will discuss some important guidelines and best practices when creating ACLs.

# ACL guidelines and best practices

Creating and configuring ACLs on a router can be somewhat complex and a bit confusing at first until you get the hang of it. In this section, you will learn about some guidelines and best practices to help you create and implement ACLs efficiently on a Cisco IOS router.

The first rule of thumb is that you need to know the three Ps when applying ACLs to a router. They are as follows:

- One ACL per protocol (IPv4 or IPv6)
- One ACL per direction (in or out)
- One ACL per interface

You cannot have two ACLs on the same interface filtering inbound IPv4 traffic. You cannot have the same ACL filtering inbound and outbound traffic on the same interface. However, you can have two different ACLs on the same interface, where one ACL is filtering inbound traffic while the other is filtering outbound traffic.

Use the following guidelines when considering the application of ACLs to a router:

- ACLs should be applied to your edge router on the network to filter traffic between your internal network and the internet.
- ACLs should be applied to a router that is connected between two or more different networks for the purpose of controlling traffic entering and leaving a network.
- Use ACLs to filter specific traffic types between networks.

The following are some best practices when creating ACLs on your network routers:

- The ACLs should be aligned with your organization's security policies.

- When creating an ACL, ensure that you use the `remark` command to insert a description and purpose of the ACL for further reference.

- When modifying an ACL, use a text editor to help you create, edit, and save ACLs.

- Before creating ACLs, ensure that they have been tested within a lab or development environment before applying them to a production network.

After you've created ACLs on your router, the next step is to apply them to the appropriate interface. The placement of ACLs is very important. The following are some recommendations based on the type of ACL:

- Standard ACLs are configured to filter (permit or deny) traffic originating from a single host or network. This type of ACL should be placed closest to the destination of the packets on the network.

- Extended ACLs are configured to filter specific traffic types on a network. Therefore, it's recommended to place this type of ACL closest to the source where the traffic is originating. This method will simply filter the denied traffic type before it is processed and forwarded by the router.

Let's take a look at the following network topology to gain a better understanding of ACL placement:

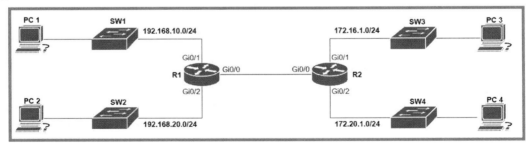

Figure 13.11 – ACL placement

Based on the preceding topology, let's create the following scenarios to better understand the most suitable place where ACLs should be applied on a router:

- If you want to filter (restrict) traffic from the source network, `192.168.20.0/24`, to the destination network, `172.16.1.0/24`, the best place to apply the standard ACL will be on **R2**'s outbound `GigabitEthernet 0/1` interface. The placement of this ACL will filter traffic that is destined only to the `172.16.1.0/24` network. If the ACL is placed on **R2**'s inbound `GigabitEthernet 0/0` interface, the ACL will filter traffic originating from both the `192.168.10.0/24` and `192.168.20.0/24` networks.

- If you want to filter FTP traffic originating from the `172.16.1.0/24` network to any destination, the most suitable place to apply the extended ACL will be on **R2**'s inbound `GigabitEthernet 0/1` interface. The placement of this ACL will filter all FTP traffic originating from the `172.16.1.0/24` network only. If the ACL is placed on **R2**'s outbound `GigabitEthernet 0/2` interface, it will filter traffic from both the `172.16.1.0/24` and `172.20.1.0/24` networks.

In the next section, you will learn how to configure and apply standard ACLs to a Cisco IOS router.

# Working with standard ACLs

When creating a numbered standard ACL on a Cisco IOS router, the ACL must first be created on the device and then applied to an interface to filter traffic. Numbered standard ACLs use the following range of numbers:

- 1 to 99
- 1300 to 1999

To create a numbered standard ACL on a Cisco IOS router, use the global configuration command followed by a number within the range of 1 to 99 or 1300 to 1999 on the device. Therefore, with this range of numbers, there can be up to 798 unique standard ACLs on a single router.

## Creating a numbered standard ACL

The following is the full syntax used to create a numbered standard ACL:

```
Router(config)# access-list access-list-number [ deny | permit
| remark ] source [ source-wildcard ][ log ]
```

The `remark` command will allow you to insert a description for the ACL and the `log` command will generate a `Syslog` message when matches are found. Additionally, there can be more than one ACE within an ACL.

The following are some examples of numbered standard ACLs:

- `Router(config)# access-list 10 permit host 172.16.1.5`
- `Router(config)# access-list 20 deny 192.168.20.0 0.0.0.255`

To remove an ACL from a Cisco router, use the following guidelines:

1. Use the `show access-lists` command within `Privilege Exec` mode to verify the exact ACL and its number that you want to remove.

2. Enter global configuration mode and use the `no access-lists` command with the ACL number. The following is an example of how to remove a numbered standard ACL:

```
Router(config)#access-list 20 deny 192.168.20.0 0.0.0.255   ①
Router(config)#exit
Router#show access-lists          ②
Standard IP access list 20
    10 deny 192.168.20.0 0.0.0.255

Router#conf t
Router(config)#no access-list 20   ③  ◄──── [ Removing ACL 20 ]
Router(config)#^Z
Router#show access-lists          ④
Router#
```

Figure 13.12 – Removing an ACL

There is no need to specify the entire ACE or ACL. Simply use the `no` command and the ACL number to delete an entire ACL from the `running-config` file.

After creating an ACL, you need to apply it to a router's interface to filter either inbound or outbound traffic. The following is the syntax to apply the ACL under `interface` mode:

```
Router(config-if)# ip access-group [ access-list-number |
access-list-name ] [ in | out ]
```

The syntax enabled you to use the `ip access-group` command to specify either the ACL number or the ACL name, and the direction to filter traffic.

The following snippet shows an example of applying a numbered ACL to an interface:

```
Router(config)#access-list 20 deny 192.168.20.0 0.0.0.255
Router(config)#interface GigabitEthernet 0/1
Router(config-if)#ip access-group 20 in
Router(config-if)#exit
```

Figure 13.13 – Applying an ACL to an interface

Next, we will learn how to implement a named standard ACL.

# Implementing a named standard ACL

Occasionally, numbered ACLs can be a bit confusing when there are many ACLs on a router. Cisco IOS allows us to create named standard ACLs, which make things easier for us.

Here are some guidelines when creating a named ACL:

- A named ACL can contain both letters and numbers.
- It is recommended to use capital letters.
- Named ACLs cannot have any spaces or punctuation characters.
- An example of creating a named standard ACL is `ip access-list standard filter-ftp`.

To create a named standard ACL, use the following instructions:

1. Enter global configuration mode and then use the following syntax to create a named standard ACL:

   ```
   Router(config)#ip access-list standard name
   ```

   You will then enter a new mode – standard (`std`) named ACL (`nacl`) configuration mode.

2. Next, use the following syntax to create ACEs within the ACL:

   ```
   Router(config-std-nacl)# [ deny | permit | remark ]
   source [ source-wildcard ] [ log ]
   ```

The following snippet shows an example of creating and applying a named standard ACL:

```
Router(config)#ip access-list standard Named-STD-ACL
Router(config-std-nacl)#permit 192.168.10.0 0.0.0.255
Router(config-std-nacl)#exit
Router(config)#interface GigabitEthernet 0/2
Router(config-if)#ip access-group Named-STD-ACL in
Router(config-if)#exit
```

Figure 13.14 – Creating a named standard ACL

Now, let's see how to delete an ACL.

## Deleting an ACL

To remove an ACL from a Cisco IOS router, take the following steps:

1.  Remove the ACL from the interface by using the no ip access-group command with the ACL number and its direction (in or out).

2.  Enter global configuration mode and use the no access-lists command with the ACL number to remove the entire ACL from the device.

Having completed this section, you have gained an essential understanding of standard ACL operations, and how to configure and apply them correctly to a Cisco device. In the following section, you will gain hands-on experience with creating and applying both standard and extended ACLs to a Cisco environment.

## Lab – implementing a standard numbered ACL

In this hands-on lab, you will learn how to implement standard ACLs to filter traffic from a source host and network. The following topology shows an organization network (left) that is connected to the internet (right) via an **Internet Service Provider (ISP)**:

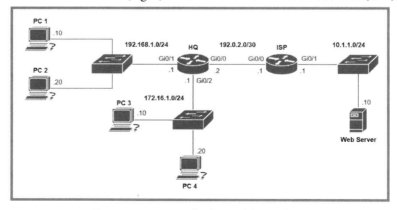

Figure 13.15 – Standard ACL lab topology

The objective of this lab is to demonstrate how to apply standard numbered ACLs to a Cisco router to filter traffic between devices and networks. We'll use a numbered ACL to restrict traffic originating from all devices on the `192.168.1.0/24` network, except **PC 1**, which is going to the `172.16.1.0/24` network.

For this lab, we'll be using Cisco Packet Tracer to simulate the Cisco environment. Additionally, ensure that you've assigned the IP addresses to each device according to the following IP address table:

| Device | Interface | IP Address | Subnet Mask | Default Gateway |
|---|---|---|---|---|
| PC 1 | Fa0 | 192.168.1.10 | 255.255.255.0 | 192.168.1.1 |
| PC 2 | Fa0 | 192.168.1.20 | 255.255.255.0 | 192.168.1.1 |
| PC 3 | Fa0 | 172.16.1.10 | 255.255.255.0 | 172.16.1.1 |
| PC 4 | Fa0 | 172.16.1.20 | 255.255.255.0 | 172.16.1.1 |
| Server | Fa0 | 10.1.1.10 | 255.255.255.0 | 10.1.1.1 |
| HQ | Gi0/0 | 192.0.2.2 | 255.255.255.252 | |
| | Gi0/1 | 192.168.1.1 | 255.255.255.0 | |
| | Gi0/2 | 172.16.1.1 | 255.255.255.0 | |
| ISP | Gi0/0 | 192.0.2.1 | 255.255.255.252 | |
| | Gi0/1 | 10.1.1.1 | 255.255.255.0 | |

Figure 13.16 – IP address scheme

Please observe the following guidelines when following this lab to ensure that you get the same results:

- Configure a default route on **HQ** to point to the **ISP** router at `192.0.2.1`.

- Configure a default route on the **ISP** router that points to **HQ** at `192.0.2.2`. This is to simulate the internet on the topology.

- Ensure that each device has end-to-end connectivity by using the `ping` utility. If you are unable to ping a certain device, be sure to double the physical connections and configurations on your devices.

Having built your lab environment, use the following instructions to implement a standard numbered ACL on your **HQ** router:

1. Firstly, let's create a numbered ACL to only allow traffic from **PC 1** on the `192.168.1.0/24` network to the `172.16.1.0/24` network while restricting all other devices:

```
HQ(config)#access-list 10 permit host 192.168.1.10
HQ(config)#access-list 10 permit 10.1.1.0 0.0.0.255
```

Please keep in mind that if we did not create a second ACE to permit traffic from the 10.1.1.0/24 network to 172.16.10/24, **PC 3** and **PC 4** would not be able to reach devices on the internet side of the topology.

2.  Next, let's apply ACL 10 to the interface closest to the destination of the traffic and configure it to filter outbound traffic only:

```
HQ(config)#interface GigabitEthernet 0/2
HQ(config-if)#ip access-group 10 out
HQ(config-if)#exit
```

3.  Using the show access-lists command, you can verify the ACEs and their sequential order, as shown here:

```
HQ#show access-lists
Standard IP access list 10
    10 permit host 192.168.1.10
    20 permit 10.1.1.0 0.0.0.255
HQ#
```

Figure 13.17 – Verifying ACLs

4.  Using the show ip interface command, you can verify the ACL that is assigned to an interface and the direction in which it is filtering traffic:

```
HQ#show ip interface gigabitethernet 0/2
GigabitEthernet0/2 is up, line protocol is up (connected)
  Internet address is 172.16.1.1/24
  Broadcast address is 255.255.255.255
  Address determined by setup command
  MTU is 1500 bytes
  Helper address is not set
  Directed broadcast forwarding is disabled
  Outgoing access list is 10          ACL 10
  Inbound  access list is not set
  Proxy ARP is enabled
```

Figure 13.18 – Verifying ACLs on an interface

As shown in the preceding snippet, ACL 10 is applied to filter traffic leaving the GigabitEthernet 0/2 interface on the router.

5.  Now, let's check whether ACL 10 will allow **PC 1** to communicate with devices on the 172.16.1.0/24 network:

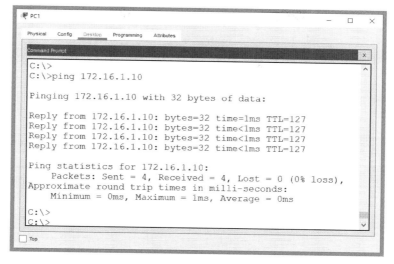

Figure 13.19 – Verifying connectivity

As shown in the preceding snippet, **PC 1** is able to communicate with **PC 3** on the `172.16.1.0/24` network.

6.  Let's test whether our ACL is working correctly to restrict other devices on the `192.168.1.0/24` network. Try to ping from **PC 2** to any device within the `172.16.1.0/24` network:

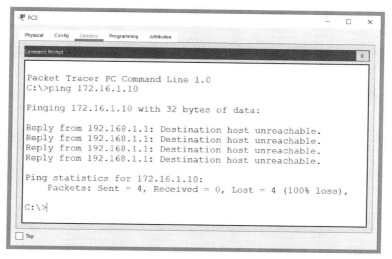

Figure 13.20 – Checking connectivity

As expected, **PC 2** is unable to communicate with devices on the `172.16.1.0/24` network simply because our ACL was configured to allow only **PC 1** with a host address of `192.168.1.10`.

7. Lastly, we can use the show access-lists command once more to verify which ACEs have been matched within an ACL:

```
HQ#show access-lists
Standard IP access list 10
    10 permit host 192.168.1.10 (4 match(es))
    20 permit 10.1.1.0 0.0.0.255
HQ#
```

Figure 13.21 – Verifying matches on ACEs

As shown in the preceding snippet, the permit ACE in ACL 10 has been matched four times simply because four ICMP messages were sent from **PC 1** to **PC 3**. To clear the ACL counters, use the clear access-list counters command.

During this lab, you have learned how to create a standard numbered ACL on a Cisco IOS router to filter traffic between networks. In the next lab, we'll use a named ACL to only permit traffic from the 172.16.1.0/24 network to access devices on the internet side of the topology.

# Lab – configuring a standard named ACL

In this lab, you will learn how to configure a standard named ACL to allow devices on the 172.16.1.0/24 network to communicate with devices on the internet side of our network topology. Our ACL will ensure that devices on the 192.168.1.0.24 network will be denied. To complete this exercise, we'll be continuing from where we left off from the previous lab.

We'll be using the following topology and the same guidelines as before:

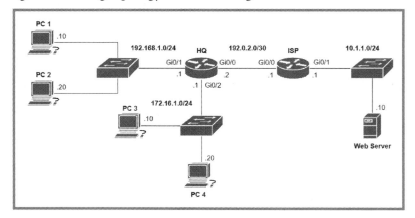

Figure 13.22 – Standard ACL lab topology

The objective of this lab is to demonstrate how to apply standard named ACLs to a Cisco router to filter traffic between devices and networks.

To get started with configuring a standard named ACL to meet our objective, take the following steps:

1.  Use the following command to create a standard named ACL with the name `INT_Access`, as shown here:

    ```
    HQ(config)#ip access-list standard INT_Access
    ```

2.  Use the `remark` command to insert a description for the ACL:

    ```
    HQ(config-std-nacl)#remark Allowing devices on the
    172.16.1.0/24 network only.
    ```

3.  Create an ACE with a placement of `10` to allow all traffic from the `172.16.1.0/24` network:

    ```
    HQ(config-std-nacl)#10 permit 172.16.1.0 0.0.0.255
    HQ(config-std-nacl)#exit
    ```

4.  Assign the `INT_Access` ACL to the outbound interface and configure it to filter traffic leaving the **HQ** router:

    ```
    HQ(config)#interface GigabitEthernet 0/0
    HQ(config-if)#ip access-group INT_Access out
    HQ(config-if)#exit
    ```

    Let's verify whether devices on the `172.16.1.0/24` network are able to communicate with devices on the internet side of the topology. On **PC 3**, perform a `ping` test to the web server:

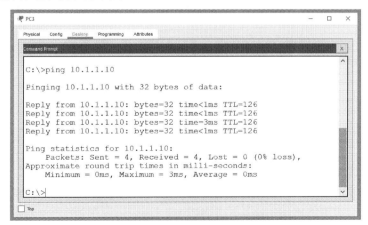

Figure 13.23 – Connectivity test

As shown in the preceding snippet, **PC 3** is able to communicate with the `10.1.1.0/24` network successfully.

5.  Next, let's verify whether devices on the `192.168.1.0/24` network are able to reach devices on the `10.1.1.0/24` network. On **PC 1**, perform a `ping` test to the web server, as shown here:

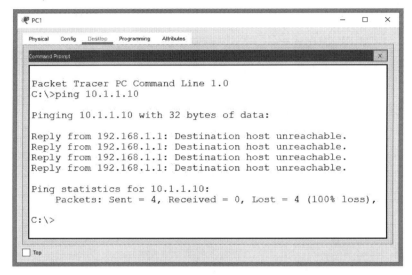

Figure 13.24 – Connectivity restricted

As expected, our new ACL is working perfectly, since devices on the `172.16.1.0/24` network are permitted to access and communicate with devices on the `10.1.1.0/24` network, while all other networks on the **HQ** router are denied.

6.  Once more, we can use the `show ip interface` command to verify that the ACL has been applied correctly to the interface as intended:

```
HQ#show ip interface gigabitEthernet 0/0
GigabitEthernet0/0 is up, line protocol is up (connected)
  Internet address is 192.0.2.2/30
  Broadcast address is 255.255.255.255
  Address determined by setup command
  MTU is 1500 bytes
  Helper address is not set
  Directed broadcast forwarding is disabled
  Outgoing access list is INT_Access          ◄──  INT_Access ACL
  Inbound  access list is not set                  applied on the interface
  Proxy ARP is enabled
  Security level is default
```

Figure 13.25 – Verifying ACL placement on an interface

7. Lastly, we can use the `show access-lists` command to verify the number of hits an ACE is receiving for an ACL:

```
HQ#show access-lists
Standard IP access list 10
    10 permit host 192.168.1.10
    20 permit 10.1.1.0 0.0.0.255 (4 match(es))
Standard IP access list INT_Access
    10 permit 172.16.1.0 0.0.0.255 (8 match(es))

HQ#
```

Figure 13.26 – Verifying ACEs

Having completed this lab, you have gained the essential skills required to configure and implement standard named ACLs on a Cisco IOS router. In the next lab, you will gain hands-on experience in terms of restricting access to VTY lines on a router.

# Lab – securing VTY lines using ACLs

In this lab, you will learn how to use ACLs to restrict remote access on your Cisco IOS router to only specific hosts or devices on a network. To complete this exercise, we'll be continuing from where we left off in the previous lab.

We'll be using the following topology and the same guidelines as before:

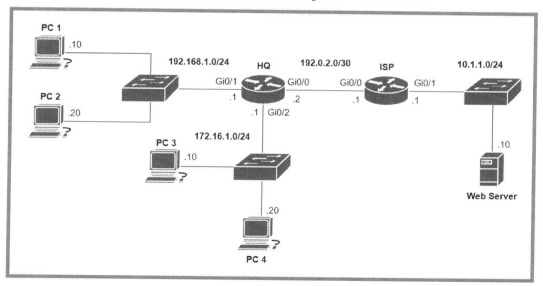

Figure 13.27 – Standard ACL lab topology

To get started setting up secure remote access and implementing ACLs on the VTY lines, use the following instructions:

1. Configure a password on the **HQ** router using the `enable secret` command to restrict access to `Privilege Exec` mode:

```
Router(config)#enable secret cisco456
```

2. Change the default hostname of the **HQ** router:

```
Router(config)#hostname HQ
```

3. Join the **HQ** router to a domain:

```
HQ(config)#ip domain-name ccnalab.local
```

4. Create a user account for remote access on the **HQ** router:

```
HQ(config)#username user1 secret sshpass
```

5. Generate RSA encryption keys to secure the SSH traffic:

```
HQ(config)#crypto key generate rsa general-keys modulus
1024
```

6. Configure the VTY lines on the **HQ** router to accept only SSH connections and check the local user database for authentication:

```
HQ(config)#line vty 0 15
HQ(config-line)#transport input ssh
HQ(config-line)#login local
HQ(config-line)#exit
```

Now that we have configured remote access with SSH on the **HQ** router, the following instructions will outline how to create an ACL to permit only **PC 3** to SSH into the **HQ** router.

7. Create a standard named ACL using the name `Secure-VTY`, as shown here:

```
HQ(config)#ip access-list standard Secure-VTY
```

8. Use the `remark` command to insert a description of the ACL and the ACEs:

```
HQ(config-std-nacl)#remark Securing incoming connections
on VTY lines
```

9. Create a `permit` statement to allow only **PC 3** access to the **HQ** router and the `host` command to specify the IP address of **PC 3** only:

```
HQ(config-std-nacl)#permit host 172.16.1.10
```

10. Insert another ACE to deny all other devices from establishing a remote session with the **HQ** router:

```
HQ(config-std-nacl)#deny any
HQ(config-std-nacl)#exit
```

11. Next, apply the `Secure-VTY` ACL to the VTY lines on the **HQ** router to filter inbound traffic on the VTY lines:

```
HQ(config)#line vty 0 15
HQ(config-line)#access-class Secure-VTY in
HQ(config-line)#exit
```

12. Use the `show access-lists` command to verify the newly created ACL and its ACEs on the **HQ** router:

```
HQ#show access-lists
Standard IP access list 10
    10 permit host 192.168.1.10
    20 permit 10.1.1.0 0.0.0.255
Standard IP access list INT_Access
    10 permit 172.16.1.0 0.0.0.255
Standard IP access list Secure-VTY
    10 permit host 172.16.1.10
    20 deny any

HQ#
```

Figure 13.28 – Verifying ACLs

13. We can use the `show running-config` command to also verify that the ACLs on the router and the interface/lines have been applied:

```
!
ip access-list standard Secure-VTY
 permit host 172.16.1.10
 deny any
 remark Securing incoming connections on VTY lines
!
!
line con 0
!
line aux 0
!
line vty 0 4
 access-class Secure-VTY in
 login local
 transport input ssh
line vty 5 15
 access-class Secure-VTY in
 login local
 transport input ssh
!
```

ACL applied under
the VTY lines

Figure 13.29 – Checking the running-config file

14. Let's now attempt to establish an SSH session from **PC1** to **HQ** to verify whether the `Secure-VTY` ACL is working as expected. Click on **PC1**, select the **Desktop** tab, and then click on **Telnet / SSH Client**:

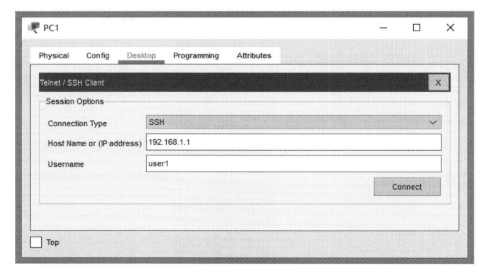

Figure 13.30 – Telnet / SSH Client

15. Insert the IP address of the router, choose the **SSH** protocol, and set the username as shown in the preceding screenshot. The **HQ** router will deny the connection from **PC1** or any device that is located on the `192.168.1.0/24` network.

The following snippet shows that the **HQ** router has terminated the SSH session because the ACL on the VTY lines restricted access to the router:

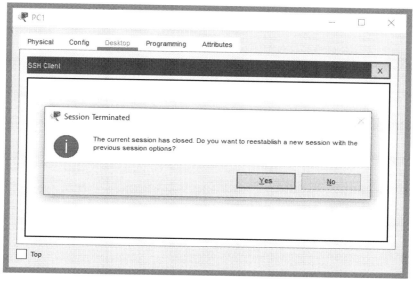

Figure 13.31 – Session terminated

16. The following screenshot illustrates an attempt to establish an SSH session from **PC3** to the **HQ** router:

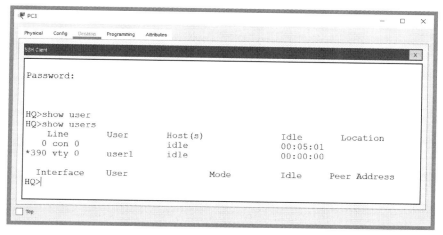

Figure 13.32 – Remote access

As shown in the preceding screenshot, **PC3** is able to remotely connect to the **HQ** router.

17. Lastly, we can use the `show access-lists` command to verify the ACLs and their entries on a router:

```
HQ#show access-lists
Standard IP access list 10
    10 permit host 192.168.1.10
    20 permit 10.1.1.0 0.0.0.255
Standard IP access list INT_Access
    10 permit 172.16.1.0 0.0.0.255
Standard IP access list Secure-VTY
    10 permit host 172.16.1.10 (2 match(es))
    20 deny any (32 match(es))

HQ#
```

Figure 13.33 – Verifying ACEs

Having completed this lab, you gained the hands-on skills to implement ACLs to secure the VTY lines on a Cisco IOS router. In the next section, we will take a deep dive into learning about the characteristics and use cases of extended ACLs.

# Working with extended ACLs

Extended ACLs are sometimes the preferred choice as they allow you to filter specific traffic types compared to standard ACLs. Extended ACLs use the following range of numbers:

- 100 to 199

- 2000 to 2699

To create a numbered extended ACL on a Cisco IOS router, use the global configuration `access-lists` command, followed by a number within the range of 100 to 199 or 2000 to 2699 on the device.

## Creating a numbered extended ACL

The following is the full syntax used to create a numbered extended ACL:

```
Router(config)# access-list access-list-number [ deny | permit
| remark ] protocol [source source-wildcard] [operator port]
[port-number or name] [destination destination-wildcard]
[operator port] [port-number or name]
```

The following is a description of the new syntax used within an extended ACL:

- `protocol`: Specifies the protocol type, such as IP, ICMP, TCP, and UDP.
- `operator`: Used to compare the source or destination ports. The `eq` operator means equal, `gt` means greater than, `lt` means less than, `neq` means not equal, and `range` allows you to specify a range of ports.
- `port`: Allows you to indicate a source or destination port number.

The following are some examples of numbered extended ACLs:

- The following command will deny all FTP traffic from the `192.168.1.0/24` source network that is going to any destination:

```
Router(config)# access-lists 100 deny tcp 192.168.1.0
0.0.0.255 any eq 20
Router(config)# access-lists 100 deny tcp 192.168.1.0
0.0.0.255 any eq 21
```

- The following command will block all ICMP traffic originating from the `172.16.1.0/24` network that has a destination of `10.0.0.0/8`:

```
Router(config)# access-lists 101 deny icmp 172.16.1.0
0.0.0.244 10.0.0.0 0.255.255.255
```

Next, let's take a look at how to implement a named extended ACL.

# Implementing a named extended ACL

Since a numbered extended ACL does not contain a description unless a comment is inserted using the `remark` command, the network engineer will have a bit of difficulty understanding the purpose of it. On the other hand, if a network engineer creates a named extended ACL, they can use a descriptive name to improve human readability.

To create a named extended ACL, take the following steps:

1. Enter global configuration mode and use the following syntax to create a named extended ACL:

```
Router(config)#ip access-list extended name
```

You will then enter a new mode, extended (`ext`) named ACL (`nacl`) configuration mode.

2.  Next, use the following syntax to create ACEs within the ACL:

```
Router(config-ext-nacl)# [ deny | permit | remark ]
protocol [source source-wildcard] [operator port] [port-
number or name] [destination destination-wildcard]
[operator port] [port-number or name]
```

The following snippet shows an example of creating and applying a named extended ACL:

```
Router(config)#ip access-list extended Ext-ACL
Router(config-ext-nacl)#permit tcp 192.168.1.0 0.0.0.255 172.16.1.0 0.0.0.255 eq 20
Router(config-ext-nacl)#permit tcp 192.168.1.0 0.0.0.255 172.16.1.0 0.0.0.255 eq 21
Router(config-ext-nacl)#exit
Router(config)#interface GigabitEthernet 0/2
Router(config-if)#ip access-group Ext-ACL in
Router(config-if)#exit
```

Figure 13.34 – Creating a named extended ACL

Additionally, you can use various keywords rather than specifying an actual TCP/UDP port number after the operator (eq) command. The following snippet shows an example of some keywords that can be used in place of a TCP/UDP port number:

```
Router(config-ext-nacl)#permit tcp 192.168.1.0 0.0.0.255 172.16.1.0 0.0.0.255 eq ?
  <0-65535>  Port number
  domain     Domain Name Service (DNS, 53)
  ftp        File Transfer Protocol (21)
  pop3       Post Office Protocol v3 (110)
  smtp       Simple Mail Transport Protocol (25)
  telnet     Telnet (23)
  www        World Wide Web (HTTP, 80)
```

Various Keywords that can be used other than port numbers

Figure 13.35 – Keywords

Please keep in mind that these keywords are only applicable to extended ACLs and their configurations. In the next lab, you will learn how to implement extended ACLs in a Cisco environment.

# Lab – implementing extended ACLs

In this lab, you will learn how to configure an extended ACL to restrict certain traffic types between networks. To complete this exercise, we'll be continuing from where we left off in the previous lab.

We'll be using the following topology and the same guidelines as before:

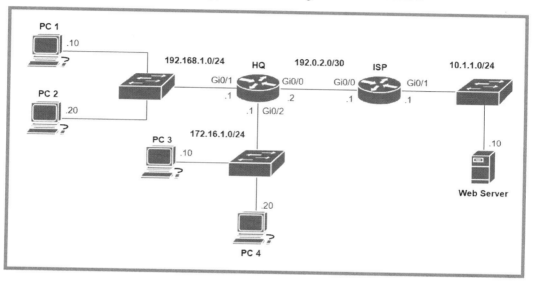

Figure 13.36 – Standard ACL lab topology

The objective of this lab is to filter FTP traffic between the `172.16.1.0/24` network and the web server. However, we want to permit only **PC 4** to use FTP while blocking all others within the network.

To get started setting up secure remote access and implementing ACLs on the VTY lines, take the following steps:

1.  Firstly, let's configure the FTP service on the server. Click on **Server**, select the **Services** tab, then **FTP**, and create a user account with the privileges shown here, and then click **Save**:

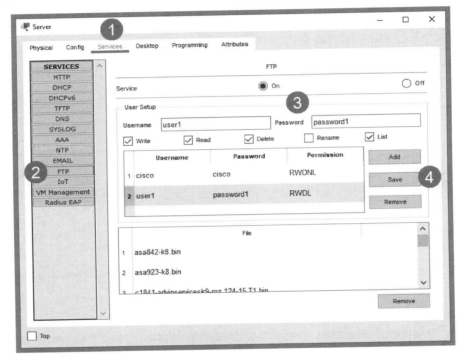

Figure 13.37 – FTP server configurations

2.  Next, let's attempt to remotely access the FTP server from **PC 4** to verify connectivity and that the FTP is working correctly:

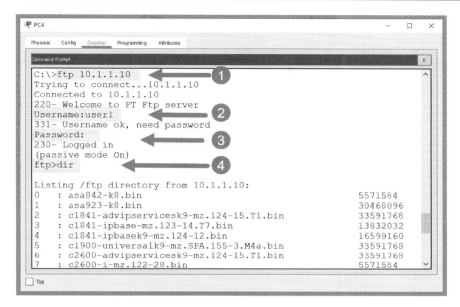

Figure 13.38 – Verifying FTP

As shown in the preceding snippet, we are able to authenticate to the FTP server and execute various FTP commands.

3.  Use the following commands to create an extended named ACL and add a description:

```
HQ(config)#ip access-list extended Restrict-FTP
HQ(config-ext-nacl)#remark Restricting FTP service to
only PC 4
```

4.  Create an ACE with a placement value of 10 to deny only **PC 3** from accessing any remote FTP servers:

```
HQ(config-ext-nacl)#10 deny tcp host 172.16.1.10 any eq
20
HQ(config-ext-nacl)#10 deny tcp host 172.16.1.10 any eq
21
```

5.  Create another ACE, using a placement value of 20 to allow all other IP traffic types originating from the 172.16.1.0/24 network:

```
HQ(config-ext-nacl)#20 permit ip any any
HQ(config-ext-nacl)#exit
```

6.  Apply the extended ACL to the inbound `GigabitEthernet 0/2` interface on the **HQ** router:

```
HQ(config)#interface gigabitEthernet 0/2
HQ(config-if)#ip access-group Restrict-FTP in
HQ(config-if)#exit
```

Please keep in mind that it's recommended to apply extended ACLs closest to the source of the traffic, while standard ACLs are to be applied closest to the destination of the traffic.

7.  Let's now use the `show access-lists` command to verify the ACLs, as shown here:

```
HQ#show access-lists Restrict-FTP
Extended IP access list Restrict-FTP
    deny tcp host 172.16.1.10 any eq ftp
    deny tcp host 172.16.1.10 any eq 20
    permit ip any any

HQ#
```

Figure 13.39 – Verifying ACLs

8.  Next, head on over to **PC 3** to verify connectivity to the server and check whether **PC 3** is able to access the FTP service:

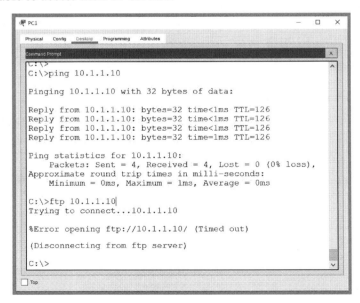

Figure 13.40 – PC3 checking the FTP service

As shown in the preceding snippet, ICMP messages and other IP traffic can be sent between the 172.16.1.0/24 network and any remote networks. However, the ACL does not allow FTP traffic from **PC 3** to any other remote devices.

9.  Now, let's check whether **PC 4** is able to access the remote FTP server:

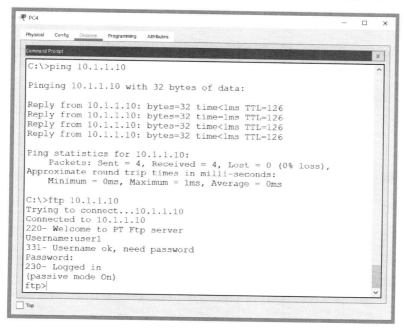

Figure 13.41 – PC 4 checking the FTP service

As shown in the preceding screenshot, **PC 4** is able to access the FTP service on the remote server. This corroborates the fact that our extended ACL is configured correctly and working as expected.

10. Lastly, we can verify the number of matches on our extended ACL by using the show access-lists command:

```
HQ#show access-lists Restrict-FTP
Extended IP access list Restrict-FTP
    deny tcp host 172.16.1.10 any eq ftp (24 match(es))
    deny tcp host 172.16.1.10 any eq 20
    permit ip any any (11 match(es))
```

Figure 13.42 – Verifying ACE matches

Having completed this lab, you have gained hands-on experience in terms of configuring and implementing extended ACLs on a Cisco network to filter various traffic types between devices and networks.

# Summary

Throughout this chapter, we've discussed the roles and functions that ACLs play on an enterprise network. We also dived into discussing the operations of ACLs on a Cisco IOS router and how they are applied to an interface. Lastly, we covered both standard and extended ACLs and how they can be used in various situations.

Having completed this chapter, you have learned how to configure both standard and extended ACLs on a Cisco router. Furthermore, you have learned how ACLs function and filter traffic based on their ACEs.

I hope this chapter has been informative for you and that it will prove helpful in your journey toward learning how to implement and administrate Cisco solutions and prepare for the CCNA 200-301 certification. In the next chapter, *Chapter 14, Implementing Layer 2 and Wireless Security*, you will learn about various Layer 2 attacks and how to implement mitigation techniques and countermeasures.

# Questions

The following is a short list of review questions to help reinforce your learning and help you identify areas that may require some improvement:

1.  Which type of ACL allows you to filter Telnet traffic?

    A. Inbound

    B. Outbound

    C. Standard

    D. Extended

2.  Which type of ACL allows you to filter traffic based on its origin?

    A. Outbound

    B. Standard

    C. Inbound

    D. Extended

3.  If a packet does not match any ACEs within an ACL, what will the router do?

    A. Allow the packet.

    B. Return the packet to the sender.

    C. Drop the packet.

    D. Do nothing.

4.  An inbound ACL has which of the following characteristics?

    A. It filters traffic as it enters a router.

    B. It filters traffic before it leaves a router.

    C. It stops a router from performing a route lookup.

    D. It filters traffic after it leaves a router.

5.  Which command can be used to verify the direction in which an ACL is filtering traffic?

    A. `show access-lists`

    B. `show access control lists`

    C. `show interface`

    D. `show ip interface`

6.  Which of the following wildcard masks is used to match all corresponding bits in an octet?

    A. 11111111

    B. 00000001

    C. 00000000

    D. 10000000

7.  Which ACL statement accurately blocks all traffic from the `192.168.50.0/24` network?

    A. `access-list 20 deny 192.168.50.0 0.0.0.255`

    B. `access-list 101 deny 192.168.50.0 0.0.0.255`

    C. `access-list 20 deny 192.168.50.0 any`

    D. `access-list 20 deny any 192.168.50.0 0.0.0.255`

8.  Which of the following ACL statements blocks SSH traffic originating from the `172.16.1.0/24` network?

    A. `access-list 101 deny ip 172.16.1.0 0.0.0.255 any eq 22`

    B. `access-list 101 deny tcp 172.16.1.0 0.0.0.255 any eq 22`

    C. `access-list 101 deny udp 172.16.1.0 0.0.0.255 any eq 22`

    D. `access-list 101 deny tcp 172.16.1.0 0.0.0.255 eq 22 any`

9.  Which command allows you to apply an ACL to the VTY lines?

    A. `ip access-group`

    B. `access-group`

    C. `access-class`

    D. `ip access-class`

10. Which command allows you to apply an ACL to an interface?

    A. `ip access-group`

    B. `access-group`

    C. `access-class`

    D. `ip access-class`

# Further reading

The following links are recommended for additional reading:

*   Configuring IP access lists: `https://www.cisco.com/c/en/us/support/docs/security/ios-firewall/23602-confaccesslists.html`

*   Commonly used IP ACLs: `https://www.cisco.com/c/en/us/support/docs/ip/access-lists/26448-ACLsamples.html`

*   Access list commands: `https://www.cisco.com/c/en/us/td/docs/routers/asr9000/software/asr9k_r4-0/addr_serv/command/reference/ir40asrbook_chapter1.html`

# 14
# Implementing Layer 2 and Wireless Security

Implementing network security practices and configurations should be like second nature to a network engineer. As a professional, it's important that you learn about various Layer 2 threats and how a threat actor can take advantage of vulnerabilities found within various Layer 2 network protocols. Our job is to make the organization's network safe and free from cyber attacks.

During the course of this chapter, you will learn about the need to use a **defense-in-depth (DiD)** approach to secure both your users and devices on a network. Furthermore, you will learn how to identify various Layer 2 threats and attacks that are used to compromise an organization. Lastly, you will gain the knowledge and hands-on experience to implement various Layer 2 security controls to prevent and mitigate such attacks.

In this chapter, we will cover the following topics:

- Types of Layer 2 attacks on a network
- Protecting against Layer 2 threats
- Wireless network security

# Technical requirements

To follow along with the exercises in this chapter, please ensure that you have met the following software requirements:

- Cisco Packet Tracer: `https://www.netacad.com`

The code files for this chapter are available at: `https://github.com/PacktPublishing/Implementing-and-Administering-Cisco-Solutions/tree/master/Chapter%2014`.

Check out the following video to see the Code in Action: `https://bit.ly/3coKE2Q`

# Types of Layer 2 attacks on a network

Throughout your journey, you will be exposed to many exciting technologies and environments. One such area an IT professional needs to know is cybersecurity and network security. As a network engineer, you won't always be designing and implementing networking technologies, but will also be responsible for the security of the network and its users. Today, newly emerging threats are surfacing – and will continue to – as hackers are developing new strategies and tools to compromise their targets.

Nowadays, hackers don't just hack for fun. Some hackers create sophisticated malware such as ransomware to encrypt all your data on your computer and request you pay a ransom to release your assets (data). Currently, there's a huge shortage of cybersecurity professionals in the world to combat the growing number of cyber threats on the internet. As a network engineer, you also play an important part in helping organizations secure their network and prevent various types of cyber threats and attacks.

In the following sections, you will learn about various network attacks and how using a multilayered approach such as DiD is used to reduce the risk of a cyber attack.

# Network attacks

Each day on various cyber news media, you read about how both large and small organizations have succumbed to some type of cyber attack. As the former CEO of Cisco, John Chambers, once said back in 2015:

> *There are two types of companies: those who have been hacked, and those who don't yet know they have been hacked.*

This statement is very accurate as many organizations do not pay a great amount of attention to their network security posture. Some have the mindset that their organization is 100% protected or that their network has nothing valuable for attackers.

In reality, no system or network is 100% secure. There are many vulnerabilities that exist – those we know about and others we have not yet discovered. The great challenge we face as security professionals is to discover all hidden vulnerabilities before a threat actor such as a hacker has the opportunity to do so.

Every system and network always holds something of value. A smartphone has gigabytes of valuable data pertaining to its user, including geolocation data, contact details, images and videos, logs relating to all their activities, and much more. On a network, your network devices and systems are storing data as they exchange messages. Your network switches and routers store **Media Access Control** (**MAC**) and IP addresses, contain user accounts for remote access, log messages of various transactions, including the forwarding of frames and packets, and so on. To a hacker, such data is very valuable.

> **Tip**
> Keeping up to date with the latest cybersecurity news can be somewhat challenging. I personally recommend checking **The Hacker News** website for the latest cyber news: https://thehackernews.com

Organizations are usually victims of the following cyber attacks:

- Data breaches
- Malware
- **Distributed Denial of Service (DDoS)**

The most valuable asset in any organization today is data. Hackers are simply not just hacking for fun anymore; well, some do, but others are evolving the game into organized crime. Threat actors are aiming to gain access to your network and steal your data. Once an attacker is able to exfiltrate data from your computers or servers, the hacker can publish or sell your organization's confidential records on the *dark web* or to your competitor.

Sometimes, a threat actor such as a hacker may develop malware to compromise your systems and networks. Some malware, such as ransomware and crypto-malware, can hold your data hostage. These types of malware are designed to exploit a vulnerability within your system, compromise the host machine, and encrypt all the data on the local disk drive except the operating system. One such ransomware is **WannaCry**, which exploited a vulnerability within the Microsoft Windows operating system and took advantage of a security weakness in SMB 1.0 as defined by Microsoft Security Bulletin **MS17-010**. Once a system was compromised, the ransomware presented a window on the user's desktop requesting a ransom be paid in bitcoins.

> **Important note**
> To learn more about Microsoft Security Bulletin MS17-010, please refer to the following URL: `https://docs.microsoft.com/en-us/security-updates/securitybulletins/2017/ms17-010`

Sometimes, threat actors may not want to gain access or compromise a system. Some hackers may want to disrupt an organization's services or resources. Hackers may execute their idea by launching a DDoS attack from multiple geographic sources. Occasionally, this may entail a coordinated attack by a group of hackers or perhaps be executed using a botnet.

> **Tip**
> To view recorded DDoS attacks around the globe, check out **Digital Attack Map** using the following URL: `www.digitalattackmap.com`

One example of such a service is an organization's website. Sometimes, hacktivists organize among themselves to take down various websites and disrupt services as a means of online protesting on behalf of a social or political cause.

Preventing all types of cyber attacks is very challenging. In the following section, we will take a dive into discussing a strategic approach to reduce the risk of cyber threats and attacks on a network.

# Defense in depth

Having a single layer of security to protect your organization is no longer efficient to stop newly emerging threats. Many organizations may implement a network-based firewall within their enterprise network and think they are well protected from all cyber threats, while some may only implement a host-based anti-virus and host-based firewall on their employees' devices and think they are safe, too. These are just some examples of using a single-layer approach to protecting assets within an organization. This method of using a single component, such as a network-based firewall or anti-malware, simply no longer cuts it when it comes to combatting cyber attacks and threats.

Using a DiD approach is where a multi-layered approach is used to help safeguard an organization and its users. A DiD approach ensures that multiple security components are implemented to protect all assets, including data and securing communication methods. In addition to using a network-based firewall and anti-malware protection, how about implementing email and web security appliances to filter both inbound and outbound threats, or **network-based intrusion prevention** (**NIPS**) and **host-based intrusion prevention** (**HIPS**) systems to detect any threats as they pass along your network?

One recommended security appliance is a **next-generation firewall** (**NGFW**). This security appliance has the ability to perform stateful packet inspection and application visibility/control for all inbound and outbound network traffic. Furthermore, with the Cisco NGFW, you can enable the **next-generation intrusion prevention system** (**NGIPS**) module for added security together with Cisco **Advanced Malware Protection** (**AMP**).

Within some companies, there are employees who work remotely and require access to the corporate network. One solution is to use either a **Virutal Private Network** (**VPN**)-enabled router or a firewall appliance with remote access VPN capabilities. Accessing the corporate network over an untrusted network is not a good thing, however. To ensure that your remote workers access the corporate network securely, a **VPN** is the solution.

In the following sub-sections, you will learn more about endpoint protection, and Cisco's email and web security appliances.

## Endpoint protection

Endpoints are commonly the most susceptible devices to malware and other cyber threats. Endpoints are host devices, such as desktops, laptops, IP phones, and servers. Some of these devices rely on traditional host-based anti-virus or anti-malware protection, host-based firewalls, and host-based intrusion detection systems. However, this is a single layer of security and, with the rise in newer and more sophisticated malware, you require a multi-layer approach such as implementing DiD.

To improve the protection of endpoints within an organization, it's better to use a combination of various security components to reduce the risk of a cyber attack. Cisco has a solution called *AMP for Endpoints*, which, as the name suggests, detects and prevents malware on endpoint devices. To help protect your users from email threats and attackers, the Cisco **Email Security Appliance** (**ESA**) can be implemented, and, to protect your user's web-based traffic, the Cisco **Web Security Appliance** (**WSA**) performs web filtering and malware protection.

## Cisco Email Security Appliance

Safeguarding your employees from various types of social engineering attacks such as phishing and spear phishing is crucial. According to the SANS Institute, in one of their reports, spear-phishing attacks account for approximately 95% of attacks on an enterprise network. Furthermore, Cisco Talos Intelligence Group also stated that approximately 85% of all email messages sent were spam, as reported in 2019.

The Cisco ESA is designed to monitor all inbound and outbound emails of an organization. It is capable of blocking all known threats on the internet, providing remediation against threats that have evaded initial detection mechanisms, blocking email messages that contain bad or malicious links, restricting access to websites newly infected by malware, and also provides the ability to encrypt outbound emails and provide **data leakage protection** (**DLP**).

The following diagram shows the processing sequence for all inbound email messages on the ESA:

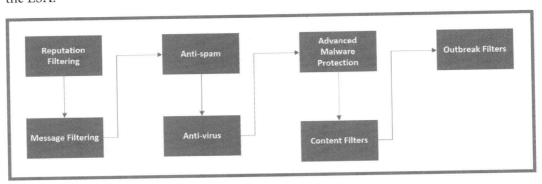

Figure 14.1 – ESA incoming mail processing

The following diagram shows the processing sequence for all outbound email messages on the ESA:

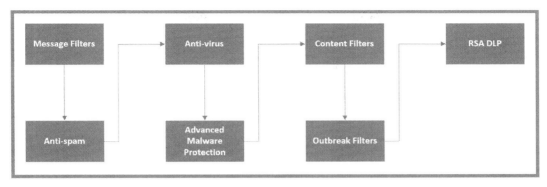

Figure 14.2 – ESA outgoing mail processing

Sometimes, a compromised system may be attempting to spread malware by sending email messages with malicious content to others. Each outbound filter is designed to prevent the spread of an outbreak on the internet and prevent users from sending confidential information outside the company's network by means of DLP.

The Cisco ESA also filters all outbound messages to ensure that malware or threat actors are not attempting to spread any malware or damage the organization's domain name. Additionally, the Cisco ESA allows IT professionals to enable DLP to prevent any confidential data from leaving the organization via email messages.

## Cisco Web Security Appliance

Protecting your employees against web-based threats is another important part of securing your organization. The Cisco **Web Security Appliance** (**WSA**) facilitates the mitigation of web-based threats while controlling inbound and outbound web traffic. The Cisco WSA enables you to control how your users within the organization access the internet.

The Cisco WSA provides the following capabilities:

- Web application filtering
- URL filtering and malware scanning
- Web access restrictions based on time and bandwidth limits

All web-based traffic leaving an organization's network is sent to the Cisco WSA before it is sent to the internet. If the Cisco WSA determines that the outbound traffic is safe and the destination is trusted, the WSA will forward the traffic. If the destination is not trusted or is unsafe, the WSA will discard the packet.

In this section, you have learned about the need to implement a DiD strategy to help protect your organization from various cyber attacks and threats. In the next section, we'll take a deep dive into discussing various Layer 2 threats that are harmful to your internal network.

# Layer 2 threats

Network professionals commonly implement various network security solutions to keep their corporate network safe from threat actors. Such network solutions may include network-based firewall appliances, IPS, and may even use VPNs for remote workers. However, such devices and components usually protect data between Layer 3 and Layer 7 of the OSI model.

If layers such as Layer 2 are compromised by an attacker, the upper layers are also compromised as well. Imagine a scenario where an attacker is able to intercept all traffic such as frames at Layer 2 within your corporate network. In such an event, the security implemented to protect the upper layers will be obsolete in preventing the attack.

The following diagram shows both the OSI reference model and the TCP/IP protocol suite:

| Layer | OSI Model | TCP/IP Stack | Layer |
|---|---|---|---|
| 7 | Application | Application | 5 |
| 6 | Presentation | | |
| 5 | Session | | |
| 4 | Transport | Transport | 4 |
| 3 | Network | Internet | 3 |
| 2 | Data Link | Data Link | 2 |
| 1 | Physical | Physical | 1 |

Figure 14.3 – Data Link layer

To protect Layer 2, Cisco has incorporated many Layer 2 attack mitigation features in their switches. As a network engineer, it's important that you learn about the various types of attacks that occur at Layer 2 and how to implement security features on Cisco switches to mitigate such attacks.

In the following sections, you will learn about various types of Layer 2 attacks that can occur on an enterprise network and how to implement countermeasures to safeguard your network.

## CAM table overflow

Switches are the networking devices that allow us to connect our end devices, such as computers, to the network and access resources. Additionally, switches are able to forward messages (frames) to their destination by simply recording the source and destination MAC addresses found in each inbound message. For each frame to enter a switch's interface, the source MAC address is populated within the switch's MAC address table, as shown here:

```
SW1#show mac address-table dynamic
            Mac Address Table
-------------------------------------------------

Vlan    Mac Address       Type        Ports
----    -----------       --------    -----

  10    0006.2a88.7218    DYNAMIC     Fa0/24
  10    00d0.ffbc.7202    DYNAMIC     Fa0/24
  10    00e0.b098.d202    DYNAMIC     Fa0/1
  20    0006.2a88.7218    DYNAMIC     Fa0/24
  20    00d0.ffbc.7202    DYNAMIC     Fa0/24
  20    00e0.f72b.9a51    DYNAMIC     Fa0/2
  30    0006.2a88.7218    DYNAMIC     Fa0/24
  30    00d0.ffbc.7202    DYNAMIC     Fa0/24
SW1#
```

Figure 14.4 – MAC address table

As shown, the `show mac address-table` command is used to view a list of MAC addresses that were learned on a specific interface and VLAN. However, a switch stores MAC addresses on its **Content Addressable Memory** (**CAM**) table. To put it simply, the CAM table does not have infinite storage capacity. Each switch has a limit in terms of the number of MAC addresses they are able to store. One such example is a Cisco switch, which may be able to store 8,000 addresses, while another model may be able to store more. Cisco IOS switches have a default aging/inactivity timer of 300 seconds (5 minutes) for any MAC addresses within the CAM table. If a switch detects no activity from a MAC address after 300 seconds, it will automatically remove it from the CAM table to make storage available for new addresses.

The following snippet shows an example of the size of the CAM table for a Cisco `IOSvL2` switch:

```
Switch#show mac address-table count

Mac Entries for Vlan 1:
--------------------------
Dynamic Address Count  : 0
Static  Address Count  : 0
Total Mac Addresses    : 0

Total Mac Address Space Available: 77818696

Switch#
```

Figure 14.5 – Checking CAM table capacity

Keep in mind that not all models of Cisco switches have the same capacity of storage on their CAM table. Even though the figure seems to be very large in the preceding snippet, it is still a finite number. One vulnerability that exists is if a switch receives more MAC addresses than it can possibly store, it will begin to flood all inbound messages (frames) out of all ports. Technically speaking, the switch becomes a hub on the network.

Attackers can flood unsolicited frames with fake source MAC addresses into a switch to fill the CAM table. When the CAM table is filled, the attacker does not stop the attack. The switch will begin to forward all inbound traffic out of all other interfaces. The attacker can capture all network traffic that is being forwarded out of the switch. This is known as a **CAM Table Overflow** attack.

> **Important note**
>
> Since each interface can be assigned to a **Virtual Local Area Network** (**VLAN**), if an attacker can flood unsolicited, bogus frames into a switch during a CAM table overflow attack, the switch will only forward traffic to all other ports on the same VLAN.

The following diagram shows an example of a network implant injecting bogus frames into a switch:

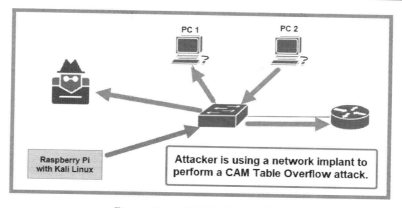

Figure 14.6 – CAM table overflow

In the preceding diagram, the attacker has implanted a Raspberry Pi with Kali Linux and is using special tools such as `macof` or `yersinia` to flood the switch with unsolicited frames.

The following snippet shows `macof` generating bogus frames:

```
root@kali:~# macof -i eth0
e1:80:f9:45:98:9 6:52:70:39:eb:a1 0.0.0.0.19006 > 0.0.0.0.4320: S 710988111:710988111(0) win 512
1c:c:8a:50:21:a7 e8:31:d7:2d:1e:37 0.0.0.0.35536 > 0.0.0.0.48231: S 1540156923:1540156923(0) win 512
ca:40:59:65:9e:45 9:df:d7:39:65:12 0.0.0.0.16661 > 0.0.0.0.43605: S 1569897595:1569897595(0) win 512
a5:1d:98:6a:e8:60 1e:14:46:61:b4:93 0.0.0.0.61026 > 0.0.0.0.52498: S 1701381115:1701381115(0) win 512
5e:fd:d1:5e:a:46 4e:0:e6:10:ef:3b 0.0.0.0.42122 > 0.0.0.0.34809: S 1692649512:1692649512(0) win 512
75:43:94:29:2f:53 3e:36:b2:7d:eb:85 0.0.0.0.63383 > 0.0.0.0.9898: S 1183917742:1183917742(0) win 512
7d:be:f8:53:7c:75 c2:c4:cc:2d:da:7 0.0.0.0.24670 > 0.0.0.0.30611: S 976029769:976029769(0) win 512
ae:9d:f7:43:a6:1e 5a:7:73:8:d9:f2 0.0.0.0.25470 > 0.0.0.0.32543: S 210634849:210634849(0) win 512
c2:a7:af:45:f8:81 5f:d8:59:b:63:21 0.0.0.0.58444 > 0.0.0.0.32636: S 982725989:982725989(0) win 512
a6:c0:7c:50:6e:2 31:2f:d7:17:b2:3 0.0.0.0.63764 > 0.0.0.0.60069: S 611132256:611132256(0) win 512
7:b1:61:3:74:29 10:f6:20:64:36:c4 0.0.0.0.53548 > 0.0.0.0.32715: S 294560344:294560344(0) win 512
```

Figure 14.7 – The macof tool

During the attack, the switch's CAM table will exceed its limitation and begin flooding all incoming traffic out of all other interfaces. In the diagram, we can see that **PC 2** is sending traffic to the switch, but the switch is forwarding it to unintended destinations and the attacker is able to capture **PC 2**'s traffic.

## VLAN attacks

By default, each interface on a Cisco IOS switch uses the **Dynamic Trunking Protocol (DTP)** to automatically negotiate the interface mode with a connection to other devices. In *Chapter 5, Implementing VLANs, Layer 2 Discovery Protocols, and EtherChannels*, we discussed DTP in further detail and how it is applied to automatically negotiate either an `Access` or `Trunk` interface on Cisco switches. Since all interfaces on a Cisco IOS switch use the default mode as `dynamic auto`, an attacker can use their machine and create an unauthorized trunk between the attacker's machine and the switch.

The following diagram shows how an attacker has enabled an unauthorized trunk on a small network:

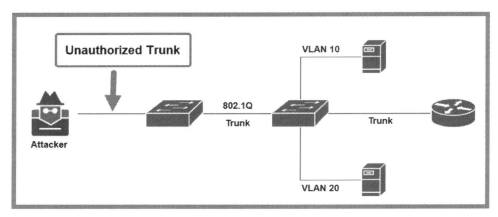

Figure 14.8 – Unauthorized Trunk

As shown in the preceding diagram, the attacker will be able to access any VLANs on the switch. Furthermore, the attacker is able to send and receive traffic on any VLANs on the switch. This is known as a **VLAN Hopping** attack.

The following snippet shows how easily an attacker can attempt to enable trunking using a tool such as `yersinia`:

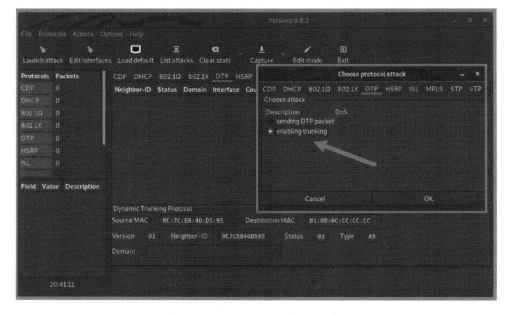

Figure 14.9 – Yersinia DTP attacks

In another scenario, an attacker can insert another VLAN tag in an already tagged frame. This is known as **VLAN Double Tagging**. In simple terms, the attacker embeds their own 802.1Q tag within a frame that already has an 802.1Q tag. To get a better understanding of how this attack works, let's take a closer look at the following diagram:

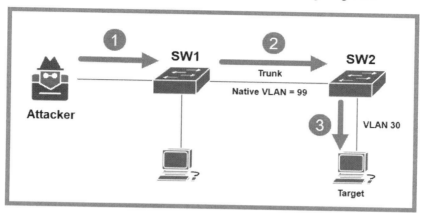

Figure 14.10 – VLAN double tagging

Based on the preceding diagram, the following is the sequence of actions that occurs on the network:

1.  In *step 1*, the attacker sends a double-tagged frame to **SW1**. The outer tag of the frame contains the VLAN ID of the interface the attacker is connected to, which is Native VLAN (99). The inner 802.1Q tag (30) of the frame is also inserted by the attacker.

2.  In *step 2*, when **SW1** receives the double-tagged frame, it inspects only the outer tag (VLAN 99) and forwards the frame out of all VLAN 99 interfaces after removing the outer tag (99). The inner VLAN tag, VLAN 30, is still intact and was not inspected by the first switch.

3.  In *step 3*, when **SW2** receives the frame, it inspects the inner 802.1Q tag that was inserted by the attacker (VLAN 30). The switch will then forward the frame to the target VLAN by flooding it out of all VLAN 30 interfaces or directly to the target machine if the MAC address of the target is known.

In a VLAN double tagging attack, the transmission is always unicast. This attack works only if the attacker's machine is connected to an interface that is assigned the same native VLAN as the trunk interfaces. Additionally, this attack allows the attacker to communicate with a target on a VLAN that is restricted or blocked by security controls on the network.

To prevent both VLAN hopping and VLAN double tagging attacks, adhere to the following recommendations:

- Make sure that you disable trunking on all your access ports on the switches. To do this, use the following interface mode command on your access ports:

```
Switch(config)#interface GigabitEthernet 0/1
Switch(config-if)#switchport mode access
```

- Make sure that you disable DTP on all interfaces by using the following interface mode command:

```
Switch(config)#interface GigabitEthernet 0/1
Switch(config-if)#switchport nonegotiate
```

- Configure your trunk interfaces manually by using the following interface mode command:

```
Switch(config)#interface GigabitEthernet 0/2
Switch(config-if)#switchport mode trunk
```

- Make sure that the native VLAN is used only on your trunk links.
- Make sure that you do not use VLAN 1 as the native VLAN.

In *Chapter 5*, *Implementing VLANs, Layer 2 Discovery Protocols, and EtherChannels*, the labs found within the chapter utilized all the aforementioned recommendations as good practice. Feel free to revisit the chapter and the labs to gain hands-on experience by applying these configurations in a Cisco environment.

## DHCP attacks

In *Chapter 10*, *Implementing Network Services and IP Operations*, you learned about a variety of IP services, including the **Dynamic Host Configuration Protocol** (**DHCP**), and its purpose and operations. Similar to many TCP/IP network protocols, DHCP was not designed with security mechanisms. On a network, an attacker can perform two types of DHCP attacks. These are as follows:

- **DHCP starvation**
- **DHCP spoofing**

In a DHCP starvation attack, the goal of the attacker is to create a **denial of service (DoS)** for any client machine that is requesting IP configurations from a DHCP server. The attacker can use a tool such as `yersinia` to generate unsolicited fake DHCP discover messages with spoofed source MAC addresses. When the DHCP server receives each DHCP discover message, it will attempt to provide an available IP address from its DHCP pool. By flooding the DHCP server with hundreds or even thousands of bogus DHCP discover messages, the DHCP pool will eventually be exhausted. Therefore, any connected client machine that requires a lease IP address will be denied and won't be able to communicate on the network without a valid IP address.

The following screenshot shows various DHCP attacks that can be performed using `yersinia`:

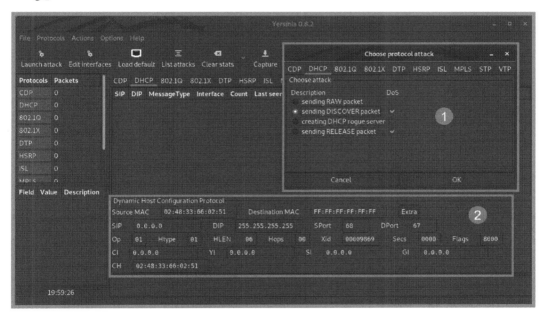

Figure 14.11 – Yersinia interface

As indicated in the preceding screenshot, window **1** allows a penetration tester or an attacker to execute various types of DHCP attacks on a network. Window 2 allows you to further customize the source DHCP messages from the attacker machine.

In a DHCP spoofing attack, the attacker inserts a rogue DHCP server on the network to provide false IP configurations to legitimate clients. A rogue DHCP server can provide the following to clients:

- **Incorrect default gateway**: This will cause legitimate hosts to forward their internet-based traffic to the attacker's machine and create the effect of a man-in-the-middle attack as well.

- **Incorrect IP addressing**: An incorrect IP address and subnet mask is assigned to clients on the network. An incorrect IP address and/or subnet mask will prevent a host from communicating with other devices.

- **Incorrect DNS server**: By providing clients with a rogue DNS server, the attacker can control the hostname to IP address lookup information. Thus, clients can be redirected to malicious websites.

To get a better understanding of what occurs when an attacker connects a rogue DHCP server to a network, let's take a look at the following diagram and scenario:

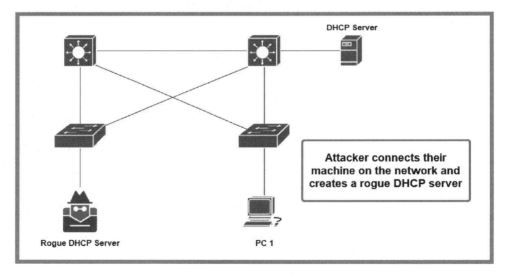

Figure 14.12 – Rogue DHCP server

Based on the preceding diagram, there is a legitimate DHCP server and the attacker has connected a rogue DHCP server to the same network. The following is the sequence of events that will take place:

1. When **PC 1** connects to the network, it will broadcast a DHCP Discover message.

2. Both the legitimate and rogue DHCP servers will receive this DHCP Discover message from **PC 1**.

3.  Both the legitimate and rogue DHCP servers will respond with their DHCP Offer message containing IP configurations.

4.  **PC 1** will respond with a DHCP Request to the first DHCP offer message it receives. **PC 1** will accept the IP configurations from the first DHCP offer message. Therefore, if **PC 1** receives a DHCP Offer message from the rogue DHCP server first, it will respond with a DHCP Request (broadcast).

5.  Both the legitimate and rogue DHCP servers will receive the broadcast DHCP Request message from **PC 1** and only the rogue DHCP server will respond with a unicast DHCP Acknowledgement message. The legitimate **DHCP server** will cease to communicate with **PC 1**, simply because **PC 1** accepted the IP configurations from the rogue DHCP server and has established trust with the device.

Additionally, an attacker can use a tool such as yersinia to create a rogue DHCP server on a corporate network. In the later sections of this chapter, you will learn how DHCP snooping can be used to prevent both DHCP starvation and DHCP spoofing attacks on a corporate network.

## ARP attacks

As we have learned throughout this book, the **Address Resolution Protocol** (**ARP**) is a Layer 2 protocol that is designed to resolve an IP address to a MAC address. As mentioned in *Chapter 1, Introduction to Networking*, switches are used to connect end devices such as PCs and servers to the network. ARP is needed as all devices within a subnet or LAN forward messages to their destination by using the MAC address of the intended recipient.

> **Important note**
> IP addresses within the Layer 3 header of packets are utilized when a host is attempting to communicate with another device on a different subnet or network.

Whenever a host wants to send a message to another device on the same network, if the sender does not know the MAC address of the destination device, it will broadcast an ARP Request message. The ARP request contains the destination device IP address and is sent to all devices on the LAN or subnet. The message is simply a request for the MAC address of the destination device. The ARP request message is received and processed by all devices on the subnet. However, only the device with the matching IP address will respond with an ARP Reply containing its MAC address.

Similar to other TCP/IP network protocols, the ARP was not designed with security in mind. Host devices such as computers are able to send unsolicited ARP replies. These are known as **Gratuitous ARPs**. An attacker can send a gratuitous ARP message to a host on the same subnet. The message will contain a MAC address and IP address mapping, which notifies the destination device to update their ARP table.

The following is the ARP cache on a Windows operating system:

```
C:\>arp -a

Interface: 172.16.17.11 --- 0x1a
  Internet Address        Physical Address        Type
  172.16.17.2             f8-54-b8                dynamic
  172.16.17.6             f8-54-b8                dynamic
  172.16.17.18            9c-3d-cf                dynamic
  172.16.17.255           ff-ff-ff                static
  224.0.0.22              01-00-5e                static
  224.0.0.251             01-00-5e                static
  224.0.0.252             01-00-5e                static
  239.255.255.250         01-00-5e                static
  255.255.255.255         ff-ff-ff                static

C:\>
```

Figure 14.13 – ARP cache

As shown in the preceding snippet, the host device will only populate its ARP cache with a device it has recently exchanged messages with. An attacker can send spoofed MAC addresses using gratuitous ARP messages to clients on a network, thereby causing them to update with ARP tables automatically. As a result, the attacker can trick clients into thinking the attacker's machine is their default gateway and create a man-in-the-middle attack.

To get a better understanding of ARP spoofing, let's take a look at the following scenario:

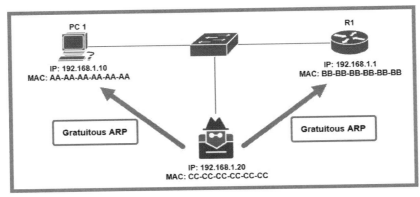

Figure 14.14 – An ARP attack

Based on the preceding diagram, an attacker connects to the network and attempts to send gratuitous ARP messages to **PC 1** and **R1**. The objective is to inform **PC 1** that the MAC address of **R1** has been updated to CC-CC-CC-CC-CC-CC. This will cause **PC 1** to update its ARP table and all traffic that is destined for 192.168.1.1 will be sent to the attacker's machine.

> **Important note**
> When an attacker is attempting to cause a victim to update their ARP cache with false ARP entries, this is referred to as **ARP Poisoning**.

Additionally, the same thing is done to **R1** as the attacker tricks the router into thinking that **PC 1**'s new MAC address has been updated to CC-CC-CC-CC-CC-CC, as shown here:

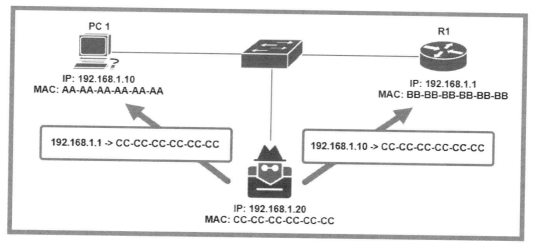

Figure 14.15 – ARP spoofing

This will ensure that all traffic between **PC 1** and **R1** will be sent to the attacker's machine and vice versa. The following diagram shows the effect of ARP spoofing in chaining a man-in-the-middle attack:

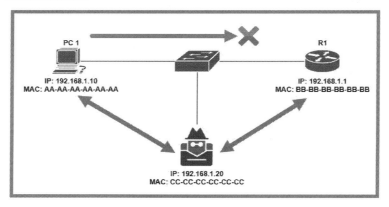

Figure 14.16 – Man-in-the-middle attack

In this attack, all the victim's (**PC 1**) traffic will be intercepted and captured. If any sensitive data is being exchanged, the messages will be compromised.

## Spanning-tree attacks

On a switch network, the **Spanning Tree Protocol** (**STP**) is used to prevent Layer 2 loops. It does this by electing a root bridge, which will then instruct all other switches within the same VLAN to block certain ports while leaving others in a forwarding state.

> **Important note**
> If you wish to recap the topics on spanning-tree, please see
> *Chapter 6, Understanding and Configuring Spanning-Tree..*

In *Chapter 6, Understanding and Configuring Spanning-Tree*, we discussed the vital role the root bridge plays on the network. One key point to always remember is that the root bridge also acts as the central reference point for all traffic within a VLAN. However, once again, STP is another Layer 2 network protocol that was not designed with security mechanisms. An attacker can simply connect their machine to a switch and inject customized STP **Bridge Protocol Data Units** (**BPDUs**) with a lower-priority value. If the attack is successful, the STP topology will change, making the attacker machine the new root bridge and central reference point on the network. Furthermore, if the attacker's machine is the root bridge, the attacker can capture all traffic on the VLAN, thereby acting as a man-in-the-middle on the network.

The following diagram shows that an attacker is attempting to become the root bridge:

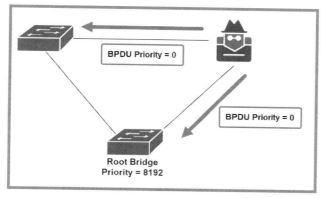

Figure 14.17 – An STP attack

To prevent STP attacks, it's recommended to implement **BPDU Guard** on all **Access Points (APs)** on your switches. In *Chapter 6, Understanding and Configuring Spanning-Tree*, we covered how to implement BPDU Guard in the lab entitled *Configuring PortFast and BPDU Guard*.

## CDP attacks

The **Cisco Discovery Protocol (CDP)** is a Cisco proprietary Layer 2 protocol that is designed to share information with other Cisco devices on the same network. CDP is enabled by default on all Cisco devices and shares information such as the device model, hostname, IOS version, device capabilities, IP address, and even the native VLAN.

CDP was designed to help network engineers with troubleshooting and determining network topology. As an example, imagine you are unable to ping a directly connected device, but you are still able to receive CDP messages from the same device. This is an indication that Layer 2 is operating properly, but that Layer 3 may require further investigation.

> **Important note**
>
> To recap on the topics and operations of the CDP, please revisit *Chapter 5, Implementing VLANs, Layer 2 Discovery Protocols, and EtherChannels*.

CDP messages are sent out of all CDP-enabled interfaces on a device every 60 seconds. These CDP messages are unencrypted. Such information found within a CDP message can be very valuable to an attacker on the network. The attacker can use the information to create a map of the network infrastructure, determine the type of devices on the network, their capabilities, IP addresses, and so on.

The following screenshot shows the contents of a CDP message using Wireshark:

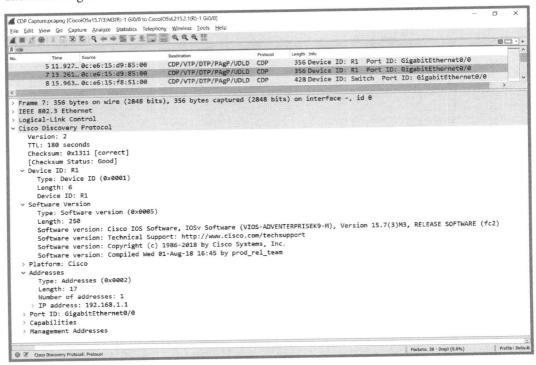

Figure 14.18 – CDP messages on Wireshark

In the preceding screenshot, the CDP messages were captured with a Cisco IOSv router and a Cisco IOSvL2 switch. The body of frame #7 contains sensitive information pertaining to the Cisco IOSv router on the network, such as its management IP address and IOS version. Since the CDP was not designed with security in mind, an attacker can also inject fake CDP messages into a network with fake information.

To mitigate such a vulnerability within the CDP, observe the following guidelines:

- Disable the CDP globally on your device using the no cdp run command.
- Enable the CDP on interfaces that are connected to other CDP-enabled devices.
- CDP-enabled interfaces should only be connected to other networking devices and not end devices.
- CDP messages should not be sent to the internet or your ISP.

Furthermore, the **Link Layer Discovery Protocol (LLDP)** is also vulnerable to the same type of attacks as the CDP. To disable the LLDP globally, use the `no lldp run` command within global configuration mode. To disable the LLDP on an interface, use both the `no lldp transmit` and `no lldp receive` commands on the interface mode.

During this section, you have learned about various Layer 2 threats and attacks that can occur within an organization's network. In the next section, you will discover various switch security controls to prevent a variety of Layer 2 attacks.

# Protecting against Layer 2 threats

Quite often, many organizations think cyber threats and attacks originate from outside of their organization, such as the internet. However, some of these threats and attacks can occur from within. These threats can be in the form of an innocent employee connecting an unauthorized device to the network, such as a switch or even a wireless router, or a disgruntled employee who wants to take down the company's network infrastructure for personal reasons. Your responsibility as a network engineer is not only to design and build networks for connectivity but also to ensure the security of the network.

In this section, you will learn how to implement security controls on your switches to prevent various Layer 2 attacks such as those mentioned in the previous sections.

## Port security

Sometimes, when implementing a newly configured switch on a production network, the network engineer may honestly forget to secure any unused interfaces/ports on the switch. Leaving unused ports active is like a doorway that is wide open, enabling anyone to access your property. Sometimes, when implementing a switch, not all ports are in use. It is recommended to disable all unused ports to prevent any unauthorized access to the Layer 2 network.

> **Tip**
> Disable all interfaces on a switch and only enable those that are required.

To secure any unused ports on a Cisco IOS switch, use the `shutdown` command within `interface` mode:

```
Switch(config)#interface FastEthernet 0/1
Switch(config-if)#shutdown
Switch(config-if)#exit
Switch#show ip interface brief
Interface          IP-Address      OK? Method Status              Protocol
FastEthernet0/1    unassigned      YES manual administratively down down
FastEthernet0/2    unassigned      YES manual down                down
FastEthernet0/3    unassigned      YES manual down                down
```

Figure 14.19 – Securing an unused port

The `shutdown` command changes the interface to an *administratively down* state, which will disable the electrical circuitry on that interface only. However, if you have to disable a range of interfaces, you can use the `interface range` command, as shown here:

```
Switch(config)#interface range FastEthernet 0/5 - FastEthernet 0/10
Switch(config-if-range)#shutdown
Switch(config-if-range)#exit
Switch(config)#exit
Switch#
%SYS-5-CONFIG_I: Configured from console by console

Switch#show ip interface brief | include administratively
FastEthernet0/1    unassigned      YES manual administratively down down
FastEthernet0/5    unassigned      YES manual administratively down down
FastEthernet0/6    unassigned      YES manual administratively down down
FastEthernet0/7    unassigned      YES manual administratively down down
FastEthernet0/8    unassigned      YES manual administratively down down
FastEthernet0/9    unassigned      YES manual administratively down down
FastEthernet0/10   unassigned      YES manual administratively down down
Switch#
```

Figure 14.20 – Disabling a range of interfaces

In the earlier parts of this chapter, we discussed many types of Layer 2 attacks, one of which was the CAM table overflow attack, which is designed to exhaust the storage capacity of a switch's CAM table. Cisco has implemented a security control known as **Port Security** to limit the number of trusted MAC addresses that are allowed on a switch's interface.

As a network engineer, this feature allows you to either manually configure trusted MAC addresses per interface or allows the switch to dynamically learn a limited number of MAC addresses. When port security is enabled on an interface, the source MAC addresses of all inbound frames are compared to a list of secure source MAC addresses. By implementing port security, you can control which devices are able to connect to an interface and your network.

Before enabling port security on an interface or a range of interfaces, ensure that the interface(s) are not using the default DTP mode, dynamic auto, since port security will not work. Ensure that your interface is statically configured as either an Access port for end devices or a Trunk port.

To enable port security on an interface, use the following commands:

```
Switch(config)#interface fastEthernet 0/1
Switch(config-if)#switchport mode access
Switch(config-if)#switchport port-security
Switch(config-if)#no shutdown
Switch(config-if)#exit
```

To verify the port security status on an interface, use the show port-security interface command, as shown here:

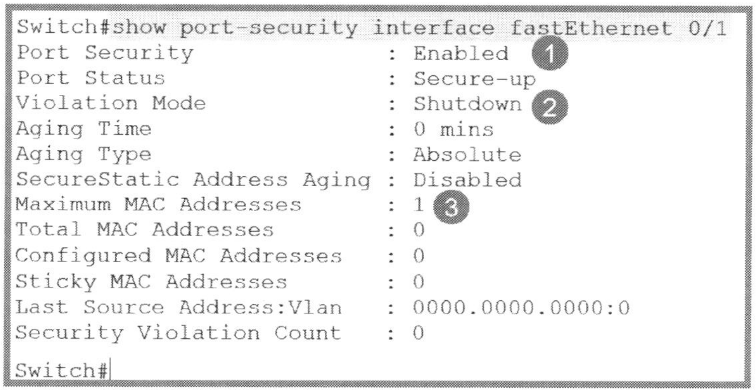

```
Switch#show port-security interface fastEthernet 0/1
Port Security              : Enabled
Port Status                : Secure-up
Violation Mode             : Shutdown
Aging Time                 : 0 mins
Aging Type                 : Absolute
SecureStatic Address Aging : Disabled
Maximum MAC Addresses      : 1
Total MAC Addresses        : 0
Configured MAC Addresses   : 0
Sticky MAC Addresses       : 0
Last Source Address:Vlan   : 0000.0000.0000:0
Security Violation Count   : 0

Switch#
```

Figure 14.21 – Verifying the port security interface status

We can determine the following key points from the preceding screenshot:

- Port security is enabled on the FastEthernet 0/1 interface.

- The violation mode is set to Shutdown.

- The maximum number of source MAC addresses that are permitted on this interface is 1. If more than one device is connected to this interface, the violation will be triggered and the interface will be transitioned into an *error-disabled* state.

- Currently, no source MAC addresses are learned on the interface. If a device connects and sends traffic to this port, the switch will automatically add the source MAC address as a secure MAC address.

> **Important note**
>
> When port security is turned on, the default configurations are as follows: the maximum number of secure MAC addresses is 1, the default violation mode is `shutdown`, and sticky address learning is `disabled`.

Limiting the number of MAC addresses allowed on an interface can prevent unauthorized devices from connecting to the network and prevent a malicious user from injecting unsolicited frames into a switch. To limit the number of MAC addresses permitted on an interface, use the following syntax:

```
Switch(config-if)#switchport port-security maximum number
```

There may be a situation that requires you to manually configure a static MAC address on a switch interface. To statically assign/associate a secure MAC address on a switch port, use the following syntax:

```
Switch(config-if)#switchport port-security mac-address mac-address
```

Manually configuring a secure MAC address on an interface ensures that only the end device with that same MAC address is permitted to connect on the same interface and send traffic. However, this task can be very overwhelming if you have to do this on all switches for the entire organization. One method is to configure the switch to dynamically learn the source MAC addresses on each interface and store them on the running configuration.

To dynamically learn and store the source MAC addresses on an interface, use the `sticky` command with the following port security syntax:

```
Switch(config-if)#switchport port-security mac-address sticky
```

The source MAC addresses learned using the `sticky` command will be associated with the interface only and will be saved in `running-config`. If the switch loses power or is rebooted, the secure MAC address will be lost. Therefore, make sure that you save the configurations to NVRAM (`startup-config`).

The following is an example demonstrating how to configure port security on an interface to limit up to two secure MAC addresses, statically configure one secure MAC address, and enable dynamic learning for additional secure MAC addresses:

```
Switch(config-if)#interface GigabitEthernet 0/1
Switch(config-if)#switchport mode access
Switch(config-if)#switchport port-security
```

```
Switch(config-if)#switchport port-security maximum 2
Switch(config-if)# switchport port-security mac-address
B881.98D3.B223
Switch(config-if)#switchport port-security mac-address sticky
Switch(config-if)#no shutdown
Switch(config-if)#exit
```

The following screenshot verifies our port security status and configurations on the interface:

```
Switch#show port-security interface GigabitEthernet 0/1
Port Security                     : Enabled
Port Status                       : Secure-up
Violation Mode                    : Shutdown
Aging Time                        : 0 mins
Aging Type                        : Absolute
SecureStatic Address Aging        : Disabled
Maximum MAC Addresses             : 2
Total MAC Addresses               : 2
Configured MAC Addresses          : 1
Sticky MAC Addresses              : 1
Last Source Address:Vlan          : bad4.e05d.fbdf:1
Security Violation Count          : 0

Switch#
```

Figure 14.22 – Verifying the port security interface status

As shown in the preceding screenshot, a secure source MAC (**Last Source Address**) address has been dynamically learned on the interface and on the VLAN. Furthermore, you can also use the `show port-security` command to verify statistics on all secure interfaces and the number as shown here:

```
Switch#show port-security
Secure Port  MaxSecureAddr   CurrentAddr   SecurityViolation   Security Action
               (Count)         (Count)        (Count)
-----------------------------------------------------------------------------
   Gi0/1          2               2              0               Shutdown
-----------------------------------------------------------------------------
Total Addresses in System (excluding one mac per port)      : 1
Max Addresses limit in System (excluding one mac per port) : 4096
Switch#
```

Figure 14.23 – Verifying port security statistics

> **Important note**
> To view the total size of the CAM table on a Cisco IOS switch, use the `show mac address-table count` command.

Since the `sticky` command was used to dynamically learn and store source MAC addresses, the `show running-config` command shows you sticky MAC addresses, if any, as shown in the following code snippet:

```
Switch#show running-config | begin interface
interface GigabitEthernet0/0
 negotiation auto
!
interface GigabitEthernet0/1
 switchport mode access
 switchport port-security maximum 2
 switchport port-security mac-address sticky
 switchport port-security mac-address b881.98d3.b223
 switchport port-security mac-address sticky bad4.e05d.fbdf
 switchport port-security
 negotiation auto
!
```

Figure 14.24 – Verifying sticky MAC addresses

When the maximum number of secure MAC addresses has been learned on an interface, if any frames with a new source MAC address are sent to a secure port, a violation will occur. There may be times when you need to manually remove a secure MAC address from a secure interface without deleting the existing secure MAC addresses. For this task, the **port security aging** feature allows us to configure an interface with an aging time limit to ensure that old secure MAC addresses remain while new MAC addresses are added.

The port security uses the following types of aging on a secure interface:

- **Absolute**: Secure MAC addresses are deleted after a defined aging time.
- **Inactivity**: Secure MAC addresses are deleted only when they are inactive for a defined aging time.

To configure port security aging on a secure interface, use the following syntax:

```
Switch(config-if)#switchport port-security aging { static |
time time | type [ absolute | inactivity ] }
```

The following is a description of each parameter for the port security aging command:

- `static`: Enables aging for a secure MAC address that is statically configured on the interface.
- `time` *time*: Allows you to specify the aging time on the interface. The time ranges between `0-1440` minutes. If the time is set to `0`, aging is disabled on the interface.

- `type absolute`: Secure MAC addresses age out and are removed from the secure address list on the switch when the specified time is met.

- `type inactivity`: Secure MAC addresses will age out only if there is no traffic from a secure MAC address for the specified time.

The following commands are an example of demonstrating how to secure MAC addresses to age out after 5 minutes of inactivity on an interface:

```
Switch(config)#interface gigabitEthernet 0/1
Switch(config-if)#switchport mode access
Switch(config-if)#switchport port-security
Switch(config-if)#switchport port-security aging time 5
Switch(config-if)#switchport port-security aging type
inactivity
Switch(config-if)#exit
```

Using the `show port-security` interface command, you'll notice that `Aging Time` has been changed to `5 mins`, and `Aging Type` has been changed to `Inactivity`, as shown here:

```
Switch#show port-security interface GigabitEthernet 0/1
Port Security            : Enabled
Port Status              : Secure-up
Violation Mode           : Shutdown
Aging Time               : 5 mins
Aging Type               : Inactivity
SecureStatic Address Aging : Disabled
Maximum MAC Addresses    : 2
Total MAC Addresses      : 2
Configured MAC Addresses : 1
Sticky MAC Addresses     : 1
Last Source Address:Vlan : bad4.e05d.fbdf:1
Security Violation Count : 0

Switch#
```

Figure 14.25 – Verifying port security aging configurations

If a secure port receives a source MAC address that is different from the list of secure MAC addresses, a violation will be triggered and the interface will transition into an *error-disabled* state. The following are the three different violation modes when configuring port security:

- `shutdown`: This is the default violation mode. If a violation occurs, the port changes to an *error-disabled* state. The violation counter is increased. To re-enable the interface, the network engineer must first use the `shutdown` command, wait a few seconds, and then use the `no shutdown` command within the affected interface.

- `restrict`: If a violation occurs, this mode drops any message with an unknown source address. The security violation counter increases and a syslog message is generated.

- `protect`: If a violation occurs, this mode will drop any message with an unknown source address. However, it does not increase the security violation counter, nor does it send a syslog message. This mode is considered to be the least secure of the three violation modes.

To configure a port security violation on an interface, use the following syntax:

```
Switch(config-if)#switchport port-security violation shutdown |
restrict | protect
```

The following is an example of configuring the `restrict` violation on an interface with port security:

```
Switch(config)#interface GigabitEthernet 0/1
Switch(config-if)#switchport mode access
Switch(config-if)#switchport port-security
Switch(config-if)#switchport port-security violation restrict
Switch(config-if)#exit
```

Using the `show port-security interface` command, you can see that the violation mode has changed to `Restrict`, as shown in the following screenshot:

```
Switch#show port-security interface GigabitEthernet 0/1
Port Security               : Enabled
Port Status                 : Secure-up
Violation Mode              : Restrict
Aging Time                  : 5 mins
Aging Type                  : Inactivity
SecureStatic Address Aging  : Disabled
Maximum MAC Addresses       : 2
Total MAC Addresses         : 2
Configured MAC Addresses    : 1
Sticky MAC Addresses        : 1
Last Source Address:Vlan    : bad4.e05d.fbdf:1
Security Violation Count    : 0

Switch#
```

Figure 14.26 – Verifying violation modes

In the next section, you will gain hands-on experience in terms of implementing port security on a Cisco IOS switch.

## Lab – implementing port security

In this lab, you will learn how to implement port security to limit the number of secure source MAC addresses that are permitted on the interfaces of a Cisco IOS switch. To get started, we'll be using the Cisco Packet Tracer application, which allows us to simulate a Cisco environment. For this lab, please build the following network topology:

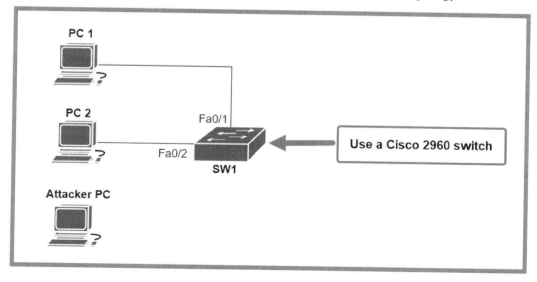

Figure 14.27 – Port security lab topology

Ensure that you've assigned the IP addresses to each device according to the following IP address table:

| Device | Interface | IP Address | Subnet Mask | Default Gateway |
|---|---|---|---|---|
| PC 1 | Fa0 | 172.16.1.10 | 255.255.255.0 | 172.16.1.1 |
| PC 2 | Fa0 | 172.16.1.20 | 255.255.255.0 | 172.16.1.1 |
| Attacker PC | Fa0 | 172.16.1.30 | 255.255.255.0 | 172.16.1.1 |

Figure 14.28 – IP address scheme

Each computer – **PC 1**, **PC 2**, and the **Attacker PC** – is using their `FastEthernet0` (Fa0) interface to connect to **SW1**.

Now that your lab is ready, use the following instructions to implement port security:

1.  On **SW1**, enable port security on the `FastEthernet 0/1` and `FastEthernet 0/2` interfaces using the following commands:

    ```
    SW1(config)#interface range FastEthernet 0/1 -
    FastEthernet 0/2
    SW1(config-if-range)#switchport mode access
    SW1(config-if-range)#switchport port-security
    ```

2.  Configure the secure ports to permit a maximum of one device per interface:

    ```
    SW1(config-if-range)#switchport port-security maximum 1
    ```

3.  Configure the secure ports to dynamically learn and store secure source MAC addresses on the running configuration file:

    ```
    SW1(config-if-range)#switchport port-security mac-address
    sticky
    ```

4.  Next, enable the secure ports only and exit:

    ```
    SW1(config-if-range)#no shutdown
    SW1(config-if-range)#exit
    ```

5.  Secure any unused ports on the switch:

```
SW1(config)#interface range FastEthernet 0/3 -
FastEthernet 0/24
SW1(config-if-range)#shutdown
SW1(config-if-range)#exit
SW1(config)#interface range GigabitEthernet 0/1 -
GigabitEthernet 0/2
SW1(config-if-range)#shutdown
SW1(config-if-range)#exit
```

6.  Ping between **PC 1** and **PC 2** to ensure that their source MAC addresses are learned and stored on the running configuration file. Use the show port-security interface command to validate the configurations on your interfaces:

```
SW1#show port-security interface fastEthernet 0/2
Port Security               : Enabled
Port Status                 : Secure-up
Violation Mode              : Shutdown
Aging Time                  : 0 mins
Aging Type                  : Absolute
SecureStatic Address Aging  : Disabled
Maximum MAC Addresses       : 1
Total MAC Addresses         : 1
Configured MAC Addresses    : 0
Sticky MAC Addresses        : 1
Last Source Address:Vlan    : 0001.C9BA.5B83:1
Security Violation Count    : 0

SW1#
```

Figure 14.29 – Validating port security

As shown in the preceding screenshot, port security is enabled on the interface, the violation mode is set to Shutdown (default), aging is Disabled, the maximum number of secure MAC addresses allowed on the interface is 1, the total number of secure MAC addresses learned is 1, sticky is Enabled and has stored one address on running-config, and the last MAC address learned is 0001.C9BA.5B83 on VLAN 1.

7. Next, use the `show running-config` command to view the port security configurations and the sticky addresses that are automatically added to the running configuration:

```
SW1#show running-config
Building configuration...

Current configuration : 1629 bytes
!
!
interface FastEthernet0/1
 switchport mode access
 switchport port-security
 switchport port-security mac-address sticky
 switchport port-security mac-address sticky 0001.966B.B95A
!
interface FastEthernet0/2
 switchport mode access
 switchport port-security
 switchport port-security mac-address sticky
 switchport port-security mac-address sticky 0001.C9BA.5B83
!
```

Figure 14.30 – Verifying the sticky address

As shown in the preceding screenshot, **PC 1**'s MAC address is bound to `FastEthernet0/1` and **PC 2**'s MAC address is bound to `FastEthernet0/2`.

8. Next, let's trigger a violation of the network. Connect the attacker PC to `FastEthernet0/2` on **SW1**. Then, attempt to ping from the **Attacker PC** to **PC 1**, as shown here:

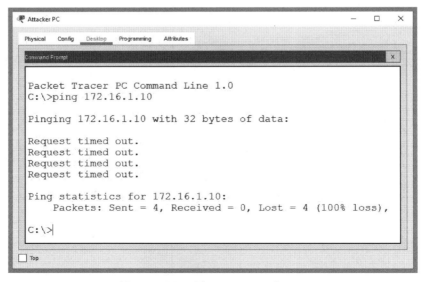

Figure 14.31 – Triggering a violation

9.  As expected, since the attacker's source MAC address does not match the secure MAC address on `FastEthernet 0/2`, the traffic is not permitted and the interface has been disabled, as shown here:

```
SW1#show port-security interface fastEthernet 0/2
Port Security               : Enabled
Port Status                 : Secure-shutdown
Violation Mode              : Shutdown
Aging Time                  : 0 mins
Aging Type                  : Absolute
SecureStatic Address Aging  : Disabled
Maximum MAC Addresses       : 1
Total MAC Addresses         : 1
Configured MAC Addresses    : 0
Sticky MAC Addresses        : 1
Last Source Address:Vlan    : 00E0.F9E9.5E39:1
Security Violation Count    : 1

SW1#
```

Figure 14.32 – Verifying violation

The port status has been changed to `Secure-shutdown`, the attacker's source MAC address is shown, and the violation counter has increased to `1`.

10. To verify which interfaces are in an error-disabled state, use the `show interfaces status` command:

```
SW1#show interfaces status
Port       Name        Status        Vlan       Duplex  Speed Type
Fa0/1                  connected     1           auto    auto  10/100BaseTX
Fa0/2                  err-disabled  1           auto    auto  10/100BaseTX
Fa0/3                  disabled 1              auto    auto  10/100BaseTX
Fa0/4                  disabled 1              auto    auto  10/100BaseTX
Fa0/5                  disabled 1              auto    auto  10/100BaseTX
```

Figure 14.33 – Verifying error-disabled interfaces

Another useful command to verify whether a port is in an error-disabled state is the `show interfaces` command.

11. Lastly, let's fix the issue by physically reconnecting **PC 2** to `FastEthernet 0/2` on **SW1** and re-enabling the interface using the following commands:

```
SW1(config)#interface FastEthernet 0/2
SW1(config-if)#shutdown
SW1(config-if)#no shutdown
SW1(config-if)#exit
```

Having completed this lab, you have gained the hands-on skills to implement port security on a Cisco environment. In the next section, you will learn how to mitigate and prevent rogue DHCP servers on a network.

# DHCP snooping

DHCP snooping is a security feature available within Cisco IOS switches that allows you to prevent and mitigate against rogue DHCP servers. DHCP snooping is not dependent on source MAC addresses as compared to port security but rather determines whether DHCP messages are originating from a trusted device or trusted source on the network. With DHCP snooping implemented on a corporate network, it can filter DHCP messages and perform rate limiting on DHCP messages from untrusted sources. Rate limiting is used to control the number of messages entering a device's interface.

On a private network, devices such as routers, servers, and switches are considered to be trusted devices. They are trusted devices simply because you, as a network engineer, have administrative control over these networking devices. However, devices that are outside of your network are considered to be untrusted. When DHCP snooping is enabled, all ports are untrusted by default.

> **Important note**
> Since DHCP clients are expected to send only DHCP Discover and DHCP Request messages to an untrusted port, if an untrusted port receives a DHCP Offer or DHCP Acknowledgement message, then a violation will occur.

A trusted port must be explicitly configured by the network engineer. Additionally, all access ports should be untrusted simply because the access layer is where an attacker can insert their rogue DHCP server. Trusted interfaces should be trunk interfaces and ports that are connected to the organization's DHCP server.

> **Important note**
> On a trusted port, DHCP Offer and DHCP Acknowledgement messages are permitted.

When DHCP snooping is enabled, the switch creates a special table known as a **DHCP snooping binding table**. This table keeps a table of source MAC addresses of devices that are connected to untrusted ports and their IP addresses that were assigned by the legitimate DHCP server. The MAC addresses and IP addresses are bound together.

To configure DHCP snooping, observe the following steps:

1. Use the `ip dhcp snooping` command within the global configuration mode to turn on DHCP snooping.

2. Configure trusted interfaces by using the `ip dhcp snooping trust` command within the interface mode.

3. Configure rate limiting on untrusted ports using the `ip dhcp snooping rate limit` *number* command. Specify a number for **packets per second (pps)**.

4. Assign DHCP snooping for either a single VLAN or a range of VLANs by using the `ip dhcp snooping vlan vlan-id` command in global configuration mode. The following is an example of entering multiple VLANs in the command: `ip dhcp snooping vlan 5,15,20-22`.

In the next section, you will gain hands-on experience in terms of implementing DHCP snooping to prevent and mitigate rogue DHCP servers in a Cisco environment.

## Lab – implementing DHCP snooping

In this lab, you will learn how to implement DHCP snooping to prevent and mitigate rogue DHCP server and DHCP attacks on a network. This lab is simply an extension of the previous exercise on *implementing port security*. For this lab, ensure that you add the additional devices to the following network topology:

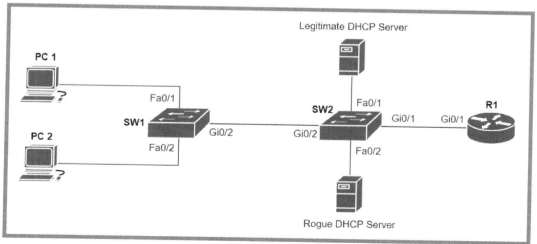

Figure 14.34 – DHCP snooping lab topology

Make sure that you've assigned the IP addresses to each device according to the following IP address table:

| Device | Interface | IP Address | Subnet Mask | Default Gateway |
| --- | --- | --- | --- | --- |
| PC 1 | Fa0 | DHCP | | |
| PC 2 | Fa0 | DHCP | | |
| DHCP Server | Fa0 | 172.16.1.100 | 255.255.255.0 | 172.16.1.1 |
| Rogue DHCP Server | Fa0 | 172.16.1.110 | 255.255.255.0 | 172.16.1.1 |
| R1 | Gi0/1 | 172.16.1.1 | 255.255.255.0 | |

Figure 14.35 – IP addressing scheme

Please observe the following guidelines when executing this lab to ensure that you obtain the same results:

- Manually configure GigabitEthernet 0/2 on **SW1** and **SW2** as a trunk port and enable the interface.

Now that your lab is ready, use the following instructions to configure DHCP snooping:

1.  On **SW1**, use the ip dhcp snooping command to enable DHCP snooping, as shown here:

    ```
    SW1(config)#ip dhcp snooping
    ```

2.  Configure GigabitEthernet 0/2 as a trunk port and as a trusted port using the following commands:

    ```
    SW1(config)#interface GigabitEthernet 0/2
    SW1(config-if)#switchport mode trunk
    SW1(config-if)#ip dhcp snooping trust
    SW1(config-if)#no shutdown
    SW1(config-if)#exit
    ```

3.  Assign DHCP snooping to the VLAN in use, VLAN 1, using the following command:

    ```
    SW1(config)#ip dhcp snooping vlan 1
    ```

> **Tip**
>
> A network may contain DHCP relay agents that will insert information about themselves (`option 82`) before forwarding a `DHCP Discover` message to the DHCP server. When DHCP snooping is enabled, it prevents the forwarding of the DHCP messages via relay agents. To prevent *DHCP relay option 82 information* from being inserted in the DHCP relay messages, you can use the `no ip dhcp snooping information option` command within the global configuration mode.

4.  Next, use the following command to enable DHCP snooping on **SW2**:

```
SW2(config)#ip dhcp snooping
```

5.  Configure `GigabitEthernet 0/1`, `GigabitEthernet 0/2`, and `FastEthernet 0/1` as a trusted port by using the following commands:

```
SW2(config)#interface range GigabitEthernet 0/1 -
GigabitEthernet 0/2
SW2(config-if-range)#switchport mode trunk
SW2(config-if-range)#ip dhcp snooping trust
SW2(config-if-range)#no shutdown
SW2(config-if-range)#exit
SW2(config)#interface FastEthernet 0/1
SW2(config-if)#ip dhcp snooping trust
SW2(config-if)#no shutdown
SW2(config-if)#exit
```

6.  Assign DHCP snooping to the VLAN in use on **SW2** and `VLAN 1` by using the following command:

```
SW2(config)#ip dhcp snooping vlan 1
```

7.  Click on the legitimate DHCP server, and select the **Services** tab | **DHCP**. Make sure that you enable the service and assign the IP details to create a DHCP pool on the server, as shown here:

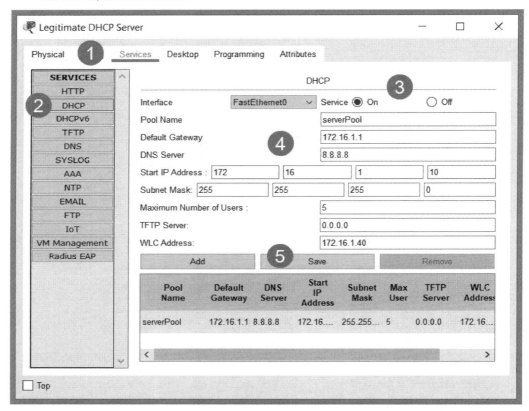

Figure 14.36 – Configuring the legitimate DHCP server

Make sure that you configure all the IP addresses: **Default Gateway** = 172.16.1.1, **DNS Server** = 8.8.8.8, **Start IP Address** = 172.16.1.10, **Subnet Mask** = 255.255.255.0, **WLC Address** = 172.16.1.40, and then click on **Save**. The WLC address will be used in the next lab on wireless security.

8.  Configure the rogue DHCP server using the following settings:

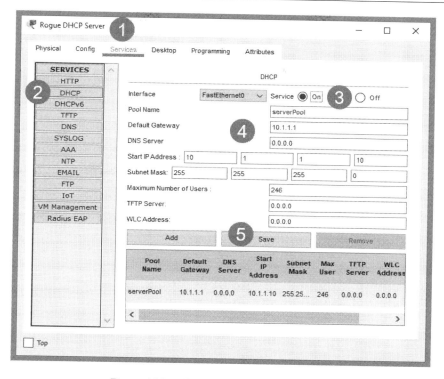

Figure 14.37 – Rogue DHCP server settings

9.  Next, enable DHCP on both **PC 1** and **PC 2**, as shown here:

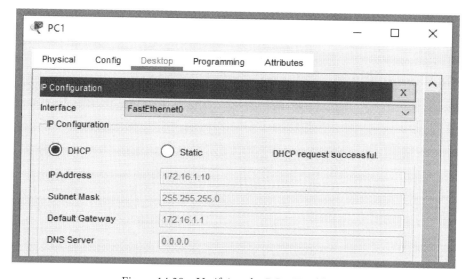

Figure 14.38 – Verifying the PC 1 IP address

If you disconnect the legitimate DHCP server from the network, you will notice that PCs do not receive any IP address configurations from the rogue DHCP server.

10. Next, use the `show ip dhcp snooping` command to verify whether DHCP snooping is enabled on the VLAN, and `Option 82` is enabled. Additionally, this command allows you to verify both trusted and untrusted interfaces on the local switch:

```
SW1#show ip dhcp snooping
Switch DHCP snooping is enabled
DHCP snooping is configured on following VLANs:
1
Insertion of option 82 is enabled
Option 82 on untrusted port is not allowed
Verification of hwaddr field is enabled
Interface                    Trusted      Rate limit (pps)
-----------------------      -------      ----------------
FastEthernet0/2              no           unlimited
FastEthernet0/1              no           unlimited
GigabitEthernet0/2          yes           unlimited
SW1#
```

Figure 14.39 – Verifying the DHCP snooping status

11. Lastly, use `show ip dhcp snooping binding` to view the DHCP snooping binding table:

```
SW1#show ip dhcp snooping binding
MacAddress          IpAddress        Lease(sec)   Type           VLAN  Interface
------------------  ---------------  ----------   ------------   ----  ----------------
00:01:C9:BA:5B:83   172.16.1.2       86400        dhcp-snooping  1     FastEthernet0/2
00:01:96:6B:B9:5A   172.16.1.10      86400        dhcp-snooping  1     FastEthernet0/1
Total number of bindings: 2
SW1#
```

Figure 14.40 – Viewing the DHCP snooping binding table

Having completed this lab, you have gained the hands-on skills to implement DHCP snooping to prevent and mitigate DHCP attacks in a Cisco environment. In the next section, you will learn how to mitigate and prevent IP spoofing and man-in-the-middle attacks on a network.

# Dynamic ARP inspection

During a man-in-the-middle attack, an attacker uses ARP spoofing to send an unsolicited ARP message with their source MAC address with the IP address of a default gateway to other hosts on the network. By implementing a **Dynamic ARP inspection (DAI)** on Cisco IOS switches, you can prevent and mitigate ARP spoofing and man-in-the-middle attacks on your enterprise network. A DAI ensures that only legitimate ARP requests and ARP replies are sent on the network.

To ensure that a DAI is effective on a network, a DAI requires DHCP snooping to be configured and enabled on the switch as well. With DHCP snooping and a DAI enabled, they prevent ARP attacks by means of the following:

- Preventing ARP request and ARP reply messages on untrusted interfaces

- Intercepting all ARP messages on untrusted interfaces

- Validating all intercepted messages that contain a valid IP-to-MAC address binding.

- Discarding and logging all ARP reply messages that are originating from invalid sources.

- Whenever a violation occurs, the interface transitions into an error-disabled state.

> **Important note**
> All access ports on a switch should be configured as untrusted interfaces. All trunk ports that are connected to other switches or routers should be configured as trusted ports.

To configure a DAI, observe the following steps:

1. Enable DHCP snooping because a DAI requires the DHCP snooping binding table to validate IP-MAC addresses. Use the `ip dhcp snooping` command in global configuration mode.

2. Assign DHCP snooping to a VLAN, using the `ip dhcp snooping vlan vlan-id` command in global configuration mode.

3. Configure the trunk links as trusted interfaces, and use the `ip dhcp snooping trust` command and the `ip arp inspection trust` command in interface mode.

4. Enable a DAI on the VLAN, and use the `ip arp inspection vlan vlan-id` command in global configuration mode.

A DAI also has the capability to inspect both the source or destination MAC and IP addresses of each message. It does this by using the following command:

```
Switch(config)# ip arp inspection validate [ src-mac | dst-mac
| ip ]
```

The following is a description of each parameter for the ARP inspection command:

- src-mac: Enables a DAI to check the source MAC address in the Layer 2 header against the sender's MAC address within the ARP body.

- dst-mac: A DAI checks the destination MAC address in the Layer 2 header against the target's MAC address within the ARP body.

- ip: A DAI checks the ARP body for any invalid IP addresses, such as 0.0.0.0, 255.255.255.255, and all multicast IP addresses.

In the next section, you will gain hands-on experience in terms of implementing a DAI in a Cisco environment.

## Lab – implementing a DAI

In this lab, you will learn how to implement a DAI to prevent and mitigate IP spoofing and man-in-the-middle attacks on a network. This lab is simply an extension of the previous exercise on *implementing DHCP snooping*. For this lab, we'll be using the same lab topology from the previous exercise:

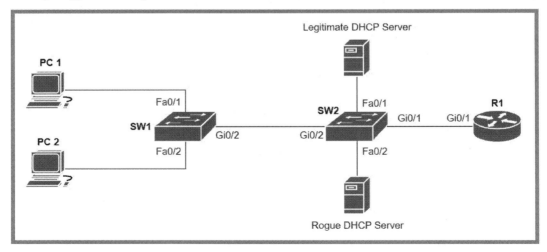

Figure 14.41 – DAI lab topology

Since we already have DHCP snooping implemented from the last lab exercise, we'll proceed to apply only the DAI configurations on the network by using the following steps:

1.  On **SW1**, configure the uplink (trunk) interface as an ARP trusted port:

    ```
    SW1(config)#interface GigabitEthernet 0/2
    SW1(config-if)#ip arp inspection trust
    SW1(config-if)#exit
    ```

2.  Enable a DAI on VLAN 1:

    ```
    SW1(config)#ip arp inspection vlan 1
    ```

3.  Configure a DAI to inspect both the source or destination MAC and IP addresses of each message on **SW1**:

    ```
    SW1(config)#ip arp inspection validate src-mac dst-mac ip
    ```

4.  On **SW2**, configure the trunk interfaces and the port connected to the legitimate DHCP server as ARP trusted ports:

    ```
    SW2(config)#interface range gigabitEthernet 0/1 -
    gigabitEthernet 0/2
    SW2(config-if-range)#ip arp inspection trust
    SW2(config-if-range)#exit
    SW2(config)#interface FastEthernet 0/1
    SW2(config-if)#ip arp inspection trust
    SW2(config-if)#exit
    ```

5.  Enable a DAI on VLAN 1:

    ```
    SW2(config)#ip arp inspection vlan 1
    ```

6.  Configure a DAI to inspect both the source and destination MAC and IP addresses of each message on **SW2**:

    ```
    SW2(config)#ip arp inspection validate src-mac dst-mac ip
    ```

7.  Use the show ip arp inspection command to verify ARP inspection
    statistics, as shown here:

| Vlan | Configuration | Operation | ACL Match | Static ACL |
|------|---------------|-----------|-----------|------------|
| 1 | Enabled | Inactive | | |

| Vlan | ACL Logging | DHCP Logging | Probe Logging |
|------|-------------|--------------|---------------|
| 1 | Deny | Deny | Off |

| Vlan | Forwarded | Dropped | DHCP Drops | ACL Drops |
|------|-----------|---------|------------|-----------|
| 1 | 0 | 0 | 0 | 0 |

| Vlan | DHCP Permits | ACL Permits | Probe Permits | Source MAC Failures |
|------|--------------|-------------|---------------|---------------------|
| 1 | 0 | 0 | 0 | 0 |

| Vlan | Dest MAC Failures | IP Validation Failures | Invalid Protocol Data |
|------|-------------------|------------------------|-----------------------|
| 1 | 0 | 0 | 0 |

Figure 14.42 – Verifying ARP inspection details

8.  Lastly, the show ip arp inspection vlan command can be used to verify
    whether a DAI is inspecting both source and destination MAC and IP addresses of
    each message:

```
SW1#show ip arp inspection vlan 1

Source Mac Validation      : Enabled
Destination Mac Validation : Enabled
IP Address Validation      : Enabled

 Vlan    Configuration    Operation   ACL Match          Static ACL
 ----    -------------    ---------   ---------          ----------
   1     Enabled          Inactive

 Vlan    ACL Logging      DHCP Logging         Probe Logging
 ----    -----------      ------------         -------------
   1     Deny             Deny                 Off

SW1#
```

Figure 14.43 – Verifying additional ARP inspection configurations

Having completed this lab, you have gained the hands-on experience and skills required to
implement a DAI to prevent and mitigate IP spoofing and man-in-the-middle attacks in a
Cisco environment. In the next section, you will learn how to secure a wireless network.

# Wireless network security

Many organizations implement a wireless network to support the mobility of their users. Implementing a **Wireless LAN (WLAN)** offers convenience to users with mobile devices, thereby allowing them to roam around the building and work from anywhere. With a WLAN, it is open to anyone within the range of the wireless signal generated by the APs and the correct user credentials to access the corporate network. WLANs create an entire landscape of threats and attacks by threat actors and even disgruntled employees.

The following are some of the threats posed to a wireless network:

- A threat actor can intercept traffic on a wireless network. The threat actor does not need to be within the building, but rather within the range of the wireless signal. It's recommended that all wireless traffic should be encrypted to prevent any eavesdropping.

- An intruder may be present on the wireless network. This is someone who is not authorized to access the wireless network or resources.

- A threat actor can create a DoS attack to prevent legitimate users from accessing the wireless network.

- A threat actor can set up an *evil twin* or *rogue access point* to capture legitimate users' traffic.

A rogue access point is where an attacker sets up their own AP outside the target organization, but close enough for its wireless signal to be reachable by employees. On the rogue access point, the attacker adds an internet connection and implements packet capture and other malicious tools to intercept and capture traffic. The idea of implementing a rogue access point is to trick victims into connecting to the AP owned by the attacker and to capture sensitive data.

The Evil Twin is an AP installed within the corporate network by a threat actor. All users who are connected are able to access the corporate resources, but their traffic is intercepted and captured by the AP owned by the threat actor.

> **Tip**
> To learn about wireless security penetration testing, you can check out my book, *Learn Kali Linux 2019*, by *Glen D. Singh*, published by *Packt Publishing* at the following URL: `https://www.packtpub.com/networking-and-servers/learn-kali-linux-2018`. The book also covers various aspects of ethical hacking and penetration testing.

One method of reducing the possibility of hiding your wireless network is disabling the **Service Set Identifier** (**SSID**) broadcast. This feature does not totally protect your network from a threat actor, since there are techniques for discovering a hidden wireless network, but it does reduce the possibility that a novice hacker may not detect it. When the SSID broadcast is disabled, the wireless router or AP will not send the SSID within its beacon messages.

The following screenshot is an example of how to disable the SSID broadcast on a Linksys 160N device:

Figure 14.44 – Disabling SSID Broadcast

Additionally, you can enable **MAC address filtering** to create an ACL of permitted or denied devices. The following screenshot shows an example of the MAC filtering interface on a Linksys 160N wireless router:

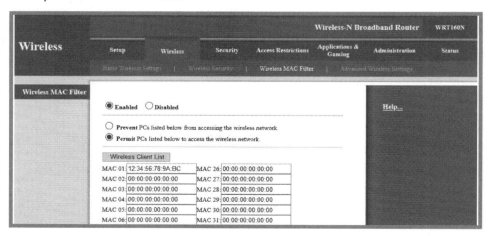

Figure 14.45 – MAC filtering

Keep in mind that an experienced hacker can find ways to bypass MAC filtering controls on a wireless network. However, it's better to have some security on your network rather than having no security at all. In the next section, you will discover various methods of authentication that can be implemented on a wireless network.

## Authentication methods

A wireless router or AP provides a few options to configure how users are authenticated onto the network. One method is **Open Authentication**, which disables any authentication mechanisms on the wireless device. This method allows anyone to connect to the wireless network freely. An authentication method such as this is commonly used in shopping malls, coffee shops and restaurants, and public areas.

> **Important note**
>
> WPA3 is currently the only wireless security standard that encrypts messages on an open network using **Opportunistic Wireless Encryption** (**OWE**). This technology allows the encryption of traffic between the client and the AP on an open network. This type of implementation is useful for public Wi-Fi deployments.

Another method involves the use of **Shared Key Authentication**. This method is also referred to as a **pre-shared key** (**PSK**). With PSK authentication, the wireless router is configured with a passphrase for the wireless network, so anyone attempting to access the wireless network will be prompted to provide the correct pre-shared key. There are various wireless security standards that use PSK. These are as follows:

- **Wired Equivalent Privacy** (**WEP**): WEP is the first official standard used to secure data transmission using the **Rivest Cipher 4** (**RC4**) encryption algorithm on an IEEE 802.11 network. Due to various security vulnerabilities found in this standard, it is no longer recommended.

- **Wi-Fi Protected Access** (**WPA**): This standard uses WEP with a more secure encryption algorithm known as **Temporal Key Integrity Protocol** (**TKIP**). TKIP applies a unique key to each packet on the wireless network, thus making it difficult to compromise. TKIP also validates the integrity of each message by using **Message Integrity Check** (**MIC**).

- **WPA2**: WPA2 is currently the industry standard for securing `IEEE 802.11` networks. This standard uses the **Advanced Encryption Standard** (**AES**) for data encryption, which is a lot stronger than those previously mentioned. AES uses the **Counter Cipher Mode with Block Chaining Message Authentication Code Protocol** (**CCMP**), which enables the destination device to validate confidentiality and integrity.

- **WPA3**: As of the time of writing this book, WPA3 is the latest wireless security standard. WPA3 uses the most up-to-date security protocols and discontinues outdated and legacy protocols. WPA3 uses **Simultaneous Authentication of Equals** (**SAE**) to mitigate vulnerabilities found in WPA2. WPA3 uses the **Commercial National Security Algorithm** (**CNSA**) in WPA3-Enterprise authentication.

The following screenshot shows an example of configuring the authentication methods on a wireless router:

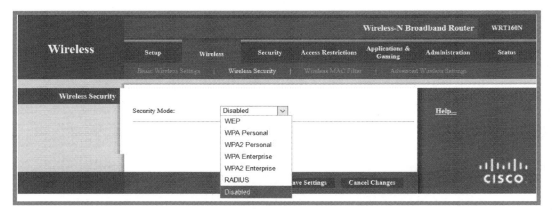

Figure 14.46 – Authentication methods

WPA and WPA2 use two additional authentication methods. These are as follows:

- **Personal**: This method is commonly used on a home wireless network and allows you to configure the PSK directly on the wireless router.

- **Enterprise**: This method allows you to associate the wireless router with a AAA server. The wireless router does not handle the authentication of users on the network but hands the responsibility over to the AAA server (RADIUS or TACACS+).

Having completed this section, you have learned about various wireless security threats and security mechanisms. In the next section, you will learn how to implement a wireless network and apply wireless security.

# Lab – implementing wireless security using a WLC

In this lab, you will learn how to implement wireless security using a Cisco **Wireless LAN Controller** (**WLC**). This lab is simply an extension of the previous exercise on *implementing a dynamic ARP inspection*. For this lab, ensure that you add additional devices to the following network topology:

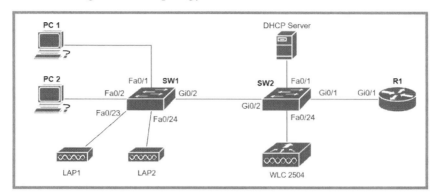

Figure 14.47 – Wireless security lab topology

Please observe the following guidelines when executing this lab to ensure that you obtain the same results:

- For the WLC, use the Cisco 2504 controller. On Cisco Packet Tracer, click on **Network Devices | Wireless** to select the Cisco 2504 controller.

- For the **Lightweight Access Points** (**LAPs**), use the **LAP-PT** devices. The following screenshot shows the location of both the WLC and LAPs on the Cisco Packet Tracer application:

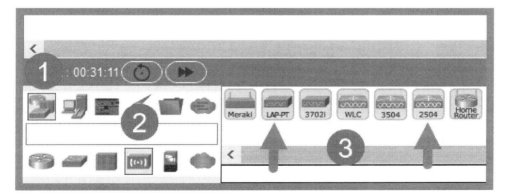

Figure 14.48 – Wireless complements

The numbered labels in the preceding diagram show the buttons to click on.

Now that your topology is ready, use the following instructions to set up the WLC and implement a wireless section on the network:

1. Click on the WLC, and then select the **Config** tab | **Management** interface to assign the following addresses, as shown in the following screenshot:

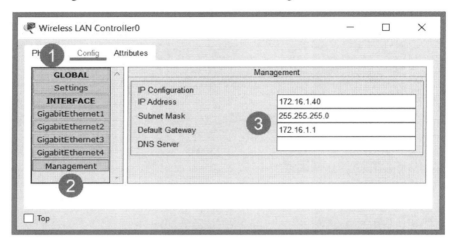

Figure 14.49 – WLC IP configurations

2. Next, click on **PC 1**, select the **Desktop** tab, and then open **Web Browser**. Enter the URL http://172.16.1.40 and click on **Go** to load the WLC home page.

3. Create a username, admin, set a password, Cisco123, and then click **Start**, as shown here:

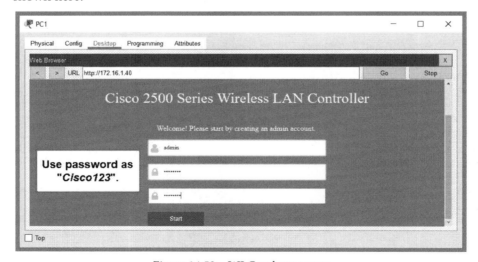

Figure 14.50 – WLC welcome page

4.  Configure the management IP address, subnet mask, and default gateway, as shown here:

Figure 14.51 – Management IP on the WLC

The IP settings are the same as defined in *step 1*. Click **Next** to continue.

5.  On the next page, create a wireless network name, WLAN-Corp, set the security as WPA2-Personal, and the passphrase as cisco456, as shown here:

Figure 14.52 – Creating a wireless network on WLC

6. Next, you will be asked to configure a virtual IP address that allows the LAPs to communicate with the WLC on the network. Leave this configuration as the default and then click **Next**:

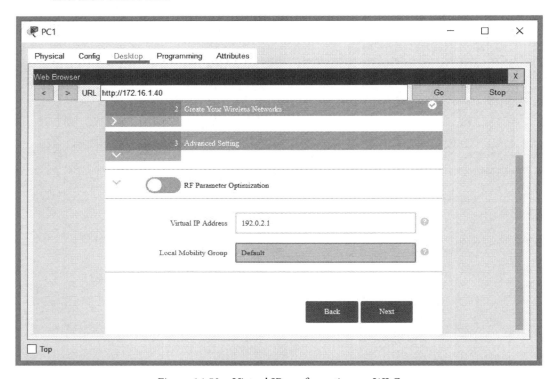

Figure 14.53 – Virtual IP configuration on WLC

7. Next, the WLC will present a summary page with the configurations you have made. Click **Apply**. The WLC will reboot. To access the WLC after it has rebooted, use the URL `https://172.16.1.40`.

8. While the WLC is rebooting, click on each LAP and drag the power adapter (**1**) to the power interface (**2**), as shown here:

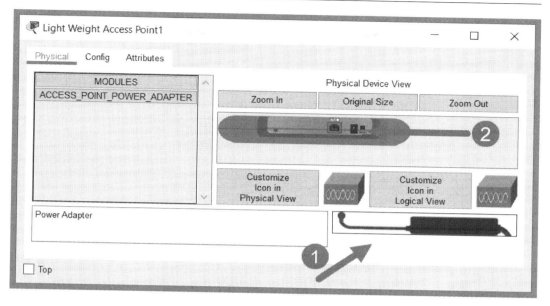

Figure 14.54 – Connecting a power adapter to the AP

By default, LAPs do not have power. Connecting the power adapter via Cisco Packet Tracer will supply power to the device.

9.  We need to re-enable the interfaces associated with the LAPs on **SW1**. Use the following commands to enable the interfaces:

```
SW1(config)#interface range FastEthernet 0/23 -
FastEthernet 0/24
SW1(config-if-range)#no shutdown
SW1(config-if-range)#exit
```

The interfaces may take a few seconds before they transition into a forwarding state.

10. It's now time to test whether the wireless network is configured properly by connecting a mobile device. On Cisco Packet Tracer, click on **End Devices** and drag the smart device (such as a phone) near to an LAP.

11. Click on the smart device (phone), select the **Config** tab | **Wireless0** interface, and apply the following settings: **SSID**: WLAN-Corp; **Authentication**: **WPA2-PSK**; and **PSK Pass Phrase**: cisco456, as shown here:

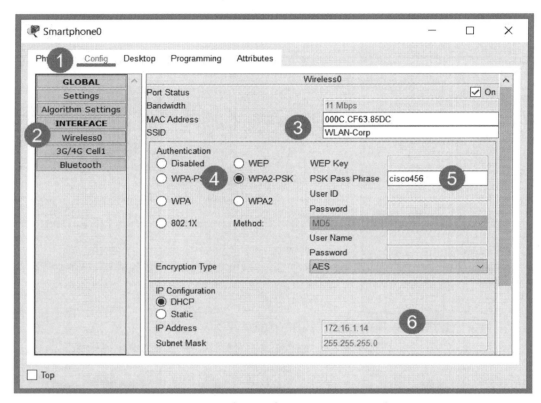

Figure 14.55 – Wireless configuration on a smart device

After applying the wireless configurations, the smart device will automatically associate itself with one of the LAPs and receive an IP address from the DHCP server on the network. If the smart device obtains an APIPA address (169.254.x.x), simply toggle back to *Static* and *DHCP* again. This sometimes happens on a network when the DHCP **Discover** message was not successfully delivered to the DHCP server on the network.

Lastly, we can validate the IP configurations on the smart device. Click on the **Desktop** tab | **Command Prompt** and execute the `ipconfig` command, as shown here:

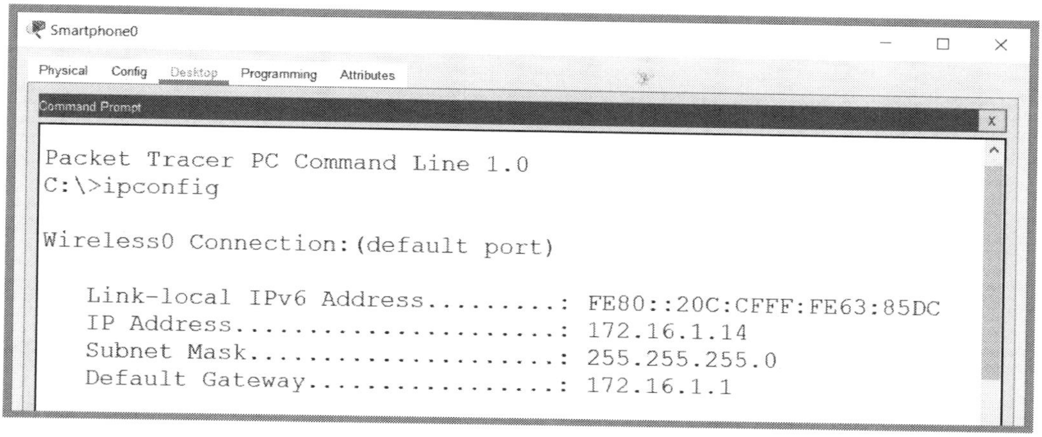

Figure 14.56 – Validating IP configurations

Having completed this section, you have gained hands-on experience of implementing a Cisco WLC and LAPs, and implemented wireless security in a Cisco environment.

# Summary

During the course of this chapter, you have learned about the need to use a multi-layered approach known as *Defense-in-Depth* to improve the security posture of your network and organization. Furthermore, you have learned how threat actors can use various Layer 2 threats and attacks to compromise our enterprise network. Next, we covered how to implement Layer 2 security controls on your Cisco IOS switches to prevent and mitigate Layer 2 attacks and wireless security to secure your network.

I hope this chapter has been informative for you and will prove helpful in your journey toward learning how to implement and administer Cisco solutions and prepare for the CCNA 200-301 certification. In the next chapter, *Network Automation and Programmability Techniques*, you will learn how automation and programmability can improve efficiency in network deployment and management.

# Questions

The following is a short list of review questions to help reinforce your learning and help you identify areas that require some improvement:

1. Which of the following is a type of malware that is designed to encrypt your data?

   A. Worm

   B. Ransomware

   C. Polymorphic

   D. Trojan

2. A security professional implements multiple security components to improve the security posture of the organization. What is the security professional trying to do?

   A. Install anti-malware on all devices.

   B. Install host-based firewalls on all end devices.

   C. Implement email security.

   D. Implement Defense in Depth.

3. A threat actor is attempting to force a switch to flood all its inbound traffic out of all other ports. What type of attack is the threat actor performing?

   A. IP spoofing

   B. CAM table overflow

   C. Man-in-the-middle

   D. ARP spoofing

4. Another attacker is attempting to gain unauthorized access to a VLAN. What type of attack is being performed by the attacker?

   A. An `802.1Q` attack

   B. A DTP attack

   C. VLAN hopping

   D. VLAN double tagging

5.   Which command is used to disable DTP on an interface?

   A. `switchport nonegotiate`

   B. `switchport mode access`

   C. `switchport mode trunk`

   D. `no switchport dtp`

6.   An attacker is attempting to connect a rogue DHCP server on the network. How can such an attack be prevented?

   A. Implement a DAI.

   B. Shut down the interface.

   C. Port security.

   D. DHCP snooping.

7.   When port security is enabled, which is the default violation mode?

   A. Protect

   B. Error-disabled

   C. Shutdown

   D. Restrict

8.   Which command can be used to enable a DAI to inspect both the source and destination MAC and IP addresses of each message?

   A. `ip arp inspection validate src-mac dst-mac`

   B. `ip arp inspection validate src-mac dst-mac ip`

   C. `ip arp inspection validate src-mac ip`

   D. `ip arp inspection validate enable`

9.   Which security appliance should you use to filter email traffic?

   A. Cisco Umbrella

   B. Cisco NGIPS

   C. Cisco NGFW

   D. Cisco ESA

10. Which is the least secure violation mode in port security?

    A. Protect

    B. Error-disabled

    C. Shutdown

    D. Restrict

# Further reading

The following links are recommended for additional reading:

- Configuring port security: `https://www.cisco.com/c/en/us/td/docs/switches/lan/catalyst4500/12-2/25ew/configuration/guide/conf/port_sec.html`

- Configuring DHCP snooping: `https://www.cisco.com/c/en/us/td/docs/switches/lan/catalyst6500/ios/12-2SX/configuration/guide/book/snoodhcp.html`

- Configuring a DAI: `https://www.cisco.com/c/en/us/td/docs/switches/lan/catalyst6500/ios/12-2SX/configuration/guide/book/dynarp.html`

# Section 6: Automation and Programmability

In this section, you will be introduced to network programmability. This is a new skill Cisco recommends for each existing and new network engineer in the field. Additionally, you will discover the many benefits of implementing techniques that will assist in network management, such as automation.

This section contains the following chapters:

- *Chapter 15, Network Automation and Programmability Techniques*
- *Chapter 16, Mock Test 1*
- *Chapter 17, Mock Test 2*

# 15
# Network Automation and Programmability Techniques

In 2019, Cisco made a huge announcement related to their certification tracks and examination structure. One notable update is the inclusion of automation and programmability within the CCNA, CCNP, and CCIE certification tracks. You're probably wondering, what does this mean for current and new network engineers? To put it simply, automation and programmability are being integrated into network engineering, thus creating a new type of network professionals, referred to as *network developers*.

During the course of this chapter, you will learn how programmability and automation are being integrated into network engineering. Furthermore, you will gain knowledge to help you understand the various data formats of programming languages such as JSON, YAML, and XML.

In this chapter, we will cover the following topics:

- Understanding automation
- Understanding data formats
- Understanding APIs
- Understanding network configuration management
- Understanding intent-based networking

# Understanding automation

Automation is any process that is self-driven without the need for human intervention. In many manufacturing plants around the world, machines (or robots) are used during the building and assembly process. Imagine a car manufacturer using machines that can operate on a 24/7/365 continuous schedule that is being controlled by a computer. The computer provides the instructions for the machines to interpret and execute on the manufacturing line. These machines are able to work continuously without the need to stop and rest, and they can perform jobs in a precise manner without errors or faults. Having machines in a production line removes the need for human workers as higher production output is achieved while reducing the risk of human error on the job.

Automation was most used within manufacturing plants, where it was more effective to implement machines to perform certain tasks and where the working environment may be hazardous to humans. Today, automation has been expanding to many industries, including **Information Technology (IT)**. An example is home automation, where you can use a Raspberry Pi with its native operating system and the Python programming language, along with a few other components, to automate various processes within the home. Automation is such an awesome topic to learn about, especially as many tasks within our jobs in network engineering and even other areas of IT can benefit a lot from it.

Have you wondered how one system is able to communicate with another system? Let's use a scenario where the computer system is managing the machines that build cars on a production line. Both the computer system and the machines are different systems altogether – they are not designed with the same operating system or applications, so natively, they are not able to work together. From our point of view, it would seem the computer system is able to communicate fluently with the machines and vice versa, as they are executing the tasks as coordinated by the computer. When the computer sends instructions to the machines, they can connect all the instructions that are received and then use them to perform a given action. The computer must send the instructions using a structured **data format**, which will contain all the information the machines need to understand for the task and to perform their jobs. In the next section, you will learn about these data formats in detail.

# Understanding data formats

Let's imagine there are two different systems on a network, such as a computer and a router. The computer wants to share data with the router but since these are two different devices altogether, the router may not understand or be able to interpret the message it receives from the computer. To solve this issue, data formats are used to ensure the data that is being exchanged between the systems is presented in a format that is easily understood by another system. Think of a data format as two people who both speak different languages using a common language such as English so that the information that's being exchanged can be easily understood by both.

Data formats go a step further to ensure computers, network devices, and applications are all able to understand data that is being shared between them. As an example, let's take a look at a simple web page written in the **Hypertext Markup Language** (**HTML**), as shown in the following screenshot:

```html
1   <!DOCTYPE html>
2
3   <html lang="en" xmlns="http://www.w3.org/1999/xhtml">
4   <head>
5       <meta charset="utf-8" />
6       <title>TEST Web Page</title>
7   </head>
8   <body>
9       <h1> This is the Heading for the webpage</h1>
10      <p>This page is simply used to demonstrate HTML coding </p>
11  </body>
12  </html>
```

Figure 15.1 – HTML code

HTML is known as one of the standard markup languages used to create web pages. The data format of HTML ensures an application such as a web browser can read and understand the data easily. Additionally, being a structured data format allows us humans to read and understand most of the data, as shown in the preceding snippet. Notice how the data is presented between tags (elements) and that the title of the web page is placed between the `<title></title>` tags. This format is used throughout the remainder of the HTML code and is an example of a structured data format.

The following screenshot shows how the preceding HTML code is rendered within a web browser:

Figure 15.2 – HTML web page

Data formats are very important to understand as they play a vital role in network automation and programmability. The following are various data formats that are used in many computer applications to assist with automation and programmability:

- **eXtensible Markup Language (XML)**
- **JavaScript Object Notation (JSON)**
- **YAML Ain't Markup Language (YAML)**

These data formats are not just for systems and applications to understand, but being a structured data format also allows humans to read and interpret the data and values just as the system does.

Data formats use the following rules and structures:

- JSON, XML, and YAML use a key-value pair to represent data. `key` is always on the left and it is used to identify the data. `value` is always on the right and the value is the actual data itself. Additionally, the key and value are always separated using a colon (`:`) in the form of `key:value`.

- Similar to programming languages, various syntaxes are used with data formats. These are square braces `[]`, curve braces `()`, curly braces `{}`, commas, quotation marks, whitespaces, and even indentations.

- The objects within a data format can be characters (a-z) or strings such as words, lists, and arrays.

Over the next few sections, you will learn and understand the characteristics of JSON, XML, and YAML and how data is formatted using each of these data formats.

# eXtensible Markup Language

The XML data format is designed for the internet as it closely resembles HTML. The challenge with formatting data using XML is in the difficulty it presents to us as humans in reading and understanding the data. This is because the XML data format was really designed to transport or carry data from one system to another, not to present or display it to humans.

The following are the important guidelines that should be used when formatting data with XML:

- XML uses tags to structure its data. These tags use the following format: `<key> value </key>`.

- XML has the capability to use attributes with a key-value pair, such as `<key name="MyName"> value </key>`.

- All whitespaces used within XML data are ignored.

- Both configuration files and websites' sitemaps use XML.

> **Tip**
> If you're interested in learning more about the XML data format, please see the relevant page on the W3 Schools site at `https://www.w3schools.com/xml/default.asp`.

The following snippet shows a simple note written in the XML data format:

```
1   <?xml version="1.0" encoding="UTF-8" ?>
2   <note>
3       <to>Alice</to>
4       <from>Bob</from>
5       <heading>CCNA Study Group</heading>
6       <body>We have received a new assignment.</body>
7   </note>
```

Figure 15.3 – XML data format

As shown in the preceding snippet, on each line, the values are placed between their corresponding keys. Additionally, some lines within the data format are indented to improve readability by humans, but this is not mandatory for systems and applications. XML is also used to store, transfer, and read data between systems and applications.

## JavaScript Object Notation

JSON is another human-readable data format that is used by systems and applications to store, transfer, and read data. JSON has gained a lot of popularity due to its use cases with many web services and **Application programming interfaces** (**APIs**) to retrieve data from publicly accessible devices.

To better understand the JSON data format, let's take a look at the output from the show interface GigabitEthernet 0/1 command on a Cisco IOS router:

```
GigabitEthernet0/1 is up, line protocol is up (connected)
   Description: Connected to Wide Area Network (WAN)
   Internet address is 172.16.1.1/24
```

The preceding output is provided via the **command-line interface** (**CLI**) we are accustomed to when working with Cisco devices. The preceding output can be represented in JSON data format as follows:

```
1   {
2       "ietf-interfaces:interface": {
3           "name": "GigabitEthernet0/1",
4           "description": "Connected to Wide Area Network (WAN)",
5           "enabled": true,
6           "ietf-ip:ipv4": {
7               "address": [
8                   {
9                       "ip": "172.16.1.1",
10                      "netmask": "255.255.255.0"
11                  }
12              ]
13          }
14      }
15  }
```

Figure 15.4 – JSON data format

As shown in the preceding snippet, each key-value pair contains a different piece of data about the device's interface such as its name, its description, whether the interface is enabled or disabled, and the IP address and subnet mask.

To better understand how data is formatted in JSON, let's take a look at the following characteristics:

- JSON uses a hierarchical tree structure that contains nested values and objects.

- JSON uses curly braces { } to contain/hold objects.

- JSON uses square braces [] to contain/hold arrays. An array is used to represent a list of data in programming. An example of a list is a shopping list.

- Data represented in JSON is written using a *key-value* pair. These key-value pairs are written in the key: "value" format. A colon is used to separate the key and the value.

- Whitespaces are ignored but used to improve human readability.

The following are key points to help you interpret JSON:

- All keys are written within double quotation marks. Values must be either other objects, arrays, strings, numbers, or Boolean expressions. The following is an example of a key-value pair in JSON:

```
{ "certification":"CCNA 200-301" }
```

Since the key-value pair is also enclosed in curly braces, the entire format is known as a JSON object.

- You can have more than one key-value pair within a single object. A comma is used to separate each key-value pair from the others.

- A key may contain more than one value. Think of it like a list of items for shopping – in the programming world, this is known as an **array**. An array is defined as an ordered list of values enclosed in square braces []. Each value within a key is separated by a comma. Each array within an object is also separated by a comma.

The following is an example of a list of IT certifications represented in JSON:

```
1   {
2     "ITCerts":[
3       {
4         "Networking":"Cisco Certified Network Associate"
5       },
6       {
7         "Cybersecurity":"Cisco Certified CyberOps Associate"
8       },
9       {
10        "NetworkDeveloper":"Cisco Certified DevNet Associate"
11      }
12    ]
13  }
```

Figure 15.5 – An array in JSON

From the preceding snippet, we can determine the following:

- The key in this code is **ITCerts**.
- Square braces [] are used to create an array (a list) of three objects. These three objects are **Networking**, **Cybersecurity**, and **NetworkDeveloper**.
- Each object is enclosed with a curly brace {} and separated by a comma. The last object within the array does not end with a comma simply because it's the last item on the list.
- Each object contains one key-value pair.

> **Tip**
>
> If you're interested in learning more about the JSON data format, please see the following page on the W3 Schools site at `https://www.w3schools.com/js/js_json_intro.asp`.

As you may have noticed with JSON, it's another human-readable data format for representing and exchanging data between systems and applications.

## YAML Ain't Markup Language

YAML is another human-readable data format that is also used to store, transfer, and read data between systems and applications. The following are the characteristics of YAML:

- YAML uses a very minimalistic format, thus making it super easy to read and write.
- YAML uses indentations to define the data structure without the need for commas or braces of any kind.

- Whitespaces are used to define the structure of the YAML file.

- YAML uses a dash (-) to represents a list of items within an array.

- It's newer than XML and JSON and is gaining in popularity.

Let's take a look at the following JSON data:

```
 1  {
 2    "ITCerts":[
 3      {
 4        "Networking":"Cisco Certified Network Associate"
 5      },
 6      {
 7        "Cybersecurity":"Cisco Certified CyberOps Associate"
 8      },
 9      {
10        "NetworkDeveloper":"Cisco Certified DevNet Associate"
11      }
12    ]
13  }
```

Figure 15.6 – JSON data format

Now, let's take a look at the same data written in YAML format, as follows:

```
 1  ITCerts:
 2    - Networking: Cisco Certified Network Associate
 3    - Cybersecurity: Cisco Certified CyberOps Associate
 4    - NetworkDeveloper: Cisco Certified DevNet Associate
```

Figure 15.7 – YAML data format

Notice how key-value pairs written in YAML do not use any commands or quotation marks and that each object within the array is indicated using a dash (-).

> **Tip**
> If you're interested in learning more about the YAML data format, please see the following page: https://docs.ansible.com/ansible/latest/reference_appendices/YAMLSyntax.html.

YAML has become the preferred data format in the networking industry, simply because it is very easy to understand for humans and systems alike.

Having completed this section, you have gained the essential skills to interpret various data formats such as XML, JSON, and YAML. In the next section, you will discover the vital role that APIs play in a network, especially in network development and operations.

# Understanding APIs

An API allows data formats to be shared between different systems or devices. APIs simply allow an application to send and retrieve data from another system. APIs are used almost everywhere, from cloud services such as Microsoft Azure and Amazon's AWS to social media platforms such as Facebook.

To understand how APIs operate, let's imagine you visit your favorite restaurant to have a dine-in dinner with your family or significant other. At the restaurant, you are given a menu so that you can choose your meal before it's prepared in the kitchen. As a customer, you won't be allowed to visit the kitchen to retrieve your meal when it's ready – a waiter or waitress is assigned this role. When you (the user) are ready to place your order, the request is made via the waiter/waitress (API), which is known as an **API call**. The waiter/waitress then goes to the kitchen with your order (the request). When the food (data) is ready, the waiter/waitress (API) delivers it to you (the response).

The following diagram shows the concept of an API retrieving data from a system for a user:

Figure 15.8 – API operations

You can think of an API as a sort of messenger that's used to request and retrieve data from a system or an application. When one system requests information from another system, an API call is used to make the request. Now, let's look at the different types of APIs.

# Types of APIs

Various types of APIs are used for specific scenarios. Each type of API has its own unique purpose and role. The following is a list of various types of APIs:

- **Open/public APIs**: Open or public APIs are designed to be used without any restrictions on a system. An example of a public API is the YouTube Data API, which allows a person to add YouTube functionality to their application or website.

- **Internal/private APIs**: An internal or private API is used within an organization by its employees. An example of this is an internal API that can allow authorized persons from the sales team to access/retrieve internal sales information on their smart devices.

- **Partner APIs**: This type of API is used between different organizations or companies. An organization is given authorization (permission from another company) to use the API to retrieve data from their application or system. As an example, your smartphone may have a weather widget that uses an API to retrieve weather forecast data from an online server.

Next, we will take a dive into **Representational State Transfer** (**REST**) APIs.

## RESTful APIs

A REST API uses HTTP to send or retrieve data for the system or application. Before diving in further, it's important to understand the fundamentals of HTTP communication between a client device such as a computer and the web server. For a client device to interface with a web server, a standard web browser is required to allow the user to view web pages in a human-readable format. When a user wants to view a web page, the user opens their preferred web browser, which then uses either HTTP or **HTTP Secure** (**HTTPS**) to request (**HTTP GET**) the web page from the web server.

The following diagram shows a client machine requesting a web page from a server:

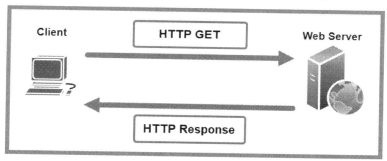

Figure 15.9 – HTTP operation

When the server receives the **HTTP GET** message, it will respond with an **HTTP status code of 200** and return the web page to the client. HTTP uses various status codes that can be used during troubleshooting. However, an HTTP status code of 200 simply means the request is *successful* and that the server will provide the data.

REST APIs are types of API that operate on top of HTTP, which means it defines the rules and instructions that developers can use to execute tasks, such as requesting data or updating or modifying records on a system or application. All of this is done using HTTP protocol messages such as GET and POST.

> **Important Note**
> An **HTTP GET** message is used to **request** data from a device such as a server, while the **HTTP POST** message is used to **update** information on a server.

APIs that abide by the rules and guidelines of the REST structure are referred to as *RESTful APIs*. The following characteristics must be met for an API to be considered RESTful:

- A RESTful API uses a **client-server** model. The client device is typically the frontend, where the user can interface with the server. The server is responsible for backend operations such as hosting applications and servers, as well as storing data. The benefit of using this model is that it allows each device to operate independently from each other, meaning that either the client or the server can be replaced.

- RESTful APIs are **stateless** by nature. Being stateless means the server does not store any data between requests from any clients. All the session information, such as states, are stored only on the client machine. An example is if a client sends an API call to a server asking *What is the weather like today?*, and the server responds with the data. If the client sends a second API call, such as a follow-up to the previous request such as *Will it be hot or cold?*, the server will not be able to respond to the second request simply because it does not keep track of any states.

- RESTful APIs are considered to be **cacheable**. Since the server is unable to store any session states, information such as responses can be cached on the client-side simply to improve the overall performance of the communication between the clients and the server.

Since RESTful APIs use HTTP to request and respond to messages between systems, it's important to understand the various HTTP methods, such as POST, GET, PUT/PATCH, and DELETE. For HTTP to request a resource, it needs to know where the resource is located, such as a web page on a web server, which is referred to by a **Uniform Resource Identifier (URI)**. An example of a URI is https://www.netacad.com/courses/packet-tracer. Web services often support various data formats, such as the ones mentioned in the previous section; that is, XML, JSON, and YAML. When a client machine wants to request a web page, it will send an HTTP GET message to the URI and, if successful, the server will respond with the HTTP 200 status code and the web page in HTML.

RESTful APIs use HTTP methods (verbs) such as POST, GET, PATCH, and DELETE to send and retrieve data formats between the client and server. These HTTP methods also correspond to RESTful operations such as **Create**, **Read**, **Update**, and **Delete** (CRUD).

The following table provides a side-by-side comparison of CRUD operations:

| HTTP Method | RESTful Operation | Description |
| --- | --- | --- |
| POST | Create | Allows a client to create data on the server. |
| GET | Request | Allows a client to request data from a server. |
| PUT/PATCH | Update | Allows a client to update data on a server. |
| DELETE | Delete | Allows a client to delete data from a server. |

Figure 15.10 – CRUD

When a client machine requests (HTTP GET) data from a system such as a server, as long as the client uses a properly structured JSON request, the server will respond with the JSON data. The JSON data in the response can then be presented in a client-side application.

For a RESTful API to interact perfectly with a system or application, it's important that the RESTful API correctly identifies web resources using a URI.

A URI has the following two specifications:

- **Uniform Resource Name (URN)**: A URN is used to identify only the namespace of a resource. An example of a resource is a web page, image, or document without specifying a protocol such as HTTP or HTTPS. An example of a URN is `www.cisco.com/c/en/us/index.html`.

- **Uniform Resource Locator (URL)**: A URL is a bit similar to a URN, except that it is used to specify the location of a resource on a network and specifies a protocol. There are many application layer protocols such as HTTP, HTTPS, FTP, SFTP, and so on. An example of a URL is `https://www.cisco.com/c/en/us/index.html`.

Additionally, a URI is made up of the following components:

- **Protocol (scheme)**: The protocol simply defines the application layer protocol that is used by an application to access a resource. Examples of protocols are HTTP and HTTPS.

- **Hostname**: The hostname simply defines the **Fully Qualified Domain Name (FQDN)**, such as `www.cisco.com`.

- **Path and filename**: The path and filename identify the location and name of the resource. An example of a path and filename is `/c/en/us/training-events/training-certifications/certifications/associate/ccna.html`.

- **Fragment**: A fragment identifies a specific area on a web page. An example of a fragment is `#~exams`.

The following is an example of a URI containing all the components mentioned here:

```
https://www.cisco.com/c/en/us/training-events/training-
certifications/certifications/associate/ccna.html#~exams
```

If you click or visit the preceding URI, it will carry you to the examination section of the CCNA page on the Cisco website.

As another example, the following shows a RESTful API request being sent from a client to Cisco DNA Center to request data on any interface with an IPv4 address of 10.10.22.253. This URI is as follows:

```
https://sandboxdnac.cisco.com/dna/intent/api/v1/interface/
ip-address/10.10.22.253
```

The server responded in JSON data format, thus providing the following response:

```
1  {
2      "response": [
3          {
4              "pid": "ASR1001-X",
5              "deviceId": "1cfd383a-7265-47fb-96b3-f069191a0ed5",
6              "portName": "TenGigabitEthernet0/0/0",
7              "ifIndex": "1",
8              "mediaType": "unknown",
9              "speed": "10000000",
10             "status": "up",
11             "adminStatus": "UP",
12             "macAddress": "00:c8:8b:80:bb:00",
13             "duplex": "FullDuplex",
14             "interfaceType": "Physical",
15             "ipv4Address": "10.10.22.253",
16             "ipv4Mask": "255.255.255.252",
17             "isisSupport": "false",
18             "mappedPhysicalInterfaceId": null,
19             "mappedPhysicalInterfaceName": null,
20             "nativeVlanId": null,
21             "ospfSupport": "false",
22             "portMode": "routed",
23             "portType": "Ethernet Port",
24             "serialNo": "FXS1932Q1SE",
25             "voiceVlan": null,
26             "lastUpdated": "2020-06-30 13:37:16.891",
27             "series": "Cisco ASR 1000 Series Aggregation Services Routers",
28             "description": "Uplink to WAN Distribution - main-switch ten 1/1/1",
29             "className": "EthrntPrtclEndpntExtndd",
30             "vlanId": "0",
31             "instanceTenantId": "5dc444d31485c5004c0fb20b",
32             "instanceUuid": "15fe6fc3-f6e7-45d8-94f9-e89a0bdba9b1",
33             "id": "15fe6fc3-f6e7-45d8-94f9-e89a0bdba9b1"
34         }
35     ],
36     "version": "1.0"
37  }
```

Figure 15.11 – Response in JSON data format

Cisco DNA Center returned all data about the interface that was assigned the specific IPv4 address, as stated in the URI. As shown in the preceding snippet, you can read and interpret almost all the information presented in JSON, simply because JSON is a human-readable data format.

The RESTful API request consists of the following parts:

- **API server**: Identifies the API server within the URL. The API server is `https://sandboxdnac.cisco.com`.

- **Resources**: Identifies the resources that are being requested by the client, such as `/dna/intent/api/v1/interface/ip-address/10.10.22.253`.

- **Query**: The query is used to specify the data format and the data that the client is requesting from the server. A query can include the **format**, which indicates whether the request is XML, JSON, or YAML. Additionally, a query can contain a **key**, which is used to identify an API key to authenticate the client to the server. Lastly, the query may also contain **parameters**, which are used to send specific information from the client to the server. This helps the API know exactly what to return to the client.

> **Important Note**
> Systems that offer publicly accessible information, such as Google Maps, allow a user to generate a public API (key) on their platform to use the services. These keys provide a form of authentication between the client and the server, which creates a number of benefits. It allows the server to track the number of persons using the API, limit the number of requests being sent by users, capture and keep track of the data requested by the clients, and gather information about the people using the API.

For a user to make a RESTful API request to a system, the user can use one of the following methods:

- **Developer website**: Many online application vendors usually have a developer website where they often maintain and publish procedures, outlining how users can create and use their systems with APIs. An example is the Cisco DevNet website (`https://developer.cisco.com`), which contains a large amount of API documentation for various Cisco platforms.

- **POSTMAN**: This tool allows a user to interact with a system using various HTTP verbs to perform actions such as CRUD. POSTMAN also allows a user to construct and send RESTful API requests with additional query parameters such as keys and format type. To learn more about POSTMAN, please see `https://www.postman.com`.

- **Python**: This programming language allows a developer to integrate a RESTful API into their code to perform actions such as automation.

- **Network operating systems**: Network operating systems use various protocols such as `NETCONF` and `RESTCONF`, which allow a network developer to interact with a network device via an API. The `NETCONF` protocol allows a user to perform network configurations, while `RESTCONF` allows the application to format the data that's passed between the client and server machines.

> **Important Note**
> To learn more about **network programmability**, check out the free course on Cisco DevNet at `https://developer.cisco.com/video/net-prog-basics/`.

Having completed this section, you have gained the skills to identify and understand the purpose and role that RESTful APIs play when you're accessing data between different systems. In the next section, you will learn about configuration management tools.

# Understanding network configuration management

At the beginning of this chapter, we discussed automation and how it helps us, as network engineers, work more efficiently when configuring, deploying, and troubleshooting issues on a large network. An important factor with network automation is that it saves us a lot of time from performing manual tasks on our network devices. When becoming a network developer, it's important to understand how various configuration management tools can improve how we automate configurations on our switches, routers, firewalls, and many other network devices.

In a traditional scenario, a network engineer will access and manage a network device such as a router or switch via a CLI. This is how we all learned to manage our devices – if there is a change that needs to be made on the network, we need to log into the CLI and manually make this change. As this method has worked for many years and it's the primary method by which we do things, it's also vulnerable to human error, where a person may misconfigure a device, and it can equally be very time-consuming if the network engineer has to apply the same configurations to multiple devices. Sometimes, you may think that copying and pasting the configurations between devices is a form of automation, but in reality, it is still a manual and time-consuming task.

In *Chapter 10*, *Implementing Network Services and IP Operations*, we covered the functionality and use cases of the **Simple Network Management Protocol** (**SNMP**). This protocol allows us, as network engineers, to manage various devices on our network, such as desktops computers, servers, networking devices, and security appliances, all on an IP-based network. A network engineer will definitely need a **Network Management Station** (**NMS**), which will function as the SNMP manager to interact with the SNMP agents on the nodes (desktops, switches, and so on). With SNMP, we can update configurations on network devices; however, it's not recommended to use SNMP for such a task simply due to the security vulnerabilities that can be found within the protocol suite. SNMP is also used to retrieve information about devices, which can help networking professionals gather useful data such as statistics and performance details on devices. This makes SNMP better for network monitoring than automating device configuration.

With APIs, a network developer can quickly automate configurations and deploy devices more efficiently over a network. Imagine that, with APIs, you can use automation configuration tools to configure changes on multiple devices simultaneously, without having to manually log into each device individually. With configuration management tools, you can use RESTful APIs to automate configuration on all your devices within your organization. These tools will help you to maintain consistency between system and network device configurations, including security settings, IP protocol settings, interface configurations, and so on.

The following is a list of several configuration management tools:

- Ansible
- Chef
- Puppet

The following are the characteristics of Ansible:

- Created by Red Hat.
- Works with the **Python** programming language and **YAML** data format.

- It is **agentless**. This means an agent is not required to be installed or configured on a network device that you want to control. Being agentless allows the user to *push* configurations to a node on a network.

- You can manage any number of devices using Ansible. As the network grows, you can designate a dedicated machine to work as an **Ansible controller**. Since Ansible is agentless, any device can be a *controller* on the network.

- All the instructions are created using a **playbook**.

The following are the characteristics of Chef:

- Chef uses the **Ruby** programming language.

- An **agent** is required to be installed on the device you want to manage with Chef. Being agent-based, the node will *pull* configurations from the Chef master.

- The device that manages all the nodes or systems on a network is known as a **Chef master**.

- All the instructions are created in a **cookbook**.

The following are the characteristics of Puppet:

- Puppet uses the Ruby programming language.

- Puppet supports both *agent-based* and *agentless* nodes.

- A **Puppet master** is used to control all the systems and devices on the network.

- All instructions are written in the **manifest**.

Having completed this section, you have learned about various configuration management tools and how each tool is different from the other. In the next section, we will take a deep dive into **intent-based networking** (**IBN**) and Cisco's **Digital Network Architecture** (**DNA**) Center.

# Understanding intent-based networking

Over the course of this chapter, you have learned about many amazing technologies that all work together to help you, as a network engineer, automate many tasks on your enterprise network. In this section, we will discuss two additional pieces of technology that bring everything together for network automation. These are known as IBN and Cisco DNA Center.

In the past, network engineers would implement a concept known as a **Software-Defined Network (SDN)** to virtualize a network and provide a new method to offer network administration and management tasks. With SDNs, the goal was to ensure network operations tasks were made simple and streamlined for network engineers.

Within network devices, there are three logical planes that exist within the operating system. Each plane has a unique role and function on the network. The following list provides descriptions of each plane:

- **Management plane**: This plane is responsible for allowing an administrator to manage a device. As a typical network engineer, we would use various protocols such as **Secure Shell (SSH)**, HTTPS, **Trivial File Transfer Protocol (TFTP)**, and SNMP to help us manage our devices. This management plane simply defines how we can access a network device.

- **Data plane**: This plane is responsible for sending and receiving messages on a network device. It's like the forwarding plane on the device itself.

- **Control plane**: This plane controls the entire network device and how it operates. This is the brain of the device. Layer 2 and even Layer 3 forwarding mechanisms, routing protocols, IPv4 and IPv6 routing tables, **Spanning-Tree Protocol (STP)**, and so on all exist in the control plane.

Since each device has all these planes, each device can think and make forwarding decisions on their own while operating on a production network. As an example, an **Open Shortest Path First (OSPF)**-enabled router is able to make its forwarding decisions for inbound packets independently, and all OSPF-enabled routers within a single area are able to establish neighbor adjacencies in order to exchange information with each other. Enabling OSPF on a router does not happen automatically; a network engineer needs to configure each router on the network with OSPF, and then they will attempt to create neighbor adjacencies. With SDN, the controller-based network allows us to automate and manage the overall deployment and configuration of OSPF within the enterprise network.

To put it simply, we are using an **SDN controller** to manage the brain of all the network devices together. Therefore, the control plane moves from the switches, routers, firewalls, and so on to the SDN controller on the network. The SDN controller enables a centralized control plane for all the devices on the network, while the data plane remains on the network devices as they will need to forward Layer 2 and Layer 3 messages.

The following diagram shows the concept of an SDN controller acting as the centralized control plane for all the networking devices in a corporate environment:

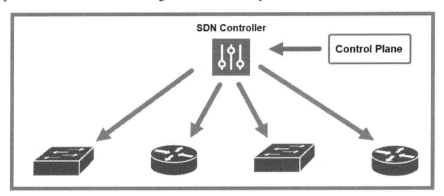

Figure 15.12 – SDN controller

The SDN controller can control all the nodes (switches, routers, and so on) by using a **Southbound Interface** (**SBI**). The SDN controller needs to use some type of method to actually manage the network devices. The following is a list of technologies that the controller uses:

- NETCONF
- OpenFlow
- A CLI
- SNMP
- OpFlex

The **Northbound Interface** (**NBI**) on the controller allows us, the network engineer, to access and control everything on the network using a *single pane of glass*. As a network engineer or network developer, you can access the NBI using either a **Graphical User Interface** (**GUI**) or RESTful APIs.

The following shows the NBI of a Cisco DNA Center instance on the Cisco DevNet platform:

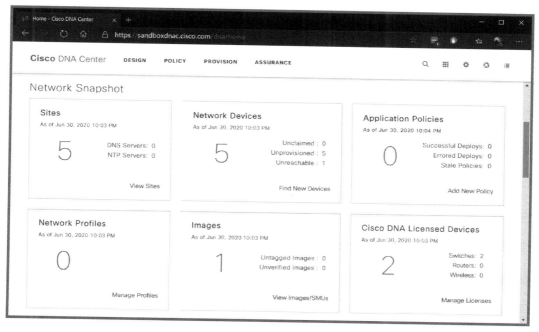

Figure 15.13 – Cisco DNA Center NBI

IBN is the latest technology that builds on top of SDN, which allows all manual and hardware-centric tasks and operations to be designed into a fully fledged automated system that is software-centric. IBN makes all this happen by using Cisco DNA Center. With IBN, you do not need to log into your routers or switches individually to configure **Access Control Lists** (**ACLs**) in order to allow or deny traffic between networks, or even manually configure the OSPF routing protocol on a group of routers. With Cisco DNA Center, as a network developer, you won't need to be worried too much about the actual CLI configuration that we are accustomed to. This is because we just need to tell Cisco DNA Center what our intent is, and it will make it happen. Cisco DNA Center, the centralized brain of the network, will automatically apply the configurations to all the devices to make our thoughts a reality regarding how we want the network to operate, hence the term *intent-based networking*.

IBN consists of the following three functions:

- **Translation**: This function is used to gather information about the business intent and translate it into policies. With this feature, a network engineer or developer can tell Cisco DNA Center their intention for the network and Cisco DNA Center will translate this into supporting policies for the network.

- **Activation**: This function takes the policies it received from the **Translation** function, then coordinates the policies and configures the network devices such as switches, routers, and so on to meet the intent of the business.

- **Assurance**: This function is used to continuously gather insights about the network, which will allow Cisco DNA Center to manage and perform any adjustments to the network as required.

The following diagram shows how these three functions all work together in Cisco DNA Center:

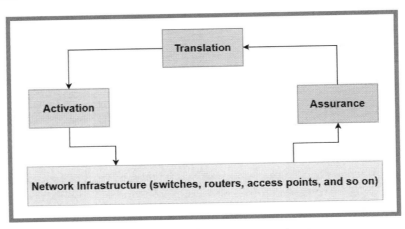

Figure 15.14 – The three functions of IBN

With IBN, the network infrastructure (including both physical and virtual devices) is known as the *fabric*. The term fabric is used to describe the entire topology of an enterprise network. The fabric is everything in a network, such as the devices, applications, and technologies used to forward traffic between networks and devices.

## Fabric, overlay, and underlay

With SDN and IBN, the Cisco DNA Center controller is not too concerned with how the network devices are interconnected or the protocols they are using to forward traffic through the network. In Cisco DNA Center, the controller uses an **overlay** to manage the logical topology.

The **overlay** reduces the number of network devices a network engineer must manually configure on the network, and it's also responsible for the services and how network devices forward traffic. To put it simply, a network engineer can specify their intent to Cisco DNA Center, which will translate it into policies, which are then applied to the devices on the network via the **Overlay Control Plane** to make it happen.

The following diagram shows a typical physical network topology without the **overlay**:

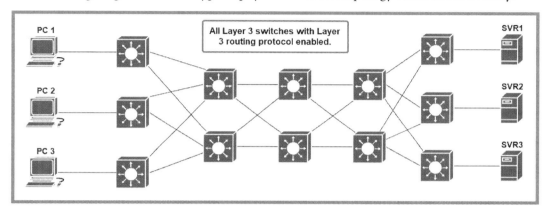

Figure 15.15 – Physical network topology

Based on the physical topology shown in the preceding diagram, there are multiple hops between **PC 1** and **SVR1**. If **PC 1** wants to communicate with **SVR1**, the traffic can take many paths. With an **overlay**, a tunnel known as a **Virtual Extensible LAN** (**VXLAN**) is established between both devices, so **PC 1** will see **SVR1** as a single hop away on the network.

The following diagram shows the concept of a VXLAN being established between **PC 1** and **SVR1** over the network:

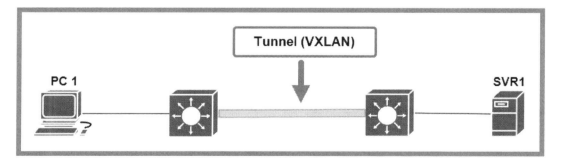

Figure 15.16 – VXLAN tunnel

With Cisco DNA Center, the controller makes it seem like **PC 1** and **SVR1** are on a network that only contains those two devices.

> **Important Note**
>
> You can think of the **overlay** as the area where the encapsulation protocols exist between a controller such as a **Wireless LAN Controller** (**WLC**) and its **Lightweight Access Points** (**LAPs**). Between the WLC and the LAPs, there's a **Control and Provisioning of Wireless Access Points** (**CAPWAP**) tunnel that allows the WLC to manage its LAPs.

The **underlay** is the actual physical network that provides connectivity for the **overlay**. This is typically the physical network topology and includes the switches, routers, servers, firewalls, and so on. Within the **underlay**, the control plane is responsible for forwarding traffic between devices on the topology.

Within a larger topology such as a data center, such technologies are used to improve traffic flow between endpoints in the network. Cisco uses their **Application Policy Infrastructure Controller** (**APIC**) to manage all the network devices within the data center network.

The following topology shows a typical data center network topology:

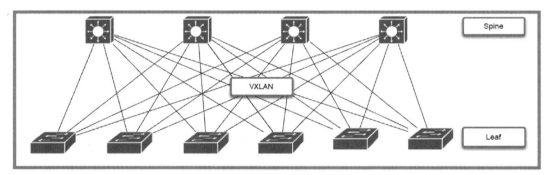

Figure 15.17 – Spine-leaf topology

The lower switches (leaves) are connected to the upper layer switches (spines) to create a full-mesh design. The lower layer is made up of access switches that operate as both the access and distribution layers, and each leaf switch is connected to every spine switch. This model, which is implementing a VXLAN, allows the network to scale easily and takes care of issues that are related to cloud deployments.

# Cisco DNA Center

Cisco DNA Center provides you with the following five key functions:

- **Design**: This function allows you to create an entire model of your intent network with buildings and office locations. You can also include both physical and virtual devices, LANs, WANs, and even cloud technologies.

- **Policy**: Policies allow the automation of network management, thus helping us reduce the overall cost and risk while rolling out new services quickly on our enterprise network.

- **Provision**: This feature enables Cisco DNA Center to provide new network services quickly and efficiently on the network. Whether it's a smaller or larger enterprise network, Cisco DNA Center gets it done.

- **Assurance**: This feature enables Cisco DNA Center to take a proactive approach toward monitoring and gathering intelligence on the network. Such information helps Cisco DNA Center predict potential network issues quickly, as well as ensure the policies that are applied to the **underlay** are aligned to the business intent.

- **Platform**: This feature allows a network engineer to use APIs to interact between the Cisco DNA Center and vendor devices.

> Tip
>
> To learn more about the Cisco DNA Center user interface, please be sure to check out the free Cisco DNA Center online sandbox from Cisco DevNet at `https://developer.cisco.com/docs/sandbox/#!networking`.

With Cisco DNA Center, you can implement IBN within your organization. As you have learned, with this controller, you can securely deploy devices on your network. Additionally, with Cisco DNA Center, you can implement the following solutions:

- **Software-Defined Access (SD-Access)**: With SD-Access, access to network resources is made available within a matter of minutes to users or devices, without security being a concern.

- **Software-Defined WAN (SD-WAN)**: This solution allows organizations to gain a better user experience when accessing their applications that are hosted in the cloud or even locally on an on-premises platform.

- **Cisco DNA Security**: Provides an entire 360-degree view of all real-time analytics and security intelligence on the network. This helps reduce the risk of threats while protecting your organization.

- **Cisco DNA Assurance**: Allows a network engineer to determine the cause of issues on the network quickly and provides recommended actions to resolve issues.

Having completed this section, you have learned about IBN, its operations, and the components required to make everything work together. Additionally, you have discovered how Cisco DNA Center becomes the brain behind all the operations of your network, as well as the functionalities it offers to improve everything on an enterprise network.

# Summary

Over the course of this chapter, you have learned about the new era of networking, where automation and programmability can greatly help network engineers improve the time they spend on deployment and configuration while reducing the need to manually perform repetitive tasks in their daily job. Additionally, you have gained the skills to understand various data formats such as XML, JSON, and YAML, as well as how they are used to request data from a system via APIs.

Furthermore, you have learned about the functions of various types of APIs and the components of RESTful APIs. You learned about the characteristics of configuration management tools such as Ansible, Chef, and Puppet and the role they play to assist us in network automation. Then, we covered how IBN and Cisco DNA Center can be used to help us fully automate our enterprise network using a controller-based model.

Lastly, I know the journey of preparing for the **Cisco Certified Network Associate (CCNA) 200-301** examination isn't an easy one and that there are many challenges along the road to success. I would personally like to thank you very much for your support by purchasing a copy of my book, and congratulations on making it to end while acquiring all these amazing new skills by learning about network engineering. I do hope everything you have learned in this book has been informative and is helpful in your journey toward learning how to implement and administer Cisco solutions, as well as prepare for the CCNA 200-301 certification.

# Questions

The following is a short list of review questions to help reinforce your learning and allow you to identify areas that require some improvement:

1. Which data format is commonly used to create web pages?

   A. JSON

   B. XML

   C. HTML

   D. YAML

2. Which data type is similar to HTML?

   A. JSON

   B. XML

   C. YAML

   D. Python

3. Which data type is the simplest to read and understand?

   A. JSON

   B. XML

   C. YAML

   D. Python

4. When using YAML, which syntax is used to represent a list of items?

   A. { }

   B. [ ]

   C. ( )

   D. -

5. While using JSON, which syntax is used to represent a list of items?

   A. { }

   B. [ ]

   C. ( )

   D. -

6.  Which type of API allows a vendor to access data within an organization's system?

    A. Partner

    B. Open

    C. Public

    D. Internal

7.  Which RESTful API operation is equivalent to an HTTP POST message?

    A. PUT

    B. Update

    C. Request

    D. Create

8.  Which component of a URI identifies a specific area on a web page?

    A. Path

    B. Filename

    C. Hostname

    D. Fragment

9.  Which configuration management tool uses a push function?

    A. Ansible

    B. Chef

    C. Python

    D. Puppet

10. Which function of Cisco DNA Center is responsible for configuring the network devices with the intention of the network engineer?

    A. Translation

    B. Activation

    C. Assurance

    D. Policy

# Further reading

The following links are recommended for additional reading:

- Ansible IOS modules: `https://docs.ansible.com/ansible/latest/modules/list_of_network_modules.html#ios`

- Cisco DNA Center Solution: `https://www.cisco.com/c/en/us/products/collateral/cloud-systems-management/dna-center/nb-06-dna-center-so-cte-en.html?oid=sowen000306`

- Learn JSON: `https://www.w3schools.com/js/js_json_intro.asp`

- YAML basics: `https://docs.ansible.com/ansible/latest/reference_appendices/YAMLSyntax.html`

# 16
# Mock Exam 1

## Questions

1. Which of the following network protocols are implemented in all modern-day devices?

   A. OSI Model

   B. TCP/IP

   C. AppleTalk

   D. IPX

2. Which technology would you use to extend a branch office network to another location many miles away?

   A. Switch

   B. WLAN

   C. Router

   D. WAN

3.  On which layer of TCP/IP does a segment exist?

    A. Transport

    B. Data Link

    C. Application

    D. Network

4.  Which layer of TCP/IP is responsible for data formatting?

    A. Application

    B. Presentation

    C. Transport

    D. Network

5.  Where is the operating system located on a Cisco router?

    A. NVRAM

    B. HDD

    C. Flash

    D. SSD

6.  What is the default method to access a new Cisco switch?

    A. VTY

    B. Console

    C. AUX

    D. Management IP address

7.  An IPv4 address is made up of how many bits?

    A. 28

    B. 30

    C. 48

    D. 32

8. You have interconnected many **Access Points (APs)** onto the same corporate LAN. This type of wireless network is known as which of the following?

A. BSS

B. ESS

C. SSID

D. WLAN

9. Which command is used to create a VLAN?

A. `vlan 10`

B. `vlan sales`

C. `vlan number 10`

D. `vlan name sales`

10. Where are VLANs stored on a switch?

A. `Flash`

B. `startup-config`

C. `running-config`

D. `vlan.dat`

11. Packets that are discarded because they are less than 64 bytes in size and are smaller than the minimum packet size are referred to as which of the following?

A. CRC

B. Runts

C. Collision

D. Giants

12. Which is the default priority value found within a BPDU message?

A. `4096`

B. `32767`

C. `32769`

D. `32768`

13. Which of the following is a port role only in Rapid-PVST+?

    A. Listening

    B. Blocking

    C. Discarding

    D. Forwarding

14. The Spanning-Tree Protocol is defined by which of the following frameworks?

    A. IEEE 802.1D

    B. IEEE 802.1Q

    C. IEEE 802.1X

    D. IEEE 802.11

15. Which command allows you to view the MAC address of a switch?

    A. show version

    B. show ip interface brief

    C. show running-config

    D. show device mac

16. If fault packets enter a switch interface, which counter will increase to inform the device administrator?

    A. Giants

    B. Input errors

    C. CRC

    D. Collision

17. Which network tool can be used to test end-to-end connectivity?

    A. nbtstat

    B. netstat

    C. traceroute

    D. ping

18. Which command allows you to see all routes on a router?

    A. show ip protocols

    B. show route

    C. show ip route

    D. show routing table

19. Which command is needed to enable IPv6 routing?

    A. ipv6 unicast-routing

    B. ipv6 route enable

    C. enable ipv6 route

    D. enable ipv6 unicast-routing

20. Which command allows you to create a default route to an ISP router that has an IP address of 192.0.2.1?

    A. ipv4 route 0.0.0.0 0.0.0.0 192.0.2.1

    B. ip route 0.0.0.0 0.0.0.0 192.0.2.1

    C. route 0.0.0.0 0.0.0.0.0 192.0.2.1

    D. ip route 0.0.0.0/0 192.0.2.1

21. The default administrative distance of OSPF is which of the following?

    A. 90

    B. 120

    C. 110

    D. 170

22. Which command allows you to view the link-state database of OSPF?

    A. show ip ospf neighbor

    B. show ip ospf

    C. show ip ospf neighbor detail

    D. show ip ospf database

23. What is the default Hello timer on an OSPF-enabled interface?

    A. 10

    B. 5

    C. 40

    D. 15

24. Which command allows you to verify the Hello and Dead timers on OSPF?

    A. show ip ospf database

    B. show ip ospf neighbor

    C. show ip protocols

    D. show ip ospf interface

25. You want to create a Static NAT map between an internal computer with an IP address of 192.168.1.10 and the edge router has a public IP of 192.0.2.10. Which of the following commands will you use to create the Static NAT map?

    A. ip nat inside source static 192.0.2.10 192.168.1.10

    B. ip nat inside source static 192.168.1.10 192.0.2.10

    C. ip nat inside source 192.0.2.10 192.168.1.10

    D. ip nat inside static 192.168.1.10 192.0.2.10

26. An organization has a single public IP address and many computers that require internet connectivity. Which type of NAT is recommended to allow the internal devices to connect to the internet?

    A. Dynamic NAT

    B. Static NAT

    C. Port Address Translation

    D. PAT with Static NAT

27. Which command allows you to verify recent NAT translations on a router?

    A. show ip nat

    B. show ip nat statistics

    C. show nat translations

    D. show ip nat translations

28. Which command allows you to determine whether Static NAT, Dynamic NAT, or PAT is being used on a router?

    A. show nat

    B. show ip nat statistics

    C. show nat translations

    D. show ip nat translations

29. You're a network administrator for a large organization and you are assigned a task to configure the time on all devices within the company. Which of the following methods is the most efficient to complete this task?

    A. Configure an NTP Server on the network and configure all other devices as NTP clients to synchronize time.

    B. Configure the time on each device within the network and ensure NTP is turned on.

    C. Configure the edge router as an NTP client only and all other devices will synchronize their time with the router.

    D. All of the above.

30. The device that has the most accurate time within a network is known as which of the following?

    A. Public NTP server

    B. Stratum 1

    C. Stratum 0

    D. NTP server

31. Which command is used to relay DHCP messages between machines on an IP network?

    A. ip dhcp helper

    B. ip helper-dhcp

    C. ip dhcp helper-address

    D. ip helper-address

32. Which application layer protocol is used to resolve a hostname to an IP address?

    A. ARP

    B. DNS

    C. DHCP

    D. ICMP

33. Which command is used to enable sequence numbers in Syslog messages?

    A. `service timestamps`

    B. `enable service-sequence`

    C. `enable service sequence-numbers`

    D. `service sequence-numbers`

34. Which network protocol allows you to perform monitoring on all of your networking devices?

    A. SNMP

    B. Syslog

    C. SolarWinds

    D. MIB

35. Which type of threat actor uses their hacking skills to perform malicious actions to serve a social or political agenda?

    A. Script kiddie

    B. Hacktivist

    C. Grey hat hacker

    D. Black hat hacker

36. An object that takes advantage of a security weakness on a system is known as which of the following?

    A. Vulnerability

    B. Threat

    C. Exploit

    D. Hacker

37. Which type of malware holds your data hostage and asks for a ransom to release the data back to the victim?

   A. Worm

   B. Crypto-malware

   C. Trojan

   D. Ransomware

38. Which of the following AAA servers is compatible with mixed vendor devices?

   A. RADIUS

   B. AAA

   C. TACACS+

   D. ASA

39. Which command is used to accept only SSH inbound traffic on a network device?

   A. `transport ssh`

   B. `transport input ssh`

   C. `transport input all`

   D. `transport accept ssh`

40. Which is the recommended command to create a secure password to prevent access to privilege mode?

   A. `enable password cisco123`

   B. `enable password secret cisco123`

   C. `enable secret cisco123`

   D. `enable secret password cisco123`

41. Which command is used to encrypt all plaintext passwords automatically?

   A. `service password-secret`

   B. `service enable-password`

   C. `service encryption-password`

   D. `service password-encryption`

42. Which security mechanism can be used to prevent an attacker from flooding bogus frames into a switch?

    A. DHCP snooping

    B. IP source guard

    C. Port security

    D. Dynamic ARP inspection

43. An attacker is attempting to flip an interface on a switch into a trunk port. What can the network engineer do to prevent such an attack?

    A. `switchport mode trunk`

    B. `switchport mode access`

    C. `switchport nonegotiate`

    D. `switchport port-security`

44. Which of the following is true when port security is enabled on an interface?

    A. MAC addresses are automatically stored in the `running-config`.

    B. The default violation mode is `Restrict`.

    C. Sticky is enabled.

    D. Sticky is disabled.

45. Which wireless security standard uses the **Advanced Encryption Standard** (**AES**) for data encryption?

    A. WPA

    B. WPA2

    C. WPA3

    D. WEP

46. Which data format was designed for transporting data rather than its presentation?

    A. XML

    B. YAML

    C. JSON

    D. HTML

47. Which syntax does JSON use to hold an object?

     A. ( )

     B. []

     C. { }

     D. -

48. Which of the following syntax is used to represent a list of items in YAML?

     A. ( )

     B. -

     C. { }

     D. []

49. Which RESTful operation is used to request data on a server?

     A. GET

     B. Create

     C. Update

     D. Request

50. Using YAML, instructions are created in which of the following?

     A. JSON

     B. Cookbook

     C. Playbook

     D. Manifest

# 17
# Mock Exam 2

## Questions

1. A packet contains which of the following in its header?

   A. IP address

   B. MAC address

   C. Port numbers

   D. CRC

2. A switch uses which of the following to make its forwarding decision?

   A. Source IP address

   B. Destination MAC address

   C. Source MAC address

   D. Destination MAC address

3.  Which transport layer protocol does not provide any reassurance of a message being sent between a source and destination?

    A. TCP

    B. IP

    C. ICMP

    D. UDP

4.  What is the size of a MAC address?

    A. 128 bits

    B. 40 bits

    C. 48 bits

    D. 32 bits

5.  A network engineer wants to verify the MAC address on a Windows computer. Which command can the network engineer use to obtain such information?

    A. `ipconfig`

    B. `ipconfig /all`

    C. `ifconfig`

    D. `netstat`

6.  When a switch learns about a MAC address, where does the switch store the newly learned MAC addresses?

    A. `Running-config`

    B. `Flash`

    C. `RAM`

    D. `CAM`

7.  Which device is primarily used to filter malicious traffic between networks?

    A. Router

    B. Switch

    C. IPS

    D. Firewall

8.  A network engineer has deployed multiple **Access Points (APs)** at various branches of an organization. Which network component will help the network engineer to manage all the devices?

    A. Wireless LAN controller

    B. Implement each AP in autonomous mode

    C. Use a console cable

    D. Set up remote access using SSH

9.  In the Cisco 2-Tier architecture, the Collapsed Core layer is made up of which of the following layers (choose two)?

    A. Access

    B. Distribution

    C. Core

    D. Routers

10. Where is the startup-config file located on a Cisco IOS router?

    A. TFTP

    B. HDD

    C. RAM

    D. NVRAM

11. A network engineer has just received a new Cisco router. Which is the primary method used to access the device?

    A. GUI

    B. Console

    C. AUX

    D. VTY

12. Which command will show you a summary of all the interfaces on a Cisco device and their statuses?

    A. `show ip interface`

    B. `show interface brief`

    C. `show ip interface brief`

    D. `show interface ip brief`

13. Which of the following syntaxes allows you to configure a banner on a Cisco IOS device?

    A. `banner motd %Keep Out%`

    B. `banner %Keep Out%`

    C. `banner motd %Keep Out`

    D. `banner motd %Keep Out&`

14. Which command can you use to verify how long a switch has been powered on?

    A. `show router`

    B. `show clock`

    C. `show status`

    D. `show version`

15. Which of the following IP address is not routable on the internet?

    A. `172.33.1.4`

    B. `172.32.1.3`

    C. `172.31.1.23`

    D. `172.15.1.5`

16. An IPv4 address contains a total of how many bits?

    A. `8`

    B. `32`

    C. `48`

    D. `128`

17. What is the number of usable IP addresses in the network `172.16.1.0/28`?

    A. `14`

    B. `16`

    C. `254`

    D. `65,534`

18. Which of the following IP addresses belongs to the network `192.168.1.64/27` (choose two)?

    A. `192.168.1.97`

    B. `192.168.1.80`

    C. `192.168.1.126`

    D. `192.168.1.94`

19. Which of the following IPv4 addresses is assigned to a device automatically when a DHCP server is not present on the network?

    A. `169.254.1.5`

    B. `168.254.1.5`

    C. `192.168.1.5`

    D. `10.10.1.5`

20. Which IPv6 address is used when devices are communicating on the same local area network?

    A. Unique local

    B. Global unicast

    C. Link-local

    D. Anycast

21. Which of the following commands is used to enable IPv6 routing on a Cisco IOS router?

    A. `ipv6 routing`

    B. `ipv6 enable`

    C. `enable ipv6 routing`

    D. `ipv6 unicast-routing`

22. Which **Access Point (AP)** mode has the capability to switch traffic between an SSID and a **virtual LAN** (VLAN) if the CAPWAP tunnel is down?

    A. `Bridge`

    B. `FlexConnect`

    C. `Local`

    D. `Flex+Bridge`

23. Which type of hypervisor is installed directly on top of the hardware of a system?

    A. VirtualBox

    B. Type 2

    C. Type 1

    D. Type 0

24. Which type of cloud service provides the user with only the application's user interface?

    A. SaaS

    B. PaaS

    C. IaaS

    D. Private

25. Which type of cloud delivery model cloud infrastructure is owned by another organization that rents part of or the entire data center to others?

    A. Community

    B. IaaS

    C. Public

    D. Private

26. When a frame enters a switch interface, which of the following tags is inserted into the message?

    A. `IEEE 802.1X`

    B. `IEEE 802.1w`

    C. `IEEE 802.1D`

    D. `IEEE 802.1Q`

27. By default, how many VLANs exist on a Cisco IOS switch?

    A. `1`

    B. `5`

    C. `0`

    D. `2`

28. VLANs that belong to the extended range are stored where?

    A. `startup-config`

    B. NVRAM

    C. `running-config`

    D. `vlan.dat`

29. Which of the following commands will allow you to configure an interface to be an access port?

    A. `switchport mode access`

    B. `switchport access port`

    C. `switchport mode access enable`

    D. `switchport enable access`

30. Which of the following commands allows you to assign a VLAN to an access port?

    A. `switchport mode access vlan 10`

    B. `switchport vlan 10`

    C. `switchport access vlan 10`

    D. `switchport access mode vlan 10`

31. Which of the following commands allows you to configure a native VLAN on a trunk?

    A. `switchport trunk allowed vlan 99`

    B. `switchport trunk vlan 99`

    C. `switchport native vlan 99`

    D. `switchport trunk native vlan 99`

32. Which of the following is the default operating mode of a switch's interface?

    A. Access

    B. Trunk

    C. Dynamic desirable

    D. Dynamic auto

33. Which command is used to disable the trunking negotiation feature on a switch interface?

    A. `switchport mode trunk`

    B. `switchport mode access`

    C. `switchport nonegotiate`

    D. `no switchport nonegotiate`

34. When configuring inter-VLAN routing, which command is used to associate VLAN 10 with a sub-interface?

    A. `encapsulation 802.1q vlan 10`

    B. `encapsulation dot1q 10`

    C. `encapsulation vlan 10`

    D. `encapsulation dot1q vlan 10`

35. Which command allows you to view a summary of all the VLANs on a switch and their associated interfaces?

    A. `show running-config`

    B. `show interface vlan brief`

    C. `show vlan interface brief`

    D. `show vlan brief`

36. Which command will allow you to view a summary of the trunk interfaces on a switch?

    A. `show interfaces trunk`

    B. `show trunks`

    C. `show trunk interface`

    D. `show ip interface`

37. Which command is used to disable CDP entirely on a switch?

    A. `no cdp`

    B. `no cdp enable`

    C. `no cdp run`

    D. `no enable cdp`

38. Which CDP command will allow you to obtain the IP address of a directly connected Layer 3 device?

    A. `show cdp interface`

    B. `show cdp neighbors`

    C. `show cdp`

    D. `show cdp neighbors detail`

39. Which of the following commands is used to enable LLDP on a Cisco device?

    A. `lldp enable`

    B. `lldp run`

    C. `enable lldp`

    D. None of the above

40. Which of the following is an interface operating mode for LACP?

    A. Active

    B. Auto

    C. Desirable

    D. Enable

41. Which command allows you to verify whether an interface is experiencing any physical issues?

    A. `show interface status`

    B. `show ip interface`

    C. `show interfaces`

    D. `show version`

42. Packets that are discarded because they exceed the maximum packet size are known as?

    A. Collisions

    B. Runts

    C. Output errors

    D. Giants

43. Which of the following standards/frameworks are designed to prevent loops on a Layer 2 network?

    A. `IEEE 802.1Q`

    B. `IEEE 802.1D`

    C. `IEEE 802.1w`

    D. `IEEE 802.3`

44. A BPDU contains which of the following components (choose 3)?

    A. Extended System ID

    B. Priority

    C. Bridge ID

    D. MAC address

    E. Hostname

    F. Interface ID

45. By default, each switch uses which of the following default priorities?

    A. `32768`

    B. `32769`

    C. `4096`

    D. `0`

46. Which version of Spanning-Tree is enabled by default on a Cisco switch?

    A. STP

    B. RSTP

    C. PVST+

    D. Rapid-PVST+

47. Which of the following port roles does not exist in PVST+?

    A. Listening

    B. Forwarding

    C. Learning

    D. Discarding

48. Which command allows you to enable Rapid-PVST+?

    A. `spanning-tree enable rapid-pvst`

    B. `spanning-tree mode rapid-pvst`

    C. `spanning-tree rapid-pvst enable`

    D. `enable rapid-pvst`

49. Which of the following commands can a network engineer use to ensure a switch is elected as a Root Bridge on VLAN 20?

    A. `spanning-tree vlan 20 priority 4096`

    B. `spanning-tree vlan 20 priority 8192`

    C. `spanning-tree vlan 20 priority 4095`

    D. `spanning-tree vlan 20 priority 8193`

50. Which command when applied to an interface prevents BPDUs from entering?

    A. `enable spanning-tree bpduguard`

    B. `spanning-tree enable bpduguard`

    C. `spanning-tree bpduguard enable`

    D. `spanning-tree bpduguard`

51. Which factor does a Cisco router use to determine the most suitable route to a destination?

    A. Number of hops

    B. Administrative distance

    C. Bandwidth

    D. Metric

52. Which of the following routing protocols uses hop count as its metric?

    A. EIGRP

    B. OSPF

    C. BGP

    D. RIP

53. A static route has a default administrative distance of…?

    A. 1

    B. 0

    C. 90

    D. 5

54. What is the default dead timer on OSPF?

    A. 15

    B. 180

    C. 40

    D. 120

55. Which command allows you to verify the process-ID of OSPF?

    A. show ip ospf interface summary

    B. show ip protocols

    C. show ip interface

    D. show ip ospf interface

56. Which command allows you to verify the OSPF process-ID on a router?

    A. show ip route ospf

    B. show ip protocols

    C. show ospf

    D. None of the above

57. You want to advertise the network 192.168.1.0/24 using OSPF. Which of the following commands will you use?

    A. network 192.168.1.0 255.255.255.0

    B. network 192.168.1.0 0.0.0.255

    C. network 192.168.1.0 255.255.255.0 area 0

    D. network 192.168.1.0 0.0.0.255 area 0

58. You want to prevent OSPF messages from either entering or leaving a specific interface on a router. Which command will you use on the router?

   A. `passive-interface`

   B. `enable passive-interface`

   C. `passive-interface enable`

   D. `passive-interface default`

59. HSRPv2 uses which of the following multicast addresses to exchange messages with other HSRP-enabled devices on the network?

   A. `224.0.0.10`

   B. `224.0.0.5`

   C. `224.0.0.2`

   D. `224.0.0.102`

60. Which of the following commands is used to verify the HSRP status between Cisco devices?

   A. `show active`

   B. `show glbp`

   C. `show standby`

   D. `show hsrp`

61. Which of the following first hop redundancy protocols is not a Cisco proprietary protocol?

   A. GLBP

   B. VRRP

   C. HSRP

   D. All of the above

62. Which type of NAT allows an organization to map multiple private IP addresses onto a single public address?

   A. Port forwarding

   B. Static NAT

   C. Dynamic NAT

   D. PAT

63. Which of the following is used to create a static NAT map with the inside address 192.168.1.10 and the outside address 192.0.2.10?

    A. `ip nat inside source static 192.168.1.10 192.0.2.10`

    B. `ip nat outside source static 192.168.1.10 192.0.2.10`

    C. `ip nat inside source static 192.0.2.10 192.168.1.10`

    D. `ip nat outside source static 192.0.2.10 192.168.1.10`

64. Which of the following commands will allow you to see NAT translations on a router?

    A. `show ip nat statistics`

    B. `show nat translations`

    C. `show ip nat translations`

    D. `show nat statistics`

65. Which of the following protocols allows you to ensure time is synchronized on a network?

    A. DNS

    B. ICMP

    C. CDP

    D. NTP

66. Which of the following ports does a DHCP server use?

    A. 67

    B. 68

    C. 53

    D. 69

67. Which command allows you to configure a default gateway as part of a DHCP pool on a Cisco IOS router?

    A. `default-gateway`

    B. `default-router`

    C. `ip default-gateway`

    D. `ip default-router`

68. Which DNS record is responsible for resolving an IP address to a hostname?

   A. NS

   B. SVR

   C. PTR

   D. A

69. In Syslog, a severity name of *Error* has which of the following severity levels?

   A. 1

   B. 2

   C. 3

   D. 4

70. An SNMP manager uses which of the following messages to retrieve information about a network device?

   A. Retrieve

   B. TRAP

   C. SET

   D. GET

71. Anything with the motivation to cause harm or damage to a person, system, or network is known as a what?

   A. Risk

   B. Threat

   C. Vulnerability

   D. Exploit

72. Which type of cyber-attack is focused on tricking high-profile employees of an organization into revealing confidential information?

   A. Whaling

   B. Spear-phishing

   C. Pharming

   D. Vishing

73. Which of the following commands is used to enable AAA on a Cisco IOS router?

    A. `enable aaa-model`

    B. `enable aaa new-model`

    C. `aaa new-model`

    D. `enable aaa`

74. Which command ensures the router accepts only SSH inbound connections?

    A. `transport ssh`

    B. `transport only ssh`

    C. `transport ssh input`

    D. `transport input ssh`

75. Which type of ACL would you use to filter Telnet traffic?

    A. Standard ACL

    B. Inbound ACL

    C. Extended ACL

    D. Outbound ACL

76. Which of the following commands will allow you to assign an ACL on your remote access lines?

    A. `ip access-group`

    B. `access-class`

    C. `access-group`

    D. `ip access-class`

77. Which of the following commands will allow you to assign an ACL on an interface?

    A. `ip access-group`

    B. `access-class`

    C. `access-group`

    D. `ip access-class`

78. Which type of security appliance can be implemented to prevent malicious emails from entering your organizations?

A. Anti-virus

B. IPS

C. Firewall

D. ESA

79. An attacker is attempting to inject bogus frames into a switch. Which type of attack is the threat actor trying to perform?

A. Buffer overflow

B. CAM table overflow

C. Packet injection

D. DoS

80. Which security mechanism can be implemented to prevent a DHCP starvation attack?

A. `switchport port-security`

B. DAI

C. DHCP snooping

D. Shutting down the interface

81. Which of the following commands is used to automatically learn and store the source MAC address on an interface onto RAM?

A. `switchport port-security mac-address sticky`

B. `switchport port-security sticky`

C. `port-security mac-address sticky`

D. `switchport mac-address sticky`

82. Which of the following is the default violation mode for port security?

A. **Shutdown**

B. **Protect**

C. **Restrict**

D. **Administratively down**

83. Which of the following commands is used to enable DHCP snooping on a switch?

    A. `dhcp snooping`

    B. `enable ip dhcp snooping`

    C. `ip dhcp snooping`

    D. `enable dhcp snooping`

84. Dynamic ARP inspection is dependent on which of the following components?

    A. Port security

    B. The contents of the CAM table

    C. The ARP cache on the local switch

    D. The DHCP snooping binding table

85. Which of the following wireless security standards uses TKIP for its data encryption?

    A. WPA2

    B. WPA

    C. WEP

    D. WPA3

86. Which of the following data formats is the simplest to read and understand?

    A. JSON

    B. YAML

    C. HTML

    D. XML

87. Which of the following attributes is used to describe a RESTful API?

    A. Stateful

    B. Stateless

    C. Non-cacheable

    D. Easy to read

88. Which of the following configuration management tools requires an agent to be installed on the client device?

    A. Python

    B. Ansible

    C. Chef

    D. Puppet

89. Which of the following are functions of intent-based networking (choose two)?

    A. Translation

    B. Design

    C. Activation

    D. Policy

90. Within a data center, which component is used to manage all the networking devices?

    A. APIC

    B. Cisco DNA

    C. Ansible

    D. Cisco cloud

# Assessments

## Chapter 1

The following are the answers to the review questions:

1. B
2. D
3. C
4. B
5. B
6. B
7. A
8. C
9. D
10. B

## Chapter 2

The following are the answers to the review questions:

1. D
2. C
3. A
4. B
5. D
6. C

# Chapter 4

The following are the answers to the review questions:

1. D
2. C
3. A
4. B
5. D
6. A
7. B
8. C
9. D
10. B
11. C
12. B
13. AD
14. C

# Chapter 5

The following are the answers to the review questions:

1. B
2. D
3. C
4. A
5. B
6. B
7. D
8. C
9. A
10. D

# Chapter 6

The following are the answers to the review questions:

1. A
2. D
3. B
4. A
5. C
6. D

# Chapter 7

The following are the answers to the review questions:

1. A
2. A
3. B
4. D
5. B, C
6. B – False
7. B – False
8. D
9. D
10. C

# Chapter 8

The following are the answers to the review questions:

1. B
2. D
3. C
4. B
5. A

6.  C

7.  D

8.  B

9.  D

10. A

# Chapter 9

The following are the answers to the review questions:

1.  C

2.  A

3.  D

4.  B and D

5.  D

6.  B

7.  A

8.  C

9.  B

10. C

# Chapter 10

The following are the answers to the review questions:

1.  C

2.  D

3.  A

4.  B

5.  C

6.  D

7.  D

8.  B

9.  A

10. B

# Chapter 11

The following are the answers to the review questions:

1.  B

2.  C

3.  D

4.  A

5.  C

6.  D

7.  B

8.  A

9.  C

10. D

# Chapter 12

The following are the answers to the review questions:

1.  C

2.  A

3.  C

4.  B

5.  D

6.  A

7.  B

8.  C

9.  D

10. A

# Chapter 13

The following are the answers to the preceding practice questions:

1. D
2. B
3. C
4. A
5. D
6. C
7. A
8. B
9. C
10. A

# Chapter 14

The following are the answers to the review questions:

1. B
2. D
3. B
4. C
5. A
6. D
7. C
8. B
9. D
10. A

# Chapter 15

The following are the answers to the review questions:

1. C
2. B
3. C
4. D
5. B
6. A
7. D
8. D
9. A
10. B

# Chapter 16 – Mock Exam 1

The following are the answers to the questions from Mock Exam 1:

1. B
2. D
3. A
4. A
5. C
6. B
7. D
8. B
9. A
10. D
11. B
12. D
13. C

14. A

15. A

16. B

17. D

18. C

19. A

20. B

21. C

22. D

23. A

24. D

25. B

26. C

27. D

28. B

29. A

30. C

31. D

32. B

33. D

34. A

35. B

36. C

37. D

38. A

39. B

40. C

41. D

42. C

43. C

44. D

45. B

46. A

47. C

48. B

49. D

50. C

# Chapter 17 – Mock Exam 2

The following are the answers to the questions from Mock Exam 2:

1. A

2. B

3. D

4. C

5. B

6. D

7. D

8. A

9. B, C

10. D

11. B

12. C

13. A

14. D

15. C

16. B

17. A

18. B, D

19. A

20. C

21. D

22. B

23. C

24. A

25. C

26. D

27. B

28. C

29. A

30. C

31. D

32. D

33. C

34. B

35. D

36. A

37. C

38. D

39. B

40. A

41. C

42. D

43. B

44. A, C, D

45. A

46. C

47. D

48. B
49. A
50. C
51. B
52. D
53. A
54. C
55. B
56. B
57. D
58. A
59. D
60. C
61. B
62. D
63. A
64. C
65. D
66. A
67. B
68. C
69. C
70. D
71. B
72. A
73. C
74. D
75. C
76. B

77. A

78. D

79. B

80. C

81. A

82. A

83. C

84. D

85. B

86. B

87. B

88. C

89. A, C

90. A

# Other Books You May Enjoy

If you enjoyed this book, you may be interested in these other books by Packt:

**Learn Wireshark**

Lisa Bock

ISBN: 978-1-78913-450-6

- Become familiar with the Wireshark interface
- Navigate commonly accessed menu options such as edit, view, and file
- Use display and capture filters to examine traffic
- Understand the Open Systems Interconnection (OSI) model
- Carry out deep packet analysis of the Internet suite: IP, TCP, UDP, ARP, and ICMP
- Explore ways to troubleshoot network latency issues
- Subset traffic, insert comments, save, export, and share packet captures

**Network Automation Cookbook**

Karim Okasha

ISBN: 978-1-78995-648-1

- Understand the various components of Ansible
- Automate network resources in AWS, GCP, and Azure cloud solutions
- Use IaC concepts to design and build network solutions
- Automate network devices such as Cisco, Juniper, Arista, and F5
- Use NetBox to build network inventory and integrate it with Ansible
- Validate networks using Ansible and Batfish

# Leave a review - let other readers know what you think

Please share your thoughts on this book with others by leaving a review on the site that you bought it from. If you purchased the book from Amazon, please leave us an honest review on this book's Amazon page. This is vital so that other potential readers can see and use your unbiased opinion to make purchasing decisions, we can understand what our customers think about our products, and our authors can see your feedback on the title that they have worked with Packt to create. It will only take a few minutes of your time, but is valuable to other potential customers, our authors, and Packt. Thank you!

# Index

## Symbols

2.4 GHz
  versus 5GHz  189-192
2-Factor Authentication (2FA)  487
5 GHz
  versus 2.4 GHz  189, 190

## A

AAA servers
  RADIUS  505
  TACACS+  505
Access Control Entry (ACE)  564
Access Control Lists (ACLs)
  about  107, 391, 461, 562
  applying, on router  573
  best practices  571-573
  guidelines  571
  operations  564-568
  recommendations  572
  used, for securing VTY lines  583-588
  using, benefits  563
  wildcard masks  568
Access Point (AP)  42, 55, 56, 187
access ports  230, 233

Accounting  504
ACL placement  573
Adaptive Security Appliance (ASA)  52
Address Resolution Protocol
      (ARP)  46, 502
administration  151
Administrative Distance (AD)  330
Advanced Malware Protection (AMP)  603
Advanced Research Projects Agency
      Network (ARPANET)  20
adware  498
AMP for Endpoints  604
amplification  500, 501
amplitude  188
Anycast transmission  140
AP modes
  about  199
  bridge mode  199
  Flex+Bridge mode  199
  FlexConnect mode  199
  local mode  199
  monitor mode  199
  rogue detector mode  199
  SE-Connect mode  199
  sniffer mode  199
API call  670

Application Policy Infrastructure
    Controller (APIC)  684
Application Programming
    Interfaces (APIs)
  about  666, 670
  internal/private APIs  670
  partner APIs  671
  Representational State Transfer
    (REST) APIs  671
  types  670
ARP attack  615-618
ARP cache
  viewing, on Linux operating system  49
  viewing, on Microsoft Windows
    operating system  49
ARP Poisoning  617
ARP Reply message  48
ARP Request message  47
array  667
AS number (ASN)  124
assets  474-480
association  194
attenuation  40
Authentication  504
Authentication, Authorization,
    and Accounting (AAA)
  about  503-506
  implementing  506-509
authentication methods, wireless
    network security
  Open Authentication  647
  pre-shared key (PSK)  647
authentication methods, WPA3
  enterprise method  648
  personal method  648
Authorization  504

Automatic Private IP Addressing
    (APIPA)  145
automation
  about  662
  uses  662
Autonomous System Number (ASN)  346
Autonomous Systems (AS)  163, 346
auxiliary (AUX) port
  about  525
  securing  525-527
AUX line
  securing  525
availability  477

# B

Backup Designated Router (BDR)
  election process  358-360
bandwidth  458
bare-metal hypervisor. See also
    Type 1 hypervisor
Basic Service Area (BSA)  191
Basic Service Set (BSS)  194
Basic Service Set IDentifer (BSSID)  194
beacons  193
binary
  converting, into decimal  129-131
  decimal, converting into  132-136
BitLocker, on Windows 10
  reference link  476
bits  36, 38
bits per second (bps)  458
black hat hacker  481
boot sector virus  496
Border Gateway Protocol (BGP)  124
BPDUguard
  configuring  291-293

Bridge Protocol Data Units (BPDUs)
  about 273, 274, 618
  Bridge ID 273
  Extended system ID 273
  MAC address 273
Bring-Your-Own-Device (BYOD) 56
broadcast domain 228
broadcast storm 272
broadcast transmission 138, 139
buffer 502
buffer overflow 502, 503
burned-in address (BIA) 36

# C

cable categories 39
CAM table 48
CAM Table Overflow attack 608
Carrier-Sense Multiple Access
     with Collision Detection
     (CSMA/CD) 44, 45
CDP attacks 619, 620
Central Processing Unit (CPU) 90
central reference point 286
Certificates Authority (CA) 488
channel bonding 192
Chef master 678
CIA triad
  about 475
  implementing 477, 478
Cisco
  URL 27, 436
Cisco 2 Tier architecture 61, 62
Cisco 3 Tier
  architecture 63, 64
  characteristics 65
  hierarchy, benefits 65

Cisco 3 Tier model
  characteristics 65
Cisco Access layer switches
  URL 61
Cisco AnyConnect Secure
     Mobility Client 543
Cisco autonomous wireless
     architecture 196
Cisco Certified Network
     Associate (CCNA) 27
Cisco Certified Network Associate
     (CCNA) certification 435
Cisco Certified Network Professional
     (CCNP) 347, 349
Cisco cloud-based wireless
     architecture 197
Cisco devices
  access control 520
Cisco Devnet
  URL 215
Cisco Digital Network
     Architecture (DNA) 58
Cisco Discovery Protocol (CDP)
  about 255, 619
  characteristics 257
  enabling 256, 257
Cisco distribution layer switch
  URL 62
Cisco DNA Assurance 686
Cisco DNA Center
  assurance function 685
  design function 685
  platform function 685
  policy function 685
  provision function 685
  used, for implementing solutions 685
Cisco DNA Security 686

Cisco Internetwork Operating
    System (Cisco IOS)
  about  90
  configuring  96-98
  network, setting up  98
Cisco IOS devices
  accessing  92-96
  boot process  90-92
  SSH, enabling  532-535
  starting with  90
Cisco IOS privilege levels
  URL  523
Cisco IOS router
  IPv6, configuring on  168, 170
Cisco lab environment
  building  71
  Cisco Packet Tracer  71-76
  Graphical Network Simulator
    3 (GNS3)  77
  physical lab  89
Cisco network
  objectives  99
  Rapid-PVST+, implementing  288-291
  setting up  98, 99
Cisco network, setting up
  administrative access, securing  108-111
  banner, setting  111, 112
  Cisco IOS, navigating  100-102
  configurations, saving  116, 117
  console, configuring to use
    local user accounts  115
  domain lookup, disabling  116
  hostname, changing  103, 104
  IOS version, checking  116, 117
  IP addresses, configuring on
    Cisco devices  104-107
  plaintext passwords, encrypting  116

  secure remote access, setting up  112
  Secure Shell (SSH), configuring  114, 115
  Switch Virtual Interface (SVI),
    configuring  108
  Telnet, setting up  113, 114
Cisco Packet Tracer
  about  71, 72
  advantages  72
  using  72-75
Cisco router
  Telnet, configuring  528-532
Cisco's DHCP configurations
  about  429
  addresses, excluding  429
  DHCP pool, creating  429, 430
Cisco SNMP Object Navigator tool  452
Cisco Validated Design (CVD)
  about  59
  reference link  59
Cisco Web Security Appliance (WSA)
  about  605
  capabilities  605
Cisco wireless architectures
  about  195
  autonomous  196
  cloud-based  197
  Split-MAC  198
Cisco wireless LAN controller (WLC)  56
Cisco WLC GUI
  accessing  201
  configuring  201, 202
Class-Based Weighted Fair
    Queuing (CBWFQ)  461
Class of Service (COS)  464
clientless VPN  544

cloud computing
   about  213, 215
   benefits  214
   cloud delivery models  216
   cloud services  215
   disadvantages  215
cloud delivery models, cloud computing
   about  216
   community cloud  217
   hybrid cloud  217
   private cloud  216
   public cloud  217
cloud services, cloud computing
   about  215
   IaaS  216
   PaaS  216
   Saas  215
collision domain  177
Command-Line Interface (CLI)  281
Commercial National Security
      Algorithm (CNSA)  648
Common Vulnerability Scoring
      System (CVSS)  494
confidentiality  476
Confidentiality, Integrity and
      Availability (CIA)  475
congestion  458
connection-oriented protocol  33
console access
   securing  520
console port
   securing  520-524
Content Addressable Memory
      (CAM)  46, 281, 607
contention-based network  44
Control and Provisioning of Wireless
      Access Points (CAPWAP)  198

controller ports, types
   console port  200
   distribution system port  200
   management interface  201
   redundancy port  201
   service port  200
counter types, on interface
   collisions  186
   Cyclic Redundancy Check (CRC)  186
   giants  186
   input errors  186
   late collisions  186
   output errors  186
   runts  186
Create, Read, Update, and
      Delete (CRUD)  672
crypto-malware  497
cyber-attacks
   about  496
   amplification and reflection  500, 501
   buffer overflow  502, 503
   Denial of Service (DoS)  499, 500
   malware  496
   Man-in-the-Middle (MiTM) attack  501
   reconnaissance  498
   spoofing  499
cyber warfare
   reference link  481
Cyclic Redundancy Check
      (CRC)  35, 186, 477

**D**

daisy chaining  60
data at rest  475

data formats
  about 663, 664
  eXtensible Markup Language
    (XML) 664
  JavaScript Object Notation (JSON) 666
  rules and structure 665
  YAML Ain't Markup Language
    (YAML) 668
datagram 27
data in motion 475
data in use 475
data leakage protection (DLP) 604
Data Link Header 36
data VLAN 230
Dead timer 353
decimal
  binary, converting into 129-131
  converting, into binary 132-136
Deep Packet Inspection (DPI) 52
default route 308, 328
Defense Advanced Research Projects
    Agency (DARPA) 21
Defense in depth (DiD)
  about 603
  endpoint protection 603
delay (latency) 459
Demilitarized Zone (DMZ) 53
denial of service (DoS)
  preventing 613
Denial of Service (DoS) 477, 499, 500
Department of Defense (DoD) 20
Designated Router (DR)
  about 356, 357
  election process 358-360
  Router ID 357, 358
developer website 675

DHCP relay
  about 430, 431
  configuring 432-435
DHCP services
  configuring 432-435
DHCP snooping
  about 634
  configuring 635
  implementing 635-640
DHCP snooping binding table 634
DHCP spoofing attack 614
DHCP starvation attack 613
Differentiated Services Code
    Point (DSCP) 464
Differentiated Services (DS) 127, 165
Differentiated Services or DiffServ (DS)
Diffie-Hellman (DH) 545
Diffusing Update Algorithm (DUAL) 316
Digital Attack Map
  URL 602
directly connected static routes 326, 327
discovery protocols
  Cisco Discovery Protocol (CDP) 255
  enabling 255
  Link-Layer Discovery
    Protocol (LLDP) 257
Distributed Denial of Service (DDoS) 500
Domain Name System (DNS)
  about 21, 123, 140, 435-437
  configuring 439-441
  record types 438, 439
  root servers 437, 438
dual stacking 340
Dynamic ARP inspection (DAI)
  about 641
  configuring 641
  implementing 642-644

Dynamic Host Configuration
    Protocol (DHCP)
  about 426
  DHCP Acknowledgement 428
  DHCP Offer message 427
  DHCP Request 428
  Discover message 427
  Discover packet 427
  of Cisco 429
  operations 426-429
  request message 428
dynamic NAT
  about 397, 398
  configuring 398, 399
  implementing 409-412
dynamic routing
  about 345, 346
  protocols 346
dynamic routing protocols
  exterior gateway protocols (EGP) 346
  interior gateway protocols (IGP) 346
  types 346-349
Dynamic Trunking Protocol (DTP)
  about 237-239, 609
  dynamic auto mode 238
  switchport mode access mode 238
  switchport mode dynamic
      auto mode 238
  switchport mode dynamic
      desirable mode 238
  switchport mode trunk mode 238

**E**

electromagnetic interference (EMI) 39
Email Security Appliance (ESA) 604

endpoint protection, DiD
  Cisco Email Security Appliance
      (ESA) 604, 605
  Cisco Web Security Appliance
      (WSA) 605
  endpoint protection 603, 604
endpoints 57
end-to-end connectivity
  testing 172
Enhanced Interior Gateway Routing
    Protocol (EIGRP) 316
error-disable (err-disabled) 139
EtherChannels
  about 259
  benefits 260
  configuring 259-262
  creating, between switches 260, 261
  implementing 263-265
Ethernet 38
Ethernet network interface
    card (NIC) 187
Exploit Database
  URL 495
exploits 495, 496
extended ACLs
  about 563
  creating 588
  implementing 591-595
  named extended ACL,
      extending 589, 590
  working with 588
Extended Service Set (ESS) 194, 195
eXtensible Markup Language
    (XML) 665, 666
Exterior Gateway Protocol (EGP) 307
external BGP (eBGP) 347

# F

Federal Communications
    Commission (FCC)  188
Fiber Distributed Data Interface
    (FDDI)  232
fiber optic cables
    modes  40
File Check Sequence (FCS)  35, 186
File Transfer Protocol (FTP)  567
firewall
    about  51
    security zone  53
firmware virus  496
first hop redundancy  370-372
First Hop Redundancy Protocol (FHRP)
    about  371, 372
    Gateway Load Balancing
        Protocol (GLBP)  381
    Hot Standby Router Protocol
        (HSRP)  372
    using  372
    Virtual Router Redundancy
        Protocol (VRRP)  378
First-In, First-Out (FIFO)  461
Flash  90
floating route  330, 331
Frame  36
full duplex method  183
Fully Qualified Domain Name
    (FQDN)  437
fully specified static routes  327

# G

Gateway Load Balancing Protocol (GLBP)
    about  381
    Active router  382
    implementing  382, 383
    Standby router  382
Gigabits per second (Gbps)  39
Graphical Network Simulator 3 (GNS3)
    about  77
    Cisco IOS image, adding  83-88
    devices, adding  88
    environment, setting up  77-89
    versus Cisco Packet Tracer  77
graphical user interface (GUI)  125, 201
Gratuitous ARPs  616
gray hat hacker  481
guest operating system  209

# H

hacktivist  480
Hard Disk Drive (HDD)  475
host-based intrusion prevention
    (HIPS)  603
host operating system  209
host route  329
Hot Standby Router Protocol (HSRP)
    about  372
    Active router  373
    implementing  374-378
    Standby router  373
    version 1, versus version 2  373
HTTP GET message  672
HTTP POST message  672
HTTP Secure (HTTPS)  460, 671

Hubs
   about 42
   broadcast messages 44
   operations 43
human vulnerabilities 484, 486
human vulnerabilities, cyber-attacks type
   pharming 486
   phishing 485
   smishing 486
   spear phishing 485
   vishing 485
   waterhole attack 486
   whaling 485
Hypertext Markup Language (HTML) 663
Hypertext Transfer Protocol
      (HTTP) 460, 482
Hypertext Transfer Protocol
      Secure (HTTPS) 28
hypervisor
   Type 1 hypervisor 210, 211
   Type 2 hypervisor 211-213

I

Identity Services Engine (ISE) 505
inbound ACLs
   using 565
Infrastructure-as-a-Service (IaaS) 216
insider threat 481
Institute of Electrical and Electronic
      Engineers (IEEE) 38
intangible assets 474
integrity 476, 477
intent-based networking (IBN)
   about 678-682
   activation function 682
   assurance function 682
   Cisco DNA Center 685

   control plane 679
   data plane 679
   fabric 682
   management plane 679
   overlay 682
   Overlay Control Plane 683
   translation function 682
   underlay 684
interactive dialog 100
Interior Gateway Protocol (IGP) 315
internal BGP (iBGP) 347
International Organization for
      Standardization (ISO) 25
internet
   evolution 21
Internet Assigned Numbers Authority
      (IANA) 123, 140, 163
   URL 21
Internet Control Message Protocol
      (ICMP) 128, 482
Internet Corporation for Assigned
      Names and Numbers (ICANN)
   about 123
   URL 21
Internet Engineering Task
      Force (IETF) 41
   URL 21
Internet Header Length (IHL) 127
Internet of Things (IoT) 162
Internet Protocol (IP) 34, 127, 163, 482
Internet Protocol security (IPsec)
   about 544
   Authentication Header
      (AH protocol 544
   benefits 544
   Encapsulating Security
      Payload (ESP) 544
Internet Protocol version 6 (IPv6) 34

Internet Service Providers
    (ISPs)  24, 123, 391
Internetwork Operating System (IOS)  72
Inter-Switch Link (ISL)  237
inter-VLAN routing
  about  231, 239-241
  configuring  252-254
Intro to Packet Tracer course  71
intrusion detection system (IDS)  199
Intrusion Prevention System (IPS)  42, 54
IP addressing
  need for  122-125
IP routing  300-306
IPv4
  characteristics  125, 126
  used, for static routing
      configuration  332-337
  using, challenges  390, 391
IPv4 addresses
  binary, converting into decimal  129-131
  classes  140, 141
  decimal, converting into binary  132-136
  Link Local  145
  loopback address  145
  private IPv4 address space  142-144
  public IPv4 address space  141, 142
  Test-Net  145
IPv4 address space  144
IPv4 default route
  configuring  337-340
IPv4 network transmissions
  Anycast transmission  140
  broadcast transmission  138, 139
  multicast transmission  137, 138
  types  137
  unicast transmission  137

IPv4 packet
  composition  126-128
IPv6
  configuring, on Cisco IOS
      router  168, 170
  configuring, on Windows
      computer  170-172
  used, for static routing
      configuration  340-345
IPv6 addresses
  about  162-165
  Anycast  167
  global unicast address  166
  Link-Local IPv6 address  166
  lookback address  166
  modified EUI 64  167, 168
  multicast  167
  types  165
  unique local address  167
IP version 4 (IPv4)  34

J

JavaScript Object Notation (JSON)
  about  666, 667
  characteristics  667
  interpreting  667, 668
  URL  668
jitter  459

K

Kiwi Syslog Server
  reference link  444

# L

LastPass password manager  487
Layer 2 attacks
  about  600, 606
  ARP attacks  615
  CAM table overflow  607-609
  CDP attacks  619
  Defense in depth (DiD)  603
  network attacks  601, 602
  preventing  621
  spanning-tree attacks  618
  types  600
  VLAN attacks  609-615
layer 2 broadcast domain  228
layer 2 loop prevention protocol  272
Layer 2 switches  45, 46
Layer 2 threats. *See* Layer 2 attacks
Layer 3 switches  50
light-emitting diodes (LEDs)  40
Light-weight Access Points (LAPs)  198
Lightweight Directory Access
      Protocol (LDAP)  484
Link Aggregation Control
      Protocol (LACP)
  active mode  262
  on mode  262
  passive mode  262
Link Aggregation Group (LAG)  260
Link-Layer Discovery Protocol (LLDP)
  about  257, 621
  configuring, on Cisco IOS
      device  258, 259
Link Local  145
local area networks (LANs)  158
local route  307

Logical Link Control  35
loopback address  145
Low-Latency Queuing (LLQ)  462

# M

MAC address
  checking, of network  37
machine learning (ML)  126
macro virus  496
malware  496
malware, types
  adware  498
  crypto-malware  497
  ransomware  497
  rootkit  497
  spyware  498
  Trojan Horse  497
  virus  496
  worm  497
Man-in-the-Middle (MiTM) attack  501
Media Access Control (MAC)  36, 601
Megabits per second (Mbps)  39
Message Digest 5 (MD5)  350, 536
Message Integrity Check (MIC)  647
Metasploit
  about  496
  reference link  496
Metro Ethernet (MetroE)
  about  24, 301
  URL  541
microflow
  differentiated services (DiffServ)  463
Microsoft Security Bulletin MS17-010
  URL  602
Microsoft Server Message Block
      1.0 (SMBv1)  495

MS17-010 security bulletin
    reference link  495
Multi-Area OSPF  361
multicast transmission  137, 138
Multifactor Authentication (MFA)  487
multi-mode fiber  41
Multiple Spanning-Tree
        Protocol (MSTP)  281
Multiprotocol Label Switching (MPLS)
    about  24
    URL  541

# N

named extended ACL
    implementing  589, 590
NAT overload. *See* also port
        address translation (PAT)
Nessus
    about  482
    reference link  482
    using, to perform vulnerability
        assessment  488-494
Nessus Essentials
    about  488
    reference link  488
network address translation (NAT)
    about  391
    dynamic NAT  397-399
    operation and terminology  393-395
    static NAT  395-397
    types  395
    using, benefits  392
    using, disadvantages  393
Network-Based Application
        Recognition (NBAR)  465

network-based intrusion
        prevention (NIPS)  603
    about  674, 675
    tools  675
network devices
    functions  42
networking
    evolution  20
network interface card (NIC)  36, 164, 186
Network Management Station (NMS)  677
network operating systems  676
network prefix  146, 148
network programmability
    URL  676
network protocol suites  25
network routes  325
network security concepts
    about  474, 475
    CIA triad  475
    cyber-attacks  496
    exploits  495, 496
    threats  478, 479
    vulnerabilities  482-484
network sizes  22
network switch functions
    about  176, 177
    physical issues, detecting  178-186
Network Time Protocol (NTP)
    about  418-421
    configuring  421-425
    stratum hierarchical structure  421
network topology  98
network topology architectures
    2 Tier  60, 62
    3 Tier  63, 64
    about  58

next-generation firewall (NGFW)  603
next-generation intrusion prevention
        system (NGIPS)  54, 603
next hop static routes  325
Nmap  498
non-root ports  277
non-volatile random access
        memory (NVRAM)  91
Northbound Interface (NBI)  680
numbered extended ACL
  creating  589

# O

Object IDs (OIDs)  451
Open Shortest Path First
        (OSPF)  138, 308, 316
Open Shortest Path First
        version 2 (OSPFv2)
  about  349
  benefits  350
  commands  360-362
  configuration, validating  366-370
  configuring  363-366
  Designated Router (DR)  356
  interface cost  355, 356
  interface states  354, 355
  messages  352
  operations  351
Open Source Intelligence (OSINT)  498
Open Systems Interconnection (OSI)  25
Opportunistic Wireless
        Encryption (OWE)  647
Organization Unique Identifier (OUI)  36
organized crime  480

OSI reference model
  about  25, 26
  application layer  27, 28
  data link layer  35
  network layer  34, 35
  physical layer  38
  presentation layer  29, 30
  session layer  30
  transport layer  30-32
OSPF, benefits
  classless  350
  efficiency  350
  open source  350
  scalability  350
  secure  350
OSPF components
  Adjacency Table  350
  Forwarding Database  351
  Link-state Database (LSDB)  350
OSPF Hello Packet  352-354
OSPF packet types
  Database Description (DBD)
        packets (type 2)  352
  Link-State Acknowledgement
        (LSA) (type 5)  352
  Link-State Request (LSR)
        packet (type 3)  352
  Link-State Update (LSU) (type 4)  352
  OSPF Hello packets (type 1)  352
outbound ACLs
  using  565

# P

packet loss  459
parent route  308

Password Authentication
    Protocol (PAP)  539
password vulnerabilities and
    management  486-488
perimeter firewall deployment  52
Personally Identifiable
    Information (PII)  475
Per-VLAN Spanning-Tree+ (PVST+)
    about  275, 281
    port states  281
    root bridge, discovering  282-286
pharming  486
phishing  485
physical access control  509
physical layer, OSI reference model
    network components  38-40
plaintext passwords
    encrypting  539, 540
Platform-as-a-Service (PaaS)  216
Point-to-Point (PPP)  539
port address translation (PAT)
    about  399
    configuring  399-403
    implementing  403-406
Port Aggregation Protocol (PAGP)
    auto mode  261
    desirable mode  261
    on mode  261
PortFast
    about  287
    configuring  291-293
port security
    about  621-629
    implementing  629-634
POSTMAN  676
Power-on Self Test (POST)  91

Preamble  36
pre-shared key (PSK)  647
private IPv4 address space  142-144
Privilege Exec mode
    securing  535-538
probes  194
program virus  496
Protocol Data Unit (PDU)  27-30
PRTG
    reference link  444
public IPv4 address space  141, 142
Putty
    URL  95
Python  676

# Q

QoS implementation methods
    classification  464
    congestion avoidance  466
    marking  464, 465
    policy and shaping  466
    queuing  465
QoS policy models
    about  462
    best effort model, advantages
        and disadvantages  462
    differentiated services (DiffServ)  463
    IntServ  463
    IntServ, advantages and
        disadvantages  463
QoS queuing algorithms
    Class-Based Weighted Fair
        Queuing (CBWFQ)  461
    Low-Latency Queuing (LLQ)  462
    Weighted Fair Queuing (WFQ)  461
Quality of Experience (QoE)  460

Quality of Service (QoS)
  about 127, 165, 564
  implementation methods 464
  policy models 462
  queuing algorithms 461
  terminologies 458, 459
  traffic classification 456-458
  traffic type characteristics 459, 460

# R

radio frequency (RF) 197
Random Access Memory (RAM) 46, 90
ransomware 497
Rapid-PVST+
  about 286
  implementing, on Cisco
      network 288-291
  PortFast feature 287
  supported port states 287
Rapid Spanning Tree Protocol
      (RSTP) 286, 288
Read-only Memory (ROM) 91
Receive Signal Strength
      Indicator (RSSI) 188
reconnaissance 498
recursive lookup 338
reflection 500, 501
Regional Internet Registries (RIRs) 123
remote access VPN
  about 543
  configuring 551-557
  configuring, in Full Tunnel mode 543
  configuring, in Split-Tunnel mode 544
Remote Administration Trojan (RAT) 497
Remote Authentication Dial-in User
      Service (RADIUS) 505

Representational State Transfer
      (REST) APIs
  about 671, 676
  characteristics 672-674
  request, making to system 675
RESTful API request
  API server 675
  query 675
  resources 675
Rivest Cipher 4 (RC4) encryption
      algorithm 647
roaming 195
root bridge 274
rootkit 497
round-robin algorithm 465
router
  about 50
  sub-interface, creating 241
router-on-a-stick 239, 252
routes 301
Routing Information Protocol (RIP) 307
routing metrics
  about 314, 315
  Enhanced Interior Gateway Routing
      Protocol (EIGRP) 316
  Open Shortest Path First (OSPF) 316
  Routing Information Protocol 315
routing protocol codes 306
routing table
  about 50
  components 306
routing table, components
  about 306
  Administrative Distance (AD) 311-314
  gateway of last resort 317, 318
  network mask 309, 310

next hop  310, 311
prefix  309, 310
routing metrics  314, 315
routing protocol codes  306-309

# S

sales  151
script kiddies  480
SCRYPT  538
SDN controller  679
Secure Hashing Algorithm (SHA)  350
Secure Shell (SSH)
  about  93
  enabling, on Cisco IOS device  532, 534
security program
  elements  509
Segment  30
Server Message Block (SMB)  483
servers  57
service providers (SP)  24
Service Set Identifier (SSID)  193
Shared Key Authentication  647
Shielded Twisted Pair (STP)  39
Short Message Service (SMS)  486
Shortest Path First (SPF)  351
Simple Network Management
      Protocol (SNMP)
  about  448-450
  community strings, read-only  451
  community strings, read-write  451
  components  448
  configuring  453-456
  Management Information
      Base (MIB)  449-452
  SNMP agent  449
  SNMP manager  448
  versions  451

Simple Network Management
      System (NMS)  448
Simultaneous Authentication
      of Equals (SAE)  648
single-mode fiber  40
Site-to-Site VPNs
  about  541, 542
  configuring  545-551
Small Office/Home Office (SOHO)  23
smishing  486
Snort
  URL  54
Social Engineer Toolkit (SET)  498
Software-as-a-Service (SaaS)  215
Software-Defined Access (SD-Access)  685
Software-Defined Network (SDN)  677
Software-Defined WAN (SD-WAN)  685
solid-state drive (SSD)  90
Southbound Interface (SBI)  680
spanning-tree
  Per-VLAN Spanning-Tree+
      (PVST+)  281
  port roles  277, 278
  port roles, determining  278-280
  Rapid-PVST+  286
  root bridge, determining  278-280
  standards  277
  states  277, 278
spanning-tree attacks  618, 619
spanning-tree, port roles
  alternate or backup ports  277
  designated ports  277
  root ports  277
Spanning-Tree Protocol (STP)
  about  270-272
  benefits  270

Bridge Protocol Data Units
    (BPDUs) 273
  root bridge 274, 275
  secondary root bridge 274, 276
spear phishing 485
spine-leaf topology 684
spin up resources 214
Split-MAC wireless network
    architecture 198
spoofing 499
spyware 498
standard ACLs
  about 563
  deleting 576
  standard named ACL,
      implementing 575, 576
  standard numbered ACL,
      creating 573, 574
  working with 573
standard named ACL
  configuring 580-583
  creating 575
  implementing 575
standard numbered ACL
  creating 574
  implementing 576-580
Stateless Address Autoconfiguration
    (SLAAC) 167
state-sponsored 481
static NAT
  about 395
  configuring 396, 397
static NAT, with port forwarding
  implementing 406-409
static routes
  about 307
  creating 323
  default route 328

directly connected static routes 326, 327
  floating route 330, 331
  fully specified static routes 327
  host route 329
  network routes 325
  next hop static routes 325, 326
  types 325
static routing
  about 322-324
  configuring, IPv4 used 332-337
  configuring, IPv6 used 340-345
  need for 324, 325
  using, situations 325
Stratum 420
subnet mask
  about 146
  identifying 148, 149
  Network ID 148, 149
  network prefix 146, 148
subnetting
  about 150-152
  appropriate IP address,
      determining 152-154
  subnets, assigning to network 157-159
  subnets (subnetworks), creating 154-157
  Variable-Length Subnet Masking
      (VLSM), performing 159-162
switch security controls, for
    preventing Layer 2 attacks
  DHCP snooping 634
  Dynamic ARP inspection (DAI) 641
  port security 621
Switch Virtual Interface (SVI)
  about 234, 425
  configuring 108

Syslog
  about  442
  benefits  442
  configuring  445-448
  severity levels  443, 444
Syslog message  418

# T

tagged traffic  235
tangible assets  474
TCP/IP protocol suite
  TCP three-way handshake  33
Telnet
  about  528
  configuring, on Cisco router  528, 529
Temporal Key Integrity
      Protocol (TKIP)  647
Terminal Access Controller Access-
      Control System + (TACACS+)  505
Terminal line (VTY)  442
Test-Net network  145
threat actors  480-482
threat actors, types
  hacktivist  480
  organized crime  480
  script kiddies  480
  state-sponsored  481
threats  478, 479
Time To Live (TTL)  127, 304
tools, network configuration management
  Ansible  677
  Ansible, features  677
  Chef, features  678
  Puppet, features  678
Top-Level Domain (TLD)  437

Transmission Control Protocol/
      Internet Protocol (TCP/IP)  21
Transmission Control Protocol (TCP)
  about  25
Trivial File Transfer Protocol
      (TFTP)  91, 679
Trojan Horse  497
troubleshooting procedures
  performing  117, 118
trunk  236
trunk interfaces
  about  236
  creating  237, 248-252
  Dynamic Trunking Protocol (DTP)  237
Type 1 hypervisor
  about  210
  applications  211
Type 2 hypervisor
  about  211, 212
  applications  212
Type of Service (ToS)  127, 461

# U

unicast transmission  137
Uniform Resource Identifier (URI)
  fragment  673
  hostname  673
  path and filename  673
  protocol  673
  URL  672
Uniform Resource Locator (URL)
  about  436, 673
  example, reference link  673
Uniform Resource Name (URN)
  about  673
  example, URL  673

Unshielded Twisted Pair (UTP)  39
user awareness  509
user credentials
    example  504
User Datagram Protocol (UDP)  34, 457
user training  509

# V

Variable-Length Subnet Masking (VLSM)
    about  159
    performing  159-162
Virtual Extensible LAN (VXLAN)  681
virtualization
    about  209
    fundamentals  209
    hypervisor  209
Virtual Local Area Network (VLAN)
    about  162, 226-232, 562
    concerns  227
    extended range, features  233
    implementing  242-247
    inter-VLAN routing  239, 241
    normal range, features  232
    ranges  232
    trunk interfaces  236, 237
    types  233-235
    used, for improving security  232
Virtual Private LAN Service
    (VPLS)  24, 542
virtual private network (VPN)
    about  540
    benefits  541
    Internet Protocol security
        (IPsec)  544, 545
    remote access VPNs  543
    Site-to-Site VPNs  541, 542

Virtual Router Redundancy
    Protocol (VRRP)
    about  378
    Backup router  378
    implementing  378-381
    Master router  378
Virtual Terminal (VTY)  109, 508, 564
virus  496
vishing  485
VLAN Double Tagging
    about  611
    preventing  612
VLAN Hopping attack
    about  610
    preventing  612
VLAN types
    about  233
    data VLAN  233, 234
    default VLAN, features  233
    management VLAN  234, 235
    native VLAN  235
    voice VLAN  234
Voice over IP (VoIP)  231, 458, 564
voice VLAN  230
VTY line access
    securing  527
    SSH, enabling on Cisco IOS
        device  532-535
    Telnet, securing on Cisco
        router  528-532
vulnerabilities
    about  482-484
    human vulnerabilities  484, 486
    Nessus, using to perform vulnerability
        assessment  488-494
    password vulnerabilities and
        management  486-488

# W

WannaCry  602

waterhole attack  486

Web Security Appliance (WSA)  604

Weighted Fair Queuing (WFQ)  461

whaling  485

white hat hacker  481

Wide Area Network (WAN)  158, 539

Wi-Fi
  about  193
  URL  193

Wi-Fi Protected Access (WPA)  647

wildcard masks
  about  568, 569
  calculating  569, 571
  using, examples  568

Windows computer
  IPv6, configuring on  170-172

Windows Hello  488

Wired Equivalent Privacy (WEP)  647

wireless bands  192, 193

wireless components
  managing  200

wireless interface cards (WICs)  192

Wireless LAN Controller (WLC)
  about  42, 197
  used, for implementing wireless
    network security  649-655

Wireless LAN (WLAN)
  implementing  645

wireless network connection  187

wireless network security
  about  645
  authentication methods  647, 648
  implementing, WLC used  649-655
  MAC address filtering  646
  Service Set Identifier (SSID)
    broadcast. disabling  646
  threats  645

wireless network, with Cisco WLC GUI
  configuring  203-209

wireless technologies  187, 188

Wireshark
  about  226
  download link  509

Wireshark 101
  about  509-513
  packets, analyzing  514, 515

Wireshark display filters
  reference link  513

worm  497

WPA2  648

WPA3  648

# Y

YAML Ain't Markup Language (YAML)
  about  668
  characteristics  668
  URL  669
  versus JSON data format  669

Made in the USA
Columbia, SC
10 May 2021